POSSIBILITIES AND LIMITATIONS OF PRAGMATICS

STUDIES IN LANGUAGE COMPANION SERIES (SLCS)

The SLCS series has been established as a companion series to
STUDIES IN LANGUAGE, International Journal, sponsored by
the Foundation "Foundations of Language".

Series Editors:

John W.M. Verhaar		Werner Abraham
Gonzaga University	&	University of Groningen
Spokane, WA		The Netherlands

* * *

Volume 7

H. Parret, M. Sbisà, J. Verschueren (eds.)

Possibilities and Limitations of Pragmatics

POSSIBILITIES AND LIMITATIONS OF PRAGMATICS

Proceedings of the Conference on Pragmatics,
Urbino, July 8-14, 1979

edited by

Herman PARRET

*(Belgian National Science Foundation;
Universities of Louvain and Antwerp)*

Marina SBISÀ

(University of Trieste)

and

Jef VERSCHUEREN

*(Belgian National Science Foundation;
University of Antwerp)*

AMSTERDAM/JOHN BENJAMINS B.V.

1981

© Copyright 1981 – John Benjamins B.V.
ISSN 0165 7763 / ISBN 90 272 3006 4

No part of this book may be reproduced in any form, by print, photoprint, microfilm or any other means, without written permission from the publisher.

ACKNOWLEDGMENTS

This book is the sediment of the conference on *Possibilities and Limitations of Pragmatics* held at the Centro Internazionale di Semiotica e Linguistica (Urbino, Italy) from July 9 to 14, 1979, and organised by the editors of this volume. Neither the conference nor the book would have been possible without the indefatigable support of Professor Giuseppe Paioni, Secretary General of the Centro, who deserves, therefore, our profoundest gratitude. Thanks are also due to the dozens of scholars who contributed indirectly to this volume by actively participating in the conference.

H.P, M.S. and J.V.
February 1980

TABLE OF CONTENTS

Acknowledgements	v
List of Contributors	viii
Introduction	1
Thomas T. BALLMER, Context change and its consequences for a theory of natural language	17
Diane BROCKWAY, Semantic constraints on relevance	57
Luigia CAMAIONI, The problem of appropriateness in pragmatic development	79
Robin N. CAMPBELL, Language acquisition, psychological dualism and the definition of pragmatics	93
Aaron V. CICOUREL, Pragmatic issues in the construction of recent history from interview narratives	105
David E. COOPER, Pragmatics and pragmatism	123
Florian COULMAS, Idiomaticity as a problem of pragmatics	139
Marcelo DASCAL, Contextualism	153
Steven DAVIS, Causatives	179
Susan ERVIN-TRIPP, How to make and understand a request	195
Nicholas FOTION, I'll bet you $10 that betting is not a speech act	211
Dorothea FRANCK, Seven sins of pragmatics: Theses about speech act theory, conversational analysis, linguistics and rhetoric	225
Beatrice De GELDER, Attributing mental states: A second look at mother-child interaction	237
Paul GOCHET, How to combine speech act theory with formal semantics: A new account of Searle's concept of proposition	251
Günther GREWENDORF, Answering as decision making: A new way of doing pragmatics	263
Hartmut HABERLAND, and Tove SKUTNABB-KANGAS, Political determinants of pragmatic and sociolinguistic choices	285
Wolfgang HEYDRICH and János S. PETÖFI, Pragmatic considerations within a text-theoretical framework	313
Götz HINDELANG, Pragmatical grammar and the pragmatics of grammar	331

Franz HUNDSNURSCHER, On insisting	343
Christian KOCK, Non-truth-conditional quantification	359
Werner KUMMER, Pragmatically based grammar	371
François LATRAVERSE and Suzanne LEBLANC, On the delimitation of semantics and the characterization of meaning: Some remarks	399
Geoffrey LEECH, Pragmatics and conversational rhetoric	413
Paolo LEONARDI and Marco SANTAMBROGIO, Pragmatics, language games, questions and answers	443
Stephen C. LEVINSON, The essential inadequacies of speech act models of dialogue	473
Guido MORPURGO-TAGLIABUE, Grammar, logic and rhetoric in a pragmatic perspective	493
Richard T. OEHRLE, Common problems in the theory of anaphora and the theory of discourse	509
Franca ORLETTI, Classroom verbal interaction: A conversational analysis	531
Domenico PARISI and Cristiano CASTELFRANCHI, A goal analysis of some pragmatic aspects of language	551
Isabella POGGI, Cristiano CASTELFRANCHI and Domenico PARISI, Answers, replies and reactions	569
François RECANATI, On Kripke on Donnellan	593
Helmut SCHNELLE, Phenomenological analysis of language and its application to time and tense	631
Viggo SØRENSEN, Coherence as a pragmatic concept	657
Dennis STAMPE, Pragmatics and causal theoretic aspects of semantics	683
Charles TRAVIS, How to be a referent	713
Jocelyne M. VINCENT and Cristiano CASTELFRANCHI, On the art of deception: How to lie while saying the truth	749
Dietmar ZAEFFERER, On the formal treatment of illocutionary force indicators	779
References	799
Index	833

LIST OF CONTRIBUTORS

Thomas T. Ballmer, Ruhr Universität, Bochum
Diane Brockway, Department of Linguistics, University College London, London
Luigia Camaioni, Institute of Psychology, University of Rome, Rome
Robin N. Campbell, Department of Psychology, University of Stirling, Scotland
Cristiano Castelfranchi, Istituto di Psicologia, C.N.R., Rome
Aaron V. Cicourel, Department of Sociology, University of California, San Diego
David E. Cooper
Florian Coulmas, Seminar für Allgemeine Sprachwissenschaft, Universität Düsseldorf
Marcelo Dascal
Steven Davis, Simon Fraser University
Susan Ervin-Tripp, Psychology Department, University of California, Berkeley
Nicholas Fotion, Emukj University, Atlanta
Dorothea Franck
B. De Gelder, N.I.A.S. and Tilburg University
Paul Gochet
Günther Grewendorf, Fachbereich Germanistik, Freie Universität Berlin
Hartmut Haberland

Wolfgang Heydrich, Fakultät für Linguistik und Literaturwissenschaft,
    Universität Bielefeld
Götz Hindelang, Germanistisches Institut, Münster
Franz Hundsnurscher, Germanistisches Institut, Münster
Christian Kock, Department of English, University of Copenhagen,
    Copenhagen
Werner Kummer
François Latraverse, Département de philosophie, Université du
    Québec à Montreal
Suzanne Leblanc, Département de philosophie, Université du Québec à
    Trois-Rivières
Geoffrey Leech, Department of Linguistics and Modern English
    Language, University of Lancaster, Lancaster
Paolo Leonardi, Instituto di Storia della filosofia, Università di
    Padova, Padova
Stephen C. Levinson, Department of Linguistics, University of
    Cambridge, Cambridge
Guido Morpurgo-Tagliabue, Università di Trieste, Milano
Richard T. Oehrle, Department of Linguistics, University of Arizona,
    Tucson
Franca Orletti, Instituto Linguistico, Facolta degli Studi di Roma,
    Rome
Domenico Parisi, Instituto di Psicologia, C.N.R., Rome
János S. Petöfi, Fakultät für Linguistik und Literaturwissenschaft,
    Universität Bielefeld
Isabella Poggi, Instituto Linguistico, Facoltà di Magistero, Università
    di Roma, Rome
François Récanati, C.N.R.S., Paris
Marco Santambrogio, Instituto di Filosofia, Università di Bologna,
    Bologna
Helmut Schnelle, Ruhr-Universität, Bochum

Tove Skutnabb-Kangas
Viggo Sørensen, Institut for nordisk sprog og literatur, University of Arhus, Arhus
Dennis W. Stampe, University of Wisconsin
Charles Travis, Department of Philosophy, The University of Calgary, Calgary
Jocelyne M. Vincent, S.S.O.M.M., Instituto Universitario Orientali di Napoli, Napoli
Dietmar Zaefferer, Institut für Deutsche Philologie der Universität München, München

INTRODUCTION

During the past decade a respectable number of pragmatic readers have been published, such as Y. Bar-Hillel (1971), P. Cole and J.L. Morgan (1975), A. Rogers, B. Wall and J.P. Murphy (1977), J. Mey (1979), and J.R. Searle, F. Kiefer and M. Bierwisch (1980), to mention just a few. In addition three periodicals have seen the light, viz. "Pragmatics Microfiche", "Journal of Pragmatics" (North-Holland Publishing Company), and "Pragmatics and Beyond" (John Benjamins B.V.). Therefore, a legitimate question would be: Why yet another collection of essays? The conference of which this volume is a reflection was organised because we figured that, exactly ten years after the publication of Searle's *Speech Acts* (with its ensuing snowball effect), it was about time to make an assessment of the achievements in the field of pragmatics and, if possible, to open some new perspectives. This explains why explicit reference is made to *possibilities* and *limitations* of pragmatics, as a uniting theme, throughout this book. *Possibilities and Limitations of Pragmatics* also differs from previous readers in the unrivalled diversity of topics and approaches presented. The diversity of the contributions necessitated their alphabetical ordering, by author, which in turn necessitated the following topical introduction.

1. The problem of the *delimitation of pragmatics* with regard to syntax and especially to semantics is, of course, of central importance

in various contributions to this volume. According to OEHRLE the trichotomy syntax-semantics-pragmatics may be totally misconceived due to the existence of linguistic phenomena (such as prosodic properties) which do not strictly belong to any of them. Be that as it may, a lot of effort is spent trying to delimit *semantics* and *pragmatics*, or to show that no clear delimitation is possible. Most of the contributors tacitly assume the validity of the distinction. Some actively defend it; GREWENDORF does so with reference to questions. According to him the task of a pragmatics of questions is to define the concept of a pragmatically significant answer, whereas the semantics of questions should define the concept of a true answer as well as the concept of the logical presupposition of a question. Others concentrate on the fuzziness of the boundary: KOCK demonstrates that a large group of lexical items, which are normally regarded as semantic units, resist analysis in terms of truth conditions and can only be explained if natural language is seen as purposive action for the furtherance of speakers' interests and needs. Whereas dozens of scholars have - usually quite convincingly - shown how pragmatic explanations are needed for semantic (and syntactic) phenomena, BROCKWAY's article is unique, as far as we know, in trying to reveal the opposite side of the coin. She opposes the common distinction between semantics as covering the truth-conditional aspects of meaning and pragmatics as dealing with its non-truth-conditional aspects. According to her, semantics is a matter of conventional aspects of meaning whereas pragmatics is a matter of its conversational aspects, consisting in a set of universal principles on the basis of which utterances are interpreted; hence contextual constraints on the use of individual lexical items are said not to belong to pragmatics (because otherwise one would have to accept two logically distinct types of pragmatic rule). She concludes that there are aspects of pragmatic interpretation (as in the case of connecting particles such as 'after all', 'actually', etc.) which are semantically determinable or that certain words impose semantic constraints on pragmatic interpretation.

Similar tensions concerning the delimitation of the domain of pragmatics are exposed by philosophers. COOPER raises the methodological issue of the pragmatic nature of semantic claims. His view of the status of semantic claims is a *pragmaticist* one, in the sense that he believes their relevance to consist in their success or failure in licensing inferences which maximally facilitate ascriptions of propositional attitudes. His pragmaticism - as a methodology - does not lead to an identification of semantics and pragmatics. On the contrary: the ascription of propositional attitudes is generated by a *semantic* theory which is autonomous with regard to pragmatics. The author rejects the claim that statements about propositional attitudes, as well as about reference, are ultimately statements about speakers, thus denying that pragmatics and semantics should be identified with each other. In fact, COOPER is concerned - just like STAMPE and RECANATI - with the so-called "causal" theories of meaning (as Kripke's and Putnam's, which have the more limited scope of theories of proper names and of natural kind terms, or, at most, theories of reference). STAMPE defends a variant of the "causal theory of meaning". Among all causal theorists, STAMPE is the one who claims the most explicitly that the pragmatic properties of a sentence *explain* its semantic properties. Pragmatics, according to STAMPE, is the study of certain regularities in the *causation* of utterances underlying the practical functions they serve. Pragmatic inference is causal inference, and therefore the relevant procedure is to insert pragmatic information in truth-conditional semantics. This is an original amendment of Kripke's suggestions, which makes STAMPE into the most pragmatically oriented of all causal theorists. RECANATI, on the other hand, while criticising Kripke's account of Donnellan's distinction between attributively and referentially used definite descriptions, introduces a distinction between the semantic and pragmatic aspect of referentiality; moreover, he argues in favor of a distinction between referentiality and rigidity, and between identifying, indefinitely-referring and potentially incongruent descriptions. All these distinctions are still semantic: the student of meaningful language use has to go along semantic lines as far as possible, even if the central notion of semantics becomes that of "perspectival truth condition".

The question of whether syntax, semantics and pragmatics are horizontally or vertically related is addressed by LATRAVERSE and LEBLANC. According to the "horizontal" view the domains of these three disciplines would be contiguous one to another, whereas the "vertical" view implies that one domain would rest, through a foundational relation, on another domain, the priority of which can be of a theoretical-logical or of a temporal-material nature. The authors opt for the second possibility, where pragmatics is foundational with regard to semantics and syntax, though this priority is rather theoretical-logical than empirical-ontological.

2. Many authors stress the *interpenetration* of pragmatics with other traditionally distinct disciplines. This interpenetration, characterised by an overlap of methods and perspectives, does not lead automatically to a unified science of language use. Contact with particular philosophical traditions such as *pragmaticism* (COOPER) and *phenomenology* (SCHNELLE) is established. COOPER's conception of the pragmaticist status of semantic claims is close to the type of view held by Peirce and other pragmaticists, whereas SCHNELLE goes back to Husserl and phenomenological theories in general in his analysis of the categories of tense, mood and aspect; he makes the phenomenological framework more explicit and more precise by "translating" this framework in terms of information processing; phenomenology, according to SCHNELLE, helps the linguist to transcend the objectivistic or even physicalistic conceptual schemes in linguistic theory.

It is remarkable that *rhetoric* revives in three of the contributions to this volume. FRANCK explicitly defends this revival, which signals a return to the age-old division of labor between grammar and rhetoric; she defines rhetoric as a repertoire of strategies, communicative principles and formal patterns of use applied by speaker and hearer in order to manage the interaction and pursue their communicative aims in varying contexts and circumstances in an adequate and effective way. MORPURGO-TAGLIABUE argues that Grice's logic of conversation is nothing else than the rules of classical rhetoric adapted by contemporary philosophical research on language use and discourse. This convincing exposition is evidently in concordance with LEECH's point of view; the aim of his *conversational rhetoric* is to reconstruct the system of principles by means of which language is matched to the communicative functions we perform in using language.

If the definition of pragmatics as the science of language use is extended to include the relationships between language and the cognitive processes of its users, then *psycholinguistics* is no doubt part of it. Anyway, several papers in this collection deal with psycholinguistic matters. CAMPBELL stresses the need to revive the old psychological distinction between conscious (phenic) and unconscious (cryptic) structures and processes; whereas linguistic knowledge has so far mainly been regarded as unconscious, phenic structures and processes do not only have a role to play in metalinguistic communication since making sense of what is said is no doubt a conscious process. DE GELDER, in her discussion of adult-child interaction, launches an attack on Bruner's "mentalism"; she maintains that a mother's assistance in bringing a child to act in a certain way amounts to more than assisting the child in articulating his own intentions - no doubt norms are being imposed in the process of interpreting the child's intentions. *Interpretation processes* are studied by ERVIN-TRIPP (who produces evidence that they rely heavily on content and depend on expectations based on repetition and knowledge of usual sequences of events and roles, as filtered by attention) and simulated in HEYDRICH and PETOFI's reconstruction of some pragmatic aspects of the process of text interpretation.

Pragmatic aspects of *language acquisition* are touched upon by ERVIN-TRIPP (who reports an investigation of children's comprehension of implicit directives) and DE GELDER, and they are the central topic of CAMAIONI's article which reports a study of how children adjust their speech style to different listeners, leading to the conclusion that even young children are able to do so. CAMPBELL formulates the hypothesis that when learning a language (as other skills!) one first goes through a conscious phenic process which leads in a mysterious way to the acquisition of short-cut procedures which adequately replace deliberate processes.

Another borderline discipline is *logical pragmatics* which comes into being either by "logicising pragmatics" or by "pragmatising logic". LEONARDI and SANTAMBROGIO, for instance, talk about the role of logic and game-theoretical semantics in pragmatics (which is said to have a non-empirical core). They are truly influenced by Lorenzen's and especially Hintikka's framework: the use in dialogues and the dialogical situation in general determine the value of expressions considered to be moves of the game; pragmatic rules are, in fact, *strategies*. In their analysis of questions and answers, the basic notion is that of doubting or attacking the partner's assertions and forcing him to defend them, and this is why the notion of truth gives way to that of *proof*. However, it is still not evident - as LEONARDI writes in an additional note - that the game-theoretical framework matches natural language phenomena adequately, and there are serious problems once (logical) game-theoretical strategies are confronted with specific natural language principles such as Grice's conversational principles. This effort of putting logic in pragmatics is turned upside down by MORPURGO-TABLIABUE's proposal to put pragmatics in logic, especially in modal logic. The introduction of pragmatics here is on the level of the postulates of modal logic: these postulates are shaped by presuppositions which have to do with a specific view of the *expectations* of the users of modal categories, as is already clear in Aristotle. Suffice it to say that next to these pleas for logical pragmatics as an interdisciplinary field we encounter in this volume good examples of formal descriptions of empirical materials. To give just three examples, GREWENDORF contends that precise descriptions in pragmatics are possible on condition that it uses theoretical apparatuses from other fields, the appropriate ones being subjective probability theory and decision theory; and ZAEFFERER's aim is to expand formal semantics to cover not only locutionary indicators but also illocutionary ones such as mood and certain particles. BALLMER insists on the necessity of a *context change logic*, and he relates it to more commonly known logics, such as propositional logic, predicate logic, indexical logic and intensional logic: context change logic formalises how linguistic expressions - particularly speech acts - *change contexts*. He outlines the general setting of so-called 'bookkeeping' where expressions to be interpreted are analysed from left to right, operating as linguistic instruments on contextual parameters. 'Context change logic' is shown by BALLMER to be powerful enough to handle intricate empirical problems of reference, such as the Bach-Peters paradox, and of syntactical ambiguity.

We also encounter applications which seem to go far beyond the realm of 'pragmatics proper' if such a thing exists. CICOUREL, for instance, addresses the following issue: Can we identify a set of pragmatic principles which specifies the way in which interview narratives and textual materials are subjected to analysis by historians? He is interested in the often unreported practical problems faced and practical knowledge assumed in field research since "Much of the information left out of reports based on the study of language structure and use delete references to socio-cultural conceptions the researcher was obliged to invoke tacitly in order to conduct his or her study". HABERLAND and SKUTNABB-KANGAS, on the other hand, show, in their comparison between Skandinavian and West German language policies oriented towards immigrant workers, how different political contents can require different interpretations of established scientific knowledge and may lead to different proposals as to how to apply this knowledge.

3. In spite of the fact that pragmatics is an area of linguistic research with fuzzy boundaries - spreading like an uncontrollable oil slick - and that at present no scholar will be so audacious as to claim that he knows what is pragmatic in the study of language and what is

not, there seems to be some sort of general consensus that pragmatics, or the study of language use, deals with matters of *appropriateness*, i.e. the adaptation to situational and interpersonal context. Hence the term appropriateness crops up frequently, as in CAMAIONI's title and in LEONARDI and SANTAMBROGIO's partial definition of the task of pragmatics as stating "what it is appropriate to say under what circumstances".

There is, however, less agreement as to the exact nature of the relationship between language and extralinguistic reality to be described. The general tendency is to believe that *rules* can be formulated which constitute linguistic institutions. Two slightly different views are represented in this collection. LEECH investigates in how far the domain of pragmatics can be defined as the domain of *principles* (similar to Searle's regulative rules) rather than of real *rules* (corresponding to Searle's constitutive rules). And CICOUREL argues that the domain of pragmatics is not so much a matter of rules as of *problem-solving behavior* (creating goals and plans, pursuing goals, implementing plans) having an impact on the world and connecting actions to what can be expected to happen in terms of consequences. PARISI and CASTELFRANCHI's *goal analysis* is closely related to this view, as well as LEVINSON's contention that conversational sequencing is not rule-based but rather *strategy*-based.

The nature of the extralinguistic world to which language is related is less subject to debate. As BROCKWAY points out, context can be described as the set of beliefs held by the person from whose point of view an utterance is being described. According to BALLMER, however, the aim of pragmatics is to study the *dynamic* relation of expressions to the context: linguistic expressions operate causally on contexts, so as to *alter* them. He stresses the *instrumental* character of natural language: the nature of linguistic *action* is to change contexts in a thoroughly orderly manner by 'bookkeeping' mechanisms running off in the context components. BALLMER's interest is not so much in the static relation of contextual factors to language, as studied by classical pragmatic theories, but rather in the *dynamic* relation of linguistic expressions to contextual parameters.

'Contextualism' or the hypostasis of the role for *context* in the theory of language is strongly opposed to in DASCAL's article. He distinguishes between 'moderate contextualism', overlooking the importance of non-contextual factors and paying exclusive attention to contextual influence upon the production and interpretation of utterances, and 'radical contextualism' claiming explicitly and holistically that there is no such a thing as a context-free literal meaning of a sentence. DASCAL himself defends 'moderate literalism' (which, in principle, is not incompatible with 'moderate contextualism'), determining in this way the autonomous domains of semantics and pragmatics. His defense of literal or context-free meaning is supported by that the fact that, in order to interpret and understand plain 'pragmatic' phenomena such as certain implicatures, one needs first to discover *semantic* relevance or even, in some cases, semantic *irrelevance*. A well balanced theory of meaning-in-language should admit *literal* meanings, not as complete entities capable to determine unambiguously truth conditions but rather as 'schematic' entities specifying conditions through which their 'gaps' might be appropriately filled by contextual information. Among the 'radical contextualisms', DASCAL ranges Olson's cognitivism, Harman's conceptualism, and above all Searle's direct attack of context-free literal meaning (Searle, 1978). DASCAL argues that Searle may have shown that literal meaning is not a *sufficient* condition for the determination of significance in every context, but that this does not have to be an argument in favor of the statement that literal meaning is not a *necessary* condition for it. Indeed, through methodological work should be done to demarcate the boundaries of pragmatics not only with semantics but also with *performance*, and relevant types of *contexts* should be distinguished here.

The search for an adequate definition of the *domain of pragmatics* can be truly foundational. Some authors go further than simply saying that pragmatics studies the system of regularities underlying meaningful language use, whether they are institutions, strategies, rules, or principles. LEONARDI and SANTAMBROGIO stress the relevance of the Wittgensteinian notion of *language game* (giving rules which constitute institutions, assigning roles to those taking part and achieving coordination) for pragmatics. The idea of language games is even the most promising for an adequate 'theory' of context and discourse, according to LATRAVERSE and LEBLANC. The notion of language game makes it possible to "pinpoint exactly where our ontological prudence has led us" in the debate on the nature of pragmatics and its relation to semantics. In a radical Wittgensteinian sense the predicate 'pragmatic' cannot even be applied to theories and objects, and it is true that many so-called 'pragmatic theories' are in fact 'extended' semantic theories. Going back to the Wittgensteinian notion of language games has at least the heuristic advantage of radically avoiding all mentalism, even when intentions, beliefs and 'attitudes' are at the core of the reconstruction.

4. Let us mention among the wide range of specific topics discussed in this volume four areas of evident interest: the nature of *speech acts* and the empirical-theoretical relevance of speech act theory; the pragmatics of *reference* or, more adequately, of the act of referring; the analysis of *suprasentential action units*, i.e. the pragmatic units *par excellence*; and the relationship between pragmatic *functioning* and particular linguistic *forms*.

4.1. *Speech act theory* as a central area of pragmatic research is referred to in nearly every contribution. The classical framework (Searle, 1969), with some minor revisions, is still accepted by some. Others offer a reinterpretation; LEECH, for instance, reduces Searle's account of speech acts to Grice's account of conversational implicature. Still others concentrate on the limitations of speech act theory. A case in point is FRANCK's paper in which it is argued that 'classical' speech act theory is not sufficient as a basic, all-encompassing framework for the pragmatics of verbal communication; in doing so she does not make the mistake of presupposing that the founders of the theory have ever intended it as such a framework. She also contrasts this limitation of the theory with a clear possibility: speech act categories can be expected to play a vital role in an empirical theory of language and communication. LEVINSON dismisses, more specifically, speech act models of dialogue because of problems such as the identifiability of unit acts corresponding to specific utterance units; the relevant unit acts are said not to be unitary assignments from a well-defined set of speech act types but n-ary assignments of intents; DAVIS' considerations on basic actions, in connection with causatives, can throw some light on the problem of the nature of 'unit acts' as well.

If the conference on possibilities and limitations of pragmatics had been held five years earlier, there would have been at least half a dozen lectures on *speech act classification*. Now there was none. This state of affairs confirms our feeling that, at present, within the framework of 'classical' speech act theory, nobody seems to be able to offer a considerably better theoretical classification than the one to be found in Searle (1976). On the other hand, in spite of the fact that, as HABERLAND and SKUTNABB-KANGAS state, there is nothing disdainful about taxonomies, nobody seems eager to undertake large-scale empirical research towards a better understanding of the diversity of things we do with words. This is symptomatic of the overly theoretical nature of pragmatics which, due to the large number of linguists engaged in it, almost threatens to strip linguistics itself of its empirical character. Here we believe to be confronted with one of the main shortcomings of pragmatics (for further discussion on this point, see Verschueren, 1979). Nevertheless, BALLMER's typology of speech acts based on context change, should be mentioned here. The conception of *context change* leads in a natural way to a typology of speech acts. Thus, the typology is based on four main groups of context change: physical context changes, mental context changes, social state changes, and linguistic context changes. This rough classification being as it may, the present volume contains a number of articles yielding interesting insights into individual speech act types. Questions and answers are dealt with by GREWENDORF and LEONARDI/SANTAMBROGIO. In their goal analysis of how questions can be answered, POGGI, CASTELFRANCHI and PARISI distinguish between answers, replies and reactions (each category including the previous one). FOTION's article is an attempt to show that *betting* is *not* a speech act type but a type of speech activity typically consisting of two separate speech acts (i.e. an offer to bet such as "I'll bet you ...." and an acceptance of the offer). *Insisting* is analysed by HUNDSNURSCHER as a step in a speech act sequence the initiative move of which is often a speech act with a directive component. *Directives* and other 'control moves' are considered by ERVIN-TRIPP who concentrates, among other things, on the boundaries or overlap between requests and offers. Some notes on requests are also to be found in DE GELDER's discussion of mother-child interaction.

Whereas *perlocutionary effects* and *perlocutionary intents* have usually been regarded as marginal to speech act theory, they are quite well represented in the following essays. MORPURGO-TAGLIABUE argues that perlocutions cannot be left out of account in a discussion of illocutionary meaning though the relationship between illocution and perlocution varies: sometimes it is definitional or semantic (as in the case of commands), sometimes it is contextual or pragmatic (as in the case of promises). Also HUNDSNURSCHER claims that perlocutionary intent is constitutive for communicative interaction and hence central in the analysis of linguistic action; what keeps communicative interaction going is trying to reach some communicative goal. Similarly, KUMMER is concerned with the verbal planning of structures of utterance goals in situation frames. A belief in the importance of perlocutionary intents is the basis of PARISI and CASTELFRANCHI's *goal analysis* which they present as a unifying and general framework of investigation (unifying speech acts, indirect speech acts, discourse, conversation, and applicable to non-linguistic as well as linguistic behavior). This goal analysis is applied to answers by POGGI, CASTELFRANCHI and PARISI and to instances of *deceiving* and *lying* by VINCENT and CASTELFRANCHI who offer an interesting taxonomy of such acts.

Some other related problems are *politeness* and *indirectness*. Politeness is touched upon by LEECH. Indirectness is dealt with by GOCHET, and PARISI and CASTENFRANCHI, to mention just a few; ERVIN-TRIPP studies indirectness in requests, which provide a particularly clear case because requests are impositions and therefore prone to being conveyed indirectly. Two specific types of indirectness, *metaphor* and *punning*, are studied by COULMAS; he concentrates on the relationship between metaphors and idioms and argues that punning on idioms (which involves a reliteralization of idioms) could be regarded as a form of communicative boycott.

4.2. *Reference*, for many scholars, constitutes the most difficult aspect of meaning to be incorporated in a pragmatic theory of language use. It is dealt with repeatedly. The most thorough treatments are those by STAMPE, RECANATI (who, as said before, distinguishes semantic from pragmatic referentiality) and TRAVIS (whose discussion starts from the assumption that it is necessary to talk about referring in terms of both words and speakers). TRAVIS makes a most useful distinction between "identification theories of reference" and "theories of reference identity"; the second type of theory, called a 'generative' theory of reference, would specify the different identities that a reference might have by providing characterisations of references adequate for distinguishing between one reference and another. TRAVIS pursues along lines of such a "generative theory of reference" and there he automatically meets pragmatic constraints which have to do, among other things, with the fact that reference *has to be understood*, and that what is thus to be understood is the 'presumptive' descriptive backing carried by the reference; both aspects of this orientation (understanding-oriented with 'presumption' as a necessary condition on understanding reference) introduce a pragmatic perspective into the very core of the theory of reference.

More cursory remarks on the *proposition* in general are made by MORPURGO-TAGLIABUE who argues that proposition, illocution and perlocution cannot be separated, and by GOCHET who insists that certain aspects of meaning do not belong to the proposition from a pragmatic point of view whereas they *do* from a semantic point of view (such as the element 'I order you' in "I order you to leave").

4.3. Probably the bulk of this volume is devoted to the analysis of units of interaction larger than the speech act. Many of the articles dealing with speech acts or speech act theory were already shown to deal, in fact, with such larger units. Remember LEVINSON's argument against speech act models of dialogue, FOTION's analysis of betting as a *speech act sequence* with a particular illocutionary force, and HUNDS-NURSCHER's definition of insisting in terms of preceding acts. Apart from HEYDRICH and PETÖFI, who attempt to reconstruct (the pragmatic aspects of) the process of *text interpretation*, most of the articles dealing with textual or conversational aspects of language approach this subject matter from the point of view of what LEECH calls *conversational rhetoric*. It is clear, according to LEECH, that the interpretation of the 'rhetoric' of discourse sequences rests upon generalisations which can be made by the speaker and the hearer in a community of language users about the functional structuring of suprasentential units. Negation, questions and politeness presuppose conversational functions attached to larger units than just the sentence.

The problem of *coherence*, which is thoroughly treated as a pragmatic phenomenon by SØRENSEN, is also touched upon by HUNDSNURSCHER (who defines discourse coherence as the relation an individual speech act in a sequence bears to the communicative goal set up in the initiative speech act), KOCK and KUMMER. A slightly wider notion is *relevance*, which does not only cover coherence between utterances (as in GREWENDORF's account of the informativeness of answers to questions, which is a matter of the relevance of those answers as answers to questions) but also between utterances and the non-linguistic context. BROCKWAY maintains that Grice's maxims of conversation can be reduced to a principle of relevance; she also offers some distinctions between different types of relevance.

Not only discourse and discourse strategies in general are investigated in this book. We also find studies of some specific types of discourse. ORLETTI, for instance, examines the turn-taking phenomena revealed in discourse in the classroom; she shows how such discourse is governed by a mixed systems of *turn-taking* which is between the logically managed system of natural conversation and the debate system in which turns are pre-allocated. Pragmatic aspects of narrative interviews are scrutinised by CICOUREL.

4.4. The relationships between pragmatic *functions* and particular linguistic *forms* are explored in a large number of articles. Some general principles are outlined by HINDELANG who describes the writing of a grammar as a language game (i.e. the pragmatics of grammar) and addresses the question of how the language game of writing a grammar can be played pragmatically, proposing a number of rules for the writing of a strongly pragmatical grammar. Another general remark is made by KUMMER who claims that a pragmatically based grammar should function as a constitutive part of a model of discourse production and comprehension along the lines developed in Artificial Intelligence.

Particular linguistic phenomena dealt with are the following: *anaphora* (OEHRLE), *causatives* (the hypothesis that verbs such as 'to open' can be analysed as the semantic feature 'cause' plus two propositions is rejected as a semantic hypothesis by DAVIS though it is admitted to be probably correct as a pragmatic hypothesis in connection with what we believe about the world), *idiomaticity* (COULMAS sets out a number of tasks for the pragmatic treatment of idioms which he regards as linguistic devices to enlarge the possibilities of a language and to adapt it to new demands without introducing new material), *illocutionary force indicators* (for which ZAEFFERER provides a formal treatment), *interrogation* and *negation* (LEECH), *prosody* (OEHRLE investigates how prosodic properties such as intonation can play a decisive role in such entrenched areas of semantics and pragmatics as the assignment of reference to anaphoric expressions), *quantification* (KOCK presents a bunch of observations on the vagueness in the quantification expressed by means of 'a bit', 'several', 'often' etc., arguing that the meaning of these items is argumentative rather than truth-conditional, and attacking the theory of the 'implicit norm'), *sentence adverb(ial)s* such as 'after all', 'actually', 'anyway' etc. (which BROCKWAY analyses as connectives linking utterances and contexts), and finally *time* and *tense* (SCHNELLE regards the objectivistic conceptual schemes on which many semantic ideas are based as inappropriate for a treatment of tense, mood, aspect, etc. and resorts to phenomenology, reformulated in terms of information processing, for help). Whereas several years ago the *performative analysis* would still have been a central topic in the discussion of grammar and pragmatics, in this volume it is only mentioned, in passing, by GOCHET.

An assessment of the benefits which *Possibilities and Limitations of Pragmatics* bestows on our field of investigation will be left to the cooperative reader who will not find it difficult to discover some new promising perspectives. However, we would like to advocate, with LEVINSON, a resolute return to the data: further abstract theorising, in most areas of pragmatics, is likely to be profitable only when we shall have more systematic information. If an empirical line of research is pursued then there is a good chance that after another ten years of hard work we shall be able to publish another collection of essays called *Advances in Pragmatics*.

Herman PARRET
Belgian National Science Foundation;
Universities of Louvain and Antwerp

Marina SBISÀ
Università di Trieste

Jef VERSCHUEREN
Belgian National Science Foundation;
University of Antwerp

CONTEXT CHANGE AND ITS CONSEQUENCES
FOR A THEORY OF NATURAL LANGUAGE

Thomas T. Ballmer

1. *Critical consideration*

The impression which one may get scanning through the literature on pragmatics is that - in an important respect - it is not quite on the right track. In a traditional and structuralistic mannerism classificatory terms are coined and rules are formulated, as if language - from a synchronic point of view - is a *static, monolithic* structure. The *kinematics* (or even *dynamics*)[1] of natural language (NL) is *not* taken care of, not to mention taken as a fundament of linguistic communication.

The aim of pragmatics - being concerned with *linguistic action* and *performance* - indicates in various manners the indispensability of a *kinematic* and/or *dynamic* analysis of NL. *First*, the *production* and *perceiving* of linguistic expressions, both in a *conceptual* and a *behavioral* sense, is *dynamic*: there is internal (conceptual) and external (behavioral) *dynamics*, i.e. there is dynamics from a phenomenologic-psychological as well as from a neurophysiologic-physical point of view. *Secondly* the *relation* of linguistic expressions to the *speech situation* is *dynamic*. Linguistic expressions operate causally on the speech situation, including the addressee, so as to *alter* it.

But the proper pragmatic standpoint to conceive speaking as a special kind of acting according to intentions, plans and goals in order to bring about certain effects is *fundamentally dynamic*, even more so when sequences of such actions are considered.

Therefore we should be wondering why there is no dynamic (or at least kinematic) theory of the various aspects of NL. *Neither* the structuralistic approaches, *nor* the Chomskyan generative grammar, *nor* the by now standard logical analysis of NL are dynamic. Procedural mechanisms are now and then taken into account, informally, by theoretical linguists (ISARD, KUMMER, VENNEMANN, BARTSCH, SCHNELLE) who are not all strictly speaking pragmaticians *and*, in a more systematic way, by researchers in AI (WINOGRAD, SCHANK). But as far as I can see, none of these approaches has acquired a state of 1. *heuristic* power, 2. *empiric* foundation, 3. *methodologic* strength *and* 4. *formal* rigor.

In this paper I shall present *some ideas* on what a fundamentally *dynamic* theory of language looks like. It is a theory which in its final state would really merit the name *pragmatics*, because it is based on the *dynamic interaction* of human beings with their environment by *instrumental* means. Linguistic expressions are conceived as special *instruments* used by human beings to *change* the *real* and *mental world*.

2. *A parable*

Let me present a parable, a parable, though imaginary, exhibiting nevertheless some traits of reality: Imagine an alien, an intelligent, adult and educated specimen of his race. Let us consider a situation of gross average as a result of which he has to stay on earth, alone without any special knowledge about men, neither about their society nor their mind. Intelligence presupposed, the question is: what will the alien find out about language? Will he be able to eventually understand what is going on among humans, will he be able to interact with them in an effective way, will he be able to get to know their culture and maybe to convey his own intentions and plans to them?

This situation, though highly speculative, merits a proper analysis. For it focuses on the basic question: what *abilities* have to be presupposed in order to enable a being, *here* an *alien*, to learn and understand a human language.[2]

One of the alien's basic observations will be that people produce sounds which may ask for a reaction. People would, especially, direct sounds towards *him* and wait briefly. Not responding - how could he, not knowing the language! - they would probably repeat the same sounds *louder*, they would *move* their arms, pointing in a certain direction, or even *grasp* and lead his limbs and body in a certain direction. The reaction would even be forced upon him bodily.

Such experiences corroborate his basic observation that humans use sounds (and certainly bodily movements) to get (other) people to do something. Sounds and movements seem to serve for humans in his terminology - stemming from a highly technological culture he may analyse this situation by corresponding concepts - as an *instrument* to get people to do something. The reactions need not be *immediate*, they may be *delayed*. But in elementary situations of teaching, *sounds* and *forcing a reaction* occur together. Accordingly, *habituation* and *insight* probably more than *reward* consolidate the connection between sound and reaction. The intelligent alien finds himself forced eventually into a system of *instrumental interactions*. Following a principle of least effort (or maximal freedom) he tries to use the sounds (and accompanying movements) in a most efficient way, as a controlling agent and as a controlled patient.

I do not defend a behavioral or even a behavioristic picture of language learning and language use here! There are some important differences between a behavioral conception and ours. *First* it is not *punishment* and *reward* but more primarily *habituation* and *insight* which stabilize the connections between sound and observable effects (including gesture and sound responses). *Secondly*, only *primary* language learning situations are of a quasi-behavioral type in which co-occurrences of sounds and their effects are more or less immediately related. As language learning goes on, the contextual knowledge forbids immediate relationships of sounds and effects. For instance the question

(1.1) Hast du Hunger?
      (have you hunger: Are you hungry?)

in the context of presenting rhubarb jam to a potential speaker establishes only in early language learning stages the link that 'Hunger' denotes rhubarb. This happens because of lacking *contextual clues* which make it clear that (1.1) is used also in the context of presenting strawberries, or even presenting nothing at all, and that (1.1) is said moreover in a situation where hunger is an easily detectable prevailing feature.

Likewise the sentence

(1.2)   Niemand kommt
        (nobody comes: Nobody is coming)

said after the ringing of a bell tempts the potential speaker to associate 'Niemand' and some definite person as, say, the postman who normally appears at this time of the day. But after some experience with sentence (1.2), he will eventually recognize his failure and reconsider his interpretation of 'Niemand'. The *contextual knowledge* forces him to digress from his "behavioristic" language learning. Other examples which illustrate the growing divergence from behavioral patterns are ironical speech, indirect speech acts, certain types of metaphor and jokes, speech about non-present situations (past, future, remote places) etc. Language learning based initially on behavioral-like patterns enables the subject to digress more and more from immediate responses, in understanding and producing language. *Context change procedures* are just the source of *overcoming* strictly behavioral patterns. The lasting effects of earlier experiences (perceptive and memorative context changes) create the basis for building up the distance to initial immediacy. But the *starting point* of every learning is "behavioristic" with respect to the hic et nunc experiences of the learner.

The basic insight that sounds get people to react in a specific way is generalized to the insight that the use of (particular) sounds *gets things changed*: the use of these sounds *enable, force* or *forbid* certain things to happen. This embraces in particular in turn the retorting production of sounds: the situation produced in part by the *previous use* of specifically shaped sounds and in part by the *prevailing physical* environment *promotes* and also *restrains* the use of other sounds.

Sounds used in physical environments change the conditions of people's reactions be they acoustic or bodily reactions, be they immediate or be they delayed. Therefore sounds of a certain shape occur to our alien as *instruments* used by humans having the potential for *more or less definite effects* determining in turn the *further use* of *instruments*.

3. *A discussion of some examples*

Let us now check, by considering phenomena of natural language (NL), how far the metaphor of *linguistic expressions as instruments* is valid. In particular, we would first like to show how a language learner, like a child, a foreigner, or an alien if you want, can find out about the instrumental character of NL.

The following is probably a most explicit and nonetheless *not untypical* example demonstrating instrumental applications of subsequent words. These words (or one word sentences) induce *each a* corresponding *reaction*:

(2) | *Words in sequence* | *Reactions in sequence:* |
|---|---|
| John! | John gets attentive and listens. |
| Come! | John approaches the speaker. |
| Take! | John takes, say, an apple. |
| Eat! | John eats the apple. |
| Sleep! | John lies down and tries to repose and sleep. |

Somebody not knowing the words would be able, other capacities presupposed, to associate the linguistic entities and their corresponding reactions. He will be able to grasp the *meaning* of these linguistic entities as the *systematic relation* to their effect.

The next example demonstrates that even in *one and the same* sentence the reaction to single words may drastically vary. This gives us a reason to attribute to every single word in a sentence an *instrument-*

al force upon the addressee:

	Wordsequences:	Reactions of hearer:
(3a)	Hello	Hearer smiles.
(3b)	Hello blockhead	Hearer does not smile.
(3c)	Hello blockhead-Paul	Hearer smiles again.
(3d)	Hello blockhead-Paul comes	Hearer gets scared.
(3e)	Hello blockhead-Paul comes hardly	Hearer smiles again.
(3f)	Hello blockhead-Paul comes hardly today	Hearer is scared again.

Saying 'hello' pleases the hearer (3a), he then mistakes 'blockhead' as an injury directed towards him (3b) and stops smiling, but then recognizes that not he, the hearer, is meant but rather somebody else: blockhead-Paul (3c). He smiles again, but gets scared then, because he is afraid of blockhead-Paul's coming (3d), his "coming hardly" calms the hearer down again (3e) but at the end, he stays scared (3f), because it is hinted that blockhead-Paul is coming another day.

Thus far we have a *heuristic* and *empirical* entrenching for the *interactive instrumental* view of NL: the application of linguistic entities *in a* situation *to the* situation induces in some clear cases immediately verifiable effects. Linguistic entities serve as *instruments* of human *interaction*.

But the assumption of *interactive instrumentalism* proves its force by the possibility to conceive it also in *more abstract* domains. Let us consider acts of reference. A very concrete way to refer to an object is to lead the addressee to the object and to *force* him to *touch* it: The most concrete act of reference is *bodily* and *sensory contact*. A little less concrete or, say, direct is *grasping from a distance* (what children typically do) or *pointing*, a conventional means of inducing reference to an object. Cases which are yet more remote from concrete reference occur in ASL (American Sign Language for deaf people): the space in front of the speaker and hearer serves as a space of reference, a spatial phantasma (Sprachtheorie, BÜHLER 1934). In this space individuals can be *first introduced* as discourse individuals, they are *secondly shifted* around; according to the actions they perform and according to communicative purposes of the signer. They can *thirdly* be *used* as discourse referents.

The case of ASL demonstrates in a perceptually intelligible way the instrumental character of reference mechanisms in NL. An individual is *introduced* (e.g.) by pointing at a place in the phantasma and spelling its name. This introduction of the individual *changes* the *state* of the phantasma. A locally irreversible change occurred. An individual exists for a certain time in the phantasma. *Shifting* an individual around by making him, say, walk from one corner to another in the phantasma has equally decisive consequences. The state of the phantasma is changed again: the place of the discourse referent is different from before.

Reference in spoken NL works in a very similar, but even *more* abstract way. This can be seen by the following type of examples:

(4)   Alf drinks.   He is sad.

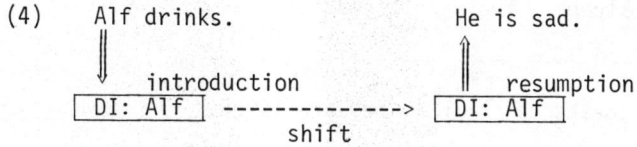

The expression 'Alf' introduces the individual "Alf" in a discourse individual set and makes it thus available for future reference as for instance by the pronoun 'he' in the subsequent sentence.

The discourse individual set is therefore comparable to the phantasma of ASL to some degree. But as we said it is more abstract. Biologically speaking, it is certainly neurophysiologically realized, maybe in a very complex way, but psychologically accessible, it is consciously or subconsciously present. The double arrow ⇓ (for: introduction) leading from the expression 'Alf' to the discourse individual set DI, the arrow -----> (for: shift) between the two occurrences of the DI-set and the double arrow ⇑ (for: resumption) leading from DI to the expression 'he' (and its interpretation) represent the kinematic flux underlying the interpretation of expression (4).

Male names introduce individuals in a *different* subset of discourse individuals than *female names*, namely in a subset which can be immediately utilized by a male *pronoun*. This is shown by the referential ambiguity of (5a) which does not occur in (5b).

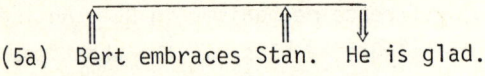
(5a)　Bert embraces Stan.　He is glad.

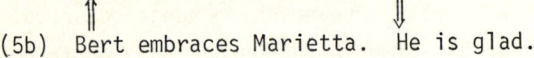
(5b)　Bert embraces Marietta.　He is glad.

In (5a) there are two individuals introduced in the male discourse individual set, whereas in (5b) only one. (5a, b, c) shows that there must be also a specific subset for reference by plural pronouns such as 'they'.

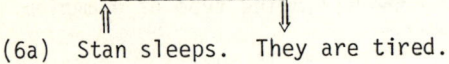
(6a)　Stan sleeps.　They are tired.

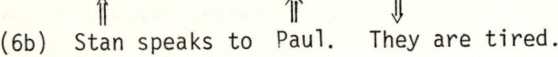
(6b)　Stan speaks to Paul.　They are tired.

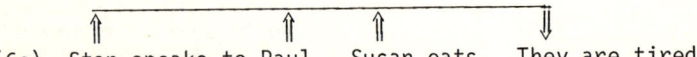
(6c)　Stan speaks to Paul.　Susan eats.　They are tired.

In (6a) no reference is established to Stan. In (6b), however, because enough individuals are introduced into the plural discourse individual set, reference is established to exactly Stan and Paul. (6c) is highly ambiguous. The three individuals introduced allow for *four* plural partitions.

In fact there must generally be assumed a discourse individual (sub)set (DIS) for each pronoun and even more generally for each proform and referential expression. This can be demonstrated by a vast number of linguistic examples. For instance we have:

(7a) *Regula* watches *herself* in the mirror.

(7b) *He* shaves *himself*.

(7c) *A motorcycle* scorches down the street. *The motorcycle* is faster than the police car.

(7d) Brahms lived in the *19th century*. He liked to live *then*.

(7e) Franklin was born in *Philadelphia*. He hated to be *there*.

(7f) Who *rang* the bell? — Thierry *did*.

(7g) *Marsha got sick*. *It* is terrible.

(7h) *Margret is pregnant*. *Therefore* she is especially beautiful.

Names and pronouns introduce individuals for reference by reflexives (cf. 7a, b). In English resumption by reflexives is restricted to single clauses, of course. Indefinite noun phrases introduce (sets of) individuals for future reference by definite noun phrases (7c). Temporal and local designation introduce times or places respectively (7d, 7e), verbs introduce actions (7f), and whole sentences introduce propositions, reasons and the like (7g, h).

A lexical classification of referential expressions can be given on the basis of the role such expressions play in the dynamical process of interpretation (and production). This point is illustrated by German spatial expressions:

(8) *A lexical classification of referential expressions*

Request	Introducing Focusing Setting up	Trans- porting	Using	Identifying Disidenti- fying
Wo?	Wo	Verbs of active	Dort	Daselbst
An welchem	Dort wo	locomotion,	Da	Am gleichen Ort
Ort?	in der CN	grasping and	An diesem	An derselben Stelle
Wo denn?	in einer CN	transport,	Ort	Anderswo
	CN: *Küche,*	shift pro-	Hier	
	Kirche,	positions	Eben da	
	...			

Paß auf
Nimm ein CN
Angenommen
Hallo
Schau her
Hör
Irgendwo
Überall wo
Es gab einmal
ein CN

Spatial expressions are very fundamental with respect to reference. Therefore all logico-linguistic problems of reference have a spatial realization as the following examples suggest:

(9) Common referential problems are also problems of local reference

(9.1) Non-substitutional cases!

Überall geht die Sonne unter.   *Dort möchte ich sein.

CONTEXT CHANGE

Überall wo die Sonne untergeht   möchte ich sein.

Irgendwo geht die Sonne unter.   Dort möchte ich sein.

(9.2) Quantifier iteration!

Überall gibt es *irgendwo* ein paar Sehenswürdigkeiten.

(9.3) Non-protected intensionality

There *is hyperspace*.   This is what I believe.

(9.4) Geach's Donkey problem

Every man who owns *a castle* loves to stay there.

(9.5) Geach-Seuren's Plato
Plato believes that there is somewhere *a nice green peninsula which is free of foreigners* and hopes that it stays like this.

(9.6) Winograd type reference selection

The cathedral is two hundred meters from *the market*.
   There there is nice fish to get.
   There there are long sermons to hear.

(9.7) Local Bach-Peters paradox

Woher Klaus dorthin sehen kann ist es schöner als *woher* wir dahin blicken können.

more explicitly:

Der Ort *woher* Klaus dorthin sieht ist schöner als die Stelle *woher* wir dahin sehen können.

more condensed:

Woher du kommst da geh' ich hin.

another turtling-down problem:

Die Stelle, von der ich weiß, daß sie gefährlich ist, hat schon vielen das Genick gekostet.

Whereas all the examples (4)-(9) belong rather strictly to the realm of reference, the following examples though very similar seem to approach the syntactical realm, i.e. the domain of combining clauses and phrases to sentences. Thus consider:

(10a) Whichever man you saw on the beach -- that man is dangerous.

(10b) Wherever you find him, that is the place.

(10c) Where you are going, there I shall go too.

(10d) When the president is leaving, everybody must leave.

(10e) Because Charles went on holiday, the whole business went bankrupt.

Clauses beginning with conjunctions (and pronouns) like 'whichever', 'where', 'when', 'because' introduce individuals, places, times, reasons. In cases like (8a, 8b), for 'whichever', 'wherever' and so forth it need not be a fixed individual which is introduced, it may rather be a "variable" individual, designated by what is best called an *adjustable constant* (cf. BALLMER 1978). The reference-using (main-) clause may syntactically be moved away from the place where the referent is introduced. Thus we may have for instance:

(11) When the president is leaving - (in lower voice) and I tell you the full truth ... (aside) Sorry I don't want a drink, I beg your pardon ... (looking straight) Oh hello Dr. Duck - (resumptive intonation and pointing with finger in the air and intensively nodding) everybody must leave.

Thus there seem to be mechanisms to store information away for latter use even for phenomena belonging traditionally more to the realm of *syntax*, and not to reference, as the previous examples (10) and (11) show.

4. *Bookkeeping, a general concept*

Let us introduce a concept, *bookkeeping*, which gives us a more coherent account of the interaction between linguistic expressions and the context relative to which they are produced or interpreted.

Let us therefore start with the presentation of the general communicative framework which we are working in:

(12) General communicative framework

(12.1)

and more abstractly:

(12.2)

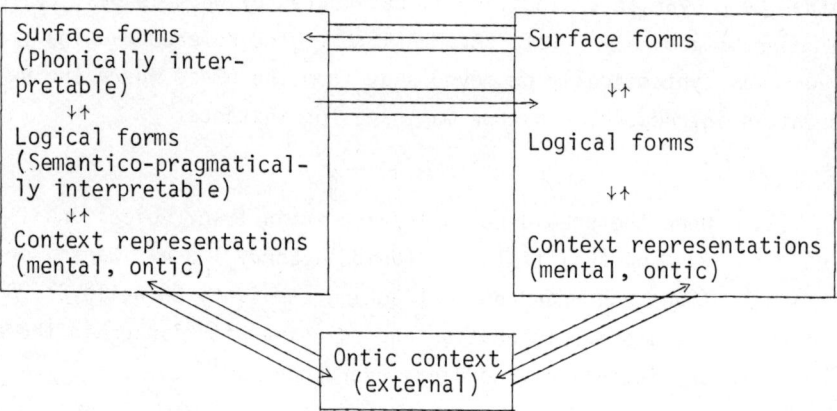

As an example how linguistic expressions with respect to this general communicative framework are analysed, consider (13) and (14):

(13) Context change: REFERENCE

(13.1, cf. 4)

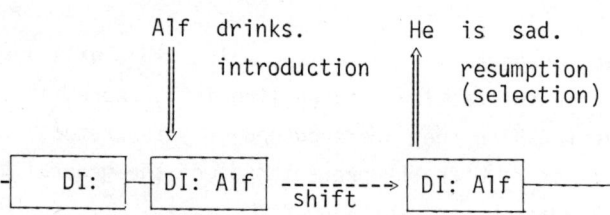

(13.2)

LRS
(language reconstruction system; syntactical head)

CCL
(context change logic)

Alf drinks.   He is sad.
↳ Drinks(Alf) ∧ Sad(he)
↳ Drinks(Alf) ∧ Sad(Alf)

(13.3) Some formal clauses of interpretation:

$h(\alpha \wedge \beta, I) \equiv h(\alpha, I) \wedge h(\beta, \xi(\alpha, I))$
$h(\delta, I) \equiv \delta$
$h(he, I) \equiv \varepsilon x(x \in I)$
$\xi(\delta, I) \equiv I \cup \{\delta\}$
$\xi(he, I) \equiv I$

The steps of interpretation pinpointed in (13.2) can be made formally explicit: In (14) the rules of language reconstruction systems [syntactical head] (cf. 14.1) and the rules of context change logic (cf. 14.2) as given in (13.3) are applied in the appropriate manner to proceed from language surface to the logical form:

(14) Application of the formal calculus!

(14.1) Alf drinks.   He is sad.
Alf $\lambda u Drinks(u)$ $\kappa\Pi_{VP}\kappa\Pi_N(\Pi_{VP}(\Pi_N))$ he $\lambda P \lambda u P(u)$ $\lambda u Sad(u)$
                             $\kappa\Pi_{Adj}\kappa\Pi_{Be}\kappa\Pi_N\kappa\Pi_S(\Pi_S \wedge \Pi_{Be}(\Pi_{Adj}, \Pi_N))$
Alf $\kappa\Pi_N[\lambda u Drinks(u)](\Pi_N)$ ...
Alf $\kappa\Pi_N Drinks(\Pi_N)$ ...
Drinks(Alf) $\kappa\Pi_S(\Pi_S \wedge [\lambda P \lambda u P(u)](\lambda u Sad(u), he))$
Drinks(Alf) $\kappa\Pi_S(\Pi_S \wedge Sad(he))$

(14.2) Drinks(Alf) ∧ Sad(he)
$h(Drinks(Alf) \wedge Sad(he), \emptyset) \equiv$
$h(Drinks(Alf), \emptyset) \wedge h(Sad(he), \xi(Drinks(Alf), \emptyset)) \equiv$
$Drink(h(Alf, \emptyset))$ ...
$Drink(Alf) \wedge Sad(h(he, \xi(Drinks(Alf), \emptyset)))$

$$\begin{bmatrix} \xi(\text{Drinks}(\text{Alf}),\emptyset) \equiv \\ \xi(\text{Alf},\emptyset) \equiv \\ \emptyset u\{\text{Alf}\} \equiv \\ \{\text{Alf}\} \end{bmatrix}$$

Drink(Alf) ∧ Sad(h(he,{Alf})) ≡
Drinks(Alf) ∧ Sad(Alf)

Examples (15) and (16) show that context change logic is powerful enough to handle sufficiently intricate problems of reference, the *Bach-Peters paradox* and *Geach's donkey*:

(15) A context change solution to the Bach-Peters paradox

The boy who loves her kisses the girl who hates him.
$\lambda P \lambda Q \text{The}^M x(Px,Qx) \lambda u \text{Boy}(u) \kappa \Pi_{CN} \gamma \Pi_{V2} \lambda \Pi_N \lambda u (\Pi_{CN}(u) \triangleright \Pi_{V2}(u,\Pi_N))$
$\lambda v \lambda w \text{Love}(v,w) \text{her} \lambda v \lambda w \text{Kiss}(v,w) \; \lambda P \lambda Q \; \text{The}^F y(Py,Qy)$
$\lambda u \; \text{Girl} \; (u) \kappa \Pi_{CN} \gamma \Pi_{V2} \gamma \Pi_N \lambda u(\Pi_{CN}(u) \triangleright \Pi_{V2}(u,\Pi_N))$
$\lambda v \lambda w \; \text{Hate}(v,w) \; \text{him}$

$\kappa \Pi^2_{CN} \kappa \Pi^2_{DET} \kappa \Pi_{V2} \kappa \Pi^1_{CN} \kappa \Pi^1_{DET}((\Pi^1_{DET}(\Pi^1_{CN}))((\lambda v \Pi^2_{DET}(\Pi^2_{CN})) \lambda w \Pi_{V2}(v,w)))$

$\text{The}^M x(\text{Boy}(x) \triangleright \text{Love}(x,\text{her}),\text{The}^F y(\text{Girl}(y) \triangleright \text{Hate}(y,\text{him}),\text{Kiss}(x,y)))$

with
$$\begin{bmatrix} h(\text{The}^M x(\Pi x, \Sigma x), A^M, A^F) \equiv \\ V_1 x(h(\Pi x \wedge x=a, \xi(\Sigma x, A^M u\{a\}, A^F)), h(\Sigma x, \xi(\Pi x, A^M u\{a\}, A^F))) \\ h(\text{The}^F y(\Pi y, \Sigma y), A^M, A^F) \equiv \\ V_1 y(h(\Pi y \wedge y=b, \xi(\Sigma x, A^M, A^F u\{b\})), h(\Sigma y, \xi(\Pi y, A^M, A^F u\{b\}))) \\ h(\alpha \triangleright \beta, A^M, A^F) \equiv h(\alpha, A^M, A^F) \wedge h(\beta, A^M, A^F) \\ h(\text{him}, A^M, A^F) \equiv \epsilon v(v \in A^M) \\ h(\text{her}, A^M, A^F) \equiv \epsilon w(w \in A^F) \\ \xi(\text{The}^M x(\Pi x, \Sigma x), A^M, A^F) \equiv A^M u\{a\} \\ \xi(\text{The}^F y(\Pi y, \Sigma y), A^M, A^F) \equiv A^F u\{b\} \end{bmatrix}$$

Translational interpretation gives with $A^M = A^F = \emptyset$
$V_1x(Boy(x) \wedge x=a \wedge Love(x,b), V_1y(Girl(y) \wedge y=b \wedge Hate(y,a), Kiss(x,y)))$
With $V_1\delta(\Pi(\delta), \Sigma(\delta)) \equiv V\delta(\wedge\gamma(\Pi(\gamma) \leftrightarrow \delta=\gamma) \wedge \Sigma(\delta))$
one finally arrives at:
$Vx \wedge vVy \wedge w(((Boy(v) \wedge Love(v,y)) \leftrightarrow x=v) \wedge ((Girl(w) \wedge Hate(w,y))$
$\leftrightarrow y=w) \wedge Kiss(x,y))$

(16) A context change solution to the Geach's donkey with adjustable constants

Every man who owns a donkey beats it.
$\lambda P \lambda Q$ Every $x(Px, Qx) \lambda u$ Man(u)
$\kappa \Pi^1_{CN} \gamma \Pi_{V2} \gamma \Pi_{DET} \gamma \Pi^2_{CN} \lambda u (\Pi^1_{CN}(u) \triangleright ((\Pi_{DET}(\Pi^2_{CN}))(\lambda w \Pi_{V2}(u,w))))$
$\lambda u \lambda w$ Own$(v,w) \lambda P \lambda Q$ One $y(Py, Qy) \lambda u$ Donk$(u) \lambda v \lambda w$ Beat(v,w)
it$\kappa \Pi_N \kappa \Pi_{V2} \kappa \Pi_{CN} \kappa \Pi_{DET}((\Pi_{DET}(\Pi_{CN}))(\lambda u \Pi_{V2}(u, \Pi_N)))$
⋮

Every $x(Man(x)$ One $y(Donk(y), Own(x,y)), Beat(x, it))$

with $\begin{bmatrix} h(\text{Every } x \ (Px,Qx),A) \equiv \wedge x(h(Px,A) \to h(Qx,A)) \\ h(\text{One } y \ (Py,Qy),A) \equiv Vy(h(Py \wedge y=b,A) \wedge h(Qy,Au\{b\})) \\ h(\alpha \triangleright \beta, A) \equiv h(\alpha,A) \wedge h(\beta,B) \\ h(it,A) \equiv \epsilon x(x \in A) \end{bmatrix}$

$\wedge x((Man(x) \wedge Vy(Donk(y) \wedge y=b \wedge Own(x,y))) \to Beat(x,b))$[3]
$\wedge x \wedge y((Man(x) \wedge Donk(y) \wedge y=b \wedge Own(x,y)) \to Beat(x,b))$
$\wedge x \wedge y((Man(x) \wedge Donk(y) \wedge Own(x,y)) \to Beat(x,y))$

For further information about the two examples (15) and (16) the reader is referred to BALLMER (1978).

As can be seen from formal analyses such as (14) to (16) the technicalities reach a point where they forbid *immediate* insight. For this reason other forms of representing contextual problems of interpretation (and generation) of linguistic expressions should be made available. An ideal situation would be one which allows us first to *visualize* the introduction, transport and resumption of individuals and which can be, secondly, *translated into rigorous formalism*, if needed.

This visualizing technique which will now be introduced we call *bookkeeping*. The individuals (and other entities) referred to in (the use of) linguistic expressions are carefully kept trace of: they are generated (say by the use of names), transferred (say during the further analysis of a text), employed (say by pronouns), eliminated (if no longer needed). The following examples referring back to (5)-(6) will illustrate some aspects of the bookkeeping technique:

(17.1) Referential ambiguity

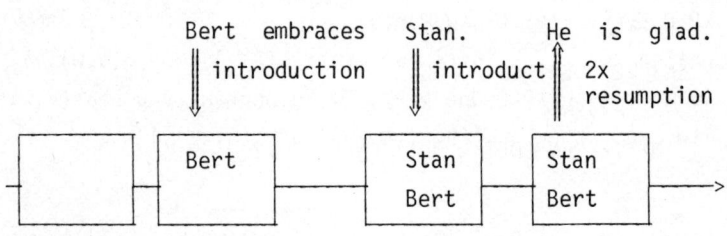

DIS:
*D*iscourse-*I*ndividual-*S*et

(17.2) Referential failure

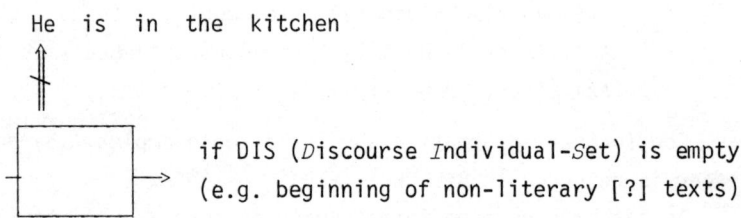

CONTEXT CHANGE

(17.3) Female names do not introduce in male DISs:

Thus referential uniqueness

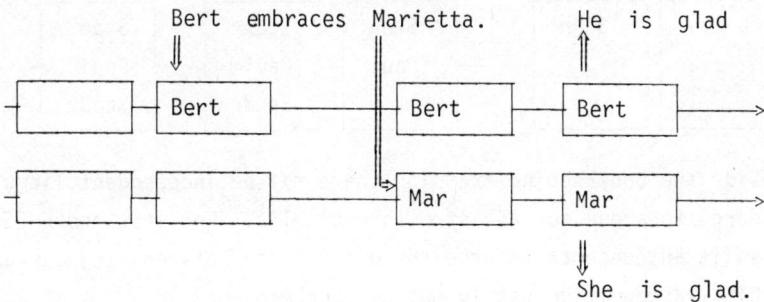

(17.4) Plural-DISs are indispensable!

(17.41)

(17.42)

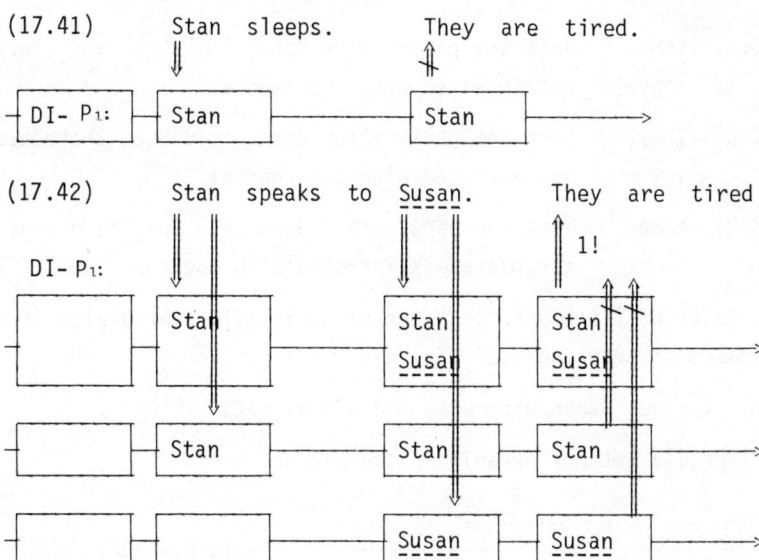

(17.43)

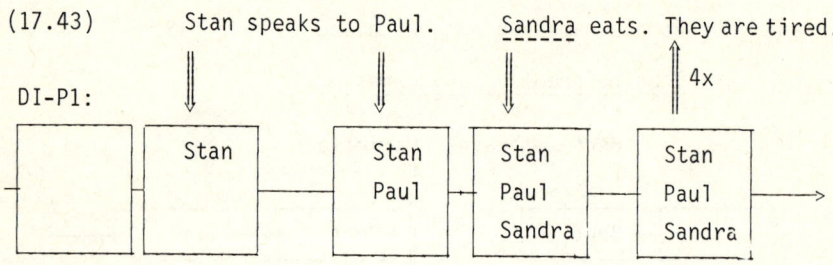

Beside the bookkeeping examples there may be independent linguistic evidence to argue for the structure of DISs. For instance EDES' (1968) split antecedents enforce the distinction between singular and plural DISs, a condition easily met by bookkeeping:

(18) A further argument for plural DISs: split antecedents

(18.1) $\begin{Bmatrix} *He_1 \\ *She_1 \end{Bmatrix}$ left the party after John$_1$ told Sue$_2$ the place was infested with cockroaches.

(18.2) They$_{1,2}$ left the party after John$_1$ told Sue$_2$ the place was infested with cockroaches.

(18.3) *They$_{1,2}$ left the party after John$_1$ and Sue$_2$ said that the place was infested with cockroaches.

The value of the bookkeeping technique is illustrated also in more general cases of reference (cf. 7a-7h):

(19) Various other discourse individual sets

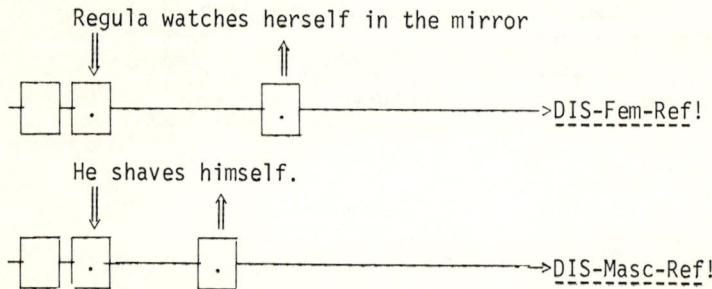

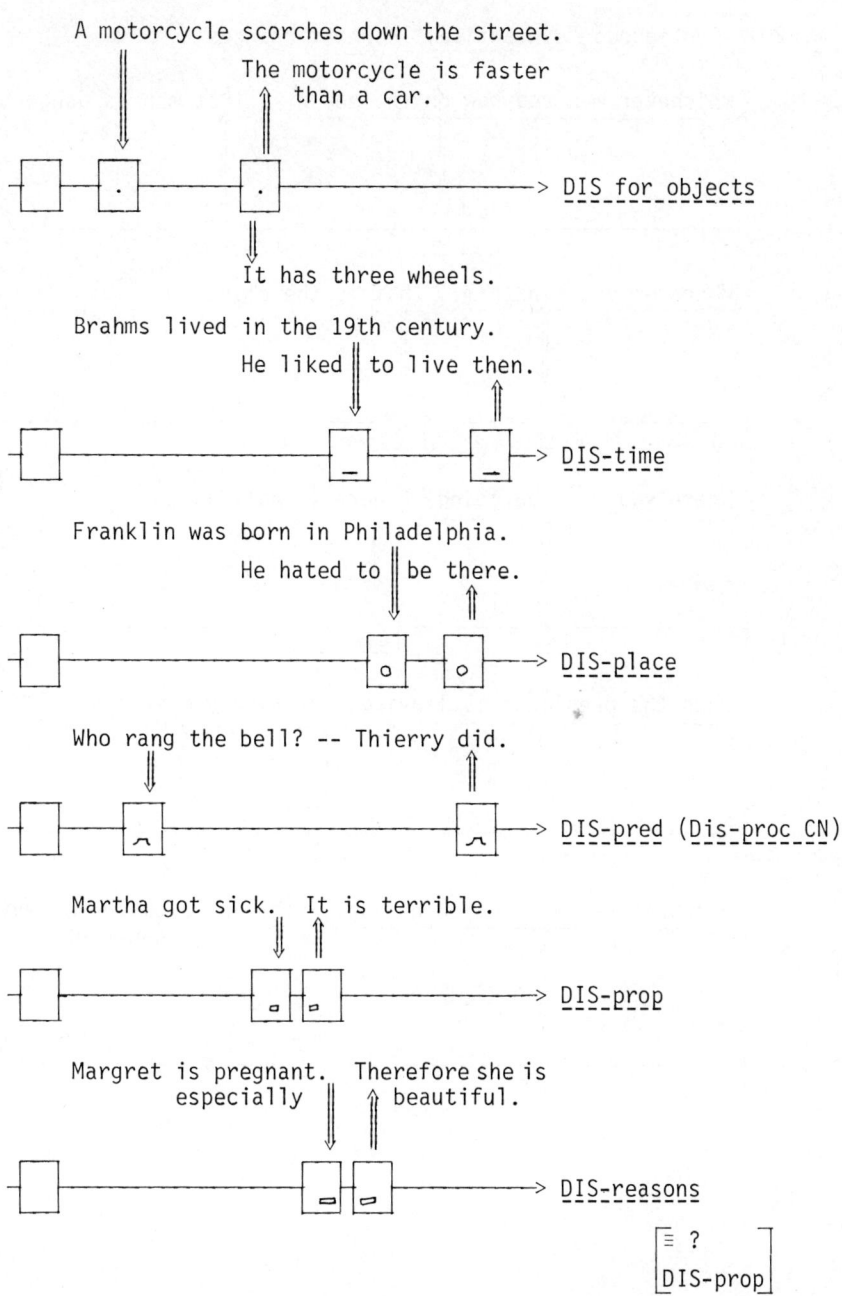

(20) Contiguous "<u>syntactical</u>" context changes

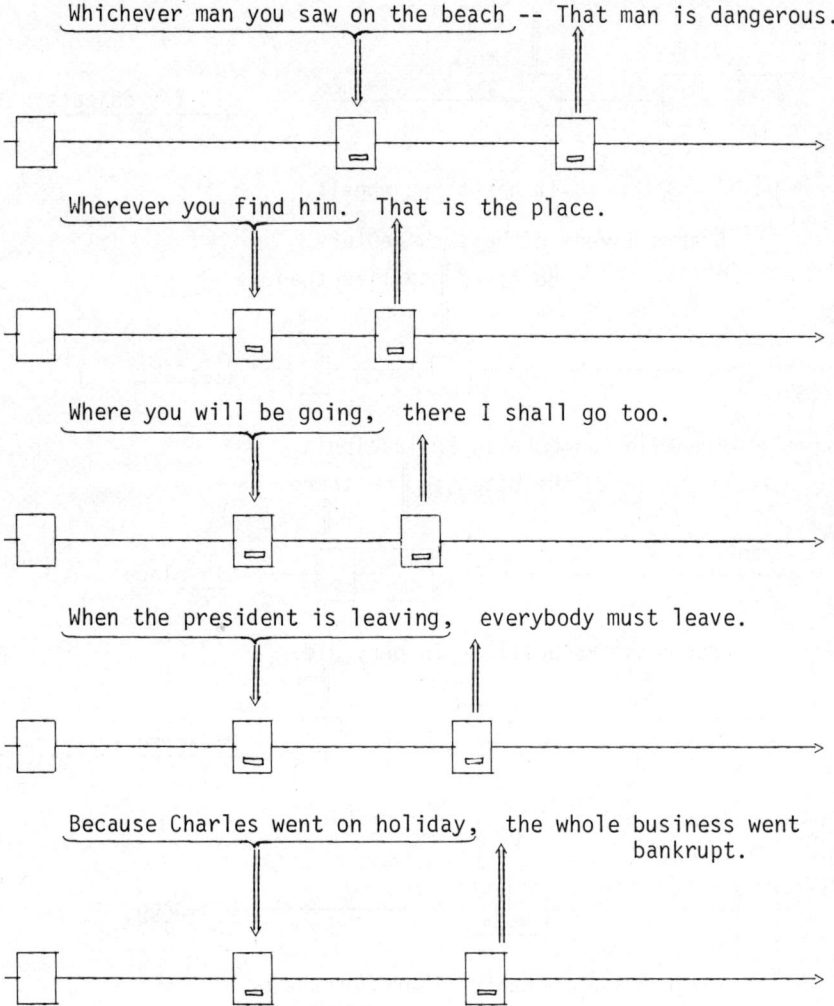

(21) Non-contiguous "syntactical" context change

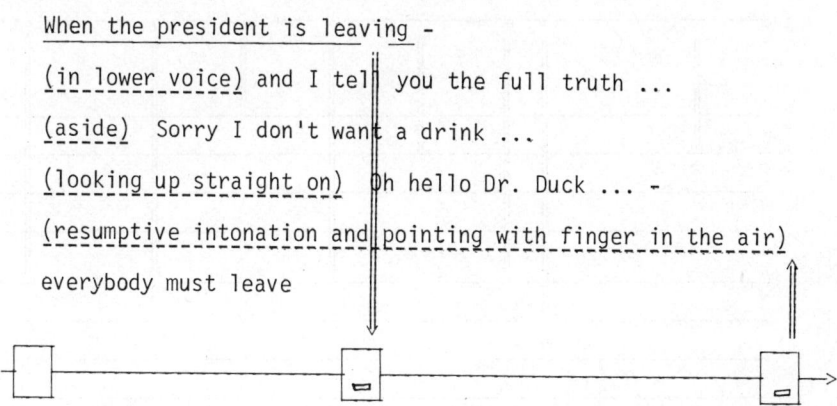

The general setting for bookkeeping is the following: linguistic expressions to be interpreted are analysed from left to right. Single words or morphemes (indicated as — in (22)) operate as linguistic instruments on the contextual aspects or parameters. These contextual aspects are conceived as sets (DISs = Discourse Individual Sets). There are various explicit or implicit changes which may be induced by the interpretation of the simple linguistic expressions (morphemes, words, maybe phrases) on the context parameters. The interpretation may (1) introduce and extroduce individuals, (2) it may transport, shift, foreground, background or cause fading, (3) it may select, take up, substitute, consume individuals. This set of operations of linguistic expressions and dynamic behavior of the context parameters is open. An empiric study of the language in question will tell what operations are basic, what are necessary and what are less relevant. The process of interpretation leads to an evaluation of the expression under consideration (or parts of it): there may be unique, void or ambiguous interpretations. Some basic features of bookkeeping are summarized as follows:

(22) Bookkeeping

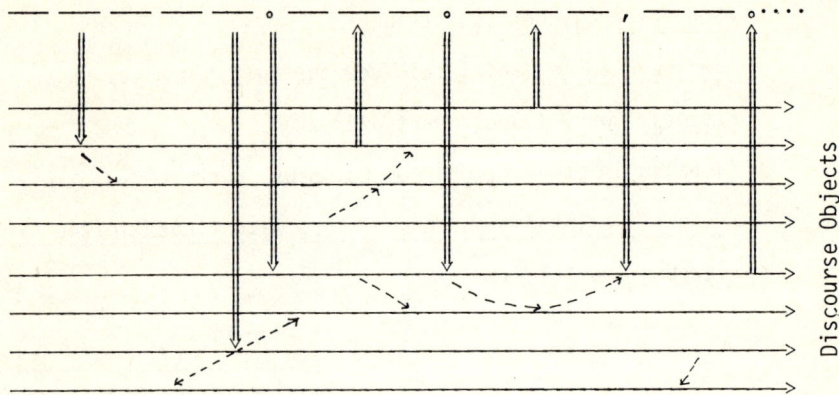

Layout:

1. Linguistic instruments
2. Contextual aspects: Discourse individual sets (≡Discourse objects)

Operations:

1. Introduction, extroduction
2. Transport, shift, fading, ...
3. Resumption (use), consumption, selection

Evaluation

1. Unique interpretation
2. Void interpretation
3. Ambiguous interpretation

Context dynamics --->

1. passive context changes (temporal)
2. spontaneous context changes
3. induced context changes
4. linguistically induced context changes: Operations!

5. *Pragmatic syntax*

5.1 Syntactic dependency

Let us branch back to the dynamical analysis of syntactical phenomena (cf. (10) and (11)). An important case in point is constituents in a sentence:

(23) Representation of <u>syntactical</u> ambiguities

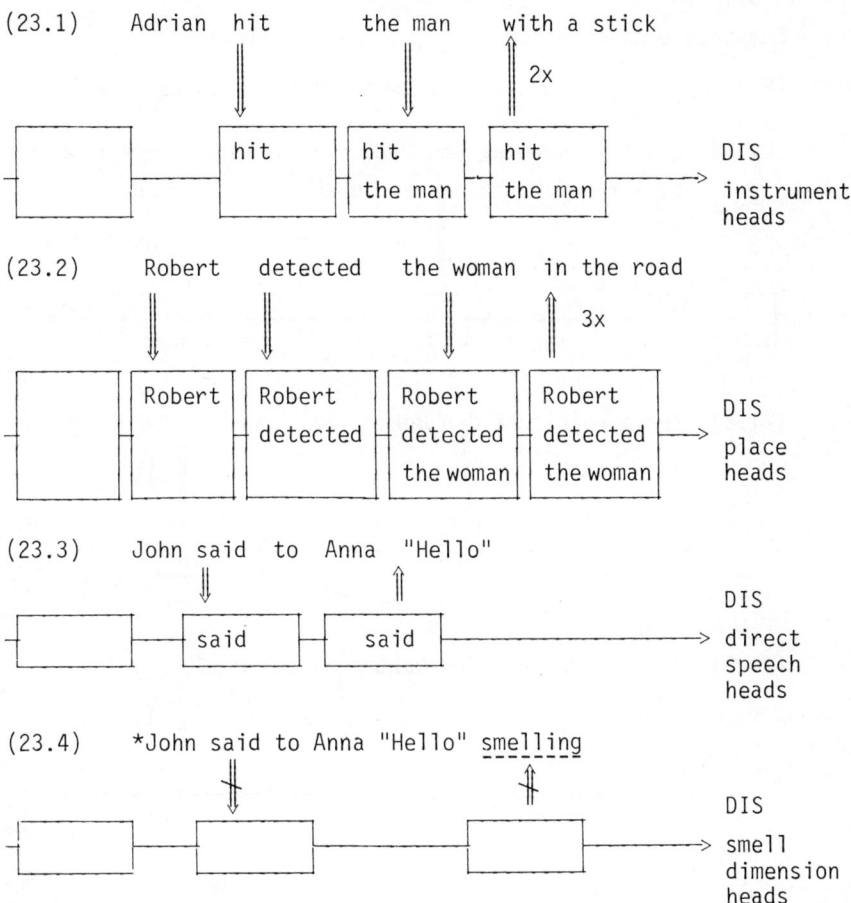

The dependency structure which accounts for the ambiguities and approximate inferences is controlled again by the instrumental character of NL. 'hit' as well as 'the man' introduce a possible referent for the phrase 'with a stick' (cf. 23.1). In (23.2) the case is even more extreme in that 'in the road' is susceptible for even more "coreferences" introduced for it. In (23.3), however, '"Hello"' takes reference only to the verb, whereas in (23.4) no appropriate "coreference" is established.

Comparable cases occur with subordinate clauses.

(24) <u>Syntactical</u> analysis of subordinate clauses

(24.1) Josef versuchte, den Doktor zu sehen ... der krank war
(Josef tried the doctor to see   who sick was)

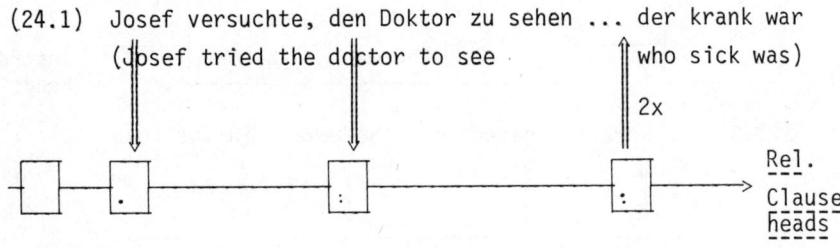

(24.2) Maria versuchte den Doktor zu sehen ... der <u>krank</u> war.

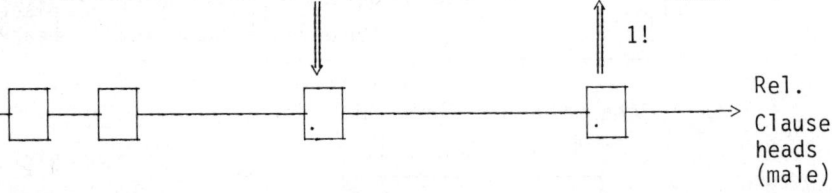

(24.3) Maria versuchte den Doktor zu sehen ... <u>die</u> krank war

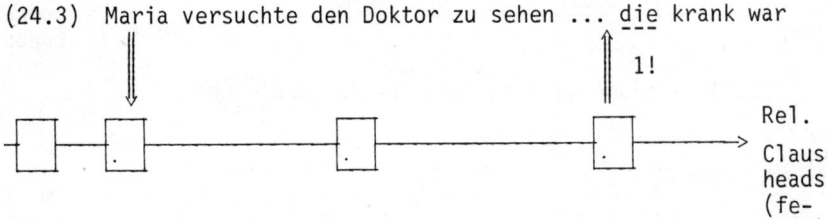

(<u>interaction between gender and syntax [dependency]</u>)

(24.4) Bennie believes Wally that California was gone.

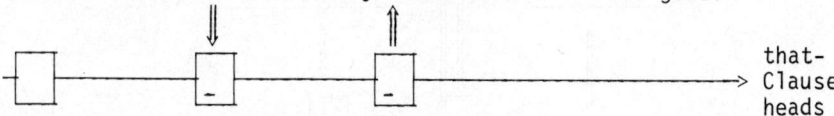

The head of the subordinate clause may be widely separated from the clause itself. The correct *dependency* is again to be established by an adequate instrumental context change mechanism. In the context in which the relative clause is interpreted the possible references (i.e. heads) must be present for immediate reference.

5.2 *Representation of classical cases of ambiguity*

In order to get an idea how we book-keep ambiguities, we shall, as an introductory example, consider classical cases of semantic ambiguity:

(25) Classical cases of ambiguity

(25.11) Everybody loves someone.

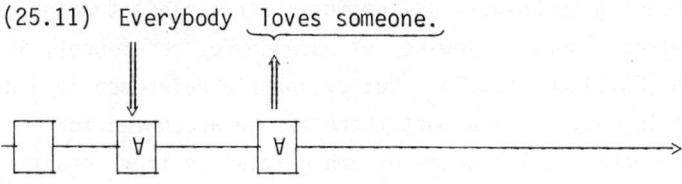

(25.12) Everybody loves someone.

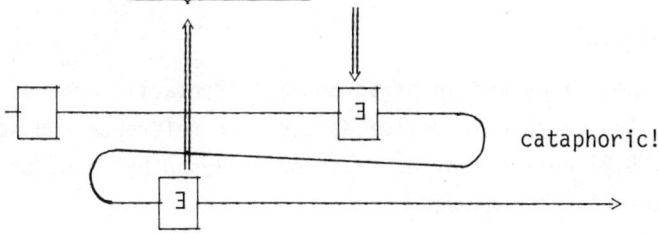

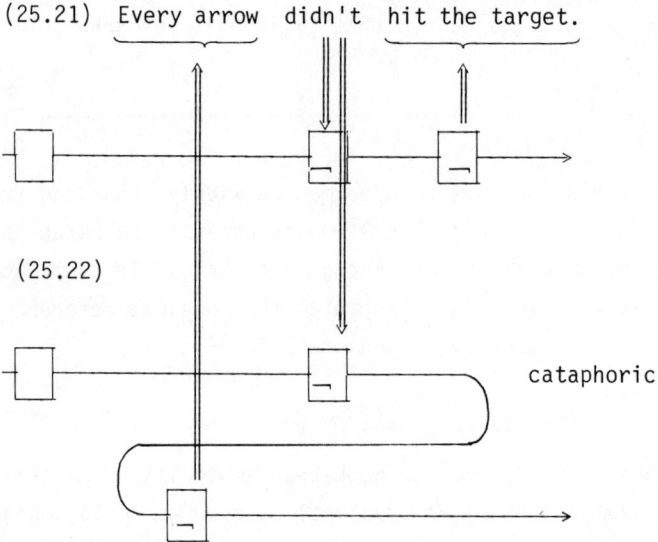

The bookkeeping technique, asking for a strict left to right analysis, requires "loops" allowing for *cataphoric* "reference", as is seen from both (25.1) and (25.2). But cataphoric reference is a device known to exist in many NLs and must therefore be accounted for in any case. Thus the more complex cases of ambiguities be they semantic or syntactic should not pose serious problems.

5.3 *Syntactic ambiguity*

Along the lines discussed in paragraph 5.1 (syntactic dependency) and according to the cataphoric device as used for reference and scope ambiguities (cf. 5.2) entire sentences can be analysed by means of an appropriate bookkeeping technique.

(26) Analysis of one whole single sentence
(Construction of dependency trees)

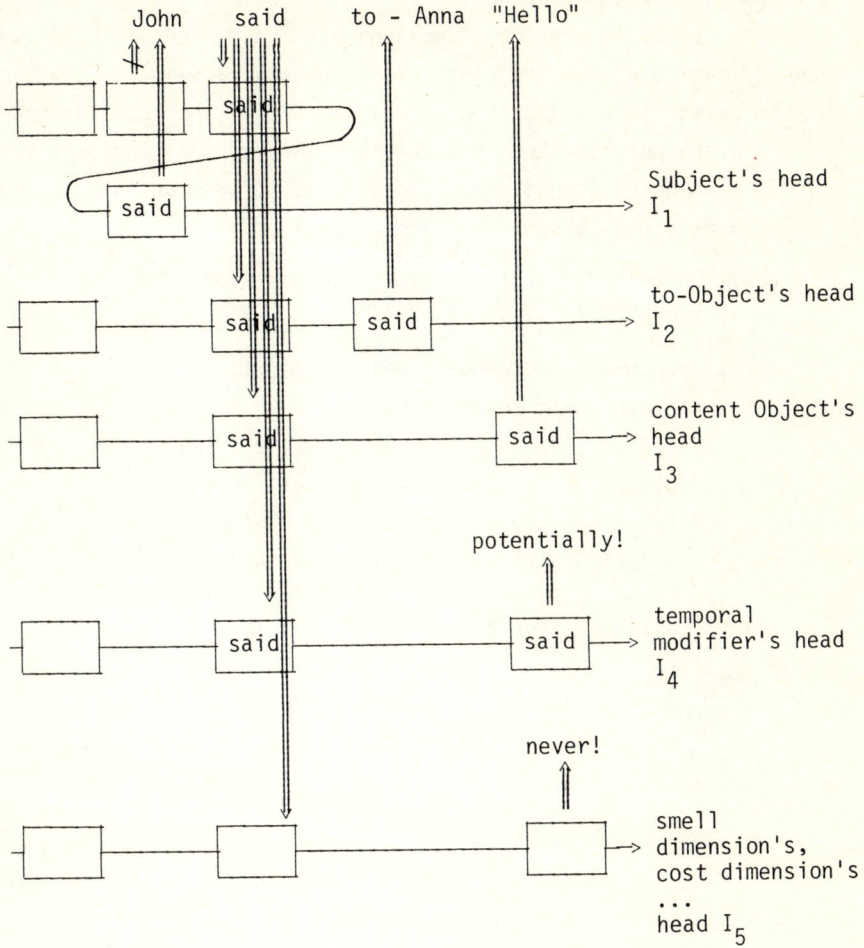

This accounts for

1. obligatory valences (null check at the end of sentence analysis)
2. facultative valences
3. impossible valences

A context change formalism can be employed to build up the appropriate dependency trees. The context $<I_1, I_2, ...>$, abbreviated as $\overline{I}$, is to be interpreted as usual, i.e. as say in (26). It is not explicitly made use of for the construction of the dependency tree (27.3) by means of the local dependencies (27.2), because a simple algebraic algorithm exists to proceed from (27.2) to (27.3): the local dependencies $\begin{smallmatrix}A_1 & A_2\\ \downarrow & \downarrow\\ B_1 & B_2\end{smallmatrix}$ ...,are put together in a coherent manner, the coherence condition being identity of nodes, so as to make up an oriented network (or as a special case: a tree).

(27) Context change formalism to account for
<u>dependency tree construction</u>

(27.1) g(John said to-Anna "Hello", $<I_1,I_2,I_3,I_4,I_5,...>$)≡
g(John·said·to-Anna·"Hello", $\overline{I}$)≡
g(John,$\overline{\xi}$(*John*·said·to-Anna·"Hello", $\overline{I}$)).
g(said,$\overline{\xi}$(John·*said*·to-Anna·"Hello", $\overline{I}$)).
g(to-Anna,$\overline{\xi}$(John·said·*to-Anna*·"Hello", $\overline{I}$)).
g("Hello", $\overline{\xi}$(John·said·to-Anna·*"Hello"*, $\overline{I}$))≡

(27.2) said   R (root)   said   said
        ↓   .   ↓   .   ↓   .   ↓   ≡
        John   said   to-Anna   "Hello"

(27.3)

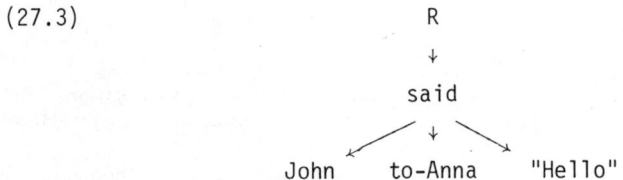

More complex dependency trees can be constructed on the same basis:

(28) A more complex dependency tree construction:
<u>"Cases" (Modification dimensions)</u>

(28.1) John said to-Anna "Hello" who was there
        g(John said to-Anna "Hello" who was there, $\overline{I}$) ≡

(28.2) said   R   said   said   was
       ↓Agent .   ↓Action .   ↓Addressee . ↓Content .   ↓Object .
       John   said   to-Anna   "Hello"   who

       (to-) Anna   was
           ↓Specification .   ↓Place ≡
            (State)
          was   there

(28.3)

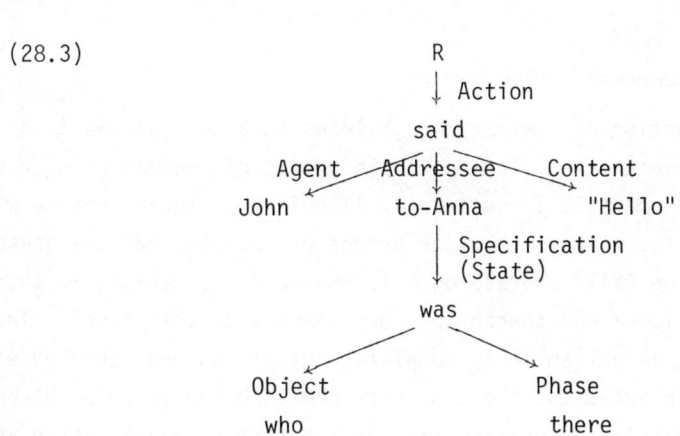

Even dependency trees of ambiguous sentences are constructible: instead of a tree a more general network with loop is obtained, cf. (29.3):

(29) **Ambiguous** dependency trees:

(29.1) Adrian hit the-man with-a-stick
        g(Adrian hit the-man with-a-stick,$\overline{I}$) ≡

(29.2) hit   R   hit   hit   the man
       ↓Agent .   ↓Action .   ↓goal .   ↓instrument/propriety ≡
       Adrian   hit   the-man   with-a-stick

(29.3)

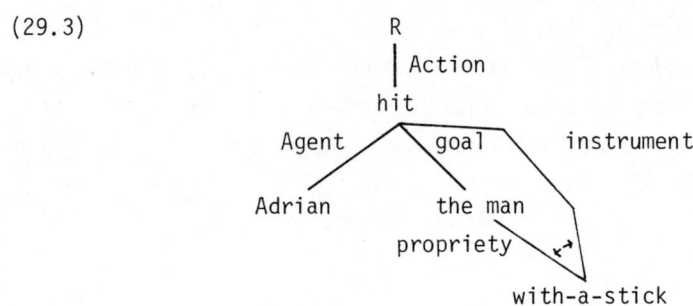

6. *Context change and speech acts*

The conception of *context change* leads in a natural way to a typology of speech acts. The four main groups of *context changes* are: 1. physical, 2. mental, 3. social, 4. linguistic. In accordance with this division there are four major groups of *speech acts*: the speech acts which essentially operate on a 1. physical, 2. mental, 3. social, 4. linguistic level and thereby perform changes on that level. The following list is not entirely complete, but it has been checked with a complete speech act classification (cf. BERLINER GRUPPE 1975; BALLMER/ BRENNENSTUHL 1981): it contains many of the most relevant speech acts.

(30) A typology of speech acts based on context change

1. Physical context changes

a. speech: repeat, reproduce, say, utter;
b. writing: note down, record, register, note down;
c. states of affairs: desire, plan;

2. Mental context changes

a. belief: inform, notify, report, say, tell;
   (knowledge) convert, demonstrate, persuade;
   instruct, lecture, preach, teach;
   ask, quest; answer, tell;
b. expectation: foretell, plan, predict;

c. attention: accentuate, emphasize, stress;
   focus, point to, present;
   scrutinize, investigate;
   admonish, remind, spur on;
   alarm, warn;
   menace, threaten;
d. emotion: curse, lament, moan;
   (ego)
e. emotion: caricature, deride, jeer, jest, joke, make a pun;
   (alter) insinuate, spit at, tease;
   cajole, coax, flatter, seduce;
   beg, implore, pray;
   surprise, shock, astound;
f. obligation: commission, send for;
   delegate, depute, mandate;
   command, direct, enact, order;
   ask, consult, question;
   agree to, commit, guarantee, warn
g. uncertainty: check, guess, test;
   clarify, elucidate;
   call into question, doubt, suspect;
h. memory: document, store;
   recall;
   remind;
i. conceptual: arrange, classify, group, mark, list, order,
   parallelize, rubrify, segment, structure;

3. Social state changes

a. institutional: advance, promote;
   expel, degrade, subordinate, suspend;
   charge, commission;
   swear;

aa. law: accuse, denounce, inculpate;
arrest, apprehend, imprison;
defend, plead for;
condemn, convict, sentence;
acquit, excuse, exculpate;
outlaw, punish;
ab. state: appoint to an office, crown, delegate, depute, elect;
exile, impeach;
ac. economy: devaluate;
sell, buy, contract;
ad. bureaucracy: countersign, sign;
factuate;
ae. church: baptize, confirm, marry;
bless, condemn, maledict;
banish, excommunicate;
af. moral: censor, disallow, filter, prohibit, screen;
b. public individual:
ba. social values: appreciate, depreciate;
attest, certify;
acknowledge, thank;
celebrate, glorify, praise;
devalue, discriminate, ignore;
bb. social structure: call together, convoke, organize;
bc. social position: argue, attack, fight, oppose;
bd. social contracts: guarantee, insure, warrant;
antedate, book, date, misdate, limit;
bc. social publicity: advertize, cry out, declare, maintain, pronounce, publish;
c. existence of institution: annul, suspend;
constitute, found, establish;

4. <u>Linguistic context changes</u>
a. expressions: verbalize;
   encipher, decipher, paraphrase, summarize, translate;
b. meaning: define, interpret, redefine;
c. reference: call, dub, name, point to;
d. discourse intensity/phase: begin, preface, start;
   converse;
   discontinue, end, finish;
e. turn: break in, call on, intervene, howl down;
   begin to speak;
   conclude;
f. theme: elaborate, mention, raise, touch upon;

7. *The logic of context change*

The formal apparatus dealing with questions of context change is *context change logic*. A rather complete account of its definition and linguistic application can be found in BALLMER (1978), *Logical grammar*. In order to relate context change logic to more commonly known logics the following synopsis (31) is given. (31.1) puts context change logic in relation to propositional logic, predicate logic etc. according to its expressive power. Context change logic is, because of its ability to express arbitrarily complex quantifier prefices, at least as powerful as branched quantifier logic. (31.2) shows some of the operators used in context change logic and (31.3) gives an idea of the semantic interpretation.

(31) Logic of context change

(31.1) - Propositional logic
- Predicate logic 1. Order/higher order.
- Indexical logic
- Intensional logic

- Branched quantifier logic
- Context change logic

(31.2) <u>Syntax</u>

special operator expressions:
↓, Я, ∧, ∀, ⇒ ...

(31.3) <u>Semantics</u>:

$h(\downarrow\phi, i) \equiv h(\phi, \xi(\downarrow\phi, i))$
$h(\alpha \wedge \beta, i) \equiv h(\alpha, i) \wedge h(\beta, \xi(\alpha, i))$
or more generally:
$h(\alpha \wedge \beta, i) \equiv h(\alpha, \sigma(\alpha, \beta, i)) \wedge h(\beta, \tau(\alpha, \beta, i))$
($\equiv$ modular logic)

(31.4) Major <u>applications</u> of the logic of context change:

Reference
Syntax
Speech acts
⋮

A summary of the topics of context change concludes this paragraph. This summary is intended to provide an overview over the various linguistic and semiotic possibilities of making use of the notions dealt with in this paper and elsewhere:

(32) Topics of context change

(32.1) <u>Grammatical topics</u>

Phonetic/Phonologic level (e.g. vowel harmony)
Morphologic level (e.g. agreement)
Word-level, Thesaurus level
Phrase-level esp. Nounphrase level
Adverbial phrase level

>   Sentence level
>   Text level
>   Dialogue level
>
> (32.2) <u>Semiotic topics</u>
>
>   Semiotics (general, bio-social)
>   Psychosemiotics
>   Grammatical
>   Categories
>   Grammatical processes
>   Logical analysis
>   Lexicologic, Lexicographic
>
> (32.3) <u>Contextual topics</u>
>
>   Context
>   Context-bookkeeping
>   "Pragmatic": Focus control, Goal dynamics
>
> (32.4) <u>Prorhematic topics</u>:
>
>   Kinematics, Dynamics
>   Action/Non-action
>   Speech act
>   Speech act sequences
>   Language learning
>   Language teaching
>   Language use/applications

8. *Conclusion*

These considerations may suffice to explain what I mean by context change and mean (and meant: cf. BALLMER 1972) by *introduction, control* and *use* of discourse worlds, or more generally *discourse parameters*. During speaking, linguistically active people construct by introducing individuals, objects, propositions situations of all kinds; and by relating them they build up a complex epistemic structure, which we call a discourse world. This discourse world may have a value *in its own*, or it may induce the agents to draw further *conclusions* (thought) and to realize certain *wishes*, *wants* and *plans* (action).

This *dynamic* process begins on the level of attention and perception, goes on to the level of grasping and reference, to the sentential level, reaches then the level of single speech acts and finally of speech act sequences both in monologue and dialogue.

This is what can be said here in favor of the instrumental character of NL which puts forward the intrinsically *dynamic*, i.e. kinematic *and* interactive, nature of linguistic *action* with its very basic task to *change contexts* in an extremely orderly manner by bookkeeping mechanisms running off in the context components: a thoroughly pragmatic view of language!

If I may add a last remark: People may think that this interactive language model is based on the precision of Swiss watches and the bookkeeping tradition of Swiss banks: I fear they may be perfectly right!

FOOTNOTES:

1. The difference between kinematics and dynamics is the following: *kinematics* deals with the temporal development of systems which do not interact and upon which no external influence exists, *dynamics* deals with the temporal development of systems which do interact and may stand in contact with the outside.

2. To consider an alien rather than a child or an adult foreigner has the advantage that the initial conditions of the learning situation have to be stated more completely and more explicitly, *much less* can be tacitly assumed.

In order to avoid problems which are irrelevant for the present discussion assume that the external appearance of the alien is roughly indistinguishable from human beings. We shall assume that he is initially charitable and reasonably cooperative. He is moreover assumed to stem from a technological culture.

The alien will thus appear among humans and try to be one of them.

3. b is an adjustable constant, cf. BALLMER (1978). A reformulation of adjustable constants in the traditional terms of classical logic can be formulated by "vector predicates".

SEMANTIC CONSTRAINTS ON RELEVANCE*

Diane Brockway

1. It is clear that, in discourse, utterances are interpreted as relating to preceding remarks, or, more generally, to certain propositions which are already believed. Unless he interprets it in conjunction with what he already knows or believes, a hearer will not be able to deduce anything from an utterance other than its logical entailments. In particular, he will not be able to judge whether it is relevant.

However, it seems that there are various ways in which an utterance may be related to background beliefs, and that its interpretation may vary accordingly. Sometimes hearers must work out the nature of the relation for themselves. However, often it is made explicit. Consider (2a-f) as said in response to (1), and (4a-c) as said in response to (3).[1]

(1) I'm going to vote for Fred Dagg in the next election.
(2) (a) He'll do the most for the farmers.
 (b) After all, he'll do the most for the farmers.
 (c) Actually, he'll do the most for the farmers.
 (d) Now, he'll do the most for the farmers.
 (e) Anyway, he'll do the most for the farmers.
 (f) Well, he'll do the most for the farmers.
(3) Fred Dagg will be the best man for the job.
(4) (a) He's a member of the Young Farmers Club.
 (b) After all, he's a member of the Young Farmers Club.

(c) Still, he's a member of the Young Farmers Club.

Among the various possible interpretations of (2a) are those suggested by (2b-f), and among the possible interpretations of (4a) are those suggested by (4b-c). It seems that there is something about each of (2b-f) and (4b-c) which instructs the hearer to interpret (2a) and (4a) in a certain way, or which puts a constraint on the possible interpretations of (2a) and (4a).

The interpretations suggested by (2a-f) and (4b-c) might be described in the following informal, intuitive way: (2b) suggests that the belief that Fred Dagg will do the most for the farmers, taken in conjunction with certain other beliefs, commits the speaker to the belief that he should vote for Fred Dagg in the next election; (2c) suggests that the possibility of Fred Dagg being voted for in the next election had been regarded as unlikely, and that the claim that he will do the most for the farmers affects this possibility; (2d) suggests that "Fred Dagg will do the most for the farmers" is being suggested as an answer to a question which has been discussed some time previously, and perhaps that this answer has nothing to do with the first speaker's proposal to vote for him in the next election; (2e) suggests that the speaker believes that there could be some objection to voting for Fred Dagg in the next election, but that this is unimportant or irrelevant in view of the fact that he will do the most for the farmers; (2f) suggests that the fact that Fred Dagg will do the most for the farmers is the only reason one could have for voting for him in the next election, and furthermore, that this is not the best reason one could have; (4b) suggests that Fred Dagg's being a member of the Young Farmers Club is a reason for his being the best man for the job; (4c) suggests that while there may be some reason for Fred Dagg being the best man for the job, his being a member of the Young Farmers Club is a reason for his not being the best man for the job.

Ultimately, some framework must be provided within which more explicit descriptions can be given. However, even on this intuitive and approximate level, a number of observations can be made.

It is obvious that the differences between (2b-f) and (4b-c) are due to properties of the words in (5):

(5) after all, actually, anyway, now, still, well

While (2a) and (4a) have a considerable range of possible interpretations, including those in (2b-f) and (4b-c), the addition to these sentences of one of the words in (5) immediately determines which particular interpretation is intended. It seems, then, that these words are used to narrow down the range of possible interpretations of the utterances to which they are prefaced.

The question is, in which component of the theory of utterance interpretation should the properties which contribute to this role be described - pragmatics or semantics? It might seem that since they determine how utterances are related to beliefs about the world they must belong to pragmatics. Alternatively, it might be claimed that they belong to semantics, since semantics deals with the arbitrary contributions of words to utterance interpretation.

It seems that the only way of accounting for the differences between (2b-f) and (4b-c) within a purely pragmatic framework would be to treat the words in (5) as words governed by context sensitive transderivational constraints in the sense of Gazdar and Klein (1977). Gazdar and Klein's account of context sensitive transderivational constraints is intended as a formal explication of the notions *pragmatic property of a word* (cf. Karttunen and Peters 1975), and *relative well-formedness* (cf. G. Lakoff 1971a and 1972). Certain words, (for example, *but, too, please*, and *therefore*) are regarded as having no (semantic) meaning, but only a 'use', described by a contextually conditioned rule. Such rules have the form, "If the context has property P, then use @." (where P is a property and @ a lexical item). The well-formedness of a sentence containing such a lexical item will depend on whether or not it is uttered in a context which has the required property.

It is not difficult to see that such rules could be formulated for any of the words in (5). Thus any criticism of the claim that these words should be treated in this way would have to be directed at the coherence of the notion of a transderivational constraint itself.

The main claim underlying the notion of a context sensitive transderivational constraint is that the well-formedness of utterances can depend on the context. Gazdar and Klein do not give an explicit definition of pragmatics. However, it is clear that they consider the definition of contextual conditions on well-formedness to be part of pragmatics, and throughout their account the term 'pragmatic' is used as if it were synonymous with 'contextual'. But, as Gazdar and Klein would agree, pragmatics cannot be defined simply as the theory of context dependent aspects of utterance interpretation. The proposals of this paper are made within a framework in which pragmatic explanations are distinguished from semantic explanations not by the fact that they invoke the notion of context dependence, but by the fact that they invoke general rules or principles which apply to all utterances irrespective of their form and content.[2] This view of the semantics-pragmatics distinction should be contrasted with that expressed, for example, in Gazdar (1979a). According to this view, semantics is a theory of the truth conditional aspects of utterance interpretation, and pragmatics is a theory of all the non-truth conditional aspects. The difference between these two approaches lies in the treatment of words whose meanings cannot be defined truth conditionally. According to the approach adopted here, the meanings of these words are defined in semantics since they are conventional properties. However, according to the other approach, they are defined in pragmatics - in terms of context sensitive transderivational constraints - since they are non-truth conditional properties. Thus the criticism of the notion of a context sensitive transderivational constraint can be understood as implying a preference for a non-truth conditional semantics over a pragmatics containing non-universal, conventional rules.

The claim that pragmatics cannot be defined as a theory of context dependent interpretation does not, of course, mean that pragmatics has nothing to do with context dependence at all. However, Grice (1975) has shown that the interpretation of utterances in context must be explained in terms of non-conventional, conversational principles which require that certain relations hold between utterances and contexts. What follows from the fact that a particular utterance has been made in accordance with such a principle depends on what propositions it conveys and what is included in the context. But the essential point is that these are *universal* principles: hearers interpret every utterance on the basis of the assumption that it has been made in accordance with them. Context sensitive transderivational constraints, on the other hand, are not universal: they are contextual constraints on the use of individual lexical items, and therefore apply only to utterances containing those items. Thus, to include both transderivational constraints and conversational principles in a pragmatic theory would be to propose two logically distinct types of pragmatic rule.

Clearly, the recognition of context sensitive transderivational constraints is inconsistent with the view that pragmatics should be based only on universal conversational principles. Moreover, the claim that pragmatics should contain transderivational constraints as well as universal conversational principles would be inconsistent with the assumption that pragmatics is homogeneous. The original point of drawing a distinction between semantics and pragmatics was to capture the non-homogeneity of utterance interpretation by distinguishing two complementary homogeneous levels of explanation. If this distinction is to be maintained, then either the notion of a context sensitive transderivational constraint must be described in some other new level of the theory, or we must dispense with it altogether, and provide some semantic account of the facts which it was introduced to explain.[3]

While it cannot be taken for granted that the theory of utterance interpretation is exhausted by semantics and pragmatics, the strategy of consigning to some other new level of explanation facts which apparently cannot be explained at either of these established levels requires considerable justification. This is especially true if this strategy is adopted with the aim of salvaging a particular theory (in this case, a particular theory of semantics) which is already threatened by counter-examples.

However the differences between (2b-f) and (4b-c) are formulated, it seems clear that they could not be regarded as differences of truth conditional interpretation - at least not in the 'standard' sense. None of the words in (5) seems to affect the truth value of the sentences in which it appears. It is unlikely, for example, that the utterance of a sentence prefaced by *after all* would be regarded as false simply because it could not be interpreted as expressing a premise in an argument which had the proposition expressed by the preceding utterance as its conclusion, or that the utterance of a sentence prefaced by *anyway* would be regarded as false just because the speaker believed neither that whatever was expressed in the previous utterance was unimportant nor that there were background assumptions that were unimportant or irrelevant. However, according to the view adopted here, these differences are semantic differences since they are due to conventional properties of words. Clearly, this claim must be supported by specific proposals about an alternative theory of semantics.[4] However, the main purpose of this paper is not so much to propose such an alternative, but to state a condition which must be satisfied by any semantic theory - truth conditional or not - in which the meanings of the words in (5) are described.

I began by suggesting that the interpretation of an utterance may depend on how it is related to the hearer's background beliefs, and that this relation may either be implicit or indicated explicitly. (2b-f) and (4b-c) were given as examples of utterances in which these utterance-background relations are indicated by the use of particular lexical items. I propose now that these relations should be understood in terms of the pragmatic notion of types of relevance. Thus (2b-f) and (4b-c) should be regarded as constraining the possible pragmatic interpretations of (2a) and (4a) respectively by indicating exactly how they are relevant.

If the differences between (2b-f) and (4b-c) are due to the properties of the words in (5), and if these properties are to be described in semantics, then the differences between (2b-f) and (4b-c) must be regarded as semantically determined. But I have just argued that these differences affect pragmatic interpretation too. If this is right, then clearly it must be accepted that there are aspects of pragmatic interpretation which are semantically determinable, or that certain words impose semantic constraints on pragmatic interpretations.

The idea that pragmatics crucially involves judgements of relevance is suggested by the Gicean view of pragmatics as a theory of conversation. Grice's theory (Grice 1975) was intended to explain how speakers may communicate more by their utterances than what they actually say, or how speakers may convey information which is not semantically specified. Since the phenomena for which pragmatic explanations are proposed are characteristically those which would constitute counter-examples to standard theories of semantics, it seems that Grice's theory might provide the basis for a full-scale theory of pragmatics which could accommodate all semantically troublesome examples.

A major objection to Grice's theory is that, as it stands, it is too inexplicit and informal to provide the basis for an adequate pragmatic theory. However, the search for more specific formulations has brought to light a much more serious objection: not all Grice's maxims are necessary for an account of utterance interpretation. Wilson and Sperber (1978) have argued that they can in fact be reduced to a single principle of relevance. They show that once the notion of relevance is properly defined, it can be incorporated in an axiom which subsumes Grice's maxims of relation, quantity, quality and manner, and thus provides a criterion for distinguishing semantic and pragmatic phenomena. In other words, according to this view, pragmatics is not merely concerned with judgements of relevance: it is *defined* as a theory of relevance.

I have claimed above that if there are words which indicate types of relevance, this means that there are semantic constraints on pragmatic interpretation. It might seem that this claim is compatible with either the standard Gricean view of pragmatics or the theory proposed by Wilson and Sperber. However, Wilson and Sperber's theory provides much stronger support for the claim, since it includes specific proposals about the nature of relevance, and a more explicit criterion for distinguishing semantic aspects of utterance interpretation from pragmatic aspects. I shall, therefore, base my proposals on Wilson and Sperber's account of relevance which I summarize below.

However, my claim is not just that there are words which indicate that the utterances that contain them are relevant; it is that there are words which impose constraints on the *way* in which their associated utterances are relevant. Grice's maxim of relation and Wilson and Sperber's axiom of relevance require only that utterances be relevant, not that they have any particular type of relevance. Can the notion of types of relevance be defined within a pragmatic theory?

It might seem, at first, that the words in (5) do simply indicate relevance. Consider examples (6) and (7).

(6) (a) A. I didn't get accepted at Oxford.
   B. Don't worry. Anyway, you always wanted to be a lumberjack.

(b) A. I didn't get accepted at Oxford.
 ? B. Don't worry. Anyway, Fred Dagg wears gumboots.

(7) (a) You must be able to say what *anyway* means: after all, you use it all the time.

 ? (b) You must be able to say what *anyway* means: after all, Daisy has drunk all the brandy.

It seems that we could explain the oddity of the (b) examples by saying that the function of *anyway* and *after all* is to indicate explicitly that their associated utterances are relevant, and that something approaching an inconsistency arises when they are associated with something that is difficult to interpret as relevant.[5]

The fact that relevance is a pragmatic property of utterances does not mean that it cannot be indicated explicitly by the use of some word or phrase. However, the fact that the (b) examples are odd even when they are not prefaced by *anyway* and *after all* suggests that the problem here has nothing to do with the meanings of these words, but rather with the fact that a maxim of conversation has been violated.

Indeed, we already have evidence that these words cannot simply indicate relevance. (2b-f) and (4b-c) all seem to be relevant; however, as we have seen, each of these utterances must be interpreted differently, and these differences are attributable to the meanings of the words in (5).

Moreover, it seems that we can construct examples of utterances which are relevant and acceptable, but which when prefaced by words from (5) become relevant but unacceptable. The (a) examples in the following triples include responses which might easily be interpreted as relevant and acceptable. The responses in the (b) examples would generally be interpreted as relevant but unacceptable. The (c) examples contain acceptable uses of *still, anyway, well, after all,* and *now*.[6]

(8) (a) A. Would Fred Dagg be the best man for the job?
        B. He's a member of the Young Farmers Club.
    (b) A. Would Fred Dagg be the best man for the job?
  ?   B. Still, he's a member of the Young Farmers Club.
    (c) A. Fred Dagg would be the best man for the job.
        B. Still, he's a member of the Young Farmers Club.

(9) (a) A. Have you returned the library books?
        B. I returned them on Friday.
    (b) A. Have you returned the library books?
  ?   B. Anyway, I returned them on Friday.
    (c) A. I forgot to return the library books.
        B. Don't worry. Anyway, they're not due until next week.

(10) (a) A. Donald escorted Daisy to the ball.
        B. She wore a yellow dress.
    (b) A. Donald escorted Daisy to the ball.
  ?   B. Well, she wore a yellow dress.
    (c) A. Donald escorted Daisy to the ball.
        B. Well, he went with her.

(11) (a) Any mathematician should be able to add up the bill.

Dick is a mathematician.
Therefore he should be able to add up the bill.

(b) Any mathematician should be able to add up the bill.
Dick is a mathematician.
? After all, he should be able to add up the bill.

(c) Dick should be able to add up the bill; after all he is a mathematician.

(12) (a) A. Who is Fred Dagg?
B. Fred Dagg is the man who will do the most for the farmers.

(b) A. Who is Fred Dagg?
? B. Now, Fred Dagg is the man who will do the most for the farmers.

(c) A. I'm going to vote for Fred Dagg in the next election.
B. Now, he's the man who will do the most for the farmers.

Since the (a) and the (b) responses differ only in that the latter contain words from (5) while the former do not, it seems that the oddity of the (b) responses must have at least something to do with the meanings of the words in (5). Furthermore, since the (a) responses might very easily be interpreted as relevant, the oddities cannot be explained in terms of the claim that the words in (5) are merely indicators of relevance.

However, I do not want to say that the oddity of the (b) examples has nothing to do with relevance at all. These examples can be accounted for in terms of the claim that there are words whose function is to indicate types of relevance. The problem in (8b-12b) is that the words with which the responses are prefaced indicate a type of relevance which is difficult to interpret as satisfied given the properties of the prefaced utterance. Of course, if the function of the words in (5) is to indicate that their associated utterances have a particular type of relevance, then, clearly, these words cannot be used in association with utterances which are not relevant at all. In this sense, but only in this sense, these words might be said to indicate relevance alone.

If an account along these lines is correct, then an adequate pragmatic theory must include not only a definition of relevance, but also definitions of different types of relevance. In the next section I show that types of relevance can be defined in terms of constraints on contexts, and that these constraints can be defined quite straightforwardly within the pragmatic framework proposed by Wilson and Sperber.

2. Utterances are relevant or irrelevant only in context. I cannot, for example, expect you to judge whether (13) is relevant without specifying the context in which it is uttered.

(13) Fred Dagg is a member of the Young Farmers Club.

Clearly, then, the definition of relevance must start from a definition of context.

Although linguists and philosophers have attached considerable importance to the fact that utterances are produced and interpreted in contexts, there have been relatively few attempts to define context explicitly. Contexts are generally introduced in terms of their various roles in interpretation, or in terms of features which are considered relevant to those various roles, or in terms of other notions which are themselves vague and imprecise. Thus a context is sometimes seen as whatever is necessary for the determination of illocutionary force, sometimes as a set of features, sometimes as a situation, sometimes as the physical environment, sometimes as the cultural or social environment, and sometimes as the sorrounding text or discourse. In the absence of central definition, a context can, it seems, be almost anything. But clearly, we do need some criterion for saying which aspects of utterance interpretation are context dependent and which are not.

It is clear that contexts play a role in the interpretation of utterances. But if contexts play such a role, then they must be defined as being available to hearers in that role. It is difficult to see how features or contextual indices might be regarded as being available to hearers. What about situations, environments and the preceding discourse? It is evident that it is not the situations, environment, or preceding discourse themselves which are available to hearers, but rather beliefs or knowledge about them. This suggests that a context should be defined as a set of beliefs, or, more accurately, as the set of beliefs held by the person from whose point of view an utterance is being described. Theories of knowledge and belief are standardly based on the premise that the objects of our beliefs are propositions. Thus we might define a context as a set of propositions believed by a given speaker or hearer.

Now, it seems unlikely that a hearer will actually use his entire belief set in the interpretation of an utterance. We might, then, distinguish between a hearer's entire belief set or available context, and the subset of beliefs which is used by that hearer in the interpretation of a given utterance. The proposals of this paper are based on a theory in which the subset of beliefs used by a hearer in the interpretation of an utterance is defined as that subset which is required for the interpretation of that utterance as relevant. Here, however, let us simply note that to say that a certain aspect of utterance interpretation is context dependent is to say that a hearer must use some subset of his available belief set in its evaluation.

The claim that a context should be defined in relation to the person from whose point of view an utterance is being described does not entail that a context does not include beliefs that are shared by both speaker and hearer. Conversely, the fact that a belief held by one person is also held by another does not make it any the less *his* belief. However, the role of a shared stock of beliefs in conversation is not captured by saying simply that a hearer's belief set may include beliefs held by the speaker (and *vice versa*). It seems that we must define the subset of beliefs actually used in utterance interpretation as consisting of beliefs shared by speaker and hearer. It is clearly essential for a theory of context dependent interpretation to explain how one speaker's beliefs become available to another for the interpretation of utterances. Moreover, it must explain how a speaker represents the knowledge that a given belief is shared by another. However, it is not the characterization of a shared stock of beliefs which is crucial for the explanation of the phenomena described in the first section of this paper, but the definition of the principle according to which speakers and hearers use their shared beliefs in the production and interpretation of utterances. Here, then, I simply suggest that the subset of beliefs related to an utterance by this principle must consist of beliefs shared by speaker and hearer, but that this subset is essentially the subset of beliefs held by the person from whose point of view the utterance is being described since it is he who must recognize that these beliefs are shared.

It is important to note that taken with the commonly held view that utterances convey propositions and a general requirement that belief sets be consistent, this definition implies that there is no need to distinguish between a background of previous utterances, on the one hand, and a background of knowledge and beliefs, on the other. Thus when talking of relevance, there is no need to distinguish between an utterance being relevant to a previous utterance and an utterance being relevant to the context: the propositions conveyed by the previous utterance are, by definition, part of the context. Belief sets may be enlarged (or otherwise modified) non-linguistically, but clearly, the fact that speakers use language to increase or modify each other's beliefs has considerable significance in a theory of contexts. In order to understand how utterances contribute to the enlargement of belief sets let us consider how hearers interpret utterances as informative.

It is easy to see that informativeness is context dependent. Very intuitively, and rather trivially, an utterance is informative if it expresses more information than the hearer already knows. Now, an utterance may be regarded as expressing more information than the hearer knows if it expresses propositions not included in his belief set. However, while the propositions expressed by an utterance may not themselves be included in a hearer's belief set, it is possible that they may be deducible from it, and clearly, an utterance which expresses propositions deducible from a hearer's belief set is not informative. This suggests the following definition:

(14) An utterance is informative relative to a belief set, C, if it expresses a proposition not deducible from C.

Equivalently, an utterance is informative relative to C if and only if the set of logical consequences of C together with the propositions expressed by the utterance properly includes the set of logical consequences of C.

According to this definition, (13) would be informative relative to the belief set given in (15).

(15) $C = \{c_1, c_2, c_3\}$

c_1 *Fred Dagg wears gumboots.*
c_2 *Fred Dagg wears a black singlet.*
c_3 *Donald is going to vote for Fred Dagg in the next election.*

(13) expresses the proposition *Fred Dagg is a member of the Young Farmers Club*, which taken together with C entails c_1 *and* c_2 *and* c_3 *and Fred Dagg is a member of the Young Farmers Club*, which clearly is not deducible from C alone.

It might be thought that the definition (14) captures the idea of an utterance enlarging a hearer's belief set. However, a belief set is clearly not enlarged in any useful sense if the new logical consequences are trivial, as they are in the above example. Typically, speakers do not make remarks if they know that their audiences will deduce no more than the mere conjunction of the propositions expressed and the propositions they already believe. Clearly, this is not captured in a theory which only incorporates the maxim "Be informative". We need a maxim which imposes a much stronger constraint on utterances.

According to Wilson and Sperber, the definition of this constraint amounts to the definition of what we intuitively think of as relevance.[7] Thus the upshot of the remarks above is that speakers typically try to make only relevant utterances, and that not all informative utterances

SEMANTIC CONSTRAINTS ON RELEVANCE

are relevant. The idea of non-trivial deduction is captured in Wilson and Sperber's definition of synthetic implication, in terms of which they go on to define pragmatic implication and, ultimately, relevance. Their definitions, which presuppose that only a restricted subset of standard inference rules are available, are summarized in (16), (17) and (18):

(16) A set of propositions $P_1 \ldots P_n$ synthetically implies a proposition Q iff $P_1 \ldots P_n$ logically imply Q and there is no member P_i of $P_1 \ldots P_n$ which entails Q.

(17) A proposition P pragmatically implies a proposition Q relative to a belief set C iff
  (a) there is a set of propositions $R_1 \ldots R_n$ which synthetically implies Q, of which at least one member is entailed by P and not contained in C, at least one member is contained in C and not entailed by P, and all of whose members are either entailed by P or contained in C
  (b) Q is neither entailed by P nor contained in C.

If an utterance U expresses a proposition P which pragmatically implies a proposition Q relative to a belief set C, we shall say that Q is a pragmatic implication of U relative to C.

(18) An utterance U is relevant relative to a belief set C iff there is at least one proposition Q which is a pragmatic implication of U relative to C.

According to these definitions, (13) would be relevant relative to the belief set given in (19).

(19) $C = \{c_1, c_2\}$

c_1 *All members of the Young Farmers Club are against banning the bomb.*

c_2 *Very few people will vote for someone who is against banning the bomb.*

From c_1 and the proposition expressed in (13) we derive q_1,

q_1 *Fred Dagg is against banning the bomb.*

which itself is sufficient for the relevance of (13). But now q_1 is part of the hearer's belief set which already includes c_2. Thus we derive q_2, which also becomes part of the hearer's belief set.

q_2 *Very few people will vote for Fred Dagg.*

Now, it is unlikely that a hearer's belief set would be exhausted by the set (19). This set is more plausibly regarded as that subset of the hearer's beliefs which are required as premises in the derivation of whatever pragmatic implications are considered to be involved in establishing the relevance of (13). Clearly, if an utterance U taken together with a set of beliefs k, pragmatically implies Q, then U taken together with any set containing k pragmatically implies Q. However, it seems that in an actual derivation a hearer will use as premises only those propositions which he believes to be necessary. That is, if a hearer derives a pragmatic implication Q from an utterance U taken together with a set of propositions k, then he must believe that there is no proper subset of k which can be taken together with U in the derivation of Q. But we have seen in the above example that the interpretation of an utterance can involve the derivation of more than one pragmatic implication. This suggests that we should regard the set of propositions which are used by the hearer in the interpretation of an utterance as the union of all those subsets relative to which pragmatic implications are derived.

Thus the effect of defining relevance is to define a particular class of subsets of contexts, namely, the class of context subsets which contain the propositions used in the calculation of the pragmatic implications of utterances. Let us call each member of this class a κ-subset. Thus for each relevant utterance interpreted in a context there is a subset of that context which is a κ-subset.

It is clear that κ-subsets themselves may be subject to different constraints. In particular, they may be subject to constraints which involve reference to the properties of the propositions which they contain. For example, it would be possible to define a κ-subset which must not include the proposition expressed in the previous utterance, or which must include a proposition believed by the hearer's grandmother, or which must consist entirely of propositions which are believed to be actually true. Of course, to say that the definition of such constraints is possible is not to say that they are actually imposed. However, I wish to introduce a constraint which is imposed on κ-subsets, namely, the constraint defined in (20).

(20) (Let U_n be an utterance relevant against a κ-subset K. Let u_n be the proposition expressed by U_n. Let u_{n-1} be the proposition expressed by the utterance preceding U_n (U_{n-1}). Let p be any proposition pragmatically implied by U_{n-1}.) K must consist of propositions which do not include u_{n-1} or p, but which can be taken together with u_n as premises in an argument which has either u_{n-1} or p as its conclusion.

That the definition of this rather unlikely looking constraint is required for the explanation of how hearers interpret utterances is suggested by the use of *after all*. Recall example (11c).

(11c) Dick should be able to add up the bill; after all, he is a mathematician.

What is the relation between the sentence prefaced by *after all* and the one before it? Consider a subcontext K against which the utterance of *he's a mathematician* is relevant. This might be the one in (21).

(21) K = {c_1}

c_1 *Any mathematician should be able to add up the bill.*

From c_1 and *he's a mathematician* we derive q_1.

q_1 *Dick should be able to add up the bill.*

But q_1 is the same proposition expressed in the sentence preceding the one prefaced by *after all*. Thus the utterance of the sentence prefaced by *after all* is relevant relative to a κ-subset which has the property required by the constraint defined in (20).

Consider now (22).

(22) Why shouldn't Donald hold Daisy's hand; after all, he is her husband.

The utterance of *he is her husband* is relevant relative to the subcontext given in (23).

(23) K = {c_1}

c_1 *If Donald is Daisy's husband, then he can hold her hand.*

From *he is her husband* and c_1 we derive q_1,

q_1 *Donald can hold Daisy's hand*

which is a proposition pragmatically implied by the utterance preceding the utterance of *he is her husband*. Thus the subcontext (23) also has the property required by this constraint.

My claim is that the use of *after all* in these sentences makes explicit the fact that their utterance is relevant against a κ-subset which has the property required by the constraint in (20), or that the use of *after all* imposes this constraint on the relevance of the utterances it prefaces. The arguments of Part 1 suggest that the fact that the use of *after all* imposes this constraint should be regarded as a fact about the *meaning* of *after all*. Thus the constraint defined in (20) is one which may be imposed by the semantic properties of a particular lexical item.

This account of the meaning of *after all* explains the oddity of (11b).

(11b) Any mathematician should be able to add up the bill.
Dick is a mathematician.
?   After all, he should be able to add up the bill.

After all can only be used to preface an utterance which expresses a proposition which is a premise in an argument. It cannot be used to preface an utterance which expresses the conclusion of an argument.

To say that the use of *after all* imposes a constraint on the subcontexts against which its associated utterances are relevant is to say that it indicates that these utterances must be interpreted as relevant against a particular type of κ-subset. Thus the use of *after all* indicates that its associated utterances must be interpreted as having a particular type of relevance.

Relevance has been defined as a relation between utterances and contexts: an utterance is relevant if and only if the propositions it expresses can be taken with a subset of that context in an argument by which some non-trivial conclusion is derived. I have claimed that different types of relevance can be defined in terms of the properties of the subsets taken in those arguments. Thus a word which indicates that the utterance that contains it has a particular type of relevance indicates a relation between that utterance and a particular subset of propositions. It seems that such a word is best regarded as a word which links utterances and contexts; that is, as a sort of connective. The idea of a connective which links utterances and contexts might, at first, seem rather eccentric. But once the definition of a context as a set of propositions is accepted, it can be developed as an extension of the standard notion of a connective rather than as a departure from it.

Notice that the analysis of the words in (5) as connectives would explain why none of them are ever used to start of conversations. Utterances prefaced with these words must be understood as being in response to, or following on from, something. One would not normally enter a room and announce, "Anyway, Fred Dagg won". Similarly, one does not begin a conversation with *and* or *but* - unless, of course, there is something in the context for these words to "refer back" to.

In this paper, I have concentrated on the analysis of *after all*. It is obvious that my proposals need to be supported by explicit analyses of the other words in (5). I believe that the functions of all these words can be described in terms of constraints on κ-subsets. For example, the function of *actually* seems to have to do with the modal properties of κ-subsets, and the use of *anyway* seems to indicate that its associated utterances are not relevant against κ-subsets which include the proposition expressed in the previous utterance. Obviously, these are only very rough indications of what the analyses might be like. However, whatever the details of these analyses may be, it seems clear that these words cannot be regarded simply as particles or interjections.[8]

The claim that words like *after all* are connectives will, no doubt, have important implications for a theory of connectives. However, the main significance of my analysis of these words lies in the claim that in connecting utterances and contexts they impose *semantic* constraints on the *pragmatic* interpretation of those utterances. Clearly, if this is right, the theory of utterance interpretation must allow for a relation between semantics and pragmatics. In particular, it must be possible for semantic explanations to refer to pragmatic properties of utterances.

It is important to understand that the claim being made here is that semantics and pragmatics are related in the sense of there being semantic constraints on pragmatic interpretations, not that they are related in the sense that semantics depends on pragmatics, or, indeed, in the sense that pragmatics depends on sematics. That is, my proposals provide neither argument against the standard view that semantics is autonomous with respect to pragmatics nor confirmation for the standard view that pragmatics depends on sematics. Rather they suggest that semantics and pragmatics are related in the less familiar sense of there being pragmatic properties of utterances which may be sematically specified.

FOOTNOTES:

* I would like to thank Deirdre Wilson for her help and encouragement throughout the writing of this paper. I would also like to thank the members of the U.C.L. study group on the syntax and pragmatics of 'mystery' particles, Penny Jamieson and François Récanati, for comments on an earlier version.

1. I assume that the interpretations of (2a-f) and (4a-c) will be the same whether they are uttered by the speaker who made the original utterance or by another speaker.

2. For detailed justification of this view, see D.L. Brockway, University College London Ph.D. thesis.

3. G. Lakoff, who introduced context sensitive transderivational constraints in 1970, did not, of course, wish to maintain the distinction between semantics and pragmatics. However, Gazdar and Klein do not see their proposals as entailing the abandonment of the semantics-pragmatics distinction, and claim that pragmatic well-formedness must be defined on a level quite distinct from the level on which semantic well-formedness is defined.

4. It is possible that these words are analysable as contributing truth conditions in a non-standard theory of truth conditional semantics. For example, in the theory proposed by Wilson and Sperber (1979) these words would be analysed as low ordered entailments.

5. It is clear that the sentences marked '?' are only odd relative to certain contexts. Relevance is context dependent, and there are contexts in which the utterance of these sentences would be acceptable, and contexts in which the utterance of the sentences not so marked would be unacceptable. I do not wish to suggest that these contexts are in any way abnormal. However, I hope that the reader will be able to construct contexts in which the utterance of the '?' marked sentences is unacceptable, and see thereby that their acceptability is not affected by the removal of the words with which they are prefaced.

6. Again the utterance of the sentences marked '?' is odd only relative to certain contexts. However, I hope that the reader will have no difficulty in constructing contexts in which the utterance of the (a) sentences is acceptable, but in which the utterance of the (b) sentences cannot be interpreted in the way that is suggested by the acceptable uses of the words from (5) in the (c) sentences.

7. R. Smaby (1975) also claims that the set of relevant utterances are amongst the set of informative utterances. However, he does not say just what this set of relevant utterances is.

8. Anna Wierzbicka (1976) analyses *well* as a 'pragmatic particle', that is, as a word whose function is to express a pragmatic meaning at min-

imal cost. She uses the term 'pragmatic meaning' to refer to bundles of assumptions, intentions and attitudes. She argues that since pragmatic meanings are represented by sentences, particles are best regarded as abbreviations for whole sentences, and that the proper way of stating their meanings is to reconstruct these sentences. For detailed criticism of Wierzbicka's treatment of *well*, see D.L. Brockway, U.C.L Ph.D. thesis.

THE PROBLEM OF APPROPRIATENESS IN PRAGMATIC DEVELOPMENT

Luigia Camaioni

The aim of this paper is to propose an analysis of appropriateness in child's speech, i.e. to investigate how and when children learn to employ language so as to suit the demands of a particular listener and the particular context of a conversation.

In a piagetian framework (see Piaget 1923) the child's communicative inadequacy or inefficiency is viewed as a consequence of his cognitive egocentrism, i.e. the inability to detach oneself from one's own point of view and to take into account the perspective of someone else. For Piaget speech is appropriate only when the listener actually does understand the intended message of the speaker.

In our view the use of a content criterion alone for judging appropriateness fails to capture the fact that social conventions pertaining to different contexts and different listeners can influence the formulation of content itself. We propose to define speech as appropriate if (a) a speaker is selecting content that a listener might understand and/or respond to; and (b) he honors the social conventions relative to status differences, listener's capacities, conversational setting, and so on. In what follows we will try (a) to show that this view of appropriateness has been the most productive one in the recent research on "speech adjustments" both in child-adult and in child-child interaction, and (b) to present and discuss some pilot data in which children ranging from 21 to 33 months of age adjust their speech style to different listeners: same-aged children, different-aged children and adults.

Let me now start with the first point, analysing briefly the most recent research on speech adjustments.

Speech adjustments in child-adult and child-child interaction

At the beginning of the seventies, a number of researchers set out to analyse the structural characteristics of the language which adults use with children, defining it as "motherese". Basically the results of this research show that adults behave in such a way as to make the acquisition of language easier for the child; they use a simplified sample of language, which consists of well-formed utterances, short and syntactically simple, and of a restricted vocabulary (Snow 1972; Phillips 1973).

Subsequent research has shown that the adult selects the linguistic input he addresses to the child on the basis of considerations whose nature is not only structural (i.e. lexical and syntactic constraints) but also contextual (i.e. sociolinguistic and conversational constraints) (Ervin-Tripp and Miller 1977; Gelman and Shatz 1977; Camaioni 1979). In other words, most of the linguistic choices the adult makes cannot be explained by the shorter length and/or syntactical complexity of the utterances produced, but rather by assuming that the adult takes into account his own role in the interaction, the role and status of the interlocutor and the social context in which the interaction takes place. This recent emphasis on the *linguistic style* adopted by the adult speaking to the child, tends moreover to show that lexical and syntactic choices are secondary to choices concerning the appropriateness, in terms of sociolinguistic and conversational constraints, of the linguistic forms produced.

Analyses of the language adopted by older children when talking to younger children (Shatz and Gelman 1973) provide us with an interesting extension of the research on "motherese". The most significant result of these studies is that even at the age of four, children are able to adjust their own language when speaking to younger interlocutors; for example, they simplify and shorten utterances, they exaggerate intonation and make use of a greater number of requests for attention (e.g. "Look ...", "Listen" etc.). Such adjustment does not occur when the same children are speaking to peers: the language used with the latter is identical to that which they use with adults. This means that children do not discriminate generically between adult and child (otherwise they would speak to peers and younger children in much the same manner) but instead they are able to perceive and adjust to the linguistic capacities characteristic of different ages and therefore of different developmental stages.

In conclusion, both the research on "motherese" and the analysis of linguistic interaction between children of different ages show how the speaker tends to "adjust" to the communicative capacities of the interlocutor. When the interlocutor is a beginning language learner, this adjustment also functions as a mechanism which facilitates language acquisition and the development of communicative competence.

The pilot study

Starting from this view Loredana Stefani, Walter Gerbino and myself carried out a pilot study aimed at analysing how social interaction is structured between different-aged children and how it differs from social interaction between children of the same age. We talk of social interaction because we do not intend to restrict our analysis to linguistic production *per se*, but rather to interpret it within the social context in which it takes place.

Two pairs of different-aged children (with about a year's age difference between the members of each pair) were examined and a comparison was made between these pairs and those formed by the same children interacting with peers. We started off with the hypothesis that the difference between same-aged and different-aged pairs of children might basically be interpreted in terms of different *interaction styles* and that it therefore implied an awareness by both participants in the interaction of their respective role and status within the interaction itself, as well as of the context in which the interaction took place.

Of course, given the difference in competence between older child and younger child (when the interaction is between different-aged children), this awareness may be more evident in the older partner. We consider it important, however, not to look at adjustment in a uni-directional manner, as though it takes place just in one direction, from the more adult and competent partner towards the younger and less competent one. It seems to us that this uni-directional view is present both in the research on "motherese", in which it is assumed that it is always and only the adult or the older child who adjusts his language to the (younger) child, and in the more recent research which interprets adjustment in terms of interaction styles but continues to consider it a prerogative of the more adult and competent partner. We think instead that adjustment should be seen as a bi-directional process: in other words, the way in which the participants in the interaction adjust to one another is always the result of a negotiation between them in which both participate, even with different competence levels and degrees of awareness.

Bearing in mind this view of adjustment we decided it would be interesting to check out the analogy proposed by some of the above-mentioned researchers (particularly Shatz and Gelman 1973) between older-younger child interaction and adult-child interaction. According to Shatz and Gelman's interpretation, this analogy would be based on the fact that both the adult and the older child assume a role which could be defined as "pedagogical" with regard to the younger child ("talk down"). Shatz and Gelman observed the adult-child and older-younger child pairs both in a "task-oriented" situation, in which the child was explicitly instructed to talk about the workings of a toy to each of his two listeners, and in an "unstructured situation".

Instead, we chose to carry out our observations (both on different-aged and same-aged pairs, as well as on the interaction of the same pairs with an adult) in the most natural situation possible, absolutely not constrained by the introduction of specific tasks or explicit instructions either with regard to the children or the adult, i.e. in a "free-play" situation. We considered that this type of context would allow the "spontaneous" child behavior towards different partners to come to light more easily.

Method of data analysis

The analysis of the interaction was carried out by evaluating which *function* the verbal and non-verbal behavior of the interlocutors serves during reciprocal interaction and therefore, by categorizing behavior on the basis of the functions so isolated. For this purpose, we partly employed the classes of functions used by Gelman and Shatz (1977) to analyse the linguistic adjustments performed both by familiar adults (the mothers) and by 4-year-olds when speaking to 2-year-olds.

Our categorization covers 15 functions, which we will now briefly describe:

1) *Requests for attention:* Serve to call interlocutor's attention, verbally or non-verbally, to an object, activity or event, or to the speaker himself.
2) *Requests for action:* Serve to induce interlocutor to carry out a particular course of action. The standard form implies the use of a verb with imperative mood.
3) *Modulation of request:* Marks the degree of a request's flexibility, i.e. gives the interlocutor the possibility of refusing the directing of his attention or the course of action requested. Modulation may be carried out, for example, by formulating the request in an interrogative form ("Shall we wash our hands?") or else by using a predicate construction introduced by psychological verbs such as *think* ("I think we'll go and wash our hands").
4) *Reply I* (to the request for attention or action): May consist of a certain type of behavior or of a verbal reply.
5) *Requests for information:* Ask interlocutor to provide information which the speaker does not possess.
6) *Testing:* Serves to elicit answers or responses the speaker knows or assumes are in the listener's repertoire.

7) *Reply II* (to the request for information or testing): In the case of a request for information, always consists of a verbal reply; in the case of testing may be a verbal or a non-verbal reply.
8) *Requests for confirmation:* Seek interlocutor's agreement or approval, i.e. ask interlocutor to confirm something the speaker has just said or done.
9) *Confirmation:* Serves to indicate that the interlocutor has performed the right action or has given the correct verbal reply.
10) *Disconfirmation:* Serves to indicate that the interlocutor has performed the wrong action or given the wrong reply.
11) *Disconfirmation and suggestion to change activity:* Serves to tell the interlocutor not to do what he is doing and to do something different instead.
12) *Demonstration:* Serves to show the interlocutor how to use an object, how to carry out an activity, etc.
13) *Clarification:* Serves to explain what the speaker or the listener has just said or done.
14) *Modulation of assertion:* Marks speaker's degree of certainty or doubt about an assertion made by him or by the interlocutor.
15) *Directing or regulating children's interaction:* Serves to direct children's interaction towards one another or to regulate it.

Using certain dimensions as a basis, these functions may be grouped together in more general categories. A first dimension makes it possible to distinguish functions which serve to direct the future behavior of the interlocutor (requests for attention, action, information, suggestion to change activity, demonstration, testing) from those which concern past behavior (confirmation, disconfirmation, clarification). The second dimension distinguishes between functions which serve to guide or regulate action (request for action, suggestion to change activity, demonstration) and functions which serve to acquire or exchange knowledge and information (request for information, testing, reply to the request for information or testing, clarification). Finally, a third dimension regards the presence or absence of marks of flexibility and makes it possible on the one hand to distinguish direct requests from indirect or modulated ones, and on the other hand, real assertions from statements whose truth can be questioned.

As stated above, it is from the analysis of interaction styles - specified by the functions we have just defined - that we expect to obtain differences as a function of different pairs of interlocutors, and in particular:

a) differences in interaction style between different-aged pairs of children and same-aged pairs formed by the same children interacting with peers;
b) differences in the interaction style of the adult with regard to the older child and the younger child in different-aged pairs and, conversely, of the two different-aged children towards the adult.

On the basis of the analysis outlined in b) we also intend to check how well-founded the analogy between the older-younger child interaction and the adult-child interaction is.

The pairs were formed by children who had been going to a day-care centre long enough (8 - 12 months) to guarantee an identical level of familiarity, both amongst themselves and with the adult care-taker.
The pairs were observed in a "free-play" situation in the room normally reserved for play activities within the day-care centre and a series of familiar toys were available.

The data consist of video-tape films, utilizing a video-tape carefully hidden by a neutral screen in a corner of the room so that it was invisible to the children. Table 1 summarizes data regarding the age and sex of the children. (See table 1 on next page.)

The video-tapes were transcribed completely and separately by the two observers present at each observation session and the two transcriptions were checked for agreement. On the basis of the first complete transcription, two more analytical tables were then elaborated, i.e.:
a table relating to the interaction style present in the different-aged pairs and in the same-aged pairs formed by the same children (table 2);

FUNCTIONS	RI - MA + FABRIZIA						AN - PA + SELVAGGIA					
	Y→←O	Y→	A→Y	A→O	Y→A	O→A	Y→←O	Y→	A→Y	A→O	Y→A	O→A
Attention requests	0	0	6	7	6	3	0	0	2	3	25	18
Action requests	1	1	13	3	0	1	0	0	11	5	1	0
Modulation of request	0	0	3	3	0	2	0	0	0	0	0	0
Reply I	0	0	0	2	2	6	0	0	7	2	3	6
Information requests	0	0	3	4	4	10	0	0	0	1	1	10
Testing	0	0	3	18	0	0	0	0	2	7	0	0
Reply II	0	0	1	5	2	13	0	0	1	12	0	1
Confirmation requests	0	0	0	1	1	7	0	0	0	0	0	6
Confirmation	1	0	5	19	1	1	0	0	12	13	0	0
Disconfirmation	0	2	2	2	0	0	0	8	4	10	0	0
Disconfirmation + suggestion	0	1	0	0	0	0	0	0	3	2	0	0
Demonstration	0	0	1	0	0	0	0	1	1	2	0	0
Clarification	0	0	0	0	0	0	0	0	0	0	0	0
Modulation of assertion	0	0	0	0	0	0	0	0	0	0	0	0
Directing interaction	0	0	0	0	0	0	0	0	0	0	0	0
TOTAL	2	4	37	64	16	43	0	9	43	57	30	41

TABLE 3

SYMBOLS: Y = Younger child
O = Older child
A = Adult caretaker

Different-aged children's pairs	Age (in months)	Sex	Adult caretaker
RI - MA	21 - 31	M-F	Fabrizia
AN - PA	22 - 33	M-M	Selvaggia
Same-aged children's pairs	Age (in months)	Sex	
RI - AN	21 - 22	M-M	
MA - PA	31 - 33	M-F	

TABLE 1

FUNCTIONS	RI - MA Y→ ←O		AN - PA Y→ ←O		RI - AN P→ ←P		MA - PA P→ ←P	
Attention requests	6	3	6	1	3	0	1	15
Action requests	7	2	0	1	3	0	1	1
Modulation of request	0	0	0	0	0	0	4	0
Reply I	6	8	1	5	1	2	9	5
Information requests	1	0	0	1	0	0	10	7
Testing	0	0	0	0	0	0	0	0
Reply II	0	1	1	0	0	0	5	6
Confirmation requests	0	0	1	0	0	0	0	0
Confirmation	0	0	0	2	2	0	7	5
Disconfirmation	0	8	0	9	0	0	10	10
Disconfirmation + suggestion	0	0	0	0	0	0	2	1
Demonstration	0	3	0	3	0	1	0	0
Clarification	0	0	0	2	0	0	5	8
Modulation of assertion	0	0	0	0	0	0	0	0
Directing children's interaction	0	0	0	0	0	0	3	3
TOTAL	20	25	9	24	9	3	57	61

SYMBOLS: Y = Younger child; O = Older child; P = Peer (same-aged child)

TABLE 2

a table relating to the interaction style adopted by the adult with regard to the different-aged children and by the latter with regard to the adult (table 3).

Analysis of the interaction styles

Table 2 shows the results of the codification of the *functions* relative both to the interaction of different-aged children between themselves (O→ ←Y) and to the interaction of the same children wiht peers (P→ ←P).

In the different-aged pairs RI - MA and AN - PA, the younger child addresses to the older child mainly requests for attention and action, and to a much lesser extent requests for confirmation (1 out of a total of nine in the pair AN - PA) and requests for information (1 out of a total of 20 in the pair RI - MA). The older child either replies to the requests for attention and/or action addressed to him or he intervenes to control the behavior or the activity of the other, particularly in a negative manner, i.e. disconfirming it. The older child also intervenes in order to guide, in a more didactic manner, to other's behavior, giving some demonstrations (3 out of a total of 25 for both pairs).

These results make more sense if we take into consideration the pairs formed by the same children interacting with a peer (i.e. RI - AN; PA - MA). In the pair formed by the two older children interacting together (MA - PA) disconfirmations are reciprocal and furthermore the number of disconfirmations is counterbalanced by the presence of some confirmations (5 and 7 respectively). In the different-aged pairs, however, disconfirmations are addressed only by the older child to the younger one but not vice versa and this fact underlines the uni-directional control nature of the behavior of the older child towards the younger one and therefore characterizes the interaction as asymmetrical.

In our opinion, also the demonstrations which the older child addresses to the younger one (but not vice versa), perform a control function, but more with regard to knowledge than with regard to actions or activities. In fact demonstrations define the uni-directionality of the flow of information, which is based on the perception of the difference in competence by the older child with regard to the younger one. This uni-directionality is absent in the interaction between peers, where the flow of information is, instead, bi-directional (in the MA - PA pair, 10 and 7 requests for information respectively, and 5 and 6 replies to the requests for information).

The asymmetry of the roles within the different-aged pairs and the perception of the difference in competence is also reflected in the considerable drop in the number of clarifications (2 addressed by PA to AN, while PA addresses 8 to his peer MA; the latter addresses none to RI, whereas he addresses 5 to his peer PA) and in the absence of regulation of the interaction between children (present, however, in the MA - PA pair). These last two functions, in our opinion, serve to mark the sharing of the interaction taking place (clarification) or to define the respective positions of the partners in it (regulation of the interaction). These positions prove to be defined *a priori* in the interaction between different-aged children, which results therefore in asymmetry from the point of view of the roles.

We shall now move on to analysing the behavior of the different-aged children towards the adult (Table 3). This behavior essentially exhibits three types of function: requests for attention, requests for information (made mainly by the older children, but also by the younger ones who, however, hardly direct any at the older child, thus showing that they differentiate him from the adult), and requests for confirmation. They also produce a certain number of replies to the requests for attention and action as well as to the requests for information and to testing which the adult addresses to them. The only difference between the older child and the younger child is that the former performs more of all these functions, with the exception of the requests for attention which are more numerous for the younger children of both pairs.

The adult's behavior clearly appears to be characterized by those functions which are complementary to the functions shown by the children with regard to the adult, i.e. replies (to the requests for attention and information), confirmations and disconfirmations and lastly, testing. Moreover, the adult also performs a greater number of all these functions with the older child; the only exception is the requests for action which are addressed mostly to the younger child.

The first impression from these results is that the older-younger child interaction is structurally different from the adult-child interaction. In our opinion, in both these cases, there is "adjustment", not so much by one single member of the pair - the more adult and competent one - towards the other, but rather by both reciprocally, in that both show that they are aware of the difference between themselves and the interlocutor and on this basis they build up expectations which are appropriate in relation to the respective roles and status in the interaction.

When the children are on their own, the younger child treats the older one as an interesting, but somewhat unwilling interlocutor whom he must try to involve at all cost in his own centres of interest and action. The older child, on his part, besides replying (though not always) to the requests of the interlocutor, perceives him mainly as someone to be kept in check, telling him that what he has done is not right and that it should be done in another way.

In the situation with the adult, however, the younger child, besides trying to involve the adult by calling insistently for his attention, also sees him as a person able to provide information and confirmations, i.e. as a teacher and judge at the same time. Basically, the older child sees the adult in the same manner, with the only difference that thanks to his higher (mainly linguistic) competence level he runs a smaller risk of losing the adult's attention.

Finally, the adult treats the younger child differently from the older one. In fact he intervenes directly in the actions of the younger one, helping to guide them, whereas he tends to intervene with the older child only *post factum*, by confirming or disconfirming. Moreover, it is mainly with the older child that the adult takes it upon himself to check or test the knowledge which he thinks the child ought to possess. Sometimes this task becomes explicit when the adult, having asked the child a question in order to test his knowledge, repeats the child's answer with an evaluative comment on it. As is well-known, this three-turns exchange - adult's question, child's reply, adult's comment on the reply - forms the standard sequence of the interaction between teacher and pupil in the school (Sinclair and Coulthard 1975). It may also be noted that adult and older child use different functions to control the younger child's behavior: the adult tends to direct the action of the younger one by prefiguring it (request for action); the older child disconfirms the behavior taking place and uses demonstration instead to prefigure the future behavior of the younger child.

In our opinion, these different interaction styles of the older-younger child pair and of the adult-child pair, may be explained on the one hand by the different age of the interlocutors and the consequent asymmetry of knowing-power, and, on the other hand, by the type of role which the situation assigns to the older interlocutor within each pair. In a free-play situation, the older child does not feel he has to play a pedagogical role with regard to the younger child and so he behaves in the same way in which an inattentive adult would behave when forced to spend half an hour with a child; he gets on with his own business, replies to the other's advances when necessary, and basically "keeps him in check". The adult on the other hand - in this case the caretaker - continues to feel invested with his pedagogical role even within an unstructured situation and therefore intervenes both to direct or to control the child's action and to test the adequacy of the knowledge and information possessed by him.

Conclusions

From our analysis some significant differences in interaction style as a function of different interlocutors, i.e. same-aged children, different-aged children, children and adult, have emerged.

First of all, the interaction style between peers proves to be qualitatively different from the interaction style between different-aged children. The difference arises mainly from the fact that, between peers, the functions shown by both members of the pair mark the interaction as symmetrical from the point of view of the roles, whereas between different-aged children the interaction is marked as asymmetrical by the fact that the older child adopts an attitude of "control" and basically shows himself rather unwilling towards the younger child. This fact, in our opinion, would indicate that the older child does not *naturally* assume a pedagogical role towards the younger child and if he does so (as the results of Shatz and Gelman's research would show), it happens because he is assigned a task instead of being in an unstructured situation. In other words, in Shatz and Gelman's research (1973), assuming a pedagogical role by the older child seems to be a consequence of the methodological choice of structuring a "task-oriented" situation.

Secondly, the adult adopts different interaction styles towards the older child and the younger one, in particular a "knowledge control" style with the first and an "action control" style with the second. On the other hand, the adult and the older child behave differently towards the younger one. The older child, basically unwilling towards the younger child, "keeps him in check" by disconfirming most of his actions; the adult, who continues to feel invested with his pedagogical role, directs him by "proposing", i.e. by channelling his actions along what he considers the most suitable lines. Lastly, also the younger child adopts towards the older child interaction styles which are different from those he uses with the adult: he tries to involve the former in his own games and activities in spite of resistance, whereas from the latter he mainly seeks confirmations and information on his immediate environment.

In sum, the ability to perceive the difference between himself and the interlocutor and to formulate appropriate expectations with respect to the latter - in other words to adjust to the interlocutor - is not a prerogative only of the more adult and competent partner. Adjustment as emerges from our data is essentially bi-directional or reciprocal: it is the result of the manner in which both interlocutors, on the basis of their respective competences and expectations, negotiate their own roles during interaction.

LANGUAGE ACQUISITION, PSYCHOLOGICAL DUALISM AND THE DEFINITION OF PRAGMATICS*

Robin N. Campbell

By way of introduction, let me say that my work has been largely concerned with first language acquisition and that, although I have kept an intermittent watch on developments in linguistics and philosophy of language over a period of 10 years or so, I make no claims to expertise in these subjects. Any opinions that I offer should therefore be regarded as very tentative. I have the feeling, however, that I am not the only one who is unsure what pragmatics is, never mind how it should be studied.

I will begin by identifying two tendencies - "results" is too strong a word - of work in my own field which I will use in subsequent argument. The first of these tendencies is that it has begun to seem (paradoxically enough) in child language research that there is no such thing as a child *language*. Rather there are only *idiolects* - at any rate in the early years. This is of course hardly surprising since, in the cultures mostly studied, it is unusual for young children to have much contact with their peers before age 3 or so. However, even within triplets, as Anne Marie Schaerlaekens (1973) has shown, there are marked divergences in the course of language acquisition. Here, of course, the important point is that the input or target idiolect is the same for each triplet. These divergences are found at all linguistic levels: they make the construction of notional proto-languages such as, say, the 3-word stage in the acquisition of English, quite impossible in my view. This has led me to doubt whether it is reasonable at all to speak - even for adults - of knowing a language where a language is thought of as a transcendental and socially-determined institution. If we know one language then we know several, it seems. Despite enormous divergences of idiolect I - a speaker of an obscure British English dialect - succeed in communicating with inexpert speakers of English as a second language, with 2 year old children and even with North Americans! It may be possible, I suppose, to argue that what makes this communicative virtuosity possible is the possession of a large variety of linguistic competences but that seems to me to be a doomed hypothesis.[1] Rather, I prefer the idea that we each have our idiolects and use our intelligence and common sense to make them fit! Surely one of the great advantages of the notion of "negotiation of meaning" - which has been so common in pragmatic writings - is that it frees us from this old idea of a language being an institution shared by a community of speakers. Of course, for certain purposes it may be useful to stick - as dictionary makers must stick, for example - to the derivative notion of a language as a union of overlapping idiolects of members of a culturally-defined community, but inasmuch as a *science* of language is possible the goals of that science should be concerned with idiolect.

The second bias which I will import from work in psychology is more personal. In my recent work (see Campbell 1979a and 1979b) I have argued, largely on the basis of certain puzzles in early language acquisition, that it is essential to revive the old psychological distinction between, roughly, *conscious* and *unconscious* structures and processes. While there has been a continuing acknowledgement of the importance of this distinction in mainland Europe, in Anglo-American psychology it has practically faded from view outside of psychoanalytic writings. Instead, the distinction has been either ignored, as irrelevant, or worse still, conscious activity has been treated as epiphenomenal - being regarded as uninvolved with the causation of behaviour. Even if that were true - which I do not for one moment believe - it is quite astonishing that such a large group of psychologists should have turned away from the task of describing and perhaps explaining this

form of mental life. I have preferred to identify these two levels of
cognitive function by means of theoretical terms, referring to effortful,
reportable cognition as *phenic* and to effortless, unreportable cognition as *cryptic*.[2] A good example of the need to distinguish them comes
from work done by Annette Karmiloff-Smith at Geneva on acquisition of
the French determiner system (cf. Karmiloff-Smith 1978, 1979). Her
work showed that 3-4 year old children assigned gender to new nouns
routinely on the basis of the phonological form of the noun ending, regardless of the sex of the denoted object or of the actual grammatical
gender of the noun. However, when faced with new nouns whose ending
favoured neither gender, these children would typically assign gender
on the basis of sex, if possible, or invented sex, if not. So, semantic-
ally-based gender assignment *was* used but only as a default procedure when
phonologically based gender failed. Of course with increasing age Karmiloff-Smith's subjects began to use semantic and syntactic information in assigning gender. However, the remarkable aspect of her results was that phonological categories - which were the first to be
utilised in the actual assignment of gender - were the last thing to be
offered as an explanation of why they had used this article or that, or this
form of an adjective rather than that. On the other hand, at the time
when phonological categories were plainly controlling gender assignment
her children typically justified their gender assignments semantically,
in terms of the real or imagined sex of the denoted objects. It seemed
to me that a natural way to resolve this contradictory tangle is to
suppose that gender-related morphological decisions are normally made
by a *cryptic process* but are defaulted to a *phenic process* whenever the
noun ending cannot be assimilated to one of the key phonological categories. Children's explanations would, naturally enough, reflect this
phenic process entirely and the phonological process not at all. Now
it might be thought that the distinction between these two levels of
cognition could be granted but that phenic structures and processes
would have a role to play only in metalinguistic communication. I think
this is false, for two reasons. In the first place, ordinary communi-

cation involves understanding what is said, which I take to mean something more - a lot more - than just figuring out what proposition is being expressed and knowing what would make it true. It seems to me that the pretheoretical notion that gives the key to what is additionally involved here is *making sense of what is said* - making adjustments to a mental representation of the universe of discourse in such a way that what is said becomes sensible. A good example of this sort of thing is what Herb Clark has called *bridging* inferences (see Clark and Clark 1977, Chapter 3). Suppose, reporting a late-night gathering someone says "And then the police arrived and so we all swallowed our cigarettes". To make sense of what was said we need a bridging inference. For example, that the cigarettes contained an illegal substance. I think it is fairly clear that in general such inferences involve real cognitive effort and hence phenic structures and processes - a conclusion which is supported by Clark's experimental work. Perhaps when communication occurs between ideal speaker-hearers obeying impeccable conversational principles it may proceed effortlessly. However this would be extraordinary communication. Ordinary communication as Schegloff, Sacks and Jefferson (1977) and Jefferson (1974) have shown is littered with all sorts of repair-sequences showing, or so it seems to me, effortful cognition at work.

My second reason for believing that such processes play an essential role in language is the following. What a speaker thinks about the meaning of linguistic elements - words, syntactic formations or whatever - may be described as prescriptions. But they can hardly be *dismissed* as prescriptions unless it can be shown that they do not affect his choice of these elements. But surely on occasion they do. Karmiloff-Smith's children entertained a false theory of their own system of assigning gender but did employ this theory in assigning gender to a small set of default cases. In English at the moment we are experiencing a wave of idiolect change where the remnant of a system of grammatical gender is being transformed into a strictly semantic system, resulting in several changes, the introduction of new pronouns, for example, *he-or-she*, the abolition of *it* as a means of referring to children and other domestic animals, and the employment of pronoun-avoiding syntactic stratagems. In most idiolects this new system is quite unstable, the old cryptic system breaking through whenever the effort of keeping selection of these elements under phenic control proves too much.

As a last example, let us assume the truth of the popular theory, due to Lawrence Horn (1972) that expressions which can be considered as intermediate on a scale, such as *some*, *possible*, the *number-names*, the *equative comparative* and *or* are for many idiolects semantically compatible with expressions denoting more extreme values on these scales so that *some* is compatible with *all*, *possible* with *necessary*, etc. Of course they may be used and often *are* used to denote values incompatible with the value denoted by the appropriate extreme. The fact that they may be used in this way is then explained by appealing to implicatures based on the maxim of quantity. Briefly, if the extreme value were applicable, the maxim generally requires the use of the extreme expression. Since the extreme expression has not been used, by implicature the extreme value is not applicable. It seems to me that investigation would show that in many idiolects, mine for example, these cryptic structures and their associated processes are in unstable conflict with phenic structures - prescriptions, if you like - which specify these intermediate expressions as ambiguous, resulting in redundant and erratic addition of what Horn has called the implicature-cancelling suspenders *only some, some or all, at least some, at least as big as, two or more, and/or*, etc.

Let me conclude this section of my paper by drawing the obvious *general* methodological moral. If you share these biases of mine, then you had better study idiolects in action! A much more awkward question will occupy me for the rest of this paper. Suppose that we do acknowledge the centrality of the idiolect and the complementary, if occasionally conflicting, roles of phenic and cryptic activity in language use. What consequences does this have for the traditional division of linguistics into syntax, semantics and pragmatics and for what we understand by pragmatics in particular? What makes this question such an awkward one is that there is no really satisfactory pre-theoretical notion of what pragmatics is, nor is there any obvious consensus amongst linguists or philosophers of language about what phenomena should be counted as pragmatic phenomena. For some it has been little more than a handy label for certain phenomena, such as thematic structure, deixis or reference. Others have employed the notion systematically, but in quite diverse ways. For some, the principles governing the process of *making sense of what is said* - of making sense of utterance meaning if you like - are pragmatic principles. For others, such principles are considered to be external to linguistics proper - belonging instead to a theory of rational cooperation. Again, for some, in relating sentence-meaning to utterance-meaning a sharp distinction is made between *syntactic and semantic principles* which together determine a propositional function for each sentence and *pragmatic principles* which specify what actual proposition is determined by the function in context: for others pragmatic principles combine first with syntactic and semantic principles to yield a literal utterance meaning and are then employed in a second cycle to yield an actual utterance meaning. Finally, pragmatic principles such as Grice's conversational maxims have been applied at quite distinct levels in the functional hierarchy; Horn, for example in his treatment of the scalars appeals to the maxim of quantity as controlling the move from sentence meaning to utterance meaning; others have chosen to apply the maxims to the determination of the *act-content* of an utterance already fully specified as to meaning - to what I have been calling *making sense of what is said*.

Now, it is appealing at first sight to employ the distinction between phenic and cryptic activity in a direct and simple manner, associating knowledge of the language (of one's own idiolect, that is) with the cryptic automatic level and knowledge of how to employ this system in speaking and understanding with the phenic level, thus retaining an analogue of the original radical distinction of Morris, (see, e.g.

Morris 1938) between syntax and semantics on the one hand and pragmatics on the other. A proposal along these lines has recently been made by Pieter Seuren (1978). However, the confusing picture of pragmatics revealed by recent work suggests fairly strongly that this view is wrong. Why? Consider once again Horn's treatment of the scalars. If A asks B, *How many children do you have?* and B answers *Two*, then, since B may be presumed to know exactly how many children he has and to be obeying the maxim of quantity, A may reasonably infer that B does not have 3 children or any larger number since he should then have said so. However, it is hard to imagine A in this situation deliberating *does B mean exactly 2 or at least 2?* and resolving the equivocality of the scalar by the inference just described. It is even harder to imagine A actually initiating a process of repair by saying to B *Do you mean exactly 2 or at least 2?* Such inferences, if Horn is indeed correct to analyse them in this way, must surely be automatic and unreportable - in my terms *cryptic*.

On the other hand, if A asks B *Do you have two children?*, it is not at all hard to imagine B thinking *Does A mean exactly 2 or at least 2?* and either resolving the equivocality in favour of *exactly* 2 by an inference involving the maxim of quantity or in favour of *at least* 2 by a different inference involving the larger context - say, that A is trying to establish thresholds for tax purposes or the allotment of housing or the like. Of course, the maxim of quantity is involved here as well, since - assuming mutual knowledge of the purposes of exchange - for A to have asked *Do you have at least 2 children?* would have been redundant. Again, in this example it is not at all hard to imagine B initiating a repair by saying to A *Do you mean exactly 2 or at least 2?* or, perhaps more likely, deciding to treat the question as a indirect request and answering *I have 4.* So my claim here is that under different circumstances a listener may be aware or unaware of the equivocality of a scalar and may resolve the equivocality by effortless or by effortful inference. So it would be wrong to make a strong direct connection between phenic and pragmatic processes on the one hand and cryptic and grammatical processes on the other. However, I do agree with Seuren (and practically everyone else) that it is important to distinguish linguistic from extra-linguistic elements in the activities of saying and understanding and if we have to make this distinction with respect to idiolects - as I am urging - then Seuren's notion that what we ought to count as *linguistic* processes are, to use Seuren's term, *underground* - fluent, effortless and unreportable - seems to me to give much the best hope of success. Accordingly, as a first step it seems necessary to distinguish between what might be called *micropragmatic* and *macropragmatic* levels. Macropragmatic processes would be analyzed in terms of explicit inferences guided by principles of rational cooperation while micropragmatic processes would be analyzed *as if* they involved such inferences. However, it may also be possible to go a little further and indeed, it is desirable to do so if one dislikes the notion of unconscious inference - as I do. It seems to me that the ontogenesis of many types of skilful performance follows a pattern of *this* sort: initially, the performance - whatever it is - is guided phenically; the results of many component parts of the performance are monitored and controlled in a deliberate and thoughtful way. However, with time and practice automatic cryptic processes are acquired - goodness knows how - which enable a smoother and more fluent performance. However, it is typically the case that these cryptic processes are merely heuristic; they deal adequately with the majority of circumstances but when they break down the control of the performance is returned, by default, to deliberate phenic guidance. Clinical diagnosis provides an interesting case in point. It is a truism of the art of diagnosis that experienced physicians can make, in many cases, an accurate diagnosis based on gross aspects of the patient's appearance - the characteristic facial appearance and gait associated with Parkinson's disease is perhaps the best-known example. Of course ethical standards require that such intuitive diagnoses be backed up by a deliberate eliminative procedure based on the results of laboratory tests and so forth. And in some cases, the "look of the patient" gives no clue. Similar heuristics are employed by those skilled in plant identification: with practice, what began as slow deliberate fumbling through a botanical key gives way to smooth effortless identification. The important point for my argument is that these intuitive cryptic procedures are based upon criteria - presumably complex and subtle perceptual properties of faces, leaf-shapes, etc. - quite different from the explicit phenic procedures which generally involve close examination of highly local properties. A slightly different example is the process of attribution of art objects, such as paintings. There, one may know a Piero della Francesca when one sees one without having any idea why. Such intuitive attributions can be contrasted in the same sort of way with the deliberate feature-by-feature attributions of a professional art historian whose judgments are subject to verification by examination of brushwork, compositional structure, iconography and historical data. It seems to me that in all these cases there is little reason to suppose that the intuitive procedure is homomorphic with the explicit one - that it is not a sequence of inferences driven underground by practice but rather an independent heuristic (i.e. operating within a more limited domain) with a possibly quite different dynamical structure.

What I want to suggest, then, is that the pattern of development just discussed occurs also in the learning of a language: that success in achieving communicative goals in speaking and understanding can lead in some mysterious way to the acquisition of short-cut cryptic heuristics which satisfactorily replace intelligent and deliberate processes of guidance and control through a large part of their domain. When these processes fail to yield a result, then control may be returned by default to the phenic level. Accordingly, it may be possible to relate macro and micropragmatic processes in roughly *this* way: a macropragmatic process is one constituted by a sequence of explicit inferences governed by principles of rational cooperation. A micropragmatic process develops as a cryptic and heuristic procedure which *partially* replaces some macropragmatic process and which defaults to it in the event of breakdown.

In conclusion, I should like to acknowledge that this has been no more than an essay in what Jerry Fodor (1975, Preface) has called "speculative psychology". That is, I have disgracefully little in the way of evidence for the position I have outlined. It is perhaps best to regard it as just one possible sketch of one way in which some aspects of linguistic knowledge could be psychologically represented.

FOOTNOTES:

*   This paper was prepared while I was a Fellow at the Netherlands Institute for Advanced Studies, Wassenaar. I would like to acknowledge their support with gratitude and also to record a debt to my co-Fellows, in particular David Olson, Herman Parret and Manny Schegloff, for many useful discussions of the topics dealt with here. My thoughts on these topics were also heavily influenced by Manfred Bierwisch's unpublished papers (Bierwisch 1979a and 1979b) and his discussions with the group at N.I.A.S.

1. For a similarly pessimistic view, see Matthews 1979.

2. A word of justification for introducing new terminology is perhaps required. It is central to my proposal that the distinction drawn should be (a) theoretical and (b) potentially applicable to other and to juvenile organisms. Thus *effortful/effortless* and *conscious/unconscious* fail since these are simply the usual empirical marks of the distinction; *reportable/unreportable* is not only empirical but also limited to language users; lastly, existing theoretical oppositions such as *higher/lower*, *inner/outer* and so forth have unfortunate anatomical interpretations. My strategy in employing the theoretical distinction has been to try to show that it solves problems for us, rather than to show that it has a direct empirical justification - since this latter route has been pursued long and hard without much success. I should expect the distinction to turn out only conditionally associated with each of its usual empirical symptoms.

PRAGMATIC ISSUES IN THE CONSTRUCTION OF RECENT
HISTORY FROM INTERVIEW NARRATIVES*

Aaron V. Cicourel

Linguistic theories invariably distinguish the rules of a language from the principles for using the language in everyday settings. But with rare exceptions (Green n.d.) linguists seldom deal with the consequences of this distinction. Green argues that grammar and pragmatics are separate systems and that pragmatics has little to do with linguistics when the latter is viewed as the rules of a language. Her use of the term pragmatics is taken from Morris (1946) and refers to aspects of users of a language in the sense of principles for doing things. This means having an impact on the world and connecting actions to what can be expected to happen in terms of consequences. Hence language use is not the key issue, necessarily, but certain speech acts are obviously pragmatic in having particular affects on people. There is a notion here of creating goals, plans, routines, and procedures, and the idea of pursuing goals, implementing plans, leading to certain kinds of actions, and projected consequences. A key aspect of pragmatics from this perspective is problem-solving behavior. For Green speech acts have little or nothing to do with grammar or some notion of strict linguistic competence. But when language is used as a tool for communicating speech acts about intentions, beliefs, goals, acts, and purposes, then language use is as pragmatic as cleaning and dressing a laceration on a person's body.

Pragmatic aspects of constructing recent history from narrative interviews presupposes that interviewer and informant can utilize the same language. This use of language further presumes that the interviewer's questions require the informant to infer the intentions and goals of the speaker in whatever is asked. The interviewer must also make judgments about the extent to which the informant's answer addresses the intentions and goals of the question. When this interview process permits clarification of the question and answer, as well as digressions that are presumed to be related to the question and answer, then what are often viewed as standardized ways of eliciting information become negotiable pragmatic practices. Certain procedures must be followed in order for the interviewer-researcher to gain access to informants in a context in which some sources of data and/or informants are blocked. Some sources of information become especially rich in detail because of unplanned relationships that emerge in the course of conducting the study. The conditions of doing field research are pragmatic issues that are integral to the analysis of narrative interview material. This point is in many respects similar to an observation made by students of folklore (Hymes, 1975; Kirshenblatt-Gimblett, 1975) in their analysis of narratives: the way a story or parable is embedded in the performance of interactional aspects of its telling is central for judging the authenticity of the material. Hence there are pragmatic aspects of the telling of a story or the formulation of an answer to a question which become part of the researcher's data base and can influence the interpretation of the narrative.

Interviewer-researchers develop pragmatic strategies for organizing a field study in which numerous contacts must be arranged and judgments made about the selection of informants. These activities include practical matters like convincing people to become respondents or informants and the ability of the interviewer to initiate, sustain, and close the interview successfully. The pragmatic conditions of carrying out the exchanges necessary to gain access, sustain this access during interviews or other recording of information about individuals or groups, and terminating the study successfully, are never described as an integral part of the analysis of data obtained. Yet these conditions make it possible to create the "edited" data base that is used for analysis and the reporting of findings. Indeed, the most difficult problem faced by students of discourse is that higher level predications or more complex levels of analysis are always presupposed in the analysis of materials, but the larger context within which tacit use of higher level predicates is invoked, is never identified in an explicit way when coding information and generating categories within which speech acts are classified.

When we confront discourse and interview narrative materials with the intention of preparing these materials for analysis, we may parse and organize them into constituent elements that can yield an analysis of data by the use of speech act categories. We may also create expansions that identify the intentions and higher level predicates of the discourse or interview narratives that may or may not lead to speech act classifications. These expansions can also provide us with a problem-solving analysis that categorizes the data base by producing propositions about goals, sub-goals, plans, acts, intentions, and purposes. The three types of analysis, however, do not address the larger ethnographic or organizational context within which the data base is embedded. When we leave out the ethnographic context we are often forced to treat all utterances as if they contained intentions to communicate. The researcher is obliged to classify each utterance under the assumption that each of then carries relevant content for the understanding of the larger episodes and events under review. The three approaches to the analysis of discourse and interview narrative materials all depend on data-driven procedures and do not seek top down or hyphothesis driven expectations unless forced to do so after finding that alternate interpretations or classifications of the same speech acts do not yield consistent explanations of the data. But the fact is that none of these data-driven approaches to the analysis of discourse and interview narratives can be accomplished unless the researcher makes tacit use of other materials from his data base. In addition, he or she must use findings from other studies, and unexplicated elements of social organization known to him or her because of being a native of the culture in which the data are obtained. Other sources include implicit impressions from actual participation with those from whom materials for the data base was obtained, and the use of theoretical concepts external to the analysis itself but where these concepts can be used in a global and often synecdochical way.

An important parallel that is often ignored in studies of discourse and interview narratives is that between the perception of those persons whose utterances we study, and the researcher's understanding of those utterances in a context of initial elicitation, organizing them for analysis and constructing an interpretation of them. The utterances of those we study depend on similarities and differences in their perception of factual conditions and circumstances at the time of interaction. The researcher's analysis also depends on the observation of acts embedded in the particular circumstances at the time of analysis of materials. In the case of the participants or informants we study, the observation of facts in a setting means that communicants perceive a setting in terms of what is *assumed* to be culturally known in common with others even if these assumptions are seldom confirmed explicitly. Following Peirce (1931-1935), the researcher also engages in a form of abduction in which an inferential step occurs in first stating and then reflecting on a hypothesis that would choose among several possible explanations of some set of facts. Particular circumstances perceived at the time of making guesses about what is happening in a social exchange are a result of the interaction between data-driven and hypothesis-driven inferences.

Field research forces the researcher to formulate hypotheses from among several, possibly ambiguous, observations whose factual status remains and was unclear at the time they were experienced. A model of the pragmatics of eliciting, organizing, and analyzing interview narratives requires that we clarify our observations by probing informants and the use of later observations or field notes. The field researcher invariably begins to build up a tacit model of what each informant is like and how each one fits into the beginnings of an overall conception of the study and the way we start the identification of general substantive themes. Various alternative themes are entertained, assessed, changed, and perhaps recorded in field notes. The interpretive work required for developing and assessing the themes may never be stated explicitly in the field notes. Many of the themes will not be stated clearly until some decision is made about how to organize the interview narratives. If the materials are coded by the use of a few categories in the form of an attribute space analysis, or some modified form that permits scaling to techniques to be used, as well as the cross-tabulation of categories, then the researcher must await the marginal tabulations in order to make substantive claims. If a thematic analysis is pursued the field notes and general tacit impressions of the researcher will provide the pragmatic conditions for creating a textual analysis.

We are dependent on an appropriate format for asking questions and the informant's ability to create or remember an opinion or judgment about an issue or activity, if we are to be successful in getting the respondent to retrieve or create information we seek. Our field notes interpret and summarize activities and thus impose particular orderings on events and settings. The field notes convert visual and auditory information into a standardized written format that is like an edited text.

A key issue of this paper is: Can we identify a set of pragmatic principles which specifies the way elicitation procedures and field notes are used in contemporary research, and which also includes the way narratives and textual materials are subjected to analysis by historians and students of literary or dramatical or artistic works? In each of these methodologies we seek the way evidence is created to form a data base which is dependent on the descriptive or categorization system used, and the theoretical concepts employed at different stages in the gathering and analysis of data. Our model, therefore, must also represent the way people in everyday life go about developing and using pragmatic principles and knowledge when they produce discourse and interview narratives. We recognize that differences exist in the actual gathering and sorting of such materials, and that differences also exist in their analysis. Some researchers are more skilled at obtaining discourse materials or eliciting narratives or engaging in participant observation, while others are more proficient in searching for or in organizing and analyzing textual materials. Our ability to produce particular types of inferences depends on the way we organize our data base. But we also seek to identify similar processes of interpreting, deleting, and paraphrasing experiences and other sources of information when we record participant observer notes and descriptions, interview narratives, and textual materials. I want to stress common elements of information processing despite the diversity of skills that can be evident in the way different scholars use research strategies.

Finding informants

It is not always possible to choose informants systematically. In my study of Sephardic Jewish communities in Spain I began looking for informants by consulting a list of households provided by community authorities in Madrid, while also choosing others known to be active leaders in the community or persons knowledgeable about community organization and history. Additional contacts in Barcelona and Málaga (and then later in Tangiers, Morocco, Izmir and Istanbul, Turkey, Tel Aviv and Haifa, Israel, and Los Angeles and Atlanta) were all done by developing a "snowball" sample based on my initial list of informants and my own personal and family contacts.

Interviewing informants in Spain and Morocco required several months of continuous field work in order to establish necessary contacts and to obtain a degree of informality which would be conducive to more spontaneous talk about personal and community experiences. My interviews, therefore, are embedded in very different contexts and produced wide differentials in the breadth and depth of information obtainable and believable. The interviews in Spain were more formal in Madrid, less so in Barcelona and Tangiers for the most part, and much more informal in Málaga. Those conducted in Turkey, Israel, and the U.S. were always more spontaneous and marked by a high degree of informality. The practical aspects of language use and non-verbal behavior during these interviews always influenced the kinds of data obtained and therefore contributed to the constraints of attributing meaning to the materials. Other confounding conditions involving the age of the informants and when they left their country of origin are discussed elsewhere (Cicourel n.d.).

Choosing substantive topics

The general issues I had hoped to address in my study of Sephardic communities seemed overhelming. I chose a few themes around which I tried to focus my interviewing. I devised a brief interview schedule which would permit me to obtain some demographic details about each family as well as more elaborate narrative descriptions about community activities. I could not devote continuous time to informants in their everyday living arrangements, nor was it possible to engage in intensive ethnographic work in each of the sprawling urban settings in which I found my informants. I was, however, invited to informants' homes and able to participate in a number of community social and religious functions as a way of gathering additional information to that gathered in the interviews.

Reconstructing recent history from interview narratives

Specific interviews often provide the researcher with a point of departure because they should embody the ubiquitous presence of general pragmatic knowledge in trying to represent a great deal of information with selective material from a few interviews. The remarks of one informant born in Tangiers proved useful for revealing a broad range of substantive issues about everyday life in Morocco, particularly the topic of language use in Sephardic communities. The issue of language use emerged in a context in which I observed the use of French at a meeting of the community leadership. When I asked the informant about the use of French I was told instead about the use of old Spanish or "Hakitia". I realized early on that a reconstruction of when the communities in Morocco stopped using Hakitia was central to my research and also an important challenge for deciding the credibility of an informant's remarks.

Figure I INFORMANT REMARKS ON LANGUAGE
SPOKEN IN MOROCCO

R: 1 Wait. We talk the same. (We are   Espéreme. Hablamos lo mismo.
    2 talking about the same
      thing (?)
    3 It is about Ladino,   Es del ladino,
    4 we speak Spanish or Hakitia.   hablamos español o hakitía.

I: 5 Ah, Hakitia, okay.   Ah, hakitía, okay.

R.   6 But why didn't we speak uh,...   Pero por que nosotros no hablamos uh...
    7 Hakitia so much in Tangiers?   la hakitía tanto en tánger?
    8 Because we were near Spain..   Porque estabámos cerca de españa..
    9 Thus our language   Entoces, nuestro idioma
  10 kept on evolving at the   fue evolucionando al
  11 same time as the language...   mismo tiempo que el idioma...
  12 Spanish, right?   español, no?
  13 But, nevertheless in the   Pero, sin embargo en los
  14 smaller villages and   pueblos mas pequeños y
  15 and [among] people with less   y la gente menos culta,
      cultural
  16 background,
  17 the people of the village   la gente del pueblo,
  18 continued speaking   seguían hablando
  19 Hakitia until recently,   el hakitia haste últimamente,
  20 until these last 20 years.   hasta estos 20 últimos años.
  21 Do you follow me?   Comprende?

22	[I: Okay] Now, the educated	[*I: Okay*] *Ahora, la gente culta*
23	[cultured] people	
24	who had learned	*que habían aprendido*
25	Spanish, Castillian (Spanish) in school	*español, castellano en el colegio*
26	and who thus went [out] with [associated, visited]	*y que frequentában españoles*
27	Spaniards,	*entonces,*
28	[for] these [people] their language evolved	*estos su idioma evolucionó*
29	with Spanish	*con el español.*
30	On the other hand, in Turkey,	*En cambio, en turquía*
31	the Spaniards were	*los españoles estában*
32	so far away..	*tan lejos..*
33	that the language remained as	*que al idioma se quedó como*
34	(it was) in the fifteenth c-ent-ur-y.	*en el s-ig-l-o quince.*
35	Do you follow me?	*Comprende?*

One dot	: 1 second pause
Dash	: abrupt stop of utterance
Hyphen	: separation of letters which are less than a word
(?)	: overlap or unclear speech
Apostrophe	: missing letter

In Figure 1, the informant (lines 1-4) insists that the Moroccan Sephardics also speak Ladino, that is, "Spanish or Hakitía". The informant suggests that Hakitía was not spoken in Tangiers because of its geographical proximity to Spain. What is not clear here is if she meant that there was contact between members of the Sephardic community in cities like Tangiers, and Spaniards from the Iberian peninsula before colonization. This line of argument seems reasonable, but the fact that the Spaniards colonized northern Moroccan cities after 1912 does not clarify the nature and extent of these possible contacts with Spaniards prior to 1912. One obvious point of contact was between Sephardics in Morocco and those in Gibraltar where Spanish was spoken. Another contact existed between Sephardics in Ceuta, a Spanish colony, and Tetuan, Morocco. This information was given to me by other informants. At the time of this interview with the informant of Figure 1, I had no way of knowing how to place the information I received into a larger context, such as the establishment in the middle of the 19th century of a series of schools called the l'Alliance Israélite Universelle ("Alianza" school in Spanish), for Sephardic Jews living throughout the Mediterranean area. Nor was I aware, at the time of the interview with the first informant, of the establishment of secondary schools in all of the major cities the Spanish occupied in northern Morocco. These were often the only secondary schools available.

The remarks in Figure 1 imply that in small villages Sephardics would continue to speak a form of Hakitía, while their more urban and/or better-off counterparts would learn modern Castillian in Spanish schools and through business and social contacts with Spaniards. No mention is made of the existence of Spanish schools in the smaller villages, nor is it clear which villages were being referenced. The idea of contacts with Spaniards is implied by the informant's remark that "the educated/cultured people who had learned Castillian (pause) Spanish in school, and who thus went (out) with (visited) Spaniards".

When I began to examine the initial transcripts of my interviews, there was no way to ignore my memory of information from prior and subsequent interviews as I began to interpret the material in Figure 1. In addition I used sources acquired by participating in the group's activities or from reading about the group. The use of these sources required an interaction between sources of information that is tacit, despite a presumed reliance on what is given by the interview narrative.

The analysis of textual material from narrative interviews, discourse, and historical and literary sources always presumes interpretations that remain faithful to the details contained in the text. At the time of eliciting the interview materials (or recording discourse or selecting historical and literary sources) I may or may not be aware of historical details related to the questions I ask, and my ethnographic experiences may be restricted or extensive. But when I attempt a close reading of the interview narratives I must assume that the materials can be viewed in a restrictive way and code them into a small number of categories. I can also expand what I perceive to be the intended meaning of utterances before categorization. Another alternative is to expand the materials as a means of identifying constituent elements that can be viewed as part of a larger story grammar (Rumelhart n.d.). In this latter case the goal would be to create a more precise model of analysis that would specify more top down or hyphothesis-driven expectations of what should be found in the materials.

The reduction of the narrative materials to a small number of categories has as its goal a restricted type of predication which can be correlated to similar levels of predication in other narrative materials as in survey research. Another strategy is to pursue several levels of predication in the recognition that open-ended questions and open textual information invite the respondent and researcher to think of several, possibly related, types of predication. For example, when the informant says, in Figure 1, "we were near Spain", this can mean that there were exchanges with Spaniards because of different geographical and commercial factors, or that cultural similarities motivated and facilitated contacts between the groups. This approach can identify elements of the narrative as speech acts, and also identify problem-solving or story grammar structures and processes.

My notes during an interview can also reveal reflexive thought about what seems to be happening that is not being marked by the speech events being recorded. Emergent conditions or spontaneous speech that goes beyond the questions asked can enhance more narrowly conceived goals operationalized by the elicitation devices used.

Based on the rather limited fragment of interview narrative in Figure 1, it is possible to produce a few propositions that can also be given the status of hypotheses with which to examine additional narratives. The propositions listed below constitute a rough combination of analyzing discourse and textual materials by remaining close to the text while also invoking other sources of information or levels of predication. The informant in Figure 1, in her brief remarks, implies the following circumstances associated with the use of Hakitía in Morocco.

1. The use of Hakitía in Morocco was influenced by proximity to Spain and contacts with Spaniards, but no specific details nor time period is given.

2. No explicit mention is made of Spanish colonization of northern Morocco as facilitating contacts between Sephardic Jews and Spaniards because of a common cultural tradition and language. Other informants noted the contacts which derived from legal and commercial activities based on colonization.

3. Educated families would associate with Spaniards and send their children to Spanish schools where modern Castillian Spanish would be learned.

4. Hakitía continued to be used in smaller villages or towns even as recently as 20 years ago, or roughly until Moroccan independence.

Additional information from the same informant and others clarified the above propositions, often altering the content considerably. These changes are reported elsewhere (Cicourel n.d.).

Pragmatics as an interactive model

Identifying and integrating different sources of information that go into the creation and use of pragmatic principles and knowledge enable a speaker to produce a network of acts designed to achieve a goal which presupposes a knowledge of grammatical rules. But as Green notes, citing work by Van Dijk (1977), the relevance and coherence of discourse or textual materials are not to be understood as linguistic properties, but as a listener's inferred consequences of a relationship between observed acts and goals, intentions, purposes, and motivations. The notion of pragmatic principles refers to the tacit ways in which we link information from different sources to create coherency and relevance in our speech acts and non-verbal and paralinguistic actions. These sources include an explicit and implicit use of knowledge that can be identified as part of a data base elicited from informants if we are talking about written summaries. These written summaries or research reports can include the sources of information previously identified as field notes, and ethnographic experiences or impressions that are not recorded. When the immediate interview narrative is being examined along with other interviews, the written summaries and theoretical concepts are used in a general or global way along with the results of other studies. The interviewer and informant must both engage in the interpretative activity we call comprehension to accomplish the goal of creating questions and responses.

The several levels of information involved here can be clarified by reference to Rumelhart's (1975) use of the nation of an interactive model to characterize the idea that several levels of information are examined in conjunction with several types of logical reasoning. The Rumelhart model can be viewed as a way to formalize earlier work by Peirce (1931-35); the form and content of the interaction between deductive hypotheses and inductive inferences or abductive reasoning. The interaction of levels occurs in a situation in which the observation of facts is linked to the particular, emerging circumstances that exist at the time of observation. In Rumelhart's model the different types of information would include the perception of speech, vowel-consonant clusters, lexical items, phrases, and sentences, and the syntactive structures and semantic domains which are used to constrain and interpret the information being received. The additional higher levels identified in the last paragraph, however, are not adequately integrated with the levels specified by Rumelhart's model. This brief paper has attempted to identify some of the initial steps that must be adressed if we are to achieve this integration when using interview narratives embedded in a larger field study.

Rumelhart's work on a story grammar model can help us understand the way we recall and summarize ethnographic experiences and other sources of information, including narrative material. For Rumelhart a reader's comprehension of a story is said to be identical to the way he or she selects and verifies conceptual schemata or knowledge of concepts when accounting for or explaining a situation or text. The idea of summarization as central to comprehension is similar to Peirce's notion of creating facts and making guesses under conditions of abductive reasoning. When we interview an informant about past events and experiences, we ask for information within a context of how well a question has been able to access a respondent's memory of prior activities and his or her world knowledge. The informant's reasoning is constrained by the question and the recoding of past events and experiences in order to fit the frame provided by the researcher. The selection and verification of schemata or modules of knowledge which can be identified as reflecting key elements of an experienced situation or event can be more complex than recalling a story or film which has been read or seen within the context of an experiment. Similar principles should be expected, however, despite changes in what is to be elicited and the material to be coded.

The use of elicitation frames for reconstructing past events and experiences requires a negotiation process between the interviewer and informant. This process will reflect pragmatic elements that are part of a model implicitly used by the researcher and informant. The model includes elements of the speaker's or listener's plan (thoughts, intended meaning) that would be consistent with his or her acts, and congruent with the emergent context.

The analysis of narrative and textual material must attempt to specify the interaction between the researcher's perception and interpretation of specific utterances or lines of prose, and the building up progressively of more abstract levels of predication or complexity through an interaction of textual perception and the researcher's own knowledge base and hypotheses or conjectures or imagery. The model of text comprehension and reading for an individual can provide a preliminary stage for depicting the way a researcher contemplates different sources of information from the narrative response, from prior knowledge, and deductive and inductive hypotheses.

The researcher's selective combination of information from several informants, creates a progressively more elaborate explanation of an identified aspect of history or some account of events, activities, and persons. This approach avoids the reduction of each informant's answers to a categorical assignment of meaning in a speech act or survey research sense. The relative assignment of meaning employed in the paper is designed to develop and refine a model that combines expansion and story grammar or schema notions.

The reader will notice that the perspective used in this paper seeks to identify the construction of historical events or experiences of informants by recognizing their limited capacity processing of information. The researcher's task is to recognize the informant's limitations as well as his or her own limits, while also revealing the reconstruction necessary to create a group's collective knowledge of some aspect of their history. The researcher must include some assesment of the informants' knowledge base as part of the elicitation and analysis of information.

Summary

In order to deal with the elusive term "pragmatics" I have followed some distinctions used by Green (n.d.) in a recent paper and have added a few of my own by linking the notion to practical conditions associated with field research. My concern with changes in language use and the sense of community identity among Sephardic Jews, particularly over the past 100 years or so, has directed my attention to the practical problems faced and practical knowledge assumed in all field research that often goes unreported. Much of the information left out of reports based on the study of language structure and use delete references to socio-cultural conceptions the researcher was obliged to invoke tacitly in order to conduct his or her study.

Throughout this paper I have argued for an explicit concern with levels of predication or complexity that are involved in all studies of language structure and use. The notion of interaction among levels of predication assumes that no reductionist argument exists here, but that several systems of knowledge are in interaction, but they are not reducible in some hierarchical sense.

The analysis of interview narratives does not follow a survey approach to language use by posing a series of questions which would reduce the informant's responses to coded expressions of use over designated time periods. Such a survey strategy would ignore the limited capacity processing capabilities and knowledge base of the informants. Each informant becomes, instead, an exemplar of possible candidate sources of information about a topic that is the result of a progressively built, data-driven, analysis that combines with hypothesis-driven information derived from other informants and historical materials.

The notion of levels of predication is an integral part of an interactive model that requires us to find a way of integrating the practical problems associated with field research into our more restricted analysis of language structure and use. My brief reference to a larger study of Sephardic communities is intended to sensitize the reader to the necessity of reporting practical problems routinely encountered in field research that influence the way we make inferences about the meaning of speech events, and how these can reflect historical activities. I have tried to underscore the fact that speech events are always embedded in socio-cultural contexts whose knowledge we often take for granted.

The researcher's folk theory of social life, his or her everyday beliefs and opinions, become an integral part of his or her interpretation and summarization of the interview materials. The pragmatics of the reconstruction process, therefore, constitutes the heart of the use and creation of knowledge processes and our claims to factual information about the world.

FOOTNOTE:

* The research which produced the materials presented in this paper was made possible by a John Simon Guggenheim Fellowship and a sabbatical leave from the University of California, San Diego.

PRAGMATICS AND PRAGMATISM

David E. Cooper

Consider these claims:

(i) Calling Bavarians 'sausage-eaters' is insulting.
(ii) By 'there' the speaker meant Bavaria.
(iii) 'Bayern' refers, in German, to Bavaria.

The first is a purely pragmatic claim, saying something about speakers and their acts, without providing information which is relevant to determining the truth of sentences. (ii) is about a speaker, but does provide information that is crucial to determining truth-value. Following Cresswell (1973;238) we might call such a claim 'semantically pragmatic'. (iii) provides vital semantic information, without mentioning speakers at all. Similar claims would include:

(iv) 'Bayerisch' applies to whatever is Bavarian.
(v) 'München ist in Bayern' means that Munich is in Bavaria.

It would be natural to call (iii)-(v) 'semantically semantic', or 'purely semantic'. Natural, but provocative. For many writers have insisted that, *au fond* and implicitly, such claims *are* about speakers. What look to be purely semantic claims are really sematically pragmatic, since they are about a three-termed relation between words, speakers, and the world.

Examples of this attitude will help. Strawson (1950) said that it is not words which refer, but we who refer with them. Taken literally, this must mean that a claim like (iii) is, implicitly, about speakers - equivalent to something like "In standard circumstances, normal Germans utter 'Bayern' to pick out Bavaria". All facts about reference become, thereby, pragmatic.

A very well-known example of the attitude I have in mind is H.P. Grice's account of meaning - according to which claims about what words or sentences mean are reducible to ones about what speakers mean (which, in turn, are analysable in terms of speakers' intentions).

As a final example, think of the so-called 'Causal Theory of Reference', of the type hinted at by Kripke (1972). According to such a view, (iii) is implicitly a claim about the causal connections holding between speakers who utter 'Bayern' and the place, Bavaria. Dennis Stampe (1977, and this volume) has recently tried to elaborate a 'causal Theory' of meaning as well; (v) would be treated as a claim about the circumstances causing utterances of the quoted sentence. Such views are often contrasted with an account, like Grice's, which emphasizes the intentions and beliefs of speakers; but to the extent that, according to both, claims about meaning and reference are taken to be claims about speakers, they belong together for my purposes. The real contrast is with all those theories which deny that claims like (iii)-(v) are, even in the final analysis, about speakers. Let those who deny this be called 'purists'; we may pit them against the 'reductionist' views just illustrated. The relevance of the distinction to the topic of this volume is obvious: if the 'reductionists' are right then the limits of Pragmatics are wide indeed, since Semantics lies within them.

The main business of this paper is to assess what is at issue between 'purists' and 'reductionists' - but first a preliminary point. 'Reductionists' should not be thought unwilling or unable to draw distinctions which, traditionally, have been characterized as ones between the semantic and the pragmatic. The need is for *re*-characterization, not abolition. For a start, Cresswell's distinction between the 'pragmatically pragmatic' and the 'semantically pragmatic' remains - between, that is, information about speakers which is, and information which is not, relevant to determining truth. Second, a distinction remains between, roughly, very general facts about speakers which are normally taken for granted and paid no explicit attention in ascertaining reference or meaning, and specific facts about particular speakers, explicit mention of which is required for such ascertainment. Between, for example, the fact that nearly all Germans nearly always use 'Bayern' to refer to Bavaria, and the fact that this speaker on this occasion referred to Bavaria by 'there'. It is because the general facts are so well-known, and stable, that no explicit mention of them figures in semantic claims, so the 'reductionist' will argue - and it is on this lack of explicitness that he will blame the illusion that such claims have no pragmatic content at all. Respect for the distinctions just mentioned is clearly compatible with the insistence that the so-called 'semantic' really is, in the last analysis, one with the pragmatic.[1]

How is the issue to be settled? Are claims like (iii)-(v) purely semantic or are they implicitly pragmatic? It is the kind of question to make the head swim, for one is unsure what sorts of consideration should count. And this is due, in part, to uncertainty about the very point and aim of Semantics.

But isn't the aim of, say, a theory of reference obvious? It is to entail, for each referring expression of the language under study, true claims of the form "'...' refers to ____". The one which does this is right; the rest are wrong. But, for us, this is an unhelpful idea. Many such claims are debatable, and it is precisely one's theory of reference - in some further sense - that motivates acceptance or rejection. For example: a causal theorist is more likely than his opponent to accept a claim like "'Santa Claus' refers to St. Niklaus". Moreover, even if we were satisfied that a set of axioms and rules entailed all and only true referential claims, there would remain the problem of interpreting these. The 'reductionist' will not be perturbed if the axioms do not *look* pragmatic, since his is a view about what they are in the final, deep analysis. Both remarks suggest that a theory which yields all and only true referential claims is insufficient. It should also provide a philosophical analysis of what these claims amount to - or, at any rate, be supplemented by such an analysis.[2]

In some recent writings, the following conception of the aim of Semantics is prominent: semantic theory is to be seen as one element in a wider theory whose job is to ascribe propositional attitudes - beliefs, desires, etc. - to speakers. A semantics is plausible to the extent that it, in conjunction with other elements in the theory (some psychology and some biology, for example) promotes a plausible ascription of beliefs etc. to speakers. For that ascription to be plausible, the beliefs etc. must be ones whose genesis, and whose role in the explanation of behaviour, are, given the empirical data, intelligible. At least two constraints must govern such an ascription. First, the beliefs etc. ascribed must not, beyond a certain point of tolerence, be inconsistent with one another; otherwise they can play no role in explaining behaviour. Second the beliefs etc. ascribed must not clash, beyond a certain point of tolerance, with what we take speakers to be *saying* (asserting, commanding, etc.); otherwise we must imagine the speakers unable to express their beliefs etc. with any accuracy which, *inter alia*, would make it impossible to understand how beliefs get transmitted in their community. (Perhaps this second constraint is a special case of the first; if someone sincerely asserts p then in *some* sense he believes that p - in which case there would be a clash in the beliefs ascribed to him if we had already decided, on other grounds, to ascribe to him the belief that not-p).

This second constraint guarantees a crucial role, within the overall theory, to some machinery for inferring what people are asserting, commanding, etc. from the noises they utter. For it is speech acts, not mere acoustic emissions, which must cohere with the propositional attitudes being ascribed. Now semantic claims, whatever else they may be, are permits for making precisely these inferences. If 'Bayern' and 'Deutschland' refer to Bavaria and Germany respectively, then we are entitled to infer, other things being equal, that someone uttering 'Bayern ist in Deutschland' is asserting that Bavaria is in Germany. A set of semantic claims, then, will pass muster to the extent that the assertions, commands etc. we infer on the basis of them cohere with a plausible overall ascription of beliefs, desires, etc. generated by the total theory.

Of course the traffic is not one-way. If a semantics has served us well in helping to ascribe beliefs within a certain, important area of discourse, we shall not necessarily revise the semantics when, put to work in some other area, it fails to facilitate a smooth ascription of intelligible beliefs. Perhaps in this area - religion, say - the speakers *are* hopelessly inconsistent, or badly self-deceived, or very poor at expressing their beliefs. Or, more likely perhaps, we shall invoke the *ceteris paribus* clause in the inference from utterance to assertion; preferring, thereby, to regard the utterances as symbolic, or metaphorical, rather than as serious, literal assertions of what is believed.

Vague as this conception of Semantics is, I am going to accept it for the rest of this paper - and to accept, therefore, the rough but real criteria of adequacy it imposes on semantic claims. Our question can now be: given this conception, how does the issue stand concerning the ultimately pragmatic nature of semantic claims? Can conceiving of Semantics in the above manner help us choose between the doctrines of the 'purists' and the 'reductionists'?

There is a strong, but unfortunate tendency among writers who espouse this conception to suppose that it *immediately* implies a 'reductionist' account. One philosopher, for example, moves briskly from 'the account which [...] locates semantical notions within the general framework of propositional attitudes' to the conclusion that 'semantics *is part of* propositional attitude psychology' (B. Loar 1976a:138-39; italics mine). But this is a *non sequitur*. From the fact that Semantics is 'located' within the framework of propositional attitudes - in the sense that its claims help us ascribe such attitudes - it does not follow that these claims are *about* these attitudes; that, for example, they are about speakers' intentions. An analogy may help. Statements of the form 'X is (il)legal' are 'located', no doubt, in the framework of social behaviour - of what men do, and refrain from, and of what happens to them in consequence. Some jurists have been tempted to construe the statements as being about the behaviour and its consequences - the 19th century thinker John Austin, for instance, according to whom 'X is illegal' means something like 'The Sovereign will do something unpleasant to anyone who disobeys his command to refrain from X'. But the much more plausible view is that such statements are not themselves about behaviour and its consequences; rather they are statements which, in conjunction with further information of a sociological sort, enable us to predict behaviour and its consequences. Given that X is illegal and the information that nearly everyone in the country respects the law, we can predict that few will commit X. Likewise, it may be best to construe semantic claims, not as themselves being about beliefs, intentions, or whatever, but as claims which, in conjunction with further information, enable us to ascribe such mental states.

It would be a *non sequitur*, too, to conclude that because speakers must be causally related to the things they have beliefs about, therefore referential claims are about these causal relations. For there remains the alternative, and perfectly intelligible, idea that information concerning causal relations belongs in a quite different part of the overall theory which generates ascriptions of propositional attitudes.[3]

So, to adopt the conception of Semantics outlined above is not, *ipso facto*, to regard semantic claims as being, in the last analysis, about speakers. But this is not to say that we should not regard them in this way. Indeed, I want now to sketch what looks to be a powerful line of argument in favour of doing just that.

For the formal semanticist, inventing an interpretation for an artificial language, no problem arises concerning the nature of the facts expressed by the axioms he lays down - axioms like "The symbol a denotes the number three". For no facts are expressed. The axioms are simply stipulations, arbitrary pairings of symbols with objects (numbers, for example). But a problem does seem to arise with natural language claims like (iii)-(v); especially when they are considered to play a role in ascribing beliefs, desires etc. to speakers. For surely they must be *true* - that is, express facts - in order to play this role successfully. Now what can these facts be, if not facts about speakers? To reply that they are special, unanalysable semantic facts sounds unappealing from the standpoint of Occam's Razor. Moreover such a reply must sound completely intolerable from the standpoint of *physicalism*, which so many of us would like to embrace. Tarski (1956) was quite right to stress that, on the surface at least, semantic facts do not fit into a purely physicalist picture of the world. A claim about a word's reference, for example, does not, on that surface, report some physical feature of the world. Reference, meaning, etc. left unanalysed would seem to be non-physical relations, dangling outside the framework of extensional relations allowed by the physicalist.

The urge to make semantic claims physicalistically respectable has been, clearly, a strong motive behind causal accounts of reference and meaning.[2] But this same motive, less obviously, can impel accounts in terms of intentions, beliefs, etc. After all, the physicalist is anyway stuck with the problem of the mental; so it is a bonus for him if one kind of unwelcome fact - the semantic - can be reduced to another kind, the mental. For if he can provide a satisfactory treatment of the mental, he will then, *ipso facto*, have handled the semantic as well.

Although I intend resisting the line of argument just sketched, there is no denying its force or the appeal it lends to 'reductionism'. Before putting up some resistance, however, I want to state why resistance is desirable; why, in other words, a 'purist' treatment of semantic claims is desirable; why, if you like, 'reductionism' should be rejected (unless there is no way of resisting the 'physicalist' line of argument).

It is important to stress that from the technical, mechanical point of view, semantic claims *need not* be treated other than 'puristically' in order to play the role allotted to them within an overall theory generating ascriptions of propositional attitudes. That role was to license inferences, *ceteris paribus*, from utterances to speech acts - the disquotational role, as it might be called. The *only* information we require, to infer from a serious utterance of 'Bayern ...' to the conclusion that the speaker asserted something about Bavaria, is the information that 'Bayern' refers to Bavaria. Any view we might have concerning the content of that referential claim is immaterial to the license it provides for the inference. I am not sure how sound the following principle is, but it has the welcome ring of methodological economy: Do not treat claims as having more content than they must have in order to play the role they are designed for! If this, or a more refined principle, is sound, it provides a reason for a 'purist' treatment of semantic claims.

The central point, though, is that any current 'reductionist' theory renders the connection between semantic claims and a particular range of facts about speakers much too *tight*. On one theory a claim like (iii) stands or falls according to facts about speakers' intentions when uttering 'Bayern'. On another theory it stands or falls according to facts about the causal connections between utterances of 'Bayern' and the place, Bavaria. It would be correct, but too shallow, to complain of the one-sidedness of such theories, of their failure to take account of the motley considerations which influence acceptance or rejection of semantic claims. For this complaint is open to the rejoinder that, while our present practice may be to consider motley facts, that practice should be reformed; just one range of facts ought to be promoted to sovereign status.

The deeper complaint, which forestalls that rejoinder, is that any one-sided diet of facts about speakers would predispose us, on many occasions, towards implausible ascriptions of beliefs, desires, etc. to speakers. Let me elaborate. We have seen that no semantic claims would *force* us to conclude that someone who utters s thereby believes that p; but if our Semantics tells us that s is true iff p, *explanation* is required if, on the occasion, that conclusion is not to be drawn. It must be explained either why, on this occasion, the utterance of s was not the assertion that p, or why the assertion that p was not a straightforward expression of the belief that p. In such explanations, facts about speakers' intentions, or about descriptions they carry in their heads, or about causal relations between them and the world, will often figure. But no facts of just one of these kinds are especially privileged; none play a sovereign role in ascribing beliefs, desires, etc. As such none should be built into the semantic claims themselves.

Let me illustrate. One reason for *not* construing a referential claim as being about descriptions in the heads of speakers is that this would predispose us to some highly implausible ascriptions of beliefs, obliging us, most unsatisfactorily, to 'explaining' why we refuse to make the ascriptions. For example: average speakers on another planet might associate with their word 'flub' just those descriptions average speakers here associate with 'gold' - even though flub is a quite different substance from gold. An overwhelming reason for denying that 'flub' and 'gold' have the same reference, despite the identity of the descriptions usually associated with them, is that the beliefs the aliens express when they refer with 'flub' are not those we express when we refer with 'gold'. How could their beliefs be ours when they have never even encountered gold? Clearly they could not have beliefs *about* gold, any more than we could have them about flub (which we have never encountered). But if we were to insist that 'flub' and 'gold' have the same reference, in virtue of the similar descriptions associated with them in the heads of speakers, we would have to *explain* something that surely does not need explaining - namely, that flub-beliefs are not gold-beliefs.[4]

The inhabitants of the other planet cannot have beliefs about gold since they have never, however indirectly, been in causal contact with it - but I am not holding a brief for a causal theory of reference. Causal theories, of the type presently available, can also predispose us towards implausible ascriptions of propositional attitudes. Consider the idea that 'a' refers to X if and only if, roughly, X was 'baptised' by the name 'a', and that a causal chain extends from this 'baptism' to present uses of 'a' through speakers' inheriting the use of the name from speakers who inherited its use from ... speakers who witnessed the 'baptism'. It would seem to follow that if I picked up the name 'Louis' in a bar-room conversation from someone who picked it up from someone who ... witnessed the 'baptism' of Louis XIII by this name, then it is to this King I refer when *à propos* of the bar-room conversation, I later remark "I hear this Louis was a bit of a pervert". And I do this, even if I have not the slightest idea who Louis is, beyond his being whoever the conversation was about. As Gareth Evans (1973), from whom I borrow the example, remarks, this would seem a weird conclusion. Surely I cannot be said to be referring to one French King rather than another, or to any King at all. And the main reason this cannot be said is that it would be absurd to ascribe to me, on the basis of my remark, any belief *about* Louis XIII. Hearing that this Louis, whoever he was, was a bit of a pervert, adds nothing to my stock of beliefs concerning 17th century French regal history.

These counter-examples are directed against particular versions of particular 'reductionist' theories - but they strongly suggest that any such theory sets off on the wrong foot. For, given the large variety of facts which are relevant in determining propositional attitudes - and I have only mentioned some of these (causal connections, descriptions in the head, etc.) - there can be no warrant for promoting any one kind of fact to the status of actually entering into the content of, or being expressed by, semantic claims. To promote a kind of fact about speakers to this status would, given the license that semantic claims give us for inferring propositional attitudes from utterances *via* speech acts, reflect unwarranted prejudice against all the other kinds of facts.

There remains the 'physicalist' line of argument for 'reductionism' sketched earlier. Those with strong physicalist predilections may feel that this argument, if left unanswered, outweighs the 'purist' considerations just rehearsed.

One way of trying to resist the argument borrows from Donald Davidson's (1970) thesis concerning the physical and the mental. His aim is to reconcile physicalism with the view (which he accepts) that psychological descriptions are not reducible to physical ones. The thesis relies on a sharp distinction between events (states etc.) and their descriptions. Physicalism holds that all events are physical - and this, says Davidson, is not threatened by the impossibility, in general, of replacing psychological descriptions ('wants a sausage', say) by neurophysiological ones. Although each event of wanting a sausage is a physical one, there is no reason to suppose those events constitute a neurophysiologically significant class; no reason, therefore, to suppose that each such event is describable by the same, significant neurophysiological predicate. And this reflects the fact that our reasons for grouping events under physical and psychological descriptions respectively are entirely different. The point of ascribing wants or beliefs is to explain behaviour as rational; and if the ascription of the same want or belief on a variety of occasions serves this purpose, it is of no consequence that, on these various occasions, no single type of neurophysiological event is occurring (nor any manageable disjunction of such types).

An analogous thesis has been applied to the relation between the physical and the semantic.[5] Semantic claims, it is agreed, are not reducible to (ultimately) physical descriptions of speakers, their noises, and relations to the world. But this, it is held, is perfectly consistent with physicalism, taken as the doctrine that all events (states etc.), including speech acts, are physical. No doubt there are plenty of (ultimately) physical connections between Germans, 'Bayern", and

Bavaria; but there is no reason to think that "'Bayern' refers to Bavaria" is replaceable by a description of these relations. And this is because the purpose of semantic claims is entirely different from that of physical descriptions. The aim of semantic claims is to license inferences from utterances to assertions; and if a claim succeeds in this aim it will be of no consequence that, on different occasions of a word's utterance, no single, significant physical relation holds between utterance, speaker, and the world. None of this shows that the utterance, the act of reference, or the assertion are anything but physical events.

If this thesis is correct, the fallacy in the line of argument being challenged by it is clear: it resides in the assumption that if semantic claims are not reducible to physicalistic statements then they must express non-physical facts. That, it is held, is no more warranted than the similar asssumption attacked by Davidson - to the effect that psychological events must be non-physical, unless 'mentalese' is replaceable by purely physicalistic talk.

Attractive as this borrowing from Davidson is, I do not think the thesis can be made to carry over from the psychological to the semantic. A reasonably clear sense can be given to the idea that psychological descriptions are, nevertheless, descriptions of purely physical events; and this is why, despite the irreducibility of 'mentalese', there is no ontological rivalry between the mental and the physical. But what is supposed to stand to semantic claims in the way that neurophysiological events stand to psychological descriptions? If there is nothing analogous, it is hard to see how physicalism can be maintained - for it is essential to Davidson's thesis that, on any occasion, a psychological description is of an event which is physical. But if there is something analogous - a complex physical relation between people, noises, and the world, say - it is difficult to see how one avoids reduction of the semantic to the physical. Certainly one cannot avoid it in the way Davidson avoided reduction of the psychological to the physical - by arguing that, on the different occasions where a sematic claim obtains, one should not expect to find physically similar events occurring. For a semantic claim is not, like a psychological description, an occasion-statement at all. It makes no sense to say that "'Bayern' refers to Bavaria" holds on some occasions, and not on others; *ipso facto* it can make no sense to say that, on the occasions it does hold, physically dissimilar events are occurring.

It seems to me that, once it is conceded that semantic claims do express facts, it is impossible to reconcile semantics with physicalism except by reduction of the semantic to the physical. If so, either the case must be conceded to our 'reductionist' opponents, or the price of 'purist' semantics is abandonment of physicalism.

There remains just one way for the physicalistically-minded 'purist' to save the day. Earlier it was agreed that no problem arises concerning the status of the semantic facts in a formalist's interpretation of an artificial language; for there are no such facts, merely stipulations, arbitrary pairings of symbols and things. My suggestion is that we look on semantic claims about a natural language in the same way: they are mere *devices* - pairings - for inferring speech acts from utterances. As such, the question cannot even arise as to the nature of the facts - physical or otherwise - expressed by the claims, since none are expressed. There will, to be sure, remain a distinction between the linguist's claims and the formalist's stipulations - namely the sensitivity of the former to empirical facts about speakers. If the ascriptions of propositional attitudes, inferred in part from a set of semantic claims, are implausible, then those claims will be altered. Like any device, a semantic claim can be scrapped if it serves its purpose ill. But this sensitivity to empirical consequences does not force us to regard the claims themselves as true or false, as expressing facts. Rules of a game will be scrapped if they have unfortunate empirical consequences; that does not render them fact-stating.

Suggestions of the same shape as mine once peppered Positivistic philosophy. One thinks of Ramsey's idea that universal generalizations are merely rules; or the idea that moral judgments are merely emotive ejaculations. Such suggestions are rightly treated with scepticism - and the problem with them (including mine) is their head-on collision with the powerful, intuitive impression that the relevant claims (moral, semantic, etc.) *are* true or false, *do* express facts. Certainly it will not do to say, merely, that they have the same grammatical form as genuine fact-stating sentences. So the obligation is on someone who makes such a suggestion to explain away, to discredit, that powerful impression.

In the case which concerns us, we would go a long way towards discharging this obligation if we identified genuine facts which it is only too easy to *mistake* as being expressed by semantic claims. Or, what comes to the same thing, if we identified some non-semantic, fact-stating claims which it is only too easy to *confuse* with semantic claims. For then, we should have an explanation of why the powerful impression just mentioned is, nonetheless, illusory.

Earlier I argued it is wrong to treat certain kinds of facts about speakers, their beliefs, causal relations to things, etc. as entering into the very content of semantic claims. That was the error of 'reductionism'. But it is surely just these kinds of facts which most of us have dimly in mind when we wrongly consider semantic claims to be fact-stating. It is sentences expressing these facts - sentences like "The average German uses 'Bayern' with the intention of talking about Bavaria" - which become confused with genuine semantic claims, and lend to the latter the illusory air of being true or false. It is a confusion which is explicit and doctrinal among 'reductionists'; but it is the same confusion, I suggest, which in a rough and non-theoretical manner is shared by all who share the impression that semantic claims must be fact-stating. It follows that any objection to 'reductionism' is, *ipso facto*, a reason for not taking too seriously that powerful impression; for it is but a dim reflection of the wrongheadedness that pervades 'reductionism'.

Why does 'Pragmat*ism*' occur in my title? A pragmatist attitude enters in at two places. First, I have discussed the 'purist' vs. 'reductionist' issue in the light of a certain conception of semantics - one which understands semantics in terms of the *role* which semantic claims play within a wider theory whose aim is to ascribe propositional attitudes. Second, my view of the status of semantic claims is pragmatist. I denied that thsese claims are to be treated as true or false; but it would be a mere verbal shift to say, instead, that their truth or falsity consists *entirely* in the success or failure they have in licensing inferences which maximally facilitate plausible ascriptions of propositional attitudes. There would then be a close connection between my view and the type of view, held by Peirce and other pragmatists, of theoretical claims in the natural sciences.

FOOTNOTES:

1. It is clear, I hope, that I am using 'Pragmatics' in the original, wide sense given it by Charles Morris - to refer to that area of language-study concerned with the relations between expressions, objects, and speakers. Narrower senses have since grown up - e.g. pragmatics as the study of indexical expressions.

2. See Hartry Field (1972).

3. See J. McDowell (1977).

4. The example, and the line of criticism, is borrowed from Hilary Putnam. See, for example, Putnam (1973).

5. See J. McDowell (1978).

IDIOMATICITY AS A PROBLEM OF PRAGMATICS

Florian Coulmas

0 *Introduction*

In 1971 at the seventh regional meeting of the Chicago linguistic society, James D. McCawley presented a paper on "The applicability of transformations to idioms", thereby establishing his reputation as a leading figure in scato-linguistics. At issue was the question as to whether or not a number of expressions referring to the satisfaction of natural needs, such as, *to take a shit*, were to be considered idioms, and whether they could undergo any syntactic transformations. I do not intend to continue this tradition, yet I could not but recall McCawley's paper when I recently came across a passage in Kurt Vonnegut's famous book, "Breakfast of Champions", which I would like to present to you, because it sheds some light on a number of pargmatic problems concerning idioms, which I want to discuss in this paper.

The following dialog takes place in a highway restaurant between Kilgore Trout, a science fiction writer, and the truck driver who has given him a lift:

> 'Excuse me', said the truck driver to Trout, 'I've got to take a leak.' 'Back where I come from', said Trout, 'that means you're going to steal a mirror. We call mirrors *leaks*.' 'I never heard that before', said the driver. He repeated the word: 'leaks'. He pointed to a mirror on a cigarette machine. 'You call that a *leak*?' 'Doesn't it look like a leak to you?' said Trout. 'No', said the driver. 'Where did you say you were from?' 'I was born in Bermuda', said Trout. About a week later, the driver would tell his wife that mirrors were called *leaks* in Bermuda, and she would tell her friends. (Vonnegut, 1975:88f.)

What has this sort of punning to do with idiomaticity and what with pragmatics? The general answer to the first part of this question is quite obvious: *to take a leak* is an idiom. As for the second part, I will now give some arguments for a pragmatic treatment of idioms.

1 *Idiomaticity*

First, let us take a closer look at this particular idiom. We all know what *to take* means, and most of us know that *leak* means something like "an accidental aperture permitting liquid or gas to flow out of or into a vessel". Yet, those who are not native speakers of English may not know the meaning of the expression composed of these two words. There is, in other words, no way to predict the meaning of the complex unit on the basis of the meanings of its parts. As with most idioms, the compositionality principle of semantics is suspended here. Nevertheless, we may very well be able to interpret the expression in question correctly if it occurs in actual discourse, even if we don't know the meaning of *leak*.

It is my conviction that the study of obstructed and in some sense abnormal or handicaped conditions of verbal communication often helps us to understand what the normal conditions are and how they govern normal verbal behavior. Let me try then to reconstruct what it takes for a non-native speaker to arrive at a correct interpretation of the driver's remark.

A distinction must be made between two different cases: a speaker who knows the meaning of *leak* and another one who doesn't. Clearly, the former has an advantage over the latter, because if he knows the meaning of *leak* he knows that a leak is a particular kind of nothingness, and as such, nothing that one can take in the literal sense of *take*. This, of course, is not enough to show the meaning of *to take a leak*, but it suffices to know that it is an idiom. On the other hand, the speaker who does not know the meaning of *leak* has to reckon with two possibilities: one is that *leak* is a noun which refers to a class of objects and that it is used as such; the other one is that *leak* does not refer to a class of objects or is not being used in this way. The first assumption will lead him to the false conclusion that it is merely one word that he doesn't know, while the second assumption allows him to conclude that *take* is not being used in its literal sense, and that the whole phrase must hence be an idiom. If he assumes that *leak* is being used as a regular noun, he will arrive at the latter conclusion only after having consulted a dictionary, and after having found out that the expression still doesn't make sense. For the non-native speaker it is always a sensible assumption that an incomprehensible expression might be an idiom. It is part of his bi- or multi-lingual competence that those expressions which are both items with higher level grammatical structure *and* lexical items, and which thus defy regular intertranslatability, are hardest to grasp.

Let us suppose now that the non-native speaker, in one way or other, has inferred that *to take a leak* is an idiom. The subsequent interpretation process makes use of two different kinds of knowledge which combine to reduce the range of possible meanings:

- the logic of everyday activity; and
- the structure of lexical phrases.

Most communicative acts take place in stereotyped social situations. This is the reason why no linguistic novelty is demanded in most situations, but rather, a combination of familiar material which to some extent is itself stereotyped, and conventionally tied to some situational constraints (cf. Coulmas 1979 for further details). The little dialog between Kilgore Trout and the truck driver takes place in an everyday situation of the commonest kind: two people are sitting at a restaurant table. One of them gets up in order to relieve himself and thus temporarily interrupts the conversation. Before he leaves, he apologizes for so doing, and he offers some explanation as to what he is going to do. In the ordinary course of events there are not many alternatives as to the content of what he is going to say. It is in this sense that I understand Halliday's remark that "from a sociological point of view, a text is meaningful not so much because we do not know what the speaker is going to say, as in a mathematical model of communication, as because we do know" (Halliday 1975:129). Not only do the participants of every normal conversation share a common context of information, they also have knowledge of what can ordinarily be expected to happen when conventional activities unfold. Hence, even if our non-native speaker's linguistic competence is too poor to allow him to venture any conclusions, he has still a good chance to infer correctly the meaning of *to take a leak* on the basis of his knowledge of everyday activities, and a "general sense postulate" (in the Griceian manner; see Grice 1975) when he encounters this phrase in a setting such as the one just sketched.

I don't want to implicate, however, that this is merely a matter of chance, and that correct interpretation is little more than guesswork. The context of situation plays an important part, and so does our knowledge of everyday activities. Language as it happens is always embedded, but for the sake of concentrating too strongly on the embedding, we should not forget that which is being embedded. A closer look at the phrase in question is thus in order. As a lexical phrase it functions like a verb, but its internal structure cannot be overlooked. It is composed of the verb *take*, the indefinite article, and the noun *leak*.

Take is what I would like to call an "idiom-prone" lexeme of English. There are innumerable lexical phrases, idioms and compound words into which it enters as a component. *Take on, take off, take after, take in, take advantage of, take a chance, take a look, take it seriously, can you take it, overtake, undertaker, take aback*, etc. are but a few examples, and it is not easy to identify a common conceptual core. This is, however, not what I am trying to do here. More important to my present purpose is the mere fact (a) that there *are* "idiom-prone" lexemes in every language (cf. Makkai 1978), (b) that speakers know of this fact, and (c) that *take* is a very typical instance of an "idiom-prone" lexeme whose counterparts in many languages function in a similar fashion. Given this kind of knowledge, the non-native speaker will not be "taken by surprise" by the fact that *take* can take a great variety of different meanings. He will realize very soon that an expression in which a noun syntactically functions as the direct object of *take* is not necessarily to be interpreted as a relation holding between an agent and an object that he takes. Various activities are labeled with expressions that are composed of *take* and several different prepositional, nominal or adverbial complements. Hence if he encounters the phrase *to take a leak* he is well prepared to interpret it correctly. Additional information is, of course, provided by the literal meaning of the lexeme *leak*, which is both a noun whose meaning can roughly be paraphrased as "an accidental aperture, crack, etc." and a verb which is partly synonymous with *drip*. These concepts are quite suggestive. But by themselves they cannot guarantee a correct interpretation. The relation between the literal and the idiomatic meaning of an expression is not altogether arbitrary (cf. Chafe 1968; Makkai 1972), yet the latter is not (mechanically) deducible from the former. *To take a leak* could very well mean "to steal away" or "to escape". Different meaning components of *leak* would be the basis of an idiom of this sort, but the relation between the literal meanings of the parts and the idiomatic meaning of the complex unit would be of essentially the same kind as in the case of the idiom being considered.

In addition to our knowledge of everyday activity, situational information, and the word meanings, there is yet another clue for its correct interpretation: namely, our cultural knowledge of the way certain bodily functions are treated and talked about, that they belong to a taboo zone and are likely to be labeled with euphemistic expressions. These different kinds of information all combine to form a *defining context* for the idiom (cf. Hockett 1956:223), providing us with a solid basis for its correct interpretation.

Assuming now that the non-native speaker has, indeed, arrived at a proper understanding of *to take a leak* by inference rather than instruction, there is one thing that he has no way of knowing: He cannot tell whether *to take a leak* is a nonce-form or an established lexical item (idiom) of the English language. I will come back to this point presently. In concluding the foregoing observations about the linguistic part of the interpretation process, and in order to counterbalance the claim that utterances are meaningful because we are familiar with stereotyped utterance situations, I want to point out that the most important ingredient of language understanding is the capacity to exhaust the meaning potential of lexical items in such a way as to match linguistic expressions with factual circumstances, both of which are never exactly the same as they recur. At the same time, this is the capacity to make productive usage of lexical items. Language is a very flexible instrument, and it is critically important to its competent employment that lexical items are used, on the one hand, to reduce the infinite variety of the perceptual world to humanly manageable complexity, and that they are, on the other hand, applied to novel experiences — a process which often leads to an expansion of the meaning potential of a lexical item. Idioms play an important part in this respect. They are a linguistic device to enlarge the possibilities of a language and to adapt it to new demands without introducing new material. Our capacity to produce new idioms and to understand them rests essentially on this equilibrium between the novel and the familiar.

The importance of a proper understanding of idioms for everyday verbal behavior is neatly summarized in the following observation by C. Hockett:

> As we go about the business of living, we constantly meet circumstances which are not *exactly* like anything in our previous experience. When we react via speech to such partially new circumstances, we may produce a phrase or an utterance which is understandable only because those who hear it are also confronted by the new circumstances. Alternatively, an individual may react to conventional circumstances with a bit of speech which is somewhat unconventional — again being understood because of context. Given any such novelty, either of expression or of circumstances or of both, the event installs special meaning into the linguistic form which is used, and the latter becomes idiomatic (Hockett, 1956:223).

2 *Punning and communicative boycott*

We are now in a position to analyse the internal structure of the initially quoted instance of punning on an idiom. According to W. Chafe, "well-formed idioms" have literal counterparts (Chafe 1968: 111). What he has in mind are idioms such as *to bite the dust* or *to be on the wagon* which can be interpreted literally as well as idiomatically. This is not so with *to take a leak* because, as we have already observed, a leak is nothing that one can take. A sentence such as **He took a leak and carried it away* doesn't make much sense. Yet, the non-compositional meaning of the phrase establishes its identity as an idiom. I think that the twofold interpretability is a general tendency rather than a defining feature of idiomatic expressions. This tendency clearly lies at the bottom of Vonnegut's pun about stealing a mirror.

The mechanics of this pun are readily described as a process of *reliteralization*, i.e. of providing the expression with a literal interpretation. This is only possible if *leak* is given a new interpretation. The author's choice is of course not arbitrary. By declaring *leak* in the meaning of "mirror" a Bermuda dialectal variant he alludes to the Bermuda triangle, Lewis Carroll, and probably a few other things which have escaped my attention. Reliteralization is the reverse of the process which leads the non-native speaker to understand that *to take a leak* is an idiom. The expression is stripped of its idiomatic meaning.

The refusal to interpret an idiomatic expression in its idiomatic meaning is the structural basis of many puns. In cases such as the one under discussion so far, a literal meaning of one of the components must be invented in order to achieve the desired effect. In other cases things are easier thanks to the actual ambiguity of the phrase. It is about time for a fresh example, I take it, so, for a change, I want to quote from another book by Vonnegut:

> The adulation that Trout was receiving, mindless and illiterate as it was, affected Trout like marijuana. He was happy and loud and impudent.
> 'I'm afraid I don't read as much as I ought to', said Maggi.
> 'We're all afraid of something', Trout replied. 'I'm afraid of cancer and rats and Doberman pinschers.' (Vonnegut 1969:114)

In this case, too, reliteralization is the basic structural mechanism of the pun. It differs from the previous example in that the literal and the idiomatic meanings are closely related. *I'm afraid* ... is a routine formula, and it is common knowledge that, in normal usage, it does not mean that the speaker is afraid of something, but that he is about to admit or disclose something unpleasant or somehow negative. It is a sort of a speech act frame or gambit (cf. Keller 1979). By reacting to the literal meaning of the formula rather than to its standard usage, Trout implicitly denies this part of common knowledge which ammounts, in fact, to a violation of a convention. It is a breach of conduct (indicated by the author, incidentally, by the epithet *impudent*). In a way, this kind of punning can be viewed as *communicative boycott*. That is, the stable course of conversational interaction is jeopardized, because one of the participants fails to recognize and to comply with the background expectations of common understanding.

It is therefore not surprising to find the same pattern of communicative misconduct in some of the inconsistency experiments which H. Garfinkel designed in order to elucidate the conditions of normal interaction. Consider the following case:

> My friend and I were talking about a man whose overbearing attitude annoyed us. My friend expressed his feeling.
> (S) I'm sick of him.
> (E) Would you explain what is wrong with you that you are sick?
> (S) Are you kidding me? You know what I mean.
> (E) Please explain your ailment.
> (S) (He listened to me with a puzzled look.) What came over you? We never talk this way, do we?
>   (Garfinkel 1967:44)

As in the previous example, the literal interpretation of *sick* in *I'm sick of* ... is again a violation of a convention. The experimenter thus deliberately undermines the basis of uninterfered interaction by not recognizing the conventional status of *I'm sick of* ... as a routine formula never to be interpreted in the literal sense of *sick*.

The general conclusion that can be drawn from these observations is this: Idioms, lexical phrases, and routine formulae play an important part in ordinary everyday conversation. Their status as fixed expressions is part of the common knowledge governing verbal behavior. Idiomaticity and linguistic routine are qualities of verbal expressions which severely influence the way they are to be interpreted. In those cases where two alternative interpretations — a literal one and an idiomatic or routinized one — are structurally possible, the choice of either one depends on the situational and verbal context of the utterance. As with so many things in language, the literal interpretability of idiomatic and routinized expressions as a real option is a matter of degree.

3   *Idioms and metaphors*

I will say a few words now about the relation of idioms and metaphors. We could argue that the difference between both simply corresponds to the difference between language and speech. According to this view, an idiom is a lexical item of a language whereas a metaphor is coined on the spot as a means of indirectly conveying meaning. Hence, metaphor qualifies as an operation ranging over utterances, while idiomaticity is a property of sentences or parts of sentences. As regards the actual processing of idioms and metaphors in discourse, this implies that with the former we have to strain our memory, and with the latter, our inferential capacities.

Recall now what we have said about the non-native speaker's efforts to interpret an idiom (cf. above p. 141 f.). In many cases the processing will not be different from the processing of a metaphor. If he does not happen to know the idiom in question, the essentially diachronic difference between idiom and metaphor is immaterial to him. This is so because many idioms *are* metaphors, or rather "petrified metaphors". The practical inferences and conversational implicatures that must be drawn in order to understand impromptu metaphors have acquired conventional status and turned into rules of use in the case of idioms. I believe that many idioms have come into existence in this way. Hence, in a sense, the processing of metaphors and idioms in actual discourse is the reverse recapitulation of the diachronic process of idiomatization. However, obviously not all metaphors become idioms, and not every idiom can be traced to a metaphor. Accordingly, we can distinguish three classes of expressions:

      (i) idioms whose metaphorical qualities were lost in the course of history;
      (ii) idioms whose metaphorical origin is still transparent;
      (iii) productive metaphors without idiomatic status.

For the non-native speaker, the latter two types are often indistinguishable. In order to interpret instances of either type he has to rely on inferences involving context, the topic of conversation, social and cultural knowledge, and expectations of what the speaker might want to convey. From a systematic point of view, the differences between impromptu expressions for the indirect signaling of speaker's meanings, i.e. class (iii) expressions, and their conventionalized counterparts, i.e. (i) and (ii), are more significant. In other words, the three types cannot always be kept apart. Rather than discrete subsets of the superordinate class of metaphors in a very general sense they mark focal points on a continuum. Owing to the simple fact taht history is a continuous process rather than a succession of discrete time segments, nobody knows exactly where to draw the line. Therefore a dictionary can never be complete. We would not want to include any nonce-form in the dictionary, but, to the extent that its use spreads throughout the speech community, it acquires lexical status. From an original utterance conveying meaning in metaphorical guise it turns into a conventional unit of the language. In a more obvious manner than other linguistic units, idioms are thus witnesses of linguistic history.

    It was observed above that idioms frequently originate in metaphor. They emerge where functional needs demand linguistic innovation, and they increase the semantic inventory of a language without introducing new material. Clearly, this is the most economical way of using the lexical recourses of a language for innovative purposes. This kind of innovation depends on the speakers' possessing the same code as well as on their shared ability to recognize the metaphorical or metonymic relation between what a given lexemic unit already denotes and what a speaker in a given speech situation wants it to denote by way of meaning extension or transfer. It is only on the basis of a common context of information and/or perception that this result can be occasioned.

4 Toward a pragmatic treatment of idioms

To conclude, a few general remarks on the pragmatic aspects of idioms are in order. Idioms abound in English and in all other languages of the world. In linguistic theory they are generally considered a nuisance rather than a challenge, because they stand where the freedom, as well as the regularity, of syntax ends, and where the semantic principle of compositional meaning fails. Most disturbing of all, they are at the same time holistic and analyzable. The fact that they are composed of freely occurring units, and that their meaning cannot be reduced to the meanings of these units is part of a competent speaker's knowledge of his language. He knows when a lexical unit is used in its own right and for its own meaning, and when it occurs as an element of a larger unit which is stripped of its literal meaning. His ability to know this rests on the contextual processing of speech, a general sensefulness postulate, and particular expectations of what his interlocutor might want to convey, and on the large "phrasicon" (to use Fillmore's term) which constitutes a large part of his linguistic memory.

The pragmatic aspects of idiomaticity become intelligible when we consider the difficulties they present to the non-native speaker. The ideal non-native speaker for our purposes is a very artificial figure whose lexicon contains, among other things, all of the lexical items that enter into idioms but not the idioms themselves. When he learns the meanings of expressions in a foreign language, he gradually acquires the ability to match them with an increasing range of appropriate circumstances. As he encounters idioms, he learns that linguistic meaning is vastly more complicated than a simple computation of the meaning

components of identifiable parts. More consciously than in his own
mother tongue, he will become aware of the polyfunctional nature of
lexical items, and, in some cases, in particular with what I have called "idiom-prone" lexemes, this will lead to a major reassortment of
meaning. The English verbs *take* and *get* stand out as pertinent examples. The non-native speaker will only gradually realize how wide
the ranges of their respective application are and in what directions
they can possibly be extended.

This brings us to yet another aspect of idiomaticity. It is well-
known that idioms, properly used, have the feel of authenticity. On
the other hand, there are also unidiomatic expressions. By "unidiomatic" I do not mean all of the well-formed expressions which are not
idioms. Rather, this notion refers to those expressions which are deviant for no obvious structural reasons. Clearly, every speech community makes only limited use of the possibilities of its language. Many
well-formed expressions never occur, because they do not conform to
the idiomatic preferences of the speech community. In Japanese, for
instance, there are two structural possibilities for the negation of
past tense adjectives. One is to build the negative into the copula,
and the other one is to have a negative affix attached to the adjective
stem. Only the latter possibility is made use of. The former, while
structurally well-formed, appears "outlandish" i.e. unidiomatic to the
native speaker of Japanese. Again, the non-native speaker can help us
to uncover the idiomatic preferences of a speech community, because
this is where he is bound to make mistakes, even if he has mastered the
grammar of the language.

The non-native speaker is a heuristic model that helps us to understand the exceptional position that idioms occupy at various levels of
a language. When I say that they occupy an exceptional place, I don't
mean that they are a rare and specialized extension which can safely be
ignored untill the more pressing problems have been resolved. Idiomaticity is a feature of language pervading everyday discourse throughout,
and it is hard to imagine a language without idioms. I believe that it

is a misconception to consider idioms only as semantic and syntactic irregularities. To be able to fully understand their functional and structural significance, we need to take a pragmatic approach.

A pragmatic treatment of idioms has to account for the polyfunctional nature of lexical units; for the relations between different meanings that are conveyable by idiomatic expressions; for the choice of an idiomatic or literal interpretation of idioms in a given context; for the occurrence restrictions of pragmatic idioms (routine formulae (Coulmas 1979), gambits, proverbs, gnomic expressions, etc.); and for the idiomatic preferences of a speech community.

CONTEXTUALISM

Marcelo Dascal

> In that Empire, the Art of Cartography achieved such a degree of Perfection that the Map of a single Province occupied a whole Town, and the Map of the Empire, a whole Province. Soon, these Enormous Maps were no longer satisfactory and the Colleges of Cartographers created a Map of the Empire which had the Size of the Empire and coincided with it point by point. The Following Generations, less adicted to Cartography, understood that such a huge Map was Useless and, not without impiety, delivered it to the Harshness of the Sun and Winters. In the Western Deserts there are still Ruins of the Map, inhabited by Animals and Beggars; in the whole Country there is no other Vestige of the Geographic Disciplines.
>
> Jorge Luis Borges

I

At the turn of the decade, everybody agrees that 'context' cannot be neglected in the study of language; and nobody denies that 'pragmatics' is the branch of the study of language that has to deal with the contribution of context to the production, structure and interpretation of utterances. Yet, these two general theses seem to be as far as agreement on these matters goes, in spite of an intensive research effort during the last decade.

To be sure, the discovery of context in linguistics and philosophy of language is not an achievement of the seventies. In the sixties, and even before, the role of context was widely recognized in many quarters. In fact, context became so pervasive in discussions about language that Max Black probably expressed the feeling of many when he proposed (in 1970) to create a special discipline - 'contextics' - to deal with all the aspects of context relevant to language.[1] But the complexities of context and the variety of ways in which it turns out to be relevant to language seemed to preclude the possibility of quick progress and successful generalization. While some scholars continued to complain about the lack of systematic discussion of the subject,[2] and some engaged in very broad theorizing,[3] others were quite skeptical about the prospects of the whole enterprise. Chomsky, for one, declared, as recently as 1979, that the formalization (hence, the systematization) of pragmatics is 'premature', for lack of sufficient 'richness' in the domain.[4] The deficiency Chomsky alludes to is not one of data nor of theories (there seem to be plenty of them in this field), but stems from the fact that, according to him, the basic ideas currently employed in pragmatics are "too elementary, vague and without an explicative character" (ibid.).

Among such dubious ideas, the more problematic are perhaps the concepts of "context" and "pragmatics" themselves. The former can be roughly divided into the linguistic environment of an utterance (the 'co-text', following Bar-Hillel's suggestion), and the non-linguistic situation of utterance (for which Bar-Hillel reserved the term 'context'). But both are vague and difficult to define. The situation of utterance was at first conceived as being describable in terms of a small number of parameters: the speaker, the audience, the spatio-temporal location of the speech event, and a few other 'indices'. But clearly many other elements of the situation may be relevant for the production and interpretation of an utterance: the surrounding objects; the non-linguistic behavior of speaker and audience; the preceding and following events; the socio-cultural environment - to mention only the most obvious factors. As Goffman puts it, "it hardly seems possible to name a social variable that doesn't show up and have its little systematic effect upon speech behavior".[5] Consider the parameter labelled "the speaker", for example. Who is she? Certainly not a mere physical entity. It must be an entity endowed with complex sets of beliefs, desires, intentions, thoughts. Among the latter, there must be assumptions about the beliefs, desires, thoughts and intentions of the audience, some of which are thoughts about the speaker's beliefs, etc. All these elements can play a crucial role in the interpretation of any utterance produced by the speaker. Not less important is the recognition of the various social functions that can be performed by "the speaker" in his capacity of "source" of an utterance. Goffman distinguishes four such functions (principal, strategist, animator and figure) which may or may not co-exist in a set of utterances. When they do, the interesting phenomenon of 'multiple-selfing' occurs (Goffman, 1974: 523). And there might be more such functions behind the 'same' speaker. To be sure, not all the facets of the speaker we have so far mentioned are to be taken into account on every occasion, since "a speaker might be considered a whole set of somewhat different things" (Goffman, 1974:519), on different occasions. But the fact that any of them *might* turn out to be relevant implies that *none* of them can be left out of an account of the linguistically relevant aspects of the context. Thus, it seems that the situation of utterance cannot be reduced to a small set of parameters, and must be equated with a whole "possible world", as suggested by Stalnaker (1978: 317-8). But it is not certain that even such a radical proposal will be sufficient, since possible worlds do not standardly include the sets of epistemic and other mental states of the individuals that inhabit them.

The co-text presents us with similar difficulties: are the silences in a conversation parts of the 'text' that constitutes the conversation? How many preceding and following utterances are to be considered a part of the relevant co-text? Under what circumstances should the insertion of an utterance in a given co-text be seen as yielding an incoherent or 'ill-formed' text, rather than as a way of demonstrating that the utterance in question has a somewhat weird meaning in that co-text?

In fact, whoever wishes to demonstrate the contextual dependency of the meaning of a sentence usually constructs a story (a co-text) depicting a situation of utterance in which the sentence means something other than its 'normal' meaning. But the imagination displayed by philosophers and linguists in devising such stories is apparently unbounded (and I know of no principled grounds to constrain it, provided they do not violate the rules of logic). Hence, if the "context" should include every factor that can ever affect the interpretation of an utterance, then 'contextics' would have to be indeed the science of everything.

One way of handling this problem is to replace the pre-theoretical, intuitive and unnecessarily vague notion of context by a more satisfactory theoretical construct. It would include only those factors which, "by virtue of their influence upon the participants in the language event, systematically determine the form, the appropriateness or the meaning of utterances" (Lyons, 1977: 572). Knowledge relative to these factors, now labelled 'context-of-utterance', would constitute the speaker's 'communicative competence', to be accounted for by linguistic theory. The rest of the real context, which would still be lurking behind our utterances, would have to be handled, on Lyons' proposal, by a theory of performance. But such a proposal, though useful, does not really provide a satisfactory way of dealing with the multifariousness of context. The decision as to whether the influence of a given factor is systematic or not will be often quite controversial and somewhat arbitrary. This is true of some of the factors discussed by Lyons himself, e.g. 'subject-matter'. The factors he discusses, by the way, certainly do not form an exhaustive list of all that should be included in our communicative competence, and it is hard to see how such a list could ever be compiled.[6] Furthermore, there is no reason to suppose that some factors traditionally associated with a theory of performance - e.g. memory limitations, perceptual strategies - are not 'systematic'. On the contrary, their influence upon linguistic phenomena obeys certain general principles and proceeds in an orderly way, as recent studies have demonstrated (e.g. Bever, 1974). Hence, systematicity alone - even supposing it may be clearly defined - will not do as a criterion for inclusion of some factor in a theory of communicative competence (as opposed to a theory of performance). Thus, though Lyons' proposal does perhaps indicate the right direction, it still requires a more convincing implementation.

Presumably, the contextual factors selected by Lyons' criterion (or by a more sophisticated one, when available) are to become the subject-matter (or part thereof) of 'pragmatics'. The previous discussion has highlighted the difficulty in establishing one of the borderlines of this discipline: the one that distinguishes pragmatics as the study of communicative *competence* from a theory of *performance*, i.e. a theory of the *use* of language (in communication). But the other borderline of pragmatics, the one that separates it from semantics, is hardly less controversial than the former. Conceptions of semantics vary broadly, so that its relationship with pragmatics can range from full identity,[7] through various degrees of overlapping, to full separation, with the line drawn at a number of different places.

Consider what has been taken by many to be a typical part of pragmatics, namely speech acts theory. One of its key notions is that of 'illocutionary force'. But, in so far as the illocutionary force of certain verbs (the so-called performatives) is a characteristic feature of their meanings, independently of the context of utterance, it certainly pertains to semantics and not to pragmatics to describe and analyze it.[8] Furthermore, since we perform speech acts not only by means of explicit performatives, but whenever we utter a sentence, some theorists have proposed to include in the underlying semantic structure of every sentence an implicit performative indicating its 'standard' illocutionary force. Such a proposal has been strongly criticized, as is well known. Among other things, it has been pointed out that the actual illocutionary force of an utterance not containing an explicit performative (and even of those containing one) depends upon the context of utterance, and cannot thus be associated with a sentence in isolation. One may try to meet this objection by resorting to the more abstract notion of an 'illocutionary act potential' (cf. Alston, 1964: 37 ff.), to be associated not only with every sentence, but also to be used as definitory of the meaning of every word. But, besides the fact that this proposal seems to raise more problems than it is able to solve (cf. Khatchadourian, 1974), it amounts in fact to the transformation of speech acts theory into the heart of semantics, with little or no room left for its treatment by an independent pragmatic theory.[9]

Or consider what is perhaps a more typical example of a phenomenon belonging to pragmatics: Grice's 'implicatures'. As has been stressed by Grice himself, it is of vital importance for his theory to distinguish between 'conversational' and 'conventional' implicatures. The former - e.g. the implicature conveyed by an utterance of "He has a good handwriting" as a recommendation for an academic position that has nothing to do with calligraphy - are mediated by the (pragmatic) maxims of conversation. The latter - e.g. the kind of contrast conveyed by an appropriate use of 'but' - are not. The former are clearly 'pragmatic', while the latter are 'semantic', in so far as they must be included in any adequate description of the 'meaning' of words like 'but', even though they do not affect, according to Grice, their truth-conditions. But, as Saddock (1978) has shown, the criteria proposed by Grice (1975, 1978) - mainly cancellability and nondetachability - are unable to provide the required distinction, and no satisfactory alternative is available so far, to my knowledge. Grice himself might argue that the lack of such a distinction does not affect the issue of the borderline between semantics and pragmatics, since both types of implicature presumably belong, on his view, to pragmatics. But others (e.g. Cohen, 1971) are not too eager to accept such a way out, so that the issue has in fact to do with the borderline in question.

One might think these are just terminological questions or, perhaps, a matter of division of labor that should not concern the theorist interested in more substantial issues. But the question of limitations and possiblities of pragmatics, which is the underlying topic of the papers in this volume, hinges on a clearer conception of what is reasonable to expect from it. And this has to do with the way its boundaries with semantics and performance are to be demarcated, at least in principle. For, if pragmatics is required to do too much on either side (i.e. either to become a complete 'contextics' or to absorb most of semantics), there is reason to fear that it will accomplish too little. Since the tendency to over-emphasize the role of context in the study of language, thus assigning to pragmatics more than it can be reasonably expected to do, is quite widespread today, there is room to examine and criticize it. This is what will be done in what follows. For convenience of exposition, I will dub such a tendency 'contextualism'.

The expansion of pragmatics can be achieved at the expense of any one or both of its neighbours, namely semantics and performance. Just as the notions of context of utterance and communicative competence (which are supposed to be studied by pragmatics) are the result of a first step of abstraction, so is the domain of semantics defined by a second step of abstraction. The former sets apart 'systematic' and 'random' contextual factors, leaving the treatment of the latter for a theory of performance. The latter is designed to separate even the systematic influences of the context of utterance from what can be properly viewed as the 'meaning' attached to linguistic expressions. Lyons (1977: 588 ff.) calls this second step 'decontextualization'; unfortunately I have not found a natural label for the first. Now, a contextualist may oppose any one of these steps or both. The interesting thing is that these two moves are not independent of each other. It turns out that there is a direct relationship between the refusal to decontextualize and the need to take into account more contextual factors within the theory. For, objection to decontextualization, i.e. to the assignment of context-free 'meanings' to linguistic expressions, usually is based on the imagination of very special circumstances in which the alleged context-free meanings cannot be assigned to the expressions in question. In order to account systematically for their meanings in such circumstances, it is therefore necessary to include among the contextual factors analyzed by pragmatic theory all the rather idyosincratic factors that characterize those circumstances. In other words, the more 'semantic' jobs are assigned to pragmatics, the more 'performance' jobs it will be required to perform. On the other hand, the very possibility of finding out which contextual factors are in fact operative in the determination of the interpretation of a given utterance depends on the availability of a context-free meaning standardly associated with the sentence used, i.e. it requires the proper functioning of a decontextualized semantics.

Given this interdependence of the two possible strategies of contextualism, my criticism will proceed as follows. I will first examine 'moderate contextualism', not because I think there is something intrinsically wrong with it, but in order to show how it substantiates some of the claims of the preceding paragraph; at the same time this will illustrate some of the important systematic contextual factors that pragmatics should handle. I will then go on to discuss a few versions of 'reductionist contextualism', whose shortcomings are more serious. A disclaimer is in order here: by criticizing 'contextualism', I am not denying a role for context in the theory of language. I am only objecting to the exaggeration of such a role. The term 'contextualism' should thus be understood as a label similar to 'psychologism', 'logicism', etc.: those who coined these terms meant to criticize not psychology or logic as such, but the attempt to reduce all of epistemology to one of these disciplines, i.e. the attempt to extend them beyond their proper domains.

II

Sometimes contextualism consists merely in overlooking the role of non-contextual factors, due to exclusive attention paid to one or more types of contextual influence upon the production and interpretation of utterances. This form of contextualism may be called 'moderate' in so far as it is not in principle reductionistic, i.e. in so far as it does not intend to account for the meaning of utterances exclusively in terms of context. One may describe this position as an attempt to account for most of the total *significance* of an utterance in terms of contextual factors, while neglecting or minimizing (though not nullifying) the contribution of the *meaning of the sentence* (or words) uttered to that total significance. (The distinction here employed is adapted from Grice (1975, 1978). He distinguishes between the 'total signification' of an utterance and 'what is said' by uttering a given sentence, and goes on to distinguish further, within the total signification, what is conventionally implicated from what is conversationally implicated. Taking into account these and other forms of what can be implicitly conveyed - as suggested for example by Ducrot (1972) - I have come to think of the total significance of an utterance as an onionlike structure, where several 'layers of meaning' (both implicit and explicit) are hierarchically superposed, and can interact in interesting ways (cf. Dascal and Katriel, 1977). These layers, however, do not simply add up to form the total significance. Some of them may merely *contribute* to its determination without being a part thereof. As will be shown later, part of the motivation for reductionistic contextualism may come from overlooking this important fact).

Versions of moderate contextualism differ in the kind of contextual factors they stress. According to the professional bias of their authors, these factors may be mainly social, psychological, cultural, co-textual, etc. Let us consider a few examples.

Labov and Fanshel (1977) try to show that, in order to "get at the 'real meaning' of conversation", one must inevitably go beyond the mere plane of 'what is said', and deal with what is in fact 'being done' by

the participants in the course of the conversation (p. 123). In order
to reach that level of understanding, speakers have to know such things
as the social roles of interlocutors, in terms of their needs, abilities, obligations and rights (p. 94), whether they have or not this or
that particular piece of information (p. 89), whether a certain action
is needed or not, and whether the interlocutor is willing to perform it
(p. 87), etc. But even before such a deeper level of interpretation is
reached, the very determination of 'what is said' requires a process
Labov and Fanshel label 'expansion', in which co-textual factors play
a preponderant role (pp. 49-50). Furthermore, the authors admit that
there are no precise rules nor limits for the production of such an expansion, i.e. that it is an open-ended process, depending to a great extent
on the interpreter's intuitions: "There is no limit to the number of
explanatory facts we could bring from other parts of the interview, and
the end result of such a procedure might be combining everything that
was said in the session into one sentence" (pp. 50-51). In this process
of interpretation, the role of the meaning of the sentence uttered is
minimal, but not null, according to them:

> "...the speaker's utterance does contribute something towards the
> state of shared knowledge that makes this recognition (of the
> speaker's intention, M.D.) possible. However, this is only a small
> part of the structure of commonly recognized social facts that de-
> termines the interpretation of the utterance. In our study... it
> will become increasingly apparent that most of the information
> needed to interpret actions is already to be found in the structure
> of shared knowledge and not in the utterances themselves" (p. 82).

Yet, no matter how small is the part played by the meaning of the sentence uttered, it cannot be entirely dismissed, because it plays a
crucial role in the process of interpretation: its contribution is not
so much that of adding a further item to the amount of information conveyed, but rather of leading the hearer to the identification of the
relevant items of information in the background of shared knowledge
(as well as in other components of context). It has thus a 'control'
function comparable to that of a feedback loop in a mechanical device:

though using only a very small fraction of the total energy involved in the process, the feedback loop is one of the major factors in determining the actual output of the device.

Notice that Labov and Fanshel are not radical enough in demonstrating how little out of the literal meaning of the sentence uttered is in fact retained as part of the final interpretation of the utterance. Consider their example of an utterance which is interpreted (through their 'Rule of Indirect Requests') as a request for dusting the room (p. 83):

2.6(b) *"Wellyouknow, w'dy'mind takin' thedustrag an' just dustaround?"*

In this case, a number of words in the sentence used refer directly to the action whose performance is requested, so that they contribute quite substantially to establishing the characterization of what the request is about. But the minimization effect could be more convincingly illustrated by examples in which no word in the sentence used designates specifically the action intended. For instance:

"Aren't you supposed to look after this place?"

Clearly, in order for such an utterance to be interpreted as a request to dust a particular room, the context must supply much more information than in the case of an utterance of 2.6(b) in otherwise identical circumstances. But even here, it is only *via* the semantic relationship linking the literal meaning of the words uttered with the intended referent that the context can be made to supply the relevant information.

Radicalizing still further, one might recall Ziff's intellectual soldier who mumbles "Ugh ugh blugh blugh ugh blug blug" in reply to a question he believes is appropriate to morons (Ziff, 1972). In the context, his 'utterance' is easily interpreted by the participants in the 'talk' exchange. This fact might suggest that interpretation has nothing to do with semantics, since nonsense sounds were used. But the message gets through only if the hearer is aware of the fact that the sounds are meaningless, i.e. that they cannot be accounted for by the system of semantic rules of the language. Only after this much is established, can the hearer go on to try to find out what is the significance of the 'utterance'. That is to say, even when no contribution at all is made by the 'literal' meaning to the total significance of the utterance, the notion of literal meaning, as defined for the language-system presumably used, plays an important role in the determination of such a significance.

A role for literal meaning, similar to the triggering effect described above, can be detected in the 'working out' of conversational implicatures. As I have shown elsewhere, the discovery of a *semantic* irrelevance is a necessary step in the process that leads to the assignment of a certain implicature as the correct interpretation of an utterance (cf. Dascal, 1977). Here too the semantic content of 'what is said' can be completely left out of the final interpretation, but without its role in triggering and guiding the process, such an interpretation could not be reached.[10]

Some artificial intelligence models of language comprehension stress the fact that a very broad range of 'knowledge of the world' is required in order to interpret the simplest sentences. Even if a program is designed to simulate a single 'frame of mind' or set of topics, a broader context is always required. A case in point is Abelson's (1975: 274 ff.) simulation of an ideolog, operating within a fixed framework of political premises:

> "...we soon discovered that the system could not interpret events (and *a fortiori* utterances, M.D.) sensibly without some reasonable level of mundane knowledge about simple physical properties of persons and objects, independent of ideological import. Thus our system, operating entirely at an abstract level, reasoned that since Latin American radical students had thrown eggs at Nixon (as Vice-President visiting in 1958), it was quite plausible that Fidel Castro might throw eggs at Taiwan. ... (The system was) innocent of the logistics of egg throwing ... as well as many other low-level facts..."

Thus, instead of associating fixed (context free) bits of information with any given expression and trying to interpret it within a single frame of reference, such programs must be able to gather the adequate information, for each particular context or task, out of a multitude of sources. The organization of such knowledge in terms of 'scripts' (Schank), 'frames' (Minsky) or similar conceptual structures is meant to overcome part of the difficulty in determining exactly which sources are relevant on each occasion. As one of the researchers engaged in devising programs that simulate language comprehension puts it:

> "...the essence of both problem solving and language comprehension lies in knowing what are the relevant questions to ask during a selection or searching activity... that is, in knowing which aspects of the environment could possibly be relevant to the attainment of some goal" (Rieger, 1976: 102).

> "... the heart of the problem of organizing world knowledge lies in encoding a knowledge of what *other* knowledge bears relevance to the solution of any given task, be it synthesizing a solution to a problem, or searching through algorithmic structures during language comprehension" (ibid.).

Now, even though such a knowledge is entirely oriented towards context, since its main function is to provide the means "to seek out context", Rieger is aware of the fact that it must be defined, at some level, in a context-free way. That is to say, there must be a set of procedures standardly associated, say, with a linguistic expression, which provides the basis for the search of the relevant data in the context. These data can in turn interact with and modify the former, but without that basic and fixed set the whole process of interpretation cannot get off the ground. For, if the system does not know, "in a context-free way, what is ultimately relevant to the functioning of the patterns among which it is selecting, how can that (system) ever be made to do different things in different environments?" (ibid.).

Other examples of moderate contextualism can be easily found in the work of sociologists (cf. Goffman, 1974; Carswell and Rommetveit, 1971), ethnomethodologists (cf. Gumperz and Hymes, 1972; Gumperz, 1974; Schenkein, 1978), 'text-grammarians' (cf. Van Dijk, 1977),[11] and others. Sometimes they may overstate their case,[12] but essentially they do not purport to eliminate the notion of a context-free, semantic, meaning; they just tend to take it for granted and, thus, to overlook its fundamental role.

All these examples clearly show that context can only play a systematic role in the determination of the total significance of an utterance if the literal meaning of the uttered sentence is available in order to lead the way in the selection of the relevant contextual features. Furthermore, they indicate that, even though the literal meaning *need* not be retained as a component of the total significance, if it happens to be retained (totally or partially), then the range and amount of contextual information required in order to 'fill the gap' is reduced. Such a reduction is roughly proportional to the 'amount' of literal meaning actually retained. That is to say: if the significance of the utterance is substantially identical to the literal meaning of the sentence uttered (or logically implied by it), then there is no need to look further into the context for a satisfactory interpretation; on the other hand, when practically nothing of the literal meaning is retained, most of the significance must be gathered from the context. These facts have a direct bearing on the question of the two borderlines of pragmatics. If all the variations in significance ought to be accounted for entirely by the semantics, then all possible contextual factors ought to be kept track of, there would be no end to the multiplication of 'senses' of the expressions, the semantic system would be enormously complicated thereby, and there would be no point at all in having a separate pragmatic component in the theory.[13]

III

There is a form of contextualism which is more radical than the one we have considered so far. It claims that there is no such a thing as a context-free literal meaning of a sentence, present in all its utterances. Contextual factors, therefore, must be made responsible for the whole significance of an utterance, with no context-free anchoring to serve as a starting point. On such a view, there can be no principled grounds for distinguishing between semantics and pragmatics, nor, so it seems, between pragmatics and the theory of performance. It represents a holistic approach to language, according to which any distinctions made among the components of a theory of language are merely a matter of convenience, with no possible claim to empirical adequacy. In what follows, I will discuss a few cases of this type of contextualism.

As in the case of moderate contextualism, versions of radical contextualism may differ in the kind of contextual factor which is considered dominant, and to which all meaning is ultimately reduced. We have mentioned *en passant* some varieties: Bloomfield's behavioristic approach (cf. note 7), Firth's socio-cultural contextualism, Austin's speech-acts centered theory of meaning (cf. note 9). Another example of a psychologically oriented, but not behavioristic, contextualism, is that of Olson's 'cognitive theory of semantics' (1970). Having observed experimentally that the choice of lexical items for the description of a given object varies with the number and properties of alternative objects present in the environment, Olson goes on to draw somewhat hasty conclusions, first relative to speech production (performance) and then relative to the nature of semantics itself. The former are illustrated by his claim that "semantic decision is based on cognition, the knowledge of the intended referent, not on the rules internal to language" (p. 259). To be sure, 'semantic decision' must rely on knowledge of the intended referent and its alternatives, but Olson presents no reason whatsoever to support his further claim that such decisions do not rely on the knlowledge of the rules of language as well. On the contrary: his examples show that if the speaker did not know the standard meanings of words such as *white*, *block*, *under*, etc., the knowledge of the intended referent would be of no help for him in the choice of the appropriate lexical item. His conclusions regarding the nature of semantics are even less founded. He proposes in fact to define all semantic properties in terms of the contextually available alternatives to the intended referent. Thus, for him

> "...ambiguity is a function of the perceived alternatives to the intended referent, not of the rules of language" (p. 260),

and

> "...a sentence is anomalous if the listener cannot imagine a context in which that sentence would specify an intended referent" (ibid.).

Recall however that there are practically no limits to the ability of speakers to imagine contexts in which the most strange sentence can be assigned a meaning, as well as contexts in which the most common sentence can acquire a meaning different from its 'normal' one. It follows that Olson's definitions are vacuous, since they imply that all sentences are 'ambiguous' and no sentence is 'anomalous'. Furthermore, it is clearly a *non sequitur* to infer anything about the relativity of meaning from the following, perfectly acceptable statement, which is almost a truism:

> "Since not all the potential information of the referent as perceived is signaled by a word, we conclude that words (or utterances) neither symbolize, stand for, nor represent referents, objects, or events. They serve rather to differentiate some perceived event from some set of alternatives" (p. 265).

Words can serve to differentiate events precisely because they have a standard meaning, independent of the various sets of events among whose members they may differentiate on different occasions. It is only by demanding too much of words (namely, that they be able to describe fully all the possibly relevant features of a referent) that one is led to conclude that they contribute little or nothing to reference.

Another, rather subtle, version of radical contextualism is the one defended by G. Harman. Instead of explaining meaning in terms of the 'external' context (social, cultural, etc.) of use, he takes the determinant contextual factor to be 'internal'. For him, the main task of semantics is to characterize the meanings of linguistic expressions in terms of their 'conceptual roles', i.e. of their function as components of thought processes (perception, reasoning, inference, etc. - cf. Harman, 1973, *passim*). This kind of functionalism, which might be expressed - paraphrasing Wittgenstein - by the dictum "sentences have meaning only in the stream of thought", is a version of radical contextualism in so far as it maintains that there are no principled grounds to isolate 'meanings' as specific components within the stream of thought-processes. Harman rejects the analytic-synthetic distinction, and argues that there is no evidence supporting the assumption (made by semanticists like Katz) that knowledge of 'language-independent meanings' can be separated from other forms of knowledge (cf. Harman, 1976). If 'pragmatics' is understood as referring not only to the uses of language in communication, but also to its uses in thought,[14] then Harman's thesis implies the denial of the possibility of establishing a distinction between a 'semantics of thought' and a 'pragmatics of thought' and, more generally, between semantics and pragmatics. Furthermore, unless the 'conceptual role' of an expression is arbitrarily restricted to certain specific cognitive functions - a move which could hardly be justified -, it is open-ended and variable with the (cognitive) context, thus yielding a similarly open-ended and variable notion of meaning, characteristic of radical contextualism. Since I examine Harman's views elsewhere (cf. Dascal, in preparation), I will make no further comments on them here.

Let us turn now to a recent direct attack on the notion of context-free literal meaning (Searle, 1978). By letting an apparently innocent sentence like *The cat is on the mat* be uttered in odd situations (e.g., when the mat is stiffened and stands on one of its edges and the cat is drugged and lies on the other edge), Searle attempts to undermine the thesis that "every unambiguous sentence... has a literal meaning which is absolutely context-free and which determines for every context whether or not an utterance of that sentence in that context is literally true or false" (p. 214). His examples are designed to show that, with the help of appropriate background assumptions, the sentence can be understood quite straightforwardly even in such odd contexts. According to Searle, in each of these cases the speaker says exactly and literally what he means, and the hearer understands him so. But if this is the case, then there is no such thing as *the* literal meaning of the sentence since what is meant and understood and, in particular, the truth-conditions associated with the sentence vary from case to case. Relative to a given set of assumptions, the truth-conditions may be such that an utterance of the sentence is literally true; relative to another set, it may be literally false; and relative to a third set, "the notion of the literal meaning of the sentence (may) not have a clear application" (p. 211). The problem cannot be solved by listing all the relevant assumptions and representing them in the semantic structure of the sentence, says Searle, because they are indefinite in number. In view of such difficulties with the notion of a context-free literal meaning, Searle proposes the following alternative account:

> "For a large class of unambiguous sentences such as *The cat is on the mat*, the notion of the literal meaning of the sentence only has application relative to a set of background assumptions. The truth conditons of the sentence will vary with variations in these background assumptions; and given the absence or presence of some background assumptions the sentence does not have determinate truth conditons" (p. 214).

Searle is very cautious in his formulations. He stresses that he is not claiming that *all* sentences are subject to a similar relativity of their literal meaning (p. 219). But, of course, by choosing sentences that are very likely candidates for having a context-free literal meaning, he intends to provide support for the more general thesis which would destroy that notion altogether. Furthermore, he declares that he is not denying that sentences have literal meaning: "literal meaning, though relative, is still literal meaning" (p. 220). But if one takes this claim literally, and combines it with his earlier remarks on the indefinite number of contextual variations, it turns out that each *sentence* (not utterance!) has indefinitely many 'literal meanings', and it is at least questionable whether such multiple entities do share with their more traditional homonyms a significant portion of their characteristic properties.

One of Searle's main reasons for relativizing literal meaning is his belief that the variations he has discovered cannot be accounted for by means of the available conceptual tools of semantics and pragmatics:

> These variations have nothing to do with indexicality, change of meaning, ambiguity, conversational implication, vagueness or presupposition as these notions are standardly discussed in the philosophical and linguistic literature" (p. 214).

Is it true that no semantic or pragmatic extant concepts can be used in order to explain Searle's examples? Consider first indexicality. As is well-known, this notion has to do, among other things, with the spatio-temporal position of the speaker *vis-à-vis* the objects and events he refers to at the moment of utterance. Now, Searle's example exploits the contextual dependence of the word *on* (p. 215). This word, although apparently on-indexical, can be reasonably assumed to contain an implicit indexical component, which is more apparent in other location words such as *up, down, behind, before*, etc. In a sense, things are *on* other things relative to the point of view of the speaker. If the speaker were to be turned upside-down, what was *on* would be now *under*, and vice-versa. To be sure, we are able to perform the necessary conceptual 'corrections' in order to compensate for our changed point of view, so that we will probably continue to say that the radio is *on* the table rather than *under* it.[15] Such corrections are based on our current knowledge (visual memories, among other things) of the things which are usually on and the things which are usually under. It is the use of such knowledge and the habitual corrections it allows for that conceals the indexicality of the words in question. Once the situation is such that things are no longer usual, we have to rely again on that indexicality in order to decide whether something is on or under another thing. Searle's first example (astronauts in a spacecraft watching pairs of cats-mats through the window) is one such unusual circumstance. Although gravitational considerations are of no use in this case, the astronauts are not free to describe the pairs as *cat on mat* or *mat on cat* indifferently. They must respect the spatial relationship obtaining between their own bodies and the pairs observed. Since these relationships are also taken into account in the more usual circumstances - the fact that they are eventually 'corrected' notwithstanding -, no change in the 'literal meaning' of *on*, and hence of the sentence uttered, has to be postulated. The example can be accounted for simply by paying attention to the *constant* role of the relevant indexical factor.

And this is not the only constant factor. Certain implications of the sentence are unaffected by the contextual changes of Searle's examples. Whenever the cat is on the mat, the mat is under the cat, the cat is not under the mat, the mat is not on the cat, etc. But consider now another of Searle's examples, the case of the stiffened mat. According to him, when the cat has been jumping from one sticking up object to another and happens to be now on the stiffened mat, *The cat is on the mat* is the correct, literal, and precise answer to the question *Where is the cat?*. However, if such background assumptions are unknown to the hearer, such an answer "is misleading at best and probably should be described as an ingenious lie" (p. 213). The relevant assumptions in this case supply the set of alternatives out of which the sentence is supposed to pick up one as describing the situation. But this phenomenon, characteristic of all or most uses of language, must be handled in terms of the available conceptual machinery of semantics and pragmatics. It has to do mainly with the 'point' of uttering that particular sentence in that particular circumstance - which is an important part of what we have called the 'significance' of the utterance. There are various devices which can be used to convey the point of an utterance. Contrastive stress is one example. If one says *The cat is on the mat*, the hearer may assume that this is meant to exclude alternatives such as *The dog is on the mat*, *The doll is on the mat*, and so on. If one says *The cat is on the mat*, the alternatives excluded will resemble more *The cat is under the mat*, *The cat is beside the mat*, etc. To be sure, the precise set of alternatives is a piece of information supplied by the context, but the linguistic devices employed (including the selection of particular words) guide the hearer in his contextual search for such alternatives. Such a procedure is necessary in 'normal' as well as in 'abnormal' situations, so that no special measures (like the relativization of literal meaning) are required in order to explain it.

In some cases, of the *cat on the mat* type, the question of the choice of alternatives is mainly pragmatic. The relevant principle may be akin to Grice's maxims, say, "Every utterance must have a point". The hearer is entitled to assume that the point - as far as the set of alternatives is concerned - is fairly perspicuous, given the cooperative principle. The misleading effect of the reply on the hearer who is unaware of the other sticking up objects can be explained by pointing out that he was not in a position to grasp the correct set of alternatives. In so far as the speaker deliberately witheld such information from the hearer, he may indeed be accused of (almost) lying. In other cases, the provision of a set of alternatives is a requirement for the semantic well-formedness of the sentence, e.g. sentences containing implicit comparatives, such as *He is big*: for a basketball player, a dog, or an elephant? Here, it is the semantic nature of the comparative that determines the relevant dimension to be looked for as characteristic of the set of alternatives. Although in both types of cases the required set can vary widely from context to context, such a variation - which is what is in fact at stake in most of Searle's examples - not only does not require a relativization of literal meaning: it shows the need for a constant literal meaning which is able to guide the search for the relevant alternatives.

I have reasons to believe that at least some of the other semantic and pragmatic notions discarded by Searle as irrelevant for the explanation of his examples might turn out to be relevant, on closer scrutiny. Certain types of vagueness, for example, are such that they prevent a clear determination of truth-conditions (Khatchadourian, 1974: 17 ff.), and a judicious use of the various available notions of presupposition might go a long way towards capturing Searle's claims about 'failure of application'.[16] But I will leave aside these possibilities now, in order to deal with the sources of Searle's extreme - and unwarranted - move.

I think the main underlying source for Searle's attack on literal meaning can be put simply in this way: he is demanding too much from literal meaning. He not only identifies the literal meaning of a sentence with full-blooded truth-conditions for that sentence. His use of the notion of 'application' strongly suggests that what he in fact requires for a literal meaning to 'have an application' is the availability of a procedure for the verification of the actual truth-value of the utterance in a given context. But both claims are unnecessarily stringent. Very few, if any, expressions can satisfy the requirements of verificationism; as for truth-conditions, even strict Tarskians like Davidson admit that they are not determined by sentences alone but by pairs of utterance-cum-context. All that Searle has shown is that literal meaning is not a sufficient condition for the determination of truth-conditions and for the verification of truth in all contexts; i.e. he has shown that contextual information is necessary in order to achieve such a determination. But in order to dismiss or relativize literal meaning, what he would have to show is that literal meaning is not even a *necessary* condition for the determination of truth-conditions - and this he has not done.

Searle's demands concerning literal meaning are excessive also in another sense. As we have seen, he assumes that the literal meaning of a sentence literally used should be able to capture the whole significance of the utterance (or a major part thereof). Since literal meaning cannot, for obvious reasons, satisfy such a demand, it is dismissed. But again, Searle merely shows that literal meaning is not a sufficient condition for the determination of significance, a claim with which I have no quarrel. We have indeed stressed the fact that the total significance of an utterance is the result of the interaction of many factors, *one* of which is the literal meaning of the sentence used. Furthermore, we have also pointed out that the role of literal meaning can be such that no part of it is finally retained as a component of the total significance. But the analysis of moderate contextualism has shown, on the other hand, that, however small its role may actually be, literal meaning is a necessary ingredient for the assignment of a significance to an utterance. What Searle would have to show in order to substantiate his claims is not that literal meaning is not a sufficient condition, but that it is not a necessary condition for the determination of significance in every context. And this he has not done.

There would be more to say about Searle's paper, especially with respect to his claim that the relativization of literal meaning does not contradict his own 'principle of expressibility' (p. 221), but enough has been said for the purposes of characterizing and criticizing radical contextualism. The obvious strategy to cope with the arguments of radical and moderate contextualists, in so far as they call attention for hitherto unrecognized forms of context dependency, is to adopt a position that might be dubbed 'moderate literalism'. Instead of considering literal meanings as somewhat complete entities, identical to or capable to determine truth-conditions and significance, such a position would view meanings as 'schematic', incomplete entities, specifying conditions, guiding principles and other means through which their 'gaps' might be appropriately filled by contextual information.[17] The study of these abstract entities would properly belong to semantics, whereas the study of the ways in which contextual information would be embedded in them, after being duly selected, would belong to pragmatics. But, in view of the interaction between them, required for the generation of the end product (language comprehension), each one of them should be developped, from the outset, with the other 'in mind'. This seems to be the best way to avoid the excesses both of contextualism and of its counterpart, 'radical literalism'.

FOOTNOTES:

1. This proposal was made, half-humorously, in the Symposium on the Pragmatics of Natural Languages (Jerusalem, 1970). Some papers inspired by the symposium are collected in Bar-Hillel (1971).

2. "...although many recent studies point to the importance of context in language, there is little in the way of a systematic discussion of how and in what ways context affects the interpretation of sentences in everyday interaction" (Gumperz, 1974: 17).

3. "It is such a framework of frameworks that we must seek out; it is some such meta-schema that will allow us to accumulate systematic understanding about contexts, not merely warnings that in another context meaning could be different" (Goffman, 1975: 33). See also Goffman (1974).

4. "Per quanto riguarda poi la formalizzazione della pragmatica, la mia convinzione è che sia davvero prematura: non c'è sufficiente ricchezza nel settore da giustificare un tentativo del genere" (Chomsky, 1979: 11).

5. Quoted by Lyons (1977: 574 n. 2).

6. Lyons of course does not suggest that his list is exhaustive. The factors he lists are: (1) the participants' role and status; (2) spatio-temporal location; (3) degree of formality of the situation; (4) knowledge of the medium (graphic, phonic) appropriate for the situation; (5) subject-matter; (6) province or domain to which the situation belongs (Lyons, 1977: 574-585).

7. E.g., Bloomfield's inclusive definition of 'meaning' in terms of S-R, which covers "relation, on various levels, of speech-forms to other speech-forms, relation of speech-forms to non-verbal situations (objects, events, etc.), and relations, again on various levels, to the persons who are participating in the act of communication" (Bloomfield, 1955: 236). This is nothing short than the whole of syntax, semantics and pragmatics, as Bloomfield himself points out (p. 272), and implies that "linguistics... depends for its range and accuracy upon the success of science as a whole" (p. 272-3). For a non-behaviorist version of the full identity thesis, see Firth's contextual theory of meaning (Lyons, 1977: 607-613).

8. See Cohen's criticism of speech acts theory (1973).

9. Such a position is assigned by Lyons to Austin, and leads him to call Austin's theory a "contextual theory of meaning" (Lyons, 1977:735).

10. For an example in which what is retained in the final interpretation from what is said is minimal, see Dascal (1981), *in fine*.

11. See Dascal and Katriel (1979) for an approach which might also be characterized as a form of 'moderate contextualism', although the fundamental role of literal meaning is there always kept in view.

12. One example is Carswell and Rommetveit's (1971: 5) reading of Uhlenbeck (1963) as saying that "language essentially is meaningless when taken out of context", while all he said was: "Every sentence needs to be interpreted in the light of various extralinguistic data".

13. It should be recalled that for some authors (e.g., Grice, 1975; McCawley, 1978) one of the advantages of explaining a number of linguistic phenomena in terms of pragmatic principles is that such a procedure allows for a semantics free from unnecessary complications.

14. Such a use of the term is grounded in the way it was used by Peirce and by Carnap. For the importance in recognizing the right to existence of a 'pragmatics of thought' or 'psychopragmatics', see Dascal (1979).

15. Stratton's famous experiments with glasses that generated inverted images, which demonstrated our ability to adapt to the new situation by 'correcting' the inverted positions of the objects, illustrates the way in which conceptual schemes can sometimes overcome the data of perception themselves (cf. Gregory, 1972: 204 ff.).

16. Cf., for example, Atlas' (1973) account of the three types of presupposition to be found already in Frege's writings.

17. "It appears reasonable to suggest that words and sentences specify some abstract conditions concerning the nature of the relations and the participating entities to be considered, and that it is the comprehender's ability to think (i.e. create situations such that the relations can be realized) that allows him to understand what the sentence might mean" (Bransford and McCarrel, 1974: 213). Similar suggestions are made by those who propose to use in semantics notions like *script, frame,* etc. (cf. Raskin, 1977, for example).

CAUSATIVES

Steven Davis

Are there causative verbs? Many linguists think that there are, but there is not general agreement on how they are to be treated. Currently, there are two kinds of theories which have been advanced to account for causatives. The first, found within generative semantics, I shall call the *syntactic-semantic hypothesis*. There is actually more than one hypothesis in this framework which differ on important points of detail. However, what I wish to say about causatives is unaffected by these differences. Consequently, I have drawn on the work of David Dowty (1972) as representative of the syntactic-semantic hypothesis.

On his view the underlying structure of

(1) John opened the door.

is

(2)

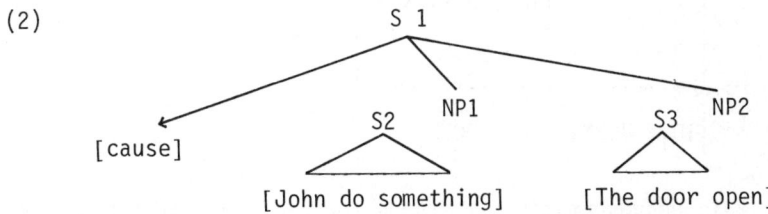

(2) represents both the syntactic structure and semantic representation of (1). Consequently, material in square brackets are semantic

representations, not lexical items.

The second account, which I shall call the *semantic hypothesis*, is found in the work of Mayayoshi Shibatani (1973). Shibatani claims that the semantic representation of (1) is

(3)
$$\begin{bmatrix} PR_1, CIP_1, CDP_1 \\ \dots\dots\dots\dots\dots \\ PR_1: \text{CAUSE} \\ \\ CIP_1 \begin{bmatrix} PR_1, ID_1, ID_2 \\ \dots\dots\dots\dots \\ PR_2: \text{MANIPULATE} \\ ID_1: \text{AGENT} \\ ID_2: \text{PATIENT} \end{bmatrix} \\ \\ CDP_1 \begin{bmatrix} PR_3, ST_1 \\ \dots\dots \\ PR_3: \text{OCCUR} \\ ST_1 \begin{bmatrix} PR_4, ID_2 \\ \dots\dots \\ PR_4: \text{OPEN} \\ ID_2: \text{PATIENT} \end{bmatrix} \end{bmatrix} \\ \\ \dots\dots\dots\dots\dots\dots\dots \\ ID_1: \text{JOHN}, \quad ID_2: \text{DOOR} \end{bmatrix}$$

In this representation *PR* stands for *predicate*, *ID* for *individual*, *CIP* for *causing phrase*, *CDP* for *caused phrase*, and *ST* for *state*. On Shibatani's account the particular predicates, individuals, *etc.* in a semantic representation are abstract semantic entities and are not to be confused with entities which a speaker refers to in uttering a sentence. There is, however, a connection between semantic representation and what a speaker would standardly be taken to be referring to in uttering a sentence. Given Shibatani's account of the meaning of (1), a speaker in uttering this sentence would be taken to be referring to the cause of the door's opening, that is, to John's doing something. The function of the CIP in (3), JOHN MANIPULATE THE DOOR, is to connect an utterance of (1) with this event.

What we wish to take from these two hypotheses is the common semantic content they attribute to causatives. In both we find the semantic feature [Cause] and two propositions, which are on Dowty's and Shibatani's views, respectively,

(4) (a) [John Do Something.]
    (b) [The Door Open.]
(5) (a) JOHN MANIPULATE DOOR.
    (b) DOOR OPEN.

According to both hypotheses, in the semantic representation of (1), (4a) and (5a) are the subject of [Cause] and (4b) and (5b) its complement. Generalizing from the above, we can say that the lexical entry of every causative verb contains

(6) (a) The semantic feature [Cause].
    (b) P, a proposition having sentential structure, which is the subject of [Cause].
    (c) Q, a proposition having sentential structure, which is the complement of [Cause].

There are several reasons why the bi-sentential or bi-propositional account of causatives is important. Its syntactic-semantic variant, an example of which is given in (2), is one of the central hypotheses used to support the framework of generative semantics. Moreover, it is part of an hypothesis which supposedly gives an account of the semantic relationship between (1) and

(7) (a) John opened the door by doing something.
    (b) John's doing something opened the door.

and of the putative entailment relationship between (1) and

(8) (a) The door is open.
    (b) John does something.

Finally, the bi-propositional hypothesis allows the utilization of the semantic models developed to account for counterfactual conditionals to provide a possible world semantic model for sentences containing causative verbs (Dowty, 1972; McCawley, 1976).

    In this paper I shall divide my attention between two aspects of the causative hypothesis. First, I shall examine the thesis that the semantic subject of sentences which contain as their main verb a causative verb is a proposition. Second, I shall consider the assumption that the lexical entry for every causative verb contains [Cause] as part of its semantic content. Dowty and Shibatani disagree on some important points. However, I shall only take their disagreements into account when they are relevant to a discussion of the hypotheses mentioned above.

    Propositions have a sentential structure which includes a subject and a predicate. The subject of the proposition, P, which is the semantic subject of [Cause], is the semantic representation of the lexical subject of the sentence which contains P in its semantic representation. However, the predicate of P is not the semantic representation of any lexical items contained in the sentence. But, Dowty and Shibatani differ on the way it is determined. Let us consider the following sentences:

(9) (a) The man opened the door.
    (b) The war frightened Sam.
    (c) The house made Mary happy.

In the semantic representation of (9a), for both Dowty and Shibatani, the subject of P is the semantic representation of *the man*. On Dowty's account the predicate of P is a function of the semantic representation of the subject of (9a), whereas according to Shibatani, it is a function, as well, of the semantic representation of other lexical items in the sentence, that is, of *open* and *door*. The predicate of P, then, differs on the semantic-syntactic and on the semantic proposals. It is, respectively

(10) (a) [Do Something.]
     (b) MANIPULATE THE DOOR.

One important point to notice about Shibatani's hypothesis is that the inclusion of MANIPULATE in the semantic representation of the predicate of P is not a function merely of the semantic representation of *open*. Photoelectric cells can open doors, although they cannot manipulate anything. Rather, its inclusion must be a function of both *the man* and *open*, since usually humans open things by manipulating them. However, there might be some question that MANIPULATE should be part of the meaning of (9a), for people can open doors by kicking or elbowing them. Because of this difficulty, I shall concentrate on Dowty's proposal in (10a).

The subjects of the P's in the semantic representations of (9b) and (c) are determined in exactly the same way as for (9a). They are, respectively, the semantic representations of *the war* and *the house*. However, their corresponding predicates cannot be either (10a) or (b), since neither houses nor wars do anything or manipulate anything. To handle cases of this sort Dowty proposes that for sentences like (9b) the predicate of P is [Come About] and for sentences like (9c) it is [State] (Dowty, 1972:113). One test for these hypotheses is that there are sentences corresponding to (9a) - (c) which contain *by*-phrases in which the main verb has as its semantic content the predicates which Dowty proposes.

(11) (a) John opened the door by doing something.
     (b) The war frightened Sam by occurring.
     (c) The house made Mary happy by being in a certain state.

For (9a) - (c) the predicates of their corresponding P's are not determined directly by any of their lexical items, but are rather a function of the semantic representation of their subjects. However, this is not the case for all sentences which have causatives as their main verbs. Consider:

(12) (a) John's snoring awoke Mary.
 (b) John awoke Mary by snoring.

In both (12a) and (b) the predicate of P would seem to be the semantic representation of *snore*, although it might be argued that the predicate of P is [Come About] and its subject the semantic representation of *John's snoring*. However, in what follows we shall not consider sentences which contain sentential subjects or *by*-phrases.

For the sentences we are considering, then, such as (9a) - (c), the semantic contents of the P's which their semantic representations are supposed to contain have a subject and a predicate. The subject of the corresponding P is the semantic representation of the subject of the sentence which contains P as part of its semantic representation; the predicate of P is a function of its subject. However, it is not completely clear how the predicate of a particular P is to be determined. Let me propose as a tentative hypothesis that

(13) P, the propositional subject of [Cause] in the semantic representation of causative verbs and sentences, contains:
  (a) [Do Something] as predicate just in case the subject of P contains [Agent].
  (b) [Come About] as predicate just in case the subject of P contains [Event].
  (c) [State] as predicate just in case the subject of P does not contain [Event].

One consequence of (13) is that it marks a sentence like (14) as being ambiguous.

(14)   The man frightened Sally.

On (13a) and (13c), (14) is semantically related to either

(15) (a) The man frightened Sally by being in a certain state.
(b) The man frightened Sally by doing something.

(13) is not a complete account of P. In addition we need a specification of its structures. However, (13) does give us a clearer picture of the causative hypothesis contained in (6). It determines the content of the subjects of the semantic representations which contain causative verbs.

Let us now turn to some criticisms of this proposal. First, it yields incomprehensible semantic representations. Consider:

(16) (a) The occurrence of the fight frightened everyone.
(b) The state of the house pleased Alice.

For these two sentences (13) gives as semantic representations something like

(17) (a) The occurrence of the fight's coming about causes everyone to be afraid.
(b) The state of the houses being in a certain state caused Mary to be happy.

(17a) and (b) entail

(18) (a) The occurrence of the fight comes about.
(b) The state of the house is in a certain state.

both of which are analytic and neither of which appear to be entailed by (16a) or (b). Moreover, on the assumption that occurrences occur and states are in certain states, it is not the occurrence of the fight's occurring or the state of the house's being in a certain state which, respectively, frightens everyone or makes Mary happy, rather it is the occurrence of the fight and the state of the house which have these consequences.

The second criticism of the causative hypothesis is that there are causative sentences in which the semantic representation of the subject expression contains [Agent], but which can be true without its being the case that the referent of the subject expression does anything. Consider:

(19) John opened his eyes.

There are two sorts of cases in which (19) can be true without John doing anything to open his eyes. The first is one in which John opens his eyes because he wants and intends to do so and the second is one in which he opens his eyes without wanting or intending to do so. The latter case should not be confused with one in which John opens his eyes, but wants or intends not to do so. Rather, it is one in which there is neither a desire nor an intention to open them nor a desire nor intention not to open them. An example of this would be John's opening his eyes, when he awakens. To distinguish these cases we shall call the first a case of intentional action and the second non-intentional. John's opening his eyes non-intentionally is a clear counterexample to the causative hypothesis in (6) and (13). For in such a case (19) is true without its being true either that John did something that caused his eyes to open or that he was in some state that caused them to open.

It might be thought that the causativity of *open* can be saved by distinguishing between intentional and non-intentional senses of the verb *open*, since John's intentionally opening his eyes appears to fit neatly into the causative hypothesis. We could take it that John's beliefs and wants cause him to open his eyes. We would, then, be able to apply (13c), rather than (13a), on the intentional reading of *open* to (19) to obtain its correct reading. However, when someone does something intentionally, we do not normally speak of his wants and beliefs as causes of his action. Rather, we cite these as his reasons which explain why he performed his actions. Despite this, philosophers have argued that the reasons for a person's actions, his wants and beliefs, are actually what causes his action to occur (Davidson, 1963; Goldman, 1970). Let us call this philosophical thesis, *RCIT*. Although I believe that the considerations advanced to establish the truth of RCIT are compelling, this does not lend support to the hypothesis that *open* is a causative verb, even if we suppose it has an intentional reading. The latter hypothesis is a semantic hypothesis. Consequently, it cannot be based merely on the truth of RCIT, nor even on its being necessarily true. What it requires is that RCIT be analytically true. But there are reasons to think that this is not so. Many arguments have been raised against the truth of RCIT which, while not establishing that RCIT is false, show at least that it is not analytic (Gustafson, 1973).

However, even if RCIT were analytic, it would not help the causative hypothesis. Consider (19) again. Suppose that it is true and that John opens his eyes because he wants to. What does John's desire cause? On the causative hypothesis it causes his eyes to open, but on the hypothesis that reasons are causes it causes him to open his eyes. There is an important difference between the two hypotheses. On the causative hypothesis what John's desire causes is that his eyes open, while on RCIT what it causes is that he opens his eyes. The reason for this difference is that the former is a semantic account of the meaning of causative verbs, while the latter is an hypothesis the purpose of which is to explain the causal conditions of actions. It follows that to prevent the circularity of the causative hypothesis, the two-place predicate *open* cannot appear in its own lexical entry or in the semantic representation of sentences which contain it. But, since RCIT is supposed to be an account of the conditions which cause John to open his eyes, there is no reason not to include the two-place predicate *open* in giving this account. Consequently, RCIT gives no support to the causative hypothesis. In addition, in the above defense of the causativity of *open*, we have made the unwarranted assumption that there are intentional and non-intentional readings of *open*. But, this is to confuse a certain kind of vagueness, lack of specificity with respect to a feature, with multiplicity of meaning. Hence, the conclusion we reach is that *open* is not a causative verb and that the causative hypothesis in (6) and (13) does not apply to sentences which contain it.

There is a class of verbs, similar to *open*, which are regarded to be causative, which includes verbs like *move, raise, bend, stretch, etc.*, verbs which are true of what philosophers call basic or primitive actions. There are many views about what constitutes a basic action. One view is that a person performs a basic action just in case it is an intentional action, but one which he does not perform by performing any other action. Our example, John's opening his eyes, is then a basic action. He opens his eyes because he wants to, but he does not do so by performing any other action. Although John's opening his eyes on a particular occasion might be a basic action, it need not be the case that whenever he opens his eyes, he performs a basic action. He might, for instance, open his eyes by lifting his eyelids with his fingertips. But, for the argument to go through against *open* being a causative verb, all that need be the case is that there be a particular occasion where John's opening his eyes is a basic action. Similarly, not every case of raising one's hand, stretching one's arm, or bending one's back is a basic action, but for each one of these action types, there are particular actions which are basic in the required way. And because of this, arguments parallel to the one above about *open* can be constructed which show that the verbs, *raise, stretch, bend, etc.* are not causative verbs.

However, there are verbs, for example, *kill, defrost, persuade, melt, bake, etc.*, which appear to be quite different from the verbs which are true of basic actions. Take *kill* for example. It seems that for a person to kill someone he must do something else, such as shoot a gun or administer poison in order to cause the person to die. Killing always seems to be done by doing something else. That is, it can never be a basic action. Consequently, we could try to save the causative hypothesis by finding a criterion for verbs like *kill* which excludes the verbs true of basic actions and by arguing that it is this class of verbs which is causative.

As we have seen, there are two related theses connected with the causative hypothesis. First, it is claimed that there is a class of causative verbs. And second, following from this, it is held that it is part of the meaning of sentences such as

(20)   John killed Smith.

that

(21)   That John does something causes Smith to die.

Hence, if (21) is part of the meaning of (20), then in every possible world in which John kills Smith John must do something which causes Smith to die. But, it follows from this that it is impossible that John's killing Smith is a basic action. That is, it is an essential feature of killings that for someone to perform one he must do something which causes a death. To defeat the semantic thesis that (21) is part of the meaning (20), I shall raise some considerations which, I hope, will cast doubt on the ontological thesis about the nature of killings. That is, I will try to show that there could be killings which are basic actions.

There is an argument of Professor Davidson which purports to show that killings are basic actions, but not when described as such (Davidson, 1971). Suppose John kills Smith by shooting him. And suppose further that he shoots Smith, by pulling the trigger of a gun. And finally, he pulls the trigger of the gun, by moving his finger. Is it the case that John's moving his finger is the same action as his killing Smith? If it is, then his killing Smith is a basic action, since it is identical to his moving his finger which is a basic action. The first premise of Davidson's argument is that John's moving his finger the way he did on that occasion is identical with his doing something which caused Smith's death. His second premise is that doing something which causes a person to die is identical with causing a person to die. And the last premise is that causing a person to die is identical with killing him. Hence, John's moving his finger the way he did on that occasion is identical with John's killing Smith.

Davidson's third premise is similar to a strong version of the causative hypothesis, namely that *kill* means *cause to die* (Lakoff, 1971b). But, it should not be confused with this hypothesis, since Davidson claims only that killing a person is identical with causing him to die. Clearly, the latter can be true without Lakoff's sematic hypothesis being true. However, some of the criticisms which have been raised against the strong causative hypothesis show, as well, that Davidson's third premise is false. One criticism is that it is possible to cause someone to die without killing him, for example by ordering his death. Thus, killing someone and causing his death are not the same. And consequently *kill* does not mean *cause to die*. We should notice in passing that this argument which cuts against the strong causative hypothesis does not affect the weaker causative hypothesis being considered in this paper. That is, it does not show that *cause to die* is not part of the meaning of *kill*.

Let us return to Davidson's argument. Even if it were free from defect, it would not show that the causative hypothesis is false. On Davidson's view it seems that an action's being basic depends upon the way it is described. Hence, to describe John's action as his killing of Smith is to describe it as being an action which John does by moving his finger, although his killing Smith is identical with his moving his finger which is, as so described, a basic action. But this is compatible with the causative hypothesis. Consequently, our task is to show that there can be killings, so described, which are not done by moving one's finger, one's arm, *etc*.

Suppose I open my eyes intentionally. In the normal case all that seems to be required is that I want and intend to open my eyes and because of what I want and intend, my eyes open. Nothing else on my part needs to be done. That is, while it is true of me that I open my eyes, it is not true of me that I open my eyes by X-ing, where *X* is replaced by some verb or verb phrase other than, perhaps, *open my eyes* (Thomson, 1977:171, 246). Now killings appear to be essentially different from my opening my eyes intentionally. It does not seem possible that someone could kill anyone without it being true of the killer that he killed his victim by doing something other than killing him. But is this really so? What I wish to propose is that is that it is possible for there to be killings which occur in a way similar to my intentionally opening my eyes in the normal way. Suppose Smith dies and his death occurs because I want and intend him to die. Moreover, there is nothing I did which caused his death. I did not stab or poison him; I did not even cast a spell on him. All that happened was that I had a desire and intention that he die and because of my desire and intention he died. In addition let us imagine that it is a general feature of the world I am describing that whenever anyone desires and intends that someone dies, then he dies because of their desire and intention and that responsibility for deaths which occur in this way are attributed to those with the corresponding desire and intention. I believe that in a world of this sort that it would be true of me that I killed Smith, but not true of me that I did it by *X*-ing, where *X* is to be replaced by some verb or verb phrase other than *kill Smith*. In this world, then, (20) does not entail (21) and hence the latter is not part of the meaning of the former.

There are several objections which can be raised against my argument. First, it might be claimed that I have changed the meaning of the word *kill*, for when a killing occurs a *how*-question is always appropriate which can be answered by a *by*-phrase. But, to the extent that *how*-questions with *by*-phrase answers can be asked about killings, it is inappropriate to ask them of someone who opens his eyes intentionally in the normal way. Now suppose that I were able to fire at will the nerve fibers which activated the eyelid muscles which caused my eyes to open. In a case of this sort it would be appropriate to ask of someone who opens his eyes intentionally a *how*-question which would have a corresponding *by*-phrase answer. However, there is no reason to think that if this were so that the meaning of *open* would change. Correspondingly, the inappropriateness to killings of *how*-questions which have *by*-phrase answers does not change the meaning of *kill*.

Second, it might be claimed that the world I have described is incoherent, because I have not provided any connection between my wanting and intending that Smith dies and Smith's death. But one can easily be provided. Imagine that my particular desire and intention that Smith dies is identical to some particular brain states of mine. And imagine further that there is a causal connection between these brain states and Smith's death. However, that there is such a causal connection has nothing to do with the meaning of *kill*. For in our world those who use and understand *open* know nothing of a causal connection between wants and desires and the opening of their eyes. Moreover, I believe that the world I have described is coherent without my providing a causal connection between my wants and intentions and Smith's death. It is as coherent as this world in which we give teleological explanations for human actions, but cannot provide causal explanations.

I have argued that *kill* is not a causative verb. Similar arguments can be given which show that other verb of the same sort, such as *melt, defrost, cook, etc.*, are not causative verbs. That is, sentences which contain these verbs and have agent subjects do not have as part of their meaning either [Cause] or as propositional subject [Cause] [Agent] [Do Something].

What motivates the view expressed in the causative hypothesis? I think what underlies it is the deeply entrenched belief that most things that happen have causal antecedents. We cannot defrost the refrigerator, melt the ice, or persuade our boss to give us a raise merely by having certain desires and intentions. What is required is that we do something to melt the ice or to get a raise. But that this is required, as Hume taught us, is not necessary. We could all have been born gods with the power that our wanting and desiring would make it so.

Where does this leave the causative hypothesis? If we take it to be an hypothesis about the semantic structure of our language, then I believe I have shown it to be false for a good many verbs commonly taken to be causative. However, if we take it to be an hypothesis about what we believe about the world, it is probably correct. But then it is not a semantic, but a pragmatic hypothesis.

HOW TO MAKE AND UNDERSTAND A REQUEST

Susan Ervin-Tripp

Introduction. Requests and other moves to influence actions have recently come under particular scrutiny. They impose on others, so that they lead speakers to conceal intent. They provide a challenge to the expectation that speakers value clarity, and that there is a direct relationship between intents and speech acts or between "speech acts" and their verbal realization.

Why are speaker's purposes so often hidden? It is not only so when they involve a major imposition. The answer is that moves to influence or control do more than one thing at a time. They affect the activities of the partner. At the same time, inevitably, they convey a social interpretation which defines the relation of the speaker and hearer. They may also, optionally, convey anger, love, or condescension. How can one utterance, even a very short one, do so much? How can so much be understood?

Social impact on conveyed intent. If one examines only certain well-defined acts, such as directives, it can be found that they are systematically related to such variables as the participants' relative rank, age, familiarity, and the key, the relevance of the task to normal roles, and even distance (Ervin-Tripp 1976). For example, explicit imperatives occurred more often than modal questions like "could you..." to familiar peers doing expected tasks, close at hand. The form taken to realize the act, then, captures some of the social properties of the interaction too.

But directives are only a part of the problem. Directives belong to a larger class of moves which affect the partner's actions, which I shall call control moves. Control moves may include efforts to encourage actions or to prohibit, slow, or stop actions already under way by another person. Control moves could include directives, prohibitions, warnings, and ownership claims having action consequences. They may also include offers, promises, permission requests, and statements of intention if they have consequences for the addressee's actions, possessions or territory.

Let us begin according to the tradition and focus on the problem of *action* rather than relationship or attitude. The same goal, the same action by the hearer, can be brought about by a variety of speech acts. The same utterance can have a variety of interpretations as to the action goal.

Suppose you walk into a friend's kitchen and see a thirty-month old child cutting carrots with a very large butcher knife. You are concerned that she might injure herself and so you speak:

(1) A-C: Can I help you?

How is this utterance to be understood? You may be making an *offer* to help, with the possibility of refusal. You may have already taken up the large knife, so your utterance merely expresses your *intention* to help. We often see such cases where offers or even directives are given after the adult speaker has already taken action. The difference between an 'offer' and an announced 'intention' is in the beliefs of viewers or participants, not in the action in view. In both cases the speaker will act, not the hearer. In the case of an offer, the hearer is the principal beneficiary and so has the right to control what happens.

Now consider the situation in which you, an adult, are slicing carrots and the same small child appears and says:

(2) C-A: Can I help?

If you consider yourself the beneficiary of the assistance of a well-trained Montessori-taught carrot-slicer, you may hear this as an *offer*. If you doubt the skill or even safety of the help, you may consider it a plea for *permission*, especially if said with a wheedling tone. The difference here is that in the case of permission requests the speaker, as principal beneficiary, wants the action more than the hearer. Yet again, in this situation there is no difference in the action itself which is in view.

Since it's very hard to tell the difference, perhaps it's not surprising that American children accept offers with *OK*, which sounds like compliance with a request. Maybe the boundaries between offers and requests are after all not well marked. For example:

(3) A-C: Do you wanna play outside?
(4) A-C: Do you wanna have more juice?

While we expect juice to be more often the desire of the consumer than the speaker, and to therefore be accepted as an offer, either (3) or (4) would be acceptable as an offer or as a directive, depending on desires and circumstances.

It must often be the case that participants do not agree as to the act intended. Since the consequences are so slight as the greater likelihood of thanks for offers, it cannot surprise us that even the participants are not always sure of intent, in speech act terms. Since the action goals are the same across these interpretations there is no sense of the collapse of communication.

But there are circumstances in which the social features even influence the view of the action goal. Picture an elderly landlady and her student tenant in conversation. The landlady says to the student:

(5) L-S: Can we move the dust bin over here?

The student will hear the utterance as a request to move the dust bin. The social features influencing this view include the knowledge that the student is younger and more capable of lifting dust bins.

There are also formal reasons to hear (5) as a request. Note that a common form in English for unexpected requests is the modal:

(6) Can you + (desired act) ?

The form in (6) has been found to be typical of requests to listeners of a different age or rank, or to mark unexpected tasks or even greater distance (Ervin-Tripp 1976).

The *we* pronoun is commonly used to designate the addressee when a superior asks a subordinate to do tasks for the common good (Ervin-Tripp 1976, Sinclair and Coulthard 1975).

(7a) Doctor - nurse: We'll get a temperature at midnight.

(7b) Teacher - pupils: Let's take our naps now.

At this conference, E. Schegloff, acting as moderator, used *we* to a questioner he thought out of line:

(8) Moderator - questioner: If we will restrict ourselves to clarification questions.

Thus for both social and formal reasons (5) is heard as a directive to the student to perform the action mentioned.

But if the social positions are reversed there is a radical change in interpretation. In (9) the student *asks permission* using a standard permission form:

(9) S-L: Can we move the dust bin over here?

In this case it is the speaker, not the hearer, who is to carry out the action; it is the speaker, not the hearer, who wants the action done and who is the principal beneficiary.

The difference in interpretation is here very overt since a different person acts. The difference depends entirely on conventions such as those about *can you* and *we* in English, and the rank relation of the two parties.

This example came to my attention because a Turkish student said (9) to an American landlady intending a directive. But the landlady replied:

(10) Why, Ayhan, I didn't know you had a roommate!

In the landlady's view, her greater age (and possibly her rank as proprietor) entitled her both to receive permission requests more than directives, and to give but not receive *we* as a second-person form in her relationship with student tenants. The landlady's reply indicated that she heard an unambiguous permission request.

Despite the fact that an explicit goal was stated, it is not only the interpreted speech act which changes according to the social assumptions, but who is to carry out the goal act, the speaker or the hearer. In cases where the goal is implicit and not stated -- such as "Is there any coffee left?" -- the diversity of interpretation is well known.

We cannot know whether an utterance is a request for permission for the speaker to benefit himself, or an offer for the speaker to benefit the hearer unless we know the participants' assumptions about skill and benefit. We cannot know whether the speaker is going to act himself or is directing the hearer to act unless we know the speaker's estimate of relative rank. In more general terms, it's not possible to have an empirically satisfactory theory of control acts that is not also an analysis of social interpretation. Because there appears to be a very complex relation between action goals and utterances, it is sometimes thought the relation is completely indeterminate. But if we include social information we have shown that there is consistency in the relation between action goals and form. It is the omission of social information which obscures the mapping system.

Foregrounding social information. In the above examples, I took the action or goal as focal. In this perspective, the social information is necessary for disambiguation of action goals, since there is no one-to-one mapping of action goals. Sometimes -- perhaps more often than we realize -- control acts are a means for conveying social information (e.g. Mitchell-Kernan and Kernan 1977a).

(5) Sup-inf: Can we move the dust bin over here?
(9) Inf-sup: Can we move the dust bin over here?

Since (5) and (9) are alike, we could say that the utterance conveys two potential messages:

(11) You will move the dust bins + you are inferior.
(12) You give permission + we will move the dust bins + we are inferior to you.

When the social relationship is perceived the same way by both and is not under negotiation, the resolution of the message with more than one axis is not a problem. The action then becomes focal and the message is informative about action.

If somebody was already busy moving the dust bin, and another participant said (5) or (9), the utterance would become an assertion about social relationships, since the action is unambiguous. Our family studies suggest that the intended action may be known to observers at least half the time. When that is the case, control acts can become at least as informative about social relationships and feelings as they are about action goals.

Looking back at the first example, we can contrast the alternatives:

(1) A-C: Can I help you?
(13) A-C: I'm going to help you.

The second alternative would explicitly specify that the adult intended to help whether the child gave permission or not. The social implication of the difference can only be correctly understood if we knew the usage distribution of explicit intention forms vs. permission forms in situations where the context makes clear that speech states intentions.

We have found in American middle class samples that many forms typically spoken by women in offices to persons different in rank -- either higher or lower -- are also spoken to children, e.g.

(14) Could you give me that?
(15) Would you please come in?

Adults in these cases appear to be signalling a rank difference and letting intonation convey the direction of the difference.

We have found that children, on the other hand, are likely to mark higher/lower by many different cues, rather than just distance or difference in rank. They often focus more explicitly on the social information conveyed, rather than the act. Andy Rogers (1979) reported an excellent example between an older and younger brother and sister:

(16) B-S: Carrie, stop sucking your fingers.
S-B: David, you're not the boss of me.

If we had unambiguous one-to-one coding of control acts they would be imperatives like *carry the dust bin* and *give me the carrot knife*. If we had unambiguous one-to-one representation of social relationships they might be declaratives like *I'm the boss, I can do that better*, or *I love you*. People do of course make such statements, and some mental health reformers think we should do it more, rather than conflating social and action messages. Real languages allow us to attend focally either to social relationships or action goals and let the other remain in the background. In such a system it is almost impossible to communicate action goals without at the same time signalling adult/child, inferior/superior, familiar/strange. Studies of pragmatics with respect to action have focussed either on conveyed intent or on social meaning and politeness. The outcome has been some despair at the possibility of discovering mapping rules that are empirically verifiable outside of the scholar's study.

The multiple mapping which includes both action goal and social claims helps us to see why there are so many communication problems. These are endemic in the differences of interpretation of speaker and hearer as to their relative skill, rank and so on, which on occasion can lead to a difference in interpretation of intended act or actor. Some speakers chronically use forms conveying greater distance or deference than hearers expect; such a speaker's control acts will be misinterpreted: her hints will not be heard as directives, her directives will be considered literal questions, her statements of intent will be heard as permission requests. While recent work suggests such chronic mis-mapping can exist between spouses, it would of course be more common to find it cross-culturally. We are usually more aware of social misinterpretations. For example, if Europeans believe the forms in (14) and (15) are appropriate only to superiors, they might assume American middle class women are deferential to children. The mismatches leading to failure to comply with an action goal are likely to be incorrectly attributed.

My analysis proposes that social assumptions affect the interpretation of speech acts -- if there is a level such as the speech act -- and that social assumptions also affect the interpretation of action goals to be accomplished by the speech act. Conversely, assumptions as to conveyed intent or action goals affect messages received about social features conveyed. The decision as to whether a speech act level is analytically necessary awaits a detailed proposal incorporating social and action aspects into one description.

Interpreting speech in context. We have recently been engaged, in Berkeley,[1] in a study of the practical problem of interpreting a system with two or more unknowns. Our empirical means have included: collecting critical instances of misunderstandings, identifying formal variation with correlated social differences, videotaping natural interaction to get context, and testing conveyed intent in situations where we can control what is known.

It is surprising to see, in everyday family interaction, how often actions are quite predictable. In order to test this intuition, we asked an audience of adults to watch and listen to the videotaped scenes. We stopped the action at critical test points and asked them what was going to happen next. They guessed the next speech act correctly half the time. These guesses were based on a few obvious principles:

(a) *Actors hold intentions over time*. When a control act fails, it will be tried again. Since the younger the child, the more limited the repertoire, the principle of repetition may apply at a low level, namely to the overt act or utterance itself.

(b) *Events have trajectories*. From the beginnings of social and physical experience, infants begin to recognize regularities of sequence. For instance, mother opens the refrigerator door, baby is fed soon. In infant games, schemes of sequence or alternation can be said to have simple trajectories. Baby throws toys out of the crib, partner puts them back. Door slams; Daddy enters the house, so that an early reported utterance is "Daddy" when a door slams.

The knowledge of trajectories makes many control utterances redundant with action. Suppose a person carrying a package enters a room and another points to a place suitable to put packages. The pointing is functionally equivalent to "put it there", but it is only intelligible because the participants (a) have noticed the package, (b) know that packages are put down, (c) agree on appropriate places to put packages, (d) on the particular occasion know that either the package or its bearer is not going further. Even pointing relies for its interpretation on prior knowledge of a course of events.

(c) *Participants know the roles in the events*. Norms like event trajectories develop out of early social experience. Infants, for example know if it is their father who supplies food, who feeds them. The combination of event knowledge and social roles can create powerful expectations about the course of actions.

Cooking can be a complex joint enterprise. Experienced adults would expect that there will be actions including the locating and adding of ingredients, and their processing. If a helper comes, they produce questions about location of food and utensils, questions about the next action, and the person who controls the resources can be expected to give directives to find, add, or process.

In such a situation, the interpretation of a particular utterance depends on assumed relative expertise.

(17) Where's the vanilla?

From an outsider (17) is more likely to be a location question; from the head cook it is more likely to be a directive.

We have studied children's understanding of implicit directives which do not state what is to be done. We showed stories with pictures in which children did naughty things like spill food on the carpet or couch. If the mother was in sight, or if her voice could be heard, even three year olds expected that the event coming next would be that the naughty children would stop and clean up, regardless of what the mother said or whether she spoke at all. She might say (18) or she might be silent.

(18) M-C: Are you spilling food?

The crucial role of the mother is apparent from the contrast in consequences when it is another child who speaks instead of the mother. Our interpretation of these data is that children learn very early that certain actions are prohibited by the mother, and that she demands specific remedial acts like cleaning up. In fact, many children supplied what the mother would be likely to say. The mother's presence either in sight or in sound suggests this normal train of events. In the sense that the scenario is already familiar, what the mother says is not critical if it is congruent with this expectation. When it was not, the children said she was silly and told us what she should have said. For instance she was silly if she said she liked to play too, which of course is a serious violation of normal roles.

In another picture story, a mother and child carry groceries from the car. The door to the house is closed, but some children are playing nearby. By seven, half of the children we tested proposed opening the door even when nothing was said. They could actively construct the trajectory without additional cues. By six, children who were told the mother said (19) nearly always reported opening the door. The question directs attention to an obstacle.

(19) M-C: Is the door open?

The importance of social roles to this development of event/role expectations can be seen in a story in which we unwittingly violated normal roles. In this story a child sits near a cake at a dinner table. Farther away is the mother who announces (20).

(20) I've finished my cake.

It was very rare that any child proposed offering more to the mother, this being a reversal of usual roles.

We propose that *before* an utterance occurs, observers and participants are engaged in projecting the event trajectory with the actions according to expected roles. The utterance then has less burden in supplying information.

In cases where the point of view or knowledge of participants differs, more explicitness is necessary. With an adult in a joint cooking activity, a child might be more interested in process, for instance in mixing or beating, than in getting a particular food cooked. In such a case, (21) would be inadequate.

(21) M-C: One teaspoon of vanilla.

The child's event projection does not include food addition at this point, only more of the present activity.

(d) *Utterances alter attentional focus*. If a listener is preoccupied with different activities than the speaker, joint focus has to be brought about. Even a shared project need not result in joint focus if roles are divided or experience is different. Parallel activity can bring the partner into peripheral focus, allowing divided attention if such complex work is possible.

Many activities require that an actor divide attention at a given time. For instance, a source of frustration reported by housewives is the chronic overlap of attention, for instance to a household task, planning a future action, helping a child with homework, monitoring the path of a toddler. In such a situation, oscillations of relative focus determine how much special stimulation is necessary to bring intensive focus on a given target. A famous central European folktale chronicles the disasters coming to a husband who was unable to maintain simultaneous attention to multiple trajectories and program his interventions in the right order, when he trades jobs with his wife.

Take a specific incident to illustrate attention division. A driver and a passenger are commuting for an hour on a complex route in which highways must be entered and left at appropriate points, not always well marked. Both have two foci of attention at least, the route and the talk. The driver also, of course, has the mechanics of driving the car, shifting, and turning. The passenger can afford to put almost all attention, perhaps all attention, on the narrative he is producing. The driver's attentional focus depends on the demands of the route, making turns at the right points and going through lights. At one point in the narrative, the passenger suddenly leaned forward, turned to the driver, waved his hand, and in an excited voice said:

(22) P-D: No, not the San Francisco Airport the Oakland Airport!

How was this to be heard by the driver?

The sudden shift in body attitude, the loud excited voice could signal an urgent warning. Or they could signal self-correction in the narrative. The content was appropriate to the narrative, but both airports were turn-offs from the route the car was on. So the content was equally relevant to the narrative and to the route.

The narrative had been relegated to secondary attention by the driver. So the effect of (22) was an initial interpretation that it was a warning. Why? If the driver's primary attention is to the route, the first scan of all messages will fit them to that framework. The accidental overlap of topic, and of kinesic and vocal cues fit the driver's primary framework of interpretation, with a disruption of driving until the secondary analysis according to the narrative was done. This was a dramatic evidence of the impact of attentional priorities in determining interpretive order.

In the videotapes of families, many control acts occur through altering attention. That change is enough to set to work the event knowledge which leads the listener to understand what needs to happen next. If one's own actions are very engrossing, or if one's abilities do not allow simultaneous attention to several trajectories at once, then special efforts to gain attention are needed. These are not just of the type to call attention to speech, though that, of course, is learned very early. In particular these attention-focussing utterances involve reference to obstacles to the successful completion of desired acts.

Context and utterance. The videotape analysis and the experimental stories have shown us that understanding starts first from context. When a listener is attending to ongoing action and its trajectory, then it is possible to understand a congruent utterance with minimal interpretive work. What is said is likely to be redundant with what is already known, or it may add specifications, as in the case of *please, hurry, there,* or *three*. Alternative interpretations are not likely to be considered at all, including "literal interpretations" unless the utterance is so unconventional as to require inference to reach a relevant interpretation. The activities in focus and trajectories of expected events to come create a field of relevance or projected relevance within which priorities of interpretation will be made.

In this view, language is needed to direct attention, to control timing, to specify, to organize action, to identify actors, to motivate or provide reasons, to reinforce or change social relationships affected by control acts. When any of these accomplishments are left undone by the prior work of the interaction or the prior knowledge of the participants, we can say that language is supplementary.

The evidence from our experimental work with children is that the calculation of the intent of the speaker is not necessary in many situations. If the partner understands the event trajectory, is aware of obstacles, and has a cooperative attitude about the removal of obstacles, understanding can occur without any inference about intent.

A standard interpretive model for speech acts makes the utterance occur first. Context is checked against possible interpretations. We can say that interpretation is retrospective to context. Our analysis of data suggests the opposite. We propose that participants become aware of inferential processes when there is incongruity or misunderstanding, and that this awareness has been the model for standard interpretation. Most of the time, language is facilitative to ongoing event projection, and merely confirms or supplements what is already known. Because so little needs to be done by language, it is available in everyday exchanges for ellipsis, for joking, or for the redundancy that instructs children and newcomers about conventions. By generalizing the structural features of these redundant instances to new occasions, learners can project an interpretation into the novel instances which supply no supportive clues.

Conclusions. The major claims made in this paper are that interpersonal control acts always involve both information about social assumptions and relationships, and information about desired acts or goals. The analysis of interpretive processes which attends only to politeness, to social meaning, or to conveyed intent is doomed to fail. Since these meanings are conveyed jointly through a complex mapping they must be included in a model of interpretation and production.

Analysis of both videotaped and experimental control acts revealed that interpretive processes rely heavily on context, and appear to depend on expectations based on repetition, knowledge of usual sequences of events and roles, as filtered by attention. Although interpretive processes can be retrospective to context when something goes wrong, it appears far more common that language is redundant with or supplementary to knowledge already available from what was going on before the utterance in question. The selective power of such prior knowledge permits extremely efficient interpreting of control acts and by-passing of irrelevant literal interpretations.

FOOTNOTE:

1. The research mentioned in this paper was funded by grant RH01-26063 to the Institute of Human Learning at the University of California, Berkeley. The "we" in the text refers to my collaborators David Gordon, Ruth Bennett, Ann Eisenberg, Susan Gelphman, Catherine O'Connor, Amy Strage, and Georgette Stratos.

I'LL BET YOU $10 THAT BETTING IS NOT A SPEECH ACT

Nicholas Fotion

1. Betting is a peculiar speech act. In fact, it is so peculiar a speech act that I am willing to bet anyone $10 that it is not really a speech act at all. "You're on," John might reply. "Of course it's a speech act. After all, the act of betting has an explicit illocutionary force formula as do many other speech acts such as promising, ordering, stating and apologizing; and certainly since the bet you just made about betting was made in my presence such that I heard, understood what you said, etc., it has to be an act performed *in* the utterance of a meaningful sentence. Betting sure looks like a speech act. Why would you suppose it isn't?"

By way of replying to John, I would like to refer to an article by Michael Hancher (1979) titled "The Classification of Cooperative Illocutionary Acts". In this article Hancher praises Searle's (1975b) classification system for (illocutionary) speech acts but argues that that system needs to be supplemented. He is particularly interested in speech acts where the actions of at least two people are needed in order for a speech act to be performed. These so-called cooperative speech acts are to be contrasted with unilateral ones. Firing someone, stating something and ordering someone about are clear-cut examples of unilateral speech acts where all that is required of the hearer is that he receive uptake (i.e., hear, understand, etc. what was said by the speaker). With a cooperative speech act, in contrast, it is "[....]

essential to the very nature of the act" that there is more than one speaker (Hancher 1979:10). You and I might pray together and thus perform what Hancher calls multiple speech acts, but such acts are not of the cooperative type. Although we *can* pray together, we need not. Betting, in contrast is a cooperative act. We do not bet together or bet separately. We either bet together or we don't bet.

If, as a speech act theorist, one accepts the distinction between unilateral and cooperative speech acts, he runs straight into a serious problem. Hancher states that problem as follows:

> [...]: how large is an illocutionary act? According to Searle [...] 'the characteristic grammatical form of the illocutionary act is the complete sentence'. On the face of it this would seem to exclude all cooperative illocutionary acts, which in their fully articulated form involve at least two sentences. And yet Searle acknowledges that 'making ... a bet' is 'performing an illocutionary act,' even as 'saying certain things constitutes getting married' [...]. These bilateral contracts, betting and marriage, both involve more than the one sentence supposed to be 'characteristic' of illocutionary acts. (Hancher 1979:7)

Hancher's solution to the largeness problem is to expand Searle's constricted notion of speech act. The speech act of betting, although larger than that of an order since it involves the actions of two people at least, is still an act. As embarrassing as it might be to Searle to include these larger units of speech into the realm of speech acts, Hancher thinks we must.

There are two separate issues which need to be distinguished in order to appreciate what is right and wrong about what Hancher is saying. The first has to do with the analysis of betting; the second with whether betting is a speech act and, as a part of that issue, what is a speech act. I will argue that with respect to the first issue Hancher is right but with respect to the second he is not.

2. Notice that if Sam says to Lucky "I bet you $10 the Yankees won't win the pennant this year", Lucky's reply can be, especially if it is already obvious that the Yankees are in trouble in the pennant race,

"OK, but you've got to give me odds". But if he says, instead, "You can't be serious", "Forget it", or "No thanks", can he be said to have rejected Sam's bet? Hancher thinks not and I agree. One does not reject bets. He may welch on one, pay up if he loses a bet or get paid if he wins. But it is an *offer* to a bet, not the bet itself, which gets rejected. We should not be misled here by the phrase "I bet you ..." into supposing that the bet has been made because Sam has uttered these magic words. Other expressions such as "I'll make a bet with you", "$10 says the Yankees won't win the pennant this year" and "Want to bet that ...", which also can be used to help make a bet, are perhaps better indicators of what is going on here. The expression "I'll make a bet with you ..." is especially instructive. Unlike "I bet you ...", which is in the classical first person, present indicative, active form with which speech act theorists feel most comfortable, "I'll make a bet ..." is in the future tense. It implies, when used, that the bet has not yet been made. The interrogative form of bet making, "Want to bet?", similarly suggests that the bet itself is still in the future and has not been consummated. So we should not be misled by the "I bet you" form of betting into analyzing betting roughly the way "I promise" and "I order you to ..." are analyzed. Indeed, "I bet you..." may be elliptical for "I'll (make a) bet (with) you" and, if it is, it is clearer still that what the speaker is doing in saying "I bet you" is not betting but offering to bet.

So in the process of making a bet, but prior to the bet being made, the speaker has uttered a perfectly legitimate speech act. It is a speech act of offering. It is as if Sam had said to Lucky, "I offer to bet you $10 that the Yankees won't win the pennant this year". Notice that this speech act is unilateral. Of course, Lucky may accept or reject Sam's offer, or he may try to renegotiate a somewhat different bet. Yet prior to his doing anything (apart from hearing, understanding, etc., it) the offer still stands. Lucky's response is to a standing offer, that is, it is a response to a speech act which is complete simply as the result of the speaker's words and the communicative setting.

Lucky has other options. He may delay his response by saying "Let me think it over", but the offer will still stand, within reason, until Lucky says "Yes" or "No" to that offer. When he does, his response will *itself* be a speech act.

It is important to contrast this speech act with Sam's initiating act since the two acts are not parallel as might be supposed. To be sure, once the bet is made, and especially if no one is giving odds, the status of the betters can be thought of as parallel. Each, by then, is equally committed to paying a debt should he lose and, at that stage, it makes no difference who initiated the bet and who consented to it in response.

Prior to that stage, however, by uttering "I'll bet you $10 the Yankees won't win the pennant this year" Sam is:

(a) committing himself by making an offer on a conditional basis (the condition being in Lucky's control)
(b) inviting (directing) Lucky to respond with a yea or nay.

This commissive-directive (Hancher's terminology) type of speech act contrasts with Lucky's commissive(-acceptance) response ("You're on"). That response requires nothing of the original speaker except, optionally, an acknowledgement in the form of a hand shake or some indication that the acceptance has been received (e.g., like a ticket stub given at a race track). To make a bet then, two separate and somewhat different (in type) speech acts are required. The bet, as it were, emerges from these two acts, not as an identifiable third act but as a creation of the cooperative linguistic efforts of the participants. On the one side, the final betting act does not magically emerge from two completely disparate acts. Rather the two prior acts are aimed at bringing about a bet. Sam's offer is after all an offer to make a bet -- not to do something else. On the other side, the bet does not emerge as a large and yet 'atomic' speech act not based upon any other smaller speech act. If betting is a speech act, it is an act built upon other (at least two other) speech acts and in this sense is 'molecular'. So far I am in basic agreement with Hancher.

However, against Hancher, I now want to argue that betting is better characterized not as a speech act but as a piece of speech activity (discourse). If a speech act can be thought of as the minimal unit of language communication (Searle 1969:16), speech activity can be thought of as a stringing together of speech acts. To be sure, most bets represent strings of only two speech acts. Nonetheless, the principle I want to defend here should be obvious by now. Sometimes it takes more than one speech act to "bring about" an illocutionary effect, that is, to satisfy certain of our linguistic purposes. It may very well be true that below the linguistic level of a sentence an illocutionary effect also can be brought about with a few special expressions or acts (e.g., "Hello", "OK"). It may also be true that in most cases the illocutionary effect is brought about within the framework of a sentence; thus also creating a speech act. However, it simply is not true that the notion of illocutionary effect (force) and speech act are even roughly correlative. If a linguistic unit of language is a (full) speech act, it has an illocutionary effect (force); but if a linguistic unit has an illocutionary effect (force) it does not follow that it is a speech act. Talking about illocutionary acts and equating 'illocutionary act' and 'speech act' only confounds the issue here. The illocutionary force of a unit of language communication is identified in terms of what gets done *in* uttering that unit. Thus, it is also not true that all the illocutionary effects that we wish to bring about with(in) language are brought about only within the framework of a single act. In fact, betting is only one example of this point. As Hancher makes clear in his article, betting is one kind of agreement of which (bilateral) contracting, and other less formal agreements, are more specific examples. Some other types here are appointing (some of which require the appointee to consent to the 'appointment' before it becomes an appointment), gift-giving (which is merely an offering until the 'gift' is accepted), and on a larger scale, marrying (Hancher 1979:8-10). More on some of these activities later.

Returning for now to betting -- why, in addition to the fact that betting is a speech unit composed of an offer and acceptance, is it better to think of this unit of language as an activity rather than an act? Consider the following betting setting. Albert thinks the Yankees will win the pennant next year and is willing to bet accordingly. Billy is willing to bet that the Yankees are a second, and Charley that they are a third place team. David completes the 'pool' bet by taking the position that the Yankees are no better than a fourth place team. Now when these four bet, are they engaged in the business of uttering a speech act? What if the betting pool includes a dozen or so employees from the office who are 'betting' on the score of the first game of the World Series? Is making the 'pool' best characterized as uttering a speech act?

Well, it could hardly be argued that the 'pool' constitutes a series of bilateral betting acts between the various participants. More plausibly it could be said that the 'pool' represents a series of bilateral betting acts made against 'everybody else'. But this kind of 'pool' betting is more than that. For one thing, each 'bet' placed affects the total amount of money in the pool and in this sense cannot be said to be independent of the others. Yet more basically, since the many acts of betting create one pool of money which one winner takes away, that betting cannot be understood as anything less than group activity. Of course, that activity can include, in addition to verbal activity (e.g., "Let me in on the pool" or "Put may name down in the pool") other things as well. It also includes, optionally (sometimes mandatorily), acts of putting one's money down and drawing a 'score' from a hat. In the smaller pool with Albert, Billy, Charles and David, money need not be exchanged. But again their bet or bets can only be seen as a single organized activity made up of, but not analyzed simply into, individual acts.

Now my point is that once we see multilateral betting as an *activity*, not an act which creates the sui generis illocutionary force betting, bilateral betting can be viewed more readily not as an act but as a minimal form of betting activity. A bilateral bet is not a bloated speech act but sparing speech activity.

Much the same point can be made about marrying. As Hancher (1979: 15) points out, marrying is a contractual arrangement and, perhaps, in its most sparing form requires only two speech acts (viz., an exchange of vows). It could be, then, that the whole marriage *ceremony* is composed of a long series of speech acts which play a variety of roles (e.g., preparatory and congratulatory), only a few of which are concerned with the business of actually getting a couple married. Yet, whether these few speech acts are minimally two, or three, four, five or more will, in fact, vary with the tradition. It will also vary with the tradition as to whether certain non-linguistic acts during that wedding ceremony need to get done, and what the role of marrying official is (i.e., whether he/she *needs* to say or do anything to get the couple married). In any case, once one views getting married as something which gets done as the result of a *series* of acts, with two being the absolute minimum, getting married more naturally gets viewed as an activity rather than an act.

3. Of course it really should make little difference whether the units of language being talked about in this paper are called (macro, etc.) speech acts or activity. One is tempted to say that the whole issue of acts or activity is merely a terminological one. What should matter is how one systematically identifies, and then analyzes, the units of language in question and not what they are called. But unfortunately terminological considerations get in the way of how we think about these matters. Under the act model there is a strong temptation to shrink the unit of language under analysis down the single sentential form. To identify the official's "I pronounce you ..." as the operative expression in a marriage ceremony, as Searle (1975b:358) does, may be an example of succumbing to this temptation. But in a sense even Hancher is not immune here from this temptation, focusing as he does mainly on bilateral units of language. After all, it only seems

like a slight extension of the speech act concept to allow for various 'acts' which are merely twice the size of normal speech acts.

A more fruitful way of looking at how language works here is to think of people as having various purposes which they wish to have satisfied through the use of language. If those purposes are to bring about an illocutionary effect, they might or might not bring off that effect by uttering a single sentence. Sometimes it might take less than a full sentence to get the job done, sometimes more. One needs, as it were, to keep an open mind about the various possibilities including one which does not permit the creation of an illocutionary effect without the utterance of six, twelve, or whatever number of speech acts.

Notice how this open-minded policy affects what one says about the following five quite different language units. Consider first bilateral contracting. Minimally such contracting requires two speech acts when *what* is contracted for (the propositional content of the contract) can be represented within the framework of one speech act. But a contract can be a complex thing containing a variety of conditions arrived at possibly through long negotiations. Thus when the parties to the contract sign it, they are, to be sure, signing one contract. Yet at the same time they are committing themselves to various conditions stated in the contract and benefitting from various other conditions. In other words, we must not forget that the *whole document* is the contract and that it is composed not only of a whole series of speech acts but of items in that series which would not have been there had not other items been there as well (i.e., certain items are there as trade off for other items). Thus, with a contract it is no longer just a matter of stretching a meaning of 'speech act' to apply to a pair of acts, but stretching it almost to the breaking point so that it now applies to long and interrelated strings of such acts.

Consider next the unit of language we call swearing *in*. It is tempting to confuse this unit with swearing. Swearing that I am telling the truth is a speech act. But when Smith is being *sworn in* as

President, he swears to many things. More than that, he is sworn in only after he has sworn to all the things contained in the swearing portion of the inauguration ceremony.

Consider thirdly the linguistic unit, and a very large one at that, of electing someone to office. Hancher talks about this 'act' and identifies it as an integrative cooperative act. It is a cooperative act for him because many people join in in order to get someone elected to office and yet it is an integrative (rather than a reciprocal) act because "[...] the cooperative acts (votes) are all parallel, and of the same sort [...]" (1979:10). It is interesting that electing and the closely related 'act' of a binding city referendum (vote) are the only really gross acts which Hancher explicitly considers in his paper, and they appear very late in his presentation, almost as if in retrospect. As was indicated earlier, it is as if he is still mainly concerned with 'acts' which are just a bit larger than the ones Austin, Searle and the other speech act theorists are concerned with and, as a result, has not as yet seen the full import of some of the things he is saying about speech act theory. However that may be, an 'act' now appears to be so gross in size so as to encompass literally millions of individual speech acts (votes). It would seem more natural to speak here of the activity of electing; or better yet of the process of electing a person to an office. Whichever word seems most appropriate, notice how both words help us to say exactly what we want to say in contrast to 'act'. They both give us a sense that the linguistic unit with which we are dealing is complex and yet is organized. To engage in an activity or process is not to perform acts of a random nature but acts which lead to one common goal as in the three activities already discussed in this portion of this paper.

Fourthly consider the activity of trying as when we try someone in a courtroom. Unlike electing someone to office, the activity of trying someone is composed of variously connected speech acts as well as other acts of a physical-linguistic nature such as the presentation of evidence. This activity is so complex in fact that it is rarely thought of in connection with talk about illocutionary forces. It is assumed that the only illocutionary forces which might be found in the process of trying someone are those associated with asking questions, making statements and the like. And yet when someone has been tried (and not yet found guilty or innocent), we can say, much as we do when someone has been married, elected, etc., that something has been done in the process of using language and, in this sense, that an illocutionary effect more than that found in individual speech acts has been brought about.

Lastly, consider praying. Praying is both an act and activity concept. Single-liners such as "God, help me", "Where are You now that I need You?" and "I pray You will help me" are examples of the act form, although I personally have a sense of reluctance in actually calling these speech acts prayers or praying. Certainly if someone said, somewhat anachronistically, to a superior "I pray you will help me", calling that speech act prayer or praying would seem odd. But whatever one calls these speech acts, they hardly exhaust the use of 'pray' and its cognates. It hardly also exhausts the use of 'pray' in the speech act sense to say, as Searle (1975b:356) does, that 'pray' is directive. It is a directive in the classic first person speech act form as when someone says "I pray You will make it rain again". But certainly, although "Let us pray" is a directive, the praying which follows is not limited to this directive function. Prayer in the activity form can include speech acts which are representatives (in relating, for example, God's deeds), commissives (in promising God that we will do better tomorrow), expressives (in thanking God for what He has already done) and even declaratives (in declaring ourselves to be on His side). On those occasions, at least, when the tradition dictates that the various kinds of speech acts are to be issued in a certain order or sequence, praying seems to be an example of getting something done in using language which transcends the speech act level.

4. These five examples of speech activity which have their own illo-

cutionary force are not isolated examples. In the Catholic church one has not been forgiven merely by having the priest say "I absolve you..." More than that is required, such as that the sinner confess to the sins which he has committed (Martinich 1975:406,408). Similarly the sacrament of the eucharist is performed, in part, because the priest has uttered a whole eucharistic prayer (id.:406). In a non-religious setting, in addition to those activities mentioned already, there are, for example, those of making a will, examining someone, conducting a hearing and divorcing.

It might be thought that in presenting this list of (allegedly) illocutionary speech activities I am confusing, in spite of what has been said earlier: (a) the actual illocutionary unit, with (b) what often accompanies that unit (e.g., certain preparatory acts). In this connection consider a proclamation by the mayor of Metro that this is Human Rights Week. This proclamation may look like illocutionary speech activity, an objector might say, since prior to saying "I proclaim..." his honor issues a series of whereases. "Whereas," he says, "it is generally recognized that there are certain fundamental human rights of ..., and whereas certain individuals and groups have been deprived of ... and whereas ... I proclaim this first week of the month of ... to be Human Rights Week". However, so the argument continues, these whereases are not actually part of the proclamation. Rather what they represent are acts which make explicit what is generally called the preparatory conditions of some speech act. Often, of course, the preparatory conditions are left implicit if for no other reason than that of convenience. In a proclamation such as the one cited, convenience is of little import. What is important is making clear (explicit) the whys and the wherefores of the proclamation so that the cause of human rights may be furthered. In any case, the proclamation itself, in contrast with the proclamation ceremony, is only an act and not an example of speech activity.

An important distinction needs to be made here in order to assess the full force of this argument. Indeed, as the argument makes clear, the whereas portion of the proclamation is largely and perhaps wholly concerned with making background or preparatory conditions explicit. Further if these and other conditions were not present, the proclamation would not be a proclamation (i.e., would misfire). In this sense then at least some of the whereases (at least those which represent preparatory conditions) can be said to be *necessary conditions for the utterance* of the proclamation even though the *utterance of these conditions* is not necessarily part of the proclamation itself.

So the objector is right. If we thought of a proclamation as illocutionary speech activity because of the whereas clauses, we would be on shaky grounds. However, what I am arguing is that there is a difference between a proclamation of the kind his honor the mayor issues and, say, a contract. The conditions of a contract are not mere preparatory conditions for the signing of the contract. They are literally part of the contract. It is similarly the case with the sacrament of penance (in a Catholic setting). The confession by the sinner prior to the priest absolving him/her of sin is not a preparatory condition, although, of course, the sinner must have sinned in order to be absolved (Martinich 1975:406). Nor is it accurate to speak of the confession as the propositional content of the priest's absolving act, although the confession contains the propositional content of the absolution (id.: 408). Rather penance is best seen as an activity which in being consummated requires both the sinner to say certain things (e.g., to actually perform speech acts of confessing) *and* the priest then to absolve the sinner.

But if I am not confusing the actual illocutionary unit, which I am claiming is often longer than a single sentence (and best characterized as activity), with what accompanies that unit, it might be thought that I am, nonetheless, confusing or at least not being clear about something else. How, it might be asked, is illocutionary activity differentiated from non-illocutinary activity? How that is to be done has not been made clear thus far, for surely the claim here is not that each form of linguistic activity yields its own illocutionary force.

Indeed not. When a speaker issues a list of promises or resolutions, no one would be tempted to say that the activity or process of making that list yields a macro illocutionary force of listing-one's-promises or some new, unique speech act. Similarly, the grocery list which a wife gives to her husband represents a series of independent requests-to-purchase rather than some larger unique single linguistic function with its own illocutionary force.

Yet when the lingusitic activity has some unitary aspect to it, it is not so easy to decide whether to assign some unique illocutionary force to the activity in question. Part of the problem is this. If an illocutionary act is conceived of as an act performed in locuting (where 'locuting' in turn is an act of putting *words* together), identifying illocutionary acts (and their forces) is pretty much restricted to what is found within the act itself. In contrast, in dealing with illocutionary activity of two up to millions of speech acts, it is not so clear where the illocutionary force indicating devices are to be found. But more importantly, in focusing on activity, it becomes clear how unclear expressions such as 'force', '*in* saying something', 'the act of saying something', 'doing something' and others like them are in telling us what 'illocutionary' means. So the objector here has a point in noting that 'illocutionary' and thus 'illocutionary activity' has not been fully clarified. The discussion of betting and other speech activities has, in fact, exposed this unclarity.

However, the main thrust of this paper has not been to give a definitive answer to the question: What are illocutionary forces? Rather, it has been to argue that some units of language utterance, most of which have been generally conceded to have their own illocutionary forces but have been reduced in analysis to acts or made to look as much like acts as possible by analysis, are not really acts at all but more complex units better labelled activity.

SEVEN SINS OF PRAGMATICS:
THESES ABOUT SPEECH ACT THEORY,
CONVERSATIONAL ANALYSIS, LINGUISTICS AND RHETORIC*

Dorothea Franck

In the first place I want to give some arguments why speech act theory is not sufficient as basic framework for the pragmatics of verbal communication. After having said what speech act theory is *not*, some considerations will be given as to what it *could* be viz. what role speech act categories could play in an empirical theory of language and communication. Finally it will be argued that a reanimation of the age-old notion of rhetoric might be fruitful and that the division of labour between grammar and rhetoric should be discussed thoroughly. Some outlines and examples will be given of what a rhetoric of conversation could be.

Speech act theory, when applied to empirical data of verbal interaction, showed the following disadvantages:[1]

(i) The attribution of speech act labels to segments of verbal behaviour seems highly arbitrary in various respects: the segmentation of the stream of speech into speech act units is the first problem. If one sticks to the sentence as unit it is often counter-intuitive to maintain at the same time that the speech acts segmented along this line are the most relevant items on the level of (inter-)action analysis. Intuitively more relevant speech acts often are carried out by several sentences or by parts of a sentence. But even if one does not pay attention to the segmentation problem a more fundamental problem remains: that - with the exception of 'indirect speech acts' - every utterance has to be labelled as one and only one speech act out of a fixed and finite repertoire of speech act types. This impedes the insight that even in the most trivial conversation speakers do a lot of things with one and the same utterance simultaneously. I do not refer here to other levels of analysis which were called acts too in speech act theory like 'locutionary' or 'reference or predication acts', but to different interactional categories which are differentiated by the contextual features taken into account by the respective label. No level or sort of abstraction is a priori more relevant than any other.

(ii) The selection speech act theory makes out of all the possible categorizations of bits of verbal communication is highly arbitrary too. The "vocabulary" of speech act labels, drawn mainly from performative expressions, restricts the range of conditions to be met by and being established by the utterance. Especiallly those 'acts' were neglected which have to do with the organizational aspects of interaction viz. the conditions which are mainly locally relevant on the very spot of its occurence in conversation. Take for instance the trivial and extremely frequent case of socalled 'minimal responses', i.e. non-interruptive short utterances of the listening participant, which do not only display interest or willingness to continue listening but fulfill a variety of other locally relevant tasks which can in no way be covered by analysing them as a speech act 'statement of agreement'.

(iii) The previous remarks concern properties of speech act theory which are associated with more fundamental assumptions making this theory incompatible with the approach of conversational analysis. Even if we concede that speech act theory gives us a rational reconstruction of some crucial types of verbal act this does not entitle us to consider it as an adequate theory of *inter*action. Human communication is interactional in a more fundamental way than is represented in the view that two or more speakers mutually address some speech acts to each other, speech acts which are defined entirely in terms of speaker's intentions.

The analysis of 'real life' - communication shows - even if cases of misunderstanding or partial misunderstanding are excluded - that the interactional meaning of the contributions to the conversation is to some extent subject to mutual negotiation. A considerable degree of indetermination and vagueness leaves room for subsequent precision and also for coexisting interpretations. This indetermination is not just an imperfection of natural communication but more often than not an essential prerequisite for smooth interaction. It is necessary for tact and politeness, for all the face work done in communication - which in fact is not a marginal but an overall and crucial aspect of practically all natural conversations. It is technically necessary for the more implicit organizational tasks as is demonstrated in the studies on e.g. conversational openings and closings.[2]

It is practically impossible to draw a sharp line between the indetermination existing only for the non-participating observer because of his lack of access to shared knowledge and to assumptions of the participants, and the indetermination experienced by the participants. But this is a less serious problem than it might seem; the difference is only a gradual one. The difficulty to categorize utterances in real-life conversation as speech act types of the usual sort results on the one hand from the fact that these categories might not cover the most important interactional functions of the utterance in question or only parts of these; on the other hand it is a consequence of the pre-fixed nature of accuracy of speech act labels. It obliges the analyzer to both over- and under-determine the interpretation of the utterance: overdetermine by filling in blancs concerning speech act conditions which are not or not yet established with certainty, underdetermine because so many other meaning aspects not covered by the given speech act notion are neglected. If one tries to apply speech act labels to natural conversation it soon becomes obvious that the accomplishment of those speech acts typically mentioned in speech act theory like requests, permissions, offers, invitations and acceptations of offers etc., is a joint and finely tuned achievement of several speakers. The delicate preparation of 'risky' interactional steps is only possible by the beforementioned indeterminacy and cannot be described adequately by the notion of indirect speech act. Consider the following trivial example (while in fact almost every piece of natural conversation could illustrate the points made above):[3]

(1) A: *Bischt du zuhaus heut?* (Are you home today?)
    B: *Mhm ich bin zuhause ja.* (Mhm I am home yes)
    A: *Ich hab überlegt ob ich einmal rausfahren soll.* (I was thinking of eventually making a ride out of town)
    B: *Ja komm doch mal raus.* (Yes why don't you come out here)

(A is the caller in the given telephone call; the sequence occurs after an extended opening phase, i.e. at a moment when the introduction of the 'reason-for-call-topic' by the caller might be expected.) For the interpretation of the 'raus', the direction indicating prefix of 'rausfahren', one has to know that A is living in the city and B in near-by village. The indeterminacy of 'raus' in A is difficult to translate: it can both be heard as 'getting out of town to *your* place in the country-side' or just as 'getting out of town'. In B it can only be heared as 'to my place'. The subtle switch in the interpretation of 'raus' is only one of the various means by which both speakers produce a well located acceptable and most probably subsequently accepted invitation. Taking into account the wider context, especially the occasion of the call, namely the first call after A's return from a journey, and the nature of A and B's relationship, it might very well be clear already in A's first utterance or even before that A wants to elicit an invitation. But to classify A's first and/or second utterance as indirect requests for an invitation would - although covering some of the intuitions about interactional functions of the utterances - mean to make a rough and uninstructive cut through the complex arrangement of meaning aspects. It would mean to petrify something as a fixed result which is rather an ongoing process of joint sense-production, doing no justice to the fine mechanics and the problem-solving nature of human interaction management. Because of the all too fast short-cut from form to speech act-meaning, many aspects of the utterances, the sequencing and the situatedness of the utterances would remain uninterpreted, while other aspects get a more fixed and definitive interpretation than the speakers themselves would agree upon at the given moment.

This general shortcoming of speech act theory - that it is not adequate as a theory of *inter*action, neither in its basic orientation nor with respect to the descriptive power of the more technical details - is intrinsically linked to all the other criticisms; therefore I will be very brief at the following points.

(iv) The viewpoint of speech act theory is a static one, falling short of the dynamic and strategic nature of natural conversation. By cutting a piece of conversation into speech acts of the usual categories one does not reveal sufficiently (if at all) the internal 'logic' in the development of the conversation, viz. the strategies of the participants to steer and anticipate this development. It is based on a fixed post factum perspective, not on the continously 'moving' perspective of the participants towards the unfolding structures of communication. The units of communication, at the moment when they are interpreted, are not yet 'faits accomplis' but *units under construction*. Besides, the fact that not just one perspective is effective but as many as there are participants, should be taken into account.

(v) This one-dimensionality in perspective has to do with the primitives which are used to explicate the results, viz. the felicity conditions for speech acts. They are stated in terms of obligations and epistemic states of mind (knowledge, belief ...) of speaker and hearer. If one wants to grasp the 'dynamic' feature of speech acts (or 'utterances in use'), one has to pay attention to the local conversational status quo before and after the utterance in question: i.e. it should be analyzed into a) what it does to the previous utterance and b) how it changes the context for the following one. If one takes 'turns' as units of analysis, this means to explicate what kind of a reaction is given to the preceding one and which configuration of options for an acceptable (coherent, conforming to indicated preferences) continuation is outlined for the next speaker.

(vi) These remarks lead us to the following point: a criticism about the way *context* is dealt with in speech act theory. This notion of context is a marginal one with a primarily remedial function. On the one hand speech act theory holds that it is more than a semantic analysis of linguistic forms but that it analyzes what is *done* with them in communication. But if one subscribes to this aim of investigation one cannot restrict the role of the context so far that it only comes in when words fail (as e.g. in the case of ambiguity or indirect speech acts'). For a linguistically and interactionally satisfactory analysis the notion of context has to be divided into two different ways of appearance in which context is experienced and used by speakers/hearers:

a) the independently given context which is present in the mind of the participants and can be presupposed without any reference to it expressis verbis; structures of the local conversational context - as far as they are unproblematic - mainly fall under this category;

b) aspects of context which become relevant and are taken into account only because of implicit or explicit indicators in the given utterance; that means that their relevance can only be attested after the utterance is made.

Since every utterance has to be and will be interpreted in the light of the given context and is designed accordingly, utterances in natural conversation appear highly 'elliptic', - 'elliptic' by a standard of verbal explicitness which can certainly not be mistaken as a norm but at the most as an orientation indicating slots for the insertion of contextual information if one wants to give a recompleted paraphrase of the utterance in the context. But the 'elliptically' formulated utterances are only more obviously, not essentially, more dependant on context with respect to their interactional meaning than linguistically 'complete' sentences.

That contextual features have to be dealt with was not in any programmatical way denied by speech act theory, but in the actual analysis its role was reduced to a very marginal one. By the fact that mainly self-made examples of isolated and exceptionally explicit speech acts were considered, the local sequential context (cf.(a)) was almost completely neglected. But in addition, when context is called upon, it is done in a way which is not devoid of circularity. It is not clear if a given utterance is taken as expressing a speech act of type X because - among other things - a (context-) condition Y is fulfilled and known to be fulfilled, or if the independently identified speech act X gives reason to infer that condition Y must hold viz. that the speaker assumes that it holds. This difference is not irrelevant because the conditions are mostly 'internal' conditions, concerning assumptions and intentions of speaker and/or hearer. Since speech act theory does not deal with the problem of interpretation and grounds the identification of speech acts mainly on the speaker's intentions independent of their recognizability, it neither has to take into account differences between speaker's and hearer's (and eventually observer's) perspective nor is it obliged to describe how context emerges and intertwines with the verbal message.

(vii) The failure to approach the problem of context-dependency in a differentiated way is intricately linked to another quite fundamental question: the linguistic theory, especially the theory of semantics, on which speech act theory is (more implicitly than explicitly) based, is a semantics modelled in many respects after logical semantics. It is true that speech act theory showed that propositional (truthfunctionally described) meaning is not the only kind of meaning expressed in natural language. But on the one hand the way in which propositional and illocutionary meaning combine remained to a large extent unclarified. On the other hand, some basic features of the given model of semantics were not challenged although they are hardly compatible with a pragmatic theory of communication. Linguistic meaning is still seen as - if not indexical - explicit descriptive meaning. At the same time, *indexicality* is acknowledged only where it is impossible to deny it: in deictic expressions. The troublesome *vagueness* expressions in natural language was either considered a general defect of natural language or an optic delusion which can be overcome by the linguist's ingenuity. The analysis of natural interactive language use makes a thorough revision of the prevailing model of linguistic semantics necessary. Vagueness then appears as an essential quality of linguistic expression, and indexicality is the rule, not the exception with natural language. Of course, vagueness as deliberate indeterminacy on the level of use has to be distinguished, theoretically, from vagueness in the sense of a general flexibility of the meaning of linguistic expressions as such, which provides for the typical adjustability to the context and the specific requirements of each situation of use. The linguist must explain these qualities - indexicality and vagueness -, not explain them away. In the broad sense of indexicality as advocated here it coincides to a fair extent with the notion of vagueness and context-sensibility. Unfortunately a fuller account of these notions and an outline of a semantics compatible with an empirical pragmatic theory of communication cannot be given here.

After having given a whole list of arguments why speech act theory is not sufficient if presented as *the* framework for an empirical linguistic theory of pragmatics (I do not contend that its creators ever made that claim!), I will add some remarks about some ways in which speech act theory or parts of it *can* be useful in linguistic analysis.

First it has to be stressed that it is by no means accidental that both philosophers and linguists chose exactly those notions as representative of basic verbal acts: 'statement', 'question', 'request', 'promise', 'baptize' etc. On the one hand there are grammatical categories corresponding intuitively with some of the speech act types:'imperative', 'interrogative', 'declarative sentence' etc.; others are notions quite often used in metacommunicative clarifications or in performative utterances - factors which provide a firm place for these notions in the conscious ideas of speakers about communication. They are all quite frequent in natural reports about past communication scenes. It is obvious that these terms bundle features of communicative events which speakers very often feel to be the most relevant. Thus, consciously or unconsciously, these notions may also play a role in the business of interpretation done by the linguist or conversational analyst, since in general they draw upon exactly the same resources. But the ideas of a speaker about his language use - interesting as they are for other reasons - are not to be confused with the empirical description of the communicative practices of the speakers. If used in a controlled way as 'member's categories' speech act notions might be innocuous and even helpful in the reconstruction of communicative functions. But first this methodological issue should be discussed in a more thorough way.

Finally I want to throw some light on the mystery of what *rhetoric* has to do with all these considerations. But let me first formulate the claim about rhetoric I want to defend. I want to suggest that a reanimation of rhetoric, the other half (besides grammar) of the age-old stock of knowledge about communication, could at least be a partial remedy for the present impasse in linguistic pragmatics. Of course the whole apparatus would have to be seriously revised and elaborated. The most important revision will consist in the adaptation of the monologue-oriented framework to the more basic form of communication: dialogue (with two or more speakers). Furthermore, what holds for speech act theory holds even more for rhetoric: a new 'rage taxonomique', to use a term of Roland Barthes, is not desirable. "Rhetoric' should rather stand for the repertoire of strategies, communicative principles and formal patterns of use, applied by speakers and hearers in order to manage the interaction and pursue their communicative aims in varying contexts and circumstances in an adequate and effective way. The different layers of meaning (and their interrelations) of an utterance-in-context can only be reconstructed if more concrete and context-dependant strategies and formal patterns and figures are accompanied by very general principles like the cooperation principle, guiding the priorities and combination of the more specific norms and strategies. The similarity between the Gricean Cooperation Principle and Conversational Maxims on the one hand and the *'virtutes elocutionis'* of rhetoric strike the historically minded investigator. The virtues ('aptum' as the most general norm of situational and contextual adequacy; 'latinitas' as linguistic correctness; 'perspicuitas' as clarity or intelligibility for the hearer; 'ornatus' as pleasant, entertaining expression; and other more specific virtues) can each be offended, at least at first sight, as long as there are *remedia* or norms and aims of a higher level providing the necessary 'licence'. If e.g. it is not clear on the verbal level whether a certain expression is meant ironically, this ambiguity can be remedied by non-verbal means. The status of the Cooperation Principle as basic guide-line in the interpretation procedure and the anticipation of interpretation is that of an a priori but revisable reciprocal assumption of hearer and speaker, which could also be called, from an interpretive point of view, Principle of Optimal Interpretation.

Closely related with this issue is the following point of revision. Traditional rhetoric was primarily conceived as instruction for the speaker. As part of linguistics, rhetoric cannot be normative in the usual sense, it has to *discover* the hidden norms of the speakers, making a difference between the norms they claim to obey and those which can be shown to be effective by a close analysis of empirical data (such as taped talk in natural situations). Since a speaker always has to anticipate the interpretation to be expected and the investigator necessarily has to adopt the position of a hearer, the heuristics of the investigator must start from the interpretation side. The interpretation procedure which has to be reconstructed is a highly complex process of problem solving that can never, by the very nature of human communication, be reduced to a mere mechanical application of rules; in character it is closer to a 'best guess' than to a logical deduction. This does not exclude logical necessity in the reconstruction of that interpretation, once a certain interpretation is assumed to be the intended one or the one the adressee in question made up, but this is a post-factum necessity, based on assumptions, e.g. about aims or convictions of the speaker, which can never be fully verified. One of the advantages of dialogue that comes in here is, that in the continuation of the talk the other participant(s) give(s) implicitly or explicitly a display of interpretation and the first speaker might react to that again etc. That kind of evidence should be used if not just the linguist's personal interpretation has to be reconstructed but that of the participants.

I will briefly mention some other points of revision and/or expansion of rhetoric if one wants to apply it to spontaneous interactive language use. First of all, in oral face-to-face communication nothing can be 'erased'; everything that is said is also heard at the same moment. This limits the possibilities of what can be undone of what was done with words, and how it can be done. Secondly, no detailed planning can be made in advance, because every contribution has to be designed after the foregoing one. Coherence and the internal structure of the conversation have to be organized locally and jointly. Up to now, very little is known about how syntactic and lexical means function with respect to the conversational organization tasks. Thirdly, the figures of speech have to be freed from the procrustes bed of taxonomic sophistry and explained in a framework of general principles of language use. The semantic figures must be seen as representative for the competence of human language users, to shift, widen and narrow down literal meaning in various ways. Syntactic patterns have to be checked for influences on the turn-taking machinery and conversational coherence; syntactic figures in the narrower sense (repetition, mirroring, special word and clause order etc.) can be shown to produce effects both on the level of 'content' and of organization.

If rhetoric and grammar can be developed in such a way that they are compatible with the requirements of an empirical theory of language use, the present scepticism of conversational analysts (especially those of the 'Sacks-direction') towards the consideration and linguistic explication of semantic and pragmatic 'meaning' might be overcome.[4] What linguistic theory owes to the influence of the ethnomethodological analysis of conversation will hopefully then be matched by the tools delivered by linguistics for the exploitation of linguistic details in conversational analysis.

FOOTNOTES:

*   Since I did not want to depart substantially from the text I presented at the conference in Urbino, this paper is little more than an enlarged abstract. A more explicit treatment of some of the problems is given in Franck 1980 and Franck and Houtkoop 1979.

1. For the sake of simplicity I refer to speech act theory mainly in the form given by Searle 1969 or the somewhat simplified 'vulgarized' version that is implicit in many studies on linguistic pragmatics.

2. I refer here mainly to the studies of Sacks and Schegloff.

3. The example is from Heutiges Deutsch 1975: p.63.

4. See for instance Schegloff 1978.

ATTRIBUTING MENTAL STATES:
A SECOND LOOK AT MOTHER-CHILD INTERACTION

B. De Gelder

The thesis that the mind is essentially a social product, "that minds and selves are essentially 'social products' or phenomena of the social side of human experience", was explicitly formulated by Mead (1934:1). The way Mead elaborates this thesis belongs to the context of what he calls "a more adequate formulation" of the fundamentally behaviorist framework for the study of individual experience and behavior. It is only natural then that Mead's emphasis on the social origin of the mind follows the same lines as the attacks, coming from Watson and from James, on consciousness and its place in psychological theories. Mead seems only too happy to note that "there has been of late in philosophy a growing recognition of the importance of James' insistence that a great deal has been placed in consciousness that must be returned to the so-called objective world" (Mead 1934:4). To this remark Mead himself, in 1924, added a note: "modern philosophical realism has helped to free psychology from a concern with a philosophy of mental states" (1934:4). Now, a good fifty years later, both parts of Mead's remark seem to have lost their validity. Modern philosophical realism, whatever that may be, has not, it turns out, freed psychology from a concern with mental states. And mentalist hypotheses have massively re-entered the scene of psychological theorizing. The metaphors of course have changed, but however nice the fabric, and however impressive the efforts at making clothes out of it, the Emperor (or should we say the Empress?) occupies the middle of the stage, but is naked. Indeed, if we may believe Bloch (1978), not even his (or her) everyday 'functional' clothes will cover him (her). And while some may then be surprised to discover a naked Emperor, there are others who see no Emperor at all.

Thus although psychologists and philosophers alike may agree on the importance of the role to be played by the mind, I think the scenario is badly in need of being re-written, and it might be time to re-write it -- not in terms of metaphysical characterization of the status, nor in terms of functional characterization of the role of the mind and of mental states.

Mental states are not unlike those white rabbits -- we all know where they come from. After they have got out of the black hat, and have walked off the scene and come to sit on our shoulder, we still believe them to be *tricky* rabbits. Mental states, I think, are tricky in roughly this sense. To approach them with sufficient care involves, I claim, that we do not build our explanation around them, but that we merely incorporate them into our explanations to the extent that they are *useful for our explanatory strategy*.

Mead's thesis apparently never inspired many psychologists. It disappeared into the limbo of sociological theorizing where it apparently belonged. Indeed, it's a long-standing conviction of most psychologists that *social* phenomena are, to a large extent, derived and therefore secondary. In this atomistic approach to the nature of *psychological* phenomena, Mead's thesis could simply not be formulated. But, remarkably enough, the recent shift towards the analysis of interaction, and the emphasis on the social context of learning, brought with it in psychological theorizing a massive reappearance of the white rabbits, or if you prefer, of mental states.

Up to now I have pointed to two epistemological orientations. First, I have said that the thesis of the *social origin* of the mind, the mind as a social product, is in itself -- vague as it may be -- an interesting thesis. Second, I have claimed that mental states should be kept around only to the extent that there can be found for them a clear *explanatory role*. A natural way to combine both approaches then is to look at how psychological data gathered in interactive situations are analyzed, and in what explanatory framework they can best be set.

1. *Behavioral intentions and acquisition*

In the following I will not elaborate these theses; I shall, on the contrary, analyze what their relevance is and discuss them against the background of some recent work done in the acquisition of language and of cognitive structures. In some recent papers, J.S. Bruner (e.g. 1979 and n.d.) has put forward a theoretical framework in terms of which, if we follow him, an impressive amount of data, and the more or less *ad-hoc* speculations that go with them, could be systematized. This framework will appear to anybody not familiar with psychological theories of action as a bunch of more or less *common-sensical intuitions*. Or, to be more precise and to say something altogether different, as the bunch of intuitions that typically depict the *common knowledge* about human actions. The way these everyday intuitions are often incorporated into what these days are called *pragmatic* theories leads to what I shall bluntly call 'mentalism'. Mentalism is a certain view on everyday and scientific psychological explanations. It is characterized by its acceptance of mental states as psychological *primitives* around which psychological explanations are built and not, as I will hold later on, the other way round.

My point of departure is a paper by J.S. Bruner (1979) on "The Organization of Action and the Nature of Adult-Infant Transaction". In this paper Bruner wants to establish the following argument. Human action is steered by intentions, otherwise our empirical data about language acquisition could not be what they are; and given what our data are and the way we descriptively analyze them, the theoretical hypothesis of there being intentions forces itself upon us. The first, and most important, distinctive trait of many of the studies to which Bruner refers are data about *mother-child interactions*. Even if we persist in using traditional labels such as 'learning', and we characterize this situation as a *learning situation*, it will come out very clearly that the learning observed in such a situation of interaction will be, by the very nature of this setting, quite different from that seen in the approaches known from what is tacitly accepted in learning theories.

It is important to notice this because one would then expect that what follows from this point of departure is that concepts offered further on in an effort to explain *what is acquired* in such a situation of interaction could well turn out to be different from the notions that are brought in to explain learning in the strictly *individual* setting, or in the setting where an individual faces a learning situation strictly as an individual.

Now, in summarizing the interpretation Bruner feels forced to give to the data, he comes up with the following: "The conclusion to which I am forced is that the mother is operating as if the child had intentions in mind. As if he were trying to deploy means to its realization, as if he were out to correct errors, as if he had a finished task in mind, but that he is not quite able to put it all together in a fashion to suit his mother." (1979:7). Given that this *is* the conclusion Bruner feels entitled to draw from the facts, he then adds that the mother is behaving *appropriately* towards an immature member of the species who does in fact operate along the lines of intentional action. Clearly, by 'appropriately' here is meant that the mother is behaving on the appropriate assumptions, or has the appropriate theory.

Let me for the time being work with Bruner's appeal to intentions and see what its problems are. How should we then define initial and final intention? The *initial intention* can, one would think, be approached from two different perspectives, namely the perspective of the mother and the perspective of the child. Such a view is moreover grounded in what theories of interaction say about initial intentions. However, does it make sense at all to talk about initial intentions in this context of interactive learning? In his conclusion Bruner says that the mother is operating *as if* the child had intentions in mind, not that she is operating on the assumption that the child *has* intentions in mind. Now this makes all the difference in the world because, if there is no such initial intention that can be characterized solely from the point of view of the child as *his* intention with which he starts the interaction, then does it make sense to talk of a final intention? And, if it does not make sense to talk about a final intention, then does it make sense to view the whole interaction process -- as Bruner does -- as a process whereby the mother is trying to deploy means to assist the child in the realization of his intentions?

How is the *final* intention characterized? Let us take a situation of interaction whereby an infant is learning to label objects. Bruner refuses to accept an explanation of the child's capacity to label objects that would rely on imitation. Close inspection of the mother's efforts to bring a child to label an object, to direct his efforts and to approve of his final achievement, indeed seem to exclude any explanation in terms of imitation. However, labelling might be far too complicated an activity to give as an example and to draw an argument from, for the simple reason that labelling is not the sort of activity that is initiated by the child himself. Bruner clearly points out that if the mother wants to engage in the sort of interaction which is meant to bring the child to learn or to give the labels for the objects, she starts by focussing the child's attention. So, in this case, the initiative is clearly in the mother's hands. And this is, I think, what adds a supplementary degree of complexity to the study of this type of interaction.

Let us therefore look not at learning labels but at simple *requests*. Requests, by their very nature, seem to be the sort of intentional behavior that is autonomously initiated by the child. Requests for objects, or reaching out for objects, seem to make up a good part of the child's early activity. Whenever the child reaches out thus for one or another object, the mother can go about clearly interpreting the child's intention by bringing the object closer or by changing something in the physical environmnet which makes it easier for the child to get hold of the object. However, is this the same sort of 'interpretation of an intention' as we have in the situation where adults interact? When Mary perceives John desperately looking around while getting wet, we are inclined to say that Mary does so upon *concluding from John's behavior that he has the intention of looking for an umbrella*. Similarly when little John tries to reach out for the red ball, Mary pushes it forward upon concluding that he was reaching out for the red ball. Now, in the first case, Mary's coming to a *conclusion as to the intention* behind John's behavior, which is a conclusion upon which she will build her own intention, has a *component of interpretation* to it. In John's case we do not have an initial and a final intention. There is just *one* intention behind his interrogative or explorative behavior, which is the intention Mary is trying to get at. (The possible lack of success in doing so has motivated the theorists of the mind to make a distinction between intentions and real intentions, whereby *real* intentions are the ones that *cause*, or have caused, the observed behavior.) In helping little John to reach the red ball, the mother has (shows) no doubts about the intention from which his requestive behavior proceeds. She is certain that it is the red ball the child wants to get at. But although her intention, which subsequently gives rise to her behavior of helping the child, is based upon a conclusion as to the child's intention, it does not, so it seems, involve a process of interpretation of the child's intention. That the child is reaching for the red ball is simply evident to her.

In this case then, it would seem that we need not distinguish between initial and final intention. Indeed, if it turns out that the child refuses to grab the red ball but keeps on requesting something, then the mother will conclude simply that it was the blue ball the child wanted and not the red one. So the intention the mother attributes to the child in helping him to grab the red ball is not a final intention, it is merely the intention about which she might still be right or wrong. But the question we have to ask here is the following. Given that most of the time the mother attributes an intention which *turns out to be* the right one in that it terminates the requesting behavior, does that entitle us to conclude that in fact the child *has* this intention, and that therefore the process by which the mother attributes the intention does *not* involve a component of interpretation? Take the case, observed often enough, where there is some hesitation in the child's acceptance of the mother's help.

If, following such a short period of hesitation, the child finally accepts the red ball and this terminates his requestive behavior, the mentalist's views on intentional behavior would run as follows. Initially the child *has* an intention, but the process of interacting with the mother is needed in order to *clarify*, or to bring out, that intention, or is needed in order to give that intention its definite formulation, the one under which the regularity of his behavior can be explained. In interacting with the child the mother has thus merely come to clarify that initial intention. And the final intention is the intention to which the needed specifications have thus been added. In this theoretical perspective, initial intentions are, then, taken to be *inarticulate* (but *not* uninterpreted) intentions while final intentions are intentions that have become clarified, in a process whereby they are given their uniquely appropriate articulation.

Now what is the asymmetry between John's intentions and little John's intentions? Mary's attributing John's intention is a process of interpretation which is open to guesses and mistakes. She can be mistaken about the intention 'really present behind' John's behavior. This interpretation, at least under the analysis given to it by many theorists of action, is not part of the process itself of attributing an intention. The process of *attributing an intention* consists merely of *making a guess at the real intention*. Here we are talking about the intention John has which causes his behavior independently of the interpretation given to it by Mary. Mary's interpretation therefore does not affect the status of the intention and does not affect the relation between the intention and the behavior. Little John's behavior and the intentions attributed to him by his mother could be treated in the same way. In assuming that little John was reaching for the red ball, his mother has attributed to him an intention. She assumes that he has that intention independently of her attributing it to him. When the child refuses to be helped to the red ball she will therefore conclude that *she* was mistaken, that she attributed the *wrong* intention. Subsequent behavior or the ongoing interaction is therefore supposed to enable her to make a *better guess at what the real intention* was. Typically, it is only after repeated failure to attribute the right intention that the mother will conclude that the child 'does not know what it wants'.

I am not here interested in the conceptual analysis of the mentalist view of behavior that underlies observation and theorization in these studies of mother-child interactions. Therefore a rough statement, trivial as it may sound, of basic axioms underlying this and similar approaches will serve my purpose well enough. A certain way of conceptualizing behavior, and more recently interaction, is to an important extent dominated by an *ideal of causal explanation*. It is this ideal, and not so much common-sensical and metaphysical views on the *nature* of the mental, that determines the characteristics and the conceptual role of mental terms and of mental states. Underlying this approach is a thesis known from causal theories of action which claims that behavior is *caused* by intentions, and which then views intentions as having a component of *representation* of the behavior that follows them.[1] In such a view there is a circularity between the definition of the causal character of the intention and the epistemological characterizations of that intention. *What is said to be the cause is thereby supposed to contain the representation of what is the effect*. Intentions are dissected into, on the one hand, an element of volition or motivation that is quickly disregarded, and on the other, a cognitive component which then must be the representation *in nucleo* of the action to which the intention present gives rise. It follows from this view that 'fuzzy' intentions, namely intentions with fuzzy cognitive contents, cannot properly cause behavior. Against this background we can now picture the importance of a major consequence this view seems to have for the theory of acquisition.

The interaction process is merely a process of clarifying this fuzzy representation and of bringing out what is already behind it as a clear representation, or the 'clear' intentional object of the behavior. It is then tempting to add the final touch to this picture by claiming that the reason why, under given circumstances, behavior is initiated by fuzzy representations, is that the child lacks the means to proceed from, or to have a clear or sharp representation of, the goal objects of his behavior, although he *has* those goals *in mind*. What we are thus attributing to the child are cartesian 'clear and distinct' cognitive states, not yet quite articulated in one or another of the publicly recognized systems of representation (e.g., first language). So the fact that expressions in the first language are not yet well-formed does in no way overshadow or interfere with the well-formedness *ab initio* of the thought or of the cognitive component of the intentions, or to use the fancy idiom, the well-formedness of the expressions in the Language of Thought.

When this theory goes together with the reduction of interaction to a series of well-attuned types of behavior that have their own internal causes, what is left to be explained by the 'pragmatics of acquisition' (to use Bruner's term) is rather minimal. Aside from the methodological difficulties (access to the intentions), such a view that gives minimal weight to the interaction itself will, among other things, find it difficult to account for the fact that the child must have the cognitive means to integrate the increasing degree of precision which is exhibited in the mother's way of interacting with him. Bruner points to a number of strategies whereby the mother guides the behavioral process. In doing so, what the mother herself is guided by is her understanding of the infant's capacities and the task she wants him to perform. Against the background of that knowledge, she systematically brings the task to be performed, or the behavior to be brought out, down to dimensions to which her perceptions of the infant's capacities correspond.

2. *Acquisition and interaction*

A number of difficulties with this framework make me think that a *stronger view of interaction* is needed, whereby it becomes clear that the mother's assistance in bringing the child to act in a certain way amounts to more than simply assisting the child in *articulating* his intentions, and helping him with behavioral support. Therefore, instead of characterizing the mother's interaction as *steering* the behavioral process, we should adopt a much stronger view whereby it becomes clear that this interaction is one in which one of the parties sets the *norms* for the other. To the extent that it still makes sense to talk in terms of initial and final intentions, we must characterize *final intentions as the intentions the mother leads the child to have*. What matters then is to bring into focus not so much the process of the growing cognitive capacities of the child himself, but the part played by the interaction in *determining the form and content of the child's cognition*. If, therefore, at the end of a particular interactive process, the child exhibits a behavior the theorist is inclined to explain by reference to underlying intentions, we cannot overlook that it was the interaction itself that brought the child to have this 'final' intention, 'to go along with' the intention attributed to him by the mother.

Now, it is the mother's cognitive definition of the task, *her* perception of the object for which the child reaches out, and *her* 'knowledge' of the cognitive content of the request, against which the child's actual performance is mapped. In other words, it is the *mother's perception of what the terminal stage of the behavioral process is about that functions in her filling-in of the intention* of the child's behavior.

But here we can no longer take the child's final intention to be merely the outcome of a process of articulation in which the child is helped by the *mother who*, at least in the standard cases of interaction, *knew* all along what the *child's* final intention was going to be.

In analyzing the mother's behavior in her interaction with the child, Bruner, as said, sees two conclusions: "Either the mother is the victim of common-sense and does not really understand action, or she is behaving appropriately toward an immature member of the species who

does, in fact, operate along the lines of intentional action." (p. 7).
In accepting the second conclusion, what Bruner does is accept that
the mother is *right* in taking the child to be an intentional system because we can safely conclude that the child *has* intentions. What I am
pointing out, however, is that there is a third alternative. Coming to
the conclusion that the child indeed acts intentionally, or has intentions, Bruner overlooks that it is the very fact of the assumption made
by the mother -- who interacts with the child *as if* the child has intentions -- that might make all the difference. In other words, in the
agreement that the mother's assumption is appropriate and true to the
facts, what is overlooked is the very interaction itself. *First*, whether these assumptions are warranted or not, the very fact that the mother *acts upon them* has some importance and should make a difference for
the theorist. Whether or not the assumption is true, the theorist
should not overlook that what actually happens in the interaction is
connected with it. *Second*, and more important, not only is it a part
of the theorist's job to explain what it amounts to that this intention-assumption is made during the interaction process; he must explain that
this might be all there is to explaining the child's *having* or *being
taken as having* intentions. Intentions then are no longer those self-explanatory fundamentals of the behavior and therefore of the interaction process, and to move swiftly from the analysis of interaction to
the existence of intentions, and to explain the interaction through intentions existing prior to the interaction, is to under-estimate badly
the *effects* of the interaction itself.

My preceding analysis, then, reveals that if we are concerned with
the pragmatics of acquisition we must integrate into our analysis of it
the role played by the interactional setting itself in which cognitive
acquisition takes place. In a *first* look at mother-child interaction,
the view is put forward that the mother attributes to the child an intention she thinks he has. A *second* look, however, brings with it the
suggestion that this attribution of intentions does not consist in offering an isolated hypothesis, but that it is part of the interaction

process itself. What I have in the first pages called 'mentalism' is then an inappropriate framework for the analysis of the effects of interaction upon cognitive acquisition, because it underestimates the theoretical importance of those effects.

How can this second look be analyzed systematically if not in the framework of the traditional, predominantly mentalistic, theories of the mind?

My proposal comes to the analysis of the attribution of intentions in the broader framework of the attribution of mental states in interactions. Attributing intentions would in this framework be one of the modalities through which interaction takes place, instead of somebody's having intentions, clear or fuzzy, being a condition for the interaction. It is only when we do not at all look at the interaction itself but theorise about it from an abstract point of view that instead of modalities of interaction we postulate mental states.

A radical view of the attribution of intentions and mental states in general will have to be developed along the following lines:

(1) In ascribing mental states and representations, we assume *rationality* on the part of the system with which we interact.
(2) This rationality is not merely a broad background against which behavior takes place but comprises a *set of assumptions* which in its totality determines the *properties of the interactive situation* -- in which such sophisticated activities as listening, questioning, and answering take place.
(3) The assumptions of rationality are sometimes made in a situation characterized by *asymmetry;* that is, they can be made on one side without necessarily being shared with the opposite side.
(4) Whenever rationality assumptions are attributed in an asymmetrical exchange situation, they thereby acquire a *regulative* character; they become rules of the behavior taking place in the interactive situation. Specific rationality assumptions become ought-to-intend, ought-to-see, ought-to-do, ought-to-say, ought-to-think rules.
(5) If it is against this background that representations are attri-

buted, and if it is through *this* process of attribution that representational systems become learned, then it must be in *this context* that the subject's behavior and the whole set of characterizing specifications which we assign to it are generated and in terms of which they have to be analyzed.

Postponing till later the detailed analysis of cognitive competence in terms of interactional modalities, I conclude by giving two reasons why I hold to this particular and unpopular view on intentionalist psychology. The *first* is that I expect it to offer more interesting perspectives on the empirical data we already have about cognitive processes, language acquisition and the acquisition of representational systems in general. The *second* reason is that this radical view on interaction allows me to establish a point which I think is crucial for a general theory of cognition and its applications in psychological practice.

Common-sense practices such as the attribution of intentions in the process of mother-child interaction can be theoretically relevant without having to be warranted by knowledge or by more or less well-established theories. More generally, the common-sense practice of dealing with somebody on the basis of treating him as rational is not a practice in need of theoretical justification. Attributing beliefs to a young child is something the mother does without realizing and without knowing that *she is entitled* to do so on the basis of a reasonably well-established scientific theory, and moreover without realizing at all that this is the sort of *practice* that is *in need of (a priori)* justification. After all, we are not at liberty to refrain from treating as rational and to refrain from attributing intentions and beliefs to those beings where the hypothesis of a rational design of their actions has become problematic, as in the case of the mentally ill. *That* we do so in those cases is precisely because we expect our ascription of intentions or our interaction to have the sort of *effects* that psychological practices such as psychotherapy and education are about.

FOOTNOTE:

1. For a systematic discussion of the interference between a certain ideal of causal explanations of action and of what representational mental states are taken to be, see De Gelder (1979). For a discussion of causal theories of action see Manninen and Tuomela (1976), and especially Frederick Stoutland (1976).

HOW TO COMBINE SPEECH ACT THEORY WITH FORMAL SEMANTICS: A NEW ACCOUNT OF SEARLE'S CONCEPT OF PROPOSITION*

Paul Gochet

The notion of a proposition is a key concept in speech act theory. According to Searle, the general form of an illocutionary act is $F(p)$ "where the variable 'F' takes illocutionary force indicating devices as values and 'p' takes expressions for propositions" (Searle 1969: 31). The exact nature of this concept, however, is far from clear. I intend to search for an analysis of Searle's concept of a proposition which would make it more precise and which would fit both speech act theory and formal semantics.

Let us first examine where the trouble lies with Searle's notion of a proposition. In fact the latter concept was first introduced by means of examples. Searle enumerates seven sentences sharing the same proposition:

1. Sam smokes habitually
2. Does Sam smoke habitually?
3. Sam, smoke habitually!
4. Would that Sam smoked habitually.
5. Mr. Samuel Martin is a regular smoker of tobacco.
6. If Sam smokes habitually, he will not live long.
7. The proposition that Sam smokes habitually is uninteresting.

Searle relates the proposition to notions well entrenched in the philosophical tradition: "I might summarize this part of my set of distinctions by saying that I am distinguishing between the illocutionary act and the propositional content of the illocutionary act [...]. The reader familiar with the literature will recognize this as a variation of an old distinction which has been marked by authors as diverse as Frege, Sheffer, Lewis, Reichenbach and Hare, to mention only a few" (Searle 1969: 30).

The problem is that the distinctions drawn by the authors mentioned seem to be fundamentally different. Searle can thus be criticized for treating the following three contrasts as variants of the same distinction:

a) Frege's contrast between assertion sign and proposition which is put to use in the analysis of an argument

        unasserted

(1) If it rains the roads are wet.
(2)   It rains. Therefore the roads are wet.

        asserted

The molecular sentence (1) is asserted, neither of the atomic sentences is.

b) Hare's contrast between neustics and phrastics as exemplified by

Sugar in my coffee	Please	(Command)
Sugar in my coffee	Yes	(Statement)
Phrastics	Neustics	

c) Austin's contrast between locution and illocution as illustrated in the following examples:

You are going to leave = Statement
You are going to leave = Command
You are going to leave = Question
    locution   illocution

What is common to both an asserted sentence and an unasserted sentence is the sentence-type "It rains", which can be a bearer of a truth-value. But Hare's phrastics cannot be the bearer of a truth-value. It is not a *sentence* but a *phrase*, hence something less than a sentence. If the *phrastic* element is something *less* than an unasserted sentence, the *neustic* element must be *more*. This conclusion has been corroborated by Hare's subsequent recognition that what he initially called *neustics* covers two things: the *tropic*, i.e. the grammatical mood, and the *neustics* which corresponds to Frege's assertion signs (Hare 1970: 20-21).

However, Austin's locution coincides neither with Frege's unasserted proposition, nor with Hare's phrastics: contrary to the latter it embodies a copula, contrary to the former it is deprived of a mood.

Searle's concept of a proposition seems to be close to Austin's notion of locution. Unfortunately the latter is itself quite puzzling. There is something common to:

    You are going to leave   (statement)
    You are going to leave!   (command)
    You are going to leave?   (question)

namely, the sentence "you are going to leave" taken as a *syntactic entity*. Searle means something more since he speaks of a *proposition*. But it is hard to pinpoint this common propositional content. One might argue that the meaning of "are" varies with the force. If this is so, the search for a common propositional content is doomed to failure just as much as the search for a common propositional content in "The bank is far from here" where "bank" can mean "the bank of the river" or "the financial institution".

Ross' performative hypothesis (in Ross 1970: 254-261) seems to offer a solution to the problem. According to Ross' analysis, the three afore-mentioned sentences should be seen as surface forms derived from three distinct deep-structure sentences in which the difference of *grammatical mood* is reduced to a lexical difference in performative verbs. According to this view, the three afore-mentioned sentences are *semantically equivalent* to the following three:

I state that you are going to leave.
I command that you are going to leave.
I ask whether you are going to leave.

It might seem that this solution would not work well in French where the difference in mood survives the lexicalization of the mood in a performative verb:

J'énonce que vous *partirez* incessamment.
J'ordonne que vous *partiez* incessamment.

This objection, however, is not fatal. The proponents of the performative hypothesis would reply that grammatically expressed mood in this case is nothing but a *redundancy* peculiar to French.

There are, however, more serious objections. Gazdar (1976) has formulated eight of them. Let us consider one.

The proponents of the performative hypothesis would maintain that the following two sentences are *semantically equivalent*:

I state that the earth is flat.
The earth is flat.

They argue that if someone replied "That is true" to either of these sentences he would *always* mean "It is true that the earth is flat" and *never* "It is true that you *stated* that the earth is flat". Gazdar (1976: 58), following Lewis (1972), observes that this argument is not at all cogent. The reply "That is true" applied to the former sentence might be ambiguous between the two interpretations.

Hausser (1978) offers an argument of his own for the same purpose. He confronts the proponent of the performative hypothesis with the following dilemma: If you treat the two sentences

I order you to leave.
Leave!

as *semantically equivalent*, you are committed either to side with Lewis who takes 'Leave!' to be a proposition on the ground that 'I order you to leave' is one, or with Austin who denies that 'I order you to leave' is a proposition in view of the fact that 'Leave!' is not.

Both conclusions are unacceptable: Lewis' because 'Leave!' is obviously *not* a proposition. Austin's because it denies

I order you to leave.
You order me to leave.

membership in the same syntactic paradigm (Hausser 1978: 176).

Hausser suggests that we should renounce the main tenet of the performative hypothesis; sentences such as "I order you to leave" and "Leave!" are not *semantically equivalent*, i.e. *synonymous*; they are merely equivalent on the illocutionary level (Hausser 1978: 175), i.e. *pragmatically equivalent*.

Hausser offers a semantic account of moods which captures not only the *semantic difference* between the *sentences* "I order you to leave" and "Leave!" but also the *semantic resemblance* connected with the use of the *same verb* in the two sentences. This is undoubtedly a major achievement. Let us first examine his account of the difference between the two sentences.

In Hausser's semantics, which resembles Montague's, the declarative sentence "I order you to leave" denotes a proposition, i.e. a function from possible worlds and moments of time to truth values; that is to say, a set theoretic object of the form $(I \times J) \rightarrow \{0,1\}$ where $(I \times J)$ is the cartesian product of the set of possible worlds with the set of moments of time and $\{0,1\}$ is the set of truth values.

The imperative sentence does not denote a proposition but something else. It has the logical form

$$\lambda x [\Gamma_2 \{x\} \wedge \text{Leave}' (x)]$$

where Γ_2 is a context-variable representing the property of being the hearer. The whole formula "denotes the properties of being the hearer (Γ_2) and to be leaving" (Hausser 1978: 183). In other words, declarative sentences differ from imperative sentences in that the former have propositions and the latter have properties as denotations.

Let us now consider the semantic resemblance between the sentences

"I order you to leave" and "Leave!" in which the same word, "leave", occurs. Hausser's semantics is strictly compositional. All categorematic terms are provided with a separate denotation. The intransitive verb "leave" denotes a property or, to follow the previous formulation, a function, of the form

$$(I \times J) \to (((I \times J) \to A) \to \{0,1\})$$

which enters as *a part* into the denotation of the two sentences "Leave" and "I order you to leave".

Admittedly, the denotation of "leave" cannot be *seen* as part of the denotation of "I order you to leave" or, for that matter, of "John is leaving", but it is there nonetheless, at least, in the mathematical sense, in so far as the denotation of, let us say, "John is leaving", is the result of applying the function denoted by John to the denotation of the intransitive verb "leave" taken as an argument.

There is, however, something in the use of "I order you to leave" and "Leave!" which Hausser does not account for, namely the *pragmatic equivalence* between these two sentences, the fact that they perform the same illocutionary act. This is not a flaw in Hausser's treatment since he wishes to give a *semantic treatment* only of surface mood, *not* a *pragmatic* account of the pragmatic equivalence between the afore-mentioned sentences or between "Could you pass the salt?" said at the dinner table and "Pass the salt".

The pragmatic problem, however, remains open. It can be formulated in these terms: "Is it possible to build a *generative pragmatics* along the lines of the *generative* semantics proposed by Montague or Hausser? If the answer is Yes, how should we conceive this generative pragmatics? What requirements is it supposed to fulfil?"

Travis (1971: 629) addressed himself to these questions: "A generative theory of illocutions will, with finite means, provide a unique representation for each of the indefinite number of acts of saying something which a fluent speaker is prepared to recognize, to recognize as an instance of using the language, and to understand in a characteristic way". J.R. Searle and D. Vanderveken (n.d.) have spelt out a *recursive pragmatics* in the full sense of the term 'recursive': The set of illocutionary forces contains a finite set of primitive forces which is closed under a finite number of operations. This enables Searle and Vanderveken to *generate* an infinite set of illocutionary acts and to provide an interpretation of the sentences which serve to perform them. They describe their undertaking in this way:

> "Illocutionary force is indeed one essential and irreducible component of the sense of a sentence of a natural language. One cannot understand the sense of a sentence without understanding that its literal utterance in a given context of use constitues the performance of illocutionnary acts of such and such forms. Thus for example, in order to understand the sense of the English sentence "Are you going to the theater tonight?" one must not only understand that in a context of use where this sentence is uttered literally, the speaker expresses a proposition that is true in the world of utterance if and only if the hearer in that world goes to a theater the evening of the day of the utterance; one must also understand that this utterance in that context of use constitutes the asking of a question".

The question I want to raise at this stage is this: to what extent is recursive pragmatics in the style of Searle and Vanderveken something *genuinely different* from recursive semantics as conceived by Hausser? Is the former theory a complement or an alternative to the latter? I contend that it is a (very important) complement, not an alternative.

A semantics of surface mood à la Hausser is sufficient for the interpretation of *direct speech acts* but it cannot account for indirect speech acts such as the use of the question "Could you pass the salt?" meant as a request. It deals with meaning, not with use. The logic of Searle and Vanderveken comes into play at this point. It supplies a systematic and recursive account of the use of forces, both in direct and in indirect speech acts.

The second question I want to take up is the vexing question of the nature of a proposition. In surface semantics, the problem vanishes. No propositional content common to statements, commands and questions is postulated by Hausser. The proposition, is not a *constituent* of a command for instance. How is it introduced in speech act theory?

There are two ways of introducing it. The first is a variety of a procedure which Ryle (1931) called "operation with identity". It consists in *abstracting* the common element of sentences having different forces such as:

You are going to leave.
You are going to leave!
You are going to leave?

There is however, *pace* Quine, a second procedure which might be called, on the basis of an analogy with mathematics, an operation of substracting.

Consider "I order you to leave" and "Leave!". They are *pragmatically equivalent*. They have the same force, the illocutionary force of a command. Let us substract the force from the act. One would expect that equals minus equals would give equals. If the remainder of the act, after the force has been removed, is the proposition, it seems to follow from the subtraction argument that the proposition *shared* by "I order you to leave" and "Leave!" is the *same*. If this is so, how can we reconcile this result with Hausser's intuition that the performative sentence "I order you to leave" is not *semantically equivalent*, i.e. *synonymous*, with the imperative sentence "Leave"? How can two instances of the *same speech act* share the *same proposition* without being *semantically equivalent*?

This surprising fact can be understood once it is recognized that the *pragmatic criterion* of propositional identity is less sharp than the *semantic criterion*.

From a pragmatic point of view "I order you" does not belong to the propositional content. From a semantic point of view it does. Once this is taken into account one understands the subtle relationship which obtains between "I order you to leave" and "Leave!". It is true that these two sentences *share* the proposition, which is expressed by "that you leave", but the point is that the latter proposition *does not exhaust* the semantic content of "I order you to leave". The latter involves not *one* proposition but *two*. The second proposition expressed by "I order you", however, is likely to escape the speech act theorist's attention since the self-verifying sentence "I order you to" is *pragmatically used*, not as a *proposition bearer* but as an *illocutionary force indicating device*.

The difference between "I order you to leave" and "Leave!" resembles, to a certain extent, the difference between "It is true that snow is white" and "Snow is white". If this comparison holds, we can say that in "I order you to leave" two sentences are involved, a sentence in use, "I order you", and a sentence in the infinitive, "to leave". This yields a solution to the problem we started with. Is the proposition in Searle and Vanderveken's sense an *unasserted* proposition, a *phrastics* or a *locutionary entity*? It is neither of these; it is a proposition *referred to*.

An opponent might object that my hypothesis ignores an important difference between statements and questions. Indirect questions are introduced by "whether" in English and by "si" in French, not by "that" or "que" respectively. Could we not infer from this that the candidate I offer as the propositional content of statements, commands and questions is not the right one?

As a counterargument[1] I could mention examples from languages where there is no such difference in syntactic construction between indirect questions and subordinate clauses introduced by verbs such as "I state", "I know", "I believe". Ancient Greek is a case in point. Indirect questions can be introduced by the Greek word for "that" namely "ὅΤΙ", either expressed as in ἐρωτήοαντα τὸ ὅσιον ὅτί ποτ' ἐίη (Plato, Euthypron 6d) (literally, "asking piety what it is) or deleted as in δίκαιον γὰρ τὴν εγηωνίδον φωνὴν τοῦτον ἐρω τᾶν (Plato, Protagoras 3416) ("On Simonides language, it is right to question him").

If the propositional content of "I order you to leave" differs from that of "Leave!" in spite of sharing the same proposition, Searle's notion of proposition is reconciled with Hausser's claim to the effect that the two sentences are not synonymous. Admittedly, Hausser does not introduce the concept of a proposition while Searle does. The reason for this discrepancy is obvious: one theory deals with surface structure, the other with deep structure. This is an additional argument to show that the two approaches are *complementary* and not *alternative* to each other and that *pragmatics* has to be recognized as a separate subject.

FOOTNOTES

* I am grateful to Reidel Publishing Company for granting me the permission to use some material from Gochet (1980).

1. I owe this argument to Professor Hubien.

ANSWERING AS DECISION MAKING:
A NEW WAY OF DOING PRAGMATICS

Günther Grewendorf

The attempt to integrate pragmatics with grammatical research has so far not yielded any remarkable results. Although a few pragmatic terms have crept into the newer German grammars, this is more a fashion than a theoretically based extension of linguistic description. Apart from some efforts within the framework of integrative linguistics (e.g. Lieb 1977) or of natural generative grammar (e.g. Bartsch 1976), the establishment of a relationship between the grammatical procedures of a language and communicative functions within a framework of a grammatical theory has hardly been tried. This deficit is due, on the one hand, to the fact that pragmatic research is not characterized by a high degree of precision, and, on the other, to the identification of pragmatics with speech act theory, discourse analysis or a theory of sign use, which has prevented the recognition of the relationship between pragmatic phenomena and the grammatical procedures of the language. One result is that, within grammatical research, pragmatics has yielded relatively precise analyses only in the form of indexical semantics. This, in turn, is connected with the fact that *semantics* has at its disposal intensional logic and set theory as "borrowed" theoretical instruments which make the precise analyses of indexical phenomena possible. Like semantics *syntax* has also made use of theoretical instruments taken from other fields: recursion theory, permutation theory, Semi-Thue systems;

all of these have made the exact description of syntactic structures possible. Why, then, should *pragmatics* be expected to renounce such support from other fields?

In the following pages I want to demonstrate that precise description is also possible in pragmatics but that pragmatics must also make use of theoretical apparatuses from other fields: I will try to show that subjective probability theory and decision theory are the appropriate apparatuses in this context.

1. *Deficient answers*

Based on his formulation of a basic *syntactic* criterion for *direct* answers Åqvist attempts to arrive at a deeper understanding of the question-answer relationship in terms of the following semantic considerations: in accordance with his deontic/epistemic theory of questions which assumes that questions are to be regarded as requests to remove the desire to know something, answers to any question Q must - directly or indirectly - have something to do with the fulfilment of the request expressed by Q. Only if the request expressed by the questioner in asking Q is fulfilled by his getting to know the truth of a statement p, does such a statement count as an answer. In this case getting to know the truth of p is a (just) sufficient epistemic condition for the epistemic statement (Core Q) contained in the formalised question Q. Since the request expressed by any question Q is fulfilled if the epistemic statement contained in the formalised question is true, Åqvist formulates the heuristic semantic criterion that a *direct answer to question Q* must constitute a (just) sufficient epistemic condition for the truth of Core Q. In accordance with Åqvist's definition of a *(just) sufficient epistemic condition*[1] the statements (2)-(6) are direct answers to question (1):

(1) In what country is the Chiemsee?
(2) Germany is a country, and the Chiemsee is in Germany.
(3) Austria is a country, and the Chiemsee is in Austria.

(4) Beckenbauer's country of birth is a country, and the Chiemsee is in Beckenbauer's country of birth.
(5) The country where the Chiemsee is, is a country, and the Chiemsee is in the country where the Chiemsee is.
(6) The number 7 is a country, and the Chiemsee is in the number 7.

The strangeness of this result does not cause undue difficulty for Åqvist. He even rejects a suggested remedy, along the lines of Belnap,[2] to restrict the set of constants admissible for the replacement of variables in formalized questions to names of countries. In view of Åqvist's analysis that (2), (4) and (5) are true, (3) is false, (6) meaningless, and in addition, (4) and (5) are *not sufficiently informative*, the request made in (1) that there should be something (viz. a country) such that the questioner knows what it is (knows its 'identity') and knows that the Chiemsee is in that country, is only fulfilled by (2). But if the request made by a question is only fulfilled by true and informative answers, then, according to Åqvist, there is no reason to regard the uninformativeness or the meaninglessness of answers as more serious defects than their falsity. If the directness of answers is not incompatible with their falsity, then it is also not incompatible with their meaninglessness or uninformativeness.

In my opinion, there are a series of objections to this analysis. First, I claim without further proof that a theory of questions according to which answer (6) to question (1) is a direct answer or according to which answer (3) to question (1) is not a direct answer, is not adequate. Furthermore, it seems that a demand which must be integrated into a theory of questions is that answers must be informative, while in addition it must be taken into consideration that (a) this is not the only (pragmatic) demand placed upon significant answers and (b) that the informativeness of answers cannot be determined with the same absoluteness that Åqvist applies to (4) and (5). (4) can be just as informative as (2), and (5) is, without any doubt, uninformative on different grounds than (4) *if* (4) is uninformative.

Åqvist's demand that a direct answer to a question Q should constitute a (just) sufficient epistemic condition for the truth of Core Q seems to me to be both too narrow and too broad. *One* reason for the former qualification lies in Åqvist's overall formulation:[3] answers need not necessarily remove the desire to know something. For a questioner it is often enough to have grounds for an assumption, conjecture, hypothesis etc. An additional reason is apparent in the following example: for someone who could only afford a summer vacation with the help of a lottery jackpot and who asks the question

(7) Who hit the jackpot in the lottery?

the answer

(8) Well, definitely not you.

is sufficient, although this answer does not supply the knowledge that, according to Åqvist, is requested by (7), and although the answer contains considerably less information than would be contained in a precise characterisation of the winner. Following Åqvist, (8) would not be a direct answer on syntactic as well as semantic grounds.

Åqvist's condition is too broad because it permits answers of types (5) and (6) as possible direct answers, although they - in contrast to (2)-(4) - can *under no circumstances* create the epistemic situation requested by the questioner.

The crux of Åqvist's analysis of answers seems to me to be that for the concept of direct answers he provides a syntactic as well as a semantic condition, while the latter is, in addition, formulated with pragmatic reference to the components of a question situation. The confusion, not peculiar to Åqvist, stems from the failure to sufficiently differentiate between a *logic of questions* and a *pragmatics of questions*. In my opinion it should be the task of a *syntax* of questions to clarify the concept of direct answers within a framework of a logic of questions, while it should be the task of a *semantics* of questions to define the concept of a true answer (question/answer) as well as the concept of the logical presupposition of a question. The semantics should also clarify whether questions entail questions or whether questions entail statements. It should be the task of a *pragmatics* of questions to define the concept of a pragmatically significant answer and, in formulating this concept, the aspect of the informativeness of questions has to be taken into account.

Given these analytic distinctions the following must be taken into consideration: the answer

(9) The murderer of John is the murderer of John.

to the question

(10) Who is the murderer of John?

certainly constitutes a *true answer* according to the logic of questions, but it should be excluded from the set of significant answers by an appropriate definition of the corresponding concept in the pragmatics of questions.

Keenan and Hull (1973) try to take a note of this consideration as follows: Based on the insight that the question

(11) Which students did Mary invite?

is answered truly but not informatively by the answer

(12) All the students that Mary invited.

a revision of the question/answer relation as a result of which (12) would *not* count as a logical answer, is ruled out. The consideration that a concept of logical informativeness should be applied to L-sentences in general (and not only to answers) leads to the definition

(D1) An L-sentence S is logically informative iff
    (i) there is a state of affairs such that S is true, and
    (ii) there is a state of affairs such that S is false.

The concept of an informative answer is then defined by means of (D1) as follows:

(D2) An answer A to a question Q is informative iff the pair <Q,A>

is informative.

It follows from the definition of the question/answer relation and (D2) that (9) is a true but non-informative answer to question (10).

In contrast to Åqvist, we find here an analytic division between the two kinds of deficient answers (falsity and non-informativeness). The question of what relevance the concept of informativeness has for the evaluation of answers remains. Although tautologies, analytic sentences as well as sentences presupposed by questions are thus included as non-informative answers by means of (D2), the *semantic* aspect of the informativeness of L-sentences with respect to answers must be regarded as more or less irrelevant, it is only from a pragmatic point of view which takes into account the information situation and the interests of the questioner, that the informativeness of answers actually becomes interesting. In this context the question of whether answers have a non-trivial semantic content is only a special case of a more general pragmatic phenomenon that cannot be dealt with by using logico-semantic apparatuses.

This is demonstrated in the case of identities that are not of a logical, but of a factual kind. The answer

(13) The murderer of John is λx (p $\to$ is the murderer of John)

to, say, question (10) would be an informative answer according to (D2),[4] which contradicts any relevant intuition concerning the informativeness of answers. Further examples: on November 1, 1978, A wants to reserve a seat on a train to Berlin and is asked by the ticket agent

(14) For what day, Sir?

Let us consider the answers

(15) For October 15, 1978.

(16) For December 6, 2001.

Or: A asks a pedestrian on a sunny afternoon

(17) Can you tell me the time, please?

Answer:

(18) It's 2 o'clock in the morning.

Or: A is asked by a pedestrian on the Kurfürstendamm

(19) Where is the Gedächtniskirche?

Answer:

(20) In Berlin.

The fact that (15), (16), (18) and (20) are informative in the sense of (D2) is completely irrelevant to their evaluation *as answers*. That they are not informative *in a sense relevant to the questioner* is decisive in this case. (18) is *too obviously false* to the questioner, (15) would involve an *absurd* action, (20) is probably *already known* to the questioner in the given situation, and the data contained in (16) is *useless* for the purposes of the question in the given action context. In general, the answers (9), (12), (13), (15), (16), (18), (20) are deficient because they are useless with respect to the purposes connected with the corresponding questions.

From this it follows:

(i) A concept of the informativeness of answers defined by means of (D1) is uninteresting for a theory of questions. The concept of an informative answer must be defined, with reference to the state of knowledge and belief of the questioner, in the pragmatics of questions.

(ii) As is shown by sentence (16) possible answers that are informative, in the sense that they tell the questioner something new, can be deficient when the information provided for the questioner is useless for the purposes of the question in the given action context.

2. *The informativeness of answers* [5]

As the above-mentioned examples have shown, it is not interesting for a theory of questions to analyse answers according to an "objective" concept of informativeness. The decisive factor is whether an answer is informative *for the questioner*, and this, in turn, depends on what the questioner wants to know and what he already knows. A significant informativeness-concept for answers must refer to the knowledge situation of the questioner. We can say, therefore: an answer is informative if - with respect to the interest expressed by the questioner in his question - the answer provides the questioner with something new, that is if, roughly speaking, the answer changes the questioner's beliefs held at the time of his questioning in a way that is relevant to the question. Consequently, it is important to explicate the concept of informativeness of answers with reference to the change brought about by the answers in the subjective beliefs of the questioner. A concept of informativeness that satisfies this requirement must, therefore, refer to the knowledge situation of the questioner at the time of questioning as well as to the knowledge situation of the questioner at the time of answering. The problem is *how* the reference to these knowledge situations should be represented.

The knowledge situation of a person X at time t can be regarded as the set of beliefs X holds at t. But since all these beliefs are naturally not of equal strength on all subjects, the foregoing must be made more specific in so far that the knowledge situation must be characterized by the degree of belief X has at t with respect to the sentences of his language, or, by the degree to which he believes that the states of affairs expressed by the sentences in his language exist.

Since the degree of partial belief that X holds with respect to the sentences of his language S can be identified with the *subjective probability* of the existence for him of certain states of affairs expressed by these sentences, the knowledge situation of a person X at time t can be represented by a probability function $P_{X,t}$.[6] Since it has been demonstrated in probability theory that such a subjectivistic programme involving the measurement of the seemingly vague concept of degree of belief can be realised,[7] $P_{X,t}$ can be interpreted as a function with the propositions expressible in S as arguments and the degree of

X's belief with respect to the truth of such a proposition as the corresponding value. The fact that the function $P_{X,t}$ would be very difficult to specify concretely does not invalidate the suggestion that we represent the knowledge situation of X by $P_{X,t}$ any more than the fact that an intension function is very difficult to specify concretely invalidates the suggestion that we represent the intension of an expression by an intension function.

Since $P_{X,t}$ is a probability measure it is subject to the structural specifications stated in the axioms of probability theory. The requirement that $P_{X,t}$ be defined on a set algebra[8] is fulfilled by the assumption that the set of *propositions* expressible in S constitutes the domain of $P_{X,t}$.[9]

Let M be the set of propositions expressible in the language L spoken by the questioner X. Let function $P_{X,t}$ defined on M represent the knowledge situation of X at time t of questioning and assign the degree of belief held by X (i.e. the degree to which X believes A is true) to every $A \varepsilon M$.[10]

Let the questioner's state of belief existing after an answer B at time t' be represented by the probability function $P_{X,t'}$ (also defined on M). If the principle of credulity (C)

(C) The questioner believes what the answerer says to be true.

applies, which we presuppose, then the following is valid: $P_{X,t'}(B) = 1$.[11] Since $B \varepsilon M$ we can define:

(D3) An answer B is informative if $P_{X,t}(B) \neq 1$.

Since under $P_{X,t}$ tautologies, as well as all the propositions already known to X, have the probability value 1, the fact that the corresponding sentences cannot be counted as informative answers is accommodated. Consider, then, such examples as answer B:

(18) It's 2 o'clock in the morning.

answered on a sunny afternoon in response to the question

(17) Can you tell me the time, please?

Following (D3), B counts as an informative answer since $P_{X,t}(B)$ is certainly not equal 1. But this is highly implausible due to the *obvious falsity of B to the questioner*. The problem lies in presupposing (C) - X's (the questioner's) credulity. In the case of (18) the questioner's credulity is being overburdened; rather than believing the answerer he will *doubt the answerer's competence* or will assume that the answerer is joking etc. Since the idealisation (C) is to be retained on methodological grounds, examples such as (18) require the following revision of (D3):

(D4) An answer B is informative if $0 < P_{X,t}(B) < 1$.

With this kind of informativeness-concept the following kinds of answers are to be regarded as non-informative:

(a) Answers that tell the questioner something he already knows (cf. example (20)).
(b) Answers that are semantically non-informative such as tautologies and analytically true sentences (a special case of (a); cf. example (9), (12)).
(c) Answers for which the a priori probability $P_{X,t}$ is equal to zero i.e. answers which are obviously false to the questioner (cf. example (18)).

The defined qualitative concept of an informative answer can be further refined into the following comparative concept:

(D5) An answer B is more informative than an answer A if A and B are informative and if $P_{X,t}(B) < P_{X,t}(A)$.

That is to say, the smaller $P_{X,t}(B)$ is, the more informative is an answer B. The degree of informativeness of an answer B is thus determined by the difference between $P_{X,t'}(B)$ and $P_{X,t}(B)$.

3. *The subjective value of answers*

If we start from the assumption that questions offer alternatives among which the answerer has to decide, two important problems arise:

Problem (1): What determines the range over which the offer of these alternatives extends? As the examples in the foregoing sections illustrated, the range is obviously narrower than the set of structurally possible answers. The relevant question can, therefore, be formulated as follows: according to what pragmatic considerations can a subset of the set of structurally possible answers be isolated such that its elements represent the alternatives offered by a particular question?

Problem (2): What are the criteria against which the answerer makes his decision?

Beginning with problem (1), let us consider the following example:

(21) Where is Lutter and Wegner?

Situation (S1): I am having a conversation with friends in Munich about taverns. A joins us and realizes that Lutter and Wegner is a tavern and he asks question (21). He receives the answer (22).

(22) In Berlin.

Situation (S2): As an out-of-towner in Berlin I get into a taxi and tell the driver "Lutter and Wegner". In response the taxi driver asks question (21), he receives the answer (23).

(23) Schlüterstraße 55.

Situation (S3): At the Wittenbergplatz in Berlin a pedestrian asks question (21), he receives the answer (24).

(24) Take the Underground to the stop Bahnhof Uhlandstaße and then ask again.

Situation (S4): On the corner of Kantstraße and Leibnizstraße in Berlin, a pedestrian asks question (21), he receives the following answer (25).

(25) Go straight ahead, take the first left turn as far as the second traffic light and then it's right there.

Situation (S5): From a point where one can see Lutter and Wegner a pedestrian asks question (21). The answer combined with a gesture is (26).

(26) Over there.

In none of the obove situations (S1)-(S5) does the given answer belong to the range of alternatives available for any of the other situations. Should one say that the question (21) in the situations (S1)-(S5) has a different meaning in each case? So, for example, in (S1):

(21') In what city is Lutter and Wegner?

In (S2):

(21") In what street is Lutter and Wegner?

In (S3):

(21"') How can I get to Lutter and Wegner?

I think that this explanation based on the vagueness of the question is inappropriate, because, at least in the situations (S3)-(S5), the question would have the same meaning, and still a small change in the situation as, for example, from (S4) to (S5) would have such a *decisive* effect on the range of answer alternatives so that (26) would be significant in (S5) but not in (S4). This means that in the situations (S2) to (S5) the questioner wants to get to Lutter and Wegner and he asks his question for that purpose, and although the *same question* is asked in each of these situations, the ranges of significant answers are different because only certain answers are *helpful* to the questioner in each particular situation. That means that answers must have a *value* or *utility* for the questioner relative to the given situation, and the extent of the range of alternatives offered by a question depends on what is useful to the questioner with respect to the desires underlying his question.

The fact illustrated by the above examples is that an action-desideratum is connected with questions which is not exhaustively described by lack of information, and this motivates the assumption that a *question purpose* Z_Q, recoverable from the question situation, is connected with every question Q. This question purpose, however, is not only the obtaining of information, rather it is the question purpose which determines what kind of information is relevant for the questioner. But since this question purpose determines the restriction of structurally possible answers, the answers can be examined from the point of view of fulfilling this purpose.

This means that possible answers can be compared on the basis of their value for questioner X with respect to a particular question purpose Z_Q. Corresponding to this value a simple preference order can be established among the set of structurally possible answers.

For reasons of simplicity the fact that answers must be judged on their utility for a certain question purpose may be represented by a *function* W_{X,t,Z_Q} that assigns to every structurally possible answer Q the *subjective value*[12] this answer has at time t for the questioner X with respect to a question purpose Z_Q (connected with the question Q). This function is defined on propositions and corresponds to the utility function in decision theory.[13] The fact that the data determining this function is only available in a comparative form, does not invalidate the presentation as function any more than not knowing the concrete specification of probability or intension functions invalidates their respective presentation as functions.

We may therefore start from the assumption that W_{X,t,Z_Q} constitutes an idealized reconstruction of the fact that questions have a question purpose and answers must be judged according to their subjective value for the questioner with respect to the fulfillment of this purpose. Based on these considerations we can give the following definition:

(D6) An answer B to the question Q posed by X at time t for the purpose Z_Q is pragmatically significant if it has a positive subjective value W_{X,t,Z_Q}.

Since the subjective value function is defined on propositions in most models of decision theory,[14] in the case of (D6) this function would have the propositions expressed by the answers as arguments. But then (D6) would - as far as the pragmatic significance of answers is concerned - lead to strange results as illustrated by the following examples:

(27) Do I have cancer? - Yes.
(28) Who will be executed tomorrow? - You.
(29) What kind of wages do I get here? - Low wages.
(30) Who is Marion's lover? - Your husband.

This problem would be avoided if (D6) is revised as follows:

(D7) An answer B to the question Q posed by X at time t for the purpose Z_Q is pragmatically significant if at least one of the alternatives (offered in the question) that has a positive subjective value W_{X,t,Z_Q} is either included or excluded (i.e. if either this alternative or its negation can be inferred).

From the answer "You" to question (28) follows, for example, the negation of the useful alternative "You will not be executed tomorrow".

(D7) describes the fact that pragmatically significant answers must have a positive subjective value for the questioner. But since the latter is certainly only the case when answers are also informative, the concept of a pragmatically significant answer must refer to their subjective value *as well as* to their informativeness. It is precisely this double dependency, this interlocking of informativeness and subjective value, that the examples presented in section 1 were intended to illustrate. We therefore must say:

(D8) An answer B to the question Q posed by X at time t with the purpose Z_Q is pragmatically significant if it has a positive subjective value W_{X,t,Z_Q} and is also informative.

In our idealised quantitative way of speaking the dependence of the pragmatic significance of an answer on its subjective value *and* its informativeness is expressed by the product of these two components. The pragmatic significance of a given answer B at t' to a question Q posed by X at t (with t and t' being subject to the corresponding time condition) with the purpose Z ($PS_{X,t',Z_Q}(B)$) can, therefore, be determined as follows:

(T1) $PS_{X,t',Z_Q}(B) = W_{X,t,Z_Q}(B) \cdot [1 - P_{X,t}(B)]$

Answers B which are non-informative because $P_{X,t}(B) = 1$ are in accordance with (T1) not pragmatically significant. For answers C which on the basis of $P_{X,t}(C) = 0$ are non-informative (cf. example (18)), the value for W_{X,t,Z_Q} can be plausibly determined as $W_{X,t,Z_Q}(C) = 0$. With (T1), however, we once again face the implausibility that was illustrated in the examples (27)-(30). In order to avoid this, we must make the following differentiation.

As has already been discussed, propositions constitute the arguments of the subjective value function; in this case these would be the propositions expressed by answers. The above implausibility proceeds from the fact that the pragmatic significance of an answer would be dependent on what subjective value the proposition expressed by the anwer has for the questioner. But the subjective value of an answer has less to do with the proposition communicated to the questioner than with the fact that the proposition has been communicated to him. The propositions expressed by the answers "yes" and "no", respectively, are, in the case of question (27), without doubt, of very different subjective value to the questioner, although they probably have the same degree of informativeness, but this should be irrelevant to the consideration of the pragmatic significance of the answer. We therefore have to distinguish between the *subjective value of the communicated proposition* and the *subjective value of communicating this proposition* and the latter is relevant for determining the pragmatic significance of an answer.

We must therefore take into consideration a distinction that has so far been ignored in our discussion: the distinction between the propositions *that it is being answered that p is the case* and *that p is the case*. In the following, answer actions as in the first kind of proposition will be represented by capitals "A", "B", ...; the proposition expressed in an answer B will be represented by a lower case "b" as in the following formula that replaces (T1) accordingly:

(T2) $PS_{X,t',Z_Q}(B) = W_{X,t,Z_Q}(B) \cdot [1 - P_{X,t}(b)]$

4. *A pragmatic postulate for answers*

The second problem formulated at the beginning of section 3 consisted in asking what considerations should constitute the basis for the answerer's decision among the alternatives made available by the question. Proceeding from what we have said so far we can make two relevant assumptions:

(a) The answerer should give a true answer - unless there are important reasons not to.[15]

(b) The answerer should give a pragmatically significant answer.

In the argument that follows I intend to show how assumption (b) can be expressed and clarified with the aid of the apparatus we have so far adopted from decision theory, i.e. the probability function $P_{X,t}$ and the utility function W_{X,t,Z_Q}. This argument is based on the presupposition that the answerer is, *in principle, willing to cooperate*.

When a person is confronted with a question, his choice among the alternatives offered by the question will, in part, depend on what assumptions he makes about the state of knowledge of the questioner. When the answerer gives answer (22) in response to question (21) in situation (S1), his answer depends, in part, on his assumptions about the questioner's knowledge about Berlin. What the answerer considers the purpose of a question to be in a particular situation, also depends on his assumptions about the state of knowledge of the questioner. Whether or not the answerer understands that the purpose of the question

(31) Where is the Eiffel Tower?

posed to him in Paris, is, that the questioner wants to get to the

Eiffel Tower, will, in part, depend on whether the answerer believes that the questioner knows that he himself is in Paris and that the Eiffel Tower is also in Paris, etc.

Apart from his assumptions about the state of knowledge of the questioner and his assumptions about the purpose of the question conditioned by the first assumptions, the answerer's response will additionally depend on what value the answerer thinks his possible answer has for the questioner, given these assumptions. Given the presupposition that the answerer is willing, in principle, to cooperate, he will decide on an answer having a positive value for the questioner in the given situation *according to his own (the answerer's) evaluation*.

In order to be able to formulate a decision criterion based on (b) for the choice among the alternatives made available by a question, I start from the assumption that the answerer is in a situation such that he can make a *decision under certainty*, i.e. I start from the assumption that the answerer believes that he knows what the state of knowledge of the questioner is at the time of asking, that he believes that he knows the purpose of the question, that he has reliable sense of what subjective value the answering possibilities under consideration have for the questioner in this situation, and - in accordance with (C) - that he assumes the credulity of the questioner.

Following (a) the answerer Y should only give answers that he believes are true. Let the set of answers which he thinks are true be $M = \{A_1,...,A_n\}$. $M' = \{a_1,...,a_n\}$ be the set of propositions expressed by these answers. Y's assumptions about the state of knowledge of the questioner, relevant to the question situation, can, then, in accordance with the discussion in section 2, be represented as a function $P^Y_{X,t}$ on M' that indicates to what extent the questioner is convinced, in Y's opinion, of the existence of corresponding states of affairs at the time of questioning. However, the function can only accomplish this if it is guaranteed that it really becomes a probability measure. We must therefore postulate that the function $P^Y_{X,t}$ be extendible to a probability measure, i.e. that it can be extended to, at least, the set algebra generated by M'.[16]

Let W^Y_{X,t,Z_Q} be a function defined on M that represents the value the answers $A_1,\ldots,A_n$ have for X in Y's opinion in view of the question purpose Z_Q as assumed by Y.

In the given situation where Y can make his decision under certainty, Y can compare and weigh the answers which he thinks are true according to their pragmatic significance for X. In our idealised quantitative way of speaking the reasoning process Y has to go through, i.e. the "calculating" of the pragmatic significance connected with particular A_i in Y's opinion, can be represented as

(T3) $\quad PS^Y_{X,t',Z_Q}(A_i) = W^Y_{X,t,Z_Q}(A_i) \cdot [1 - P^Y_{X,t}(a_i)]$

As a decision criterion for choosing among the particular answers the following pragmatic postulate can be formulated which constitutes a clarification of (b):

(P1) Choose among the answers which you think are true the one for which the assumed (by you) pragmatic significance is greatest.

But the situation in which the answerer has to make his decision for one of the alternatives made available by the question is not always such that the answerer has firm beliefs about the knowledge situation of the questioner, about the question purpose, about the value of possible answers for X etc., i.e. the answerer's situation is not always such that he can make a decision under certainty. In conclusion I want, therefore, to reconstruct briefly what the situation of the answerer is like if he does not have the firm beliefs mentioned above, if he is in a situation in which he has to make a *decision under risk*.

Again I presuppose that the answerer is, in principle, willing to cooperate and that he assumes the credulity of the questioner. In the situation assumed here the answerer Y is uncertain which one of a series of possible assumptions about the state of knowledge of the questioner applies, and he is also uncertain which one of a series of possible hypotheses about the subjective values of answers has to be entertained.[17] We must therefore assign a degree of probability to these assumptions and hypotheses themselves, which indicates *to what degree* Y is convinced of their correctness. In this situation where Y has to choose among different A_i, he can only assign a pragmatic significance to the particular answers *relative to the degree* to which he thinks his assumptions about the state of knowledge and value situation of the questioner are correct, i.e. he can only reason about what pragmatic significance *is to be expected* for the particular answers. Now one has to consider

$\mathcal{W}$ = the set of all probability functions $P_{X,t}$ on $\{a_1,...a_n\}$ as thought possible by Y[18]

and

$\mathcal{M}$ = the set of all subjective value functions W_{X,t,Z_Q} on $\{A_1,...A_n\}$ as thought possible by Y.

Let P^Y be the probability measure defined on $\mathcal{W} \times \mathcal{M}$ that represents what (subjective) probability Y assigns to the existence of particular probability functions $P_{X,t}$ (states of knowledge of X) and value functions W_{X,t,Z_Q} (subjective values of the answers for X). On the analogy of the determination of the expected utility in decision theory [19] Y's *expected pragmatic significance* (EPS) of the answers he thinks are true can be determined as follows (as the weighted arithmetic mean of particular $PS(A_i)$ with the probabilities for W and P as weigths):

(T4) $EPS^Y_{X,t',Z_Q}(A_i) =$

$= \sum_{\substack{P_{X,t} \in \mathcal{W} \\ W_{X,t,Z_Q} \in \mathcal{M}}} [W_{X,t,Z_Q}(A_i) \cdot (1-P_{X,t}(a_i))] \cdot P^Y(W_{X,t,Z_Q}, P_{X,t})$

On the analogy of Bayes' rule[20] a pragmatic postulate for answers in situations in which someone has to make his decision under risk can be formulated as follows:

(P2) Choose among the answers which you think are true the one for which the expected (by you) pragmatic significance is greatest.

FOOTNOTES:

1. Åqvist (1975:142); in order to avoid the situation in which only trivial answers such as "a is a" are direct answers to identifying questions such as "who is a?", Åqvist revises his definition of a (just) sufficient epistemic condition of Core Q (1975:150).

2. Belnap (1963:18-20).

3. Cf. in this context my critique in Grewendorf (1978).

4. If p is valid, it is trivially true; if p is false, it is probably false on the basis of the non-referentiality of the right definite description according to usual definite description theories.

5. For the following analysis of pragmatically significant answers I naturally presuppose that the concept of a syntactically correct and sematically true answer has been clarified.

6. I am naturally not referring to the normative interpretation of probability but rather to the empirical-descriptive interpretation.

7. Cf. Stegmüller (1973), volume iv, part ii, section 5 and 6, as well as appendices ii and iii, where it is shown that the subjective probability concept can be specified with mathematical precision, insofar as one is prepared to accept certain basic idealisations in the form of rationality criteria.

8. In order to avoid unnecessary complications, in the following we always proceed from the finite case for which it is not required that the domain of $P_{X,t}$ is a σ-algebra.

9. Concerning the interpretation of propositions as sets, see Carnap (1971). A presentation of the Carnapian reconstruction of propositions as set-theoretical entities can be found in Stegmüller (1973:446ff) and Spohn (1978:90ff).

10. The time index t refers here and in what follows not only to a time point t but to the situation determined by this time point.

11. In my critique of Åqvist (cf. section 1) I have already pointed out that the questioner need not always be placed in a state of *knowing* something new through answers, rather he is frequently sufficiently satisfied by being given reasons for his assumptions, conjectures etc. This fact can be accounted for by allowing a smaller value than 1 for $P_{X,t}(B)$ and by modifying accordingly the informativeness concepts in what follows. In order to simplify the following representations I continue to assume that $P_{X,t}(B) = 1$.

12. Following Spohn (1978:36), I prefer the concept "subjective value" to the concept "utility" incorporated into decision theory.

13. I.e. it is subject to the so-called desirability axiom that relates the concept of subjective value with the probability concept (cf. Jeffrey (1967:94ff), Stegmüller (1973:305ff)) as well as to stipulations concerning the norming of this function (cf. Jeffrey (1967:116ff), Stegmüller (1973:327ff)).

14. Cf. in this respect the presentation in Spohn (1978).

15. On the grounds of foreseeable injurious effects on the questioner it can, in certain cases, be irresponsible "to tell him the truth".

16. The set algebra generated by M' (on M) is the smallest set algebra (on M) that contains M' as a subset. This requirement is unproblematic. It demands only that this function should satisfy the Kolmogoroff axioms, such that, for example, the number 2 cannot be assigned to any argument, and that the degree of belief assigned to propositions that contain elements from M' depends on the values of these elements, etc.

17. This includes Y's uncertainty about the purpose Z_Q that must be assumed for the question.

18. For these functions it must be valid that they can be extended to a probability measure.

19. Cf. for example Stegmüller (1973:296-297).

20. A presentation of the Bayesian principle can be found, among other places, in Jeffrey (1967, chapter I), Stegmüller (1973:297); details about controversies arising from this principle are given by Spohn (1978:39).

POLITICAL DETERMINANTS OF PRAGMATIC AND SOCIOLINGUISTIC CHOICES*

Hartmut Haberland
and
Tove Skutnabb-Kangas

One might ask what this paper has to do with pragmatics. If we consider pragmatics as something which has to be delimited from semantics, this question seems to make sense. Many a linguist struggles with this delimitation problem, and we do not deny that this is a serious effort and not just a matter of terminology. On the other hand, it seems as if this question overlooks that Carnap's famous definition of pragmatics ("If in an investigation explicit reference is made to the speaker; or, to put it in more general terms, to the user of language, then we assign it to be the field of pragmatics." Carnap 1968:9) opens up for two different conceptions of pragmatics. One of them is the usual syntax-semantics-pragmatics pragmatics, and this is not what we have in mind here. The other concept of pragmatics, which "is the basis of all linguistics" (Carnap 1968:13), could be characterized as "the science of language use" (Haberland and Mey 1977:1). Carnap tells us what he considers to be examples of "pragmatical investigations": "a physiological analysis of the processes in the speaking organs and in the nervous system connected with speaking activities; a psychological analysis of the relations between speaking behavior and other behavior; a psychological study of the different connotations of one and the same word for different individuals; ethnological and sociological studies of the speaking habits and their differences in different tribes, different age groups, social strata; a study of the procedures applied by scientists in recording the results of experiments, etc." (1968:13). Since the main exemplification of our thesis is by way of discussing the second generation immigrants' language problems in the country of production (the term is Swetland's (1979)), we think that our investigation naturally falls into the field of investigations to be called pragmatics.

We want to claim that there is an impact of society on science (here linguistics). And we want to show that this connection in a more specific sense implies that different political contexts can require different interpretations of established scientific knowledge and may lead to different proposals as to how to apply this knowledge.

The first part of the thesis has already been taken for granted. Investigations of the history of natural science in general have shown this (Bernal 1954). For philosophy we can refer to Borkenau (1932), Grossmann (1935) and Tomberg (1973), for physics to Boris Hessen (1931). These are just examples. We find a striking passage to this effect in Wunderlich (1974:31f.) on the relation between society and linguistics[1], and in the Editorial of the newly reorganized journal "Linguistics": "We should emphasize our concern for the social relevance of language studies. Our understanding of the character and effects of internal and external immigration, for example, has been enormously enhanced by sociolinguistic investigation; and there are many issues of social and political consequence where language studies can play a part. Conversely, language studies themselves may embody particular social and political biases (e.g., nineteenth century theories about the complexity of the languages of 'civilized' as compared with 'savage' peoples; or more modern theories about the comparative expressive powers of working and middle-class dialects). We would thus welcome and encourage papers of social relevance." (Butterworth 1979:2).

Of course, "impact of society on science" is a very vague term. Few will deny that there is some connection, but what matters is the precise nature of this connection. One of us once had the pleasure to come into a discussion of this problem with the late Yehoshua Bar-Hillel. He was strongly opposed to any idea of this type (and he even thought that this problem wasn't very attractive or interesting; "there are", he said, "110 millions of problems in the world. Why do you want to solve this one?"). He said, "it's silly to claim that the US Air Force has had anything to do with research on Machine Translation, except perhaps that they paid for it. I worked on MT at MIT for eleven years, and I never met a person wearing uniform there who told me what I had to do."

In a paper written in 1935, called "Linguistics and Language Struggle" (Målvetskap og målstrid), the Norwegian linguist Hans Vogt (known as a specialist on American Indian languages) has characterized the history of linguistics in the 19th century in the following way:

> European history during the 19th century is marked by language struggle and language oppression. Small nations rise against foreign oppression and fight for freedom and democracy. Everywhere re-establishment of the vernacular is the living symbol which fighters for freedom rally around. At the same time, European capitalism gains new markets in Africa and Asia. Coloured people are oppressed and toil to keep up with European machines. Against this double background, modern linguistics came into being in the Europe of the last century. On the one hand, increased interest in the national vernaculars, as opposed to the classical languages (Latin, Greek), on the other, interest in the non-European languages of the colonies.
>
> Even though it is easy to see this connection, it would be a mistake to think that the foremost men [sic] in linguistics consciously thought of themselves as fighters either for the vernaculars or for imperialism. Here, as so often, scientists do not know too much about their objective role in society. They cannot see the connection between their science and the political and economic development of their society. While they sit in their studies and believe that they are high above the daily struggles and fights, they have been instruments in a social process without knowing it. (Vogt 1973:89)

Although Vogt only talks about the 19th century, what he says is right for the 20th century, too. After the October Revolution many languages in the Soviet Union were developed as written languages for the first time. Many of the languages in Africa and Asia, which had been investigated as the languages of the colonized in the first place, were later developed as tools for all kinds of coordination and interaction. After independence, many of them became national languages. In the United States, interest in American Indian languages grew in the latter half of the 19th century, at a time when there was still hope of integrating and assimilating the native Indians. (See Darnell (1969) for the history of anthropology in the US, which started as a "government science", and went through a process of "professionalization". The emancipation of linguistics from anthropology was part and consequence of this process.) When this hope for intergration became obsolete - the Indians had been wiped out - other minorities caught the interest of the researchers, like the Blacks and the Chicanos.

But over and above the two reasons mentioned by Vogt - the rise of national consciousness, and colonialism - two other reasons were relevant for the development of linguistics: interest in technological development, and the problem of qualification of labour power.

As regards technology, the 19th century was not only the century of the steam engine. It was also the century when information processing machines came into use. In 1805, a Frenchman, Jacquard, constructed a machine which could be used to weave cloth with quite complicated patterns. This machine was controlled by small pieces of cardboard which resemble the computer punched paper tapes of today. What this means can be seen in the light of the following quotation from *Capital*: "A spider conducts operations that resemble those of a weaver, and a bee puts to shame many an architect in the construction of her cells. But what distinguishes the worst architect from the best of bees is this, that the architect raised his structure in imagination before he erects it in reality. At the end of every labour-process, we get a result that already existed in the imagination of the labourer at its commencement." (Marx 1970:178). What Jacquard made possible was to punch the "plan" which the human architect bears in his (and we have to add: or *her*) head into a piece of cardboard. Thus, the plan as the content of the architect's or weaver's imagination, becomes material as dead, transferable information, which a machine is able to read. However, this pattern on

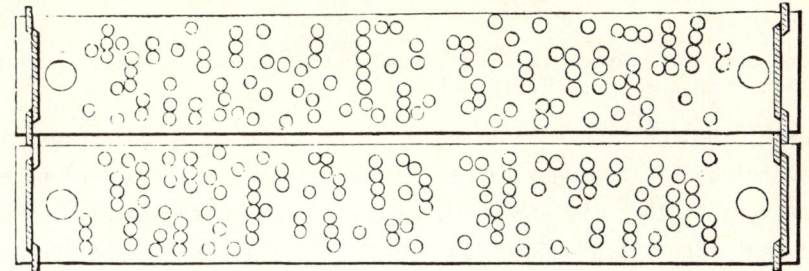

Fig. 23. Karten zur Jacquardmaschine.
from: Meyers Konversationslexicon, 5.Auflage, 17.Band,
Leipzig und Wien 1897

Jacquard's cardboard pieces had nothing to do with language in an ordinary sense. It was only the invention of artificial extensions of, and substitutes for, natural languages, namely, programming languages, which made it possible to *tell* the machine what it had to do. Today, the development of computer software strives to make this *telling* more and more similar to a natural language conversation.

This has important consequences not only for the use of computers in the labour process, but also for their use in connection with a lot of other information handling processes outside material production. The following is a quote from a paper by Newmeyer and Emonds (1971), who relate what an USAF colonel said when asked why the Air Force paid for syntax research at UCLA.

> The Air Force has an increasingly large investment in so-called 'command and control' computer systems. Such systems contain information about status of our forces and are used in planning and executing military operations. For example, defence of the continental United States against air and missile attack is possible in part because of the use of such computer systems. And of course, such systems support our forces in Vietnam.
> The data in such systems is processed in response to questions and requests by commanders. Since the computer cannot 'understand' English, the commanders' queries must be translated into a language that the computer can deal with; such languages, as you probably know, resemble English very little, either in their form or in the ease with which they are learned and used. Command and control systems would be easier to use and it would be easier to train people to use them if this translation were not necessary. We sponsored linguistic research in order to learn how to build command

and control systems that could understand English queries directly.
(Newmeyer and Emonds 1971:288f.)

Of course, the idea that syntax research could be of immediate use in war technology, is somewhat naive, but this is not what matters here. What matters is that the Air Force colonel in an quite unambiguous way states that there is a connection between the military's need for advanced natural language processing and their support to linguistic research. (It is not reported whether the colonel wore uniform when he gave this interview.)

Another function of linguistics not mentioned by Vogt in 1935 stems from the relevance of language studies for the qualification of the labour power. This becomes clear form a look at the investigations made in England and Western Germany as follow-ups to, and criticisms of, the proposals made by Basil Bernstein. Studies of the complexity of the language of working class children, and later the investigation of discourse in the classroom bear a clear relevance on the education in school; the fact that this research started in the early 1960's has an obvious connection to what economists have called the end of the reconstruction period after World War II or "the end of the *Wirtschaftswunder*".

Our main thesis can be challenged in different ways. On the one hand by those who do not believe in *any* connection between society's demands and (linguistic) research activity. But those are few. On the other hand, the exact nature of the relation between society and science can be seen in many different ways, even if you admit this relation to begin with. Some might claim that linguistics has a mere feeder relation to society: linguistics works on solutions to problems and sells them on the market. This seems to be the philosophy behind the recently established information handling agency "The Press" which David G. Hays started at Twin Willows near Buffalo, N.Y., last year, and which combines the efforts of microcomputer hardware technology ("chips and buses"), high-level, problem-oriented programming languages, and linguistics. Akin to this philosophy is the opinion of those who contend that a science first has to go through a stage of self-controlled development before it can be "finalized", i.e. subjected to demands form outside. This concept is taken from Böhme et.al. (1974); they oppose the idea that a science can develop from "pure" to "applicable" science. Rather, a science will in the beginning of its history control its development by itself, since unsolved inner-theoretical problems will set the tasks for the researcher. Only if, after these problems have been solved, the scientists cannot develop relevant tasks from inside their field, extra-scientific determinants will take over, connected with a tendency to drop causal explanations in favour of the statement of correlations. Since it is easy to see that linguistics hasn't reached a stage where it can be finalized according to Böhme et al.'s definition, it is impossible that both we, Hays, and Böhme can be right at the same time. If linguistics is not ripe to be finalized, and if Hays can sell linguistics, then the use which society can make of linguistics is a pure accident which has no consequence on the further development of linguistics (see also Kanngiesser 1976). Another objection may come from those believe that linguists tend to develop strategies of "immunization" (Ballmer 1976) which will ensure that they can abide with their science even if it has no relevance for society. In this case, linguists are seen as developing grammar as a science which cannot be understood by anyone else and which has no purpose but to provide an easy living for the priests who worship the Great Goddess of immaculate grammaticality (part of this is implicit and explicit in the writing of Utz Maas, e.g. Maas 1976:170ff). And there are those who claim the relevance of societal demands put upon science, but who see its function in the case of linguistics merely in the field of production of ideology (as is claimed in Lang 1976; see also Eisenbergs rejoinder (Eisenberg 1976)). In this case, only the two points made by Vogt above are acknowledged as determining factors for the development of linguistics.

If we want to establish our claim that society determines at least part of the decisions which the researcher has to make in his or her work, we immediately face the difficulty that many scientific theories do not look very much like answers to problems outside science (in our case, linguistics). We have to realize that not only are the problems the linguist works with different form the problems discussed in public and in political decision-making, but problems of a different kind. Terms like "fundamental research" or "pure research" somehow seem to have to do with this difference[2]. But we want to go further, and argue for a two-level model of *real* vs. *theoretical* problems. Applicability or success in the usual sense cannot be the decisive criterion for the impact of society on science. But neither do problems outside science directly determine which problems scientists work on. The connection between the two levels must be of a more indirect kind. People who get an ontological headache when they read the words "reality" or "real", might think of Carnap's distinction between observational and theoretical concepts (Carnap 1956). We see a vague analogy between our two-level concept of problems and Carnap's two-level concept of the language of science. At least the correspondence rules must have a similar status: the reality content of a theoretical problem (its significance) is established by the real problems it can be related to.

One type of real problems are problems that technicians are concerned with. For example, you might have the problem "We have to get 5 million people to work every morning", and someone proposes this solution: "Build a subway". Another problem might be, "We have to secure Denmark's energy supply without being dependent on imported oil and political extortion", and the solution might be, "Build nuclear power plants". Or, "We need a lot of high-speed high-quality translation from Russian to English", with its solution "Build translation machines!". Or, "We face problems with minority children growing up without sufficient abilities in both the country's language and their own first language", and the solution some people might propose is, "Submerge their first language by giving them all their school education in the majority language". (It should be clear from the examples that at least some of the solutions are fake solutions.)

To decide which solutions to real problems are fake, and which will work, we have to anticipate the future. Science is a means of doing this, and, looked at in this way, it is merely an extension of language, whose function, among others, is to store and anticipate experience. But the generalizations we are looking for (and which will help us anticipate) are answers to questions that are *not* normally formulated like "Which theory of grammar is good for machine translation?" Rather, the question will be: "Which way do we have to restrict deletion rules in order for the set of generated sentences to be decidable?" (the example is taken from Haberland and Mey 1977:4). That is an illustration of what we quoted Vogt for on page 287 above, namely that linguists normally "cannot see the connection between their science and the political and economical development of their society". (Vogt 1973:89). Thus, scientific questions are often put as questions regarding theoretical problems, and not as questions having to do with the correspondence between theoretical and real problems. This insight shows us the connection between many theoretical issues of the past years and problems discussed outside linguistics proper. Thus, algorithmization of transformational grammar provides the link between the problems of transformational grammar and the practical problems of machine translation. A relativistic view of cultural difference, which fits well together with a concept of constant meaning expressed in variable ways, provides a link from Labovian variable rules to racial politics in the USA. The insight that discourse administration is a culture-dependent skill whose exertion bears cultural meaning in itself connects research in discourse analysis with the problems faced by teachers in multicultural classrooms (see the contributions on the "silent Indian child" in Cazden et al. 1973 and Malcolm 1979).

Earlier we have mentioned the problem that many scientific theories do not look much like answers to problems outside science. We have tried to show that solutions to theoretical problems may in fact contribute to solving real problems. Sometimes however, we find divergent practical strategies and political proposals which base themselves on identical theories or research results. We do not consider this to be a paradox, since different political conditions can indeed lead to different interpretations of research results. We want to show this by way of comparing the discussions between researchers in West Germany and Scandinavia about the best means to educate immigrant children. In both areas researchers have been working with the problems, and some of them have influenced the political decisions made about different educational programs quite a lot.

Recommendations how best to educate immigrant children so that they become bilingual and obtain satisfactory school achievement and, later on, work opportunities, differ from Scandinavia to West Germany and West Berlin. With some unfair generalizations one can say, that the researchers in West Germany and West Berlin (WG) recommend the currently prevalent Scandinavian model, namely a more or less direct integration into German classes, or some type of bilingual education with German as the dominant language. This model most Scandinavian researchers and most of the Scandinavian immigrant organizations are strongly opposed to. These Scandinavian researchers recommend a model which is now very common in WG, but which many progressive German researchers and immigrant organizations reject, namely that of national classes at least during elementary school. Both Scandinavian and German researchers claim that they are right.

The Scandinavians use a *more theoretically based interdisciplinary argumentation, backed up with empirical evidence*, and supported by the opinions of the immigrant organizations. To a certain extent they have also got the support of the officially articulated opinion, especially during the last months (cf. Invandrarna och utbildningsväsendet 1979). The opposition towards national classes in Scandinavia comes from the political bodies, both from the right and from the left, from Swedish administrators, often on the intermediate level, and from a few, mostly Swedish-speaking scientists. The common denominator for the opponents seems to be that they favour an assimilation policy towards immigrants.

The German researchers in part seem to use a *narrower linguistic argumentation, together with practical-political arguments*. Both the support and the opposition seem to us to be too full of nuances to be characterized in any fair way.

Even if Scandinavian and German scientists recommend opposite models for the educational treatment of immigrant children, both seem to be right, given the *present* political situations in the countries concerned. In order to see how both opposites can be right at the same time, we have to give some background. First we say something about the situation of the adult immigrants in connection with the goals of the governments, as far as the immigration policy is concerned. Then we go on to the situation of the children, and finally we will come back to the research again.

First we'll compare the situation of the immigrants in Scandinavia to that of the "Gastarbeiter" in WG, with respect to the goal of the governments and the methods to realize that goal. When we speak of the governments' goal, we look at it both as it is seen in the official and semi-official documents, but also as it is seen in the measures which are taken - or, often, are *not* taken - to implement those goals. Very often there is a wide gap between the official goals and what is done in reality to implement them, especially when the education of the children is concerned (Skutnabb-Kangas 1979a).

In the sixties, when the big companies in Scandinavia and in WG lacked labour power, the organized import of labour power began on a *large* scale. What was important for the companies was to get young and healthy labour, such as the industrialized countries could use with minimal expenses for their social security systems, and send back when they were not needed anymore (FIDEF 1978). From their point of view the exporting countries thought that emigration was a good thing, too: they calculated that they could use the remittances, sent home by the people who were working abroad, to create new working opportunities at home. They also thought that the workers could get a good training abroad, and use it in building up the industry in their own country when they came back. Both these assumptions turned out to be wrong (Widgren 1975;1978). There has been a free labour market in Scandinavia ever since 1954, and now there is in the European Community, too; therefore, the receiving countries (or countries of production) could not prevent whole families from moving, if the move was inside these countries. But for workers that were citizens in countries outside these blocks, severe restrictions were introduced in order to prevent their families from coming along. It was a way to save the money which would have been needed to build up a whole new infrastructure to take care of the families.

While at first, all the industrialized countries had a shared ideology, Sweden fairly soon changed its policy. For linguists it might be interesting to notice how this change of attitudes immediately reflected itself in the words used to refer to the people who came. Here, like in many other respects, too, Sweden's attitudes in its official policy, in Government reports, etc. were much more progressive than either the attitudes of the Swedish people in general, or Swedish praxis. (In many other countries, the opposite is true.) As to Sweden, people were at first (in 1945) called "imported labour" *(importerad arbetskraft)*; then they became "foreign workers" *(utländsk arbetskraft)*; then "foreigners" *(utlänningar)*, and since 1965, "immigrants" *(invandrare)*. This development took 20 years (Öberg 1979). But the development continues: if you are called "immigrant", you stay at the border, without ever really coming into the new country, many immigrants feel. Therefore, many groups now call themselves Sweden Greeks, Sweden Finns, Sweden Yugoslavs etc. *(sverigegreker, sverigefinnar, sverigejugoslaver)*.

The other Scandinavian countries, except Finland, have followed Sweden. Norway seems to be even more positive, haven taken up the discussion of *mutual* adjustment earlier than Sweden. In Sweden, it mostly still is the migrant only who has to adjust to Sweden, even if the leading persons in the National Immigration and Naturalization Board and the Commission on Immigration Research have tried to start the discussion on the necessity of mutuality. Denmark, the only Scandinavian country which doesn't have any official immigrant policy, seems to vaccillate somewhere between a *Gastarbeiter* approach and an immigrant approach, but it will, hopefully, join the rest of the Scandinavian countries in a short time.

The Scandinavian approach means that the immigrants are allowed and expected to stay: they have the right to stay, and the measures taken have as their basic assumption that most of the immigrants *are* going to stay. Sweden's official goals submitted to Parliament in 1975 and setting out the threefold principle of "equality, freedom of choice, and partnership", "should imply continued efforts on behalf of the Swedish society to assure the immigrants of the same social standard and opportunities, and the same rights and duties, as the rest of the population. It also implies that all ethnic groups in the country must be given the same possibilities of developing their native language and of indulging in cultural activities. The goal *freedom of choice* implies that immigrants must be assured a genuine choice (whereby the State stands neutral) between retaining and developing their original cultural identity and assuming a Swedish cultural identity. Measures for the preservation of links with the culture of the country of origin also make it easier for immigrants and their children to choose between staying in Sweden and being re-integrated in their country of origin" (Widgren 1978:17, quoted in Kuusela and Skutnabb-Kangas 1978:80-81). The goal of *partnership* also should include "greater opportunities for immigrants to influence decisions concerning their own situation" (Widgren 1978:17).

Immigrants are very well organized in Sweden, but less so in both Norway and Denmark. In Sweden, many immigrants are active in different political parties, and some parties, mainly the Social Democrats and Communists, even have local branches which function in the mother tongues of some immigrant groups. The national organizations of different groups are very active in Sweden, and all the large groups have nationwide Central Unions for the local national associations. Since they participate in the hearings on official suggested policy, these Central Unions can influence decisions concerning immigrants a lot. In Sweden there are very few common immigrant organizations covering all or several countries of origin, and such organizations seen to have had some difficulties in getting state support. The national Central Unions, however, have developed a very close cooperation, and they often produce joint resolutions. In Denmark and Norway, the national associations are less well developed, and there are no Central Unions, but the different groups have some joint organizations. The first Nordic contacts between the organizations are just in the process of being built up.

In Sweden, trade union membership is required by many employers, and most gainfully employed immigrants join the unions.

Immigrants in Sweden can vote in municipal elections after two years, but state elections are only for Swedish citizens. On the other hand it is fairly easy to get naturalized, to obtain Swedish citizenship; Nordic citizens can apply after 3 years, others after 7 years. The first two immigrant members were elected to the Swedish Parliament in September 1979, but there should be close to 30, if the immigrants are to be granted proportional representation. Neither Norway nor Denmark have any immigrants in their Parliaments.

All gainfully employed adult immigrants are entitled to 240 hours of Swedish language instruction during paid working hours.

The situation in WG is very much different. The Government stated in April 1977 as a matter of principle that the Federal Republic of Germany is *not* an immigration country (Bundesminister für Arbeit und Sozialordnung, Drucksache II a-24 200/22, cited in Rieck and Senft 1978: 22). Accordingly, foreigners are treated as *Gastarbeiter*, guest workers, and the official policy reflects this.

Immigrants have very few legal rights. As Fritz Franz (according to Rieck and Senft (1978:95) Germany's leading authority on legal matters concerning foreigners) points out, they are "not under the protection of legal procedures *(Rechtsordnung)*, but under the control of police regulations as if they all represented a danger for public security and order" (quoted in Rieck and Senft (1978:95); for an excellent overview, see Franz 1975). A legal claim to an unlimited residence permit and the right of residence did not exist until a few months ago, and naturalization (attaining German citizenship) is almost impossible.

Immigrant workers have nearly no possibilities of political participation, and foreigners are not entitled to vote, not even in municipal elections. So their possibilities of changing their conditions are almost non-existant.

Language instruction in German as a foreign or second language for adults is mostly very poorly organized, and the courses are not specifically planned for foreign workers. Most of them take place in leisure time, and the immigrants have to pay for them themselves. In 1977 the state financed courses for 0.6% of the foreign workers.

When one looks at the *practical implementation of the official goals*, the differences between Scandinavia and WG become less pronounced. Many of the measures taken in Sweden and in Norway, and to a certain extent also in Denmark, show that even if these countries have in a way accepted immigrants and do not intend to throw them out (even if this is more uncertain in the case of Denmark), they have done so on their own premises: in order to become accepted the immigrants have to be assimilated to the majority societies. They have to become New Swedes, New Norwegians, New Danes (Hammer 1976). Even if the official goals say that the children should be given the possibility to develop their mother tongue and their own culture, the children do not get any real chance to do it. There seem to be many ways to accomplish the unofficial goal of assimilation, and the educational system seems to serve this goal. Through their educational systems, the Scandinavian countries see to it that the occupational structure and the class structure of the immigrants is reproduced. As a Greenland eskimologist, Robert Petersen, puts it: "the dominant society structures the education according to the demands of the majority itself." (Petersen 1978).

This is even more true for WG. The school sees to it that the immigrant children are sorted out and left outside the higher education system. Western societies will even in the future need non-qualified workers at the assembly lines, and they educate the immigrant children to meet that need. At the same time, it is of course important that the children accept their future place in the society without protest. Therefore, it is important in Sweden that the official goal is equal opportunity. In this way, the children are at the same time given the massage that it is their own fault if they fail.

At the same time the educational system also imposes the Scandinavian majority ideology onto those immigrant children who do succeed in the system, thus ensuring that they are not going to oppose the exploitation of other immigrants. Those who succeed, are co-opted, and the symbolic violence in schools and the structural violence in a post-industrial society are not discussed, because the beautiful official phrases are such that the immigrant organizations can agree with them, and this sweet harmonious consensus prevents criticism (for examples, see Skutnabb-Kangas 1978).

Some of the weapons for legitimizing the continuation of exploitation come from researchers who either do not know or do not care whether they are being used. The repressive tolerance, typical for countries which think of themselves as pluralistic, also makes it more difficult to see the real conflicts in the immigrant issue in Scandinavia, and to discuss them openly. From this point of view it becomes clearer who the opponents of national classes among the researchers are in Scandinavia: those who favour the assimilation policy, who work *against* the interests of the immigrants, and *for* the continuation of the present system of exploiting immigrants (Skutnabb-Kangas 1979b).

In WG, the official policy of *Gastarbeiter*-type is in a way honest: the exploitation is an admitted fact. In order to reduce the social expenses in the country of production, WG aims at a quick circulation of foreign labour power. It is hoped, ideally, that young, healthy male workers come alone, ready to start work immediately, stay a few years in factories and barracks, and go home when they have used their best years, before they become old and sick, to be replaced by new young and healthy workers (FİDEF 1978). It is, then, one of the main goals of the school system to keep the immigrant children non-integrated, ready to go home whenever their parents are not needed anymore (FİDEF 1978).

Compared to Scandinavia, this is a policy of direct violence and segregation, and it openly contains many violations of human rights, like the many restrictions on the movement of immigrants, etc. (Rieck and Senft 1978:94).

Some of the countries of origin take part in the oppression of those immigrants who try to criticise the official general and school policy. Ways in which the exploitation is kept alive are, for instance, control of the teachers by the countries of origin, direct importation of teaching materials with in some cases openly anti-democratic political content, and cooperation between the WG police and that of the countries of politically active immigrants, resulting in various negative consequences for their relatives at home (FİDEF 1978).

Some WG researchers, in their turn, contribute to the continuing exploitation of the immigrants, too.

Next, we will present the various current models used in immigrant education in West Germany and Scandinavia. As we said in the beginning, in both WG and Scandinavia the progressive researchers oppose the model prevalent in their own countries. But their recommendations are at opposite ends: while the Scandinavians want to have the model which the Germans oppose, the Germans want the model which the Scandinavians oppose. For reasons of space, our presentation will have to simplify and generalize on a number of points. In WG, there are basically two models (with lots of modifications in different directions) for the education of immigrant children: different types of *preparatory classes* and *national classes*.

The most important criterion for the *preparatory* classes is that their official *aim* is to prepare the students for a transfer to German-medium classes, where they are supposed to get their instruction in German, along with German children. Over the past few years, however, there has been a tendency for these classes "to become separative national schools of low quality", where "the additional German language instruction has been reduced" (Stölting 1978:100). Rather than transferring the immigrant children to German classes, the aim of these classes, according to Turkish organizations, now is twofold: first, to keep German classes free from foreigners, and to define the foreigner classes as something outside the regular school system; second, to save as much money as possible by maintaining a lower material standard in foreigner classes (FİDEF 1978). Another way of saving is, of course, to allow children to stay out of the school system completely, without even trying to enroll them in the schools or to keep them there. According to official statistics, in 1976/77 there were ca. 50,000 foreign children of school age in Nordrhein-Westfalen, who did not attend school. Adding up the teacher salaries for one year, which Nordrhein-Westfalen did not pay for these children, we see that ca. 100 million DM was "saved" out of taxes which the foreign workers had paid (FİDEF 1978:16).

Preparatory classes can have immigrant children of one or several nationalities. The language of instruction is mostly German, which the children do not understand, and don't seem to learn beyond an elementary skill to communicate about the most essential everyday needs, which is not enough to be able to follow instruction in German. This is partly a result of the fact that until 1977 there had not been *any* training for teachers in teaching German as a second language to immigrant children (Meyer-Ingwersen, Neumann und Kummer 1977; Stölting 1978).

The main difference between preparatory classes and *national* classes seems to be the medium of instruction. This is even more the case ever since the aim of the prepatory classes ceased to be the transfer of the children. From national classes, where the instruction is given through the medium of the children's mother tongue, transfer after grade 6 to German classes is *obligatory* in Länder such as Nordrhein-Westfalen. This very often means that the children simply drop out after grade 6, since they cannot follow the instruction in a German-medium school anyway. In other Länder, the transfer is *optional*, which also means that very few children are actually transferred. Very often neither the national teachers (controlled by the country of origin) nor the German teachers seem to favour a transfer; however, they may be differently motivated. The national teachers don't favour the transfer because they lose their jobs if the children go to German classes. The German teachers don't want it, because they do not have any training in teaching immigrants, and because they feel that they have failed; also, all-German classes are so much easier to teach than multinational classes with may children who do not understand the instruction. Also, there is pressure from many German parents to keep the classes foreigner-free.

Concluding then, the education of immigrant children in WG right now seems to be a low quality education, quite regardless of what it is called:

— A *separate* schooling, such as the Scandinavians advocate, seems to fail in WG. This is partly because it gets less material support than German-medium schools: the facilities are old and bad, there is less money for teaching materials, the teachers' job situation is insecure. Partly, too, separate schooling seems to fail because the teaching of German as a second language to immigrants is almost non-existent and the overall quality of the teaching is very low. And finally, it fails because both the children and the teachers (as well as the parents) are discriminated against. The result is that the children don't learn too much of their own language, they don't learn German, they don't learn very much of the subject matter, and there is always the risk of their forced return to the country of origin. Especially Turkish parents in West Germany fear also that separate schooling will facilitate right-wing indoctrination, since it implies that the Turkish Government organizes the teaching and that the teachers are directly imported from Turkey. Many of the Turkish teachers employed by the Turkish Government sympathize with the fascist organization of the "Grey wolves". There are similar objections against the so-called Koran schools (a type of religious instruction), too (Abadan-Unat 1975:319; Rist 1979). (Both these fears seen to be prevalent among Turkish parents in Denmark, too, where national classes are now debated.)

— *Integrative* (ultimately, *assimilationist*) schooling fails partly for the same reasons as in Scandinavia: namely, that the children lose their mother tongue which leaves them without a basis for acquiring German, also, they become bilingual in a *subtractive* way (in Scandinavia we call this semilingualism): they don't know *any* language on the same level as monolingual children. They either don't understand the language of instruction, or understand it only in a superficial way. They have a linguistic façade, they sound fluent and their accent is perfect, but as soon as they have to discuss something outside the concrete everyday situations, their communicative competence is not sufficient. And since they can't follow the instruction, they of course fail in school. Integrative schooling is often also insufficient for the same reasons as separative schooling: the quality of instruction, especially of the instruction in German, is low. Discrimination is a reality in these classes, too.

According to Stölting (1978:102), the battle is now on between
"1. those advocating separative schooling, where reactionary and leftist forces meet, led by different motives, and
2. those advocating integrative schooling - German trade unions, German Communist Partly, many good-willed German teachers. Under the necessity of securing a modern and qualified instruction for the foreign children the integrative and ultimately assimilationist position has survived and gained ground."

What a few very progressive researchers (like Stölting, Menk, et al.) try to do is to "break up the tie between separative instruction and low quality of instruction, and finally to make possible a bilingual schooling without isolating foreign from German children" (Stölting 1978:103).

Researchers advocating a bilingual and bicultural schooling "under the given conditions of power" (Stölting 1978:103) must, among other things, "publicly state the deficiencies of the existing models especially in contrast to what could be done, the underlying motives of the authorities, their disregard of the parents' wishes, and the *way in which scientific findings are being distorted in order to justify the decisions of the authorities*" (Stölting 1978:103; our emphasis).

As long as WG's official policy is a "Gastarbeiter" policy, with all its consequences for the foreign children's educational goals, the *best* means to educate the children seems to be some type of *bilingual* schooling, where possible; however, in very many places the authorities oppose this. The *next best* seems to be an *assimilationist, integrative* schooling, as long as it is the only way to guarantee at least some resources to the classes. Under the present circumstances, *separate* schooling seems to be the one *least likely to succeed*.

It is important to note that this kind of recommendations and decisions are *not* at all based on sound scientific knowledge of what might be best for the children from a linguistic, psychological, social psychological, pedagogical, or sociological point of view. They are solely based on a (maybe realistic) knowledge of the political facts in WG right now, and a wish to guard the children from damage as much as possible. In other words, a truly defensive strategy. Accepting the existing conditions in such a way could lead to the death of the Utopian; we can only hope that it doesn't.

Although all the Scandinavian countries have slightly different models, the models now prevalent in both Norway and Denmark also exist in Sweden; hence we'll concentrate on the Swedish situation.

"The instruction can primarily be given *through the medium of Swedish*, in a Swedish-speaking class, together with Swedish pupils, with or without different types of auxiliary instruction, with or without a companion teacher (either Swedish-speaking or a native speaker of the child's mother tongue)" (Kuusela and Skutnabb-Kangas 1978:83), and with or without a few hours' instruction per week in the mother tongue as a subject. Most of the WG researchers and many immigrant organizations in WG want to have this (integrative or assimilationist) model. It is very strongly opposed by immigrant organizations in Sweden, as well as by most of the researchers.

Looking at the people who oppose this model and those who favour it, one notes several interesting differences. *Some* of those in favour of the assimilationist model belong to a minority themselves; but often they come from old minorities which by now are almost completely assimilated. These persons are often more Swedish than the Swedes, and they often show an open contempt towards recent immigrant workers, as can be seen for instance in many articles and interviews in the newspapers. However, *most* of the supporters of this model come from the majority society, and know very little about the immigrants. Their openly expressed goal is not balanced bilingualism, but a bilingualism with Swedish as the dominant language. One of them, Lars Henric Ekstrand, argues that "for some migrant children, the optimum might well be to keep the level [of mother tongue proficiency] a bit above the risk level for complete decay" (1978:12). On the other hand, many of those researchers who *oppose* the assimilationist model come from minority groups themselves, and/or cooperate very closely with the minorities. Many of them also have quite a lot of practical experience in teaching minority children.[3]

The instruction can also take place in classes with *two* teachers, with both Swedish pupils (with a Swedish teacher) and immigrant pupils (from one nationality only, with a teacher from that nationality). The pupils are taught separately part of time, each group in its own mother tongue. The proportion of Swedish-medium instruction increases quite rapidly, until all instruction takes place through the medium of Swedish.

This model is the Swedish authorities' answer to the demands for mother tongue classes. One of the main reasons for recommending this type of model, rather than pure national classes, seems to be the fact that the authorities want to be able to control what is happening in the classes, and to force the classes to use Swedish teaching material (with a Swedish ideological content). This nervousness about teaching materials and about things happening in national classes seems to be groundless in Sweden (even if this may not be the case in WG), since the state not only controls teacher training for bilingual teachers, the employment of teachers etc., but also since the country which provides most of the pupils and teachers in national classes nowadays, namely Finland, is very much like Sweden itself in culture and ideology. A two-teacher model where the status of the immigrant teacher almost necessarily becomes lower than that of the majority teacher, is ultimately an assimilationist model, even if the assimilation is more indirect than in the earlier model.

The two-teacher model is the one favoured by the more progressive West German researchers. According to Scandinavian researchers, it is better than direct integration; however, if there are enough pupils to form a national class, that model should be preferred.

When instruction is primarily given in the native tongue of the pupils, with Swedish as a second language, we have the so-called *national class*. This is the type of instruction which all National Central Unions of Immigrants in Sweden (except the Estonians, who already have two schools of their own) unanimously demand. It is also favoured by several political parties (among others the Communist parties), but not by the Social Democrats. The Trade Unions do not unanimously support it either. The model is supported by the immigrant teachers' organizations (the immigrant teachers are selected, trained, and paid by the Swedish state, even though many of them have a teacher's training from their countries of origin).

This is also, in our opinion, the model supported by research, both theoretical and empirical. The experiences from this type of schooling are extremely good, and form a striking contrast with the bad results from other types of education. In the largest longitudinal study about national classes hitherto (in Södertälje, directed by Göte Hanson) the children are bilingual by grade 6, their school achievement is on a par with their grade, and they seem to be happy and harmonious, with a stable bicultural identity. These are results that the other two models favoured by the WG researchers have not been able to come up with, at least in Sweden (Hanson 1979).

In summary, then, the model which seems to work *best* in Sweden is that of *national classes*. The *next best* seems to be the *bilingual education with a two-teacher system*, and the one which seems to be the *least recommendable* is *the integrative assimilationist model*.

The model of national classes is a far cry from what is realistic as a political goal in Western Germany, as the situation is. Very few researchers would advocate this model for Western Germany without qualifications, although it seems to have worked out best in Sweden. This is not so much a consequence of disagreement about what we know, and what we ought to do since we know. Rather it suggests how different political conditions can affect the use and interpretation of research results. This lack of "objectivity" in linguistic research might be considered a temporary defect, something that can be remedied by developing better and more objective linguistic methods. Lang (1976) argues that some sciences have a "technology buffer", by which he means a set of properties characteristic for a well-developed science. As a first property, the results of a well-developed science go far beyond what people normally learn during higher education. This property seems to be rather trivial, but Lang's second and third property are of more importance here, viz. incompetent interference may result in damaging lossess in the productive sector of society (what Lang has in mind are obviously cases such as Lysenko's); and acceptance of such a theory can more or less be reduced to an acceptance of non-verbal actions.

According to the second property, a change in the theory, if accepted by those who work inside the science as well as by those who are dependent on its results, will have consequences for real life. As to the last property, accepting the theory is not just a matter of beliefs or subscriptions, but rather of *doing* something.

It is rather questionable whether linguistics has a technology buffer. Physics certainly has, as do most hard-core natural sciences. But whereas people to a very high degree would rely on bridges built by using knowledge which we owe to physics, it is not at all clear to what degree people would risk their lifes (or other people's futures?) on the basis of results from the language sciences.

If this is true, linguistics is still an underdeveloped science. But in the light of Tomberg's thoughts (referred to in footnote 2), it seems questionable to assume that this underdevelopment can be remedied by letting linguistics become more like physics. And regardless of how we want the language sciences to develop, it is questionable whether that development can wait at all. It has been said that linguists should stop talking about applied linguistics, until they know more about language. This may be true for certain technological problems; think of the notorious ALPAC report (ALPAC 1966). This report was delivered by the Automatic Language Processing Advisory Committe, which had to assess the relative can and cant's of Machine Translation. Among the members of the committee were the linguists Charles F. Hockett and David G. Hays. While the committee in 1966 said, "We can't do it, and we can't do it in the near future either", in 1979, two authors of the Postal Service of The Press at Twin Willows (edited by David G. Hays) tell us, "Now we can"[4]. But whereas many technological problems can wait, provided they are not too urgent, most social problems cannot wait. Thus we cannot wait to solve the problem of the second and third generation of immigrant workers in Western Europe until we know all about bilingualism, minorities, attitudes, etc.

This means that pragmatics and other linguistic disciplines cannot wait for all their research programs to have been carried out, and then provide a corpus of knowledge which would be applicable to the social problems of twenty years before. If pragmatics is to be a socially engaged science, we have to look for possible (even if only partial) answers to important problems which have to be solved right away thus giving ethnic, social class, etc. groups a chance to decide what they are going to do in pursuit of their goals (cf. Petersen 1978). In the long run, those branches of linguistics which could be related easily to problems external to linguistics, have been the most fruitful anyway. Many theoretical developments have been abandoned, not by politicians, who didn't want to pay for them, but by linguists themselves, as soon as they found out that their research interest concentrated on mere intra-theoretical problems.[5]

Theoretical and methodological sophistication (which is not the same as soundness) are of lesser importance here. For us it is clear that pragmatics (in the broad sense of Carnap's) has become less sophisticated and more interesting during the past few years, in particular in fields like speech act analysis and discourse analysis, where most workers still use distributionalist (taxonomist, if you will) criteria. In fields where technical sophistication has been highest (e.g. analysis of variation in natural languages), the results have been comparatively meager. Hence, we should not be afraid of taxonomies. The kind of linguistics developed by Noam Chomsky was methodologically as sophisticated as one could imagine. But its empirical results have been scant; maybe one could say that Chomsky's main contribution lies in the development of elaborated and rigorous methods for refuting his own theory. His tools have thus been used by other linguists for what they were designed to do in the first place, and this has been an exciting adventure in the history of linguistics. Perhaps linguists should try some adventures in real life next.

FOOTNOTES:

*   We would like to thank Marcelo Dascal for his constructive critism, and our indefatigable friend, Jacob Mey, for many suggestions which we did not always follow.

1. For a more detailed account, see Eisenberg and Haberland (1972).

2. What makes the situation more difficult, is the dichotomy of natural vs. social sciences which runs straight across linguistics. But if we follow Tomberg (1973), we can argue that this dichotomy - in spite of all attempts to form a unified science - corresponds to a certain developmental stage in philosophy of science which may be associated with what Tomberg calls bourgeois science (*Bürgerliche Wissenschaft*). At this stage, attempts to make use of the forces of nature have been successful, at least to a certain extent, but science as a rational means of building a more just society is not accepted by those who rule this society. This implies a very narrow concept of rationality, viz. one that is modelled on natural science, and leaves the social sciences outside rationality, thus understood. This reminds one somehow of the Medieveal theory of the division between a sublunary and a superlunary world. All things sublunary are subject to change, hence God's own rationality, i.e. mathematics, applies only to the world above the moon in a perfect form. It was Galilei's observation of the movements of the moons of Jupiter that for ever did away with this world-view.

3. Here we would like to make a small excursion to Greenland. Robert Petersen says (in an article about scientists as intermediate persons): "The administration body has a sort of power, connected with its organization, its situation within the community, and having own experts, while the Greenlandic community has in fact no experts of its own to help it both with argumentation and formulations. The Greenlandic community has to use the experts of the administration as its expertise. Without trying to throw suspicion on the administrative staff, it is obvious that it, as a part of a body with a certain policy, cannot be neutral. We may state that any people has a right to access to alternative expertise, which is independent of decision-making bodies" (1978, no pagination). It is easy to see the parallels with the immigrant education question. A good discussion about researchers as intermediate persons in a rehousing project for immigrants in Copenhagen can be found in Ekegren, Hecht and Hansen (1979).

4. This has, of course, to be taken with a grain of salt, as the authors themselves indicate. The concept of Machine Translation has undergone important changes in the meantime, and what The Press is aiming at is rather some kind of interactive, machine-aided translation:
    "Machine Translation is an idea whose time is about to come. Africa and Asia need Western science and technology; we need their modes of cultural play. Hence much translation is to be done. Doing it rapidly will require machine aids. And if those aids are to be of real value

then designing them will require our best knowledge of linguistics, computation, cognition, and man-machine interaction. MT is thus intellectually rich as well as urgently practical.

In the most plausible approach, human translators make decisions too difficult for the machine to handle. We call this HRT - Human Regulated Translation. The trick is to partition the translation process in such a way that the machine gets to do all the dull and easy work while the human is given only the subtle and challenging work. It hasn't been done yet, but science and technology are now ripe for a try." (Benzon and Fritzson 1979:5)

5. This is obviously partly i dependent of the actual possibility of application. The connection link is rather that a guidance of *Erkenntnisinteresse* by external problems is a most stimulating heuristic help for the working researcher.

PRAGMATIC CONSIDERATIONS
WITHIN A TEXT-THEORETICAL FRAMEWORK

Wolfgang Heydrich
and
János S. Petöfi

1. *Some basic aims of text theory*

Among the things in the world there are objects that can be classified as texts. What does it mean for an object to be a text? Among other things it certainly means that the object has some properties that allow another kind of object in the world e.g. people with certain linguistic abilities to recognize some specific (semiotic) relation between the object and the world. In short: they can interpret these objects as signs. This interpreting seems to be a precondition for the use of the objects as means for the transmission of information, for the orientation of behaviour and for some additional purposes.

It seems to be one of the basic tasks of every general theory of texts to establish necessary and sufficient conditions, which must be met if objects are to be understood as texts. It may, of course, be questioned, whether the specification of such objects reveals anything interesting at all. In principle, many objects - and very different ones indeed - can function as texts and the mere fact that such objects meet our conditions does not at all mean that they would be regarded as texts by someone in a concrete situation. (We want to call such a person an "interpreter") *Objects with properties characteristic for texts must be understood as signs if they are to be used as texts.*

In this respect we must face one central task of text theory: the explicit and - as far as possible - formal reconstruction of the interpreter's bringing a text to bear upon the world, i.e. his understanding of an object of the world as a sign.

In this paper we want to give a brief presentation of some of the components of such a reconstruction as proposed within the framework of the so-called Text-Structure World-Structure Theory (TeSWeST).[1] We do not want the reconstruction of text-interpretation to be a model of some process or event, but rather a detailed analysis of the result of such a process. In particular we deal with a complex of representations which are interconnected. Two types of connexion may be distinguished: on the one hand, there are such devices as transformation and translation, i.e. certain arrangements which can be described purely combinatorially on the level of the manipulation of symbols. And on the other hand, the different representations are interconnected insofar as they are determined by a complex of states of affairs, which constitutes the situation of the interpreter. With respect to this kind of connexion between the representations we can speak of a *pragmatic dimension* within the reconstruction of text interpretation. This means that there is no one isolated component within the theory, which by itself would play the role of 'pragmatics', rather the central components are constructed relative to the interpreter's situation.

We will not discuss individual pragmatic questions in this paper, our aim is rather to take some steps towards the presentation of an integrative semiotic theory of texts, which provides a framework for discussing the whole complex of questions about the relation between text and context. In the following paragraph we are going to characterize some of the most important parts of the TeSWeST in terms of their composition and function. The third paragraph is devoted to the general discussion of the relation between text and context within the framework of the TeSWeST, and we will outline three strategies for dealing with the problem of formalizing this relation.

2. Some components of the TeSWeST

Let us assume that in the world at a certain period of time, there are two objects J and T and also other objects, among which we may possibly find some objects A and B.

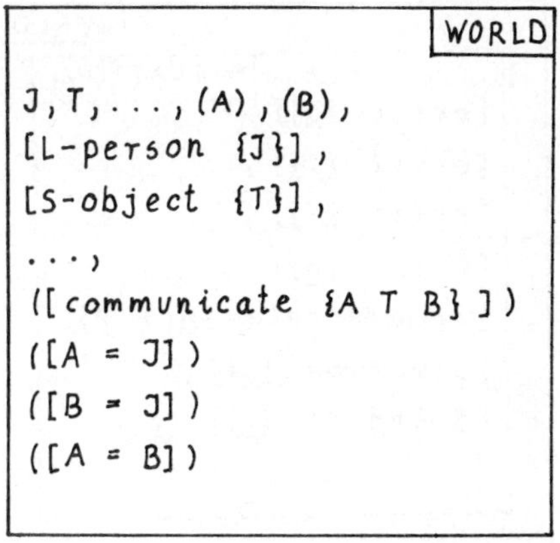

```
                                              WORLD
J, T, ..., (A), (B),
[L-person {J}],
[S-object {T}],
...,
([communicate {A T B}])
([A = J])
([B = J])
([A = B])
```

Figure 1

Parentheses indicate optionality in figure 1.

Let J be a person with certain linguistic abilities. (This is expressed in semi-formal notation as "[L-person {J}]") and let T be a text, which means that as long as it is regarded independently of some process of understanding and information-processing, it can be identified with any object that serves as a sign-manifestation ([S-object {T}]). It is possibly also the case in the world, that A communicates T to B (([communicate {A T B}])), that A is identical with J (([A = J])), B is identical with J (([B = J])) or A and B are the same person ((([A = B])). In addition to the preceding, other states of affairs may certainly obtain in the world. For the sake of simplicity we do not want to discuss here the temporal relations among the objects in the world and among the various states of affairs.

Insofar as J is an interpreter and since he is linguistically capable, he has some relation to a complex of states of affairs which can be imagined as the sum of what J is ready to accept. J has as it were at his disposal a picture of the world to which he belongs, a picture that partly coincides with and partly diverges from the world. Let us call this complex of states of affairs the "situation of J".

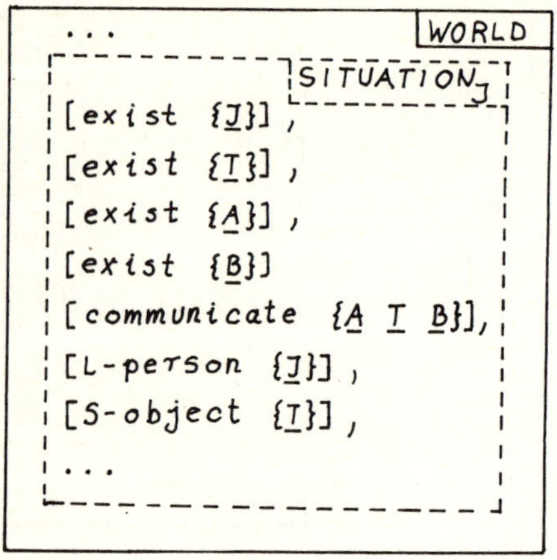

```
                              ┌─────────┐
      ┌ · · · ───────────────│  WORLD  │
      │ ┌ ─ ─ ─ ─ ─ ─ ┌──────┴─────┐ ─ ┐│
      │ │[exist {J}], │ SITUATION_J│   │
      │ │[exist {T}], └────────────┘   │
      │ │[exist {A}],                  │
      │ │[exist {B}]                   │
      │ │[communicate {A T B}],        │
      │ │[L-person {J}],               │
      │ │[S-object {T}],               │
      │ │...                           │
      │ └ ─ ─ ─ ─ ─ ─ ─ ─ ─ ─ ─ ─ ─ ─ ┘│
      └───────────────────────────────┘
```

Figure 2

Among these states of affairs we can include, among other things, the states of affairs that J, T, A und B exist. J, T as well as A and B (if they exist) are objects in the world, whereas J, T, A and B are to be regarded as their respective pictures in the situation of J, as objects as seen by the interpreter. Furthermore, the state of affairs that A communicates T to B is in the situation of J as well as the states of affairs that J is linguistically capable and that T is usable as a sign-manifestation. The graphic representation of J's situation in figure 2 does *not* entail that this complex of states of affairs is a part or a section of the world. Instead, identity of geometrical form (square) together with a broken borderline should be seen as symbolizing the image-relation between the world and the interpreter's situation which will not be explicated in this paper.

J's interpreting T as sign can now be expounded within the framework so far developed by analyzing the relation between T i.e. the text *as it is perceived by the interpreter* and his situation, i.e. the world *as seen by him*. The plan however to give an explicative analysis of this kind involves at least two difficulties.

1. It must be assumed that the situation of J - as this concept has been explained here - contains more states of affairs than are of interest for J's interpretation. What counts seems to be only a portion of this probably very comprehensive complex of states affairs - a portion for which one wants to say that it is activated by the perception of T within J as the interpretation of $\underline{T}$. Let us use the term "text correlate" to refer to this portion.

2. Neither $\underline{T}$ (the text as perceived by J) nor the text correlate (the portion of J's situation just introduced) are immediate parts of the world. One might call them "intensional entities", thus alluding to the terminology of some logicians. Consequently, they are not really given and cannot be described directly by theorists interested in the sign-character of texts.

We can try, however, to develop representations which constitute objects of the world and with which one can operate as within the frame of the theory.

The most important representations we deal with in TeSWeST are:
- the representation of $\underline{T}$ ($\underline{T}$R)
- the representation of the transformed text ($\underline{T}$TrR)
- the canonical text ($\underline{\tilde{T}}°$)
- the representation of the text-world ($\underline{T}$wR)
- the sequence of model-representations (<...mR...>)
- the representation of the text-correlate ($\underline{T}$cR)

(It should be noted that representations of this kind are objects usable as sign-manifestations just as T which was our starting point here. It should likewise be possible to submit these representations to text-theoretical analysis as outlined in this paper.)

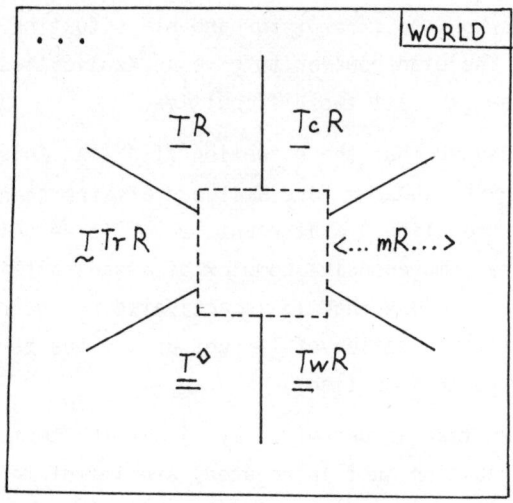

Figure 3

Figure 3 is a diagram of the global structure of TeSWeST. Within this diagram it's main components are gathered around the square in the center, which is meant to symbolize the interpreter's situation.

In the rest of this paragraph we try to give some explications concerning the different representations.

Let us assume, for example, that T is a written sentence-token of a natural language. In this case we would consider the tape-recording of an utterance of this sentence (which, among other things, specifies the intonation) as an approximation of $\underline{T}$, if it is produced by J himself. By using a representational language based e.g. on a phonetic alphabet and a means of representing intonation patterns, we should be able to provide an optimal representation of $\underline{T}$ with a minimal loss of information. We are using "$\underline{T}R$" to stand for the "representation of $\underline{T}$". The representation of the corresponding text correlate (the correlate of $\underline{T}$) cannot be developed by an equally direct procedure. Before this can be done in the theory, we must face the task of establishing a complex of description of states of affairs, assignable to $\underline{T}R$ in such a way that the interpreter's choosing a portion of his situation as a correlate can be analysed in relation to the properties of TR. At this point we are confronted with the problem that representations of type TR must as a rule remain underdetermined with respect to information indispensible for assigning correlates. Consider phenomena such as vagueness or ambiguous lexical units and syntactic constructions. In addition there is frequently a lack of specificity with respect to local and temporal information.

We also find that text utterances are usually underdetermined with respect to the modal embedding of the states of affairs exhibited, i.e. it is unspecified whether they are to be taken as the content of the speaker's beliefs, expectation, guess or knowledge etc. Or consider the margin for interpretation left by utterances with respect to their illocutionary roles.

Let us consider as an illustrative example an utterance such as

(i) It's going to rain tonight.

To understand (i) as an utterance, i.e. to relate it to the world as he sees it, the interpreter has to make some assumptions. What place is being talked about here? What period of time does the vague description "tonight" refer to? What exactly is meant by "rain"? Furthermore, the following question has to be clarified: Does the speaker of an utterance such as (i) regard the state of affairs that it is raining at a specific place during a specific period of time to be within the scope of his knowledge, his conviction, his wishes, his simple expectation or some other attitude. An finally: Who is the addressee of the utterance? Does the speaker merely transmit some neutral information, does he make a statement, does he give a warning? It may be the case that we find some more or less explicit indicators in TR, especially if we look for the marking of particular intonation, and thus make explicit some necessary information. In principle, however, we have to take into account that TR remains unspecific at least with respect to some of the dimensions referred to above. Consequently, we introduce a further representation within the framework of TeSWeST, which results from several transformations and supplementations of $\underline{TR}$ and which is maximally determined in the sense that it contains explicit information that reduces unspecificity in every dimension stated above. This representation is called "representation of the transformed text ($\underline{\tilde{T}TrR}$)". Because of the unspecificity of $\underline{TR}$-s, different $\underline{\tilde{T}TrR}$-s correspond to one and the same $\underline{TR}$, each of which can be considered as one way of rendering it precise.

A representation of type $\underline{\tilde{T}TrR}$ can now immediately be transformed into a representation of a canonical text-grammatical language which functions independently of any particular natural language and within which we can construe representations, without a fixed linear order, for atomic texts ($\underline{T}$) and texts ($\underline{T}^{\circ}$) which are complexes of atomic texts linked to each other by connectives.

The canonic language operates with canonic lexical units which are either primitive in the frame of this language or which are introduced by definition and which bear the relation of explicans to explicandum to the lexical units of the language of $\underline{TR}$-s. $\underline{\tilde{T}TrR}$-s mediate between the non-linear representations $\underline{T}^{\circ}$ of the canonical language and the linear representations $\underline{TR}$ of the phonetic representation language. They provide a linear order for the atomic texts from $\underline{T}^{\circ}$ and can be constructed with canonic units as well as lexical units which are taken from particular natural languages. (The tilde-mark below the first "T" of "$\underline{\tilde{T}TrR}$" is meant to symbolize this position between the two representation languages.) We do not intend to discuss any further details of the relation between $\underline{TR}$ and $\underline{T}^{\circ}$ in this paper.

We said above that one has to first map $\underline{TR}$ onto some complex of descriptions of states of affairs in order to be able to see how the determination of a portion (as text correlate) of J's situation works. By correlating $\underline{TR}$ with $\underline{T}^{\circ}$ we have come closer to this aim, because atomic (canonical) texts consist of hierarchies of embedded descriptions of states of affairs. The hierarchic structure results from the explicit determination of modal units (indicating propositional attitudes) and performative units (determining illocutionary roles), such

A TEXT-THEORETICAL FRAMEWORK

as we have considered briefly above.

The TR of an utterance such as (i) may be correlated e.g. with an atomic text in the canonical language which - in a grossly simplified notation - looks like this:

(ii) A communicates to B at time t_1 and at place l_1 that
A expects at time t_2 and at place l_2 that
it is raining at time t_3 and at place l_3.

(Among the simplifications of this notion we note that A and B remain unspecified and that there is no information about the relation among t_1, t_2 and t_3 on the one side and l_1, l_2 and l_3 on the other side.)

What is important for us here is simply the fact that a TR for an utterance such as (i) is mapped by means of a well-formed canonical text-representation onto three states of affairs which correspond to the three lines of (ii).

(iii) [a]: A communicates something to B at t_1 and l_1
[b]: A expects something (to be the case) at t_2 and l_2
[c]: it is raining at t_3 and l_3

If we want to construct text interpretations at this level of analysis as comparisons between descriptions of states of affairs as given in I^o-s and such states of affairs which belong to the situation of J, we face the difficulty that states of affairs such as [a], [b] and [c] do not obtain independently of each other according to a canonic text such as (ii). They are interrelated instead, because the 'something' referred to in [b] is [c], and [b] is the 'something' referred to in [a].

Let us therefore look at some states of affairs which are in fact independent of each other and which are related to [a], [b] and [c] in the following informal way:

(iv) $[s_1]$ = [a [b [c]]]
$[s_2]$ [b [c]]
$[s_3]$ [c]

Now it becomes clear that the atomic text illustrated by (ii) does not yet determine a specific complex of states of affairs, because it can be regarded as a description of any of the following complexes:

$$p \begin{array}{cccc} (a) & (b) & (c) & (d) \\ [s_1] & [s_1] & [s_1] & [s_1] \\ [s_2] & \neg[s_2] & \neg[s_2] & [s_2] \\ [s_3] & \neg[s_3] & [s_3] & \neg[s_3] \end{array}$$

Figure 4

The notation "$\neg[s_i]$ is supposed to indicate that the state of affairs $[s_i]$ does not belong to the complex. A representation of a complex of states of affairs (as indicated here by each of the combinations (v) (a)-(d)) clears up the opacity caused by the hierarchic structure of embedding canonical representations. It is referred to here as a "text-world representation ($\underline{T}$wR)". This text-world representation provides a picture of the world and shows which complex of states of affairs is exhibited by $\underline{T}$ according to the interpreter or, in other words: it explicates what the interpreter assumes to be the content of utterance $\underline{T}$. As the representation language for $\underline{T}$wR (as well as for $\underline{T}^o$) the canonical language of text grammar may be used. (In this paper we ignore the specific problems connected with the relativization of complexes of states of affairs to individuals or to groups as well as aspects of the treatment of complexes of states of affairs as fictive, which must likewise be dealt with in connection with the construction of $\underline{T}$wR-s.)

The interpretation of text T by the interpreter J can now be represented as a comparison between relevant states of affairs in the situation of J and that complex of states of affairs which has been correlated with $\underline{T}$ by $\underline{T}$wR. In effect, the interpreter examines the relation between the states of affairs given by $\underline{T}$wR and certain states of affairs which belong to his situation. In order to carry out such a comparison within text-theory, it is necessary first to give a representation of the relevant portions of J's situation. Such representations can function as models on the basis of which the complex of states of affairs given by $\underline{T}$wR will be examined.

Let us assume that the interpreter of our illustrative example would accept some $\underline{T}$wR like (v) (d). This means that he assumes that there are $[s_1]$ and $[s_2]$ among the states of affairs that belong to the complex which provides a picture of the world which is - according to $\underline{I}^\circ$ - valid for $\underline{A}$, but that $[s_3]$ is not among these states of affairs.

The interpreters' model, however, may conform to (v) (a). This means that according to the interpreter's own picture of the world in addition to $[s_1]$ and $[s_2]$, $[s_3]$ also obtains, perhaps because he has some definite information from some source independent of $\underline{T}$, that it is raining at place l_3 during the period t_3. Furthermore, the model should contain assumptions about the compatibility of the complex state of affairs $[[s_1]$ AND $[s_2]]$ with the possibility that $[s_3]$ does not obtain.

The representation of models of this kind is a sequence of so-called model-representations <...mR...>, which can be stated (like $\underline{T}$wR and $\underline{I}^\circ$) by means of the canonical language.

As a rule, constructing *sequences* of model-representation is necessary because (in contrast to our simplified example) we have to take into account not only states of affairs which are the content of J's own convictions, but also those complexes of states of affairs which are assigned by J in his situation to $\underline{A}$ (the assumed speaker), to $\underline{B}$ (the assumed hearer), and to potential actors referred to in $\underline{T}$ as assumptions made by $\underline{A}$, $\underline{B}$ and/or these potential actors. The evaluation of $\underline{T}$wR on the basis of <...mR...> is performed as a text-theoretical operation and leads eventually to a representation of the complex of states of affairs we referred to above as J's interpretation of $\underline{T}$ or the text correlate.

This final representation is called "representation of the text-correlate".

As for our illustrative example the $\underline{T}$wR we chose would be evaluated as true on the basis of the given model.

3. *The pragmatic dimension of the TeSWeST*

We said above that texts are (among other things) objects that can be understood as signs. They are understood as signs only if an interpreter recognizes certain (semiotic) relations between them and the world. Insofar as the interpreter does not look at the text in isolation from other objects of the world, but sees the text in connection with its environment in the world, his interpretation is pragmatically determined. In principle every section of the world containing T as one of its parts may be an environment of text T. Let us subdivide such a text environment into three parts: first, the context of the production of T, secondly the context of the reception of T, and thirdly, the context of the interpretation of T. As the three different contexts of any sign-object T can be identified with sections of the world which are temporally far apart, they may differ from one another considerably. On the other hand, it is possible - as mentioned above - that the interpreter J is identical with the producer A or with the recipient B (or A is identical with B). Consequently, these three contexts may be collapsed pairwise.

We can now ask the question: Where is the border of contexts? It seems to be difficult to find an answer to this question because this would amount to defining what kind of relations sign-objects have to those parts of the world which belong to their contexts. It seems to be difficult, if not impossible, to provide any convincing restrictions here. Probably, however, such a demarcation is not of much interest, because for the reconstruction of a text interpretation the only important question seems to be what *the interpreter* is likely to include in the text environment, i.e. how the contexts of T are constituted as (sub-) complexes of states of affairs in the interpreter's situation. His situation includes a picture of the text-environment consisting of certain assumptions decisive in setting up the interpretation.

Let us now mark in our general diagram those components of the theory for which the construction of various representations is influenced by assumptions about the environment of T.

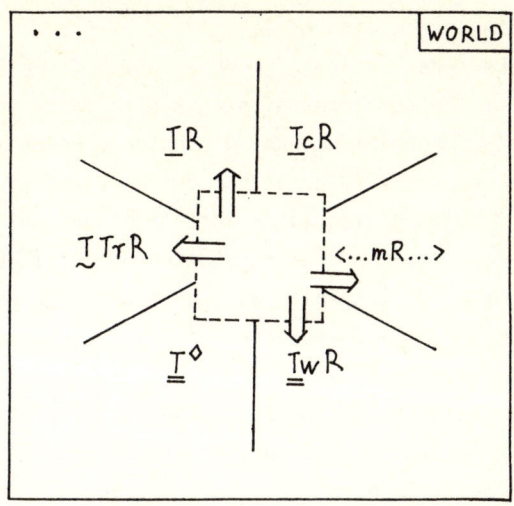

Figure 5

First, the representation of $\underline{T}$ (as the result of some perception of J) is dependent on what J considers to be the context of interpretation. In particular, as far as the assignment of intonation patterns to written text-tokens is concerned, the creation of $\underline{T}$ is closely connected with how the interpreter views his context.

Secondly: if - as outlined above - $\underline{T}R$ is transformed into $\underline{T}TrR$ by explicit marking, e.g. performative, temporal and local information, we have to take into account, among other things, both assumptions about the context of production and the context of reception. Transformational processes of this kind must be considered in close relationship with the theory of speech acts as well as with the theory of indexicality, which form at present the supporting pillars of pragmatic research.

Thirdly: whereas there is no reference to the interpreter's concept of the text-environment in the construction of $\underline{T}^{\circ}$ (it is produced as a notational variant of $\underline{T}TrR$ in the canonical language), the choice among possible $\underline{T}wR$-s is influenced by the interpreter's assumptions, especially those which concern the convictions of the producer within the context of the production of T.

Finally, the construction of models, which form the background of the evaluation of the complexes of states of affairs represented by $\underline{I}$wR-s is strongly dependent on what J considers to be the text environment - and this means, it is dependent on that complex of states of affairs which (in view of the interpreter's situation) is the context of production, reception and interpretation of $\underline{T}$. In contrast with the construction of models, $\underline{T}$cR which is the result of certain operations in $\underline{I}$wR and <...mR...>, is constructed without reference to J's situation.

As we have attempted to suggest, TeSWeST tries to provide a reconstruction of text interpretation by establishing several interrelated representations. We have just commented briefly on four points where the relations among representations are decisively mediated by a complex of states of affairs which varies considerably with different J-s and T-s. At this point we may consider how relations of this kind can be dealt with explicitly within the theory itself. Is it possible to formulate algorithmic rules for the construction of representations with reference both to other representations *and* to the interpreter's situation? Can we formalize the pragmatic dimension of the theory? The first idea which comes to mind in this connection seems to be to replace the center of our diagram (the interpreter's situation) by a representation and then to develop the whole algorithm of construction on the level of the manipulation of symbols. Certainly this proposal is impractical because, in principle, everyone of J's assumptions may be relevant for text interpretation; the proposal presupposes that the whole system of J's assumptions during the period of interpretation must be represented - which seems to be a rather unpromising enterprise, even if we consider interpreters with severely restricted competence.

Finally, let us consider instead three other possibilities which we want to refer to as pragmatic strategies of text interpretation.

Strategy 1: Let us suppose we have a text-theoretical apparatus at our disposal which contains systems of rules for the different representation languages to be taken into account and specifies conditions of well-formedness for the different types of representations. Furthermore, the apparatus contains a system of lexica which determine the relations among the lexical units of particular natural languages on one side and units of the universal canonical language on the other. Such a system of lexica might be set up, for example, as the representation of some complex of stereotypical world-knowledge, as a collection of that information which is 'usually' used by an interpreter in understanding utterances in 'normal situations'. (Another possibility might be to incorporate not only stereotypical but also different variants of specialized world-knowledge into the lexica.) A combinatorial algorithm can be defined on such an apparatus as a rule-system for the construction of the different representations of the theory. Thus the concrete person J and his situation would be replaced in a sense by a stipulated potential of interpretation accomodated to a certain standard of linguistic convention which is postulated as universal and also accomodated to an array of encyclopedic knowledge which remains more or less variable. For any given $\underline{T}R$ every $\underline{T}TrR$ constructable in a combinatorially admissible way, could be translated into a $\underline{I}^{\circ}$ which, in turn, should be supplemented by any of the combinatorially possible $\underline{I}wR$-s. The model representations are also to be constructed solely according to a criterion of combinatorial admissibility provided by the apparatus; and every pair of a sequence of admissible model representations with an admissible $\underline{I}wR$ would define at most admissible $\underline{T}cR$. Objections to the first strategy are obvious: it is impossible to manage the proposed combinatorial explosion in practice. In particular, if we provide for all of the combinatorially possible model representations, the construction of an interpretation cannot parctically be terminated. On the other hand, such a combinatorics is still even too limited. It is restricted to interpretations which make use of only that information derived from the array of language-dependent and encyclopedic knowledge provided by the apparatus. Consequently, according to this strategy, we can deal in a combinatorial way with characteristics of text environments, which are located in a level of extreme generality, but the more specific traits of concrete text-environments and interpreters cannot be dealt with here.

Strategy 2: In order to take these specific traits of concrete text-environments into account, we might think of a procedure which would in some respects restrict the rigid combinatorics but would make it more flexible in other respects. For if we look at some concrete text environments, many of the possibilities which are admissible according to the apparatus can be excluded immediately and other possibilities of interpretation which are even combinatorially inadmissible become probable after all. (Consider, for example, the variety of possibilities for the realization of speech acts in concrete situations which probably cannot be dealt with in a combinatorial way.) Our second proposal leads to some kind of interaction between interpreter and apparatus, whereby the interpreter has the right to restrict as well as to extend the combinatorial frame, delimited by the apparatus in constructing each of the four representations marked by arrows in figure 5. In restricting or extending he may use any context-relevant information given his situation.

In accordance with this strategy we dispense with a complete formalization of the theory. We gain the advantage of being able to reconstruct the flexible way in which interpreters make use of conventional and stereotypical knowledge (as provided by the apparatus). It may be questioned, however, whether this conception does not prematurely preclude to our formal treatment certain areas in the field of text interpretation.

Strategy 3 proposes, therefore, some form of division of labour between strategies 1 and 2. Wherever possible the theory operates with representations which are algorithmically constructable on the basis of a combinatorial apparatus. First of all we think here of those parts of the theory which are primarily concerned with text structure (indicated by "TeS" in figure 6).

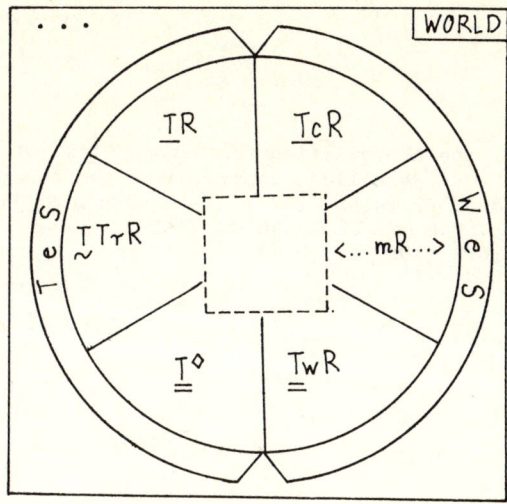

Figure 6

But wherever it appears to be inevitable, representations are constructed through interaction between an interpreter and the apparatus. Take, for example, the construction of model-representations which form the center of that part of the theory primarily concerned with world-structure (cf. "WeS" in figure 6).

FOOTNOTE:

1. "TeSWeST" is the abbreviation for German "Text-Struktur Welt-Struktur-Theorie". A detailled exposition of the theory can be found in: C. Biasci and J. Fritsche (1978), (see also J.S. Petöfi (1979)), H.J. Eikmeyer, W. Heydrich, J.S. Petöfi (1980), and K. Dorfmüller-Karpusa, J.S. Petöfi (1981).

PRAGMATICAL GRAMMAR AND THE PRAGMATICS OF GRAMMAR

Götz Hindelang

I want to explore the possibilities of a pragmatic approach to *grammar* and to the *theory of grammar*. Whereas the need for a pragmatically motivated grammatical description of a language has been felt by many linguists, it may sound strange - even to a true follower of pragmatics - that the theory of grammar could be part of pragmatics. I therefore want to begin with some general remarks about a pragmatical theory of grammar or, as I rather want to put it, about the *pragmatics of grammar*.

The main idea behind the concept of pragmatics of grammar is that writing a grammar is a language game. It is, of course, a much more complex language game than the examples mentioned by Wittgenstein in his "Philosophical Investigations" or the everyday language games we play when we order in a restaurant, when we welcome friends or when we fill in forms, but it can be compared with the language games of writing a poem or writing a letter. A pragmatical theory of grammar will have to formulate the rules that constitute the language game of 'writing a grammar' and to specify which moves are obligatory, allowed and forbidden within certain subtypes of the game, such as traditional grammar, structuralist grammar, transformational grammar, grammars for second language learning, to name just a few members of the family of grammatical language games.

In order to find out the rules of the language game 'writing a grammar' it is useful to ask: "What kind of linguistic actions do linguists perform, when they write grammars?". Doing grammatical analysis is a complex action that can be divided into two stages. In the first stage, which I will call the *methodological stage*, the grammarian plays little language games with informants or, if the rules of his game allow it, with himself. In this period he collects data and applies his discovery procedures. In the second phase, which might be called the *textual stage* he will sit down and write a text, in which he formulates his results. This text, whether it is a ten-page paper or a grammatical handbook, will have certain textual and pragmatical structures. It is important to realize that both stages consist of linguistic actions. A pragmatical theory of grammar will describe these linguistic actions in terms of speech acts and language games.

In recent linguistic research it has become a must to state the rules for the language games played in the methodological stage. It is therefore not difficult to find descriptions of language games which linguists play in the first phase. Let's look, for example, at the language game Chomsky recommends in "Syntactic Structures" to find out whether 'metal' and 'medal' are phonemically distinct in a certain English dialect. Chomsky (1957:96) suggests the following procedure:

> A careful field worker would probably use the pair test, either with two informants or with an informant and a tape recorder. For example, he might make a random sequence of copies of the utterance tokens that interest him, and then determine whether or not the speaker can consistently identify them. If there is consistent identification, the linguist may apply an even stricter test, asking the speaker to repeat each word several times, and running the pair test over again on the repetitions. If consistent distinguishability is maintained under repetition, he will say that the words 'metal' and 'medal' are phonemically distinct.

A detailed description of the language game that Chomsky sketched in the above paragraph would have to specify all linguistic and non-linguistic actions which the careful fieldworker has to carry out. Chomsky gives the above example in order to justify one of the rules of his grammatical game. He wants to exclude all linguistic actions from the methodological stage that contain reference to meaning. In other words, Chomsky does not allow his fieldworker moves like 'asking what X means' or 'asking if there is a difference in meaning between X and Y'.

Now let's look at the second stage when the linguist sits at home and writes his paper. What kind of linguistic actions will he perform there? He will do things such as

(1) announcing the topic of a paragraph
(2) give a summary of what has been said so far
(3) quote other scholars
(4) introduce and define new symbols and abbreviations
(5) give example sentences
(6) judge some sentences ungrammatical
(7) develop a linguistic argument
(8) recommend the use of a certain linguistic form
(9) advise the reader not to use certain constructions because they count as bad style
(10) compare linguistic units of a language A to corresponding units in language B

This catalogue is, of course, heterogeneous and by no means complete. Some linguistic actions like (1) and (2) occur in many written language games, others, like (3) and (4) are characteristic of scholarly prose. Only linguistic actions like (6)-(10) are typical for linguistic texts. Some of the linguistic actions that occur in the textual stage depend upon the rules of the methodological stage. A purely descriptive grammar will, for example, not contain moves like (8) or (9), which occur in normative grammars only.

Little work has been done yet to describe the language game of presenting a grammatical analysis. As one important exception, the linguistic action 'developing a linguistic argument' has been studied by Rudolf Botha. His books and articles on this topic (Botha 1970, 1973, 1976) contain a very detailed description of the way transformational linguists present their views. But, as Botha (1976:3) points out, the reconstruction of linguistic argumentation as he conceives it "is not a sort of linguistic analysis. It is essentially a sort of philosophical analysis". The study of the pragmatics of grammar aims, however, directly at the description of the linguistic acts performed by linguists when they do their job. We will return to this problem in the last part of the paper where I will try to analyse some examples taken from linguistic texts. But I first want to discuss the second topic announced in the title of this paper and give a sketch of a *pragmatical grammar*.

If we adopt the framework developed in the first part of this paper one may pose the question as follows: "How can the language game of writing a grammar be played pragmatically?". It will be useful, to distinguish *strongly* and *weakly* pragmatical grammars. A grammar is weakly pragmatical if the methodological rules allow reference to information about the context of the utterance, the speaker and his intentions, the relation between speaker and hearer and other pragmatic conditions. Some examples of weakly pragmatical grammars are traditional grammars, transformational grammars that make use of performative hypersentences and approaches that use pragmatical arguments when syntactic or semantic considerations fail to give a satisfactory explanation. A grammar can be called strongly pragmatical if pragmatics is the central component of the grammar. In a strongly pragmatical grammar syntactic, semantic and morphological descriptions are built around pragmatical concepts. To say that a grammar is strongly pragmatical is to make certain claims about the rules of the methodological stage. Now, what are the principles we have to follow if we want to write a strongly pragmatical grammar? I would recommend the following rules:
- Start out with the analysis of speech acts. Speech acts are the pragmatical units of language.
- Make up a speech act taxonomy. (If you don't want to do that, take the classification suggested by Searle (1976).)
- Find and define the relevant subtypes of the basic speech act groups.

- When the subtypes are defined, study the linguistic forms that count as the performance of those subtypes.
- Organize the linguistic forms according to semantic, syntactic and morphological principles.

Although I fear that there is not enough space to explain this program in full detail,[1] I will try to illustrate it by giving an example.

Let's take the easy way and start with one of the speech act classes proposed by Searle (1976), for example with the group he called *directives*. We must now define the relevant subtypes of this class in terms of situational and communicative conditions.

The lines we draw to distinguish the different subtypes must not necessarily coincide with the clusters of situational conditions lumped together in the semantics of speech act verbs. So if we have, for example, subclasses that are labeled with terms like ORDER, COMMAND, REQUEST, ADVICE, SUGGESTION, RECOMMENDATION, DEMAND, INSTRUCTION, BEGGING, ASKING and so on, it would be wrong to identify these names directly with the semantics of the corresponding speech act verb. The vernacular verbs are just convenient names which might also be substituted by an awkward terminology based on Latin or Greek words.

One of the relevant subtypes of DIRECTIVES might be characterized as follows:

> The speaker S_1 and the speaker S_2 are both confronted with a practical problem T. S_1 and S_2 have decided to cooperate on the solution of the problem. S_1 and S_2 are equal in status and are both equally interested in the solution of the problem. If S_1 utters a directive speech act under such circumstances it will be called a SUGGESTION, if S_1 thinks the suggested action will contribute to the solution of the practical problem T.

It is easy to see that only a few aspects of the verb 'suggest' are captured by the label SUGGESTION. We do not cover examples like (11) or (12) (quoted from Lee 1976) or the use of 'suggestion' described by Wellman (1961:233) in (13).

(11) It suggested a fine Italian hand to me. (Lee 1976:110)
(12) I suggest that Cora did it. (Lee 1976:111)

(13) "In suggesting, it is assumed that the agent would welcome some suggestion because he is bored or undecided and that a verbal cue will set him off."

We will now ask: "How can SUGGESTIONS in the sense defined above be expressed?" or "What semantic and syntactic options do we have in English if we want to make a SUGGESTION?. First, we have the possibility of expressing SUGGESTIONS performatively or by means of 'let's ...' like in (14) and (15).[2]

(14) I suggest (that) we do X.
(15) Let's do X.

But there are other ways to formulate SUGGESTIONS. We can do things like (16a)-(16j)

(16) a. saying that it is desirable to do X
      b. asking if it is not desirable to do X
      c. asking why X-ing is not desirable
      d. saying that it is possible to do X
      e. asking if it is not possible to do X
      f. saying that it is necessary to do X
      g. asking if it is not necessary to do X
      h. saying that T will be solved by doing X
      j. saying that S_1 and S_2 will do X

Expressions like (16a)-(16j) might be called 'semantic patterns'. They are a kind of semantic generalization over a number of linguistic forms. We can now say that a communicative pattern like SUGGESTION can be performed by various semantic patterns like (16a)-(16j) and that semantic patterns can be realized by various grammatical patterns; and this is where the formal aspect of language comes in. In order to illustrate this concept I will first give one example for each semantic pattern under (16) and then present a variety of examples for one selected pattern.

Let's imagine Jack and Jill coming home from a party. When they want to go in, they realize that neither of them has a key. That's the practical problem T. This situation fits into the general frame sketched above. Now, what can Jack say, if he wants to suggest breaking a window in order to get in? If he wants to use a linguistic form that conventionally counts as the performance of a SUGGESTION he can utter sentences like (17), (18) or he can use sentences like (19a)-(19j) which correspond to the semantic patterns (16a)-(16j).

(17) Let's break a window!
(18) I (would) suggest (that) we break a window.
(19) a. I think the best thing (to do) is to break a window.
   b. Wouldn't it be a good idea to break a window?
   c. Why don't we just break a window?
   d. We could break a window.
   e. Couldn't we just break a window?
   f. I think we (will) have to break a window.
   g. Isn't it inevitable to break a window?
   h. If we break a window, we can climb in.
   j. We will simply break a window.

If we now look at a semantic pattern more closely we will see that there are many different ways to express that pattern. Let's take (16b) for example. There are many lexical and grammatical options open to the speaker who wants to make a SUGGESTION of that type. He can say:

(20)
a. Wouldn't it be
b. Isn't it
c. Don't you think (that) it is
} a good idea to break a window?

Instead of 'think' one could use 'believe' or 'agree'. Realize that in this special context these lexical items are roughly synonymous; the same is true for expressions such as 'good idea', 'the best thing', 'the only solution' which are only synonymous as parts of realizations of SUGGESTIONS. In (20c) the speaker can choose between indicative and subjunctive: 'Don't you think it is a good idea?' vs. 'Don't you think it {could, would, might} be a good idea?' He can also use different ways of formulating the suggested action. He may say:

Don't you think it is a good idea ...

(21) ... for $\begin{Bmatrix} a.\ me \\ b.\ us \end{Bmatrix}$ to break a window?

(22) ... that $\begin{Bmatrix} a.\ I \\ b.\ you \\ c.\ we \end{Bmatrix}$ should break a window?

(23) ... if $\begin{Bmatrix} a.\ I \\ b.\ you \\ c.\ we \end{Bmatrix}$ break a window?

(24) ... if $\begin{Bmatrix} a.\ I \\ b.\ you \\ c.\ we \end{Bmatrix}$ should break a window?

The different grammatical options can be represented in tree-like figures. It's there that the grammatical description in the traditional sense starts. For (21)-(24) we might get a representation like (25).

(25)

```
       ┌── infinitive constr. ─────┬── 1. pers. sing. ── (21a)
       │                           └── 1. pers. pl.   ── (21b)
       │          ┌─ 'that'- subj. ──┬── 1. pers. sing. ── (22a)
       │          │                  ├── 2. pers. sing. ── (22b)
       │          │                  └── 1. pers. pl.   ── (22c)
   ────┤          │
       └── clause │              ┌─ind. ──┬── 1. pers. sing. ── (23a)
                  │              │        ├── 2. pers. sing. ── (23b)
                  │              │        └── 1. pers. pl.   ── (23c)
                  └─'if'─────────┤
                                 └─subj. ──┬── 1. pers. sing. ── (24a)
                                           ├── 2. pers. sing. ── (24b)
                                           └── 1. pers. pl.   ── (24c)
```

This diagram may demonstrate what I meant when I said that syntactic and morphological information is built around pragmatic units. In that approach, the focus is not on the semantic and pragmatic functions of certain grammatical patterns, but on the different grammatical patterns that are conventionally used to express a certain speech act. From this position it will be possible to develop both a linguistically oriented speech act theory and a pragmatically based grammatical description.

In this last section of the paper I will, as promised, return to

the problem of the pragmatics of grammar and discuss examples taken
from two linguistic texts. These texts are Marina Burt's "From Deep
to Surface Structure" and the German DUDEN-Grammatik. Burt (1971) has
been chosen as an example because in this book the rules on the textual
level are relatively simple. The quotations from DUDEN-Grammatik have
been selected to show that it is important to take into account the intentions and needs of the user of a grammar in order to explain the
speech acts in the grammatical text. Burt's book consists mainly of
questions, answers and phrase-markers. There are some other ingredients
too, but the basic form of her text can be illustrated by the following
quotation:

> Q. What S will this structure give us?
> A. After *Affix Hopping* this will give us the unacceptable
>   *There is a devil among us, isn't he?*
> Q. How can this derivation be avoided?
> A. By applying the rules in the reverse order [...] (Burt
>   1971: 24)

The language game that Burt plays in her text is modeled after the everyday language game of oral instruction. It also contains speech
acts like commands (25), definitions (26), announcing (27) and recapitulating a certain topic (28), but the basic rule that underlies her
text could be formulated as follows: "Use only questions-answer sequences in your text!".

> (26) Compare now the phrase structure rules [...] (Burt 1971: 35).
> (27) A simplex sentence is a sentence which does not have another
>   sentence embedded in it [...] (Burt 1971: 138).
> (28) We will now consider a sentence in which the order is [...]
>   (Burt 1971: 138).
> (29) Thus far, we have been considering only simplex sentences
>   (Burt 1971: 67).

We will now look at some examples from the German DUDEN-Grammatik.
The quotations show that the language game that the author of this

grammatical text plays is completely different from the games played by structuralist and transformational grammarians. The writer presupposes a reader who is uncertain about the use of a certain word, phrase or construction and wants to consult a grammar in order to find out what is correct or incorrect, good or bad German. So the language game that is played is comparable to the everyday language games of counseling, advising and recommendation. The writer takes the part of an expert who can tell the layman what is right and wrong because he has more experience and knowledge about the subject. Here are some speech acts that belong to that counseling language game:

(30) Die Trennung vom Bezugswort ist dann möglich und stilistisch zu empfehlen, wenn der Relativsatz Satzteile trennt, die eng zusammengehören. (DUDEN 569)

(31) Der relativische Anschluß an das letzte von mehreren Substantiven mit *welch letzterer* usw. ist sprachlich unschön. (DUDEN 569)

(32) Diese Einleitungswörter (welcher, welche, welches) wirken immer etwas schwerfällig [...].
Gut: Die Lerche, *die* im Äther singt.
schwerfällig: Die Lerche, *welche* im Äther singt. (DUDEN 570)

(33) Im Kaufmannsstil wird das Subjekt gelegentlich ausgelassen, [...].
Dies ist jedoch eine Unsitte. (DUDEN 586)

The writer gives a stylistic recommendation ('stilistisch zu empfehlen') in (30), criticizes the use of a construction as unpleasing ('unschön') in (31), judges constructions as 'good' or 'awkward' in (32) and censures the use of a construction as a 'bad habit' in (33). In order to develop an analysis of the pragmatics of grammar we must not only analyse the language games that linguists play in the methodological and textual phase, we also have to take into account how the grammar will be used by the reader. We have to ask: "How and when do people use grammars?", "What is the role grammatical texts play in everyday life?"

and "What kind of linguistic or grammatical texts could be useful for which group of readers?".

FOOTNOTES:

1. For an application of the program see Hindelang (1978).

2. Note that there are also expressions with "How about ...." and "What about ...." like in (i).

(i) $\begin{Bmatrix} \text{How} \\ \text{What} \end{Bmatrix}$ about playing a game of pinball?

Such forms are, however, mainly used in suggestions of the type defined in (13).

ON INSISTING

Franz Hundsnurscher

1. *Speech act theory: a theory of singular speech acts*

A great deal of work in traditional speech act theory has been devoted to the main question: What do people do when they talk? If it is reasonable to say that when people talk they perform certain speech acts, it is certainly important to find out what types of speech acts there are and what a description of speech act might be like. This means drawing up taxonomies of speech act types, establishing criteria for distinguishing them, analysing the conditions and formulating the rules for the felicitous performance of the various speech acts.

There are a number of heuristic and methodological reasons why speech acts should be analysed and described in isolation, and nothing can be said against that as long as it is kept in mind that the isolation of speech acts is a matter of method, not of fact. There is a parallel situation in syntax where isolated sentences form the units of linguistic description whereas sentences in use are normally found to be incorporated in texts.

Speech acts are, of course, incorporated in discourse, and we communicate in performing speech acts that are linked to other speech acts in systematic ways. If as linguists we want to find out how language works and if we do this in a pragmatic perspective, we are bound to investigate the structure of speech act sequences as incorporated in discourse. The question to answer is in fact: What do people do when they talk *to each other*? The complaints of conversational analysts against speech act theory in its present form may have their justifications in this point. The complaints are neither new nor exciting, but they become an interesting issue when we look for their theoretical and practical implications. Being restricted to the analysis of speech acts in isolation, as present-day speech act theory on the whole is, its findings and their applicability to the analysis of authentic discourse are also limited in several important respects. The setting out of rules for the successful performance of an illocutionary act gives us a lot of valuable insight, especially into the relation between utterance form and the illocutionary act performed, which is determined by the semantic conventions of a language. But all this leaves us wondering whether that is really all there is to what we do when we talk to each other. Should we really be content with insight into the illocutionary mechanism of singular speech acts only? In standard speech act theory a distinction is made between the speech act viewed under the aspect of its illocutionary force - the illocutionary act - and the speech act viewed under the aspect of its perlocutionary effect - the perlocutionary act. Examples given for perlocutionary effects are mainly of this type: being persuaded, being convinced, being frightened, feeling annoyed, feeling pleased and so on. The perlocutionary effect of a speech act is obviously considered to be a kind of mental reaction in the hearer.[1] There may be some point in the observation that the perlocutionary effect of an illocutionary act like REQUESTING consists in the hearer's being prepared to do what he is told to do, or of an illocutionary act like REPROACHING in the hearer's feeling ashamed about what he has done. Although there may be speech acts that aim prominently at such types of perlocutionary effects, e.g. insults or laments, this description in general falls short of capturing the full range of what the speaker tries to bring about by the performance of his speech acts.

2. *Making one's illocutionary point: a harmonious model*

In the case of REQUESTING the illocutionary point may well be "to get the hearer to do something",[2] and the hearer may well have realized the illocution, but as long as he does not perform the action predicated of him, the speaker cannot be said to have achieved his speech act goal. On occasion we have the situation of a felicitous performance of an illocutionary act together with its complete failure with respect to the intended perlocutionary effect.

Traditional speech act theory stops here, pointing out that whereas the relation between locution and illocution is governed by the conventions of language, illocution and perlocution are not related to each other by way of convention.[3] What may seem paradoxical in speech act theory, is not uncommon at all in everyday communicative interaction: It fairly often happens that in connection with requests the hearer is not prepared to do what he is told to do, or in connection with blames put on him is not in the least ashamed of what he has done but sets forth good reasons why he is not to blame. This is in fact the point where communicative interaction sets in. Instead of simply asking what people do when they are talking to each other the question why people should talk to each other in the first place and why they should go on to do so ought to be taken into consideration also.

If we restrict ourselves to a speaker-centred model of communication where the attention is focussed on how the speaker releases his speech act and where the effect it has on the hearer is of marginal interest only, we miss one crucial point of communicative interaction: People talk to each other and go on to do so because they want to attain their respective communicative goals, and they are well aware of the fact that this cannot always be achieved with one single move. There is, on the other hand, no great inducement for them to go on talking if all their orders are complied with, their wishes granted, their proposals accepted, their assertions agreed with and their reproaches met with excuses. This type of 'minimum interaction' could be represented by a graph like (1).

(1)

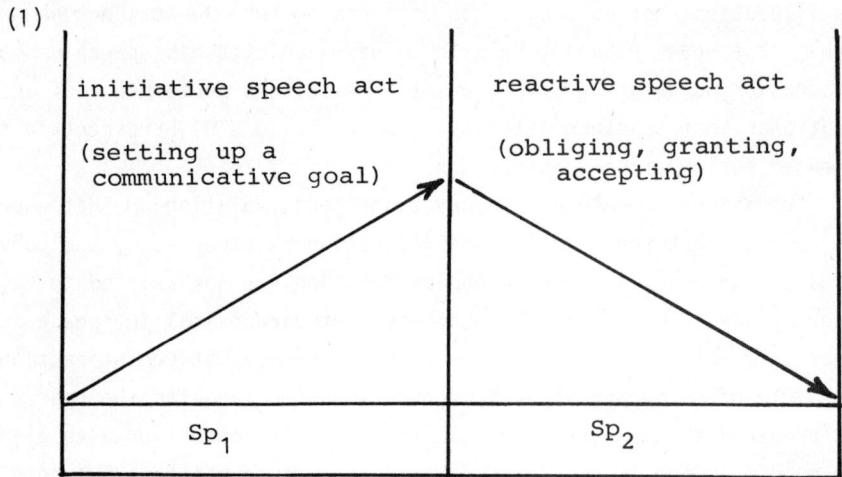

To be sure, communicative interaction does not stop altogether when the communicative goal of a speech act has been reached, but it is equally true that most likely people will go on talking in spite of having been thwarted in their first attempt of reaching their communicative goal. A speech act theory in a pragmatic perspective and with the ambition of being applicable to the analysis of authentic discourse cannot ignore the question of what happens after and beyond the felicitous performance of an illocutionary act, nor can it really be interested in a model of harmonious and one-sided communicative interaction of the type mentioned, because this is only part of the picture. In performing an initiative speech act the speaker sets out a frame for communicative interaction by establishing his communicative goal. The harmonious model shown in (1) represents the minimum extension of the communicative interaction frame: In his countermove, speaker two (Sp_2) is prepared to do exactly what speaker one (Sp_1) wants him to do and will possibly say so.

One of the problems of speech act theory lies in developing a systematic way of talking about communicative goals. In the standard description of illocutionary acts the communicative goal turns up in the guise of the so-called 'illocutionary point of a speech act'.[4] If we refer to it as 'the intended perlocutionary effect of a speech act' we take into consideration both the speaker's and the hearer's perspective. What the perlocutionary effect is going to be is in fact to a great extent up to the hearer. The felicitous performance of an illocutionary act on the side of the speaker puts the hearer into a position to react according to his own interests and with respect to the communicative goal set up by the speaker. An illocutionary act may have all sorts of perlocutionary effects; the speaker, once he has issued his speech act, can only hope for the best. On the other hand, the speaker is not bound to be satisfied with any particular reaction it calls forth in the hearer; he will most likely be interested in one question only, namely whether the reaction of the hearer conforms with the communicative goal set up by the speaker himself or not. The view of perlocutionary effects as a range of mental attitudes established in the mind of the hearer by the illocutionary act of the speaker will only lead us into a psychological maze and divert our attention from what really keeps communicative interaction going: trying to reach communicative goals.

3. *Insisting: a simple model*

I suggest model (2) for communicative interaction:

(Table (2) see next page)

If, for instance, the speaker (Sp_1) issues an order, the perlocutionary effect on the hearer (Sp_2) may be that of exhileration, derision, annoyance, anger or what not. All these reactions are of no primary importance for Sp_1 who wants to achieve his communicative goal, namely that his order be complied with. If it is not complied with, i.e. if Sp_2 refuses to do what he is told to do and tells Sp_1 so, the speech act will be considered by him as a failure, and this is one of the perlocutionary effects on Sp_1.

There is now an alternative situation for Sp_1: He may either RESIGN or INSIST. Resignation means abandoning the communicative goal set up in the initiative speech act and acknowledging the failure. In insist-

(2)

1st move	1st counter-move	2nd move	2nd counter-move
initiative speech act e.g. ORDERING	negative reactive speech act e.g. REFUSING positive reactive speech act e.g. COMPLYING	INSISTING RESIGNING	BLOCKING OFF GIVING IN
Sp_1	Sp_2	Sp_1	Sp_2

ing the speaker makes clear that he is not going to abandon his goal, he confirms it and at the same time acts on the hearer to revise his decision not to comply.

There are two alternatives open to Sp_2 then: He may either GIVE IN, thus permitting Sp_1 to attain his communicative goal after all, or he may BLOCK OFF the speech act sequence by making it quite clear that there is no chance for Sp_1 to attain his goal, with all the implications mentioned in connection with the resigning/insisting pair. GIVING IN means resignation on the part of Sp_2, i.e. abandoning the position taken in refusing to comply and acknowledging the failure to keep it up. BLOCKING OFF means holding tight to the position taken up in the counter move; it might also be viewed as INSISTING on the part of Sp_2.

The model allows us to group together a family of speech act sequences (or discourse types) that have in common an orientation towards a communicative goal. They are opened up by speech act types with a sort of directive component; the profile of the sequence is determined by the characteristics of the initiative speech act type.[5] The sequences can be given special names.

a) One group which is listed under (3) consists of sequences initiated by directive speech acts proper, i.e. REQUESTING and its subtypes:

(Table (3) see next page)

A special type of discourse is constituted by a sequence of reminders, for instance, continued requests to pay. Reminders are connected with PROMISING. The communicative goal of a request can intermediately be attained by getting Sp_2 to commit himself to a certain course of action which is in the interest of Sp_1: The structure of this type can be represented by (4):

(Table (4) see next page)

(3)

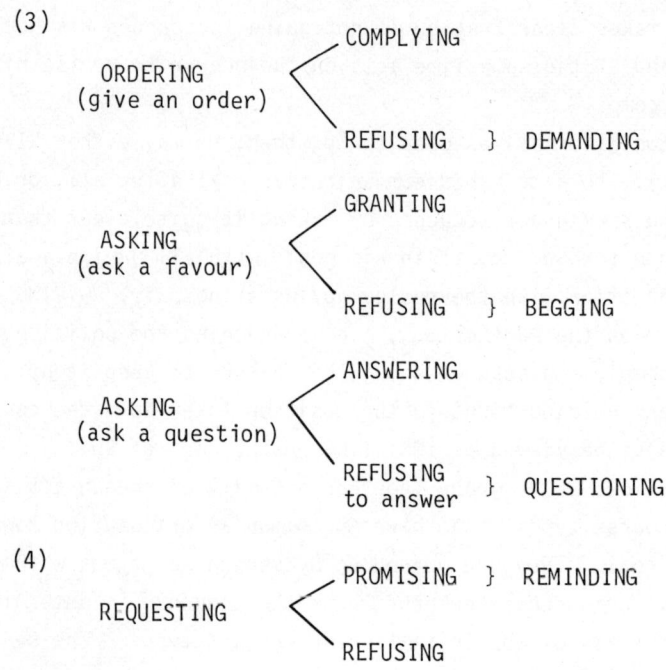

(4)

REQUESTING ⟨ PROMISING } REMINDING
            REFUSING

b) A second group listed under (5) is characterised by initiative speech acts that are not exclusively oriented towards the interests of Sp_1 but imply some sort of cooperation:

(Table (5) see next page)

There are a few more initiative speech act types that may open up insisting-sequences, for instance ADVISING and WARNING. Only under a special interpretation can the criterion of "the communicative goal is in the interest of Sp_1" be applied to these speech acts. They can nevertheless be insisted upon to "secure uptake".

c) A third group consists of assertions and assertive subtypes. Examples for members of this group are given under (6). When making an assertion one claims the truth of one's belief and tries to get the hearer to share this belief. There is no such direct connection between the communicative goal of Sp_1 and a special course of practical action on the side of Sp_2 as in the other types mentioned above.

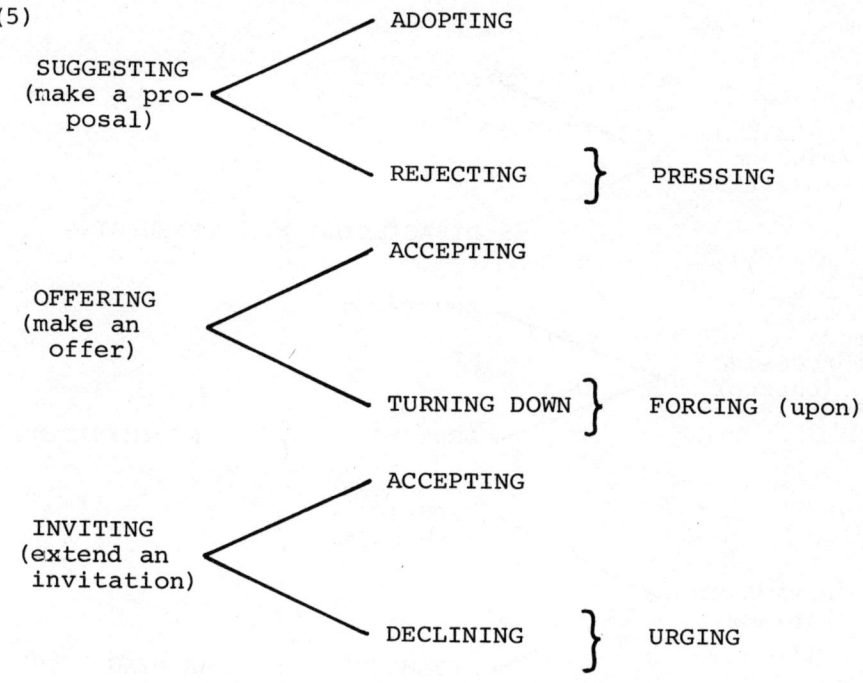

(6)

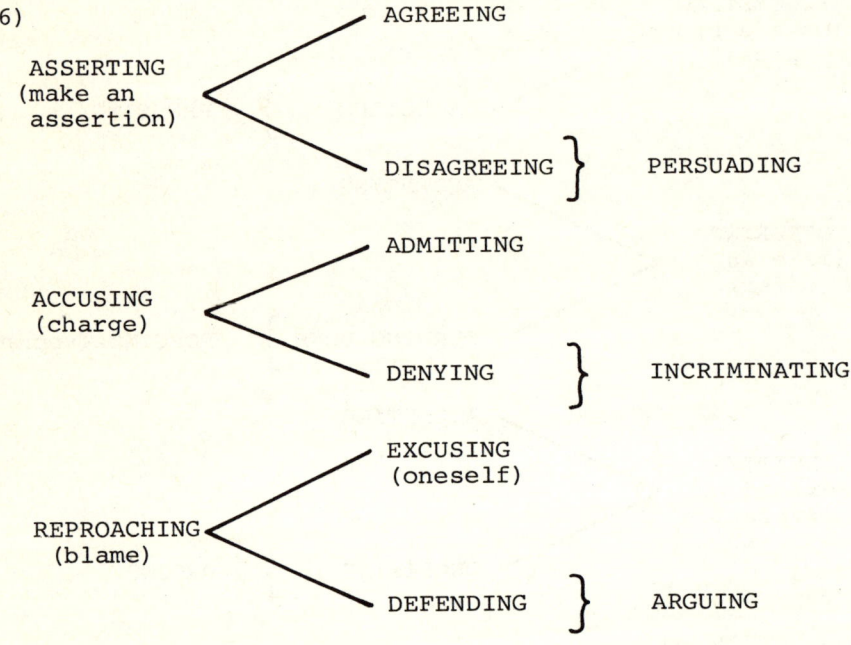

In the semantic description of quite a number of speech act verbs of natural languages reference will have to be made to the sequence type, to the relative position a speech act occupies in the sequence and the relation in which the speech act stands to the initiative speech act concerning the communicative goal.

The positions in the sequence are also characterised by special utterance forms. The speaker will phrase his utterance according to the conditions under which he thinks he can reach his communicative goal. If the speaker can foresee or actually meets resistance on the side of the hearer, he will put additional strength into his utterance. However, the success of communicative interaction will not simply depend on an extensive use of 'degree-showing devices',[6] but there are a lot of extralinguistic factors that lend weight to our words and contribute towards reaching the communicative goal.

4. *Extending the model*

The simple model marks off the crucial phases of certain types of coherent discourse.[7] Discourse coherence is based on the relation the individual speech acts in the sequence bear to the communicative goal set up in the initiative speech act. This relation can be used as a basis for the classification of discourse types.

The model provides for two pairs of move and counter-move only. In authentic discourse, it is true, it is not always clear which is the initiative speech act and what precisely is its illocution; types of moves and counter-moves do occur apart from the positive/negative reaction types in our model; more often than not it is the case that Sp_2 tries to avoid being pinned down to a clear positive or negative reply but resorts to *evasive speech acts*. Sp_1 in pursuance of his goal might try to work towards a clear positive or negative reply but is at times thrown off his track and loses himself in side sequences; but as long as he does not abandon his communicative goal or is blocked off, discourse coherence obtains.

The model may be extended to incorporate *sequences of clarifying speech acts* that are indirectly linked to the primary communicative goal. Take for instance REQUESTING or SUGGESTING as initiative speech acts of a sequence. There may be some interaction aimed at establishing what sort of request actually is made, or what is the nature of the problem that is to be solved by the suggestion. Our model could be extended to incorporate this type of 'preliminary' clarifying discourse that leads up to the initiative speech act with which the request is explicitly made or the suggestion is clearly stated.

Once the ground is cleared the various types of evasive speech acts can be tackled. According to the possible replies to the directive initiative speech act "Do this", namely "I can't do it" or "I don't know how to do it" versus "I simply cannot get myself to do it" or "I see no point in doing it", there seem to be two main subtypes of 'internal' clarifying discourse: IMPLEMENTATION DISCOURSE and MOTIVATION DISCOURSE. The distinction rests on the relevant problems that are subjected to clarification with respect to the communicative goal: Practical difficulties that stand in the way of carrying out what is requested of Sp_2 and psychological difficulties respectively. Evasive speech acts can be performed by Sp_2 in the first, the second, and even the third countermove, thus extending the sequence. But provided Sp_1 holds fast to his communicative goal and sifts Sp_2's counter-moves with regard to the relation they bear to his goal, the issue will be decided one way or another, thus ending this subtype of discourse and leading up to either resigning or insisting on the side of Sp_1: "Do it, please" or "Well, leave it then".

In the case of suggesting one possible counter-move is a counter-suggestion.

(7)

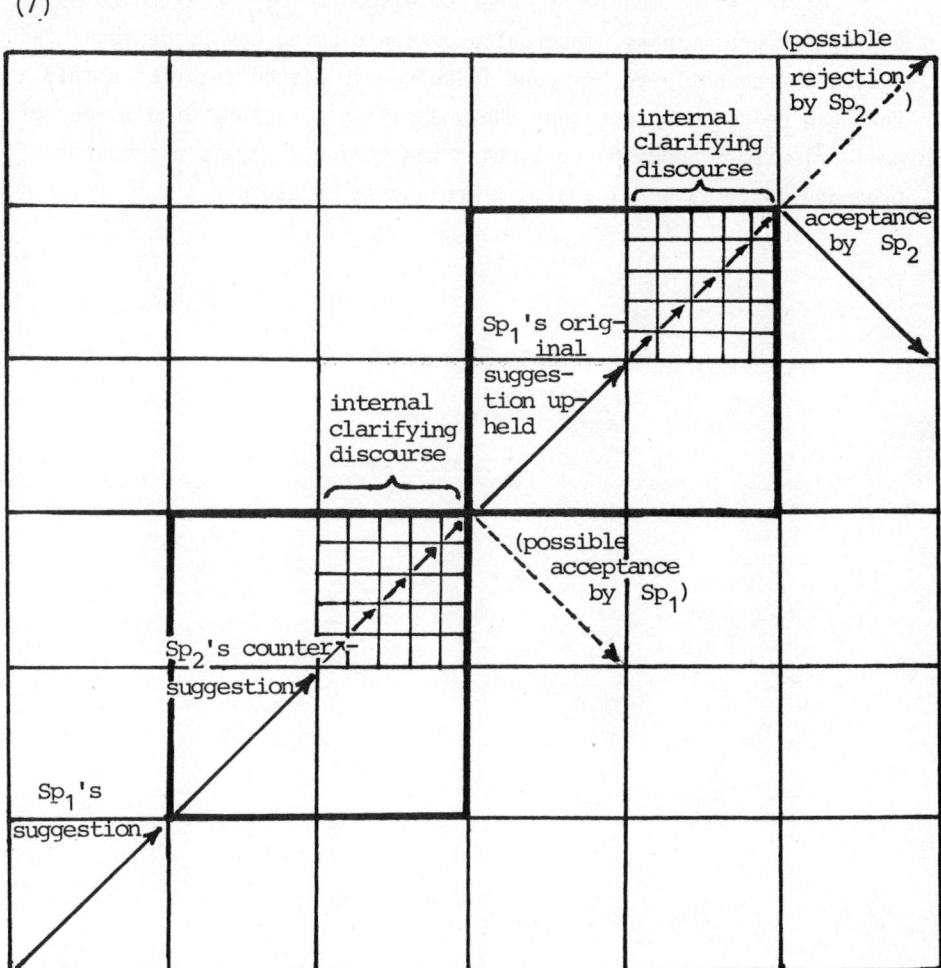

As our model (7) shows this simply means that embedded in the sequence opened up by Sp_1's initiative speech act, a similar sequence opened up by Sp_2's counter-suggestion takes place: After the counter-suggestion has been tested as to its relevance, its practicability and its preferability and so on and has been decided upon, Sp_1's initiative suggestion can be taken up and treated in the same way, leaving Sp_2 with a binary choice at the end.

The insisting model for coherent discourse may be extended by providing for preliminary, internal and even closing down side sequences that are frequently to be found in authentic discourse. Its simple form can be used to represent the underlying structure of a number of goal-oriented discourse types which the string analysis procedures of ordinary conversational analysis are unable to capture.

FOOTNOTES

1. Austin (1962: 108): "Thirdly we may also perform *perlocutionary acts*: what we bring about or achieve *by* saying something, such as convincing, persuading, deterring, and even say, surprising or misleading."

2. Searle's (1969: 66) essential rule for requests: "Counts as an attempt to get H to do A".

3. Austin (1962: 105): "(i) When the speaker intends to produce an effect it may nevertheless not occur [...]. To cope with complication (i) we invoke as before the distinction between attempt and achievement; [...]".

4. Searle (1975: 345 f.): "It is important to notice that the terminology of 'point' or 'purpose' is not meant to imply, nor is it based on the view that every illocutinary act has a definitionally associated perlocutionary intent. For many, perhaps most of the most important illocutionary acts, there is no essential perlocutionary intent associated by definition with the corresponding verb, e.g. statements and promises are not by definition attempts to produce perlocutionary effects in hearers." In this paper I try to argue for the opposite: It is the perlocutionary intent that is constitutive for communicative interaction.

5. A similar notion can be found in Fotion (1971: 235): "Each master speech act can control, and in all likelihood does control more than one aspect of the speech acts which follow."

6. Furberg (1971: 236) restricts his use of the term to devices "which a speaker uses for committing himself or avoiding to commit himself to all the implications of a discourse without signalling, what the discourse is". But the change in 'degree' is also typical of the utterances found in insisting sequences.

7. Cf. Fritz (1978).

NON-TRUTH-CONDITIONAL QUANTIFICATION

Christian Kock

This article - or rather, this collection of rambling remarks - allows itself an amount of irreverence which calls for some apology. The motivation behind it is certain simple observations I believe to have made and wish to communicate. They have been made by others, but those treatments of them which I have seen have, I feel, tried to explain away these observations rather than to take them seriously. The observations I mean all involve what has been called *vagueness* in quantification, either of amounts or degrees, in natural language. I believe there are countless cases of vagueness in quantification in natural language where the vagueness is crucial and unresolvable. Now if my linguistic intuition tells me about all these cases of unresolvable vagueness, I look for a theory to explain *why* the vagueness is there, not for one that tries to say that it isn't. I make the assumption that a truth-conditionally based semantics cannot put up with unresolvable vagueness in quantification. If this is not the case, my remarks become inoperative as far as truth-conditionalism is concerned. However, the claim that unresolvable vagueness is common in natural language remains, and my wish is to make it implausible to say that it isn't. I confess that I am either unfamiliar or unimpressed with existing attempts to resolve vagueness in quantification - mostly because they employ an amount of logical formalism that make them opaque to me. For example, there is Altham and Tennant (1975), whose "sortal quantification", as far as I understand it, has recourse to the classes-and-norms idea discussed below; and there is Kamp (1975), which, for the student who can comprehend that sort of thing, might contain something that refutes my claims. Be that as it may, I still think somebody has to make new observations about natural language. Logicians may then try to explain the mechanisms in what they have seen, not to explain it away. It cannot be satisfactory to let logicians set up a theory of natural language based on "The king of France is bald" and other bits and scraps made up to illustrate what they are looking for in the first place.

Currently, logically oriented semantic theorists are much attracted by the project of accounting for meaning in terms of truth conditions. This seminal idea is the sort of notion that is capable of grabbing hold of the minds of a large body of students within a subject, while others in the same subject, who are in the hold of some other seminal idea, tend to be impatient with it, and conversely. It will be no secret in the following that the present writer, not exactly a linguist and much less a logician, belongs to the class of impatients as far as truth conditions are concerned. In a general way, I think that linguists and other researchers in academic fields to a large extent have their views dictated to them by the *charm* that various seminal ideas exercise over their senses.[1] And the charm that certain ideas have to certain people is again derived from certain ruling instincts in their conscious and unconscious minds. This is no less true, I believe, of logicians than anybody else. Furthermore, the whole point of the following remarks is coherent with the idea that the primitive function of natural languages is to help satisfy the conscious or subconscious needs of individuals, as dictated by certain basic instincts.

As a believer in this, I am likely to say things like "The contribution made by truth conditions to the meaning of utterances in natural languages is small, while the contribution made by other mechanisms is large", whereas believers in logical semantics would put it the other way round. For instance, Ruth Kempson (1977:41), after conceding that areas of meaning like non-indicative sentences may not be describable in terms of truth conditions, adds a footnote saying: "A small and unhomogeneous group of lexical items also seems to resist analysis in terms of truth conditions. These include *even, but, deplore*, and some uses of *if*." (!) What I want to suggest is that a *large* group of lexical items seems to resist analysis in such terms. And in anticipation of what I have to say, let me direct your attention to the first sentence in the quote, and to the first sentence of my own following it. The final, and boldest, claim I am going to make below is precisely that the meaning of such uses of *small* and *large* as we find here cannot in any respectable way be accounted for truth-conditionally, but only if natural language is seen as purposive action for the furtherance of speakers' interests and needs.

Thus, a great many adjectival and adverbial quantifiers appear to be much more easily accounted for in terms of speaker's purpose than in truth-conditional terms. Take a sentence like

(1) The dictator had several clergymen arrested

This would typically occur in a newspaper report, e.g. about social riots in some Latin American country. It would be evidently suitable to support the reporter's statement as to what sort of a country it is, or what sort of man the dictator is. But it does not give the reader much idea of just *how* many clergymen were arrested. However, if it was substituted with a sentence that does, such as

(2) The dictator had 117 clergymen arrested.

it would probably be of much less use in conveying the reporter's idea, and the reader might be inclined to ask: "So what? What do you *make* of that?" On the other hand, the item *several* would not be of much use to the dictator himself in the situation where he wants his National Guard, or whatever, to go out and arrest a certain number of clergymen taking part in a demonstration or something. The order:

(3) Arrest several of those clergymen!

would be rather inappropriate here and probably put the National Guard into a state of disorientation. The point is that the purpose of *several* is not so much truth-conditional as it is *argumentative*, in the sense suggested by Ducrot (1973), Anscombre and Ducrot (1976, 1978). Leaning on their formulation of argumentative properties of items like *almost (presque)*, we might say that the most important lexical feature of *several* is the following: It may be used in a sentence S_1 to support any sentence S_2 which is such that S_2 receives stronger support the *more* members of a class are referred to in S_1. It is not important, in a sentence containing *several*, to know just *how* many members of a class it refers to. The important thing is that the kind of statement it is meant to support is the kind just defined, e.g. the statement "The dictator has taken a harsh course on political dissent within the church". Now in a situation where, say, 1,000 clergymen have been demonstrating and 117 arrested, one reporter might write "The dictator had several clergymen arrested", whereas another might write "The dictator only had a few of the clergymen arrested". The meaning of *several* and *only a few* is non-truth-conditional in the sense that there is no saying whether the actual state of affairs described by the two statements fulfils the truth conditions of one or the other. But so much is certain to any reader familiar with the lexical properties of the two items in question: Only the writer of the first statement may, with coherence, go on to say "The dictator has taken a harsh course on political dissent within the church".

An interesting adverbial quantifier is *a bit*. Suppose I say

(4) Scotland is a bit rocky.

Again it is quite unclear just what degree of rockiness I wish to predicate of Scotland. I am not saying anything that you could go to Scotland and test to see if Scotland satisfies the truth conditions of it. Truth-conditionally, I am probably only saying that there *are* rocks in Scotland. But I *am* saying more than this. I am saying that *whatever* degree of rockiness can be truthfully predicated of Scotland, it is *too much for my taste*. A typical situation for (4) to occur in would be a discussion with my wife over where we ought to go on holiday. A likely reaction to (4) would be to say, "What do you mean? Rocks are *lovely*!" Such a reaction would be a purposive act - trying to get me to see the nice side of rocks - against the purposive act represented by (4), which is an attempt to *avoid* going to Scotland on holiday.

Consider now a statement like (5), which is quite likely to be heard in the current debate over nuclear energy:

(5) Nuclear plants often have uncontrolled radioactive blowouts.

As before, my claim is going to be that the quantifier contained in this sentence, *often*, carries a kind of meaning that cannot be described in terms of truth conditions. It should begin to be clear by now that if this claim can be validated the carpet is drawn away under the truth-conditional account of an enormous amount of quantifying expressions. As far as I can see, the only notion truth-conditionalism can rely on to keep the carpet under its feet against attacks of this sort is the notion of implicit *norms*. The idea is that apparent vagueness in adjectives or adverbials is resolved in each individual case by looking at what class, or sort, of thing, or event, the vague expression applies to. The argument is usually advanced in connection with what Lyons (1968:465) calls "implicitly graded antonyms", i.e. pairs like *small* vs. *big*, where the apparent vagueness of "This elephant is big" is resolved by implying that the elephant is bigger *than the norm* for that sort of thing, i.e. elephants. I wish to return to items like *big* and *small* below, but I would like to take a first skirmish with the 'norm' theory now. In the case of (5), what norm could one adduce in order to resolve the vagueness of *often*? The example is chosen expressly with a view to exclude such a resolution, yet I claim that (5) is a perfectly natural and meaningful sort of thing to say, as in fact we all do all the time. You can't explicate *often* by saying that radioactive blowouts happen often in nuclear plants compared to the 'norm' for, e.g., power plants in general, for in other power plants radioactive blowouts do not occur at all. Hence there is no such norm. It is interesting that (5) is a statement that one would very likely hear from an opponent of nuclear power, whereas it would probably never come from one of its advocates. The case is quite analogous to that of *several*. Two opposed participants in a hearing or panel discussion on nuclear power might be quite agreed as to just *how* many radioactive blowouts have occurred in nuclear plants within a given period, e.g. 117; yet one will probably maintain that they happen *often*, while the other will maintain that they do not - or perhaps that they do happen often, *but* represent no danger. The meaning of *often* is thus argumentative, not truth-conditional, in the sense that the basic bit of lexical information about *often* is that it may be used to describe a certain state of affairs if you have a certain kind of conclusion you want to support in doing so; if you reject this kind of conclusion, you may only use it if you follow it up with a sentence containing *but* or a synonym of *but*.

I would ask the reader, without further comment, to consider the functioning of items like *repeatedly, again and again* and *all the time* in terms similar to those just suggested.

Now consider (6):

(6) Uncontrolled radioactive blowouts from nuclear plants are frequent.

It would take a great deal of hair-splitting to claim that (5) and (6) are not synonymous. That is to say, if my argument about *often* in (5) holds good, it also applies to *frequent* in (6). And in that case it will turn out that an enormous amount of utterances in daily communication involve non-truth-conditional predication, *viz*. all those where adjectives of the type *frequent/rare, small/big* are operative in the predicate. These are Lyons's "implicitly graded antonyms", or, in the terminology suggested by P.T. Geach (1956), "logically attributive adjectives". These he distinguishes from "logically predicative adjectives" like *red* or *round* which apply to any individual in the same way regardless how it is specified. In contrast, it is characteristic of a logically attributive adjective that the individual it applies to must be specified as a member of some class for which some norm may be indicated (regarding size, or whatever it is). Fink (1973:26) also calls such adjectives "logically comparative" because the positive form of such an adjective is "logically dependent on its comparative and not vice versa. A big mouse is not bigger than other mice because the property *bigness* is realised in it in a specially high degree; it is a big mouse simply because it is bigger than most other mice". This, as far as I can see, amounts to saying that there is a norm for bigness in mice which can be defined as a degree of bigness such that half the mice in the world are bigger and the other half smaller. Lyons makes essentially the same point when he remarks that "such words as *big* and *small*, or *good* and *bad*, do not refer to independent, 'opposite' qualities, but are merely lexical devices for grading as 'more than' or 'less than' with respect to some implicit norm" (1968:465-6).

But whereas this idea is nicely applicable to paradigmatic cases like "This mouse is big", it is hard to see how it can apply to (6). The application of an implicit norm regarding the quality attributed to the subject is, as we have seen, dependent on the reference of the subject to some class. While it is easy enough to refer an individual like *this mouse* to the class of all existing mice, what is one to do if the subject is not an individual, but a whole class in itself? The only way seems to be to regard it as a subclass of some super-class - but what is that to be? As we have already seen, we cannot in (6), any more than in (5), have recourse to a super-class of "uncontrolled radioactive blowouts in *all* kinds of plants", for this super-class would have no more members than the sub-class. If pressed, we might try to establish as super-class either "*all* radioactive blowouts in nuclear plants", or "*all* accidents in *all* kinds of plants", or an unlimited number of other super-classes, none of which are in any way suggested by (6) itself.

It is possibly the case that in *most* sentences with a logically attributive in the predicate the subject *may* be referred to some class with some implicit norm. But the point is that this operation is not possible in *all* such sentences. Hence I claim that the cases where a class and a norm may be appropriately adduced are special cases of a more general phenomenon. The more general phenomenon is that predicates with logically attributive adjectives in them are basically argumentative, not truth-conditional; however, they may be so directly, or *via* some norm.

In order to salvage the 'norm' account as a general ploy to resolve vagueness, one might, in a last desperate move, suggest that each occurrence of a logically attributive adjective in the predicate either refers to some pre-existent implicit norm, *or*, if this is not possible, sets up an idiosyncratic, ad-hoc norm. In order to test this suggestion, let us consider one more example of the kind that resists the simpler analysis. Let us imagine a man and a wife who have to part from each other for a certain period, say, three weeks. In parting they tell one another to cheer up and not be too sad about it, and one of them says,

(7) Three weeks is not long.

Now in many such cases it would be implausible to suggest that the couple already have, in their shared background knowledge or whatever we want to call it, an implicit norm regarding the length of periods of separation according to which three weeks is not "long". At any rate, one cannot in such a situation, along the lines suggested by Fink, interpret *not long* to mean "shorter than most periods of separation"; it may be the couple's first and even their only period away from each other. Now the "last desperate move" consists in saying that the utterance of (7) *establishes* a norm where none existed before; that is, we now have to do with a 'norm' that is *not* implicit. But all we know about this very ephemeral, ad-hoc norm is that according to it, three weeks = "not long". Now if we wish, as a logical semanticist would, to resolve the vagueness and find the truth-conditional meaning of (7), this is all we have to work with, and hence all we can do is to substitute, for the phrase *not long*, the phrase *three weeks* in which case we end up with "Three weeks is three weeks". On a pragmatic account this might indeed have some meaning, but certainly not the same as the original utterance. On any account, "Three weeks is three weeks" is, on the face of it, tautological, and on a truth-conditional account it would then have no meaning at all.

As we see, the truth-conditional account in cases such as this only manages to evacuate any meaning the utterance might have had. An alternative account, which I am not in a position to develop fully here, ought instead to interpret the meaning of the utterance in terms of what sentences it may *cohere* with. "Three weeks is not long" in the given situation may cohere with any sentence that serves to encourage mental fortitude in the hearer and/or to discourage sorrow. Thus the speaker, in saying "Three weeks is not long", is not making an assertion as to how long three weeks are in relation to any norm, but he/she is acting to encourage fortitude etc. in relation to the length of the period of separation, *such as it is*. This interpretation is of course situation-dependent (in that it assumes, among other things, that the speaker and hearer are unhappy about being separated). But it may be made independent of such contextual factors if we say the following: The meaning of the utterance is that it may cohere, in a supporting function, with any sentence which is such that it receives stronger support the *shorter* the period of absence is. Conversely, there will be no coherence with any sentence which does not fulfil this condition. Thus, in terms of coherence, the meaning of "Three weeks is not long" may be understood and described without vagueness even though there is no actual sentence for it to cohere with, and without making it circular by imputing to it a reliance on any volatile, ad-hoc 'norm'. The meaning of the utterance, if truth-conditional, is void.

Such a radically non-truth-conditional use of logically attributive adjectives is not limited to situations of the emotional nature suggested in the above example. On the contrary, it is found all the time in such allegedly non-emotional, matter-of-fact types of communication as newspaper reporting and political debate or statement. To illustrate this, let me choose just one example, quite randomly, from a newspaper I picked up on my way to the pragmatics conference at Urbino, *The International Herald Tribune* from Thursday, July 5, 1979. One of the cover stories of this issue is headed "EEC Aides See OPEC

Drive to Set Oil Ceiling" and reports on talks held in London between high-ranking EEC and OPEC representatives. The reporter, Joseph Fitchett, writes: "In the London talks, the European team, which apparently did most of the talking while OPEC listened, concentrated on conveying 'confidence-building measures' aimed at demonstrating the intentions of industrial countries to cooperate over energy matters. The French industry minister, for instance, reportedly spent much of his time trying to convince the OPEC team that the U.S. commitment at the Tokyo summit to a ceiling on oil imports until 1985 was a sincere, important step by the Carter administration to promote energy-saving." Consider the adjective *much* in the second period. The function of this period, which gives it coherence with the first, is to establish a support for the assertion made in the first - the sort of conjunctive relation that Halliday and Hasan (1976:248) would call exemplificatory apposition and place under the heading of internal additive relations. My point is that *much* cannot be referred to any norm that gives us any clue as to just *how* much of his time the French minister spent trying to convince the OPEC team. The contribution made to meaning by *much* is not truth-conditional. Its purpose is simply to get the reader to accept the assertion contained in the first period, not to supply information on the actual amount of time spent by the minister doing this or that.

Further down in the article, the reporter quotes Mr. Guido Brunner, the EEC commissioner for energy, on the outcome of the talks: "Despite the inauspicious start in London, Mr. Brunner said that 'we stand a fair chance to continue' some form of dialogue, perhaps in another framework." Consider the word *fair* in the quote from Mr. Brunner. Just how big a chance could he have meant there was for a continuation of the talks? 25%? 50%? More than 50%? There is no way for the hearer or the reader of Mr. Brunner's statement to assess this. Most likely Mr. Brunner himself did not have any figure in mind at all. The function of his statement is simply what we might call *persuasive*; its meaning emerges when one considers the various continuations it might thinkably cohere with in a supporting function. All we know about these is that they must be such that they will receive *stronger* support, the *fairer* the chance is.

We may now revert to the quarrel as to whether the group of lexical items unaccountable for in truth-conditional terms is "small" or "large". The difference between logical semanticists and more instinctive ones like myself is that I would say it was large, and they would say it was small. I have tried above to show that it is certainly larger than they think. But even if they concede that some of my points are correctly taken, they will probably still say it is small, and I will still say it is large. Both statements are vague when interpreted truth-conditionally; in fact there is no deciding whether the actual state of affairs, if it could be agreed upon, comes closer to satisfying the truth conditions of my statement or those of theirs. My whole point is that this is quite as it should be, if you believe in the sort of theory of language that I think ought to be developed; but *not* if you believe in theirs. People who believe that all sentences, or even all *declarative* sentences, have a statable truth-conditional meaning, ought to be slapping theirs mouths a lot of the times they use predicates involving words like *big* or *small*; the rest of us may go on using them unabashedly, as we always have. The use of unresolvably vague, non-truth-conditional quantification in natural language is, I believe, as omnipresent as people's attempts, in whatever they do or say, to further their interests, dictated by instincts.

FOOTNOTE:

1. Cf. Wittgenstein (1966: 24-28) for remarks on how it may be the *charm* of a certain 'style of thinking', or of a certain explanation of something, that causes people to adopt it - rather than the obviousness of its truth, which may not be obvious at all. As examples, he cites the theories of Freud and Darwin. However, it is probably just as true in linguistics and philosophy that one chooses to believe in a certain style of thinking about a subject because one happens to find it charming. In a striking way, Wittgenstein applies the word 'propaganda" to what one does in trying to persuade someone to adopt one's theory of something: "I am in a sense making propaganda for one style of thinking as opposed to another. I am honestly disgusted with the other" (1966: 28). What he says here is, I believe, consistent with the tendency of what I try to say, namely that people when they speak are not so much concerned with representing true states of affairs as they are with influencing each other.

PRAGMATICALLY BASED GRAMMAR

Werner Kummer

The task of a pragmatically based grammar is not to enumerate the infinite number of grammatically well-formed sentences in a language L, but to function as a constitutive part of a model of discourse production and discourse understanding along the lines developed in recent work in Artificial Intelligence. While some of the basic structures of speech act planning and recognition of speaker intentions in language understanding have received relatively frequent treatment, the processes involved in the grammatical aspects of verbal planning or speech understanding are still unclear. Computer models like the one in Cohen (1978) either end at the stage of an abstract speech act representation or use domain-specific prefabricated utterances. Parsing and Generation models generally used in AI research have to my knowledge until now not tackled the problem of the pragmatical determination of utterance-production or understanding, but have relied on algorithms relating semantic structures to morphological (=phonologico/morphologico/syntactical) structures. In order to pinpoint the place of a pragmatically based grammar in a model of discourse production and discourse understanding it is necessary to outline roughly a schema of a communication process as modelled e.g. in T. Winograd's "A Framework for the Understanding of Discourse".

```
                        ┌─────────────────────────┐
                        │ Problems of Coordination│
                        └────────────┬────────────┘
                                     ↓
                        ┌─────────────────────────┐
                        │ Interaction Goals       │
                        └────────────┬────────────┘
                                     ↓
                        ┌─────────────────────────┐
                        │ Filter of Goals:        │
      Speaker           │ Context Model           │
                        │ Model of the Interpreter│
                        └────────────┬────────────┘
                                     ↓
                        ┌─────────────────────────┐
                        │ Utterance Goals         │
                        │ in Situation Frame      │
                        └────────────┬────────────┘
   ┌──────────────┐                  ↓
   │ Available    │    ┌─────────────────────────┐
   │ verbal means │ →  │ Verbal Planning         │
   └──────────────┘    └────────────┬────────────┘
                                     ↓
                        ┌─────────────────────────┐
                        │ Produced Utterance      │
                        └────────────┬────────────┘
                                     ↓
                        ┌─────────────────────────┐
                        │ Perceived Utterance     │
    Interpreter         └────────────┬────────────┘
                                     ↓
   ┌──────────────┐    ┌─────────────────────────┐
   │ Available    │ →  │ Reconstruction of Speaker's│
   │ verbal means │    │ Verbal Planning         │
   └──────────────┘    └────────────┬────────────┘
                                     ↓
                        ┌──────────────────────────┐
                        │ Reconstructed Utterance Goals│
                        │ in Situation Frame       │
                        └────────────┬─────────────┘
                                     ↓
                        ┌────────────────────────────────────┐
                        │ Goal Inferring Filter:             │
                        │ Context Model                      │
                        │ Model of Speakers Model of Interpreter│
                        └────────────────┬───────────────────┘
                                         ↓
                        ┌─────────────────────────────┐
                        │ Reconstructed Interaction Goals│
                        └────────────┬────────────────┘
                                     ↓
                        ┌──────────────────────────────────┐
                        │ Reconstructed Problems of Coordination│
                        └──────────────────────────────────┘
```

In this model the reasons for verbal interchanges lie in practical problems of coordination confronting members of a group. If these problems cannot be solved by a member of the group in isolation, it develops interaction goals directed at other members of the group making it necessary to communicate with them. How much of the interaction goals need to be verbalized (I disregard for the purposes of this exposition the possibilities of nonverbal communication) depends on the interaction planner's model of the context and of his interlocutor. If the interaction goals have been filtered through these constructs, the interaction goals have changed into utterance goals embedded in a situation frame specifying the relevant parameters of the context and the interlocutor. Verbal Planning is a problem-solving procedure using the verbal means available to the speaker for the expression of his utterance goals; the product of the execution of the verbal plan is the produced utterance. In the interpretation process verbal understanding proceeds from a perceived utterance via a reconstruction of the speaker's verbal planning using hints in the perceived utterance to a filtering of the reconstructed utterance goals of the speaker through the reconstructed context model and interpreter model. By this process the interpreter can infer the interaction goals of the speaker and the coordination problems they are supposed to help solving. The reaction of the interpreter depends on his own interaction goals and starts the process over again. It is unnecessary to fill in the details of such a model in order to spot the place of a pragmatically based grammar in it: a pragmatically based grammar is a device allowing:

a) the verbal planning of any structure of utterance goals in situation frames
b) the reconstruction of the utterance goals in situation frame of any perceived utterance.

It is obvious that this definition implies the usual idealizations of a perfect speech producer and a perfect interpreter, but it is a matter of empirical research to analyse the actual limits in speakers' or interpreters' discoursing competence.

In this paper I will deal only with the a) part of a pragmatically based grammar. For a modelling of this part the following questions must be answered:
1) What is the form of a structure "utterance goals in situation frames"?
2) Is there an algorithm for the enumeration of all possible structures of this kind?
3) Which form must the "available verbal means" have in order to be usable for verbal planning?
4) What structure has the problem-solving algorithm used in verbal planning?
5) How is an utterance constructed from a plan?

The analogous problems for the interpreter's side of a pragmatically based grammar as well as the general structure in which such a grammar is embedded have been outlined in my "Grundlagen der Texttheorie" (Kummer 1974) and need not be elaborated here.

1. *The structure of "utterance goals in situation frames"*

Instead of a theoretical description of utterance goals in situation frames I will use Philip R. Cohen's example for a coordination problem: the speaker S is outside a room in which the interpreter U is situated and which is closed and locked. S wants to get into the room, but the key is on the inside of the lock. Via a chain of reasoning using the context model and the model of the interpreter the speaker develops the following utterance goal:

USER BELIEVE SYSTEM BELIEVE SYSTEM WANT UNLOCKDOOR (USER).

From this goal description Cohen uses a shortcut to the planning of the following verbal act:

REQUEST (SYSTEM, USER, UNLOCKDOOR (USER))

and to the alternative:

INFORM (SYSTEM, USER, SYSTEM WANT UNLOCKDOOR (USER))

The shortcut is effected by a regressive planning strategy in which the system knows that the effect of a request to the user, that ... is that the user believes that the system believes that the system wants the user to ... or that the same effect can be attained by informing the user that the system wants the user to .... The translation of the planned speech act into an utterance happens in Cohens case by simple fiat, i.e. by matching a speech act formula to a fixed utterance, in the first case:

(1) Can you unlock the door?

and in the second case:

(2) I want you to unlock the door.

Although Cohen's solution bypasses all of the problems of a pragmatically based grammar it illustrates the necessary elements of such a system: a relation between a speech act or a series of speech acts and an utterance goal in a situation frame such that the speech act or speech act sequence is a solution to the problem posed by the goal in the situation and a translation system producing a situationally adequate realization of the speech act or sequence. Generalizing on these elements we must require that first of all the specification of the situation as it exists in the speaker's mind before the planning of the speech act(s) must be provided in order to choose the right speech act(s). This problem is trivialized in Cohen's case, because he treats only two of the basic types of illocutionary acts distinguished by Searle: directives and representatives. In any linguistically interesting model the choice of speech acts as operators transforming beliefs-nestings of an interlocutor must be part of the verbal planning algorithm and not a simple matter of matching speech acts to goal-states. Another problem involved in Cohen's system is the multiplicity of possible verbalizations for the same planned speech act(s), which he ignores. For a linguist this aspect of verbal planning is an area of central interest, and its treatment requires a rich specification of elements of context and interpreter's representation.

In order to arrive at a pragmatically based grammar it is therefore necessary to embed Cohen's utterance goals in a situation frame specifying all the relevant assumptions of the speaker about situation features either in the context or in his model of the interpreter. The situation frame will guide the problem-solving process of verbal planning for the given utterance goals.

I will now sketch some of the problems involved in constructing all possible UGSFs:
a) problems of the language used in modelling UGSFs
b) possible UGs
c) the coherence problem for UG and SF in a UGSF structure
d) the cut-off problem for SFs in a structure
e) domain-specificity vs. domain-independence of UGSFs

a) Problems of the language used in modelling UGSFs

Basically there are two modelling techniques available for the construction of UGSFs, both illustrated in Cohen's thesis: procedural techniques directly implementable in a computer system; e.g. partitioned networks with a system of spaces like those proposed by G. Hendrix, or systems of logic using operators for propositional attitudes like 'believing', 'knowing', 'intending', 'wanting' etc. Following the tradition of theoretical linguistics I will use systems of logic as a modelling tool, counting on their recently proved translatability into partitioned network structures.

The language used in modelling UGSFs has the following structure:

1. Symbols used:
a) an infinite set of individual variables: $x, y, z, x_1, x_2 \ldots$
b) an infinite set of event variables: $e, f, g, e_1, e_2, \ldots$
c) an infinite set of individual constants: a, b, c, a_1, a_2
d) an infinite set of set variables: $X, Y, Z, X_1, X_2 \ldots$
e) an infinite set of set constants: $A, B, C, A_1, A_2 \ldots$
f) an infinite set of individual predicates: P, Q, R, ..., HAUS, ...
g) an infinite set of event predicates: U, V, W ... SCHLAFEN, ...

h) a set of case labels: A (=agent), O (=object), U (=undergoer), INSTR (=instrument), LOC (=location) etc.
i) a set of operator symbols operating on individual predicates and event predicates respectively
j) a set of modal operators: e.g. FUT = future, PAST = past, DUR = duration, $\Box_a$ = necessary for a, $\Diamond_a$ = possible for a etc.
k) quantifiers binding individual variables or set variables or predicate variables
l) the abstraction operator "λ" binding individual variables, set variables or event variables
m) the identity sign
n) a set of operators for propositional attitudes: B_a = a believes that, ...; D_a = a does ...; I_a = a intends that, ...; K_a = a knows that, ...; etc.
o) the connectives: "." = and, "v" = or, "∿" = negation, "⊃" = material implication

2. Well-formed formulae:
1) a sequence of an individual predicate, "(", $\begin{Bmatrix} \text{an individual constant} \\ \text{an individual variable} \\ \text{a set constant} \\ \text{a set variable} \end{Bmatrix}$
2) if an event predicate is of type ∅, then a sequence of the predicate symbol, "(", an event variable, and ")" is a wff if an event predicate is of type n 1, then a sequence of a wff for a predicate of type n followed by ".", "C", "(",
$\begin{Bmatrix} \text{an individual variable} \\ \text{an individual constant} \\ \text{a set variable} \\ \text{a set constant} \end{Bmatrix}$, ", ", the event variable used in the wff for the predicate of type n, ")" is a wff

where C is a variable ranging over the case labels.
3) if ϕ is a wff starting with an individual predicate, then O (ϕ) is a wff of the category of
where O_1 is a variable ranging over operators operating on event

predicates;

if ϕ is a wff starting with an event predicate, then $O_1(\phi)$ is a wff of the category ϕ

where O_1 is a variable ranging over operators operating on event predicates.

4) if ϕ and ψ are $\begin{Bmatrix} \text{two individual variables} \\ \text{two individual constants} \\ \text{two set variables} \\ \text{two set constants} \\ \text{two event variables} \end{Bmatrix}$, then $(\phi = \psi)$ is a wff.

5) if ϕ is a wff, then the sequence of a modal operator, "(", ϕ, ")" is a wff of the type ϕ;

6) if ϕ is a wff, then the sequence of an operator for propositional attitudes, "(", ϕ, ")" is a wff of the type ϕ;

7) if ϕ is a wff containing $\psi = \begin{Bmatrix} \text{a free variable} \\ \text{a free set variable} \\ \text{a free event variable} \end{Bmatrix}$, then the

sequence of "(", a quantifier symbol, ψ, ")", (ϕ) is a wff and the sequence of "(", the abstraction operator, ψ, ")", (ϕ) is a wff.

8) if ϕ and ψ are two wffs, then "$\phi \cdot \psi$", "$\psi \vee \phi$", "$\psi \supset \phi$", "$\phi \equiv \psi$", "$\phi \vee \psi$" and "$\sim \phi$" are wffs.

9) any expression is a wff if it is constructed by rules 1 to 8.

These rules are not intended to give a detailed description of the syntax of the language needed for representing UGSFs because it is still an open empirical question, how rich the language for representing UGSFs has to be in order to capture all the relevant parameters of goals and situations. But at least the apparatus given in the preceding rules is necessary for such a task.

Most of the features of the model-theoretic interpretation of this language are well-known, so I will only concentrate on the treatment of operators for propositional attitudes. Notice, that the language allows quantifying into contexts of propositional attitudes, i.e. formulas like:

(Ex) $B_a I_b B_a K_b (P(x))$

B_a (Ex) $I_b B_a K_b (P(x))$

$B_a I_b$ (Ex) $B_a K_b (P(x))$

etc.

Following Hintikka's concept of model systems and model sets we will define a belief world as the set of wffs in the scope of the same belief operator; analogously, a knowledge world is the set of all wffs in the scope of the same knowledge operator, and an intention world is the set of wffs in the scope of the same intention operator. The basic interpretation rules for propositional attitude prefixes are:

1) if $B_x(\phi)$ is a wff in the world $\emptyset$, then ϕ is a wff in the world B_x
2) if $K_x(\phi)$ is a wff in world $\emptyset$, then ϕ is a wff in the world K_x
3) if $I_x(\phi)$ is a wff in world $\emptyset$, then ϕ is a wff in world I_x
4) if $B_x(\phi)$ is a wff in world n, then ϕ is a wff in world $B_x(n)$
5) if $K_x(\phi)$ is a wff in world n, then ϕ is a wff in world $K_x(n)$
6) if $I_x(\phi)$ is a wff in world n, then ϕ is a wff in world $I_x(n)$
7) if (Ex)$B_x(\phi)$ is a wff in world n, then (Ex) (ϕ) is a wff in world $B_x(n)$
8) if (Ex)$I_x(\phi)$ is a wff in world n, then (Ex) (ϕ) is a wff in world $I_x(n)$
9) if (Ex)$K_x(\phi)$ is a wff in world n, then (Ex) (ϕ) is a wff in world $K_x(n)$

Using these rules the formula (Ex)$B_a I_b B_a K_b(P(x))$ can be represented in the following space structure, using Cohen's framework of representation

```
┌─────────────────────────────────────
│ B_a
│
│  (Ex) I_b B_a K_b (P(x))
│ ┌───────────────────────────────────
│ │ B_a I_b
│ │
│ │  (Ex) B_a K_b (P(x))
│ │ ┌─────────────────────────────────
│ │ │ B_a I_b B_a
│ │ │
│ │ │  (Ex) (P(x))
│ │ │ ┌───────────────────────────────
│ │ │ │ B_a I_b B_a K_b
│ │ │ │
│ │ │ │  (Ex)  (P(x))
│ │ │ │
```

Every space in this structure is equivalent to a Hintikka type model set, and the set of spaces defined by a formula or a set of formulas is equivalent to a model system.

I will not try to specify all the inference rules valid for the propositional attitude markers used in the language, but will only talk about the important properties of the intention operator as used in the system. The basic rule for the operator is:

(1) $B_x I_x (\phi) \rightarrow B_x I_x D_x (\psi)$. RESULT (ψ, ϕ)

The rule says that if a system has a conscious intention to reach the goal ϕ, then it has the conscious intention to do a sequence of actions ψ leading to that goal.

The second rule connects the conscious intention to do a sequence of actions and an enabling condition for the actor to the execution of the sequence of actions:

(2) $B_x I_x D_x (\psi)$. RESULT $(\psi, \phi) \diamondsuit_x D_x (\psi) \rightarrow D_x (\psi)$

Take the following example for the application of the rules:

$$B_a I_a B_b B_a(P(x))$$

The formula can be represented as the following nesting of spaces:

```
┌─────────────────────
│ B_a
│
│    I_a B_b B_a(P(x))
│
```

Applying Rule (1) the formula is changed to:

$$B_a I_a D_a(\psi). \text{ RESULT } (\psi, B_b B_a(P(x))$$

corresponding to the space structure:

```
┌─────────────────────
│ B_a
│
│    I_a D_a(\psi). RESULT (\psi, B_b B_a(P(x))
│
```

After the application of rule (2), in case the enabling condition is fulfilled, we get:

```
┌─────────────────────
│ B_a
│
│    I_a D_a(ψ). RESULT (ψ, B_b B_a(P(x))
│
│    ◇_a D_a(ψ)
│
│    D_a(ψ)
│
```

The basic rule for the action operator defines a context change effected through an action:

$$D_a(\psi). \text{ RESULT } (\psi, \phi) \to B_a(\phi)$$

Applying the rule to our example we achieve the following context change:

$$\boxed{\begin{array}{l} B_a \\ \quad I_a D_a(\psi).\ \text{RESULT}\ (\psi,\ B_b B_a(P(x))) \\ \quad \Diamond_a D_a(\psi) \\ \quad D_a(\psi) \end{array}} \implies$$

$$\boxed{\begin{array}{l} B_a \\ \quad B_b B_a(P(x)) \end{array}}$$

Using this apparatus it is possible to define the structure of UGSFs:

Definition: A UGSF is a sequence of two sets of wffs:

(i) the UG part consisting of a set of wffs beginning with the operator prefix $B_x I_x$,

(ii) the SF part consisting of a set of wffs beginning with the operator prefix B_x not immediately followed by I_x

where x is the interlocutor having an utterance goal in a situation frame.

Notice that the definition of UGSFs guarantees that every UGSF has a context change via action programmed in its structure, following the intuition that intensions lead to action if a possibility for action, expressed in the enabling condition, is fulfilled.

b) Possible utterance goals

The definition of UGSF allows in its part (i) any combination of consciously intended utterance goals; obviously this will allow for a huge number of impossible utterance goals, and it is necessary to restrict the class of possible combinations of utterance goals. It is difficult to give a priori limitations to the class of possible utterance goals, because the following aspects of the problem must be considered:

(i) There are no a priori upper bounds to the number of wffs included in the UG part of an UGSF. A UG, e.g. for a long and complex speech or for an intricate narration, can be very complex, because the apparatus of utterance goals does not correspond to any small-scale linguistic units like speech acts or utterances of sentence length.

(ii) There are no a priori conditions on the coherence between the wffs in a UG. It is perfectly possible, e.g. for a news speaker, to talk about a range of unconnected topics in the same utterance.

(iii) It is not obvious whether a condition of logical consistency can be postulated for the set of wffs in the UG part of an UGSF. Logical consistency of UGs would be given, if the set of results of the intended actions or action sequences would not contain at the same time a formula p and its negation. But in cases like double-bind communication this exactly seems to be the case.

For the reasons given in (i)-(iii) the class of possible utterance goals will not be restricted a priori in this model. It is a question of the empirical study of domain-specific forms of discourse to find out the restrictions on utterance goals valid for these forms.

c) The coherence problem of UG and SF in a UGSF structure

Obviously the situation frame for an utterance goal does not consist of everything a speaker believes to be the case or believes his interlocutor to believe, but selects from these beliefs only the ones directly relevant to the utterance goal. It is difficult to find the right criteria for coherence between elements of UG and elements of SF. If e.g. the speaker intends to make the hearer notice that he wants him to unlock and open a specific door, it is not necessary for him to confront his utterance goal with all his beliefs about doors or the specific door he wants to be opened, or with his beliefs about the hearer's beliefs about the door. He only has to deal with elements in his belief world dealing with the specific problem at hand. In the simplest cases this problem can be solved by restricting the SF to elements involved in a specific frame or script outlining the general features of the problem to be dealt with. If a frame or script is represented by a sequence of state descriptions connected by arcs marking possible actions connecting the states, or alternatively by a schema of sets of wffs representing states connected by action descriptions, then the state in which the speaker is at the time of the formulation of his utterance goals determines which elements will make up the SF of his UGSF, namely the elements in the state description constituting the state in the script he is in. In more complex cases, if there is no specific frame in which the discourse is embedded, the problem of coherence between UG and SF is more complicated. For this presentation I will not go deeper into this interesting problem.

d) *The cut-off problem for SFs in a structure*

Every utterance goal can be verbalized in many different ways, and it is one of the major difficulties for a pragmatically based grammar to cut down the number of possible verbalizations of utterance goals in specific situation frames. One possibility for this is a rich specification of the situation frame: the more detailed the information contained in the situation frame, the more restricted is the number of possible verbalizations for a given utterance goal. With this strategy a new problem arises for the determination of the cut-off point for situation frame elements. At the present state of the art it is probably impossible to determine for complex utterance goals the exact cut-off point determining a specific verbalization, and in this paper the issue will just be dodged by concentrating on very simple examples.

e) *Domain-specificity vs. domain-independence of UGSFs*

Artificial Intelligence programs often simplify the problems of simulating verbal planning by concentrating on a restricted set of domain-specific problems. For a linguist this strategy is unacceptable, because he starts from the assumption that the verbal abilities of a speaker or interpreter constitute a unified system allowing him to verbalize or understand any given UGSFs. Although the rigid conception of a unified grammar and lexicon used in every utterance situation and speech understanding situation has been shaken in the last years by the recognition of different variants making up a speaker's or hearer's repertoire, probably all linguists would agree that it is wrong to assume completely different domain-specific algorithms for the verbalization or understanding of UGSFs. It is a matter of empirical research to decide on the variability of a speaker's or hearer's systems for verbalization or understanding.

In the present outline I will assume an ideal speaker who is able to use a domain-independent algorithm for verbalizing any UGSF, but I will illustrate his abilities only with simple examples.

2. *The form of the verbal means used in verbal planning*

As several people have noticed, speech act types can be analyzed as operators transforming states in the nested belief structure of speakers into other states, the felicity conditions defining the necessary features of the two states. Asa Kasher's "Mood Implicatures" (1974) or my "Pragmatic Implications" (Kummer 1973) are different formalisms dealing with this insight. Here I want to argue that the propositional attitude operators necessary for the formulation of felicity conditions are 'believe', 'know', 'intend', 'prefer'. Consider the following sequences of utterances:

(1) I will see you tomorrow. But I don't want you to believe that I will see you tomorrow.
(2) I will see you tomorrow. But I think you believe that anyway to be the case.
(3) I will see you tomorrow. But I think you prefer me not to see you tomorrow.

In case the first utterance in the sequences (1)-(3) is supposed to constitute a promise of the speaker to see the interpreter, then the sequences are in the sense of Hintikka's "Knowledge and Belief" self-defeating, because the second part of the sequence contradicts one of the felicity conditions of the first utterance in the sequence. Using this test of common indefensibility of two utterances, we can isolate the felicity conditions of a speech act type, and it appears, that all the felicity conditions are built on the notions of belief, knowledge or intention. Formalizing this insight, we can characterize the speech act of promising:

$$\text{if } B_a \sim B_b I_a D_a(P(x))$$
$$B_a \text{PREFER}_b((P(x), \sim P(x)))$$
$$B_a I_a B_b I_a D_a(P(x))$$
$$\text{then } D_a(\text{PROMISE}(a, b, P(x)))$$

The "if - then" condition in this description specifies a possible context change according to the already given rules for intentions, the first two formulas in the "if" part functioning as the enabling condition. I will rewrite the speech act description in this format:

$$B_a I_a(B_b I_a D_a(P(x))) \rightarrow B_a I_a D_a \quad (\text{PROMISE}(a, b, P(x))).$$
$$\text{RESULT}(\text{PROMISE}(a, b, P(x)), B_a I_a D_a(P(x)))$$
$$B_a \sim B_b I_a D_a(P(x)). \quad B_a \text{PREFER}_b((P(x)), \sim P(x))) \rightarrow \Diamond D_a(\text{PROMISE}(a,b,P)$$

Notice that speech act descriptions have the structure of UGSFs. In order to see the context change implied in the description it is necessary to translate the description into a space structure:

$$\left| \begin{array}{l} B_a \\ \\ I_a(B_b I_a D_a(P(x))) \\ \sim B_b I_a D_a(P(xx)) \\ \text{PREFER}_b \ ((P(x), \sim P(x))) \end{array} \right.$$

By the rule for intentions this space structure gets changed to:

B_a
$\quad I_a D_a$ (PROMISE (a, b, P(x))).
$\quad$ RESULT (PROMISE (a, b, P(x)), $B_b I_a D_a (P(x))$)
$\quad \sim B_b I_a D_a (P(x))$
$\quad$ PREFER$_b$ ((P(x), $\sim$ P(x)))

Checking for the enabling condition we get:

B_a
$\quad I_a D_a$ (PROMISE (a, b, P(x))).
$\quad$ RESULT (PROMISE (a, b, P(x)), $B_b I_a D_a$ (P(x)))
$\quad \Diamond_a D_a$ (PROMISE (a, b, P(x)))

Using the rule for the action operator we arrive at the following context change:

B_a
$\quad I_a D_a$ (PROMISE (a, b, P(x))).
$\quad$ RESULT (PROMISE (a, b, P(x)), $B_b I_a D_a$ (P(x))))
$\quad \Diamond_a D_a$ (PROMISE (a, b, P(x)))
$\quad D_a$ (PROMISE (a, b, P(x)))

$\Longrightarrow$

B_a
$\quad B_b I_a D_a$ (P(x))

The description of speech act types as operators involving context changes does not include the social status of these operators as conventional knowledge of a group of speakers, how to affect intended context changes. In "Grundlagen der Texttheorie" this aspect of speech act descriptions was treated at length, following the analysis of conventions given by D. Lewis, S. Schiffer and others. The gist of the analysis is that the conventions regulating the use of speech acts are utterance conventions (Mitteilungskonventionen) on the one hand and interpretation conventions (Interpretationskonventionen) on the other hand, both based on the concept of mutual knowledge. The utterance convention regulating the use of promise can be specified along these lines as:

For nearly every member of a group G including a and b it is true:

$$UGSF = B_a \sim B_b I_a D_a (P(c)). \; B_a \; PREFER_b \; (Px)), \; P(x))).$$
$$B_a I_a B_b I_a D_a (P(x)))$$

then: $D_a (PROMISE (a, b, P(x))$

and:

1. In group G there is a precedence case of the form:
   $B_x \sim B_y I_x D_x (P(x)). \; B_x \; PREFER_y \; ((P(x), \sim P(x))). \; B_x I_x B_y I_x D_x (P(x))).$
   $D_x \; (PROMISE \; (x,y,P(x)). \; RESULT \; (PROMISE \; (x,y,P(x). \; B_y I_x D_x (P(x)))$
2. for nearly every member of G it is true:
   B_x (for nearly every y and z) if UGSF holds for y and z, then
   $D_y \; (PROMISE \; (y,z,P(x)))$
3. for nearly every x and y in G it is true: if UGSF holds for x and y, then $D_x \; (PROMISE \; (x,y,P(x)))$
4. for nearly every x and y in G it is mutual knowledge, that conditions 1. to 3. hold.

The mutual knowledge condition defines the infinite regress of mutual knowledge typical for human interaction and known in the formalism of game theory.

The conditions 1 to 4 explain the status of speech act types as conventional tools for the solution of coordination problems in a specific group of people; their exact formulation can vary according to one's philosophical views about the genesis and structure of conventions; the present set of conditions is based on Schiffer's analysis of conventional behavior. For the simulation of verbal planning the exact form of the conditions 1 to 4 is unimportant; the analysis of verbal means as conventionalized tools for context changes guarantees that

they are modelled in a form compatible with the structure of UGSFs on
the one hand and the structure of an algorithm for verbal planning on
the other hand. If all "grammatical rules" have the form of utterance
conventions and interpretation conventions, then the description of
linguistic structure is changed into the description of rules regulating
verbal behavior. In "Grundlagen der Texttheorie" I argued for a complete paradigm change transforming all aspects of grammar-writting into
the description of utterance conventions; here I will not take a definite stand on the question of which aspects of utterances are controlled
by pragmatic features of the UGSFs and which aspects can be treated in
a simple semantic-to-surface translation schema following the lines of
a Montague-type grammar or the methods of ATN parsing and generating.
I will only give examples showing that many aspects of utterances can
be explained by features in the underlying UGSF. Let us take up Cohen's
example of the utterance (4)

(4) Can you unlock the door!

in a context in which the door is locked from inside and the speaker
wants to get in. The door-opening procedure is part of a frame specifying the relevant situation features and actions for entering rooms; I
won't specify the frame in detail, because it can be found in Cohen's
thesis. In this frame the speaker considers himself to be in the situation characterized by the parameters:

- he wants to get inside;
- the door is locked;
- the key is on the inside of the lock.

In addition he has the following assumptions about his interlocutor:

- the interlocutor is inside;
- the interlocutor does not know that the speaker wants to get inside;
- the interlocutor can recognize the speaker's voice;
- the interlocutor does not presently intend to unlock the door;
- the interlocutor is cooperative: if he knows that the speaker wants
  to come inside, he will try to remove the obstacles for such an action

etc.

Many of these elements function already in the derivation of a UG from an interaction goal; as this process has been described by Cohen I will for the moment assume the UG to be given as:

$B_a I_a B_b I_a I_b D_b$ (Ee) (UNLOCK(e) . A(b,e) . O(c,e) . DOOR(c))

Notice that "the door" is represented by using an individual constant, because in a given frame there is only one door to be talked about and the speaker knows the identity of the door.

The SF part available for the utterance goal we assume for the moment to be identical with the situation elements specified in the frame and the elements in the speaker's image of the interlocutor already used in deriving the utterance goal from the interaction goal.

In order to find a verbal operator usable in the given UGSF we will assume an utterance convention for the speech act type 'to ask for' ('Bitten um'):

UGSF:

$B_a I_a B_b I_a I_b D_b$ (Ee) (P(e) . A(b,e))
$B_a \sim I_b D_b$ (Ee) (P(e)   . A(b,e))
B_a COOPERATIVE (b,a,)
then: D_a(BITTEN (a,b,(Ee) (P(e) . A(b,e,))))

(the convention conditions won't be enumerated here)

Checking in the UGSF we find that it matches the structure of the UG and the enabling conditions of the SF; therefore by rules already illustrated we can derive:

$B_a I_a$ ASK FOR (a,b,(Ee) (UNLOCK(e) . A(b,e,) . O(c,e) . DOOR(c)))

We now must ask for the elements in this formula that require SF specifications to be verbalized, i.e. for elements that need a definition of the verbal means used as utterance conventions.

One obvious candidate is the relation between a speech act type and the illocutionary force indicators in the utterances. There are many alternative realizations of the speech act "ASK FOR", using different sets of indicators. I will assume for the construction "can you ..." the following utterance convention:

UGSF: $B_a I_a$ ASK FOR (a,b,(Ee) (P(e) . A(b,e)))
B_a POLITE RELATION (a,b,)
then: D_a<"Can" ((T/S)/(T/S)) , "you" (T)>

The then-part of the convention states that the speaker is uttering a token of the type "can" with the syntacto-morphological category (T/S)/(T/S) followed by a token of the type "you" of the category T.

If this convention is used for verbalizing the speech act, we have as a result the sequence "can you" with the given categories and the unverbalized part of the UG: UNLOCK(e). O(c,e) . DOOR(c). In order to confront this part with the lexicon we can use the rule of λ-extraversion first on the constant "c" and derive:

(λ x) (DOOR(x)) . c

The lexicon translates (λ x) (DOOR(x)) into the type "door" with the category N/S, but it says nothing about the relation of the extraposed constant to its verbal realization. We need an utterance convention specifying the SF features responsible for the choice of determiner. I will assume that the speaker's belief that the hearer can identify the entity talked about is a sufficient cause for using the determiner "the". This analysis mirrors Strawson's analysis of definite descriptions, but does not assume that hearer identifiability is a necessary condition for the use of "the". The utterance convention embodying this analysis can be written as:

UGSF: $B_a I_a$ (λ x) (P(x)) . a
B_a(Ex)B_b (x=a)
then: D_a <"the" (S/N)/T "φ" (S/N)>
where: "φ" is the lexical translation of (λ x) (P(x))

The application of this convention in the case analyzed leads to the utterance parts "the" (S/N)/T and "door" (S/N). The rest of the UG is after the lambda-extraversion on "c":

(λy) (UNLOCK(e) . O(y,e) . c . The lexical translation of
(λy) (UNLOCK(e) . O(y,e)) is the type "unlock" of category T/(T/S)

With this translation the UG has been exhausted, leaving the following morpho-syntactic units and their categories:

"Can" ((T/S)/(T/S))
"you" T
"unlock" T/(T/S)
"the" (S/N)/T
"door" S/N

These parts can be combined to form a well-formed utterance of the type S in English:

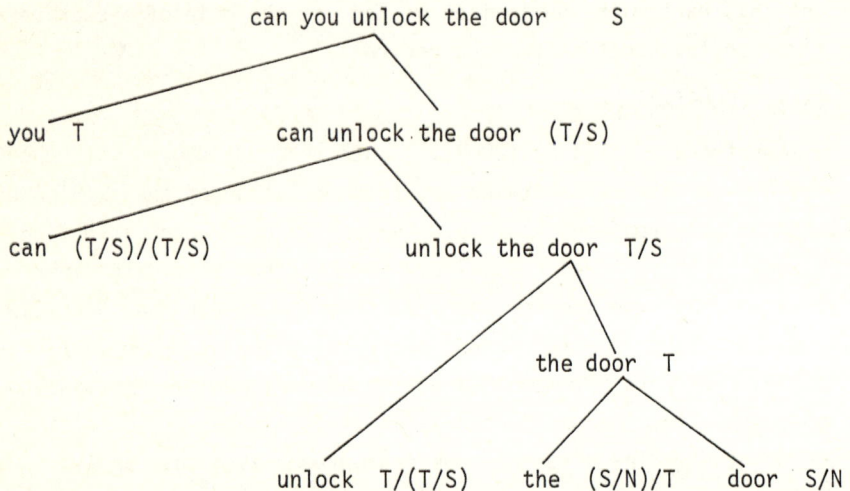

The example gives a rough idea of the form of the verbal means used in planning an utterance: pragmatically based aspects, i.e. aspects dependent on the prefix of propositional attitudes in the UG or on elements of the SF, must be represented by utterance conventions, and semantically based aspects, i.e. aspects not dependent in this way, can be handled by lexical or operational translation rules. It is a matter of the structure of the problem-solving algorithm used in verbal planning, how these verbal means are used in planning utterances.

3. The structure of the problem-solving algorithm used in verbal planning

While in artificial intelligence research the systems for parsing are relatively well developed, there does not exist to my knowledge a pragmatically based system for generating a wide range of utterances. The usual generators are either purely domain-specifically based simple algorithms or pattern-matching procedures. Psycholinguistic research in this area, as e.g. that of A.A. Leontjew, is also not sophisticated enough to handle the procedures of verbal planning for reasonably complex utterances. The following remarks therefore are tentative proposals for work in a relatively new field.

The problem-solving algorithm for verbal planning has to guarantee at least the following properties:

a) It must allow the verbalization of all the information in a given UG;
b) in verbalizing it must use all the relevant information in the SF for the part of the UG it is just working on;
c) it must guarantee that the result of the verbalization is a coherent stretch of grammatically well-formed discourse;
d) it must be able to decide between verbalizations fulfilling conditions a) to c).

While for parsing algorithms a left-to-right strategy seems to have a plausible basis in the mainly linear sequencing of perceived utterances, there is no a priori reason for choosing between one or the other list of priorities in verbalizing parts of UGSFs. Pending further empirical research in this area I want to propose that the algorithm shall start with the speech act dependent features of utterances and then work on the verbalization of the propositional content using information of the SF. This strategy has a certain plausibility, because the speech act dependent properties include such overall properties of utterances like basic word order, sentence type etc. Therefore the processing of the speech act dependent properties gives a specific frame for an utterance, into which the verbalizations of the propositional content have to be fitted. Usually there exist alternative indicating devices for a speech act and therefore different constraints on the realization of the same UG. If the sentence type has been decided on by choosing a speech act indicating device, the propositional context is worked on by using the event predications and their case frames as a basis. This strategy is traditional in artificial intelligence generators. Finally, the rest of the UG is verbalized checking the result for coherence. Notice that in the notation chosen the categorial labels indicate only necessary conditions on coherence, not, as usual in categorial grammars, the conditions on the linear order of elements. These conditions are part of an apparatus of morpho-syntactic rules.

We can now indicate the basic structure of the problem-solving algorithm:

1. The goal state of the algorithm is the UG part of a given UGSF transformed completely into a coherent utterance.
2. The start state of the algorithm is the given UGSF.
3. The algorithm starts by choosing a sequence of speech acts bridging the gap between the goal indicated in the UG part and the given situation model in the SF part (this process has already been illustrated).
4. The algorithm then takes the first speech act and chooses in the utterance conventions for speech acts one of the possible indicating devices for the given speech act.
5. Then the algorithm works on the event predications in the proposition dominated by the speech act and chooses a verbalization via the utterance conventions and lexical lookup procedures. The verbalization must be guided by the SF part of the UGSF.
6. Then the rest of the UGSF is verbalized in accordance with the utterance conventions and lookup procedures available.
7. A coherent utterance is formed from the parts derived via procedures 4 to 6.
8. The process 3 to 7 is repeated choosing alternative realizations by

the utterance conventions and lookup procedures.
9. The alternatives are evaluated by any criteria and one realization is chosen.
10. The chosen alternative is edited by linearization and other morpo-syntactic processes.

I will now illustrate the use of this algorithm with an example.

UGSF: $B_a I_a B_b I_a (Ex)\ D_b K_a (PERSON(x)\ .\ PAST(GIVE(e)))\ .\ A(x,e)\ .$
$B(h,e)\ .\ O(c,e)\ .\ BOOK(e))$
$B_a K_b (Ex)\ (PERSON(x)\ .\ PAST(GIVE(e))\ .\ A(x,e)\ .\ B(h,e)\ .$
$O(c,e)\ .\ BOOK(c))\ .\ B_a (Ey)\ K_b (y = x)$
$B_a (Ex)\ K_b (x = c)$
$B_a \sim I_b (Ex)\ D_b K_a\ (PERSON(x)\ .\ PAST(GIVE(e))\ .\ A(x,e)\ .$
$B(h,e)\ .\ O(c,e)\ .\ BOOK(c)$

Let us assume that there exists an utterance convention for speech acts involving "who-questions" of the following form:

UGSF: $B_a I_a B_b I_a (Ex) D_b K_a (PERSON(x)\ .\ P(e)\ .\ A(x,e)\ ...)$
$B_a K_b (Ex)\ (PERSON(x)\ .\ P(e)\ .\ A(x,e)\ ...)\ .\ B_a (Ey) K_b (y = x)$
$B_a \sim I_b (Ex)\ D_b K_a (PERSON(x)\ .\ P(e)\ .\ A(x,e)\ ...)$
then: D_a ASK WHO (a, b, P(e) ...)

The convention specifies roughly the felicity conditions of "who-questions". The utterance goal is the speaker's intention to make the hearer believe that the speaker intends to make him do something that will make the speaker know who the agent of a certain event is. The enabling conditions specify that the speaker believes that the hearer knows that there is an event with an agent of the specified class, and that the hearer knows who this agent is, and that the speaker believes that the hearer does not intend in the present course of events to inform him about who the agent of the event is. The validity of these conditions on "asking-who" can be seen using the following tests:

(1) Who gave you the book, but I don't want you to believe that I want you to make me know who gave you the book.

(2) Who gave you the book, but I don't believe you know that somebody gave you the book.
(3) Who gave you the book, but I don't believe you know who it is that gave you the book.
(4) Who gave you the book, but I believe you want to tell me anyway who gave you the book.

The utterance sequences (1)-(4) are self-defeating, which proves the status of the conditions in them as felicity conditions. Probably the set of conditions for "asking-you" must be refined, but for our purposes the enabling conditions are complex enough.

Matching the UGSF of the example with the UGSF part of the utterance convention leads to success for step 3 of the algorithm. The speech act found as a means for bridging the communication gap is a "who-question" and the new UGSF is:

UGSF: $B_a I_a$ ASK-WHO $(a,b, PAST(GIVE(e)) . B(h,e) . O(c,e).$
$BOOK(c)) B_a(Ex) K_b(x = c)$

Following the algorithm we must now find an indicating device for "who-questions". Let us assume the following utterance convention:

UGSF: $B_a I_a$ ASK-WHO$(a,b, P(e))$
then: D_a <"who" T , $((\phi_{Ve}) \psi)$ T/S>

The convention specifies that a "who-question" can be realized by first uttering a token of the type "who of category T" and then uttering a stretch of discourse of category T/S starting with a verbal element.

The application of the convention to the UGSF of the example leads to a match, so that we get the following elements of the utterance plan:

$B_a I_a D_a$ <"who" T, $((\phi_{Ve}) \psi)$ T/S>

and the new UGSF:

UGSF: $PAST(GIVE(e)) . B(h,e) . O(c,e) . BOOK(c)$
$B_a(Ex)K_b(x = c)$

Step 5 of the algorithm advises us to work on the event predication of the proposition. In order to do that we have to dismantle the proposition by using lambda-extroversion on the two constants in the benefactive and object roles, resulting in:

UGSF: $(\lambda y) (\lambda x) (PAST(GIVE(e))) \cdot B(x,e) \cdot O(y,e) \cdot h) \cdot c)$
$B_a(Ex)K_b(x = c)$

Lexical lookup leads to the following translation:

$B_a I_a D_a$ <"PAST("give"), T/(T/(T/S)), $(\phi)_T$, $(\psi)_T$>

Choosing this realization we remain with the UGSF:

UGSF: h, BOOK(c)
$B_a(Ex)K_b(x = c)$

We can try now via step 6 of the algorithm to verbalize these remaining parts. Lexical lookup for the constant "h" gives us the translation as "you". In order to arrive at a translation of the remaining part we have to use again lambda-extroversion and the rule for definite determiners used already and repeated here for convenience:

UGSF: $(\lambda x) (P(x)) \cdot c$
$B_a(Ex)K_b(x = c)$
then: "the" (S/N)/T, "ϕ" S/N
where "ϕ" is the lexical translation of $(\lambda x) (P(x))$

Matching this utterance-convention with our UGSF we receive:

$B_a I_a D_a$ "the" (S/N)/T, "book" S/N

We have now finished verbalizing the parts of the original UGSF and we can go to step 7 of our algorithm, checking if we can derive a coherent utterance form our verbalized parts. These parts are:

$B_a I_a D_a$ <"who" T, ((ϕ_{Ve}) ψ) T/S>
$B_a I_a D_a$ <PAST "give" T/(T/T/S), $(\phi)_T$, $(\psi)_T$>
$B_a I_a D_a$ "you" T
$B_a I_a D_a$ <"the" (S/N)/T, "book" S/N>

If we start with the highest-level verbalization, the one for the speech act marking, we can substitute the verbalization of the event predicate in its frame:

$$<\text{"who"}\ T\ ((PAST(\text{"give"})_{T/(T/(T/S))})\ (\phi)_T\ ,\ (\psi)_T>$$

We can now substitute "you" T for one of the two terms necessary for the verbalized event predicate and the sequence $<\text{"the"}\ ,\ \text{"book"}>_T$ for the other term. Checking for coherence we get a well-formed unit:

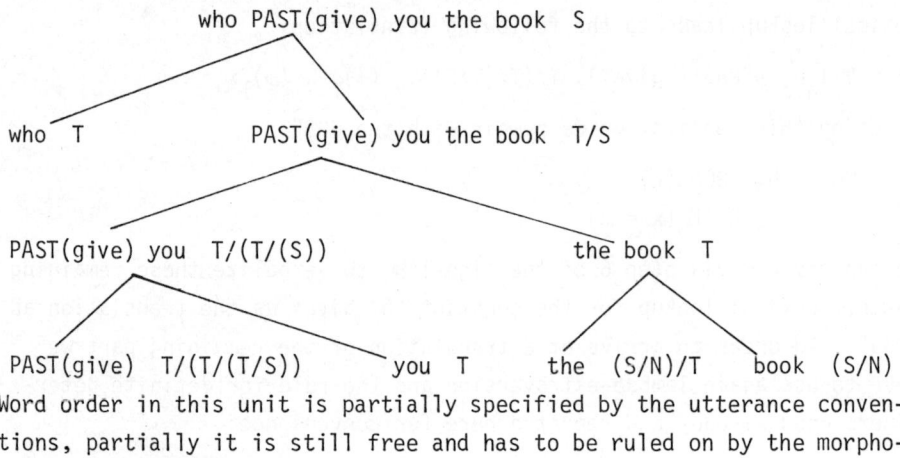

Word order in this unit is partially specified by the utterance conventions, partially it is still free and has to be ruled on by the morpho-syntactic component.

For reasons of space I will not illustrate step 8 of the algorithm, the construction of alternative realizations for the speech act, but will assume that the speaker chooses to realize the coherent unit constructed.

Step 10 of the algorithm requires the editing of the chosen alternative by linearization and morpho-syntactic adaption. In our example "PAST(give)" is morphologically realized as "gave" and a linearization rule specifies that:

$$<T/(T/(T/S)),\ (\phi)_T\ ,\ (\psi)_T>\qquad \text{where}\ \phi = \text{pronoun}$$

is linearized either as this sequence or alternatively as:

$$<T/(T/(T/S))\ ,\ (\psi)_T\ ,\ (\text{"to"}(\phi))_T>.$$

ON THE DELIMITATION OF SEMANTICS
AND THE CHARACTERIZATION OF MEANING:
SOME REMARKS

François Latraverse
and
Suzanne Leblanc

1. *On the notion and problem of delimitation*

The purpose of this volume is to define the possibilities and limitations of pragmatics*. In most of the contributions this question is touched upon in the context of particular problems, but it is rarely examined in its full theoretical dimension. The present paper is an attempt to articulate some considerations — in fact some remarks, which are still somewhat fragmentary — on some of the theoretical aspects of these broad matters.

Obviously, there are a number of ways to think of this subject, according to the various trends, however practical, that intuitively determine the borderlines of the discipline. However numerous these may be, we shall consider, for the time being, only the following two interpretations.

First, it is possible to think that the aim of our discussion is what we shall call a "prospective delimitation", in the course of which one would consider, on the one hand, some "assets" of pragmatics, corresponding to the possibilities of the discipline, and, on the other hand, what brings it to a halt, in front of which it stands puzzled, corresponding to its (perhaps temporary) limitations. Given that pragmatics is still *in statu nascendi*, though some of its fundamental traits

are almost ancient, this kind of recapitulative and prospective survey
may be useful, interesting and even fun, but from a theoretical point
of view it is extremely dangerous to narrow down our evaluations to
that single approach, since it entails a position that we shall call
the *"deus ex futura* position", according to which the development of
pragmatics would simply follow the stream of successive discoveries,
through the prospecting and opening of unknown and perhaps unthought-
of teritories. Moreover, if there is one thing on which a minimal
agreement has been reached, it is the impossibility of defining pragmatics in an inductive manner, by means of the perspicuous summing up
of its presumed realizations and characteristics. On the contrary, it
seems that pragmatics itself corresponds to multifarious and often
divergen directions, such that the definition of a common core would
simply amount to the neglect of the essential diversity of the, so to
speak, *pragmatic language games.*

According to a second interpretation, the one that will be retained
in what follows, what is to be dealt with is the articulation of pragmatics with something that it is presumably not, its other self, its
siamese twin, its shadow, that is to say semantics. It is in itself
most remarkable that the three "disciplines" ("domains", "branches",
"sciences", "sub-sciences", "fields", etc.)[1] of syntax, semantics and
pragmatics, within semiotics, within the general study of language or
something even more general, have devoted and are still devoting a
great deal of their efforts to the negotiations of shared boundaries,
often in an almost diplomatic manner, sometimes in a kind of borderline guerilla warfare, according to the objects and phenomena rightly
pertaining to each discipline.

More precisely, those relations have been discussed on two axes,
according to the type of theoretical space that one prefers. The first
family of discussions has to do with a vertical axis: in this perspective, the results or, more generally, the objects of one domain would
rest, by means of a foundational relation, on another domain, the priority of which can be of a theoretical-logical or of a temporal-material

nature. The second family of discussions concerns an horizontal axis, according to which some objects would be contiguous to another class of objects, in a relation of complementarity, on which it would be possible to give a ruling.[2]

But the development of pragmatics in the contemporary theory of language corresponds first and foremost to the idea or the intuition that the relation of correspondence that lies at the foundation of semantics is not satisfactory, as far as a proper theory of meaning is concerned, and that one should make up for what it lacks by taking into account some other relations, the nature and number of which are still undetermined. From a more strickly linguistic point of view, pragmatics can be seen as a reaction to what can be broadly called 'structuralism' if that term designates an apporach according to which language — as a form and as an activity — manifests uniform and autonomous structures. The effect of the modality of this (quite sober) irruption of pragmatics in the theory of language is that, as far as a conciliation of pragmatics with its neighbours matters, it is not with an empirical contiguity between objects that we have to deal, but rather with multi-leveled articulations, the various points of which have the multiplicity and complexity of what is aimed at, and of the postulates required by each theory.[3]

2. *Realism and methodologism*

In front of the inflation of pragmatic studies, pushing in a variety of still unconciliated directions, we are prone to think that a certain reflective point of view, that we shall term "methodological", might turn out to be fruitful for the examination of the joint questions of the possibilities and limitations of pragmatics. In particular, such a point of view would enable us to avoid what can present itself as an aporetic situation for some semantic theories developed to date, for which the 'ptagmatic question' became crucial. This aporetic situation can be somehow stated as follows: inasmuch, on the one hand, as some theories of semantics have given that question a mentalistic formulation (using, for instance, concepts like 'intentional states', 'beliefs', etc.) and inasmuch as we subscribe, on the other hand, to the opinion that mentalism is the onto-theoretical reduplication of the linguistic face of the signitive correspondence (onto-theory recapitulates grammar, so to speak), the situation becomes aporetic when the systems of intentional states or the systems of beliefs that we would like to use in order to represent the pragmatic phenomenon in its entirely are objects which, in essence, escape from their theory and carry it along in their flight. Any attempt to specify them further can only take place by losing, in an ulterior specification, its conclusive character. The pragmatic phenomenon is thus elusive, because it is regressive, and a theory of semantics that appeals to it in order to solve some of its problems might well narrow its own scope instead of widening it.

It might seem that the only semantic position that would enable us to avoid such a situation would simply be to abstain from asking the question that gave rise to it. Pragmatics would thus become theoretically useless, given that it never could pass the threshold of theory. It would then be relinquished, at most, to a pervading but trivial presence.

One can nevertheless persist in acknowledging this fact, while trying to get hold of it by other means than those presented by the mentalistic framework. It could be thought that the only way to handle the question of those other means would be to define (discover?) some, but, in our opinion, it is important to stress the fact that the methodological point of view here taken is not on a par with some other realistic position. This methodological stance solely amounts to the provisional renunciation of the craving for a starting point that would belong to an extension of a semantic theory or that could be inductively construed through the thorough and fragmentary gathering of a pragmatic "empeira". This position is one of prudence, for we believe that

the ontological suspension that it allows has the advantage, at least
negatively, of not entangling us, at least not in the short run, in
the mentalistic trap that works essentially by the projection of the
elements of our semantic analyses onto an abstruse substratum which is
but the shadow of language. Theories of language often provide then-
selves with the ontology that suits their formal apparatus and this is
how one can reach a perfect adequation between a theory of language and
a theory of linguistic description, which, for example, will introduce
in ontology exactly the distinctivity which is required by the theory.
This situation has been particularly severe in theoretical linguistics,[4]
but one should not be led to believe that it has not occurred in Philosophy. For instance, one may think that the category of intentional
states is a by-product of these approaches that try to give a foundation to the order that they have recognized in language: an intentional
state is the necessary corollary of the production of a semantic unit
if we are to give it a pragmatic orientation.

Given the doubling to which it leads, this kind of grafting can
hardly enable us to see how a pragmatic specificity could be defined,
if the supposed externality of language serves only the recapitulation
of the various theoretical options that we have taken concerning the
nature of language.

3. *The fallacy of externality and pragmatic pseudo-objects*

These questions lead us to a schematic treatment of the make-up of
the object of a pragmatic theory. The effect of the projectivist reification, as well as its epistemological realism, is that an internal
object is defined, relative to which all the rest will be considered
external. In this perspective, semantics would first define its externality through the exclusion of what escapes the control of truth-
functionality.[5] The consequence of that situation will be that no
theory of "external" objects will be analytically articulated on semantics and that pragmatics will be doomed to be an explicative theory
that will only set forth the various states of language (an open

account-book), in different disciplinary perspectives. Pragmatics would thus be an empirical science as Carnap[6] once thought it necessarily was when, making a distinction between pure and descriptive semiotics, following Morris, he states that he could not conceive a pure pragmatics and that all linguistics, that is to say any study of the ocntingent factuality of language, was based on pragmatics. This position, which perhaps cannot be avoided, will only accentuate the divorce taking place between the theoretical approaches of syntax and semantics, within a genuinely general theory of language, and a pragmatic theory that could only acknowledge and codify the external factuality of language.

But it is perhaps not that obvious that the objects of pragmatics must be (seen as) external, which is to say that pragmatics is perhaps not necessarily an explicative theory. Another way to conceive a pragmatic theory could be to think of it as an anlytical theory whose elements, viewed as external in the explicative version, would now be considered internal, their conjunction to semantic elements being otherwise provided.

The question would then be : what are these elements, once external, that would be retrieved in an analytical pragmatics? The question is somewhat important since it is the defects of the classical idea of a semantic theory that are at stake. When one examines the different candidates that various approaches propose, one realizes immediately that they are impressively numerous and that some arbitrariness can prevail in their choice. We will just mention intentional states, beliefs, knowledge of the world and a certain cultural know-how, things that are rooted in a subject that is not specified otherwise. Even if we have reasons to think that these categories belong to a fallacious conceptual vocabulary, we may make the hypothesis that this vocabulary aims at some reality, which is not totally blurred or undifferentiated. The question is then: how are we to conceptualize this reality?

It seems that the notion of 'context' is wide enough, and open enough, to leave intact the prospective character of the question and to preserve the pragmatic intuition on which everybody now seems to agree. The problem is that, so conceived, context is rather a mega— or a proto-concept since, in every case, it is crucially in need of some specification, without which it is somewhat hollow. But it corresponds to some formal necessity, which backs up its obviousness, both from a theoretical point of view (the theoretical use of 'context' in our semantic theories) and from a natural one (its use in communication).[7] The theoretical expression of this necessity is, minimally, that one ought to construe the concept of context as an analytical concept of meaning. The question is then: what can be said about it?

The first thing that strikes us is that we still have no theory of context at our disposal or, more accurately, no theory that has construed context in its analytical relation to meaning outside the correspondence framework.

Intentional states, analyzed into beliefs, desires, etc., are challengeable in that they infinitely regress in the specification of some "same" instead of reaching the "other" that they were presumably aiming at.

As for the concept of index, which precisely aims at a formalization of context, it seems at first sight that its merit is that is satisfies two requirements of a methodological position: on the one hand, it has no psychological commitment whatsover and, consequently, it does not belong to the "language side" of the correspondence relation, and, on the other hand, it is not something in the world either. A plausible idea is then that it does not fit into the exclusive representational pattern of the correspondence relation. But a closer look shows that it does in fact reproduce this relation, since, being established both on the "language side" and on the "world side", it contributes to the articulation of meanings with their references by the restrictions that it applies on the domain of the references. There is nothing, in the onto-theoretical pattern which determines the semantics in which it functions, that can brim over even in the form of a lost externality.

Nevertheless, this concept has been coined to account for the phenomenon of deixis, while context is not limited to indexicality, even in the problematical situation that we know, in which deixis can be considered an intermediate case for the distinction between semantics and pragmatics. It must also be borne in mind, in this respect, that John Searle in "Literal Meaning", claims that most statements of natural languages are subject to a set of 'background assumptions' that cannot be expressed in the semantic structure of the statements considered. Background assumptions are beliefs about or knowledge of the world, and the truth conditions of the statements that work under a presumably literal mode of meaning follow the variation of such background assumptions.

But the problem is that, although one admits the necessity to appeal to a third element, one is simultaneously brought to deny the possibility to submit this element to any theoretical treatment whatsoever. Indeed, inasmuch as background assumptions are independent of the semantic structures of the statements, it becomes very difficult to determine their number and to define their content. This difficulty takes the form of an infinite linguistic regress, in which "[...] each specification of an assumption tends to bring in toher assumptions, those that determine the applicability of the literal meaning of the sentence used in the specification" (Searle 1978:215).

Another possibility is the idea of language games,[8] which, in our opinion, is the most promising for the elaboration of an adequate "theory" of context. Its main advantage is that it accounts for the relation of correspondence by referring to a type of autonomous entity, which cannot be identified with any of the single terms that make it up, that is to say by fulfilling the need for a third term and by escaping traditional isomorphism, and this, beyond what is easily given to intuition, is what is interesting in Wittgenstein's idea. The notion of language games makes it possible, in that debate on the nature of pragmatics, and particularly on its relations with semantics, to pinpoint exactly where our ontological prudence has led us. It seems, in effect, that the question to be asked is whether the predicate 'pragmatic' (or 'pragmatical') applies ot theories or to objects. It is sufficient to open the "Philosophische Untersuchungen" to see that, when one uses the conceptuality of the language games, the neutrality of the various objects offered to reflection is never trespassed. A language game is not a new type of ontological atom, the theory of which would simply have to be realized in order to structure the world in a brand new way.

In fact, most analyses that present themselves as pragmatical do so in virtue of an extension of the traditional objects of semantic theories, but the treatment that they apply to this "new" object is nevertheless isomorphic. Many 'pragmatic' theories are thus semantic theories which, far from redefining a renewed mundane elementarism, apply themselves to something resembling an "extended meaning", using, as has been said, an ontological trickery related to their own language in order to articulate extension analytically.

Now, this is not *even* the idea of pragmatics that Charles Morris developed, however summarily, because, although one finds in Morris a complexification of the objects eternally sanctioned by the various analyses of meaning, a theoretical quest is nevertheless prescribed. For a long time, one has believed that his Grail would be found at the end of a transaction with psychology and sociology, because this quest itself has been besieged by the rationality of representation. Since the object foreshadowed by Morris' behaviourism could not be reached through the analytical projection of the semantic, one had to look for languages whose conceptual differences would satisfy the necessity of some theorization, even if the price to pay was the externalization of what was universally recognized as relevant. Since the third term could not be defined in the isomorphism holding between language and the world, it has been construed as an object of the world for which systems of representation were already available.

In that respect and for whoever thinks that the pragmatic phenomenon is a fact of meaning, a theory of language games would have been preferable. It would be untimely to abandon that intuition of Wittgenstein is by directing toward objectivity what questions the very nature of a theoretical act. For, if any such objective theory was to be found, it would invariably be inadequate, always missing a member of the family of its objects, on account of its meaningful difference.

This blind alley manifests what we shall call the "strict semantical commitment" of the epistemological category "theory", in virtue of which the failure of the isomorphic conceptualization accredits the limitations of the theoretical. If a pragmatic theory of meaning is to be possible, it must react against this commitment by satisfying the following constraints:

(1) All theory construction is itself a language game.
(2) No language game is in a relation of regulation or rationalization with another language game (that is to say: there are no meta-language-games).
(3) All meaning relations must be related to a language game.

The question as to whether or not, in the actual state of the reflection on these matters, such a theory is conceivable from an epistemological point of view remains quite open. Let it be sufficient to say, perhaps temporarily, that the Wittgensteinian way of thinking seems to be at the confluence of prudence and of conceptual possibility of investigation. On the question of the possibility of a theory of language games, one may adopt one of two positions.

The first position would be a radical Wittgensteinian one, according to which a descriptive theory of language games is impossible in principle, because of the infinite grammatical regress that it implies, where one can only partically grasp grammatical[9] effects, which fluctuate with the fluidity of the properly, though enigmatically, so-called 'forms of life', and which manifest themselves in an immediate obviousness, eluding descriptivity. According to this position, the best that we can do is to apprehend the "hardness of the soft" (Wittgenstein 1969:44e), that is to say certain forms that can be identified within language games, but for which one can only give examples, without any hope to give complete accounts (Wittgenstein 1967b:§465). Besides, Wittgenstein called "the real discovery" the one that allowed him to put an abrupt end to the series of examples, thus pacifying philosophy

(Wittgenstein 1958:§133). This position corresponds to a global philosophical, even intellectual attitude which, inviting to see what is obvious, to surrender to it, ruins metalanguage and questions everywhere the mentalistic reification.

A methodological position such as the one defended here may be considered as a 'reasonable' or 'muted' Wittgensteinian position. This position makes the hypothesis that it is possible to describe some of the determinations that constitute language games, even if this description, or this specification, is relative. To specify those determinations is to establish what we shall call the "pragmatical parameters of meaning". Conceived in terms of what they succeed to capture from the language games, those parameters are necessarily partial, but they must be exhaustive when seen from the point of view of the finality of theory construction. The exact nature of those parameters is an open question that echoes the openness of our theoretical undertakings. However, one thing must be clear: we must be very circumspect as to the attribution of those parameters to any mental substratum.

The finality of the definition of these parameters is distinctivity, but it is important not to think that the ground on which this distinctivity is set would be of an external nature: there is no externality relative to which a pragmatic theory would draw the boundaries of its domain. The residuum of any definition of pragmatic parameters is a necessary product and it cannot be salvaged by any ulterior empirical investigation. To put it briefly, from a methodological perspective on meaning, there is nothing that can be considered an externality. What could be viewed as "other" to defined structurations is not what resists analysis, what would still remain to be conquered, a challenge issued to them, but only their condition of possibility. Between them, there is no discontinuity, since they belong to the same level of reality. Their apparent difference simply indicates the limits of meaning, without there being any other territory beyond these limits.

FOOTNOTES:

*This paper was presented in French in a somewhat shorter version at the Urbino conference. Our thanks go to Terry Myers, Sheila E. Keene, Jean-Pierre Paillet and Jacques Poulain for their assistance on some points of the English translation and on some more fundamental questions.

1. For some indications on the richness and the looseness of this vocabulary in general semiotics, see H.H. Lieb (1971).

2. Even if such a ruling seems to be quite an undertaking as is exemplified by the abundant literature on the question of delimitation, the idea of respective belongings is nevertheless maintained. The general opinion expressed here is that only a foundational analysis is possible, even if the analysis reinforces the aporetic character of the problem.

3. The neglect of this relativity explains some of the questions that we quite naively ask ("Is *that* really pragmatical, isn't there any way to straighten it into *some* semantic theory?), which amounts to an odd reification of the products of our theoretical approaches. One should try not to be tortured by one's own creatures.

4. The best example being the tendency, within the transformational-generative framework, to find psychological correlates to the phenomena described by syntax, if not the tendency to invite psychologists to learn something from linguistics while defining linguistics as a branch of psychology.

5. This is to be understood as a minimal requirement for the definition of pragmatics: we are not saying that the impossibility of defining the truth conditions of a statement is a sufficient condition for its being held as pragmatical, but only that if pragmatics is to have some characteristic whatsoever, its ideas on truth-functionality must matter. Besides, from an almost 'historical' point of view, pragmatics has always (in particular in this volume) defined itself relative to some conception of truth.

6. See, for instance, R. Carnap (1968).

7. This distinction is quite important since it can enable us to avoid one confusion that often takes place, namely the confusion that occurs when one esteems that the use of context in ordinary communication resembles, even remotely, the use it has in our theories. One might well say that context is "over-determined" in everyday communication because the appeal to context is always minimal since it is directed by some function in communication (if you are asked "In what context did she say "bla bla bla"?", you usually know perfectly well what can be counted as a relevant element of context, all the rest being taken for

granted), while context, in its theoretical use, is "under-determined" since the appeal to context serves mainly to warrant the distinctivity of meanings, which, on the one hand, often *depend* on the specification of context and, on the other hand, are so construed that context can never be fully specified or even presented. (This might be used, in some way or another, in the appreciation of the role of examples in the study of language.)

8. Those who are not familiar with the notion are invited to read Wittgenstein's "Philosophical Investigation". Although, in the case of Wittgenstein's writings, one cannot understand much of it if one is not acquainted with the totality of the work, this is the best shortcut that one can take.

9. In Wittgenstein's sense of 'grammar', which is not at all obvious. To put it very briefly, the term 'grammar' refers to the conditions (indifferently seen as necessary or arbitrary) that permit our statements and, more generally, our representations. The interesting fact is that Wittgenstein's use of 'grammar' and 'grammatical proposition' is perfectly neutral as to the traditional distinction between empirical and formal questions, grammar being interpreted equally well from the point of view of factuality and from taht of the form of representation since it indicates points where it becomes impossible to tell the one from the other. ("A whole cloud of metaphysics condensed in a drop of grammar". (Wittgenstein 1958:222e)).

PRAGMATICS AND CONVERSATIONAL RHETORIC

Geoffrey Leech

1. *Introduction*

Principles (like Grice's Cooperative Principle) are different from rules (like the syntactic rules for negation and interrogation in English) although both are constraints on linguistic behaviour. I am interested in investigating how far the domain of pragmatics can be defined as the domain of principles, rather than of rules. I use the term 'Conversational Rhetoric' for the set of principles by means of which language is matched to the communicative functions we perform in using language. My aim here is to show in outline how this strategy for delimiting pragmatics works in the case of English negative and interrogative sentences. I shall start with syntax, move on to semantics, and finally end up in pragmatics. But first, an apology and some preliminary assumptions.

The names Grice and Searle tend to crop up in pragmatics more frequently than other names, although neither of these philosophers, so far as I know, makes use of the term *pragmatics* itself. What I shall say will owe a great deal to both of them, although neither would be likely to acknowledge my ideas as legitimate offspring. Roughly speaking, I shall try to reduce Searle's account of speech acts (1969, 1975a) to Grice's account of conversational implicature (1975). For this enterprise I shall give only a skeleton justification. In particular, I shall not be overcareful in observing Grice's second Maxim of Quality: "Do not say that for which you lack adequate evidence" (1975: 46). But then, I am a linguist rather than a philosopher; and one may claim that in linguistics, this maxim is more honoured in the breach than in the observance.

2. *A set of postulates*

I shall therefore start by presenting a set of postulates for the purposes of this paper. By the end, I shall have given some grounds for accepting these postulates. For the present, I merely give some face-value reasons for giving them credence.

> P1: The semantic representation (or logical form) (SR) of a sentence is distinct from its pragmatic interpretation (PI).

In other words, there is a valid distinction between meaning and use, the sense and the force of an utterance, between semantics and pragmatics. I assume that formal linguistics includes semantics, but not pragmatics. My face-value reason for accepting this distinction is that contrary positions tend to lead to absurdity. On the one hand, there have been attempts to reduce pragmatics to formal linguistics. This attempt manifested itself as 'the performative hypothesis' in the early 70s, and led to some obvious absurdities, particularly when it was applied to indirect speech acts. The *reductio ad absurdum* of this approach, to my mind, was Levin's proposal that underlying every poem there is a deleted performative which reads: "I imagine myself in and invite you to conceive of a world in which ..." (1976: 150).

On the other hand, there have been attempts to reduce linguistics to pragmatics; to show, as Searle did, that "a theory of language is part of a theory of action" (1969: 17). This has probably not led to such manifest absurdities, but it reached a certain degree of implausibility in Searle's suggestion (1969: 25) that in addition to illocutionary acts, acts of predicating, acts of referring, etc., one might want to talk about phonetic acts, phonemic acts, morphemic acts, and so on. There are things that we do with language, but that doesn't mean that language is all a matter of doing.

P2: Semantics is rule-governed (= grammatical); pragmatics is principle-constrained (= rhetorical).

The distinction I make here between 'rules' and 'principles' corresponds to that which Searle makes between 'constitutive rules' and 'regulative rules'. Linguistics has generally assumed that its subject-matter is rule-governed. Examples of constitutive rules are transformational rules in syntax and rules of inference in logic: these define the nature of the language system, and are assumed to operate, under appropriate conditions, without exception. If you find my use of 'grammatical' in P2 uncongenial, I can only plead that this matches the usage of transformational linguists when they talk about 'the grammar' as the total language system: syntax, semantics, phonology. 'Rhetoric' I use in the traditional sense of 'the art or skill of using language effectively'.

The canonical case of a rhetorical principle is Grice's Cooperative Principle (CP). Searle also recognizes the existence of principles when he talks (1975a:72) of the 'generalizations' which relate indirect to direct illocutionary acts. Principles, like generalizations, admit of exceptions, and operate under a *ceteris paribus* condition; further, I would claim that they are relative rather than absolute. One can be relatively informative or uninformative, relatively truthful or untruthful, relatively polite or impolite. Principles can also compete with one another, and one principle can be overridden by another. In general, however, P2 is in conflict with Searle's account of speech acts, for Searle claims that illocutions are defined by constitutive rules: a speech act, for him, on the whole either 'counts as' a promise/order/request or it does not.

P3: The rules of grammar are primarily conventional; the principles of pragmatics are primarily non-conventional, i.e. motivated.

Again, there is a conflict between this postulate and Searle's view of illocutionary acts. Searle says that the rules for performing and interpreting illocutions are conventional. For example, under stated conditions, an utterance will count as a promise; but if we ask *why* does it count as a promise, the only answer must be: "Because the rules say so". I would argue, in contrast, that we *can* give reasons, in terms of general principles of motivated discourse, as to why a certain kind of utterance may function as a promise - as a means of assuring a hearer, that is, that a particular action will be carried out in the future. In fact, I would say that a promise is recognized as a promise not by means of rules, but by means of a recognition of the speaker's motive.

Here I have assumed an association between the conventionality of rules, and the linguistic notion of arbitrariness, as opposed to motivatedness. Saussure's notion of the arbitrariness of the linguistic sign is one of the foundation stones of modern linguistics, and in general, linguists, in expounding the rules of grammar (e.g. the rules for negation and interrogation in English) have taken it for granted that their task is to state what the rules are and how they work, rather than to say what functions the rules perform, or what is the motivation for their being what they are. I use, in preference to the word 'intention', the vaguer and more neutral words 'motivation' and 'function', because I follow Popper (1972) in believing that just as knowledge can be objective, lying outside the individual and inhabiting the public domain, so can the functionality of language. There is continuity (particularly clear in the child's development of language) between biological and social functionality, and the point where intention breaks into the picture is not clear. So there is a natural extension of the use of 'motivated' from individual speech acts to general principles of language use, as exemplified in the CP. It take it that the hallmark of statements in pragmatics is that the reasons for them, as Grice says of conversational implicatures (1975: 50), "must be capable of being worked out" by reference to principles which go beyond the structure of the language system itself.

Having said this, one must admit that the question of conventionality is more complicated. Forms of behaviour can have an explanation

which is both conventional and motivated at the same time, and I would
want to claim that many grammatical rules and categories, while being
strictly conventional, are also susceptible, in part, to a functional
interpretation. More important, from the present viewpoint, is the
observation that pragmatic strategies can become to a greater or lesser
degree conventionalized. Indirect speech acts such as "Why don't you
listen" become institutionalized or idiomatized in specific languages,
but not in others. This institutionalization is well illustrated in
Figure 1 (from Debrett's *Correct Form* (Montague-Smith 1979:287)).

Figure 1

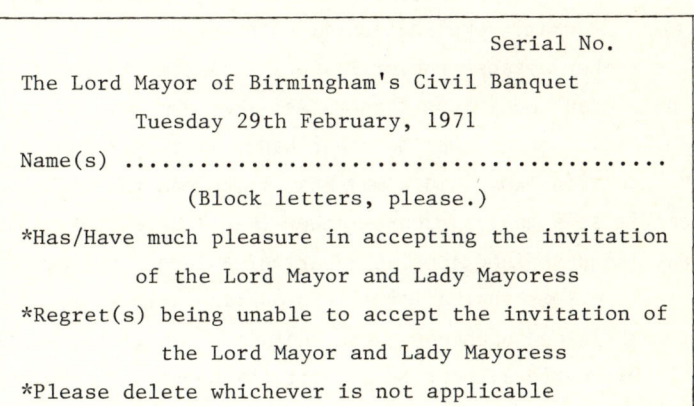

Here, as in other cases, institutionalization takes the form of an elimination of semantically well-formed options, and may therefore be called PRAGMATIC SPECIALIZATION. There are many possible ways of replying
to a formal invitation, but only two are conventionally allowed. There
is a vast excluded middle between 'X has much pleasure in accepting'
and 'X regrets being unable to accept'; for example: 'X has little
pleasure in accepting', 'X has much displeasure in accepting', 'X regrets being able to accept', 'X regrets being unable to decline', etc.
But these are excluded by the principle of politeness. Thus although
the number of responses is conventionally reduced to two, this reduction is motivated, in that it is possible to give a general explanation

of why other responses would be less acceptable or appropriate than
these. The conventions of pragmatic specialization presuppose a more
basic functional explanation. This brings us to:

>P4: Grammatical explanations are formal;
>pragmatic explanations are functional.

Roughly speaking, a grammatical theory provides an explanation of a set
of linguistic facts by specifying a system of rules, categories, conditions on rules, etc., by virtue of which the occurrence of this set of
facts, rather than another, is predicted. The rules constitute the explanation, and are evaluated by formal criteria of economy, predictive
strength, etc. Pragmatic explanation is both weaker and stronger than
this. It is weaker because rhetorical priciples impose weaker constraints on language behaviour than rules: they can only be predictive
in a probabilistic sense. On the other hand, it is stronger because it
answers the question 'why?' in a way that is beyond the goals of formal
explanation: it says that X occurs rather than Y because X is in accord
with the way language functions as a part of a larger system of human
behaviour. It follows that a formal explanation will always leave a
residue of unexplained phenomena, and that if a functional explanation
is available we should attempt to give it, as being more explanatory
than a purely formal explanation. In this way, Searle (1975a) gave a
functional explanation of one of Gordon and Lakoff's conversational
postulates (1975), and I would like to attempt to go further, and provide a functional explanation of Searle's rules for speech acts (1969).

>P5: Grammatical characterizations of language phenomena are
>largely determinate; pragmatic characterizations of language
>phenomena are substantially indeterminate.

Once again, the distinction implied here between semantics and pragmatics is relative rather than absolute. Grammatical rules are subject
to various forms of indeterminacy, whether this is a matter of socio-
lectal variation, or of the fuzziness of categories (as in the cases of
Ross's 'noun phrase squish', 1973). But one can go a long way with

phonology, syntax, and semantics on the assumption that characterizations are uniquely assignable to sentences. Pragmatic inferences (implicatures) have been distinguished from logical inferences on the grounds that they can be cancelled in appropriate contextual conditions; furthermore, in pragmatics one is often dealing with continuous rather than discrete variables. For example, the difference between an offer and a request, or between a threat and a promise, is in the degree to which the uptake of an illocution will benefit or penalize the hearer; the difference between an order and a request, or between a promise and an offer, is a matter of the extent to which speaker or hearer is understood to be committed to a future action (Leech 1977a). Hence it is a widespread feature of illocutionary acts that they are uncategorizable in a yes-or-no way, and we often trade on this indeterminacy:

(1) Here, take a seat.
(2) I order you to take a seat.
(3) I invite you to take a seat.
(4) I advise you to take a seat.
    etc.

It is surely impossible, in many circumstances, for either the speaker or the hearer of (1) to decide whether it is to be interpreted as equivalent to (2), (3), (4), etc. Just because we have the means to make illocutionary force explicit by performative verbs, we should not assume that all utterances are as neatly categorizable as performatives. For this reason, I do not accept Searle's assumption (1969: 21-2) that one can always make explicit, and presumably determinate, the force of a speech act.[1] Speech acts do not fit into neat pigeon-holes, as speech act verbs do. Speech acts, that is, belong to pragmatics, while speech act verbs belong to grammar.

P6: (General) pragmatics relates the SR of an utterance to its PI; this relationship may be relatively direct or indirect.[2]

Taking the argument one stage further, P5 claims that semantic and pragmatic characterizations are two different kinds of thing. Following Grice, I believe that the relationship between them can be stated in the form of an argument which takes account of (a) the principles of conversational rhetoric, (b) factual and contextual information, and (c) the application of informal reasoning processes, such as are used by human beings in solving commonsense problems. This informal reasoning is what Searle has in mind (1975a: 82) when he says that the way we arrive at the indirect illocutionary point of an utterance does not fit any of the usual explanatory paradigms: "The problem seems to me somewhat like those problems in the epistemological analysis of perception in which one seeks to explain how a perceiver recognizes an object on the basis of imperfect sensory input". It is recognized, of course, that such solutions become automatized: there is no claim that the human interpreter laboriously constructs a step-by-step argument in order to recognize that a table is a table, that a promise is a promise. For both cases, the appropriate paradigm seems to be that of problem-solving theory. From the speaker's point of view, the problem is: "Given that I want the state of the hearer to change or remain unchanged in such and such respects, how do I frame my utterance in order to make that outcome most likely?". From the hearer's point of view, it is "Given that the speaker said so-and-so, what is the most likely reason for his saying so-and-so?". An appropriate problem-solving model, from the hearer's point of view, is that of HEURISTICS (Hunt 1975: 331): we employ strategies which deliberately sacrifice completeness in order to get a rapid solution most of the time. We go for the most likely solution first, and if that proves incompatible with a preliminary scan of the evidence, we go for the most likely solution which resolves this incompatibility, and so on. Grice's conversational implicature obviously fits into this paradigm, as a means of resolving incompatibility with face-value evidence.

My aim is now to give an example of how this approach works out, by applying it (necessarily in an informal way) to the pragmatics of negation and interrogation in English. The method will be to start with syntax and to work towards pragmatics. This means three stages of analysis: syntactic, semantic, and pragmatic.

3. Some aspects of negation and interrogation in English

3.1 Syntax

All of the following combinations, except (6), are possible in English:[3]

(5) *George is sometimes late.*   declarative affirmative
    The train has arrived already.   assertive
(6) *George is ever late.   declarative affirmative
    *The train has arrived yet.   non-assertive
(7) George isn't sometimes late.   declarative negative
    The train hasn't arrived already.   assertive
(8) *George isn't ever late.*   declarative negative
    The train hasn't arrived yet.   non-assertive
(9) Is George sometimes late?   interrogative affirmative
    Has the train arrived already?   assertive
(10) *Is George ever late?*   interrogative affirmative
     Has the train arrived yet?   non-assertive
(11) Isn't George sometimes late?   interrogative negative
     Hasn't the train arrived already? assertive
(12) Isn't George ever late?   interrogative negative
     Hasn't the train arrived yet?   non-assertive

On the other hand, only the sentences in italics (5), (8), (10), and possibly (12), are in any sense 'usual'. The usual cases can be accounted for by the syntax redundancy rules:

(13) Rule I   negative   ⟶ non-assertive
     Rule II   interrogative   ⟶ non-assertive
     Rule III   otherwise   ⟶ assertive

But this analysis on the syntactic level does not account for the 'unusual' cases (7), (9), and (11), nor for the fact that the relation between the affirmative and negative questions (10), (12) is not parallel to that between affirmative and negative statements (5), (8).

3.2 *Semantic analysis*

These facts can be accounted for on the level of logical/semantic structure. On this level, the three syntactic oppositions correspond to three logical oppositions:

(14)   *Syntactic oppositions*   *Logical oppositions*
     affirmative : negative $pos\ (X)$: $neg\ (X)$
     declarative : interrogative $pos/neg\ (X)$: $?\ (X)$
     assertive : non-assertive X^+ : X^o

Here X represents the predication ('propositional content') shared by each member of a set of sentence types. The superscripts of X^+ and X^o represent respectively the factuality operators 'fact' and 'non-fact' which are expressed, for example, through the choice of *some* and *any*, or between *sometimes* and *ever*. The question mark $?$ is the question symbol which is a free variable ranging over $\{pos,\ neg\}$ in *yes/no* questions. That is, the question mark indicates that the truth value associated with some X is undetermined: it is what Searle (1969: 31) calls a propositional function.[4] The 'standard' sentence-types (5), (8), and (10) can thus be associated with propositions and propositional functions as follows:

    (5) George is sometimes late. $[pos\ (X^+)]$
    (8) George isn't ever late. $[neg\ (X^o)]$
   (10) Is George ever late? $[?\ (X^o)]$ ·

These formulae exemplify logical restrictions on the combination of $\{pos,\ neg\}$ with $\{^+,\ ^o\}$: positive affirmative propositions are factual (that is, they incorporate the claim that x corresponds to some state of affairs), whereas negative and interrogative sentences do not. These restrictions may be expressed by an appropriate reformulation of the redundancy rules in (13) as a set of logical rules:

   (15) In any proposition [p], *pos* cooccurs with X^+,
      neg cooccurs with X^o, and $?$ cooccurs with X^o.

This explains why (6), combining *pos* with x^o, is ill-formed. The formulae for (5), (8) and (10) also exemplify the mutually-exclusiveness of *pos*, *neg*, and *?*: naturally *pos* and *neg* are contradictory, and *?* is the variable which leaves *pos* and *neg* unspecified. A third point about these formulae is that they are enclosed by [ ], which indicates that the whole formula has the format of a proposition, something which may act as an argument of the predicates TRUE, FALSE. However, since strictly speaking only (5) and (8) represent propositions, it will be convenient to use the cover-term 'propositional' for all three formulae (5), (8) and (10).

In terms of this analysis, all questions fall into the category of 'propositional functions'. Thus a unitary definition of questionhood, as a logical type, applies to both *yes-no* questions and *wh*-questions. According to this definition, all questions are 'defective propositions', and the logical answer to a question is one which completes the proposition by supplying the missing information; i.e., which supplies a value for the propositional function. For example:

(16) Who killed Cock-robin?   [*pos* (KILL x, cock-robin$^+$)]
(17) The sparrow killed Cock-robin. [*pos* (KILL *sparrow*, *cock-robin*$^+$)]

(17) is the logical answer to (16), because it assigns a value to the free variable x, and in a similar way, (5) and (9) are logical answers to (10), because they assign a value to the free variable *?* in (10). These are 'answers' in a logical sense, which is not to deny, of course, that there may be other *pragmatically* appropriate responses to a question, such as 'I don't know', or 'No one did'. I am assuming, that is, that question and answer are logical rather than pragmatic categories; I am also assuming a distinction between a logical answer, and a syntactic realization of it, which may take such abbreviated forms as *Yes*, *The sparrow*, in accordance with general rules of ellipsis.

The problem to be considered now, however, is how to provide a logical analysis of the remaining sentences (7), (9), (11), and (12). In providing an answer, I shall try to show that a satisfactory solution from the logical point of view is also the key to the pragmatic interpretation of such sentences. By way of anticipation, it is as well to notice here the rather special pragmatic implications of these 'less usual' sentence types by considering further examples. Suppose that a customs official, instead of asking his routine question (18), asks instead one of the questions (19)-(21):

    (18) Have you anything to declare?   Cf. (10)
    (19) Have you something to declare?   Cf. (9)
    (20) Haven't you anything to declare?   Cf. (12)
    (21) Haven't you something to declare?   Cf. (11)

Immediately the relationship between the customs official and his interlocutor is placed on an abnormal, non-routine, and perhaps rather sinister footing. Here are possible contexts:

    (19) Customs official sees a woman hovering uneasily between the 'Nothing to Declare' and the 'Something to Declare' exits. He suspects that she has something dutiable in her luggage, and wants to encourage her to make a clean breast of it.
    (20) Customs official sees the woman struggling past with vast quantities of suitcases, etc. He cannot believe that amongst all that luggage she has nothing that should not be declared. He challenges her.
    (21) Customs official sees the woman walking through the 'Nothing to Declare' exit with jewellery spilling out of her handbag. He is as good as accusing her of smuggling.

Further examples show that these special question-types are closely connected with politeness:

    (22) Will you have anything to eat?
    (23) Will you have something to eat?
    (24) Won't you have anything to eat?
    (25) Won't you have something to eat?

If these are invitations from a hostess to a guest, (22), although it is the most regular kind of question, is the least polite, whereas (25) is the most polite. Here the implications of personal disposition are the opposite of those of (18)-(21). On the other hand, when the hostess addresses her guest as follows, only (27) can count as an expression of polite regret, and (28) is downright rude:

(26) Are you leaving yet?
(27) Are you leaving already?
(28) Aren't you leaving yet?
(29) Aren't you leaving already?

To explain such overtones, let us first return to the logical analysis. An initial attempt to formulate the 'unusual' types of sentence would be a mechanical translation of the syntactic features into their logical correspondents:

(7a) George isn't sometimes late. $*[neg\ (X^+)]$
(9a) Is George sometimes late? $*[?\ (X^+)]$
(11a) Isn't George sometimes late? $*[?\ neg\ (X^+)]$
(12a) Isn't George ever late? $*[?\ neg\ (X^o)]$

These formulae have asterisks, because they are clearly ill-formed according to the logical constraints mentioned: (7a), (9a), and (11a) combine *?* or *neg* with factuality; (11a) and (12a) combine *?* with *neg*. This face-value ill-formedness is, in fact, an explanation of why they are 'less normal'. Their logical form has to be more complicated, and their pragmatic implementation more oblique, than those of more regular sentences such as (5), (8), and (10).

A clue to their logical form is that some, at least, of these sentences, have the nature of what have been called SECOND-INSTANCE utterances; that is, they presuppose a context in which they make reference to some previous utterance. This is clearest in the case of (7a), which could be contextualized as follows:

(30) *A*: I'm sorry to hear that George and Bill are sometimes late for work.
    B: George isn't *sometimes* late, he's *always* late!

Similarly in (19), the smuggler might angrily retort to the customs official

(31) No, I *don't* have something to declare!

But in the other examples, it is not necessary that a second-instance utterance should repeat, in whole or in part, a previous utterance: it is only necessary for the proposition 'resurrected' by the second-instance speaker to have been believed or entertained in the relevant context.[5] In this broader sense, such utterances are 'metapropositional' rather than 'metalinguistic': they express a propositional about a propositional.

Once it is accepted that propositionals may make reference to other propositionals, the logical analysis of these sentences proceeds according to the rules:

(32) a. X^+ must occur within the immediate scope of *pos*.
  b. If two symbols from the set $\{pos, neg, ?\}$ occur together in the same propositional, one of them must be attached to the main propositional, and the other to an included (embedded) propositional.

In fact, these are minimal extensions of the logical constraints mentioned earlier. Rule (a) simply repeats the logical constraint mentioned in (15) - that X^+ can occur in the same propositional as *pos*, but not in the same propositional as *neg* or *?*. Similarly, (b) is a way of making sense of the already-mentioned mutual-exclusiveness of *pos*, *neg*, and *?*, by attaching them to the different propositionals, such that one propositional is included within the other. With these two rules, we get the following revised formulae:

(7b) [*neg* [*pos* (X^+)]]   (11b) [? [*neg* [*pos* (X^+)]]]
(9b) [? [*pos* (X^+)]]   (12b) [? [*neg* (X^o)]]

Included propositions are delimited by [ ]; notice that the rule has applied twice in the case of (11b).[6]

This analysis, however, is still less than satisfactory. Firstly, it postulates a dual interpretation of *?* and *neg*, in line with the well-known distinction between internal and external negation. It has been argued that this distinction is unnecessary, and indeed it would be a pity not to give a unitary definition of negation and interrogation. This distinction arises because *?* and *neg* have two kinds of operands: in the most usual case they operate on predications (X^O) and in the less usual case they operate on propositions. We can, however, make the less usual case into a special case of the more usual, by recalling that propositions are defined as taking the predicate *TRUE* or *FALSE*. The insertion of *TRUE* between each included proposition and the preceding operator, so that (*TRUE* [p]) becomes a predication (an instantiation of (X)), reduces the two kinds of negation/interrogation to one. Such an analysis is what underlies sentences such as (33):

(33) It is true that I drank your beer. [(*TRUE* [p]$^+$)]

And we note, in corroboration, that (33), like (7), (9), (11), and (12), is a second-instance sentence, assuming that the proposition "I drank your beer" has already been entertained in the context. This now means that the formulae (7b)-(12b) can be finally rewritten as:

(7c) [*neg* (*TRUE* [*pos* (X^+)]^O)]
  "It is not true that George is sometimes late."
(9c) [*?* (*TRUE* [*pos* (X^+)]^O)]
  "Is it true that George is sometimes late?"
(11c) [*?* (*TRUE* [*neg* (*TRUE* [*pos* (X^+)]^O)]^O)]
  "Is it true that it is not true that George is sometimes late?"
  (i.e. "Isn't it true that George is sometimes late?")
(12c) [*?* (*TRUE* [*neg* (X^O)]^O)]
  "Is it true that George isn't ever late?"

This reformulation, incidentally, deals with another weakness of the analysis of (7b)-(12b): there was no explanation, in that analysis, of why the operators *pos*, *neg*, and *?* only occur in one scope-ordering, viz. '*pos* within (*neg* within) *?*'. This ordering, under the new formulation, is the only one which is well-formed according to the rules: *pos* must be innermost when X is factual (X^+), and *?* must always be outermost, because *TRUE* must be predicated of a full proposition, not of a propositional function.

I therefore judge that (7c)-(12c) are the simplest, in the sense of most general, rule-governed analyses of logical types that they represent. But as written formulae, they are far from simple, and so for convenience of reference, I shall abbreviate them as follows (adding a further example of each sentence-type):

Abbreviations:

(5d)	*pos X*	e.g. She bought some flowers.
(7d)	*neg TRUE pos X*	e.g. She didn't buy some flowers.
(8d)	*neg X*	e.g. She didn't buy any flowers.
(9d)	*? TRUE pos X*	e.g. Did she buy some flowers?
(10d)	*? X*	e.g. Did she buy any flowers?
(11d)	*? TRUE neg TRUE pos X*	e.g. Didn't she buy some flowers?
(12d)	*? TRUE neg X*	e.g. Didn't she buy any flowers?

3.3 *Pragmatic analysis*

3.3.1 *Positive statements*

I shall begin the pragmatic analysis with the straightforward cases (5d), (8d), and (6d). For maximum generality, no specific prior knowledge will be assumed about the context. Nevertheless, certain minimal pragmatic assumptions may be made: e.g. that the utterance has both a speaker (s) and a hearer (h), that both s and h understand its conventional linguistic meaning. A further assumption is that s is observing the CP. Thus, for (5d), the most direct pragmatic interpretation is roughly as follows:

(5e) A. *pos X* (given)
  B. s says to h that X (minimal communicative assumption)
  C. s believes that X (Quality)
  D. B has the function of making h fully aware (i.e. informing h) that X (minimal illocutionary assumption)
  E. s believes that h is not aware that X (Quantity: corroborative condition)

(5e) F. s believes that it is desirable for h to be aware that X
(Relation: corroborative condition)

C is derived from B and the second Maxim of Quality. The illocutionary assumption D, which is the most important part of the interpretation, is derived from the combination of the other statements B, C, E, and F, again assuming the CP. It corresponds to Searle's 'essential condition', just as C corresponds to his 'sincerity conditon'. E and F, which in Searle's terms would be 'preparatory conditions', make use of the Maxims of Quantity and Relation. These are 'corroborative conditions' because they are ancillary conditions which, if they obtain, confirm the assumption in D. That is, if the function of B is informative (which is the most likely assumption), then s must believe that h is not aware that X, and that it is desirable for h to be aware of X. The CP here constitutes a background assumption from which the more specific assumptions C, E, and F are made. These assumptions may be called 'context sensitive' in the sense that contextual evidence may cause them to be abandoned. I am suggesting that they are likely to be the least risky assumptions that can be made, and that they are accepted 'by default' if there is no evidence to the contrary. B, C, D, E, and F are all 'default assumptions' in this sense. They are manifestations of what Garfinkel calls the '*et cetera* assumption' by which speaker and hearer 'fill in' common understandings and perspectives. The chain of reasoning can be diagrammed as in Figure 2:

Figure 2

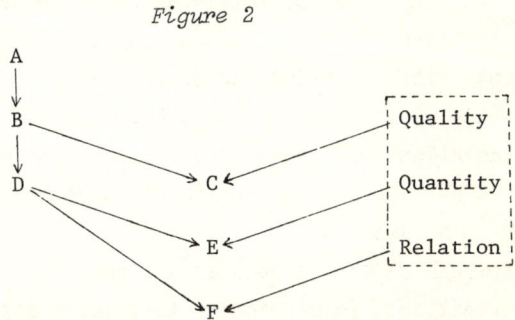

The arrows here bear no realation to logical inferences: what I am describing is more like an amateur detective procedure, in which the obvious guess is made first, and then checked for contrary evidence. The default hypothesis represented by the diagram could be rejected on grounds of counterevidence to any of its constituent statements (except A). Suppose, for example, that A were "It's noisy in here". We would then reject D on the grounds that if s were aware of the noise, so would h, unless h happened to be deaf. Therefore E ("s believes that h is not aware that X") would be rejected, and D would not hold.

This analysis draws on Grice's conversational implicature and on Searle's speech acts, but involves some reinterpretation of both. As far as Grice is concerned, C-F can be considered implicanda, using Grice's broad sense of implicature, although they are not of the kind that he most discusses - those implicanda involving an apparent violation of the CP. Moreover, I have extended the second Maxim of Quantity (in a way suggested by Pratt 1977) so that it applies to the choice of whether to say anything at all. "Do not make your contribution more informative than is required" means, in the limiting case, "Do not assert anything unless you have some information to impart". Therefore the fact that s makes an assertion is in itself grounds for assuming E. This is one reason for speaking, and the other makes an appeal to the Maxim of Relation, in the following way. One possible interpretation of this hard-worked Maxim is that the context should provide a motive for the utterance. Ryan (1974:135-6) says, proposing a further maxim, "One must not say what there is absolutely no point in saying". His example is of a man who stands up in a crowded restaurant and says "I am wearing all my usual clothes". But the extra maxim is unnecessary, since such an utterance would normally violate both the Maxim of Quantity and the Maxim of Relation. In cooperatively informing h of X, s should believe that h is not aware of X, and should also believe that it is desirable for h to be aware of X.

The statements of (5e) also bear a strong resemblance to Searle's speech act definitions, in particular to that of assertion (1969:66). In effect, A corresponds to the propositional rule or condition; C corresponds to the sincerity condition; D to the essential condition; and E and F to preparatory conditions. A major difference is in the essential condition, which Searle states as a convention: e.g. for requests, "Counts as an attempt to get h to do A (=Act)". The equivalent statement in (5e) is more like a 'fulfilment condition' or 'success condition': it interprets illocution in a way that Searle rejects, as an intended perlocution. But Searle's argument against this interpretation (1969: 42-50) is based on the assumption that speech acts are rule-governed, and that their rules do not admit of exceptions. If this requirement is not made, there is no problem in associating the pragmatic force of an utterance with the description of what it would mean for that utterance to be communicatively successful - assuming, that is, that the success condition is what it appears to be on available evidence. What I have tried to do, then, is to fit speech acts into a modified Gricean paradigm, and to suggest that some of the conditions on speech acts are predictable from others, given the CP.

3.3.2 *Negative statements*

Negative propositions follow the same interpretative pattern as positive ones, except that for X in (5e), the negation of X is substituted in each line of the interpretation, and except that an additional implicature is derived. This additional implicature is derived from the first Maxim of Quantity, via what may be called the principle of NEGATIVE UNIFORMATIVENESS (cf. Givón 1978). Negative propositions are generally far less informative than positive ones, simply because the population of negative facts in the world is far greater than that of positive facts. Consider the sentences:

(34) a. Bogota isn't the capital of Peru.
  b. Bogota is the capital of Colombia.

Both statements are true, but assuming a current United Nations membership of 132, a. is 131 times less informative than b. Hence to reconcile such a negative proposition with the first Maxim of Quantity, we must assume a context in which the negation of X is precisely as informative as is required. This will be the case if s believes that h prior to the uttering of *neg X* has a disposition to believe that X. Thus we add, in the case of a negative proposition, the implicature:

(8ė) G. s cancels h's assumed disposition to believe that X.

3.3.3 *Ordinary yes-no questions*

Straightforward questions such as (10) may be pragmatically interpreted as follows:

(10e) A. ? X
- B. s puts the question ? X to h (minimal communicative assumption)
- C. s does not know whether X is the case (Quantity)
- D. B has the function of getting h to inform s whether X is the case (minimal illocutionary function)
- E. s believes that h knows whether X is the case (Relation: corroborative condition)
- F. It is desirable for s to know whether X is the case (Relation: corroborative condition)

Since the logical analysis of yes-no questions characterized them as 'defective propositions', propositions lacking a positive or negative sign, it is reasonable to argue, via the first Maxim of Quantity, that unless s does not know whether X is the case, s is breaking the CP. Hence C, which Searle treats as a preparatory condition for questions, is a natural implicature. There may, of course, be other reasons for leaving the positive-negative value of x unspecified. This will be true of cross-examination questions in court, classroom elicitation questions, examination questions, and rhetorical questions. Searle, by way of justifying C as a condition for questions acknowledges a difference between 'real questions' and 'exam questions'. But this oversimplifies and overcompartmentalizes in a way which is avoided if the word 'question' is restricted to a logical sense. All that is claimed in (10e) is that a *yes-no* question, as a logical category, finds its most likely implementation in circumstances where s does not know the answer.

C will fail in those more specific contexts (e.g. examination rooms and courtrooms) where there are other reasons for asking questions.[7]

With the provisional identification of a question as an information-seeking device in D, the Maxim of Relation does double duty in checking this assumption, in E and F.

3.3.4 *Loaded yes-no questions*

Leaving aside the assertive negative proposition (7) (which is a rather different problem - see Note 5), I turn now to the more complex 'loaded questions' (9), (12), and (11) - in that order. Some general strategy for interpreting second-instance sentences is required for all these cases, and the correct approach seems to run roughly as follows. Second-instance questions contain a face-value infringement of the Maxims of Manner, in that regarded purely as information - elicitations, they are logically more complex and oblique than is necessary. This is because there is a logical equivalence between every one of these second-instance questions and a simpler question in which the predicate *TRUE* does not occur. Consider:

$$(9f) \; ? \; TRUE \; pos \; X \longrightarrow \begin{cases} pos \; TRUE \; pos \; X = pos \; X \\ neg \; TRUE \; pos \; X = pos \; X \end{cases}$$

In (9f) the two propositions to the right of the arrow are the alternative logical answers to the question on the left of the arrow. And these two answers are logically equivalent to the simpler propositions *pos X* and *neg X*. The situation is the same for (12) and (11), except that the positions of *pos X* and *neg X* are reversed:

$$(12f) \; ? \; TRUE \; neg \; X \longrightarrow \begin{cases} pos \; TRUE \; neg \; X = neg \; X \\ neg \; TRUE \; neg \; X = pos \; X \end{cases}$$

$$(11f) \; ? \; TRUE \; neg \; TRUE \; pos \; X \longrightarrow \begin{cases} pos \; TRUE \; neg \; TRUE \; pos \; X = neg \; X \\ neg \; TRUE \; neg \; TRUE \; pos \; X = pos \; X \end{cases}$$

If we define questions as 'logically equivalent' if there is a one-to-one relation of equivalence between their answers, then all these questions are logically equivalent to the simple question *? X*. That is, nothing can be elicited by these questions which cannot be equally well elicited by a much simpler question. According to the Maxims of Manner, therefore, we expect to find some reason for this wilful obliquity. What can it be? What distinguishes these from ordinary questions like (10) is that they refer to one or more propositions. A reference to a proposition presupposes that the proposition exists, viz. exists in somebody's mind. Hence a minimum pragmatic assumption about second-instance questions is that the propositions to which they refer 'exist in the context'. This must generally mean that they exist in the speaker's or the hearer's mind, as an assumption. I shall call this the SECOND INSTANCE IMPLICATURE.

The analysis of (9) proceeds along these lines. Since (9) is a special case of (10), the analysis repeats that of (10), substituting *TRUE pos X* for *X* throughout. However, since *TRUE pos X* is logically equivalent to *X*, we can reverse the substitution process by replacing *TRUE pos X* simply by *X*. The extra second instance implicature G is added:

(9e) A. *? TRUE pos X* (e.g. *Did she buy some flowers?*) is equivalent to *? X*. Therefore B-F in (10c) apply to *? TRUE pos X* as well. IN ADDITION:
G. s assumes or believes h to assume that X (Manner, second instance)

G explains why assertive questions such as (9) tend to be called 'questions with a positive bias', or 'questions expecting the answer Yes'.

Similarly for the negative question (12) (*? TRUE neg X*). In this case, the included proposition is negative, and so the second-instance implicature takes the form of G':

(12e) A. *? TRUE neg X* (e.g. *Didn't she buy any flowers?*) is equivalent to *? X*. Therefore B-F in (10e) apply to *? TRUE neg X* as well. IN ADDITION:
G' s assumes or believes h to assume that *neg X* i.e. that X is not the case (Manner, second instance)
H G' cancels a disposition in s or an assumed disposition in h to believe that X. (Quantity, negative uninformativeness)

The further implicature H is added by virtue of the principle of Negative Uninformativeness. Thus a negative question such as *Didn't she buy any flowers* expresses two contrasting expectations: one (the cancelled expectation) that she bought some flowers, and a second (the actual expectation), but she didn't buy any flowers. It is for this reason that such questions typically connote surprise, or even disbelief in what appears to be the case (e.g. *Aren't you ashamed of yourself?* - "I would expect you to be ashamed of yourself, but apparently you're not".)

The negative assertive question (11) "Didn't she buy some flowers?" adds yet one further degree of obliquity. Once again, the implicatures of ordinary questions apply here too, *? TRUE neg TRUE pos X* being mutually substitutable with *? X* in A-F. To these we add the three implicatures G', H, and I:

(11e) A. *? TRUE neg TRUE pos X* (e.g. *Didn't she buy some flowers?*) is equivalent to *? X*

G' *s* assumes or believes *h* to assume that *neg TRUE pos X* i.e. that *X* is not the case. (Manner, second instance)

H G' cancels a disposition in *s* or an assumed disposition in *h* to believe that *TRUE pos X* (Quantity, negative informativeness)

I H conflicts with assumption by *s* or *h* that *X* (Manner, second instance)

The negative assertive question is treated in the same way as the negative non-assertive question, except that the additional second instance implicature I is derived from the second included proposition. Pragmatically, the main difference between the two is that (11) expresses a stronger commitment to the positive proposition, the 'assumption' in I being stronger than the 'disposition to believe' in H. There is a stronger connotation of disbelief, and moreover (11) tends to occur where the proposition *pos X* has actually been asserted or presupposed in the context. The difference is brought out in (28) and (29): "Aren't you leaving yet?" could be an exasperated question to a guest who has outstayed his welcome: "I hoped/expected that you would have left, but it appears that you haven't", whereas "Aren't you leaving already?" could not be used in that context: its user assumes that "You are leaving already" is likely to be true, rather than just a fervent wish. It is understandable, in this light, that negative assertive questions like (11) and (29) often effectively cease to become information-eliciting utterances (questions in Searle's sense), and become an indirect and slightly tactful way of expressing disbelief in what h has said or implicated.

4. *Politeness*

This leads back to the question of politeness. Questions such as (22)-(25) are, for reasons we must ignore here, typically interpreted as offers, and it is noticeable that the loaded questions (23)-(25) are more polite as offers than (22):

(22) Will you have anything to eat?   *? X*
(23) Will you have something to eat?   *? TRUE pos X*
(24) Won't you have anything to eat?   *? TRUE neg X*
(25) Won't you have something to eat?   *? TRUE neg TRUE pos X*

Although we cannot consider politeness in detail, we may observe that politeness is frequently a function of 'polite beliefs' and 'impolite beliefs'. 'Polite beliefs' are those which are favourable to the hearer, (or sometimes to a third party), while 'impolite beliefs' are those which are unfavourable to the hearer. There is an essential 'Asymmetry Principle' of polite behaviour, in that whatever is a polite belief for the speaker tends to be an impolite belief for the hearer, and vice versa. This asymmetry is exemplified in the very nature of offers: it is polite to offer someone something, but it is also often more polite to decline an offer than to accept it. As the term 'polite belief' itself suggests, such beliefs are what a speaker purports to believe, rather than what he actually believes, which may be quite different.[8]

The assertive question (23) is more polite than the ordinary question (22), because it implicates (see G in (9e)) a polite belief:

(23a) s assumes [or believes h to assume] that h wants something to eat.

(The material in square brackets may be ignored for the present - see below.) Typically, (24) is also more polite than (23), for reasons which are more complex. A negative question, as we have seen, implicates an actual negative assumption and a cancelled positive belief. These two implicatures correspond to the hearer's 'polite belief' and the speaker's 'polite belief' respectively. Thus (24) is doubly polite because it pays the hearer the compliment of assuming he is being polite. It gives the hearer a chance to withdraw or suppress a polite refusal:

(24a) s [assumes or] believes h to assume that h doesn't want anything to eat. This cancels a disposition by s [or an assumed disposition by h] to believe that h does want something to eat.

But (25) is even more polite, because it countermands the hearer's polite assumption (or the hearer's anticipated refusal) by an equally strong polite assumption on the part of the speaker: the speaker refuses, as it were, to accept the politeness of the hearer, since to do so would involve himself in being impolite at a further remove:

(25a) s [assumes or] believes h to assume that h doesn't want anything to eat. This cancels a disposition by s [or an assumed disposition by h] to believe that h does want something to eat.

This conflicts with an assumption by s [or an assumed assumption by h] that h does want something to eat.

The words in square brackets in (23a)-(25a) are in practice excluded from the interpretation of these polite questions, although according to my previous account of the second instance implicature, they should be a possible component. The significant thing is that these are in practice excluded because they represent *impolite beliefs*. Here we see how the politeness principle interacts with the CP, causing an impolite part of the interpretation to be suppressed.

Another significant point is that these analyses show a connection between politeness and obliquity (indirectness). Because (23a)-(25a) are in effect restricted to the implicature of polite beliefs, we can observe how every additional implicature adds an extra degree of politeness. A principle at work here is that of 'reciprocity of perspectives' as well as asymmetry of politeness: to be really polite, one must assume that the hearer is also being polite, and must forestall his politeness. This leads in theory to an infinite regress of politeness, of which the first three stages are represented in (23a)-(25a). Thus we may derive from the progressive addition of implicatures in (23a)-(25a) a corresponding set of 'politeness implicatures':

(23b) s is observing the politeness principle.
(24b) s is observing the politeness principle.
s assumes that h is observing the politeness principle.
(25b) s is observing the politeness principle.
s assumes that h is observing the politeness principle.
s assumes that h assumes that s is observing the politeness principle.

Without anlysing in detail the customs official examples (16)-(19), we may note that in this case obliquity works in the opposite direction: because 'You have something to declare' is an impolite belief, the more indirect kinds of question are progressively more impolite, more threatening, than the ordinary *yes-no* question.

5. *Conclusion*

The separation of semantics from pragmatics is justified if it can be shown that there are different kinds of regularities to be observed on each of these levels, and that the relation between these two kinds of regularity can be explained in a principled way. This is what I have tried to demonstrate in this paper.

On the semantic level, rules can be formulated to account for the logical relātions between affirmative and negative, assertive and non-assertive, declarative and interrogative sentences, and to account for the apparent asymmetry of these categories in syntax. On the pragmatic level, generalizations can be made about the way in which the CP and the politeness principle determine the form of linguistic behaviour in relation to communicative function. It is clear that these two classes of regularity are of a very different nature, and yet their synthesis through the problem-solving strategies of pragmatic interpretation is able to show how sentences which are syntactically alike (such as negative questions) may have widely varying and contrasting pragmatic interpretations.

FOOTNOTES:

1. For a more guarded position, see Searle (1975b); e.g. "Differences in illocutionary verbs are a good guide, but by no means a sure guide, to differences in illocutionary acts" (p. 345).

2. I use the term "general pragmatics" here because I believe that there is a whole area of pragmatic investigation (e.g. much of what is termed conversational analysis) which is not covered by the rubric of P6. One should perhaps draw a distinction, therefore, between "general pragmatics" and "sociopragmatics", which is less abstract, and is concerned with the instantiation of pragmatic principles in specific social settings.

3. "George is ever late" is not ungrammatical if *ever* is interpreted, archaically, as an assertive adverb (= 'always'). It should also be noted that the syntactic characterizations of (5)-(13) ignore the possibility of combinations of assertive and non-assertive forms occurring in the same utterance, e.g. "Some people don't send any Christmas cards". I am not concerned in this paper with those occurrences of assertive quantifiers which are to be interpreted as outside the scope of negation.

4. The crucial difference, however, is that in Searle's analysis only *wh*-questions are treated as propositional functions. Cf. the logical analysis of questions in Keenan and Hull (1973).

5. More carefully considered, second-instance utterances include two quite different categories: those repeating the content of a proposition, and those repeating or quoting its form (see Leech 1977b for these and other categories of 'metareference'). My concern in this paper is with the former type (which may be called *metapropositional*) rather than with the latter (which is properly *metalinguistic*). It will be noted, however, that the most likely (but not the only) second-instance interpretation of (7) "George isn't sometimes late' is metalinguistic. This is the interpretation that can be captured by enclosing *sometimes late* in quotation marks: "George isn't 'sometimes late'". In this sense, its truth conditions are quite different from those of the corresponding non-assertive sentence (8) "George isn't ever late".

6. The formulae of (7b), (9b), (11b) and (12b) are not in themselves derivable from the rules of (32): another rule specifying a hierarchy of scope inclusion ? > neg > pos appears to be required. This ordering is, however, determined independently by cooccurrence constraints, as will be seen below in the discussion of (7c)-(12c).

7. See Levinson (1979) for a detailed analysis of questions on these lines, and a consequent critique of Searle's dichotomy of 'real questions' and 'exam questions'.

8. In other words, linguistic behaviour may be polite 'on the record', but not 'off the record' (see Brown and Levinson 1978). Naturally in pragmatic interpretation we are concerned with the beliefs implicated by what is said, rather than what beliefs are sincerely held by s and h. The politeness principle (see below) may be said the overrule the CP in the sense that an implicature that s is being polite brings into doubt the extent to which the belief-statements implicated through the CP are to be taken at face value, i.e. in accord with the Maxim of Quality.

PRAGMATICS, LANGUAGE GAMES, QUESTIONS AND ANSWERS*

Paolo Leonardi
and
Marco Santambrogio

1. It is one of the businesses of pragmatics to state what it is appropriate to say under what circumstances. In order to do this, pragmatics has to state the *rules* of linguistic institutions. There are many such institutions, not all of the same importance: when it comes to the very basic ones, it is difficult to distinguish the tasks of pragmatics from those of other disciplines. Take the institution of assertion: as an influential pragmatical maxim goes, one should be prepared to give support and reasons for what one asserts. But it is logic that tells us what counts as a reason for what, which sentences one can justifiably utter after which other sentences. There is some sort of dependence here of pragmatics on logic.

But we would like to claim more than this. At a very high level of generality, logic and pragmatics seem not to be distinct at all. Pragmatics has a non-empirical core; one might call it "logical pragmatics".

Apparently there is a vast difference between the ways pragmatics and logic look at linguistic phenomena. The prototypical pragmatic situation is one in which at least two people are involved and the basic relation is that of influencing each other's (linguistic) actions. Logical semantics, on the other hand, seems to abstract from the speakers and to take into account only sentences and their relations with the world, the basic relation being that of satisfaction of reference (which means truth when it comes to sentences).

But it is not necessarily so. There is another way of setting up logic, so that it becomes pragmatical in character, while still yielding all the familiar systems and results. Paul Lorenzen has developed a game-theoretical approach to quantification theory in which pragmatical ideas are prominent; Wolfgang Stegmueller, Kuno Lorenz and, above all, Jaakko Hintikka[1] (in a different philosophical perspective) have further explored it, and made the basic ideas widely known so that we can assume some familiarity with it.

Let us mention only some of the basic concepts. These dialogical games for assertions are two-person, zero-sum games. As a sentence is given, a game starts between two players: one of them may be regarded as the speaker or Proponent, who utters the sentence in the appropriate context and is interested in showing that it is true; the other may be regarded as his Opponent: he is interested in showing that the Proponent is wrong or at least in subjecting to criticism the support provided by the Proponent for his own utterances. If you wonder what the Opponent's point could be in behaving in such a way, you might think of the critical conscience of a Popperian scientist.

At each stage a subsentence of the main sentence is considered. For example, if a sentence of the form $'(Ex)A(x)'$ is asserted by the Proponent during the game, then he has to find a suitable member -- say, c, to give it a name (if it does not already have one) -- of the domain, D, of the individuals considered; and the game continues with the Proponent asserting $'A(c/x)'$. If it is a universally quantified sentence, it is the Opponent who searches for the individual c, and the Proponent then has to assert $'A(c/x)'$. In a negated formula, the Proponent and the Opponent exchange their roles. For instance, a game on such sentences as the following:

(1) There is a number with no predecessor
(2) There is a person with no parents

having the logical form $'(Ex)(Uy) -A(x,y)'$, runs as shown in table 1.

$(Ex)(Uy) - A(x,y)$	
$(Uy) - A(c_0,y)$	c_1
$- A(c_0,c_1)$	$A(c_0,c_1)$

Table 1

In a finite number of moves an atomic sentences is reached which is either true or false in the given domain D. If it is true, whoever has asserted it has won, and his partner has lost. This is just one version of such games. We shall later use another, slightly different one.

The moves in such games are made according to rules, depending on the logical form of the sentences uttered by the players, i.e., on the logical constants occurring in the sentences. That this game-theoretical interpretation of the logical constants yields a proper theory of first order logic is seen as soon as one *defines* the notion of truth of a complex sentence S in terms of our games, as follows: S is true if and only if its Proponent has a winning strategy in the associated game. The truth of S is thus the existence of a winning strategy of the appropriate kind.

Now, why are these games pragmatics? The idea at work here is that the meaning of a logical sign is not determined with the help of truth conditions, but by stating its *use* in dialogues. To use a sentence by asserting it makes sense only if there is or there can be someone on the other side, who denies the asserted proposition. This is why the dialogical situation is essential. Monologues will not do, even less sentences taken *per se*. No doubt this is related to what Wittgenstein said about the social character of rules and the absurdity of private language. The fact that one cannot abstract here from the roles of the users of the language is what makes such games pragmatical in character. The basic notion is that of doubting or attacking the partner's assertions and forcing him to defend them. The notion of truth gives way to that of proof.

That one has to give reasons for one's assertions is the main rule of the institution of asserting. It is also the leading idea of the game; when consistently developed, it is sufficient to produce the usual logical systems. But there are large epistemological differences between this approach to logic and the standard one: "The dialogical approach justifies the logical intuitions of Brouwer and Heyting" (Lorenzen 1969: 39). As Lorenz put it, if logic is conceived of as a science of truth, then one is led to the construction of a system of truths which hold universally, in all possible worlds, independently of special facts of the actual world. This can be done by first stating some such truths and providing ways of generating the others -- as in Hilbert-like axiomatized systems.

> On the other hand, effective logic (explicitly in its operative interpretation), must be looked at as a system of 'universal' rules which are accepted whenever a system of rules of action, e.g. rules for producing proofs or rules for producing arbitrary strings of signs, has been laid down. In this case, the field of application for the rules of logic is not the world as the totality of facts, but rather the world as seen in terms of specific kinds of scientific human activities. Within mathematics, for example, the rules of effective logic may be used without restriction. And this obtains, because mathematics is not viewed at as a system of truths, even less logical ones, but it is treated as an independent scientific activity which, together with its intrinsic rules, may use the rules of logic as additional 'admissible' ones. (Lorenz 1973: 354-355).

This is very much what Brouwer, who showed how to make sense of mathematical activity without regarding it as an attempt to elaborate a true story of what there is, seems to have had in mind. It might be interesting to note that B. van Fraassen has suggested that such an account of mathematical activity *qua* activity should really be called *pragmatical*. Also, for the kind of verificationist or non-realist semantics Dummett advocates, which takes the notion of proof as central in the theory of meaning and is closely related to the intuitionists' ideas, "it would be much more accurate to say that semantics is foresaken in favour of pragmatics". It is not a mere coincidence, therefore, that the systems of logic naturally arising from dialogical games are intuitionistic (although some additional rules would yield the classical ones), and pragmatical in the sense of explicitly formulating the rules which guide our linguistic praxis of asserting sentences, stating what we are allowed and what we are forbidden to do (our rights and duties).

We shall come back later to the problem of showing the relevance for pragmatics of language games. First we want to consider an extension from assertions to questions and answers, as the institution of questioning is by itself of considerable pragmatical interest.

Nuel Belnap (e.g., in Belnap 1969) has distinguished two approaches to the logic of questions and answers, and two distinct explicanda: the epistemic (such as that of Hintikka and Åqvist) and the linguistic (such as that of Belnap himself). The difference lies in the fact that the former, unlike the latter, sees questions as containing an epistemic operator and as having the logical form: "Bring it about that I know ...". We shall adopt the linguistic approach, but we shall try to show that the game-theoretical framework can be of some help with epistemic and pragmatical problems.

Hiż and Hintikka[2] seem to us to be absolutely right on an important point: interrogative pronouns are near relatives of what logicians call *quantifiers*. A question -- as Hiż states -- can be obtained from a sentence by replacing a phrase in it by a variable and prefixing a 'questioner'. Thus it consists of two parts: a questioner and a *datum questionis*. From a *datum questionis* an answer is obtainable by replacing the free variable by a phrase of the proper syntactic category. It is the questioner (examples being: *who, where, which bank, about whom,* etc.) that behaves as a quantifier, at least in wh-questions. This is our starting point. We take questions to be in general of the form '$(?x)A(x)$', and their direct answers to be all sentences of the form '$A(c/x)$'. Here A need not be in the language of first order logic, and x need not be a quantifiable *individual* variable. Sentence (3)

(3) What did John do with the knife to Peter?

can be put in the form

(4) For which x, John $x$ed Peter with the knife?

With the quantifier '?' binding a variable in the role of a two-place predicate. If the variable of quantification can range over sets, kinds and even sentences and truth values, one can put yes/no questions, some why-questions, some how-questions, etc., into the same form. E.g.:

(5) How did he do it?

can be rendered as

(6) For which x, he did it $x$ly?

where x ranges over adverbs;

(7) Does it rain?

can be rendered as

(8) For which x, x is the truth value of 'It rains'?

and so on. But no attempt is made here to give a complete account of all the possible interrogatives.

However, we shall restrict ourselves to first-order languages. As one can here quantify over individuals only, the form '$(?x)A(x)$' can express only some which-questions; but we shall also need yes/no questions and whether-questions. For these we introduce two more kinds of interrogative formulas:

a) $?(A,B)$ — for whether-questions (to be read as "Which of A and B is true?"), having as direct answer A and B;

b) $?A$ — for yes/no questions, having A and $-A$ as direct answers.

Some questions have a *presupposition*. We say that Q presupposes a statement P if and only if the truth of P is a logically necessary condition for there to be some true answer to Q.[3] It is easy to see that a which-question has the following sentence as its presupposition: '$(Ex)A(x)$'. If one asks

(9) Which positive integer is the smallest prime greater than 45?

one presupposes that there is such a prime number.

Sometimes such a presupposition is missing from a which-question. Many people feel that

(10) Which member of the club have you met?

does not presuppose that you have met at least one member of the club, so that "None" would be a perfectly good direct answer to it and not the negation of its presupposition, or a *correction* (as it is usually called). These cases do not create new problems, however, as they can simply be met by dropping some of the conditions to be given later.

A whether-question '$?(A,B)$' presupposes that at least one of A and B is true: its presupposition is therefore '$A \lor B$'. A yes/no question '$?A$' presupposes only that A has a truth value or that it is either true or false: '$A \lor -A$' is therefore its presupposition. A yes/no question is thus seen to be *safe* in the classical framework, since it presupposes a tautology. Intuitionistically, or in other deviant systems, things are more complicated and perhaps more interesting too, but we will not go into this.

This is all there is for the time being to our syntax of questions.[4] It is a rather radical simplification over Belnap and Steel's complicated syntax: for one thing the completeness and distinctness claims have been entirely disregarded, so that our proposal could be seen as relevant to only one-example which-questions plus yes/no and whether-questions. It is our feeling, however, that Belnap and Steel are putting too heavy a burden on erotetic syntax and that the treatment of those two claims does not properly belong to it. According to Belnap and Steel, to the question

(11) Which are the prime numbers between 10 and 20?

one cannot give as a direct answer

(12)   13 and 17 are

since a completeness requirement, which should be syntactically expressed in a formalization of the question, would be violated. The question itself requires that *all* the primes be given between 10 and 20, not only *some* of them. However, the reason why (12) does not do is precisely the same as for the assertion

(13)   13 and 17 are the prime numbers between 10 and 20

which is false because it too contains such a claim as well. It is the assertoric logician who should accommodate for the completeness claim when finding the logical form of some assertive sentences containing it. In the special case of (11) a modicum of set-theoretical notation could do the job: question (11) should be taken to mean

(14)   For which x, x is the set of all primes between 10 and 20?

which has the form

(15) $(?x)(Uy)(y \in x \leftrightarrow y$ is prime and $10 \leqslant y \leqslant 20)$

just as

(16) $(Uy)(y \in \{x_1,\ldots,x_n\} \leftrightarrow y$ is prime and $10 \leqslant y \leqslant 20)$

is a logical form of

(17) $x_1,\ldots,x_n$ are the prime numbers between 10 and 20.

Similarly

(18)   Cicero and Tully denounced Catilina

is certainly not a direct answer to the question

(19)   Who denounced Catilina?

since a distinctness claim is violated, Tully and Cicero being the same person; but for the same reason

(20)   Cicero and Tully denounced Catilina

is false or at least odd in some way even in assertoric logic. Finally, we feel that assertoric logic is where all problems related to category restrictions belong. Were these matters settled at that, our proposal to take which-questions as invariably of the form '$(?x)A(x)$' could be seen as encompassing more than just one-example which-questions.

Now, what is the precise semantical and pragmatical status of the interrogative quantifier? Hintikka's proposal amounts roughly to this: it is like an existential quantifier in every respect. It would be more accurate to say, however, that it behaves only in part as an existential quantifier: in part it is similar to a universal one. In order to see this, consider a questioner Q who asks

(9) Which positive integer is the smallest prime greater than 45?
$((?x)A(x))$

and a member R (for Respondent) of his audience. Let us suppose it is a genuine question, not an examination question. Q presupposes that there is at least one such number, and he is responsible for his presupposition, but he is not able to find such a number and wants some help. If R wants to interact with Q at all, there are *at least* two (in fact more) things he can do. He can either *correct* Q, denying his presupposition and asserting '$-(Ex)A(x)$'; or he can help Q and find himself an n such that $A(n/x)$ holds, and assert this sentence. But it is not enough to give a direct answer: he who asserts it is also taking on himself the responsibility of showing it is true -- according to the general maxim that one should give reasons for one's assertions. Of course the same holds for the correction to the presupposition.

Thus, as soon as a question is put, a game starts between two players, who alternatively put forth either an assertion or a question, to which the other responds by putting forth another according to rules. Such a game is more general than the assertoric games considered so far, since it contains them as subgames. Now, our *?* is very much like an existential quantifier in so far as an interrogative formula starting with it can be attacked or corrected by asserting the negation of an existentially quantified formula; but it is like a universal quantifier in so far as the choice of the appropriate individual is left to the Respondent, who also takes on himself the proof of the substitution instance of the matrix.

$(?x)A(x)$	$A(c/x)$ (direct answer)
	$-(Ex)A(x)$ (correction)

Table 2

Corrections and direct answers are not the only moves one is allowed in response to a question, however. Suppose that back home from Urbino someone asks you:

(21) Was Smith at the conference?

Now, suppose that Smith was in fact there and you saw him, without knowing that he was Smith. Then it would be unwise of you to answer either "Yes" or "No", if you have to prove what you say. You should simply abstain from playing the game. Too many questions would then go unanswered which do in fact receive an answer if there were no other moves available besides those mentioned so far. But it is clear which kind of move is appropriate in such cases: you should ask a *counterquestion* such as

(22) What is Smith like?

We should also allow a Respondent to postpone an answer or a correction to Q's question until he has got an answer to his own question. So a subgame starts with the same rules as the main one, but with inverted roles, with the Respondent as (local) Questioner. After a subquestion has been answered (but notice that Q himself should be allowed to ask subsubquestions, and so on) the situation is not the same as before. One player has elicited some assertion from the other, who has also provided some justification for it; that assertion has become public knowledge in that game, and the partner himself can make use of it. By means of questions, Q and R are pooling together part of what they know, so to speak. So either player, in answering to the other's questions, has a right to take advantage of what his partner has asserted. In assertoric games, hypotheses from which the player can prove a sentence take the form of sentences for which the Opponent is responsible and which can be attacked.

Can we allow any number of subquestions? No, for otherwise our games could have no end in a finite time. We shall allow the players themselves, however, to choose at the outset the number of questions they will ask, the only restriction being that the Questioner has at least one more question available than the Respondent, in order to prevent the latter from asking back the very same questions. At this stage we put no constraint on the content of the subquestions. It is reported that Bertrand Russell proved that he was the Pope, starting from the hypothesis that 2+2 = 3. We may thus imagine a dialogue like this: "Are you the Pope?" - "Is 2+2 = 3?" - "Yes" - "Then, yes, I am the Pope". One can find many other examples to show what clever people can do with apparently odd questions. Still we might feel that a subquestion should be asked only if the answer to it will be *used* at some later stage and it has something *in common* with the main one. These would be the *relevant* subquestions. But Belnap himself (one of the founders of relevant logic) does not say anything about this, and we feel entitled to ignore it.

Before giving the full set of rules, there is one final problem. People usually say that the difference between examination questions and proper questions is pragmatical. We agree; and since our claim is that language games are pragmatical, we should be able to express the difference in terms of them. And in fact the game played in the exam situation is not the same as that played with ordinary questions: the former is purely competitive, whereas the latter is not. Students tend to see the examiner as an opponent who wins if they cannot answer or if they involve themselves in contradictions. This is also the way the game of questions and answers was played in the Platonic Academy:

> The Proponent began by asking a question: A or *not-A*? He persuaded the Opponent to make a choice. Let us say the Opponent asserted *not-A*. Then the Proponent took as his thesis A, but he did not say so. Instead he began to ask the Opponent seemingly harmless ques-

tions: what about A_1? What about A_2? ... He tried to get a sufficient system of hypotheses. If he attained such a system, he performed the final stroke by saying: Well, my dear friend, now you have admitted A_1, ..., A_n: therefore you must admit A, the contrary of your original assertion. (Lorenzen 1969: 30)

We shall give the rules for this purely competitive game first, since it naturally generalises the assertoric games (which are also purely competitive). We shall use Lorenz's machinery, which is in terms of attacks and defences. *An examination question can be seen as an attack against no assertion of the partner.*

Structural rules[5]:

(i) Dialogues on questions consist of arguments which are put forth alternatively by a Questioner and a Respondent, according to the special rules.

(ii) Each argument either *attacks* prior ones of the partner (or the null argument of his ones) or *defends* one's own in the face of such an attack.

(iii) Attacks *may* be put forth at any time during the play of the game.

(iv) Defences *must* be put forth in the order of the corresponding attacks, yet may be postponed as long as attacks can still be put forth; always the argument that has been attacked last but has not yet been defended must be the first to be defended.

(v) Whoever cannot, or will not, put forth any further argument has lost that play of the game, and the other has won it.

(vi) (Additional rule to guarantee that each play terminates in a finite time.) Any argument, including the null one, may be attacked by the Respondent n times at the most, by the Questioner m at the most, with $m<n$.

Special rules: The special rules are schemas of attacks and defences which specify the behaviour of logical particles -- among which we now include "?", of course. We have already mentioned those concerning "?", but we can now give a uniform treatment to all logical constants. This is shown in table 3.

	Attacks	Defences
null assertion	?A (yes/no question)	A
		-A
	?(A,B) (whether-question)	A
		B
		-(A v B) (correction)
	(?x)A(x) (which-question)	A(c/x)
		-(Ex)A(x) (correction)
-A	A	
A & B	?A	A
	?B	B
A v B	?(A,B)	A
		B
A → B	A	B
(Ex)A(x)	(?x)A(x)	A(c/x)
(Ux)A(x)	?A(c/x)	A(c/x)

Table 3

One sees that in the simple case the Questioner asks only one initial queation and the Respondent none (apart from those he is allowed in response to Q's assertions); immediately after the initial question an assertive game begins which the Respondent wins if he gives either a direct answer or a correction *and* manages to defend it against the attacks of Q. Q wins if R gives either an answer or a correction he cannot defend. But ordinary questions are not strictly competitive games. A person is usually happy when he gets an answer to his perplexities; it would be unreasonable to say that he has been *defeated* by a true answer. It is only by a (proved) correction that a Questioner is defeated. Rather, if a question gets a true answer (thus being a true question, as somebody says) both Q and R should win. *This is a non-zero-sum game.*

In order to represent our games as non-zero-sum, all we have to do is to see them as composed of several rounds. To simplify matters, let us consider just one-question games. There are then only two rounds: the first starts with the question and closes almost immediately as an answer or a correction is given. The Questioner wins this round if an answer is given, loses if a correction is given. As soon as the Respondent makes an assertion, he has to justify it. So the second round starts, with the usual assertive rules. What it means to say that the Questioner gets a good answer is this: he wins the first round whereas the Respondent wins the second. In this case they both score three points; in any other case each of them scores one point for each round in which he wins. The matrix of the game is shown in table 4.

	R loses round two	R wins round two
Q wins round two	2 0	3 3
Q loses round one	1 1	2 0

Table 4

This is not too satisfactory, however. Maybe in round one the Respondent should score zero both in the case when he gives an answer and in the case when he gives a correction; but the main difficulty is with round two: having had an answer, why should the Questioner try hard to put it to test? Intellectual honesty, according to Popperian standards? Maybe, but if he plays carelessly, accepting an answer which is in fact not true, he can profit and score three. We could then require that the second round be repeated with inverted roles and that if the Questioner now loses, he will get a penalty of -3, thus losing all he has got. It is not a very elegant solution, but is is justified in that it corresponds to the fact that we should be prepared to be asked by others in the future the very same questions as we ourselves have asked.

Here one can define logically-interesting notions; for example, one can say that a question implies another one when any direct answer to the former implies a direct answer to the latter. Our games suggest a precise way of putting this: $?A$ implies $?B$ if from any winning strategy for $?A$ one can obtain a winning strategy for $?B$. "Which is a prime number between 10 and 20?" implies in this sense "Which is a prime number between 10 and 30?".

Conditional questions are most simply accounted for in the present framework. A conditional question like

(23) If the tide is in, is the rock covered?

which is *inoperative* if the tide is not in, according to Belnap (1969), has the following form:

(24) $?(A \rightarrow B)$

where A is "the tide is in", and B is "the rock is covered". Suppose A does not hold and R knows it. Then R can avoid saying either B or *not-B* and defending them, as he can answer simply: "$A \rightarrow B$". The game starts as in table 5: to R's answer $A \rightarrow B$, Q's attack can consist of only asserting A; but *ex hypothesis* R has a winning strategy against A. He has therefore given a direct answer and has an easy way of defending it without having to defend (still less to have a winning strategy for) either B or *not-B*.

Q	R
$?(A \rightarrow B)$	$(A \rightarrow B)$
A	

Table 5

This also explains why one can use relativized or conditional questions in order to guard oneself against corrections. If one asks

(25) If anybody killed Caesar, who did it?

then intuitively one cannot be corrected by saying

(26) Nobody killed Caesar (he fell on his sword by accident, say).

This is accounted for in our games: (25) has the form

(27) $(?x) ((Ey)A(y) \rightarrow A(x))$

a correction to which has the form

(28) $-(Ex) ((Ey)A(y) \rightarrow A(x))$

which is easily seen to be equivalent, by ordinary predicate logic, to

(29) $-((Ex)A(x) \rightarrow (Ex)A(x))$

which is a contradiction; anybody claiming this would easily be defeated. But, as before, if one knows that nobody killed Caesar and is in the position of being able to defend an answer to this effect, one can still give a direct answer, say, $"(Ey)A(y) \rightarrow A(c/x)"$. One does not have to worry about the choice of the c to be substituted for x, since one will never have to defend $A(c/x)$.

Conditional questions, which are to be rendered as $"?(A \rightarrow B)"$, should be sharply distinguished, however, from a different kind of hypothetical question, which is close to (if not identical with) the given-that-question in the sense of Belnap (Belnap 1969) and Åqvist (Åqvist 1975). Questions

(30) Given that the tide is in, is the rock covered?

and

(31) If the tide were in, would the rock be covered?

cannot be met by denying that the tide is in fact in: the Questioner is asking us to assume that, and our refusal to do so counts as a refusal to answer at all. They cannot therefore have the form $"?(A \rightarrow B)"$.

Rather they should be rendered as

(32) $A \to ?B$

the only response to which is the assertion A by the Respondent, followed by $?B$ by the Questioner; here the Respondent is assuming precisely what he was supposed to assume. The trouble is that "$A \to ?B$" is not a formula of a kind acknowledged so far, as $?$ occurs not in front of an entire formula but in front of a subformula. The present approach can be generalized, however, in such a way that $?$ behaves like a proper sentential operator, standing in front of any subformula. It could even be reiterated, much as a negation sign. The difficulty with the generalization is that of showing that the formulas so obtained admit of a natural reading, even if some are not normally in use in ordinary language. This can be done, however, and it is interesting to discover how many interrogative forms we have at our disposal, with subtly different meanings. Multiple questions, such as

(33) Who remembers where she bought which jewels?

(34) Which girls are engaged with which boys?

which Hintikka has shown to play an important role, can also be naturally accomodated in this framework. The nice thing about it is that no rule has to be changed in our games, besides allowing any A or B to stand for either assertoric or interrogative formulas.[6]

2. Let us now look back to what we have done: we have adopted the "purely linguistic approach" of Belnap, that is, we are not reading an epistemic operator into every question, as suggested by Hintikka, who reads

(35) Who is the President of Italy?

as

(36) Bring it about that I know who is the President of Italy.

We feel Hiż (1978) is right when he remarks that if I ask a question like:

    (37) Who planned this menu?

I am not saying anything about myself -- I am not saying that I do not know, I wonder and want to know who planned this menu.

> It would be perverse to read a book of algebra inserting at the beginning of every sentence 'I state that'. It would become an autobiography rather than a book of algebra. (Hiż 1978: 212)

Having disregarded at this stage epistemic operators, we accept as a genuine answer to question (35) a sentence like

    (38) Sandro Pertini is the President of Italy

which of course has to be proved. Hintikka would object to this in certain cases: he requires that an answer should entirely relieve one's intellectual anxiety. The *desideratum* of (35), what the answer should bring about is

    (39) (Ex) (I know that x is the President of Italy)

But (38) does not do this; it does not allow one to assert (39) unless one can also say

    (40) I know who Sandro Pertini is

which is not always the case (e.g., if some of you would now ask us (35) and we answered "Sandro Pertini is", it would be unlikely that you could truly say: "I know who Sandro Pertini is"). In Hintikka's words, a possible answer to a simple question of the form "Who is such that $F(he)$?" is of the form $F(a)$, *provided that the Questioner knows who a is*. We have chosen instead to drop the last clause and we therefore regard as genuine many more answers than does Hintikka. Our main reason for this is that if someone answers (38) to (35), we feel that he has given a perfectly good answer -- he has done just what he could and what was required of him, in a sense. This has the advantage that some questions which have but partial answers according to Hintikka (Hintikka 1974: 149-150) do have a direct answer for us. For instance,

(41) What does John want?

does not have any conclusive and full answer according to Hintikka if John merely wants a sloop, but not any specific sloop (just relief from slooplessness). We on the other hand feel that there is no reason to be unhappy with such an answer, if this is the way things are, and it should not be ranked lower than the answer "Your sloop", in the case where John in fact has his eyes on your sloop. Hintikka has noticed this problem; as a solution, he suggests that "A sloop" can be taken as a full and conclusive answer, if not to (41), then at least to

(42) What kind of thing does John want?

There seem to be two difficulties with this proposal. First, one may doubt that "A sloop" is a full and conclusive answer to (42), entirely relieving one's intellectual anxieties, as there are many kinds of sloops: long, short, new, second hand, made in Japan, etc., and one may still want to ask: "But what kind of sloop does John want?", and there is no more conclusive answer to this question than to (41), if John has not yet made up his mind. Second, it has the effect that the particular meaning of an interrogative sentence turns out to depend on what John has in mind. (No doubt, the meaning of "What kind of thing does John want?" is different from "Which object does John want?" which is the natural reading of (41).) Now, it is certainly plausible that in some cases the circumstances determine which proposition a sentence conveys, but it seems implausible that what John has in mind determines it.

Still, we think Hintikka is right in this respect: there are epistemic problems in the logic of answers. We did not merely require that a direct answer be given to a Questioner, we also required that the Respondent be able to defend it in a game. If, for assertions, one defines truth as the existence of a winning strategy in a dialogue starting with an assertion, then for the Respondent to be able to show the truth of his answer it is necessary and sufficient that he has a winning strategy for it. To be able to answer a which-question is, disregarding corrections, like being able to verify an existential statement, in that one has to produce an individual satisfying its matrix. But an arbitrary member of the domain is not enough -- as Hintikka stresses: "Typically one has to look around among the members of the domain for a suitable one" (Hintikka 1973: ch. III). One should perhaps "express the existential quantifier by the locution 'one can find'".

But how can one find the appropriate individual, if one does not *know* that individual, in the sense of *knowing who or what* it is? We are here seeing our games as *outdoor games*, "played out there in the fields" among the entities (individuals belonging to the domain D) of which our applied language speaks, and they consist of sequences of searches for suitable entities of this kind. Challenges and responses are connected "with those activities we are engaged in when we are using language to some extralinguistic purpose", whereas in indoor games we "apparently introduce a representant of an individual -- that is a free singular term denoting it -- without having found one" by *fiat* or a stroke of the pen (Hintikka 1973: ch. III). Thus to be able to play and win our interrogative games it is not sufficient to give names to individuals: one also has to find them in a more substantive way. In the game starting with the question "Who is the President of Italy?", if the Respondent answers "Sandro Pertini is", and has a winning strategy for it, then he can do more than baptizing Pertini or creating a name for him at a stroke of the pen; he also knows who he is, as he can find him.[7]

To sum up, if our extended games reflect the structure of the human activity of questioning and answering -- or perhaps rather of the rules that govern it -- just as the assertoric games reflect those governing the justification of an assertion, then in order to have a winning strategy to answer a who-question, a necessary and sufficient condition is to know who that person is. Hintikka is right therefore that a knowing-who condition is involved, but it concerns the Respondent, not the Questioner. After the answer has been given, what does the Questioner know? In each single play of the game, the Respondent does not disclose his strategy even if he has one; he simply applies it. But if the Questioner tries hard to defeat him and loses, then he has some reason to believe that the Respondent does have a winning strategy for the answer and therefore knows who is the individual who satisfies the question. The Questioner does not know Pertini himself, but he has reasons to believe that the Respondent does know. This is not too bad and it is not an uncommon situation.

There are many things we do not know ourselves, but it is enough for our language to work (maybe this is why we have a language at all) that there are others who know them -- if they are willing to cooperate with us. There is social division of linguistic labour, as Putnam says.[8] Personally we cannot tell an elm from a beech, but we know of others who can, and this is enough for us to use such words -- provided that there are botanists around who are willing to cooperate with us, answering questions on elms and beeches. Sometimes we use questions in order to know whether somebody is a good and reliable botanist, but there are other uses of questions. What is essential for the division of linguistic labour not to be a serious hindrance, is that the possibility exists of asking questions and getting answers.

We can now be a little more specific about the general relevance of language games to pragmatics.

> The linguistic potential of an act of uttering a sentence in a context arises from a related linguistic institution, that is, a system of nonnatural rules that govern that kind of activity [...]. Institutions have [...] properties that should be mentioned. First institutions are means of coordination between diverse goals of different persons [...]. Second, institutions assign roles to diverse people under diverse circumstances. (Kasher 1977: 229)

But this is precisely what our language games do. They give rules which constitute institutions; they assign different roles to those taking part in them, and achieve some coordination. They acknowledge that different persons are usually in different positions with respect to what they know. But they do more than this: they give them the means and the rules for overcoming this difference, and making common what they know.

To put dialogues in game-theoretical form can be illuminating in still another respect: it shows what cooperation, which plays an important role in pragmatics, amounts to. In a very general sense, he is cooperative who agrees to participate in a game of any kind. A child will consider any other kid who is willing to play with him as cooperative, even if they are going to play football one against the other. And there is a more specific sense of the term cooperation; namely, as it occurs in play in a non-competitive game, or even in a coordination game. Two people cooperating in the first sense need not share a purpose (apart from that for which they agreed to play). Socrates and Crito did not; they were in fact engaged in a zero-sum game. Thus, when one requires that conversational contributions be made such as are required, at the stage at which they occur, by the accepted purposes of the talk exchange, one need not think of purposes shared by the participants "inside the game", so to speak, for there might be none if it is a zero-sum game. Still, it holds for any sort of game that in a very general sense the players have a purpose in common and are therefore cooperating: they are willing to play that game, the rules of which state what kind of contribution is required at each stage. This seems to explain, to some extent, why Grice (1975) is able to hold that in conversation we always have cooperation, while Kasher (1976) stresses that there are many cases in which it would be difficult to find any specific purpose aimed at by all the participants in a conversation. The distinction between two senses of cooperation, a global one and a stricter local one, seems to account for this contrast and to put it in a more definite form.

Finally, let us say a few words about Sacks and Schegloff's work on the sequencing of questions and answers (as a part of the sociological analysis of conversation). We assume here acquaintance with their work (but for a detailed discussion of what follows, see Schegloff 1972: 76-79 and 106-114).

Questions and answers, they contend, constitute a typical example of a sequence (or of an utterance pair, or of an adjacency pair). That is: the occurence of a question Q provides for the relevance of the occurrence of an answer A. Looking at this the other way round: A is *conditionally relevant* on Q. Then, when, after a question has been put, no answer is forthcoming, an absence is felt. In terms of our games this relevancy is clear: after a question has been put -- leaving aside for the moment the counter-questions issue -- the only move which can follow is the giving of an answer (or of a corrective answer, a correction) to it. This is the only *relevant* move *because it is the only move which carries on the game*. The absence of an answer, then, amounts to there not being anyone entering the playing of the game opened by the question. If one wishes, one might even think that our games take care of what could follow the giving of an answer, i.e. of a longer sequence. There could follow the checking of the answer, because the questioner is looking for a *true* answer rather than just for an answer.

But, as Sacks and Schegloff have remarked, often an answer can be missing after a question without any feeling of an absence. An important example, is the case of *counterquestions*, i.e. the occurrence of questions and answers subgames. Sacks and Schegloff call these subgames "inserted question and answer sequences", meaning sequences occurring between the two parts of an adjacency pair (a question and answer sequence). They have proposed to explain such insertions as presequences. "Pre-sequences are utterances introduced as specifically prefatory to some activity." Inserted questions and answers are prefatory to the giving of an answer to the main or the basic question. Sacks and Schegloff allow for indefinitely many insertions, even if empirically they say they have not found "indefinite extensions of insertion sequences". As we have already recognized, our games need to be implemented to deal satisfactorily with counterquestions: there is a need to constrain possible counterquestions in order to admit only the relevant ones. But even if in need of such an implementation, our games deal with the problem of how many subgames are allowed: counterquestions are themselves considered attacks, and structural rule (vi) blocks an indefinitely long counterquestioning since it places a limit on the number of possible attacks.

FOOTNOTES

* Though both authors assume responsibility for the whole, part 1 has been written for the most part by M.S., while part 2 is primarily the work of P.L..

1. See Lorenzen (1961, 1962, 1969), Lorenz (1973), Stegmueller (1964), Hintikka (1973).

2. See, e.g., Hiż (1962) and Hintikka (1974).

3. This is not Strawson's notion of presupposition, although it is related to it; we are using the term "presupposition" in the same sense as Belnap and Steel (1976: 109-121).

4. We shall later on sketch a tentative generalization of this, the details of which are left for another paper.

5. These rules are taken from Lorenz (1973) almost word for word. We feel that the fact that we did not have to change much in the assertoric games to adapt them to questions and answers reveals the naturalness of our treatment -- that assertoric language games provide a natural treatment of the semantics of large fragments of natural language has been convincingly argued for by Hintikka and his associates in a number of publications.

6. Details of this will be shown in a later paper.

7. This might be obscured by the fact that "Pertini is the President of Italy" looks superficially like a prime sentence, which cannot be formally attacked. But you might know that the President of Italy is that person who has been voted by a majority of *all* senators *and all* deputees, who have in turn been elected in *some* political party by *at least n* voters in *at least one* district in the country. If you have a strategy for defending the assertion that Pertini is such a person, finding your way through so many quantifiers and sentential operators, then one cannot deny that you know a lot about Pertini.

8. See, e.g., Putnam (1975).

NOTE by Paolo Leonardi

In the preceding paper Marco Santambrogio and myself have briefly discussed the general relevance of language games to pragmatics. In this note I will instead point out some problems for our approach to pragmatics. To do this I will discuss more directly and in more detail Grice's "Logic and conversation" in relation to our language games. There are, I think, three points to be made. Since this is just a note,

I will deal with them very sketchily, after having restated Grice's original theses.

Grice has had recourse to his conversational machinery to show that the alleged divergences in meaning between some formal devices (such as '-', '&', 'v', etc.) and their natural language analogues (such as 'not', 'and', 'or', etc.) are not really divergences in meaning. Those alleged divergences are nothing more than implicatures derived from an interaction between what the speaker literally says -- its literal meaning -- and: (a) the assumption that he is following the Cooperation Principle (CP) and its maxims; (b) the context, linguistic or otherwise, of his utterance; (c) the background knowledge shared by the participants in the talk exchange; and (d) the assumption that all these facts are known to all the participants. The CP reads: "Make your conversational contribution such as is required, at the stage at which it occurs, by the accepted purpose or the direction of the talk exchange in which you are engaged". The four maxims, the following of which fosters cooperation, read: (1) (quantity) tell (a) no less and (b) no more than is required; (2) (quality) try to make your contribution one that is true, i.e. do not tell (a) what you believe is false, and (b) what you lack adequate evidence for; (3) (relation) be relevant; (4) (manner) be perspicous, i.e. (a) avoid obscure expressions, (b) avoid ambiguities, (c) avoid prolixities, and (d) be orderly. To give an example of how such a machinery works, take the following case. The ordinarily alleged divergence in meaning between the formal '&' and natural language 'and' (which is considered roughly synonymous to 'and after' when there is a temporal difference between the events spoken about by the first and the second of the two conjuncts) disappears and is explained, assuming that in such a case the speaker follows the maxim of manner, or more precisely that he is orderly.

The alleged divergences, then, are not semantical, they are not divergences in meaning. They depend upon some features of discourse; and Grice's characterization of some of those features can be thought of as a "theory" of discourse, or as a part of such a "theory".

Now I can proceed with the discussion of my three points.

(i) Do our dialogical games fit Grice's general features of discourse? On one hand, it is easy to say that our formal dialogues fit Gricean maxims. (Here the occurrence of 'formal' has nothing to do with the opposition formal/natural which Grice points out at the beginning of "Logic and conversation"). Inasmuch as they are formal, they give a completely explicit and rigorous formulation of the moves possible at each stage of a dialogue, each of them saying no more and no less than is required (quantity), being relevant (relation) and perspicous (manner). (For the maxim of quality, see below.) For instance, in our games, to the move $?A$, one can respond either A or $-A$: one is not allowed to say less nor more than this, and both the moves are perspicous, because it is clear what the possible moves following them are. Only these two moves are relevant at this stage because the person who made a different move from these would be thought of as not playing the game anymore: (leaving aside the counterquestions issue) those moves are indeed the only ones which carry on the game. More than this: since our games make precise, at least within the rather severly restricted limits within which they are applicable at this stage, what is to count as "being as informative as is required", "being relevant" and "being perspicous", they may be regarded as ideal conversations or as providing the standards which are implicitly used by conversationalists.

On the other hand, this optimistic start seems to me problematic for two reasons: first, it forces a precise meaning upon the key expressions of some Gricean maxims, and I wonder whether this is useful and whether this does not change the function the maxims have to fulfil. (I do not know, however, whether Grice would agree, at least in part, with what I am going to say on this.)

One can look at the maxims as if they were regulative principles, and as such they would be near platitudes, all depending on what counts as "as informative as is required", "relevant", "perspicous", etc. However, they may still guide: the maxims may be such that they are to be given a precise form only at each occasion in which they are set to work; then one may make any change whatsoever in their formerly used forms just to make sense of the occasion in which one is applying them. In such a case, I always have to assume that my coconversationalist has said exactly as much as was required -- by the way, he is certainly proposing to take what he says to be as much as he was required to say -- and I have to develop a frame in which things are exactly this way. This may force me to make factual assumptions (e.g., that he knows that ..., that he believes that ..., etc.), but even other assumptions, as e.g. that maybe he is not using a two-valued logic, so that the answer he has given to my question $?A$, even if different from both A and $-A$, is still a possible direct answer, is still the right quantity and is still relevant etc. (Think of what what Copernicus told forced Feyerabend's Galileo to do!) If I fail to make sense of the conversation I am in, however, I may charge my coconversationalist with having opted out of the observation of the CP and of its maxims, and he may do the same against me: this is the last resource, but can even be a lazy one. This is a suggestion for why it may not be useful to make the maxims precise, and it is at the same time a suggestion for what their function could be. However, one can entertain a quite different attitude towards rules, believing that they have to be independent of the context in which they have to be applied, and of the content of the situation to which they have to be applied. General, precise rules are exactly of this kind.

The second reason for not being that much optimistic is that going back to Grice's original problem -- the alleged divergences in meaning between some formal devices and their natural language counterparts -- it seems to me that our games do not solve, as they stand, such a problem. Grice's solution on the contrary could, I think, be extended to solve some possibly alleged new divergences in meaning to which our games are liable. This matter will be discussed at length under (iii).

(ii) However, looking at our games as dialogues one sees that there is a difference between the maxim of quality and the other maxims. The observation of the other maxims is guaranteed, as has been shown, by the rules of the games. The submaxim (b) of quality tells one that, since one has to give a contribution that is true, one has to tell only what one has adequate evidence for. In our games then one has to try to win the game. But to try to win in a game is the point of it, and it cannot be the content of any specific rule. (This then is another case where I feel that our game-theoretical approach shows to be relevant to pragmatics.)

Nonetheless, the submaxim (b) of quality is problematic from the point of view of our games. When what is at stake is a logical or a mathematical truth (and suppose it is a relatively trivial one), the proof of it can be carried out in a dialogical game framework only supposing that there is a (fictitious) Opponent, but it would be quite unreasonable to assume that he thinks to have any hope at all to win, i.e. to assume that he believes to have any evidence at all for what he says. The submaxim then may need to be reformulated, perhaps in the sense that one has to be able to argue for what one says and that one has to do it at one's best. On the other hand the range of Grice's 'theory' may be restricted to natural discourse (even if I think a different argument to the same effect could be put here again against the submaxim (b) of quality). (Note that nothing here depends upon what is to count as adequate evidence, which is by itself a very complicated matter.)

(iii) It is a common assumption that a condition for questioning is that the Questioner does not know the answer to his question (c.f. e.g. Searle 1969: 66, first preparatory condition for the speech act of questioning). (It is likely that other standardly assumed conditions for natural language questioning may be dealt with in the same way. For instance, the condition stating that one is required to put a question only to a person who knows, or is supposed to know the answer may perhaps be dealt with working on the maxim of relation.) A condition like this is normally taken as being proper at least to natural language questioning. Our question and answer games, however, do not require this as a condition; rather it has just been noticed that on the part of the Respondent there is the condition of having a winning strategy for the assertive game associated with the answer he gives, if he wants to be sure to get the maximum possible win for himself. Could this suggest that there exists a divergence in meaning between the interrogative quantifier '?' of the formal games and its natural language analogue? If it does, I think that an extension of the Gricean maxims to question and answer talk exchanges could deal with such an alleged divergence. Indeed, in such a case, a rephrasing of the maxim of quantity -- a naive one would be: "Make a contribution or ask for a contribution as informative as required" and "Do not make a contribution nor ask for a contribution more informative than required" -- would be enough to show that such an alleged surplus meaning of the natural language interrogative quantifier is just a (general) implicature of natural question and answer talk exchanges. Perhaps these problems can be dealt with also developing further the rules of our games. But then a decision would have to be taken on which way has to be preferred; then the solution hinted at above might still be more than a viable alternative. However, if this cannot be done, our games do not embody Grice's 'theory' of discourse, since they still need to be implemented by it, or by something like it.

These remarks are not meant to deny that our game-theoretical approach can be used for a general treatment of questions and answers, and that the different way of setting up logic, which backs it, cannot change the usual distinction between semantics and pragmatics. I wished only to moderate the perhaps too enthusiastic tone about it which I felt in rereading the paper by Santambrogio and myself.

THE ESSENTIAL INADEQUACIES OF SPEECH ACT MODELS OF DIALOGUE

Stephen C. Levinson

1.0 *Speech act models of dialogue*[1]

There is a simple and attractive model of dialogue that is widely if often implicitly subscribed to, which goes roughly as follows: conversations cohere or are held together not at the level of what is said, but at the level of what is *done* by what is said, by virtue of rules governing the sequencing of speech acts. Now there are many different versions of such a theory, as in Labov (1972), Sinclair and Coulthard (1975), Clarke (1978), Labov and Fanshel (1977), Power (1977), and many other works,[2] but we can isolate one whole class of such models that share the following criterial properties:

(1)   (i) There are unit acts, *speech acts*, that are performed in speaking.

    (ii) Utterances are segmentable into unit parts - *utterance units* - each of which corresponds to a unit act.

    (iii) There is a *speciable procedure that will assign unit acts to utterance units*, or at least there is a function whose domain is the set of possible utterance units and whose range is the set of possible speech acts.

    (iv) Conversational sequences are primarily regulated by a

set of sequencing rules stated over speech act types.

The kernel idea behind such models is this: since sequential constraints are clearly not easily stated on the form or meaning of what is said, we should translate utterances into the underlying acts they perform, because on this deeper level rules of sequencing will be straightforwardly describable. The idea is appealing because it promises to capture some of the obvious regularities of the sort that questions tend to be followed by answers, greetings by greetings, offers by acceptances or refusals, apologies by forgivings and so on. A very first approximation, then, to a model of dialogue along these lines can be represented as (2):

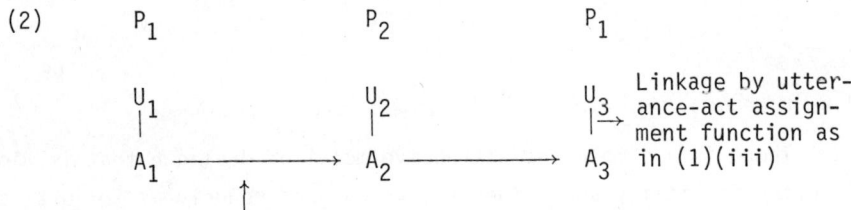

where P_1 and P_2 are the participants, U_n is an utterance unit, A_n the unit act achieved by that utterance unit.

Although as a model (2) can only be described as crude, notice that closer approximations to reality can be achieved without essentially changing its nature.[3] For example we could define the notion of a *turn* at speaking and allow each turn to contain more than one utterance unit each achieving one unit act, as in the response in (3):

(3) A: Well, how are you?
    B: Oh very well thanks. And you?

In addition we could allow for embedded sequences of a sort we shall describe in a moment (see example (4) below); and to accomodate indirect speech acts we could provide an additional 'layer' distinguishing the 'literal' speech act from the 'conveyed' or indirect one. But all these frills[4] would not change the basic features of such a model, outlined in (1) above.

Now if this view is correct we can treat conversational structure as a formal language, whose terminal vocabulary consists of utterance units, and whose non-terminal or auxiliary alphabet consists of speech act categories. We can then rapidly arrive at various important theorems about the nature of conversational structure.[5] For example, due to the existence of examples like (4), where one question-answer sequence is embedded within another, we can state the fundamental theorem 1 in (5):

(4)   A: Excuse me can you tell me where Woolworths is?   Q1
       B: Ah, do you know Penney's?   Q2
       A: Sure.   A2
       B: Well it's just around the corner from there.   A1

(5)   Theorem 1: the syntax of dialogue is essentially self-embedind and requires an infinity of substitution classes; it cannot therefore be generated by a finite state device.

To those who subscribe to any model of dialogue that has the properties outlined in (1) this would be an important result, establishing where on the familiar hierarchy of formal languages or automata the 'syntax' of dialogue must lie. We could look forward confidently to further such results.

However I believe that this apparently attractive approach is in fact quite inappropriate as a model of natural conversation. Indeed I would like to state a counter-hypothesis:

(6)   dialogue has no syntax, speech act types are not the relevant categories over which to define the regularities of conversation; there exists no other finite alphabet over which to define the regularities; and there are no concatenation rules of general application even if there were such an alphabet.[6]

To see why I maintain the counter-hypothesis let us review the properties of speech act models of dialogue outlined in (1).

2.0 *Problems for each of the cardinal properties of speech act models of dialogue*

If we examine the four basic assumptions, stated in (1) above, that underlie speech act models of dialogue, it soon becomes clear that there are overwhelming problems with each of them. Let us take them one by one.

2.1 *The existence and identifiability of unit acts corresponding to specific utterance units*

The first problem that arises here is that utterance units often seem to involve more than one speech act in a number of different ways. Simple examples are indirect speech acts like (7), which is both a question and an offer, as shown by the possible response 'yes I would thank you' where the 'yes' answers the question and the 'thank you' acknowledges the offer:

(7) Would you like another drink?

Less obviously perhaps the first utterance in (8) is not just a question:

(8) A: What are you doing tonight?
    B: Nothing, why?
    A: I was thinking of going to a movie, wanna come?

It is also as Sacks, Schegloff and associates have pointed out, a *pre-offer*. If we were to characterize A's first utterance as just a question, we would have to consider B's 'nothing' palpably false, which it isn't of course under the interpretation that it is a response to a question that is a pre-offer and that it therefore means essentially 'nothing that would make the offer of an evenings entertainment irrelevant'.

Now utterances doing more than one speech act at a time are not in and of themselves overwhelmingly problematic for speech act models of dialogue, but they are recurring difficulties. It can be shown that multiple functions arise in many different ways, that the set of speech act categories that thus arise (pre-pre-offers etc.) may be indefinitely large, and that the source of such multiple assignments of force actually lies not in the utterance taken singly, but in the slot it occupies in a conversational sequence (see Sacks and Schegloff 1974, Schegloff 1976). Thus the first utterance in (8) is a pre-offer by virtue of its placement in a recognizable offer-sequence. Finally, if a unitary utterance may achieve more than one 'act' simultaneously, shouldn't we change the terminology? For an action is a composite formed from a chunk of behaviour and a set of intentions. The multiplicity of simultaneous functions is really an assignment of more than one intention to the utterance, a chunk of behaviour. The change of terminology is apposite because it reminds us that intentions are not units in the way that behaviour chunks can be; intentions can have hierarchical organization (one being the raison-d'etre for another) and linear relations (one being a precondition to another), and for an interactant another interactant's intentions are only likely to be determinable up to a certain point, which raises the second major problem for speech act unitization.

Related to multiple-duty utterances, but ultimately more problematic is that on occasions speakers seem to have great chains of motives or perlocutionary intents that issue forth in a single utterance. Take this simple case: I'm not enjoying the party that I have gone to with my companion Mildred, so I wish to leave, so I want to suggest that we both leave, so I say to her,

(9) It's getting late, Mildred

To which Mildred may felicitously reply with any of the following utterances;

(10) a. It's only 11.15 darling
       b. But I'm having such a good time
       c. Do you want to go?
       d. Aren't you enjoying yourself dear?

where only the first one seems to respond directly to what is said. The others seem to respond to higher levels in the hierarchical chain of motives that led me to say (9); thus (10b) is addressed to my desire that we both go, (10c) to my wish that I go, (10d) to my ultimate motive in saying what I did.

There's no difficulty in showing that this is a very general phenomenon and underlies in fact many of the cases where one utterance does many speech acts, as in (7) above. It follows that speech act models of dialogue have serious problems: first, we have shown that responses can be based on perlocutionary intents, often quite remote; yet speech act theory is founded on a basic distinction between illocutionary and perlocutionary acts, and has nothing interesting to say about the latter. Secondly the speech act theorist is not in a position to simply extend his theory to cover perlocutions: due to the infinity of possible perlocutions his model does not and cannot have anything to say about them. So already the original idea of reducing the immense variety of surface utterances to a limited set of speech act types over which sequencing rules can be stated, is beginning to lose some of its charm.

2.2 *The existence and identifiability of utterance units corresponding to unit acts*

If we are to map unit acts onto utterance units, as the speech act model requires, the utterance units must be identifiable independently of the functions (the act units) they perform. This proves to be a problematic assumption. A first guess at the relevant utterance unit would be the sentence. But (11) seems to be both an order and a threat, and (12) both a statement and a question (see Lakoff 1974 for dicussion):

(11) Shut up or I'll beat you
(12) Fillipino Lippi's are delightful aren't they?

Besides we have already seen that a single unitary clause (as in (7) and (8)) can perform more than one act at once. Furthermore just about any sentence part above a bound morpheme can operate as a full conversational contribution (see discussion in Morgan 1973):

    (13) A: How do you want your coffee?
             B: Light, with sugar, to go.

In addition what are we to say of (14), which was said by way of introducing:[7]

    (14) Bill, Marry; Mary, Bill

Here the relevant utterance units are either one, two or four and it's hard to say which; we are also at a loss as to whether one, two or four acts took place. Our decision about utterance units though will determine our decision about act units, and vice-versa, clearly indicating that we do not independently identify act-units and utterance-units.

The functional (or act-based) identification of the relevant utterance units is made most clear, though, by facts like attributable silence (see Sacks n.d.). For example if a teacher presents a child with an utterance like (15), and the child remains mute, this can be 'heard' as an affirmative reply:

    (15) Johnny, did *you* smear Susie's face with paint?

So the relevant utterance units that can function as conversational contributions can be just about anything, including nothing.

One should note too that responses may be non-verbal, requests being complied with by actions for example, the ramifications of which are nicely dealt with by Goffman (1976). Further, there are some utterances that, although formally identical to others that carry functional loads, do not perform full blown speech acts, for example *okay* said in pre-closing position before a final *bye-bye* sequence (see Sacks & Schegloff 1974). To distinguish this *okay* from one that signals compliance with an order, or answers the question 'how are you', we will once again have to appeal to the functions it performs.

Utterance units then are very variable, ranging from sets of sentences through sentence fragments to single lexemes, non-verbal actions or even silence. Which unit is the relevant unit for speech act assignment cannot be determined in advance, for utterance units seem to be identified on functional grounds. How then is speech act assignment to be achieved?

2.3 *The existence of a specifiable function or procedure that will assign utterance units to unit acts (speech acts)*

We have discussed two of the basic properties of speech act models and have concluded that a) the relevant unit acts are not unitary assignments from a well-defined set of speech act types, but rather an n-ary assignment of intents, where these are linked in specific ways, from an indefinitely large set of possible perlocutionary intents; and that b) utterance units are very varied in kind and must be functionally defined, partly in terms of the acts to be assigned to them.

We now turn to the third basic property of such models, namely the assumption that there is at least a specifiable function, and more ambitiously a specifiable procedure or algorithm, that maps utterance units into speech act units.

Given conclusions a) and b) we see immediately that we are faced with problems. First the domain of the function is defined in part in relation to the range - significant utterance parts are not identifiable without reference to the speech acts that will be assigned to them. Secondly, and crucially, since neither the domain nor the range of the speech act assignment function are well-defined, and indeed seem likely to resist attempts at precise specification, there is every reason to doubt the possibility of properly specifying such a function.

Let us suppose that, somehow, these difficulties can be overcome, and that speech act theory can be purged of its present incoherencies along the lines suggested in Gazdar (1979b). Then we would still be faced with overhelming problems concerning the adequate specification of an actual procedure that would adequately implement the abstract function that maps utterance units into speech act units. Perhaps the major problem here is the fundamental prevalence of *indirection* in human communication.[8]

Attempts to solve the speech act assignment problem fall prey, more or less swiftly, to the facts of indirection. The simplest solution, which loosely following Gazdar (1979b) we may call the 'literal meaning hypothesis', would simply be to assign a unique illocutionary force to a sentence on the basis of its performative prefix (if overt) or its sentence type (often held to be a reflex of a covert performative prefix). This of course fails because of the phenomenon of indirect speech acts (see e.g. Gordon & Lakoff 1975): sentences like (16) indicate that there is no such simple relation between sentences and the speech acts they perform:

(16) Can you please pass the salt.

Searle (1975) would like to maintain that sentences like (16) continue to perform questions, but happen in addition to serve as (perlocutionary?) acts of requesting. However, sentences like (17) are counterexamples to the claim that 'literal' illocutinary force is always retained:

(17) May I remind you that your account is overdue

since it cannot possibly function as a request for permission to remind, since reminding is done in uttering the sentence without such permission being granted (see also Gazdar 1979).

Abandoning the literal meaning hypothesis one could still hope to handle indirect speech acts by means of a limited set of illocutionary force conversion rules ('conversational postulates'), along the lines pioneered by Gordon & Lakoff (1975), Labov (1972) and developed by Labov & Fanshel (1977), Sinclair & Coulthard (1975) and others. The problem here is that such an approach can only be partial.[9] In (18) for example, B (correctly) interprets A's remark as a compliment on the cake she had baked, but not by virtue of any general rule of the sort 'saying that you can eat the whole of X counts as a compliment on X':

(18) A: I could eat the whole of that cake.
       B: Thanks. It's quite easy to make actually.

The understanding of such utterances is not based on some huge set of ad hoc conventional rules for constructing and interpreting indirect speech acts, but some small but powerful set of general principles of inference to interlocutors' communicative intentions in specific contexts. In the long run then the conversion rule hypothesis fails for just the same reason that the literal meaning hypothesis fails: it attempts again to minimize the role of context in determining the acts or intents that are assigned to utterances (for many examples see Levinson 1979).[10]

Many further difficulties could be adduced here, for example one can easily show the main import of utterances is often presupposed, implicated or even more remotely implied (see Levinson 1978), but we have come far enough to present the speech act theorist with a fundamental dilemma. Either he retreats to his original position in which illocutionary force is assigned on the basis of surface sentence type, in which case assignment is a relatively simple affair but largely irrelevant to how conversation proceeds; or he is faced with accounting for speech act force and content that are often only tenuously linked to what is actually said by mechanisms that are not simply a set of conventional rules, but rather a powerful set of little-understood inference principles that take many aspects of context into account.

2.4 *The assumption that sequences of utterances are regulated by conventional sequencing rules stated over speech act types*

We come now to the final, and indeed the motivating, property of speech act models of dialogue. For the point of modelling a translation procedure from utterances to acts was to reduce the problems of sequencing in dialogue to a statement of regularities in sequences of acts.

The initial attraction of the program probably stems from observation of adjacency-pair organization (see Sacks & Schegloff 1974:238-41), the way in which, for example, questions set up expectations for answers, greetings for greetings, offers for uptakes or declinings and so on. But the bulk of conversation is not constructed from adjacency pairs, and it is easy to conceptually overemphasize the constraints on tying between consecutive utterances. Compare for example what can follow an assertion: another assertion, a question, a bet, a promise, a back-channel cue (*huhuh*, *hmm* etc), an offer, and so on indefinitely and without clear preference for one of these types of response over another.

In any case, responses to first parts of adjacency pairs are a lot freer than the question-answer stereotype would suggest. Questions can be happily followed by questions, partial answers, statements of ignorance, denials of the relevance of the question, denials of its presuppositions and so on, as illustrated in (19):

(19) A: What does Joe do for a living?
     B: i. Do you need to know?
        ii. Oh this and that
       iii. I've no idea
       iv. What's that got to do with it
        v. He doesn't.

To some extent, as I have shown elsewhere (Levinson 1979), what a question is, and hence the nature of the set of relevant responses, is dependent on the peculiarities of the particular language game (social activity) it is embedded within. Thus one cannot expect to find context-invariant sequencing rules even within the highly constrained adjacency pair organizations. Further, some apparently tightly organized adjacency pairs, like compliment and response, turn out to be something other than adjacency pairs on close examination (see Pomerantz 1978).

An entirely different problem for the idea that sequencing constraints in dialogue can be largely captured by rules stating possible concatenations of speech act types, is the problem of topic. In order for sequencing rules to have generality they will have to be stated over illocutionary force types, ignoring the variety of propositional contents. Besides, apart from general constraints that particular forces put on propositional contents, speech act theory has nothing interesting to say about content. But then how can topical coherency be guaranteed, even between questions and their particular answers, not to mention bets and their particular uptakes, assertions and agreements with those particular assertions, and so on? Obviously we would need an additional and independent theory of topical dependencies across propositional contents, and this of course is not provided by the theory in question; and there are in fact reasons to doubt that such an independent theory could be provided.

Apart from these general difficulties for rule-based approaches to sequencing constraints, there are a range of examples that seem to me to indicate that conversational coherence is not essentially rule-based at all. These are exchanges in dialogue where responses are aimed not at what has been said, but at the broader motive, or higher level goal, that is seen to lie behind what has been said. A simple example is (20)

(20) A: Is John there?
B: You can reach him at extension thirty four sixty two

where B's response is not an answer, and yet constitutes an eminently co-operative response on the understanding that the motive behind A's question is A's wanting to get in touch with John. Similar examples are raised by Robinson and Hobbs (1978), who discuss examples like (21)

(21) A: What's the metric torque wrench nipple extractor look like?
B: It's on the bench in front of you

where B's response is only co-operative on the assumption that the reason for A's question is that he wishes to identify and find the wrench and that B reckons that a statement of its location will serve A's purpose better than a description of the instrument itself.

Take a slightly more involved example:

(22) A: Can you give me Mr X's phone number?

B: Hmm. Have you a number where I can ring you back?
A: Thanks, but I'll be seeing him later anyway so it's alright.

Now note that this might equally have gone a slightly different way, as in (23):

(23) A: Can you give me Mr X's phone number?
B: Hmm. Have you a number where I can ring you back?
A: Yes, it's 60185.
B: Good I'll find out and ring you back this afternoon.
A: Thanks a lot.

We can think of B's responses in (23) as being directed by a hierarchical plan organizing a set of sub-goals as in (24):

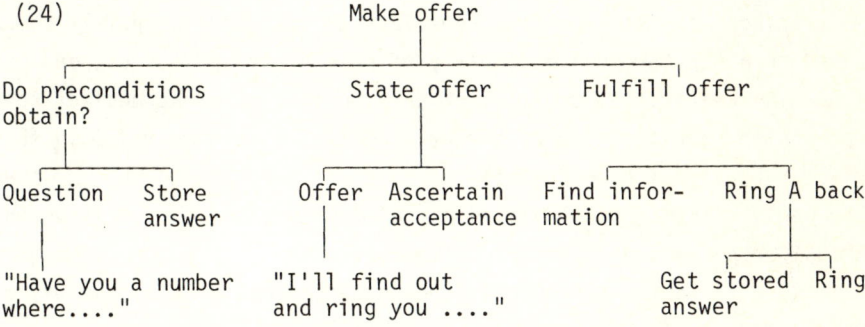

This structure of goals is implemented, up till 'Fulfill offer', in (23) but not fully in (22). But the interesting thing about (22) is that A's response in the last line is not to the immediately preceding question by B, but rather to B's unstated higher level goal ('Make offer' in (24)) of offering to ring A back. We know this because A responds to B's question with 'thanks', even though no offer ever took place. This is not simply capturable in a speech acts model of sequencing, say in terms of an embedded structure like (Request (Question-Answer) Offer to comply with Request) because the offer in question never actually took place.

This in fact appears to be a very general phenomenon: given an utterance which is merely the first in a sequence predicted by a hierarchical structure of goals, one is free to respond to any of those higher level goals.[11] In doing so there is no appreciable sense of violation, although a sequencing rules model would predict that in examples like (20), (21) and (22) violations of rules would have occurred, with the consequent expectations of repair mechanisms, sanctions and so on.[12] Examples such as these seem to me to be knock-down counter-examples to rule-based analyses of conversational sequencing.[13]

2.5 *Conclusions re speech act models of dialogue*

My strategy has been to raise the possibility of treating the structure of dialogue in terms of some formal language, with all the obvious advantages that would thereby accrue. I then set up what I take to be the most plausible sub-class of such models, namely those based on a non-terminal vocabulary of speech act categories, and outlined the criterial properties of such models. A great deal of recent work on conversation can be directly equated with some model in this class. Finally I have devoted the bulk of the paper to showing that the whole class of models is in principle incapable of modelling the actual properties of natural dialogue.[14]

Despite their inadequacies speech act models of dialogue may capture a number of observable regularities like those for example to be found in adjacency pair organization or ritualized sequences like greetings (see e.g. Irvine 1974). In limited domains, then, like question-answering systems, such models may appear to be quite successful, and we should not be misled thereby into the belief that they will offer a general account of how conversation proceeds.[15]

3.0 *Where now? Some implications of the failure of speech act models of dialogue*

The failure of speech act models of dialogue leaves us in something of a theoretical vacuum. If cohesion in discourse is not founded on rules governing sequences of acts, what is it founded on? The answers must no doubt await future research. But which directions should we look in?

There seem to me to be just two promising avenues for future research. The first is this: instead of rushing in to fill the theoretical vacuum, we should turn back resolutely to the data, for we need to have a lot more systematic information about the basic nature of conversation before abstract theorizing is likely to be profitable. Intuitions are simply not reliable in this area, as Schegloff nicely illustrated at the conference from which this volume emanates. And we may turn to the work by Sacks, Schegloff, Jefferson and associates not only for some basic findings but also for some methodological tools that have amply proved their worth (see the representative collection in Schenkein 1978).

Another quite distinct potential avenue of research has been opened up by Artificial Intelligence, namely the possibility of analysis by synthesis. The discipline of producing programs with the appropriate output puts the kind of constraints on theory that will tend to make theory construction in this area more than mere *post hoc* rationalization of how dialogue is achieved.

But the approach *via* synthesis faces the theoretical vacuum noted above, and in this context it is worth speculating in what general area adequate models of dialogue are to be found. My own hunch is that the correct approach is to be found within some general theory about the nature of inter-personal interaction. For interaction, verbal and otherwise, is based on an interlocking of goals or objectives in a way that generates sequences of highly co-ordinated inter-dependent acts. Such a theory, which I have sketched elsewhere (Levinson 1978), does not fall prey to the many objections that I have raised against speech act models of dialogue. Crucial to such a theory would be the ability of interactants to reconstruct the hierarchical plans or goals of other interactants, and thus the ability to respond to goal-structures like those in (24) above. The multiplicity of acts (or perlocutionary intents) that can be achieved by a single utterance, the indefinite nature of utterance units, the context-sensitivity of act (or goal) assignment, and the *strategy*-based rather than rule-based nature of sequencing constraints, the nature of topic, can all be given some natural characterization along these lines (again, see Levinson 1978).

But any theory of this kind takes us into novel and uncharted areas of theory about human behaviour. To appreciate this it is important to see that there is a fundamental difference between a speech act and rule-governed model of dialogue and one based on a goal-driven theory of co-ordinated interanction (a difference of a sort that makes inappropriate, I think, the theoretical amalgams in e.g. Morgan 1978a, Perrault, Allen & Cohen 1978). As Chomsky (1976) has emphasized,[16] all the recent successes in the understanding of human behaviour have come about essentially by divorcing the study of the structural properties of behaviour from the motivational system that drives it (thus for example, perlocutionary intents can be claimed to be irrelevant to semantic analysis). But in the case of conversation, although there are important structural constraints of a sort exemplified by turn-taking systematics (see Sacks, Schegloff & Jefferson 1974), it does not look as if we can make this basic methodological banishment of motives, goals and intents - not at least if we are in the business of analysis by synthesis. For goals or plans are actually required to *drive* an A.I. system of the appropriate kind, as the only existant program that generates both sides of a dialogue clearly demonstrates (see Power 1977). We thus find ourselves in quite unfamiliar theoretical ground.

To fill this theoretical vacuum what we seem to need is both a sophisticated theory of how humans construct goals and co-operatively implement them, and a metalanguage for talking about plans, goals, subgoals and the like. Some help here can be gleaned from the philosophy of action and the growing literature on 'practical reasoning' (see Brown & Levinson 1978 for an application to aspects of language usage). Another important potential source for theory and formalism here is the mathematical theory of games.[17] But by far the most promising line of approach seems to be in the development of programing languages like PLANNER (see Power 1977 for an application to models of dialogue).

But all this is speculation. In the meantime the interesting work on the nature of conversation is being conducted within the first line of approach - the careful analysis of natural occuring talk using the methods pioneered by Sacks and Schegloff.

FOOTNOTES:

1. This paper is an abbreviation of the first part of Levinson (1978) which was written in response to a confrontation with Bill Woods and David Clarke in a special session of the Semantics Conference held in Cambridge in April 1978. I am very grateful to Jay Atlas, Penelope Brown, Gerald Gazdar, David Good and Marion Owen for useful comments.

2. See also e.g. Allwood (1976: chapter 15.4). Note that the well known paper by Goffman (1976) also seems to espouse this view, while simultaneously raising many difficulties for it.

3. See Labov (1972) for the most explicit version of this model. The later work in Labov & Fanshel (1977), although obscured by sheer complexity and internal inconsistency, retains a basic model of exactly the same sort, as the following quotes and references should make clear: "obligatory sequencing is not found between utterances but between the actions that are being performed" (1977:70); "The rules of discourse that we present here are like the rules of syntax in their unconscious, *invariant* character" (1977:75, italics added); "The rules of production and interpretation that we have been disussing [...] are quite complex; the sequencing rules are relatively simple' (1977:110).

4. Another important refinement would be to use the limited set of speech act types suggested by Searle (1976), in the hope that sequencing rules could be reduced by stating them over *classes* of speech acts. A certain indeterminacy clearly enters here: see the entirely different kinds of categories used by e.g. Sinclair & Coulthard (1975) and Labov & Fanshel (1977).

5. The idea of doing this occurred independently to myself, Jens Allwood, Gerald Gazdar and no doubt many others; it seems to have been most extensively explored by David Clarke (1977, 1978).

6. This position suggests the following argument. Everything that's computable can be treated as a formal language; human processing capacities can be equated with some (as yet unknown) finite machine, which is capable of computing whatever it is that goes into constructing a dialogue; *ergo* dialogue-producing capacities must in principle be treatable as formal languages. The argument collapses because of the failure to distinguish between the structure of a domain under investigation and the structure of the language best used to describe it. One can for example *describe* the structure of a steam-engine in a formal language, but that doesn't mean that a steam-engine has the structure of a formal language. So the knowledge or abilities can be phrased in a computable language, without having the essential structure of that language.

7. I owe this example to Andy Rogers.

8. For a discussion of the motivation behind indirection, and a catalogue of means for being indirect, see Brown & Levinson (1978).

9. Gordon & Lakoff (1975) themselves discuss examples like "It's hot in here" used to attempt to get the addressee to open the window, without being able to offer 'conversational postulates' for how they work (clearly, for this example, all sorts of background knowledge about the relative temperatures of inside and outside, who is obliged to look after the comfort of whom and so on, is relevant, and there simply are no context-independent force-conversion rules that will do the trick). Likewise Searle (1975a) discusses indirect speech acts based on, for example, *reasons* for doing requests (e.g. "I can't reach that suitcase") although these make no reference to felicity conditions, a fact he does not appear to notice.

10. For a recent review of speech act theory that discusses these issues in detail see Levinson (n.d.).

11. Here is a further example (cited in Atkinson & Drew 1979:142):

    M: wuhddiyuh doing wh dat big bow-puh-tank. Nothing?
        (0.5 sec)
    V: (COUGH)
    V: Uh-h-h
        (1.0 sec)
    V: I'm not intuh selling it or giving it. That's that.

    There are other kinds of examples that would be much more resistant to an 'ellipsis' analysis (see footnote 13 below), but which would take too much space to cite and discuss in full.

12. Example (22) for example would be an instance of a violation of the rule that questions should be followed by answers. *Re* sanctions see Sacks, Schegloff & Jefferson (1974).

13. Clive Holes has pointed out to me that example (22) and similar examples might not constitute knock-down counter-examples to the conventional sequencing rules approach, if we take into account the sort of conversational 'ellipsis' suggested by Goffman (1976) and Merritt (1976). However, firstly there are examples of responses to 'perlocutionary intents' that are completely resistent to such an analysis. Secondly, there are serious methodological objections to such analyses. For example, on such an account, the offer in (22) would be generated by the rules but then 'deleted' as it were. But unless such deletion rules were precisely governed by some kind of recoverability condition, conversations could not (on the speech act model view) be understood. But recoverability is obviously a context-dependent issue: it will depend on features like the precise sequential context (see e.g. Sacks & Schegloff 1974) and the kind of activity the talk occurs within (see e.g. Merritt 1976, Levinson 1979). And in that case we are once again outside the purview of simple conventional sequencing rules. The meth-

odological objection that thus arises is that without precise formally-definable conditions on deletion, such a rule-based account with ellipsis would be unfalsifiable and thus essentially vacuous.

14. There are many further problems for speech act models of dialogue that I have ommitted for lack of space. Probably the most important of these is a proper consideration of the effects that different contexts have on (i) speech act assignment (see Levinson 1979), and (ii) sequencing rules (see Levinson 1978, Merritt 1976). The implications of these facts are that there would in fact have to be as many speech act models of conversation as there are distinct kinds of social activity or significant speech contexts. So what ever such models appear to gain in rigour, they are likely to lose in generality. A somewhat different set of problems is raised by Goffman (1976); he shows that responses in conversation are also determined by 'frame', e.g. by whether the prior utterance was a joke, a quote or example, or both a quote and an here-and-now contribution to the present action sequence - and so on. Labov & Fanshel (1977) utilize the notion of 'frame' without appearing to notice the difficulties it raises for the speech act model of dialogue that they subscribe to.

15. In attacking speech act models of dialogue, I hope it is clear that I am not *directly* attacking the notion of 'speech act' itself. All I have done is undercut one possible motivation for being interested in the notion, namely the motivation of giving an account of conversation. Well, not quite all - I have also argued that it looks impossible to define a well-formed function, let alone an algorith that would map utterances into speech act categories. Since any theory of speech acts, including the new context-change theory, will have at least to specify such a function, if my arguments are correct they do effectively undermine the viability of the concept of a speech act itself. For further pessimistic remarks on the future of speech act theory, see Levinson (1979), Levinson (1980). But for me, the failure of speech act theory to tell us anything interesting about conversation (and thus about the prototypical form of language usage) is damning enough.

16. Chomsky darkly alludes to the possibility that models of human motivation, plans, intentions and the like may be *innately* beyond our grasp: "It is not excluded that human science-forming capacities simply do not extend to this domain, or any domain involving the exercise of will, so that, for humans, these questions will always be shrouded in mystery" (Chomsky 1976:25). Goal-driven A.I. systems though seem to promise a peek under the shroud.

17. However the most relevant part of Game theory is that to do with 'games of pure co-ordination', that is co-operative games, which is the least developed branch of the theory. For some important initial steps, though, see Schelling (1960).

GRAMMAR, LOGIC AND RHETORIC
IN A PRAGMATIC PERSPECTIVE

Guido Morpurgo-Tagliabue

1. *The pragmatic phenomenon of illocutionary meaning*

We want to undertake an examination of three aspects of pragmatics, which is here considered to be the interlocutors' contribution to the semantic accomplishment through their beliefs, intentions and expectations: in the three areas of the grammar, the logic, and the rhetoric of communication.

The first and the simplest case concerns the proposition. It can be considered a sense with a way of referring added to it. Ways of referring are the two linguistic acts of ILLOCUTION and PERLOCUTION, which are always complementary and not mutually exclusive. They are constitutive of the proposition, even though didactic scruples induced Austin to separate them from the proposition as well as from each other. In the same way as there exists no locution without illocution, and vice versa, there exists no illocution without perlocution, and vice versa, each of these components being able to be either explicit or implicit (but the locutionary factor, too, could have been implicit: the silence of Ajax).

Of the three linguistic acts, our investigation may therefore concentrate on the illocutionary, assuming that it is included in the first and implies the third.

Austin (1962: lecture IX) determined three conditions to be satisfied by the illocutionary act: (i) to secure *uptake*, (ii) to *'take effect'* in certain ways, (iii) to stimulate a response. He stressed the first point, which has since then been developed by Grice (1957:377-88) with the utmost carefulness, Strawson (1964: 73 and 439-60), Searle (1969), and D. Lewis (1969). He attached even greater importance to the second, later developed immoderately and inappropriately by G. Warnock (1973) (see Morpurgo-Tagliabue (1980)); he has been deficient on the third. Due perhaps to the didactic concern to keep illocution well distinguished from perlocution, he excluded in fact that illocutionary nomenclature should include any "additional reference to some of the consequences of the locutions, i.e. [...] that his saying them [certain words] had or perhaps was intended to have certain consequences" (1962:113-14). Yet in this case the *response* of the interlocutor in (iii) would be simply a COGNITIVE response, i.e. the *uptake* in (i),[1] or a BEHAVIOURAL response, either explicit and effective in which case we are already in the midst of perlocutions, or to be understood as intentional, as a purpose in sight (which is the case that really interests us). In fact, it has been noted that the grammar of the illocution has to make explicitly allowance for the perlocution (Cohen 1973; see also, Sbisà 1972).

With Anaxagoras (Diogenes Laertios, IX:53-54) we may distinguish two principles, synthetized in two pairs: the SEMANTIC principle of *expectation-response* (*erótesis - apócrisis*) and the PRAGMATIC principle of *need-satisfaction* (*eukolé - entolé*): the first pair centers on the *uptake* (the 'response' which is ensured if one understands the illocutionary force of the utterance; cf. Strawson 1964), the second on the behavioural response (disposition or action), that is, on the effect aimed at or achieved (Morpurgo-Tagliabue 1975). In the former case we could be said to remain on an illocutionary level, whereas in the latter we move to a perlocutionary one; but a perlocutionary dimension is present in both cases.

As is well known, not everybody shares this opinion: Searle (1969) denies that the finality of the illocutionary act could be extended to a perlocutionary object, even if only as to an "object in view". He writes:

> [...] it could not be the case that in general intended effects of meant utterances were perlocutionary, because many kinds of sentences used to perform illocutionary acts have no perlocutionary effect associated with their meaning. [...] there is no perlocutionary effect of, for example, promising which will distinguish promises from firm statements of intention and emphatic predictions (1969:46).

And why not? In definitions of assertions and promises one can leave out of consideration perlocutionary EFFECTS but not ATTEMPTS to achieve effects nor, therefore, intentions, even in the most formal way; as a result, according to Searle's own definition, a promise should predicate an act in favour of the interlocutor, otherwise it is a threat (Searle 1969:58).

From our point of view, the imbrication of the two acts is essential; otherwise one remains within the limits of a simple didactic abstraction. There exists no speech act which is not an act "in view of" an accomplishment to be described in perlocutionary terms. Illocutionary and perlocutionary acts have a similar molecular structure, with the difference that in the first the (perlocutionary) consequent is implied while the second implies the (illocutionary) antecedent: "I promised her ....". (In view of what? Of which effect-response? To discharge my obligation? To make her happy? To pay her off? The intention is always the intention to attain a result); "I persuaded him to ..." (By means of which acts? Describing, debating, flattering, threatening?)

This does not mean that illocution do not offer various degrees of perlocutionary force. But the structure does not change: the difference is simply prospective. To simplify the matter, let us try to reduce the possible differences to two extremes, as reflected in 'to promise' and 'to command'. What appears to be the effect of the corresponding acts? And what effect do we really achieve?

Seemingly, if I say "I promise you to come ...", the effect of the promise on the interlocutor - i.e. the perlocution - is extraneous to the utterance, is inexplicit, and is pragmatically determined by the context. If I say "I command you to go out ...", the consequent effect in view is inherent in the utterance, is explicit; the dichotomy command-obedience, order-execution forms a simple notion. Whether the addressee submits himself to the order or infringes it, the order, by definition, entails execution, obedience; on the other hand the effect of the promise is implied only by presumption, it is not entailed. Certainly, the promise too is never without a purpose, but this purpose is not specified by the term 'promise'; it is only specified *per accidens*. By definition, one commands 'in order to make someone to fulfil', but one promises 'for ...(?)'.

Distinguishing the fine shades of perlocutionary strength inherent in the illocution would constitute at most an academic-inconclusive contribution to synonymy. It is advisable to be content with the simple prospective distinction already considered between two types of combination of the two speech acts, the one more definitional and the other more contextual, the one more semantic and the other more pragmatic.

Let us not deceive ourselves and admit that we have in fact been dealing with a distinction of convenience, an oversimplified concept. By definition the command entails the issuing of a response on the hearer's part (the execution), the promise the issuing of a response on the speaker's part (the commitment), no matter whether it deals with a would-be result or a real one. We have therefore complete symmetry. Each intrinsic would-be result will be followed in both cases by a perlocutionary sequel, constituted by one or more perlocutionary acts, which will have specific characters conditioned by the context: "He ordered him to go out, wishing to impel him to go out - and thus he impelled him to go out - and thus he humiliated him, he excluded him from the group, etc."; "He promised her to come intending an exacting engagement to meet her - and thus he gave her the security of a next meeting - and thus he reassured her". Naturally, the relation between the illocutionary antecedent and the perlocutionary consequent is reciprocal: "He admonished him - in order to warn him - and to discourage him"; "He discouraged him - having warned him - giving him an admonishment".

It is difficult therefore to say where illocutionary force ends and perlocutionary force starts. The criterion, adopted by Austin, of a possible performative use of the corresponding verb, has been disputed; but one does not see better ones. The fact that on certain occasions this norm meets some idiomatic difficulty of application (in English, e.g., it is not possible to say "I boast myself", cf. Searle 1975b, whereas in Italian it is), is a fortuitous and negligible issue. And that in some special cases it rouses an "illocutionary suicide" (Vendler 1967) is a logical issue, not a linguistic one (if I say "I insinuate", I contradict myself in the same way as when I say "I lie", by way of the well known paradox of Epimenides: we then use a preterition as in "I would not like to insinuate that ....").

Less convincing from our point of view appears another distinctive norm offered by Austin: the illocution is conventional, the perlocution is not. Of course illocutionary verbs respond to the rules of grammar and of vocabulary; still, on the basis of simple linguistic conventions the cognitive uptake would not be in a position to distinguish a promise from a threat: it has to consider a potential associated perlocution, which can only be suggested by the context. And this confirms that only pragmatic aspects specify the semantics of the proposition, specifying the intention of the speaker with respect to a likely responsive behaviour of the hearer.

To establish a scale of the different ways in which the perlocutionary object could be inherent in the illocutionary act by means of Austin's five illocutionary classes, would be a very haphazard attempt. One could propose the following regressive order: exercitives, behabitives, commissives, verdictives, expositives; but not without many exceptions.

In any case, it is not possible to separate the imbrication *erótesis-apócrisis* proper to the semantic uptake, from the binomen *eucolé-*

entolé of the perlocutionary pragmatic object.

2. *The foundation of the logical squares*

If the linguistic acts offer an example of pragmatic intervention in the grammatical space from the propositional point of view, we can recognize another one from the rational point of view, in the space of logical connections. We will list only two episodes concerning (i) the orientation of the matrix, (ii) the interrelation of the logical categories.

It is well known that the structure of the four logical operators (AOEI) is the same for the existential, for the modal, for the epistemic, and for the deontic matrix. But between the first three and the last one there are some differences, explained perhaps by the fact that the first three contain apophantic rules, while the last one is not apophantic, but axiologic. This difference does not concern categorial structure, which is always the same, but its possibility of orientation, therefore its foundation.

It is also known that each square (or at least the first three) can be constructed starting from the first category as well as from the last one, from A as well as from I: both (but only those) can be recognized as *Grundformen*. I can take *totality* as well as *particularity* as original category, and thus *necessity* or *possibility*, *certainty* as well as *admissibility*. I can determine all categories from (x), the last one being $\exists x \sim (x \sim)$, and thus from Lp, to derive $M = \sim(L\sim)$; or vice versa, from $\exists x$ I can derive $x = \sim(\exists x)\sim(fx)$, or $Lp = \sim M \sim p$ from Mp.

No logical reason is essentially connected with this choice (beside technical preferences of elegance), but there are easily recognizable extralogical ones. Given the classical square AOEI, to start from A, i.e. to privilege the universal, the necessary, the certain, means to privilege an a priori rationalistic point of view; to start from I, from the particular, the possible, implies an a posteriori point of view, and empiristic one; in the moral field this would mean a rational rigorism or an emotive spontaneousness; in the epistemologic field, in the former case a demonstrative research, an analysis, in the latter an explanatory research, through confutations of confutations (the method of Galileo's "Diàlogo dei massimi sistemi") or through observative classifications. What is at issue is indeed a very elementary and traditional polarity, a very compendious one, but there is no doubt that it sends us back to extra semantic needs which look for satisfaction in semantic answers. There is no need to leave the philosophical notions in order to enter into the pragmatic ones; certainly, of the two attitudes polarized above, one sends us back to the satisfaction of an axiological aspiration and the other rather to the satisfaction of naturalistic information.

The hypothesis is confirmed by the case of deontic logic, which, though constructed upon the pattern of previous ones (of modal logic in accordance with von Wright, of quantified logic in accordance with Kalinowski and Hintikka), nevertheless turns away from them under the aspect we are interested in. In this case the foundation of the categorial system can only start a single *Grundform*, the A. Even if other filiations have been attempted it is easy to recognize them as illegitimate.

In particular the foundation from I, which may have been the most legitimate in the other cases (after all, we do not know exactly what the universal, the necessary, the certain are, but we do know what the particular, the possible, the simply admissible are), cannot be supported by the deontic point of view - and this can be verified in the juridical field, the principal field of application of deontic logic: it would mean to derive the whole juridical system from the category of the *permitted*; but this already implies by definition the notion of *prohibition* (it is the non-prohibited), i.e. of the obligatory; for a very fine attempt see A.G. Conte (1962). Indeed, attempts have been made to derive all deontic categories of law from *prohibition* (supplied with sanctions) (cf. Anderson 1956), a proposal which would have been able to collimate deontic logic with juridical dogmatics of Kelsen (1960) (based on the primacy of prohibition). But not even prohibition (E) is an original category: it is still obligation; and as for sanction, it is a secondary norm which refers in its turn to a primary norm, the one which prescribes to the judge to apply sanctions; hence everything comes back to *obligation*, in A. It can be added that finally a logic of sanction as well as one derived from permission is even no longer a deontic logic, but still a modal logic: G.I. Lewis' modal logic and G.H. von Wright's system of deontic logic can stand on a juridical notion of permission; they are no longer normative but descriptive, sociological definitions of behaviour, implying descriptions of other behaviours. Only in a descriptive deontic, prohibition and sanction could be considered original operators: inherent the *Natur der Sache*, and not derived from applications of obligations.

This last difference explains also the diversity pointed out above between the first three logics and the last one. Strictly speaking also these squares should be led back not to two but to a single possible generative category, the I. The particular, the possible, the admissible, all of them forms in I, are primary, descriptive concepts; the corresponding A, the various forms of 'absolute' are really not a notion, they are not describable; each of them represents an aspiration, a must be, exactly like an obligation: totality can be derived from the existential particular (I) only as its inexhaustible application, as well as the infinite numerical subsequent; it is a whole, a necessity, an absolute always open, temporary, an indefinite. Deontic obligation on the other hand is a closed whole, a definite necessity. Therefore it could correspond to a modal system, like the system T in R. Feys (1937), or the one in E.J. Lemmon (1957), or in R. Carnap (1947); it is a deontic system like the New System in von Wright (1964) or in E.J. Lemmon (1965:8). Only this setting seems from our point of view to be coherent with the nature of deontic logic, depending on the logic of norms (cf. G. Kalinowski 1975). Thus we could also say that the first three matrixes originate legitimately only from the category of the particular, and the fourth from the universal: the former capable of an open perspective, the latter one closed (like every regulation), the former descriptive, the latter normative.

In this panorama exceptions are more interesting than rules. Therefore what we have seen is significant: whilst from the point of view of practice and of juridical theory tendencies towards openness revealed themselves, some attempts of foundations in I were not lacking, according to a spontaneistic conception of the law (Cossio 1944); and when the doctrine tried to give a strictly technical setting of positive law, it tried to build up a deontic logic in E (perhaps unconsciously inspired more by the strictness of the state of law than by the conceptual rigour of the law; cf. Kelsen 1943). In this field logical options too arose not from logical but from ideological presuppositions, from pragmatic interests.

3. *The problem of the subcontraries*

Another logico-syntactical field affected by pragmatical constraints can be identified in the very singular knot of the categories of logic formed by the interrelation of subcontraries.

When G. Frege (1892), with the intention to offer an example of the distinction between *Sinn* and *Bedeutung* and of the confusions which it sometimes arouses in ordinary speech, quoted the example of *Morgenstern* and *Abendstern* which both correspond to the referent planet Venus, he did not notice that he said something true and false at the same time (it is a question of the same planet, but at different times and places and constellations, and for these the principle of non-contradiction cannot be applied: it is a question of two referents). He could have quoted as an equally problematic example, the logical *subcontraries* which either can or cannot have the same referent, according to the sense in which they are considered (in the same way as for *Morgenstern* and *Abendstern*). To say, 'not-nobody' (somebody) and 'not-everybody', to say 'possible' and 'not-necessary', to say 'only admissible' and 'not-certain', to say 'allowed' (not-prohibited) and 'not-commanded', can have the same referent, in the same way as the positive and the negative of a film; but they may also dissolve in their subalternates ('everybody' and 'nobody', 'necessary' and 'impossible', and so on) in which case we no longer have either subcontraries subordinates or contradictories, but only contrary-contradictories.

To be brief, since we are dealing with an elementary question, we can start from a test-sentence which I also found in an acute essay by H. Parret (1975). I cannot say "I know that p and it is possibly not p". Indeed the assertion "I know" corresponds to "I am sure", "it is verified in every case", "necessarily", "obligatory"; therefore the sentence would fail to observe the principle of non-contradiction; I cannot say at the same time $(x)p$ and $\sim(x)p$, $\sim M \sim p$ and $M \sim p$, Lp and $\sim Lp$. Moreover, a contradictor would object that $(x)p$ implies $(\exists x)p$ as a subordinate, and this implies $(x)p$ as a subcontrary. How do we consider it? - It will be sufficient to interpret those relations exactly, i.e. literally, etymologically.

The relation of contradiction is a relation of LIMITATION (according to the diagram of Venn), not of EXCLUSION as is pointed out by the terminology. If I say "not all (où pàs) people are clever" (O), this means that there are some who are stupid, but in this case the proposition covers the clever people, the stupid constitute the set forming an exception with respect to the whole; if I say "it is not true that nobody is clever" (I) (oú pàs oùk) I mean that some clever people do exist, but as exceptions in a sea of fools. And indeed the wolfian logicians, Lambert, Crusius, and later Kant, joined both classes in a single category, that of *limitation* (to which the parallel category of the singular corresponded). In this way one avoids the sophistic equivocation mentioned above. Under the guidance of Democritos and Pythagoras, the $\exists x$, the 'only one', the 'possible', may, to some extent, come nearer and nearer to the 'all (x)', the 'necessary', without ever reaching it, like Achilles and the tortoise: always a fraction remains. It is excluded that while saying 'not-all' (O) one could mean 'nobody' and saying 'not-nobody' (I) one could mean 'all'. 'Not-all' is subordinate to 'nobody'; the same can be said of 'not-nobody' (at least one), which is subordinate to 'all'. I and A, and O and E, are subordinates but also contradictories: there always exists a limit which hinders equivalence and maintains contradictoriness. This is why logic is destined to be expressed in mathematics, possibility in probability, in degree; and degree is always a choice, a valuation in conformity to a context; where a possibility of choice of a degree is not given, there is no possibility but only necessity, a simple analytical implication. The norm of limit constitutes a presupposition already in the Aristotelian nomenclature, but its application in the shape of degree, measure, its transition from logic to mathematics, is modern; in one way Aristotle simply maintained the definition: if one defines the possible as "that what is not necessary not to exist ($\_L\_p$)", one will get a notion at the same time subordinate and subordinating to the necessary (De interpretatione XIII:22b, 10-20), but in which two homonymous notions of the possible co-exist. He did then explain it by means of a norm drawn from his own metaphysics. He distinguished a 'possible' of that which potentially is, i.e. the common possible, the simple one (*aplōs*), and a 'possible' of that which is in fact, of "what is when it is": (*tò òn ótan eî*) ex hypothesis (De interpretatione XIII:23a,6). The one is the 'possible' of that which is happening and is going to happen (*genésthai*) which is simply (*aplōs*) a not-impossible (*oùk adúnaton*); the other is a 'possible' of that which did happen (*gegonós*) and which by definition could not have not happened, an impossible-which-not. In the first case the being able to be will never reach the not being able not to be. It would go beyond its own limit. When it reaches it, it dies. And thus it happens in the second case.

In this last case indeed no doubts exist; here the principle of non-contradiction is of use (Metaphisica III:6, 1011b20), it is a question of a possibility which corresponds to the existence by definition (De interpretatione XIII:19a, 23-24; 22b, 11); it is not a 'to be possible-to be not possible'; it has no subcontrary, and it is not in contradiction with its subalternatives. Here possibility is reabsorbed in necessity, the concept of limit disapears; and with it, strictly, possibility itself.

But what about that which happens and is going to happen? In chapter IX of the "De interpretatione" Aristotle did not agree - contrary to Diodorus Cronus - to extend that possible *ex hypothesis* to future events which are contingent (*endekómena*; not necessary). Sextus Empiricus admitted it even less; and David Hume took this refusal as the principle of his epistemology. I cannot say "I am sure that the sun did rise, but it is possible that it did not rise". (Here the possible, being such by definition of the *factum*, is a necessary.) But I can say "I am sure that to-morrow the sun will rise, nevertheless it may not rise". The sentence "I know that p and it is possible that not p" is therefore legitimate.

Don't let us take away from Ceasar what belongs to Ceasar. It is obvious that all these implications are semantic. A matter of pragmatics is the choice of the postulate: Aristotle refused the postulate which was accepted by Diodorus; and Kant rejected Hume's postulate; and both, Hume and Kant, admitted methodically to do so by inclination, the former because he was inclined to give credit to empirical arguments, the latter because he could not give up the need of the universal.

If one wished, one could also include the case just considered, the choice of *Grundformen*, in the pragmatic casuistic of the former paragraph. In order to keep very close to the principle of non-contradiction one has privileged A and sacrificed I. In conclusion, just as the grammar of linguistic acts, also the syntax of logical categories is conditioned by presuppositions, that is, is chooseable on the basis of the expectations of the users.

4. *Rhetoric as hermeneutics*

In the previous section we have neglected another pragmatic presupposition which regulates logical syntax, viz. the one related to telling the truth, to bewaring of sophistic games to which logical syntax lends itself in the most easy-going manner (as has been hinted). Our mind is averse to ambiguities, and since these are nestled in the generic character of logical notions, it will strive to find a remedy by transforming these into scientific notions (as has been mentioned,

I will not speak any longer of possibility but arithmetized possibility, of probability), or else one will commit oneself to the evidence (which can also be an evident non-evidence) of rhetorical speech.

I consider the recent success of Grice's (1975) *conversational implicatures* to be actually attributable to this phenomenon. Grice again proposed nothing else than the rules of classical rhetoric adapted to the modern position of speech.

Modern speech does no longer distinguish between the canonically distinguished varieties of style and genre to which the antique rhetoric adhered (epidictic, juridical, epistolary, dialogical, historical genre; see Morpurgo-Tagliabue 1967, 1980). This results from the generic character of the rules as described by Grice, which concern any argument. As such they should not be axiomatized.

Ignoring the rather comic whim of the author, of wanting to call his principles "categories" and to put them into the Kantian classes of categories (what do the stylistic ways of rule IV have to do with the logical-transcendental modality of Kant?), it is easy to notice that his four principles are actually reduced to three (I and III almost coincide), and it is not difficult to lead them back to the three dimensions of classical rhetoric: *inventio, dispositio, elocutio*.

We thus have three rules:

A - rule II: to stick to the truth. This is in accordance with the Aristotelian sense of the *éndoxa* (agreed truths) from Book I of "Rhetorica", with Cicero's *argumenta ad faciendam fidem* (Partitiones oratoriae, I,5), i.e. with the rhetorical task of *docere*. The goal of classical rhetoric was persuasion, and persuasion can be directed toward the thruth as well as to falsity (the "deceit" of Gorgias), but the truth has never been the only object of the *techne rhetoriké*. It is its presupposition.

B - rule I + III: to say what is required and no more (I), to be relevant to the argument rather than to avoid it (III). This corresponds to the advice of appropriateness (*prépon*) and to functionality *(téleon)*, indispensable to the effect which has to be reached, according to Book II of "Rhetorica"; it is the *ordo* proper of the *dispositio*, proceeding to the *movere*.

C - rule IV: the 'perspicuitas', which is basically clarity, transparency, *saphéneia*, required by the *lexis* from Book III of the Aristotelian "Rhetorica" and by all the antique rhetoricians. "Extreme clarity and maximum conciseness" was Cicero's norm (De oratore, 2:51-54); starting from the stoics, conciseness and clarity are not missing in any master of rhetoric (such as Demetrius etc.). And even if literary advice has been put aside, we still remain in the dimension of *delectare*.

Two aspects constitute the originality of Grice's rules in comparison with antique Rhetoric.

(i) The rules are formulated as a conversational code, i.e. as a code of economical transmission of presupposed true information. But as such it is applied on the level of the proposition (*propositio*) sooner than on the level of the statement (*enunciatio*): he deals with meanings which make the addressee assume other meanings; conventionality centers around the meanings, not the signs. The code can also be applied to merely behavioural meanings (which are neither linguistic nor gestural). It is a code on the basis of which everyone anticipates, presumes or implies some behaviour on the part of others, just as a cryptographic lattice permits to decipher actions, gestures, words and to reply to them on a normal level (it would be of no use in artificial cases).

With that we have already passed on to the second characteristic of this code.

(ii) Grice's index gives no suggestions to the speaker, if not by means of an expositive expedient; it is not propedeutic but hermeneutic. The norms considered retrace traditional humanistic rhetoric but they retrace it the other way round; not from the point of view of the speaker but from the receptor. On the assumption that the speaker should follow this social code of communication, the interlocutor - who is assuming it - may legitimately deduce certain unexpressed meanings. Summing up, Grice presents a rhetoric not of convincing somebody but of convincing oneself, a classical rhetoric seen from the reverse.

Naturally, the poetics and the rhetorics of the past also had a reverse; they assigned precepts to the authors in order for the readers to know how to respond to them, but this is rather to estimate them than to interpret them, in an axiological rather than a semantic function. However, this attitude also allows Grice to approach certain aspects which for the ancients in particular had a literary value: rhetorical expedients of indirect meaning, non-exposed meanings which are only hinted to be assumed, i.e. meanings of the not-said such as the stylistic forms of metaphor, litotes, hyperbole, irony, ambiguity, "calembour", periphrase, implication etc. The ancients, facing such *schémata léxeos*, also decided to place themselves more or less on the side of the audience (for example, consult chapter eleven of Book III of Aristotle's "Rhetorica"); but Grice does so according to reason. His originality consists neither in the choice, nor in the discovery and even less in the systematisation of the rhetorical figures of presuppositional implication which he sets afloat, but in the methodical awareness by which he carried out the overturning of perspective. Thus he illuminated the hermeneutic aspect of the antique precepts.

Ultimately it is not accidental that the author dealing in such detail with the phenomena of *implying*, did in absolutely no way deal with the philosophical aspect of the problem, i.e. with the cognitive mechanism peculiar to all these forms of implication, which is the logico-inferential mechanism. He did so only, so to speak, in the field. This corroborates the rhetorical direction of his research.

According to habit, we will not draw general conclusions from an episodical investigation. Without claiming to have drawn a map of Pragmatics, we have shown, however, that grammatical presuppositions are more accidental and unforeseeable or contextual than the alternatives of logic and with the rules of rhetoric; there is a progress of a more and more accurate choice. In any case the cognitive connexion of expectation-response reveals itself to be a transactional finality corresponding to a relation *eukolé-entolé*, of need-satisfaction.

FOOTNOTE:

1. It is a mistake not even avoided by J.R. Searle (1975b) to deny that an illocutionary act would be associated with a perlocutionary aim: the aim of a promise would already be that of commitment. And 'to promise' may certainly mean to commit oneself, or even only to make the hearer believe that the speaker commits himself: in both cases there is a certain purpose, to be formulated in terms of a possible emotive or behavioural answer from the interlocutor, not extrinsic to the act, and without which not even the two cases of sincerity and of fiction could be distinguished. A 'promising' which would have the aim of promising (the engagement - warned Austin - is not following the promise, it is the promise) or a commanding with the illocutionary aim of commanding, would be like whistling the sake of for whistling (without other purposes, conscious or unconscious).

COMMON PROBLEMS IN THE THEORY OF ANAPHORA
AND THE THEORY OF DISCOURSE

Richard T. Oehrle

0. One difficulty in assessing the possibilities and limitations of pragmatics lies in the very diversity of the term's application. Particularly problematic is the fact that 'pragmatics' is at times used as a methodological term -- to designate the study of a language in relation to its users -- and at times as a theoretical term -- to designate investigations of language use in such areas as indexical expressions, speech acts, discourse structure, and, in general, almost anything which doesn't seem to belong to accepted categories of syntax or semantics.

As a methodological term, 'pragmatics' is unproblematic, but not particularly interesting, in that it fails to define any particular object or any particular method. As it presupposes no characterization of the notion 'language', one cannot help but wonder what exactly it is that is to be studied in relation to its users. Carnap (1968), in fact, subsumes the entire field of linguistics within pragmatics in this somewhat vacuous sense, and if we follow him, there can be little doubt that the only limitations on the possibilities of pragmatics are those imposed by the insight and imagination of its practitioners.

If, on the other hand, we construe pragmatics as a proper subpart of the study of human language -- namely, the study of the ways in which language is used and the influence its functions have upon its form and interpretation -- it is impossible to assess its prospects adequately without assessing as well its relation to such notions as language, syntax, semantics, and so forth. This is no simple task, and it is exacerbated by the fact that many (though by no means all) contemporary models of human language suffer from a fundamental inadequacy: they contain no analogue of one of the basic properties of speech -- its prosodic structure. While the importance of prosody to the analysis of illocutionary acts is apparent, in this paper I wish to demonstrate by the examination of a small set of examples, how prosodic properties can play a decisive role in such entrenched areas of semantic and pragmatic research as the assignment of reference to anaphoric expressions.

1. In general, anaphora involves a judgment that two expressions have equivalent values. There are a variety of considerations which constrain the anaphoric-identification of two expressions, including not only the inherent morphological and semantic properties of the expressions in question and their syntactic relations, but also their intonational properties, though the exact nature of such prosodic constraints seem to have received less attention than the study of the morphological, semantic, and syntactic constraints on anaphoric compatibility.[1]

To illustrate the dependency of anaphoric-identification on intonation, let me begin with a deceptively simple linguistic problem, which is based on a consideration of the following sentence:[2]

(1) Măry hĭt Bĭll, aňd thèn hĕ hĭt Hárry.

What is puzzling about this sentence is that the pronoun *he* cannot be anaphorically-identified with *Bill*. In fact, if we make no assumptions about the discourse conditions in which it occurs, we can accept the sentence only if we anaphorically-identify *he* with *Mary*. Why should we be forced to anaphorically mate *he* and *Mary*, violating our assumptions about anaphoric-compatibility, when there exists another expression in the first conjunct of the sentence that is anaphorically-compatible with *he* in a seemingly straightforward way.

2.   There is a simple solution to this problem: if we examine the possible stress contours of the second conjunct of the sentence frame (2),

(2)   x̌ hít y̌ and then w hĭt z.

relative to a discourse frame compatible with the stress of the first conjunct but otherwise neutral -- meaning that a satisfactory interpretation of any instantiation of (2) cannot depend on any discourse information other than the existence of a set of available referents -- there exists a simple rule which relates anaphoric-identification and stress, which I shall call 'rule R'.

(R)   If either w or z corresponds to an anaphoric expression[3] in an instantiation of schema (2), then
   (i) w is unstressed iff w and x are anaphorically-identified.
   (ii) z is unstressed iff z and y are anaphorically-identified.

Rule R provides a principled basis for such judgments as the following:

(3)   Jŏhn hít Bĭll and then hĕ hĭt Geórge.
      (he=John, he≠Bill)
      Jŏhn hít Bĭll and then hé hĭt Geórge.
      (he=Bill, he≠John)
      Jŏhn hít Bĭll and then Geórge hĭt hím.
      (him=John, him≠Bill)
      Jŏhn hít Bĭll and then Geórge hĭt hĭm.
      (him=Bill, him≠John)
      Jŏhn hít Bĭll and then hĕ hĭt hím.
      (he=John, hence him≠John; him≠Bill)[4]

Indeed, it is not difficult to see that the problem we began with -- the puzzling restriction on anaphoric-identification noted with regard to sentence (1) -- is merely an instance of a particular case of rule R.

   Yet in spite of rule R's apparent generality within the domain for which it is defined, one cannot help noticing that this domain is itself rather narrow. The restrictions on the domain of rule R stem from two distinct conditions: the first restricts the discourse contexts in which the rule applies; the second consists in the specification of particular words, e.g. the occurrences of the word *hit*. We consider the justification of these restrictions in turn in §§ 3 and 4 respectively.

3.0 Perhaps the simplest way of observing the influence of discourse factors on anaphoric-identification involves adding the phrase *as for Bill* to the beginning of sentence (1), yielding:

(4) Às fŏr Bíll, Mǎry hít Bȉll ǎnd thèn hĕ hȉt Hárrў.

Here a remarkable thing happens: whereas with (1) in isolation it appears to be impossible to anaphorically-identify *Bill* and *he*, with (4) the pronoun *he* apparently must be anaphorically-identified with *Bill*. This remains the case even when the subject of the first conjunct is an expression anaphorically-compatible with *he*, as in (5):

(5) Às fŏr Bíll, Jŏhn hít Bȉll aňd thèn hĕ hȉt Hárry.

One might conjecture that this shift in anaphoric-identification is due to some special property of the expression *as for x*. But while this is no doubt correct, it is nevertheless somewhat misleading, for the same effect can be achieved by a wide variety of linguistic means, one example of which we give in (6):

(6) A: Can you give me an exact description of Bill's role in the fight?
     B: Jǒhn hít Bȉll aňd thèn hĕ hȉt Máx.

A second way in which discourse-context governs anaphoric-identification is obvious enough: suppose that A and B are two individuals who already know (and each knows that the other knows) that Bill was the only one who hit Max. Under such circumstances, if the dialogue presented in (7) were to occur, B's utterance would be compatible with an analysis on which *he* and *Bill* are anaphorically-identified:

(7) A: Do you have any idea why Bill hit Max?
B: Nòt reállỹ. Àll wĕ knów iš thăt Jŏhn hít Bĭll and thèn hĕ hĭt Máx.

A third case involves the correction of mistaken suppositions, as, for example, in the dialogue given in (8):

(8) A: As far as I understand what happened, Jŏhn grábbed Bĭll rìght bĕfóre Bĭll hít Săm. Is that right?
B: Nòt quíte. Jŏhn hít Bĭll ănd thèn hĕ hĭt Máx.

Here again, the influence of discourse-factors on interpretaion demonstrates the necessity of restricting the domain of rule R.

In the cases thus far examined, we have shown how in contradistinction to (3) in isolation, certain discourse-contexts allow unstressed *he* to be anaphorically-identified with *Bill*. It is equally possible to construct cases in which stressed *he* or unstressed *him*, corresponding to w and z respectively in instantiations of schema (2), can be anaphorically-identified with *John*, construed as schema (2)'s x. A typical case of this occurs, for example, if we emend (8) so that B's response is as in (9):

(9) B: Nòt qúite. Jŏhn hít Bĭll ańd thèn hé hĭt Săm.

Such examples demonstrate unequivocally that judgments concerning the anaphoric relations within a certain expression are in certain cases subject to manipulation by a suitable choice of discourse frame. Where these judgments are subjectively well-defined, a satisfactory account of the cases they rest on can, by turning the problem on its head, be taken to be a criterion of adequacy for theories of discourse structure. In other words, we can evaluate competing theories of discourse structure in part by assessing their ability to deal with the demonstrated cases of the dependency of anaphoric-identification on discourse context, relative, of course, to the intonational properties of the expressions in question.

3.1 Many linguists have assumed that it is useful to analyze sentences in terms of such notions as 'topic', 'comment', 'theme', 'focus', and so forth, with the evident expectation that such analysis would not only lead to an explanation of certain intra-sentential properties of utterances, but would do so in terms of a vocabulary oriented toward the range of discourse-functions a given utterance could be used to satisfy. Although I don't wish to consider in any detail here the numerous and quite varied attempts that have been made to define such terminology nor to question the desirability of providing an account of the phenomena for which such terms have been proposed as an analytical vocabulary, it is all too obvious that in many cases, such terms are either defined inadequately (e.g. the topic of a sentence -- N.B. the presumption of uniqueness -- is what the sentence is 'about') or misapplied (e.g. it is a category mistake to say of a noun phrase or its value that it is 'old information' or 'new information', though the mistake is, in many cases, a harmless one). More seriously, however, such a vocabulary fails to bear on our cases in a deeper respect, in that there is, so to speak, no obvious discourse-logic definable over it: even supposing a satisfactory procedure by which utterances could be analyzed in terms of such notions, they seem ill-adapted to the requisite task of mediating between intra- and extra-sentential properties. The cases we have been considering of the discourse-dependency of anaphoric-identification, relative to fixed intonational properties of the utterances in question, provide an excellent opportunity to investigate this theoretical question within an empirical context of non-trivial and relatively well-defined problems.

3.2 The various examples adduced in 3.0 to illustrate cases which fall outside the domain of rule R share a common property: it is always possible to anaphorically-identify the pronoun in the second conjunct violating the stipulations of rule R with an expression external to the first conjunct. Our problem, then, is to show how it is possible under certain circumstances that a pronoun is anaphorically-identified with one discourse expression rather than with any of a number of other possible choices. The obvious way to resolve this problem is by definition of a discourse structure, consisting of an analysis of the elements of a discourse together with a set of relations defined over such an analysis, in which it can, furthermore, be shown that consistency with the chosen relations forces the observed local properties of anaphoric-identification.[5] In order to account for the cases presented above, we shall hypothesize the existence of two such structures which, though based upon seemingly rather different concepts, are not incompatible.

3.2.1 Consider example (6). Informally, suppose we reason as follows: insofar as we take B to be complying with A's request, his assertion must be construed as a whole as a description of Bill's role in the fight. Anaphoric-identification of *he* with *Bill* is intuitively consistent with this requirement, since, on this interpretation of the pronoun, both of the sentences joined by the connective *and (then)* may easily be construed as expressing propositions which describe Bill's role in the fight. If, however, we were to identify *he* with *John*, then the entire second conjunct of B's utterance would be irreconcilable with this characterization, and, as a consequence, if we construe the connective *and (then)* in such a way that it requires that each of the expressions it joins be in compliance in this case with A's request, B's utterance, on this interpretation, would intuitively violate the requirement that the second conjunct serve, in part, to satisfy A's request.

The reasoning involved here is not especially difficult, but it rests on premises which in turn depend on a variety of difficult concepts, including, at a minimum, the following:

  a) A's utterance can be construed as a request for a description of Bill's role in the fight.
  b) If B's utterance u_B satisfies A's request for a description of Bill's role in the fight, than u_B is a description of Bill's role in the fight.
  c) u_B is to be construed as satisfying A's request for a descrip-

tion of Bill's role in the fight.

d) If u_B is a description of Bill's role in the fight, and u_B is analyzable as 'S_1 and then S_2', where 'S_1' and 'S_2' are variables ranging over sentences, then S_2 must be construed as describing Bill's role in the fight.

e) The proposition expressed by *he hit Max* describes Bill's role in the fight if *he* is anaphorically-identified with *Bill*.

I shall not attempt to justify each of these premises here, although I think that each one of them is intuitively compatible with the discourse represented by (6), and in fact seems necessary if we are to consider the discourse coherent and complete. What I would like to emphasize, however, is the character of the reasoning involved: the premises require not only that the utterances of the participants in the discourse be amenable to analysis at certain levels -- i.e. syntactic structure, propositional content, illocutionary force, illocutionary point -- but that there exist significant ways of relating these various levels of analysis. These two properties together justify the appellation 'discourse structure'.

3.2.2 The details of the analysis we have given of example (6) clearly depend heavily on factors idiosyncratic to this particular case. In a more general setting, we would seek clarification of the concepts involved in the analysis of the sequence of utterances which make up a discourse at each of the levels analyzed, as well as some insight into the question of which of the many relations definable over the analysis at these levels is empirically justified. Such questions of theory clearly rest in part on the degree of precision we attain in analyzing particular utterances relative to the postulated level, together with the extent to which it can be shown that the postulated relations play a significant role in accounting for such observed properties as the disambiguation or semantic reanalysis of particular utterances in a given discourse.

Although the number of concepts involved here might be considered a theoretical drawback, the very variety of concepts involved provides a necessary flexibility in analysis -- it is evident, for example, that the analysis of (4), (5), and (7) must diverge from the analysis given for (6) in certain crucial respects: (4) and (5) depend on assumptions concerning the use of the expression *as for x*, and not on the logic (or gamesmanship) of requests and the means by which particular requests may be satisfied (in whole or in part), whereas in an explicit analysis of (7), one must take into account the ramifications of B's denial that he can satisfy A's request, with respect to the ultimate assessment of the propositional content of his next sentence (though obviously this, in turn, may be mediated, within the framework we have suggested, by various steps of reasoning which bridge the distinct levels of analysis).

In this way, relative to the distinguishability of each of the levels of analysis postulated, we can attempt to justify each level of analysis by providing cases whose analysis depends crucially on appeal to a particular level.

3.3 The levels of analysis that we relied on in our analysis of (6) included syntactic structure, propositional content relative to that structure, illocutionary force (relative to propositional content), and illocutionary point (relative to illocutionary force), and the crucial step in our reasoning concerning this example resided in the fact that the concept illocutionary point provided a bridge between the analysis of A's utterance and the analysis of B's utterance. If this analysis is a valid one, in the absence of alternative accounts, we may consider each of the levels referred to as necessary to an adequate theory of discourse. Such considerations raise in turn the corresponding question of whether the postulated levels of analysis and relations over them are sufficiently rich to provide a satisfactory account of any arbitrary discourse. Although it may be impossible in principle to definitively provide a positive answer to this question on either theoretical or empirical grounds, it is easy enough to show that a given theory is analytically too weak. In fact, this is the case for the set of levels we discussed above relative to the analysis of (6), for we have thus far failed to consider the role of prosodic properties. I will mention two ways in which the influence of prosodic properties cannot be disregarded in an account of discourse structure and develop a third way in considerably more detail.

3.3.1 First, the syntactic domain of certain operators can be delimited by such prosodic factors as pitch and relative timing. If we compare example (5) with (10), where the orthographic distinctions between the two examples represent distinct prosodic properties.

(10) As for Bill, John hit Bill. And then he hit Harry,

we find that judgments concerning the anaphoric-identification of *he* less certain. This difference can be attributed to the intonationally-governed distinction in the two cases of the domain of the expression *as for Bill*.

3.3.2 Second, differences in the pitch contour of utterances affect the ways in which the contribution of the utterance to the discourse is assessed. Consider the example of Grice (1975) in which A says, "Smith doesn't seem to have a girlfriend these days", and B responds by saying, "He's been spending a lot of time in New York lately". Grice's analysis of this case, on which B's remark is construed as a suggestion that the reason Smith is spending time in New York might have something to do with his having a girlfriend there, depends on B's utterance have a rising pitch over both *New York* and *lately*. Relative to this intonation contour, B's utterance can be construed as a suggestion that bears on the doubt expressed by A. If B utters his statement with falling intonation, however, and if we suppose that not having a girlfriend might lead one to spend a lot of time in New York, then B's utterance might be taken to confirm A's suspicions. Although the analysis of this distinction is rather crude, it suggests that intonation contours serve to distinguish not only the illocutionary force of an utterance, but, more subtly, they serve in the identification of illocutionary point as well in ways that clearly deserve much further investigation.

3.3.3 In the examples thus far considered, the influence of prosodic properties on discourse structure can be confined to the relation of different levels of analysis within individual intonational phrases. In the phenomenon of contrastive accent, however, we find a case in which prosodic properties play a more direct role in the establishment of a discourse structure which can bind together distinct utterances. The reason for this, of course, is intuitively a very simple one -- for if part of an expression is taken to be contrastive, then there must be something it contrasts with. We shall attempt an explicit statement of this simple idea.

3.3.3.1 Let us assume first that, in utterances which contain no contrastive accent, the intonation contour is smooth and either rises or falls on the syllable which bears the nuclear accent. Although this is a simplifying assumption in a number of respects, the details we gloss over do not crucially affect the problem we are addressing. Second, we identify contrastive accent relative to such a smooth intonation contour, as a perturbation in pitch consisting of either i) a rise-fall in pitch if it falls on a non-nuclearly accented syllable or, when the intonation curve is falling, on the nuclearly-accented syllable, or ii) a fall-rise in pitch if it falls on the nuclearly-accented syllable and the intonation curve is rising. Our third assumption requires that the interpretation of a syntactically complex expression be analyzable in such a way that elements of this semantic analysis may be associated uniquely with the syntactic analysis of the expression.[6] Moreover, relative to this last assumption, we require the following definition: two expressions E_1 and E_2 will be said to be propositionally congruent if i) there are two proposition P_1 and P_2 which localize to E_1 and E_2 respectively, and ii) there exist syntactic partitions of E_1 and E_2 such that the elements of these two partitions can be placed in a one-one association in such a way that the corresponding values localized to each pair of associated syntactic constituents are of the same semantic type.

Suppose we have identified a contrastively-accented constituent C in an utterance. We assert that there is an expression E_1 which contains C and an expression E_2, disjoint from E_1, such that relative to a partition of E_1 which includes all contrastively-accented constituents of E_1, E_1 and E_2 are propositionally congruent. Moreover, the value of any contrastively-accented constituent in the partition of E_1 is taken to be distinct from the value of the element of the partition of E_2 with which it is associated, while the values of all other elements of the partition of E_1 are taken to be equivalent to the values of the elements of the partition of E_2 with which they are (respectively) associated. Although this formulation of the problem may seem technically forbidding, and although it leaves open a number of loose ends, if it is essentially correct, it reveals the power implicit in the prosodic mechanism of contrastive accent: contrastive accent is an operator on the values of two propositionally congruent expressions such that the non-contrastively-accented parts are identified as equivalent in some way while the contrastively-accented parts must be construed as distinct. In this way, the phenomenon of contrastive accent has the essential property of a discourse structure: it can force the disambiguation or reanalysis of particular utterances within its domain. Let us apply the concepts we have developed to the analysis of examples (8) and (9).

Although the normal interpretation of the acute accent over *hit* in the typographical representation of B's utterance in (8) is that *hit* is contrastively-accented, the accent over *Max* can be interpreted in two ways: if there is a rise-fall in the intonation of this syllable, then *Max* is contrastively-accented; whereas if there is no rise in pitch, but only a fall, then *Max* is not contrastively-accented. We shall take up these two interpretations of the typographical representation in turn.

Suppose that both the first occurence of *hit* and the occurence of *Max* are taken to be contrastively-accented. Then take E_1 to be "John hit Bill and then he hit Max", take E_2 to be "John grabbed Bill right before Bill hit Sam", and take the associated pairs of the respective partitions of these expressions to be *(John, John)*, *(grabbed, hit)*,

(Bill, Bill), (right before, and then), (Bill, he), (hit, hit), (Sam, Max). On this interpretation, it is easily seen that our account of contrastive accent requires that of these pairs, *grabbed* and *hit*, and *Sam* and *Max* must be construed as the localizations of distinct values, while all other pairs, including *Bill* in A's utterance and *he* in B's utterance must be taken to be equivalent. This accords correctly with intuitive judgment.

Suppose, however, that we take only the first occurrence of *hit* to be contrastively-accented, and that the acute accent over the word *Max* represents only the nuclear (falling) accent. Then we can take E_1 to be the expression "John hit Bill", E_2 to be the expression "John grabbed Bill", and the association of propositional congruence between these two examples to be exactly the same as in the last example restricted to these expressions. This leaves open how to anaphorically-identify the word *he* in B's utterance, and rightly so, for its intuitive anaphoric-identification is vague and, as a result, open to manipulation by other discourse factors.

If we interpret B's response in (9) to the request of A in (8), we must take B's response to contain two contrastively-accented constituents: *hit* and *he*. In this case, we take E_1 to be "John hit Bill and then he hit Sam", and we take E_2 to be "John grabbed Bill right before Bill hit Sam", and the association between the two expressions is as follows: *(John, John), (hit, grabbed), (Bill, Bill), (and then, right before), (he, Bill), (hit, hit), (Sam, Sam)*. Since *hit* and *he* are construed as contrastively-accented, *hit* and *he* must be construed as having distinct values from *grabbed* and *Bill* respectively. Again, this accords correctly with intuitive judgment.

Although the examples we have analyzed provide rather trivial examples of propositional congruence, the power of this discourse structure can perhaps be better appreciated by considering the following example, various versions of which have been attributed to George Lakoff:

(11) George cálled Sálly ă Fáscĭst aňd theň she ĭnsŭltĕd hím.

In this example, according to the definition we gave above, both *she* and *him* are construed as contrastively-accented. Take E_1 to be *she insulted him* and E_2 to be "George called Sally a Fascist", and take the association between the partitions of E_1 and E_2 to be as follows: *(George, she)*, *(call ... a Fascist, insult)*, and *(Sally, him)*. In this case, the force of contrastive accent is manifested not only by the fact that the members of each of the pairs *(George, she)* and *(Sally, him)* must be taken to be distinct (as is easily intuitively justifiable and in fact required on other grounds), but also by the fact that the values of the respective members of the non-contrastively-accented pair *(call ... a Fascist, insult)* must be taken to be equivalent in this discourse context. This non-trivial consequence of our definitions is also in accord with intuitive judgement, and, moreover, is remarkable in that such equivalence cannot be justified on semantic grounds alone.

Our account thus far leaves a number of questions open. Of these, let us address briefly the question of what exactly is meant by equivalence of value. In the case of referential expressions, the answer is a simple one: two expressions have equivalent values if they have the same referent. In the case of non-referential expressions, the problem is more difficult, and what I have to say about it is little more than speculative. If we consider only an example such as (11), we might think that the answer to this general question would be to say e.g. that calling someone a Fascist (pragmatically) entails insulting them -- in other words that calling someone a Fascist is a (pragmatic) species, if you will, of insulting them. But this account does not seem to be correct. Consider the following three sentences:

(12) a) Gĕorge hít Sălly, aňd thĕn she slúgged hĭm.
b) Geŏrge hít Sălly, aňd thĕn shé slúgged hĭm.
c) Gĕorge hít Sălly, aňd thĕn she slúgged hím.

In (a), we are merely told that two events occurred in sequence. In (b), we may consider both *she* and *slugged* as contrastively stressed, and thus, taking the necessary propositional congruence to hold between the expressions *she slugged him* and *George hit Sally* in the nearly obvious way,[7] *she* must be distinct from *George*, and *slugged* is equally distinguished from *hit*. In (c), the necessary application of the structure of propositional congruence forces us to construe *she* as distinct from *George* (which is easy enough), *him* as distinct from *Sally* (no problem), and *slugged* as equivalent with *hit*. In this last case, however, we need not believe that hitting is a (pragmatic) subspecies of slugging or that slugging is a (pragmatic) subspecies of hitting. Rather, we may construe both hitting and slugging as common subspecies of some more comprehensive action of which both may constitute (pragmatically) special cases. In the case at hand, for example, both hitting and slugging may be taken as ways of attacking. In this way, the notion 'equivalence' comes into its own, for it is clear that in such cases as (12c) we are concerned neither with identity pure and simple nor with such particular relations as 'x is a special case of y': rather, if we find such an utterance acceptable and interpretable, we must be able to specify an (interesting) equivalence class among members of the semantic type instantiated by hitting and slugging to which both concepts belong.

Thus, it is clear that contrastive accent defines a discourse structure in the sense that it necessitates a relation between two disjoint parts of any discourse in which a contrastively-accented constituent can be identified, with observable consequences in the respective interpretations of these parts. Moreover, the consequences that such relations have are of particular interest to pragmatics in that they necessitate discourse-particular analysis of the relative values of individual constituents.

4 The notion 'discourse structure' defined and exemplified in § 3 provides a rationale for the first restriction on the domain of rule R noted at the end of § 2, but it leaves open the problem of the second restriction noted there. In this section, we shall attempt to provide an explanation of this restriction in a general setting.

Note first that when its domain is satisfied, rule R states necessary and sufficient conditions for the interpretation of the pronoun or pronouns in the second conjunct. If it is possible to interpret the accentuation in such cases as contrastive, then it is easy to see that the sufficiency of rule R can be explained by treating it as simply a special case of propositional congruence across the connective: take E_1 to be *he hit him* and E_2 to be *John hit Bill*; then if *he* is stressed (and counts as contrastive), *he* cannot be anaphorically identified with *John*, whereas, if it is unstressed, it must be; a similar argument holds for *him* and *Bill*. Thus, relative to the definition of propositional congruence and the assumption that stress in the cases in question is to be interpreted as contrastive -- i.e. as obligatorily invoking the discourse structure of propositional congruence -- then the observed interpretation of the sentences for which rule R was designed in discourse-neutral contexts follows as a special case of the discourse-structure of propositional congruence.

Suppose now that we vary the content of the second conjunct of schema (2), in such a way that propositional congruence is difficult to achieve merely because it is difficult to find an equivalence class for the verbs in question. A possible instance of this is (13):

(13) Jŏhn hít Bÿll, aňd thèn ȟe gíggľed.

Although it is simple enough to construct discourse contexts which render the anaphoric-identification of the pronoun in the second conjunct unambiguous, if I have chosen the example judiciously, then it should be difficult to fix the interpretation of *he* unambiguously in isolation. I believe that this is indeed the case with the interpretation of (13). Note, furthermore, that in such cases, stressing the pronoun does not render the anaphoric-identification of the pronoun unambiguous -- which is an exact consequence of our account, relative to the presumption that propositional congruence cannot be reasonably defined across the connective in (13). In other words, the application of the discourse-structure of propositional congruence across the connective in instances of schema (2) not only provides an explanation of the sufficiency of rule R in such cases, it also suggest an explanation for the existence of lexical restrictions on the domain of this rule.

Although it is satisfying to discover that the sufficiency of rule R follows as a special case from our definition of propositional congruence, rule R's necessity is more puzzling, particularly so in view of the fact that it has been a standard assumption in much recent work on anaphora (though there are exceptions)[8] that, cases of bound anaphora aside, an anaphoric element can be anaphorically-identified with any previous discourse expression which is compatible with its referential properties. Examples we have discussed in this paper show that this assumption is either wrong entirely or, in some cases at least, is subject to the intervention of other, more powerful, principles.

We may resolve this question as follows: suppose that an anaphoric element which is uniquely compatible with a previous discourse referent may in fact be anaphorically-identified with it. When there is more than one possible previous discourse referent compatible with a given anaphoric element, however, the discourse as a whole is satisfactory only relative to unambiguous anaphoric-identifiability of the anaphoric element. In the framework of this paper, the unambiguous anaphoric-identification of the element in question can only be justified by reference to some discourse structure which forces this choice and rules out all other possibilities. Whether or not such a view is correct depends on access to a larger amount of data than we have been able to consider here. Nevertheless, consideration of examples like (14) is instructive:

(14) Jóhn hít Mǎry, and then she hit him.

If we construe *him* as merely stressed, but not contrastively stressed, and *she* to be neither contrastively stressed nor unstressed, then *him* is naturally and unambiguously anaphorically-identified with *John*, and *she* with *Mary*. If we take *him* to be contrastively stressed, however, and *she* to be unstressed, then, as in the case we began with example (1), propositional congruence forces the identification of *she* with *John* (if we accept the sentence at all).[9] The exact interpretation of the phonetic properties which we are attempting to represent is obviously a delicate issue worthy of further investigation. Nevertheless, the situation is distinct from cases in which *he* replaces *she*, and a name normally used to refer to a male replaces *Mary*, for, in this latter case, the anaphoric-identification of the pronouns cannot be unambiguously interpreted on a phonological interpretation in which *him* is not contrastively stressed.

Thus, given the assumption that satisfactory communication requires the unambiguous anaphoric-identification of anaphoric elements (which is not unreasonable, since one can find many instances of discourses which go awry in its absence) and the assumption that in isolation sentences which violate the stipulations of rule R are not unambiguously interpretable (for which there is the evidence of intuitive judgment) we not only have an explanation of the sufficiency of rule R, but an explanation of its necessity as well. And, given this much, we may assert that we have found a solution to our original puzzle. It should also be clear, however, that this solution in turn rests on the satisfactory resolution of a number of issues: adequate justification for the phonetic identification of contrastive stress; clarification of the domain, in any given discourse, in which propositional congruence is definable; satisfactory definition of such concepts as illocutionary force, illocutionary point, and related notions, together with greater insight into their discourse consequences and relations; validity of the general notion discourse structure as here defined and exemplified; and, no doubt, other issues as well. In any case, whether or not the account I have given of the problems discussed here is ultimately correct, the satisfactory resolution of these problems may be considered a criterion of adequacy for theories of anaphoric-identification and theories of discourse: the two are intertwined.

5. In this effort to unravel the seemingly simple linguistic puzzle we began with, I have tried to demonstrate implicitly two general morals: first, that judgments of anaphoric-identifiability provide a useful test for abstract theories of discourse. And second, that since the prosodic properties of expressions play a significant role in their in-

terpretation at several distinct levels of analysis, models of natural language based on non-intonational formal constructs can provide only an incomplete, and hence possibly misleading, account of natural language structure and function. An obvious corollary of this second point is that insofar as prosodic properties do not strictly belong to any of the members of the traditional semiotic trichotomy syntax-semantics-pragmatics as these have been taken to apply to natural languages, the possibility that this division does not constitute a useful framework, but rather a Procrustean one, must be seriously considered. And, given this possibility, it is possible as well that definitions of pragmatics based on opposition to standard notions of syntax and semantics are entirely misconceived.[10]

FOOTNOTES:

1. For a summary of recent research on syntactic constraints on anaphora, see Reinhart (1976). A seminal work on the relationship between prosodic properties and anaphoric-identificability is Akmajian and Jackendoff (1970).

2. It is difficult to represent suprasegmental properties typographically and I run the risk of neutralizing the various phonetic means in English by which prominence on a given syllable is attained. Nevertheless, I use the mark ' ˘ ' over an unstressed syllable, the ' ´ ', over a stressed syllable, and ocassionally the mark ' ` ', over a non-nuclearly stressed syllable. Such a simple symbolism requires, in some cases, a good deal of indulgence on the part of the reader. Those who find themselves unwilling to grant such indulgence, or do not find the symbolization readily interpretable may obtain a copy of a tape-casette on which I have recorded the examples I discuss, at minimal expense (i.e. cost of the casette and mailing costs). If this were a general practice, it would greatly facilitate the interpretation of results concerning such suprasegmental properties as relative pitch, relative timing, relative stress, and so on.

3. To clarify this definition somewhat, we need to distinguish between at least three classes of referential expression: a) those whose reference is intrinsic in the sense that the reference of the expression may be determined on the basis of its meaning alone; b) those whose reference is deictic in the sense that the reference of the expression depends on the physical context in which reference is achieved; c) those whose reference is what we have termed anaphoric in that the reference of the expression depends entirely on the reference of some other expression in the same discourse. It is this last category that we are interested in, although this semantic category cannot be defined in any interesting syntactic fashion, since it includes some uses of definite pronouns, but not all (since definite pronouns can be used deictically), and some definite descriptions, but not all (since some definite descriptions carry intrinsic reference and some are used in situations in which their reference is determined relative to non-linguistic contextual factors, as in the examples of Donnellan (1966)). We shall not pursue the details of this classification here.

4. Certain parenthetical remarks on rule R and its consequences are necessary. First, the restriction of the rule to anaphoric elements only is justified by the fact that whereas (i), in which each of the referential expressions is intrinsically referential in the sense of note 3, is easily interpretable, substitution of appropriate anaphoric expressions relative to the same intonational contour yields unacceptable results in a discourse-neutral context, as illustrated in (ii).

We return to this problem in §4.

(i) Jóhn hít Bĭll and thèn Bĭll hít Jóhn.
(ii) Jóhn hit Bĭll and then he hit him.

Second, by rule R, an instantiation of schema (2) in which w and z are unstressed anaphoric elements identified, respectively, with the instantiations of x and y, should be acceptable, though in fact it is not, as, for example, (iii) is not under this interpretation of the pronouns:

(iii) John hit Bill and then he hit him.

The unacceptability of this case may be imputed to the unacceptability of (iv), for which I have no explanation, though both (iii) and (iv) are rendered acceptable by the addition of the word *again*, as is illustrated in (v) and (vi) respectively.

(iv) John hit Bill and then John hit Bill.
(v) John hit Bill and then he hit him again.
(vi) John hit Bill and then John hit Bill again.

Finally, it is amusing to consider the interpretation of non-pronominal epithets, in the sense of Jackendoff (1972), in the context of the examples for which rule R is defined, for example, the following:

(vii) Jóhn hít Bĭll, and then Máx hĭt the bắstard.
 (the bastard = Bill)
(viii) Jóhn hít Bĭll, and then the sŏnŏfabĭtch hĭt Máx.
 (the sonofabitch = John)

So far, so good; but if the 'epithets' are stressed, problems develop:

(ix) Jóhn hít Bĭll and then the bástard hĭt the sŏnŏfabĭtch.
 (the bastard = ?; the sonofabitch = ?)

This isn't a problem for rule R: we need merely stipulate that such expressions are anaphoric elements only when they are unstressed.

5. The general point of view I adopt here stems from discussions over a number of years with Leon Shiman, though whether he would be pleased with the use I have put our discussions to, I do not know. In particular, the vocabulary I use is adapted from his work on stable visual perception (cf. Shiman 1978). He and I have extended the basic methodological principles of his work on vision to the study of natural language in unpublished work (Oehrle and Shiman 1976), as well as in a series of envisioned joint papers.

6. Here again, the concepts on which my exposition owe much to my discussions with Shiman (cf. note 5).

7. Nearly obvious, because we cannot take propositional congruence to be defined over the respective syntactic triples <*she, slugged, him*> and <*George, hit, Sally* >. If we did, given our characterization of propositional congruence, we would have to say that *she* and *George* are not equivalent (which is reasonable), *slugged* and *hit* are not equivalent (which is not unreasonable), and *him* and *Sally* are equivalent (which is

problematic). If we take the propositional congruence to be defined over the pairs <*she, slugged him*> and <*George, hit Sally*>, however, we avoid this problem at the apparent expense of weakening our general account of anaphoric-identification. Although we cannot develop a complete account of such cases, implicit rationalization of their existence appears in §4.

8. Most notable among these is Kuno (1975). Cf. also the discussion of this problem in Reinhart (1976) and the references she cites.

9. Note that if we were not replacing rule R with a more comprehensive account, we would have to modify it in several respects to attain consistency with such examples.

10. I would like to acknowledge the benefit I have received from discussing the questions addressed in this paper with Adrian Akmajian, Leon Shiman, and, especially, Susan Steele, and to thank Dean Paul Rosenblatt of the College of Liberal Arts, University of Arizona, for material assistance.

CLASSROOM VERBAL INTERACTION:
A CONVERSATIONAL ANALYSIS

Franca Orletti

A common feature of most studies in the field of "conversational analysis" seems to be that of discovering the organization underlying verbal interaction, in spite of the apparent fragmentation of natural conversation. These studies can therefore be considered contributions to the construction of "an empirically based grammar of natural conversation", as Schenkein (1978: 3) puts it.[1] A way of looking at conversation as a structured unit of communication is to analyze it in terms of an alternation of turns which are exchanged according to a well-defined system of rules. The turn-taking model proposed by Sacks, Schegloff and Jefferson (1974) was presented as both a context-free system and a context-sensitive one, that is to say, as a model that has "a general abstractness and local particularization potential" (p. 700). This should make it possible to describe a conversation as a structured unit without requiring reference to aspects of the context in which verbal interaction occurs such as participants' roles, assumptions, and so on. The application of the conversational approach to different speech-exchange systems, such as classroom verbal interaction, seems to demonstrate the need of taking into account those pragmatic factors that appear to determine the structure of the communicative exchange, including the turn-taking system. I will discuss this point by examining data taken from transcriptions of classroom verbal interaction, with particular regard to the "questioning" situation.

Turn-taking system for classroom verbal interaction: data discussion and analysis. According to Sacks, Schegloff, and Jefferson, two types of turn-allocation techniques are found in conversation:
a) those where the next speaker is selected by the current speaker;
b) those where a next turn is allocated by self-selection.
The alternation and construction of turns is governed by the following set of rules:

> (1) For any turn, at the initial transition-relevance place of an initial turn-constructional unit:
> (a) If the turn-so-far is so constructed as to involve the use of a "current speaker selects next" technique, then the party so selected has the right and is obliged to take next turn to speak; no others have such rights or obligations, and transfer occurs at that place.
> (b) If the turn-so-far is so constructed as not to involve the use of a "current speaker selects next" technique, then self-selection for next speakership may, but need not, be instituted; first starter acquires right to a turn, and transfer occurs at that place.
> (c) If the turn-so-far is so constructed as not to involve the use of a "current speaker selects next" technique, then current speaker may, but need not continue, unless another self-selects.
> (2) If, at the initial transition-relevance place of an initial turn-constructional unit, neither 1a nor 1b has operated, and, following the provision of 1c, current speaker has continued, then the rule-set a-c re-applies at the next transition-relevance place, and recursively at each next transition-relevance place, until transfer is effected (1974: 704).

Such a set of rules permits conversation to be a system which is:
a) "locally managed",
b) "party administered", and
c) "interactionally managed",
in that the allocation of turns is accomplished in each turn for a next turn and each interactant can step in both to check the length and the order of turns, and in doing this must take into account the contributions the other speakers make to the conversation.

Not all systems of turn-taking where "one party talks at a time" organize the allocation of turns one at a time, i.e. locally. In some cases turns are pre-allocated, and in others there is a mixture of "pre-allocational" and "local-allocational" means. Using this as a basis it is possible to construct a "linear array" where the different organizations occupy different positions in agreement with their allocational arrangement. At one end we find the type of organization to which conversation adopting "local allocational means" belongs. Mixed forms are given a middle position, and the type using pre-allocation of all turns is placed at the other end. The various systems placed in linear arrangement are not independent but can all be considered subsequent transformations of the basic system of conversation. Such transformations supply the various functional needs of communicative systems.

In the analysis which follows I will try to pick out those modifications which must be made to the conversational model of "turn-taking" in order to explain the exchange of turns in classroom verbal interaction. Particular reference will be made to the necessity of introducing different parameters taken from the context of communication into this description.

In the transcriptions[2] analyzed in this study I found that there is a marked tendency to adopt "current speaker selects next" techniques in turn allocation. The almost complete exclusion of self-selection techniques is probably determined by the number of interactants. The adoption of "current speaker selects next" techniques makes it possible to avoid different contemporary starts leading to an overlapping of turns in multi-party interaction. This leads to greater fluency which is entirely necessary in a learning situation. The first type of technique is adopted by both teacher and pupil, if the pupil is speaking the next speaker is always the teacher. Of all the analyzed data only on one occasion do we have a pupil addressing a shool-mate during his own turn, thus indicating that he is choosing him as successor in the conversation, as we can see in example (1). (See appendix 2 for the original Italian data and appendix 1 for the notational conventions.)

    (1) T. -   Let's see, now who wants to be tested?
        Rossi -   Me.
        T. -   OK, come on then Rossi, your marks aren't up to

(1)   standard
    Ermelinda -   Miss, when are you going to test me?
    Giuseppe -   But your marks are already satisfactory, and
                   mine aren't.
    T. -   Alright, you can both come afterwards.

Here, while explicitly talking to Ermelinda Giuseppe is implicitly asking his teacher to test him. He is then, indirectly making a request to be tested by asserting a reason for such an action, this is the same reason which the teacher considered valid when calling Rossi. Searle (1975) has pointed out ways in which directive speech acts may be made indirectly by stating or questioning the felicity conditions of the speech acts and the reasons for doing these acts. While saying that he has low marks, Giuseppe is pointing to the necessity of his being tested and, indirectly, is asking the teacher to do so. The closing of the interactional sequence corroborates this interpretation, because it then becomes the teacher's turn to reply to Giuseppe, even though there is no explicit request. In this example too, the student chooses the teacher as the speaker of the next turn. This is done rather subtly since the social identity of the teacher is used as a basis for selection,[3] since he is the only one who has a right to test. The student covers up his choice of a different successor by another and more superficial selecting device, that of a possessive pronoun.

There was very little evidence of self-selection in the cases of verbal interaction that were considered. Those that were found may be defined as "embedded self-selection". Here I am referring to two types of phenomena: first, when self-selection occurs during a pause within a turn previously assigned to another participant by means of the "current speaker selects next" techniques; second, when after a regularly completed turn the self-selecting speaker starts an interactional sequence that interrupts the flow of previous conversation thus breaking both the sequential order of the speech acts and the topical cohesion of the discourse. In this way there begins, through self-selection, an interactional sequence with its own structure (for example: question/answer; giving offense/apologizing/accepting apology; asking for permission/giving permission, etc.) embedded in another sequence which is suspended until the completion of the one that was started through self-selection. At the end, the suspended sequence starts again.

The first kind of self-selection is only used when the current speaker is a student and it may be adopted both by the teacher and another student. The data considered also point to the existence of another condition which permits the application of this form of turn-taking. If it is a student using it, it may be adopted only to finish the turn previously assigned to the other, as long as he maintains topical cohesion. When self-selection occurs at the beginning of the turn or half way through, repair mechanisms are activated, as we can see in the following examples, particularly in (4).

(2) T. -   Right then, Marina, what does map mean?
    Marina -   Map means that=
    Another pupil - =that it's got rivers drawn in=
    Another pupil - =and mountains=
    Another pupil - =and lakes.

(3) T. -   Now, will you let Antonio speak, come on then, the tides...
    Antonio -   When the moon goes round the sea goes down. This is because the effect of attraction=
    Another pupil - =of the moon.
    T. -   Of the moon. OK.

(4) T. -   Alessio, Alessio, why don't you tell me something about what we did last time?
    Alessio -   We talked about rocks.
                    [
    Another pupil - We saw some rocks
    T. -   Yes, but I was asking Alessio.
    Alessio -   You talked about rocks, Miss.

(5) T, -   Giovanna, will you read your summary, please?
    Giovanna -   The knife grinder went calling throuhg the

(5) Giovanna -   ⎡streets. All the women came running out.
    Francesco - ⎣Oh, let's go outside!
    T. -   Be quiet, Francesco. OK, Giovanna, what about this knife-grinder?

While the behaviour in numbers (2) and (3) is considered "regular", in numbers (4) and (5) the teacher intervenes reassigning the turn to the original student, as shown in (4), thus restoring topical cohesion, as we can see in (5).

The reasons for the teacher accepting the self-selection techniques adopted in (2) and (3) and refusing those used in (4) and (5), are determined by the aims the teacher has in mind in each of the instances examined. The teacher wishes to verify her students' knowledge, and this stimulates the students into showing what they know. The number of students in the classroom and the limited time at their disposal strongly condition the fulfilment of the teacher's needs and those of the students which are closely connected to them. The use, on the part of the teacher of "current speaker selects next" techniques only, which allows only one student to speak at a time restricts the possibility the other students have to speak even more. By adopting the embedded self-selection form described earlier, it is possible to satisfy both the students' needs to show their own knowledge and those of the teacher to verify the knowledge of as many pupils as possible. In examples (2) and (3) we can see that all students, the one questioned by the teacher and those who intervene after the beginning of the turn, are able to demonstrate their capability to answer since their interventions are not juxtaposed but complete each other and are all directed towards the same interactional aim, which is to verify the knowledge of the whole class. This doesn't happen in example (4) where the child who takes over the turn previously assigned to Francesco prevents him from speaking, and in (5) Francesco's interruption is actually aimed at modifying the course of the interaction by proposing an activity which has nothing to do with testing knowledge. Here we have a modification of the rule of natural conversation according to which, given a turn, only the person chosen by the previous speaker has the right to speak. In classroom verbal interaction, at least in the "questioning" situation, it is possible to intervene in the midst of another person's turn provided that the speaker is given the chance to satisfy, at least partly, the purpose of the interaction, and provided that the interruption is directed towards this end. Here then a new parameter is introduced as regards the basic system of natural conversation, that of the interactional aim.

The second form of embedded self-selection causes the interactional sequences to be contained within others. This phenomenon is not only characteristic of classroom verbal interaction, but is very common in natural conversation. Schegloff (1972) and Jefferson (1972)[4] have described this kind of sequence. Two fundamental types of embedded sequences emerge from Jefferson's analysis: the "subsidiary" sequence, which is always generated by the suspended sequence, and acquires significance only within the context of the main sequence; and the "competitive" one where the inserted sequence is opposed to the main one and brings it to an abrupt conclusion (1972: 312). This happens for example when one of the participants introduces a new topic and tries to orientate the conversation towards it. In classroom verbal interaction there is the tendency to begin embedded sequences which are, however, subsidiary, and not competitive with regard to the main sequence. In particular these sequences have a regulating function as regards the developing interaction, which consists either in restoring the preconditions of interaction, seen as an information exchange, or in reasserting the role-distribution in the classroom. Most of the sequences started by the teacher belong to the first type, and those started by the students to the second. In fact, if we observe the following examples, in which the embedded sequence is started through self-selection by the teacher, we can see that she steps in in (6) and (7) to reduce the noise which prevents the proper development of the interaction and in (8) to ascertain the degree of actual contact between speaker and listeners.

(6) T. -   Antonio, tell me about the tides
    C. -   ((noise))
    T. -   OK, are you going to let Antonio speak?
    C. -   ((silence))
    T. -   OK, come on then, what about these tides?
    Antonio - When the moon...

(7) T. -   Last time we looked at different types of rocks
    C. -   ((noise))
    T. -   Will you be quiet please? What's going on over there?
    Child -   I can't find my exercise book.
    T. -   Hurry up and find it then
    C. -   ((noise))
    T. -   OK, are you all ready? You, Marina, can you remember the rock that=
    Marina - =Sedementary rock.

(8) T. -   OK, then, start reading your summary.
    Ugo -   The knife grinder was going along and calling out from the street.
    T. -   Just a minute, do you think they can hear you over there?
    Mirella - ((from the back of the room)) No, we can't hear a word.
    Ugo -   Well, do I have to start from the beginning again?
    T. -   Start again but face that way.

The sequences started by the teacher are therefore related to what Goffman (1976) calls "system requirements" of conversation, this being understood as a communication unit, that is to say the existence of an open channel, the possibily of keeping contact, the presence of signals for turn yielding, the request for turn repetition in case of incomprehension, etc. The embedded sequences generated here by the students usually have the following structure:

    Student -   Asking for permission
    T. -   Giving permission

as can be seen in the following examples:

    (9) T. -   What kind of rocks were they?
        Student -   Miss, may I be excused please?
        T. -   Yes.
        Antonio -   Volcanic and metamorphic rocks

    (10) T. -   Does anyone want to come up to my desk and be tested?[5]
        Francesco - I do.
        Giovanni -   Miss, may I be excused, please?
        T. -   Yes, go on. Come on then Francesco and bring your work.

Only rarely are the teacher's utterances followed by students' requests for further explanation. Similarly, a further type of embedded sequence, the "misapprehension sequence" is also rarely found. This may be explained by the fact that students are usually embarrassed about showing themselves unable to follow, and therefore not up to the standard in a situation where they are constantly being judged, and in this case afraid of being judged negatively. The following was the only case in the material that was collected that showed a sequence where further information was asked for.

    (11) T. -   So the poet uses a metaphor, he doesn't want to to talk about=
        Giovanni -   =This is something that I haven't got yet, a metaphor
        T. -   What do you mean ((horrified tone))? We've been studying this poem and the use of the metaphor for a month!
        Giovanni -   Yes, I know.

(11) T. -   OK then, a metphor is a word that means some-
                  thing different from what you normally mean by it
    Giovanni -   Yes, saying foxy when you mean cunning
    T. -   That's right, so the poet in this poem doesn't
                  say explicitly what he means, but indirectly.

These sequences remind us of the "time outs"[6] of games because they allow one to predict their structure and length. They confirm that interactants share the same interpretation of the situation since they bridge the gap between the person who has the right to give permission and the one who must ask for it, and that between the person who knows and the one who doesn't. Both the teacher and the students base their interaction on the asymmetry of roles. Interchangeability of points of view, and also the sharing of the interpretation of the communicative situation, is a fundamental prerequisite for social interaction,[7] and the subsidiary sequences started by the students are, during the interaction, a kind of check on the existence of such a situation.[8] We can say, then, that both the embedded sequences started by the teacher, and those started by the students, have a regulating function on the classroom communication. Those started by the teacher operate on the communicative exchange, regarded as transmission of information, while those started by the pupils operate on communication considered as a moment of social interaction. It is interesting to consider example (12), where the embedded sequence started by a student through self-selection shows that the condition of identity of perspectives is not always present, especially when it concerns the social roles. In that case, this situation has to be reached through a negotiation between the interactants.

(12) T.   Listen Marina, I'd like you to start off by
                  telling me where France is.
    Another pupil - The neighbouring countries=
    T. -   =That's right.
    Marina -   The neighbouring countries are Belgium, Germany
                  and Great Britain....

Here the student takes over a pedagogical role by rephrasing what the teacher has already said, and thus upsets the asymmetry of roles. By stepping in and closing the embedded sequence, the teacher restores the situation and shows who is the examiner and who is to be tested.[9] These sequences show that there must be moments for checking the existence of the condition of the identity of perspectives which has been mentioned earlier. In this example the fact that the typical roles expected in a classroom are not adopted, allows the student to select himself and begin a sequence which is different from what I call the "regulating" ones so far described. It is as if the flow of verbal interaction of the class was interrupted by a fragment of conversation between equals (with its own structure and rules). In actual fact it must be considered an exchange of roles where the student plays teacher rather more than an equal relationship existing between the two. This is shown by the type of repair the student makes, which in order to be a correction of another person's linguistic production, does not have any mitigating characteristics, i.e. "modulation" which is typical of the type of repair between equals, where the correction "is not asserted, but is proffered for acceptance or rejection".[10]

From the foregoing analysis we see that in a classroom situation the alternation of turns is predetermined by the social roles of the persons concerned, and the aims of the interaction, and that the negotiation of these roles within the interaction tends to re-establish the former asymmetry. The exchange of turns is as follows:

T. -
Student -
T. -
Student -
T. -

where the teacher always begins the communicative exchange, and checks its progress by choosing the next speaker. The pupil can take a turn by self-selection, but only in order to produce a subsidiary sequence, as has been seen so far. Examples of real self-selection are usually a result of lack of comprehension. In example (8) for instance Mirella follows the teacher's turn interpreting it as an actual request for information whereas it was intended for Giuseppe as a request for action. If the last person to speak was a student, only the teacher can select himself and where another student joins in the teacher always takes over and the student gives way, as can be seen in the following:

(13) Student -   Is the geography program long?
     T. -   Well, it might be, if we take two months
                  to do this part here.
Another student - All of it (the book).

The fact that the teacher is the one who controls what is said, both by beginning the exchanges, and completing them, is extremely important when considering the thematic organization of the conversation. The theme, or themes, around which the whole interaction is developed is introduced only by the teacher, and any modification proposed by a student can only become the argument of a conversation if the teacher brings it into the territory of the main theme. The typical progress of conversation among equals where there is thematic continuity brought by the enlargement and subsequent transformation of the original theme is altogether missing in classroom interaction. Deviations from the main theme are generally not admitted and when this happens certain repair mechanisms are put in action (see example 5). In classroom verbal interaction as opposed to ordinary conversation, the content of each turn is controlled as is the range of what is considered to be an appropriate theme.

We must now look at a further technique of turn-selection in the classroom: here the teacher doesn't select one student to answer, but speaks to the whole class. This can be seen in the following examples:

(14) T. -   Last time, apart from volcanic and metamorphic
               rocks we spoke about another kind, these were=
   Student -   =sedimentary.
   T. -   Sedimentary.

(15) T.　　　　　　　Do you remember what we said about fossils?
　　　Student -　　　　Fossils?
　　　　　　　　　　　[
　　　Another st. -　　Yes, Miss.
　　　T. -　　　　　　Tell us then.
　　　Student -　　　 Fish, shells.
　　　Another st. -　　You had a shell last time

(16) T.　　　　　　　Who can tell me about England then?
　　　Student -　　　　Me
　　　　　　　　　　　[
　　　Another st. -　　Me, me.
　　　T. -　　　　　　One at a time please.
　　　C. -　　　　　　((The class put their hands up))
　　　T. -　　　　　　Do you want to tell me?
　　　Student -　　　 ((shows that he wants to))
　　　T. -　　　　　　Go on then.

Selection of a whole class can occur by using various linguistic mechanisms: generic address forms which include the whole class; the second person plural of the verb in languages, such as Italian, where there is verbal inflection to distinguish singular and plural forms, addressing an indefinite someone, but with a certain indication given by the gaze direction, who is found within this visual space. One of the effects of using this technique is that the rule which states that only one person can speak at a time is violated and that repair mechanisms follow as a result of its violation, as in (16).

　　The function of such forms of address does not seem to be real selection. The teacher uses this technique in order to find out how the class has taken in and developed certain information and in order to have an idea how many in the class are able to answer. In this way there are fewer people to choose the next speaker from. Here the teacher is not making an actual choice, but is in fact going through a preliminary process only to see first, perhaps, how well the class have studied their lesson, basing her judgement on the willingness of the students to reply.

Conclusion. On the basis of the data analyzed it can be stated that verbal interaction in the classroom is governed by a mixed system of turn-taking which lies on the "linear array" between natural conversation, which is completely locally managed, and that of debates, which implies the pre-allocation of all turns. Speakership in the classroom is largely pre-determined and in the cases where the alternation of turns is established on the basis of a turn by turn system, it is the teacher who co-ordinates the turn-transition by taking on the role of "head" of the interaction.[11] Teachers and pupils seem to have internalized this behaviour pattern and accept the variations of the original scheme as long as what they consider the aim of the interaction, i.e. the verification of knowledge in the communicative situation examined here, is respected. The interactants evaluate on the basis of this parameter whether the sequences which break the original scheme are within the norm. On the other hand the same distribution of roles between teacher and pupils within the communicative context is based on such an end and consequently also the distribution of the possibility of access to the right of taking and giving up speakership.

In a formulation of rules of turn-taking in the classroom situation the two roles must be differentiated, and the aims of the interaction born in mind. In addition to the interactants' shared assumptions as regards the above-mentioned aims of interaction and the distinction of roles thereby established, other pragmatic factors must also be considered in order to understand how the exchange of turns occurs. We can include among these factors the interactants' knowledge of what topics and actions are relevant in an educational field and which causal relationships hold between the events in this context.[12] This is the type of knowledge implied in the exchange between Ermelinda and Giuseppe in the first example studied. Taking these factors into consideration we can understand how the participants in classroom verbal interaction locally manage the alternation of turns and do not follow a completely pre-allocated ordering of turns based on the asymmetry of roles.

It might be thought that the inclusion of so many different pragmatic factors in the description of the structure of verbal interaction, even though they are necessary for descriptive adequacy, would lead to excessively *ad hoc* analyses, restricting the possibility of constructing general models of verbal interaction. In order to avoid such "ad hocness" it is necessary to identify types of discourse and construct models for each type. This should be one of the goals of a grammar of verbal interaction.

FOOTNOTES:

1. Schenkein argues this point with reference to the conversational studies collected in his reader.
2. The data discussed here was taken from 18 verbal interactions tape-recorded in a class II of a middle school (13-14 year-olds) in a rural area. The material was collected during that part of the lesson devoted to testing the students' knowledge.
3. See Sacks, Schegloff and Jefferson (1974: 718).
4. Jefferson analyzes what she terms "misapprehension sequences" in detail, where the embedded sequence begins directly after a statement and is aimed at clarifying any obscurities of that statement.
5. All the material that was collected for this study came from classes where traditional teaching prevailed. This was also reflected in the actual organization of the classroom were the teacher's desk stood on a platform.
6. See Jefferson (1972: 314).
7. See Cicourel (1972: 252).
8. The symbolic use of interactional aspects has been noted by Mitchell-Kernan and Kernan (1977) in a role-playing situation of children of about the same age as those studied here. At the beginning of a role-playing activity directive and reactions to them are used to define and reaffirm status and rank.
9. Sinclair and Coulthard (1975) show that interaction between teacher and student must be analyzed on the basis of an exchange of 3 moves:

   T.: Query
   P.: answer
   T.: evaluative comment

and not two as in a conversation between equals.
10. Schegloff, Jefferson, and Sacks (1977: 379).
11. Mchoul (1978) notes the same fact in the analysis of formal talk in the classroom.
12. Sinclair and Coulthard (1975) note the importance of the students' knowledge of which actions are appropriate in the classroom in order to understand indirect directives.

APPENDIX 1: Notational conventions

1. ⌈[Simultaneous utterances
2. [Overlapping utterances
3. =   Contiguous utterances
4. (())   Details of the conversational scene or characterizations of the talk.
5. ...   The utterance is reported only in part.
6. T.   Teacher
7. Class Either all students or a large number of students talking at once.

APPENDIX 2

(1) I. -   Vediamo chi viene volontario.
    Rossi -   Io.
    I. -   Vieni Rossi, non hai ancora la sufficienza
    Ermelinda -   Professoré, quando mi chiama?
    Giuseppe -   C'hai la sufficienza, io non ce l'ho per niente.
    I. -   Va bene, poi venite anche voi.

(2) I. -   Intanto, Marina, che cosa vuol dire carta fisica?
    Marina -   Carta fisica vuol dire che=
    Altro bambino -   =che ci sono disegnati i fiumi, i=
    Altro bambino -   = i laghi

(3) I. -   Allora, lasciate parlare Antonio. Su, questa marea..
    Antonio -   Quando gira la luna il mare si abbassa. Questo per effetto d'attrazione=
    Altro bambino -   =della luna
    I. -   Della luna. Va bene.

(4) I. -   Alessandro, Alessandro, senti un po', mi parli un pochino di quello che avevamo fatto l'altra volta?
    Alessandro -   ⌈Abbiamo parlato delle rocce
    Altro bambino -   [Abbiamo visto le rocce.
    I. -   Si, ma io l'avevo chiesto ad Alessandro.
    Alessandro -   Ebbé, professoré, aveva parlato delle rocce.

(5) I. -   Giovanna, leggi il riassunto.
    Giovanna -   L'arrotino andava per le strade e lanciava il suo

(5) Giovanna -   richiamo di casa in casa. Tutte le donne accor-
                   revano
    Francesco -   [- Ma andiamo fuori!
    I. -   Zitto Francesco! Allora Giovanna, questo
                   arrotino?

(6) I. -   Antonio, parlami delle maree
    C. -   ((Rumore))
    I. -   Allora, lasciate parlare Antonio?
    C. -   ((Silenzio))
    I. -   Su, queste maree?
    A. -   Quando gira la luna...

(7) I. -   L'altra volta abbiamo visto diversi tipi di rocce
    C. -   ((Rumore))
    I. -   Allora, fate silenzio? Che succede lì?
    Bambino -   Non trovo il quaderno.
    I. -   Su, fate uscire questo quaderno!
    C. -   ((Rumore))
    I. -   Allora tutto a posto? Tu, Marina, ti ricordi di
                   quella roccia che=
    M. -   = La roccia sedimentaria.

(8) I. -   Allora, comincia con il riassunto
    Ugo -   L'arrotino andava e gridava dalla strada
    I. -   Senti un po', si sente fino laggiù, secondo te?
    Mirella -   No, 'nse sente niente.
    Ugo -   Allora devo cominciare da capo.
    I. -   Ricomincia da capo ma volto in là.

(9) I. -   Che rocce erano, intanto?
    Bambino -   professoré, posso andà al bagno?
    I. -   Si.
    Antonio -   Vulcaniche e metamorfiche.

(10) I. -   C'è qualcuno che viene volontario?
     Francesco -   Io
     Giovanni -   Professoré, posso uscire?
     I. -   Si vai. Allora, Francesco, vieni con la relaz-
                   ione

(11) I. -   Beh il poeta usa una metafora, non vuole parlare
                   di=
     Giovanni -   =Io questa cosa non l'ho capita, la metafora.
     I. -   Andiamo proprio bene! E' da un mese che studiamo
                   questa poesia e che parlo di metafore!
     Giovanni -   Eh!
     I. -   Vabbé! La metafora è una parola che significa
                   qualcosa di diverso da quello che normalmente
                   vuol dire.
     Giovanni -   Si, si come faina per dire furbo.
     I. -   Eh! Allora il poeta in questa poesia non parla
                   esplicitamente ma in modo indiretto

(12) I. -   Senti un po', Marina, io vorrei che tu però ini-
                         ziassi col dire dov'è la Francia.
     Ragazzo -   I confini=
     I. -   =Esatto.
     Marina -   Confina a nord con il Belgio, la Germania e la
                         Gran Bretagna...

(13) Ragazzo -   E' lungo il programma
     I. -   Sì, se ci mettiamo duo mesi a fare questa parte
     Altro ragazzo -   Tutto (il libro)

(14) I. -   L'altra volta, oltre alle rocce metamorfiche e
                         vulcaniche abbiamo visto un altro tipo, quelle=
     Ragazzo -   =Sedimentarie
     I. -   Sedimentarie

(15) I. -   Vi ricordate cosa abbiamo detto dei fossili?
     Ragazzo -   ⌈I fossili
     Altro ragazzo -   ⌊Sì.
     I. -   Di allora
     Ragazzo -   Pesci, conchiglie
     Altro ragazzo -   Lei aveva una conchiglia l'ultima volta.

(16) I. -   Chi può dirmi qualcosa intorno all'Inghilterra?
     Ragazzo -   ⌈Io
     Altro ragazzo -   ⌊Io, io
     I. -   Uno alla volta per favore
     Classe -   ((Gli studenti alzano la mano))
     I. -   Vuoi dirlo tu
     Ragazzo -   ((fa un cenno di assenso))
     I. -   Forza, allora

A GOAL ANALYSIS OF SOME PRAGMATIC ASPECTS OF LANGUAGE

Domenico Parisi and Cristiano Castelfranchi

0. The aim of this paper is to describe a framework for analyzing a number of aspects of language which are often studied under the heading of pragmatics: speech acts, so-called indirect speech acts, discourse, conversation. We are not sure we know what "pragmatics" is. Nevertheless, by proposing a definition of pragmatics within the present framework, we hope to contribute to the present debate aimed at clarifying this notion.

Two properties of the framework should be underlined at the outset: it is a *unified* and a *general* framework. By *unified* it is meant that the same set of basic concepts is used for analyzing *all* the above-mentioned different aspects of language, in such a way that the relationships among them may be revealed. By *general* we mean that the same set of concepts may be usefully applied to all behavior, not only linguistic behavior. This implies looking at the pragmatic aspects of language behavior as particular phenomena within a general theory of behavior.

The framework is based on the concept of goal which, with exceptions, has not been particulary popular within the social sciences this last century. The position taken here is that one of the best ways, perhaps *the* best way, of understanding and explaining the behavior of organisms, including talking humans, is to find out about the goals which are pursued through that behavior, how the organism pursues these goals, taking account of what conditions, and so on. We will introduce four basic concepts for a general analysis of behavior in terms of goals. Additional concepts will be defined in the course of the paper as they become necessary.

A *goal* is a state which regulates the behavior of an individual (more generally, of a system). To regulate behavior means that behavior is selected and executed so as to reduce the discrepancy between the actual state and the regulatory state. A unit of goal-regulated behavior is called an "action". In Figure (1a)

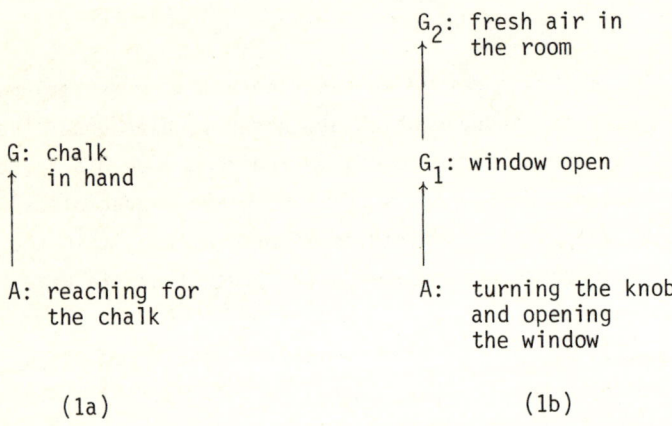

Figure 1. Actions and their goals and supergoals.

the action of "reaching for the chalk" (think of the actual movements of the arm and hand) is regulated by the goal of "having the chalk in the hand". However, the notion of a goal, as here defined, is a very general one. It includes both conscious and not conscious goals, newly formulated goals and behavioral routines, biological functions and institutional goals.

A *supergoal* is a goal of an action in respect to which another goal of the same action is a means. Consider the action of "turning the knob and opening the window". Its direct goal is "to have the window open". But this goal is only a means to the supergoal of "having fresh air in the room". This is represented in Figure (1b).

A *hierarchy of goals* is a set of connected goals and supergoals governing two or more actions, where "connected" means that two or more actions in the hierarchy have goals or supergoals in common. Consider the two actions of "reaching for the chalk" (A_1) and "making certain gestures with the hand near the blackboard (writing)" (A_2). The direct goal of A_1 is "to have the chalk in the hand". The direct goal of A_2 is that "certain marks be made on the blackboard". But the latter goal is also a supergoal of A_1, thus A_1 and A_2 have a goal in common:

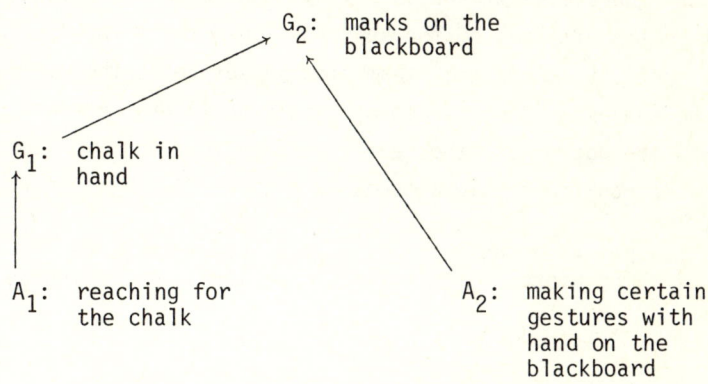

Figure 2. A hierarchy of goals.

To *adopt* a goal is to become regulated by a goal because of its being another's goal. Adopting a goal implies two individuals, A and B. A has a goal. B comes to know that A has such a goal. Because of this knowledge, B becomes regulated by the goal that A may reach his goal, i.e. he becomes regulated by A's goal. There are many ways through which B may come to know that A has a goal. For instance, B may discover A's goal by looking at A's non linguistic behavior, or B may be told by C that A has the goal. If A asks B to adopt his goal, so that

B comes to know about A's goal through A telling him, and then B adopts A's goal, we say that B *adheres* to A's goal.

1. As has been mentioned, we believe that the above set of basic concepts may be revealingly applied to all kinds of behavior (see for instance Parisi (1978), and Parisi and Castelfranchi (1978), for an application to the analysis of affective and power relationships, respectively). What is of interest here is its application to language behavior. If we take the behavior of uttering a sentence as an action like all others, we may ask ourselves about the direct goal of this action, its supergoals, the hierarchy of additional actions in which it may be inserted, what goals of other individuals its utterer is adopting, what goals its utterer is asking other people to adopt.

Take the uttering of the sentence "Open the window". This is an action that has as its goal that "the hearer opens the window". Or take the sentence "John is coming", said to inform someone. This action has the goal that "the hearer assumes that John is coming". The analogy to non linguistic actions is clearly displayed in Figure 3.

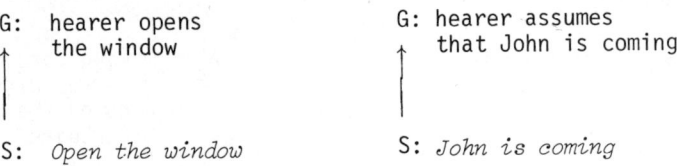

Figure 3. Sentences as actions.

Two properties of the direct goal of a linguistic action (= uttering a sentence) may be noted. It is a *social* and a *communicative* goal. A social goal is a goal of individual A whose description mentions another individual B. A goal is said to be communicative if (1) individual A (the speaker) wants his goal to be known to individual B (the hearer), and (2) the speaker intends to reach his goal through the hearer knowing and adopting it. A goal may be social but not communicative. For instance, if A wants to kill B, he has a social but not a communicative goal.

On the basis of the above definition of a communicative goal we can revise our representation of the direct goals of sentences in Figure 3, making it more analytical and precise. The new representation is shown in Figure 4. The direct goal of a sentence is now being

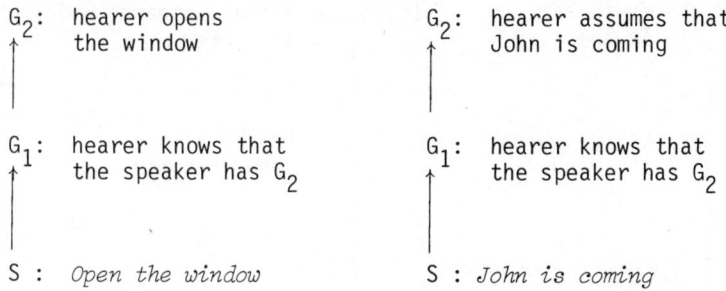

Figure 4. Goals of sentences are communicative goals.

articulated in two goals. For reasons which will become clear below, we will not call the super-ordinate goal (G_2) a supergoal of the sentence, even if it is technically one (see our definition above).

It is interesting to ask how the direct goal of a sentence is communicated to the hearer. The answer, of course, is through the linguistic competence that the speaker and the hearer share, i.e. through the speaker and the hearer knowing the lexicon and the syntax of the particular language which happens to be used. This implies that the direct goals of sentences, as defined here, do not generally vary with the context. Linguistic competence uniquely defines them for each specific sentence.

2. In addition to pursuing a direct goal by uttering a sentence, the speaker has a number of further goals he intends to reach with that sentence. These are the sentence's supergoals. Understanding language necessarily implies reconstructing these supergoals both in the sense that the hearer has to recover them if he has to really understand what is being communicated to him, and in the sense that a scientific ana-

lysis must include supergoals if it is to understand what goes on in a linguistic exchange.

As opposed to the direct goals, the supergoals (1) vary with the context, (2) are not necessarily social, and (3) are not necessarily communicative.[1] Consider the examples in Figure 5. As we know,

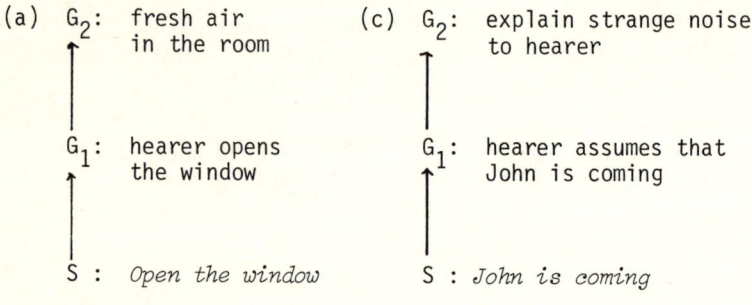

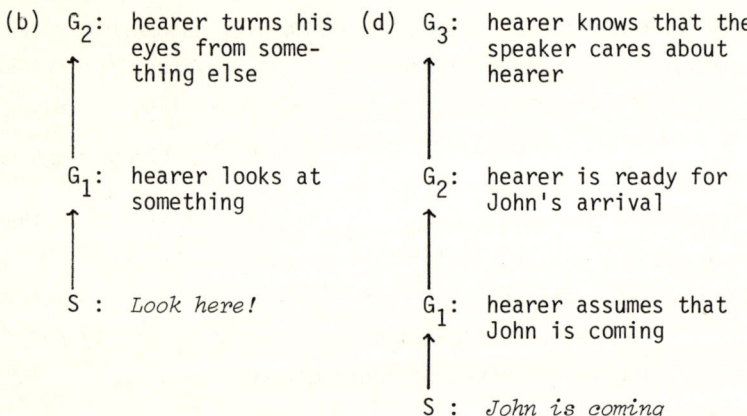

Figure 5. Types of supergoals.

the sentence "John is coming" has, in all contexts, the direct goal that "the hearer assumes that John is coming". But on a particular occasion, its utterer may have the supergoal of "explaining the hearer a strange noise", having noticed an expression of surprise or alarm in the hearer's face, and on another occasion the hearer's supergoal in uttering the sentence may be that the "hearer be ready for John's arrival", as in warning someone. Therefore, supergoals vary with the context. Consider now the sentence "Open the window". Whereas its direct goal is necessarily social, i.e. the hearer is necessarily mentioned in it, its supergoal may not be social. For instance one may utter that sentence with the supergoal of "having fresh air in the room", a goal not mentioning any individual. Finally consider the sentence "Look here!", said with the supergoal of having the hearer turn his eyes from something (rather than *to* something) without telling him directly. Here the supergoal is not communicative, since the utterer doesn't want his supergoal to be known by the hearer (see condition (1) for a communicative goal, above).

Supergoals may be classified in at least four different classes as a function of the particular manner in which the hearer wants to pursue them. *Communicative* supergoals are defined in the same way as communicative goals, so their definition will not be repeated here. As an example of a communicative supergoal, take the sentence "John is coming" uttered with the supergoal of explaining the strange noise to the hearer. Such a supergoal would not be reached unless the hearer himself understands that such is the supergoal of the speaker in uttering the sentence. The speaker knows this, and therefore he pursues his supergoal as a communicative one. *To-be-communicated* supergoals are goals the utterer wants the hearer to know, but the reason for this is not that he believes that the goal will be reached only if the hearer knows it. In the other words, the speaker wants the supergoal to be known by the hearer, but this is an independent goal, not a means for reaching the supergoal. A to-be-communicated supergoal is G_2 in the sentence "John is coming" (see Figure 5d), i.e. the goal of "having the hearer ready for John's arrival". The speaker may believe that this goal will be reached even if the hearer doesn't recognize it as one of the speaker's goals, and nevertheless he may be interested in having the hearer recognize it as such, for instance as a means for the further goal (G_3) of "having the hearer know that the speaker cares about him".

Neutral supergoals are supergoals the speaker is not interested as to whether the hearer knows or ignores them. For instance, one may ask someone to open the window with the supergoal of "having fresh air in the room", and does not care very much whether the hearer understands or not that it is his supergoal.

Concealed supergoals, by contrast, are supergoals which the speaker intends to be kept hidden from the hearer. The reason for this (i.e. a further supergoal) is usually that the supergoal itself may otherwise not be reached any more. Consider the sentence "Look here!", said with the supergoal of "having the hearer turn his eyes from something". In these circumstances it is usually the case that, if the hearer knows that what the speaker really wants is for him not to see something, the hearer will not turn his eyes and the supergoal will not be reached. This is why the speaker wants his supergoal to remain unknown to the hearer.

A somewhat interesting classification of sentences may be obtained of one considers how sentence goals and supergoals may vary along two dimensions: valid vs. not valid (for goals), and transparent vs. not transparent (for supergoals). A goal (direct goal) is valid or not valid as a function of whether it is still actually pursued by the sentence's utterer, or whether it is, so to say, atrophied, i.e. not actually pursued any more. A supergoal is transparent or not transparent as a function of whether the physical shape of the signal (at least partially) communicates the supergoal, or the supergoal is completely communicated though other means.

In the sentence "Is Bill going to be married?!" the goal (to know or to receive confirmation) is valid, and the supergoal (to express surprise)[2] is transparent: the particular intonational contour of the sentences communicates it to the hearer. In the sentence "Can you please pass me the salt?", the goal (to know whether the hearer can do something) is not valid, and the supergoal (to get the salt from the hearer) is transparent: the word *please* shows that the sentence is no simple question. In the sentence "It's hot in here", said in order to have the window open, the goal (to inform the hearer of something) is still valid, but the supergoal (window open) is not transparent: nothing in the physical properties of the sentence reveals it. Finally, in the sentence "Do you know what time it is?", the goal (to know whether the hearer knows the time) is not valid, and the supergoal (to know the time) may be not transparent.

As we have seen, supergoals may be transparent, i.e. they may be communicated to the hearer through the physical properties of the sentence. In so far as they are transparent, linguistic competence as a set of rules for systematically linking sound and meaning is the key to their communication and they are on the same plane as direct goals. However, non-transparency, rather than transparency, is the rule for supergoals. In other words, usually nothing in the physical shape of the sentence systematically reveals the supergoals pursued by its utterer, and the hearer recovers them through his inferential capacity rather than through his linguistic competence. A supergoal is the conclusion of an inferential process which takes the direct goal of the sentence and some information already possessed by the hearer, as its premises.

3. Discourse is defined as a sequence of two or more sentences produced by a single person which have supergoals in common and are therefore governed by a hierarchy of goals. Very simple two-sentence discourses are called micro-discourses. Microdiscourses can be classified according to the relationship of the goal of one sentence to the goal of the other. In one case ("aids to decoding") one sentence has the supergoal of aiding the hearer in decoding the other sentence. For instance, in "John has been treated with isotopes. Isotopes are ....", the second sentence has the goal of informing the hearer about what isotopes are, and the supergoal of increasing the probability that the first sentence be understood by the hearer. The micro-discourse may

be represented as in Figure 6.

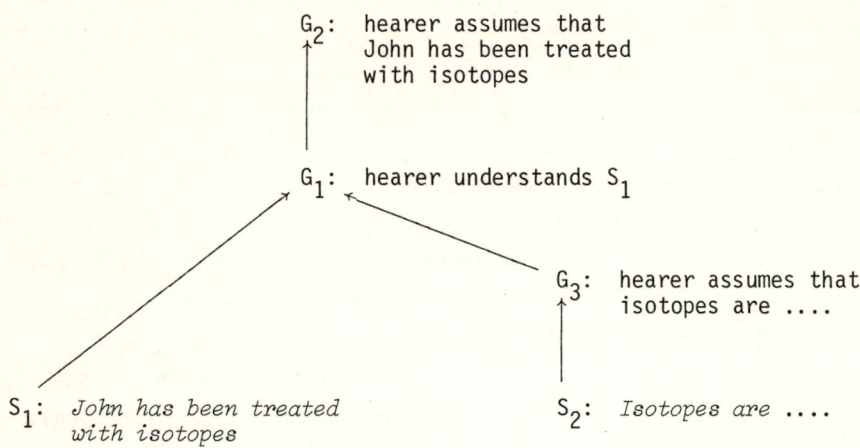

Figure 6. An example of an "aid to decoding".

In another type of microdiscourse ("supports"), one sentence has the supergoal of increasing the probability that the hearer adheres to the speaker's goal, i.e. that he does the action which is asked of him. So, in "Give me 100 dollars - I have a debt to pay", with the first sentence the speaker is asking the hearer to do a specific action (give him 100 dollars); the second sentence has the goal of informing the hearer of a specific fact (the speaker has a debt to pay), and the supergoal of increasing the probability that the required action be done. This is represented in Figure 7.

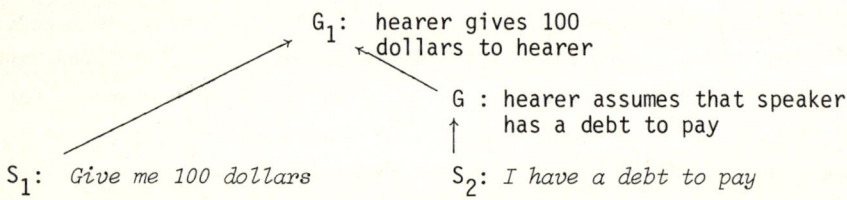

Figure 7. An example of a "support".

Other examples of supports are the following:

What time is it? My watch is broken.
Peter must be out. The windows are all closed.
Mary is very clever. She can solve 3 algebra problems in 1 minute.
Nixon is taking a sleeping pill right now. I can see it in my mirror.

In a third type of microdiscourse ("aids to integrating") one sentence has the supergoal of integrating the other sentence. "To integrate a sentence" is to provide an item of knowledge that explains the information contained in the sentence. For instance, in "John is sleeping - He works during the night" (said at 11 a.m.), the second sentence has the goal of informing the hearer about a specific fact (John works during the night), and the supergoal of explaining why John is sleeping at 11 a.m. To have an integrated map of knowledge, i.e. a map whose items are explained by other items, can be taken as a permanent goal of all individuals. In linguistic communication the content of a sentence tends to be assumed (i.e. the sentence is believed) by the hearer only if this content can be integrated into his map. It therefore becomes a goal of the speaker to provide the hearer with the means for integrating sentences if he believes that these means are not yet available to the hearer. A representation of the above microdiscourse on John sleeping at 11 a.m. is provided in Figure 8.

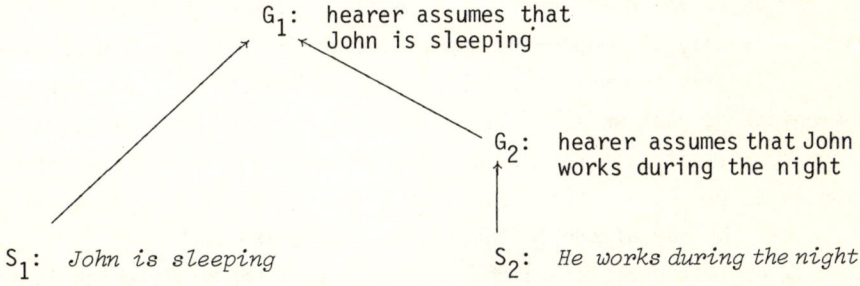

Figure 8. An example of an "aid to integrating".

In some cases the hearer may already possess the knowledge item which explains another item, but he has not get discovered the link between them. In these cases the speaker may be interested in mentioning the two items (not *informing* the hearer of them, since he already possesses them) and in explicitly indicating the explanatory link which connects them. Such is the case in "You know that the earth rotates - That's why we have day and night".

The integrated character of a knowledge map is largely responsible for the ability of drawing inferences, i.e. new knowledge items, from it. In fact, if X explains Y, and you know that X, you may infer Y. If "John lives in Italy" explains "John speaks Italian", and you know that "John lives in Italy", you may infer that "John speaks Italian". In some cases, however, this is not the case, i.e. the inference is not valid. A speaker may be interested in blocking unvalid inferences based on knowledge items he has provided to the hearer. *But* is a word to signal to the hearer that an inference is not valid and should be blocked. This gives origin to another sub-type of microdiscourses. An example is "John was born in Italy, but he doesn't speak Italian".

As we have seen, the direct goal of single sentences is communicated through the linguistic competence of the speaker and hearer, i.e. it is directly expressed in words, whereas their supergoals are mostly communicated through the inferential capacity of the hearer, i.e. only indirectly expressed in words. It is interesting to observe that in a discourse what is a supergoal for one sentence (indirectly communicated) may be the direct goal for another sentence (directly communicated), even if usually the higher or superordinate goals in the hierarchy are only indirectly communicated. In so far as higher goals are directly communicated, what we may call the "goal structure" of a discourse becomes explicit, as when we say "What we shall do in the present section is to ....", or "After explaining the reasons why ...., we will ....", or "By way of conclusion, we may say that ....".

By definition, a hierarchy of goals has a top goal, which is the supergoal towards which all other goals in the hierarchy converge as its means, or mediating goals. It may be hypothesized that titles of discourses, e.g. of an article, are direct expressions of the highest goal in the hierarchy governing the discourse. In other words, titles may communicate, through the linguistic competence of the speaker and the hearer (and not inferentially), at least part of the content of the top goal. A number of specific predictions can be derived from such an hypothesis which seem to be consistent with some observed facts. For instance, it is well known that providing the title of a text improves the comprehension of the text. If the title directly informs the reader about the top goal of the hierarchy which he has to reconstruct if the text is to be understood by him, the enhancing of comprehension can be explained by the facilitation in the reconstruction of the hierarchy obtained through knowing its top goal in advance. This improvement effect is much less marked if titles are given *after* the text, when the hierarchy has already been reconstructed. Similarly, if the title is presented to the reader as the first sentence in the text, no significant improvement in text comprehension is obtained, since the reader does not interpret it as the title, i.e. he is not helped by that sentence in reconstructing the top goal of the hierarchy and, consequently, the overall hierarchy.

4. Conversation is defined as a sequence of two or more sentences (or discourses) produced by at least two persons, such that each sentence adopts at least one goal of another sentence produced by another person. A paradigmatic case of a conversation is the question-answer exchange. Eg. A: "What time is it?", B: "It's 5 o'clock". A's goal in saying his sentence is that "A knows what time it is". The direct goal of B's sentence is that "A knows it's 5 o'clock", and a supergoal of this goal is that "A knows what time it is". As can be seen, the two sentences have a goal in common, in that in saying *his* sentence B adopts a goal that A had in saying *his* sentence. The situation is depicted in Figure 9. Attention should be paid to the

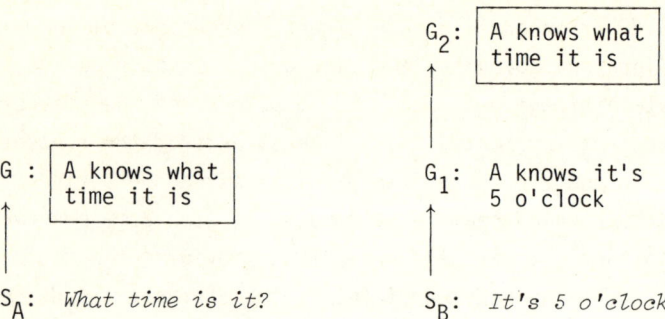

Figure 9. Sentences "make conversation" if they have a goal in common.

fact that in discourse, if two sentences have a goal in common, this refers to one and the same goal in the mind of the speaker. In conversation, on the other hand, if two sentences (uttered by two different participants) have a goal in common, this refers to two separate goals, in the minds of two different persons, that are made identical through the mechanism of adoption. In both cases, however, the linking of sentences to make larger connected units is obtained through their pursuing the same goal.

What is the key factor in conversation, however, is the adoption by B of A's goal, not the fact by itself that there is a common goal. Consider the case in which A asks B: "What time is it?", B does not hear A's sentence, but for independent reasons informs A that "It's 5 o'clock". In this case A and B's sentences have a common goal (in addition to having a common topic, to being temporally contiguous, etc.), but they cannot be taken as making a conversation. In fact, their having a common goal is not the result of B's adopting A's goal (see the definition of goal adoption in the first section of this paper); therefore they do not make a conversation.

In many cases sentences are connected in what we could call microconversations (in analogy to micro-discourses) through a special class of goals that are pursued in uttering sentences: control goals.

Anytime a goal is being pursued, another goal is simultaneously pursued, i.e. the goal to know whether the first goal has been reached or not. For example, if I do something (e.g. move my hand and arm) to reach the goal of "having the chalk in my hand", I simultaneously pursue the goal of knowing whether I have actually reached this goal. To pursue *this* second goal (a control goal) I may do such actions as looking at my hand and arm moving. In uttering a sentence, at least the following control goals are pursued: to know whether the hearer (a) has heard the sentence, (b) has understood the sentence, (c) has adhered to the sentence's goal. Consider the following three exchanges:

    A: John's gone out
B_1: Mm?
B_2: John who?
B_3: I don't believe it

B's replies to A's remark "make conversation" with that remark in that B adopts one or another of A's control goals: in saying *Mm*? he adopts A's control goal of knowing whether B has heard his sentence (in fact, "Mm?" communicates to A that B did not hear it); in saying "John who?" he communicates to A that he did not understand A's sentence; in saying "I don't believe it", he communicates to A that he cannot adhere to A's goal that "B assumes that John's gone out".

    The common goal that connects sentences in a conversation may be located higher in the goal structure of the conversation than in the cases we have seen so far. Take this example. A and B are arguing about the climate of La Spezia (an Italian town). A gives arguments for saying that La Spezia has a nice climate; B gives arguments against it. There is more than one way of conducting this discussion. A and B's highest common goal may be to determine what La Spezia's climate is like, i.e. to establish the truth. In some cases B in only trying to help A to assume what is true. E.g. A: "John is at home". B: "How is that possible? I rang him up just now, and no one answered!" But A and B, in the La Spezia example, may be conducting their discussion as an aggressive exchange. Each one has the goal that the other not reach his goal, i.e. demonstrating that he is right. In such a case, there would be no high common goal keeping together the whole exchange. A and B's sentence would be only linked through lower common goals, such as the control goals of each sentence. Alternatively, one could modify the general definition of a conversation (see above) by saying that two or more sentences, by different speakers, make a conversation also in the case where they have a *reciprocal* (not identical) goal, where "reciprocal" means that A and B's goals are identical except that A and B's roles in them are interchanged.

Various properties of conversations can be clarified by looking at the inter-speaker links as common goal links. Conversations may differ in their overall cohesion as a function of whether their common goal or goals are high and comprehensive, or not. Groups of sentences by different speakers may be more cohesive than other groups because they have more or higher common goals. A specific sentence may be linked to only one other specific sentence (through a common goal) and be unrelated to the rest of the conversation (or only related through the specific sentence it is linked to). A sentence within a conversation may be completely unrelated to the conversation (cfr. the idea of a "digression" in discourse as a sentence or group of sentences which are outside of the hierarchy because they do not converge as means toward the top goal). Finally, the goal analysis of conversations allows one not to consider temporal contiguity of sentences by different speakers as an instrinsically important parameter. Contiguous sentences may be weakly linked or not linked at all; non-contiguous sentences may be more or less strongly linked by having goals in common.

As a final remark, we think that pragmatics can be usefully defined within the present framework as the study of language (or of any other communicative system) from the point of view of the goals that are pursued, the different ways of pursuing them, and the conditions under which these goals are pursued and reached.

FOOTNOTES:

1. We do not consider the super-ordinate goals (G_2) in Figure 4 as supergoals because they do not satisfy conditions (1) and (2) above.

2. In this case reaching the goal is a condition of reaching the supergoal. In this sense the goal is still a means for reaching the supergoal.

ANSWERS, REPLIES AND REACTIONS

Isabella Poggi,
Cristiano Castelfranchi
and
Domenico Parisi

Our aim in this paper is to examine from a theoretical point of view the ways in which questions may be answered, and to compare speech acts that may be called answers, in a pragmatic sense, with those which are just replies, or even non-answers to a question. Since answering is but one aspect of conversing, for our analysis we need a model of conversation. The one we choose is the "goal analysis" model elaborated by Parisi and Castelfranchi (this volume) which views discourse as a hierarchy of goals (Parisi and Castelfranchi 1976), and conversation as the adoption of goals (Parisi and Castelfranchi 1977). According to such a model, two speech acts, two discourses or two sentences, uttered by two persons, even if uttered within an immediate spatio-temporal sequence, cannot be considered a conversation if the second speech act does not adopt at least one of the goals of the first speech act.[1] To adopt another's goal means to pursue another's goal as if it were one's own goal. Thus, one can say that B is conversing with A if, and only if, among the goals of B's sentence or discourse, at least one of the goals of A's sentence or discourse is mentioned. In order for it to be a conversation, however, it is not necessary for B to adopt the central goal of A's speech act: the adopted goal may also be one of those side goals, that Goffman (1976) calls "system constraints", and Parisi and

Castelfranchi (1977) "control goals"; they are the goals of checking whether your listener has heard and understood your last uttered sentences, whether he agrees, and so on. In this sense, not only is such a sequence as

(1a) A: Where is Mario?
      B: At home.

a conversation, but so is a sequence such as

(1b) A: Where is Mario?
      B: What?

The speaker A, in asking his question, has at least two goals: one of knowing where Mario is, which we call a communicated and a communicative goal, and one of knowing whether B has heard his question, which is neither a communicated nor a communicative goal. By "communicated" we mean a goal which a speaker makes clear through the meaning of his own sentence; and by "communicative" we mean a goal such that communicating it is a means of reaching it. As far as actions performed by speech are concerned, one who speaks, that is one who pursues a social goal by means of speech, "must first of all have the goal of having his own goal known by the listener, and this first goal is but a means of reaching the real goal: having the listener do something" (Castelfranchi and Parisi 1979). Very often, a control goal is not a communicative goal: in our example, if the speaker has the control goal of knowing whether the listener has understood his question, communicating the control goal is not necessary to reach it; while, on the other hand, communicating that he wants to know where Mario is, is necessary to have the listener tell him. Thus we can say that some goals of sentences are communicative, while others, and among them control goals, are not. To distinguish between these two cases, we will define "adoption" as getting oneself regulated by another's goal, and "adhesion" as the adopting of another's goal, independently of whether he has communicated it to you, and therefore asked you to adopt it. As far as adhesion is concerned, on the other hand, the listener performs an action he was requested to perform (to act, to answer, to believe etc.): the speaker believes that making his listener know he has a goal is useful for getting it fulfilled; in this sense we say the speaker makes a request.

We shall, now, define the notions of reaction, reply and answer,[2] in terms of the concepts thus far presented. We define a "reaction" as any behaviour with which you react to a question. You "react" to a question, first of all, by "acting", that is, when your behaviour is directed to a goal, and secondly by "re-acting" because the goal of this behaviour is determined by the fact that you were presented with a social action. However, when you react to a question (which is but a particular kind of social action) it is not necessarily the case that you realize you were presented with a question; it is sufficient that you realize you were presented with a social action. A reaction may be verbal or non-verbal, and it may be communicative or not; it does not necessarily "make a conversation" with its preceding speech act, since it does not necessarily entail an adhesion to or even an adoption of the interlocutor's goals. An example of a reaction may be the following:

(2) A asks B: When is Gianfranco coming?
B's only answer is to get out of the room.

In this example, B did react to A's action, i.e., he did consider A's sentence a social action; he may have taken it as indirect information about Gianfranco's probable coming, and as he didn't want to see him, he went away. We can call it a reaction also if, for example, after A's question, B starts cursing because he was distracted and the house of cards he was building fell down.

The class of reactions includes that of replies, and this in turn includes the class of answers, as shown in Figure 1.

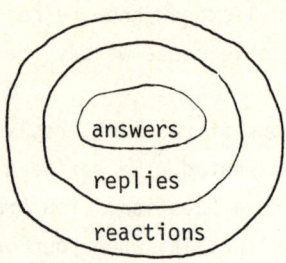

Figure 1

Let us now examine those reactions which can't be called "answers", but nonetheless do "make a conversation", and therefore may be called "replies". We define a reply as an action which adopts any of the questioner's goals. A reply may be communicative or not, and if it is communicative it may be verbal or non-verbal. Typical instances of verbal replies are sentences adopting control goals, such as

(3) I didn't understand.

(4) I can't speak Italian.

(5) What did you say?

(6) But what are you saying?

What control goals do such replies adopt? (3) adopts the goal "to know whether the listener understood the question", (4) "to know whether the listener can answer" or, again, "to know whether he understood". (5) adopts this goal too, but in an indirect way, for whoever asks "What did you say?" lets you infer he didn't understand. Finally, the "blame question" (6) [3] has the supergoal of warning: "your question is stupid", and thus it inferentially adopts the control goal "to know if your question is adequate".

Before defining our notion of an answer, let us see what a question is. A question is a request for information, that is a sentence whose goal is to request the listener to provide the speaker with an item of knowledge, or a piece of information. The information requested is supposed to be assumed by the listener, and to be necessary, pertinent and sufficient for the questioner's goals. In other words, the answerer is supposed to respect the Gricean maxims of being sincere, complete, non-redundant (Grice 1975). Thus, an answer will be a communicative verbal or non-verbal action, whose goal is to adhere to a request for information, that is, to provide the requested information. (7a) shows an example of a verbal answer.

(7a) A: What time is it?

B: Twenty past four.

And (7b) shows a non-verbal answer.

(7b) A: What time is it?

B just shows his watch to A.

Just as with any kind of sentences, questions often have, behind their literal goal, one or more supergoals.[4] Let's take a real example.

(8) A has been following a diet, for two months, because her cholesterol score is too high. After undergoing a new blood test, she is going to get the results back from the doctor and asks him:
"How is my cholesterol level?"

In this case, the literal goal of this sentence is to know how high the cholesterol level is. This goal, however, is but a means for a supergoal, which is the only really interesting information to A: to know whether she may stop her diet. In such a case, the best answer should be one which adheres to both the goal and the supergoal, for instance:

(8a) B: "It's a bit lower now. You can stop your diet."

But if a goal of economy is also present, and thus one wants to answer as briefly as possible, which of the two, goal or supergoal, must an answer adhere to, so as to be a more adequate answer? In our view, directly to answer

(8b) B: You may stop your diet.

is more adequate than, say, just to answer

(8c) B: Your cholesterol is at 170.

In the actual situation where the question was put, such was the doctor's answer, and immediately A asked again: "So ... what ...". The doctor again missed the supergoal and went on: "Well, it's lower ...", till finally A made her supergoal explicit: "Well, then ... may I stop my diet?". That A kept asking means that the first and second answer were not sufficient for her. Such a rule stating that a more adequate answer is one which adheres to a higher goal, implies that, before answering, it is sometimes convenient to ask the questioner what his supergoal is. This is a very common case:

(9) On the bus, A asks the driver: "What's your route?"
B, the driver: "Where do *you* want to go?"
A: "To the Pantheon".
B: "I'm going that way".

For the driver it would be very inconvenient to describe the whole bus route. Instead it's better to ask A where he wants to go, and then tell him whether the bus goes there or not. Not always, however, is the answer which adheres to a higher supergoal the better answer; in fact, the contrary is true when two or more separate goals contemporarily underlie the same sentence. For example, suppose A asks about the bus route both because of the supergoal of going to the Pantheon, where he has a date, and because of the supergoal of doing a research project on the town's bus service: in this case, just to tell him that the bus goes to the Pantheon would not be a completely adequate answer. However the problem of the best answer can be solved, we can at least say when an answer is not adequate. An answer is not adequate if at lest the question's communicative supergoal is not adopted. In fact, you do not adequately answer if you only say "Yes" to a question such as

(10) A: Do you have the time?

We shall now recapitulate our definition of an adequate answer. The goal of an answer is to adhere to a request for information: since the adequacy of the information depends on the goal, that is, it depends on the use for which the information was requested, then an answer is adequate to the extent to which it serves the goal of the question. This, indeed, is how we apply to answers the Grician maxim of pertinence. The maxim of "telling the truth" also applies to answering. A speaker who answers with a lie leads the questioner along a wrong route, that is, he gives him inadequate information: this is why a lying answer is an inadequate answer.[5]

Conditions of answering

From our definition it follows that three conditions are necessary for someone to give an adequate answer.

a) Understanding the question

The first condition is that the answerer should understand the question, not only at the phonological, syntactical, or lexical but also at the pragmatic level; he must have understood not only the literal goal, but also all of the supergoals really intended by the questioner.

b) Knowing the answer

Secondly, if answering means providing some requested information, it is necessary for the answerer to possess this information. Thus, according to our definition, such sentences as

(11) I don't know.
(12) How should I know?
(13) Why do you ask *me*?

and the like, will fall out of the class of answers. We consider them as merely replies.

c) Having the goal of answering

The third condition is that the questionee (that is, the person who has been asked a question) will pursue the goal of answering. Answering implies adhesion to another's request for information, and sometimes one may not have the goal of adhering to another's goal: this may happen either because one does not want to, or because one cannot. Condition c) is probably the most crucial of the three, for if this condition is fulfilled the others can be fulfilled too, while the opposite is not true. In fact, if I have the goal of answering and I did not understand the question (and, in some way of course, if I realize I did not understand it), then I may try to understand it better; or, if I do not have the information requested of me, I may try to obtain it. But, if I have no intention of answering, neither the best comprehension of the question, nor the surest possession of the requested information can force me to answer.[6] When I do not want to answer, I may use one of the various kinds of non-answers we shall be examining later. For now, we shall just note that sometimes, along with the goal of not answering, one has the goal of not letting you understand one does not want to answer; for if one's listener understands one does not want to answer, he might by inference reconstruct what one's answer could be.[7]

Pre-answers

We define as "pre-answers" those replies which are not answers themselves, but whose goal is the fulfilment of the prerequisite conditions for answering. To this class belong such replies as:

(14) I didn't understand, could you repeat your question, please?
(15) Just a moment, I can't remember ....
(16) Why do you ask?

These replies respectively adopt the questioner's control goals "knowing whether the questionee has understood the question", "knowing whether he knows the answer", "knowing whether he has made the decision to answer". In fact, to know if the answering conditions are fulfilled is one of the most typical control goals. Besides, not only are such replies adoptions: they are also "pre-adhesions", since through them the prospective answerer communicates his willingness to adhere to the questioner's request for information.

For the condition "to understand" to be fulfilled, the prospective answerer is supposed, first, to have phonologically perceived the question clearly enough. If this is not the case, he may reply with such sentences as:

(17) I didn't hear you.
(18) Could you repeat your question, please?
(19) What did you say?
(20) What?

Secondly, the prospective answerer is supposed to know all of the syntactic and lexical rules needed to translate the sounds he heard into the question semantic representation. If he lacks some of such rules, the comprehension process will stop, and he may ask, for instance:

(21) What does 'apodictic' mean?

A further level of comprehension implies the capability of reconstructing the eventual supergoals of the question. Before answering, the questionee may want to verify whether, say, the supergoal he inferred was actually intended by the questioner:

(22) A: Did you go to John's?
B: Do you want to know if I gave him his book back?

Another very similar kind of comprehension - pre-answer has as its goal "having the question better defined".

(23) On entering a clothes shop.
      A: Do you sell trousers?
      B: For men or women?

This we define as a sub-case of the last case, since when people put a generic question they often have the supergoal of putting a specific one: thus, B's asking for a specification has the goal of having A's supergoal made explicit.

With a second kind of pre-answer, the prospective answerer communicates his intention to fulfill the condition of "knowing the answer". For example:

(24) A: Is Robert there?
      B: Just a minute, and I'll have a look.

Here the questionee does not possess the requested information, but since, as far as possible, he wants to adhere to the questioner's requests, he communicates his willingness to do so. This is quite a clear demonstration, we think, that "wanting to answer" is the most decisive condition of the three to be fulfilled, since whether the other two may be fulfilled depends on whether this one is. Our definition of pre-answers does fit these two kinds of reply, since by means of them the prospective answerer confirms his willingness to answer. However, the following replies are somewhat different:

(16) Why do you ask?
(25) Why do you want to know that?

Not necessarily do such replies precede an answer, for when the questionee knows the reason why the question was put, he may decide not to answer.

Non-answers

A non-answer is defined as a reaction whose goal is "not to answer", that is, not to adhere to the questioner's request for information. A non-answer may be a mere reaction, or it may be a reply, that is, an action adopting at least one of the questioner's goals, although not the question's communicative goal. Suppose A asks B an unpleasant question and B, who doesn't want to answer, leaves the room. Of course, from B's action A may infer he does not want to answer; but whether such an action is a reaction or a reply depends on what B's goals are. We would classify B's action as a reply if B did have the goal of making A know he does not want to answer, and a reaction if he did not. Thus, we say a non-answer is a reply if B cares about adopting at least some of A's goals (typically, some control goals). Non-answers belonging to the class of replies are of two kinds since, besides not wanting to answer, you may, or may not, want the other to understand you don't want to answer. Communicating you do not want to answer may be sometimes useful in preventing your questioner from going on with his questioning. The most direct way to communicate this is to say it explicitly:

(26) I won't tell you.
(27) I can't tell you.

You can also communicate it in more inferential or impolite ways:

(28) It's none of your business!
(29) Mind your own bloody business!
(30) I'll get into trouble if I tell you.

Other more allusive ways exist, such as changing the topic or being reticent.[8] Here is an example of the first way,

(31) Mhm ... nice day, isn't it?

which is used to let you understand you picked an unwelcome topic. Reticence does not simply mean keeping silent: it entails B letting A notice he is keeping silent, and letting him understand he cannot, or does not want to speak.[9] This is why we place reticence among those kinds of non-answers that are replies, that is: non-answers which adopt the questioner's goal of knowing whether you have the goal of answering.

Finally, another way exists of reaching one's goal of not answering while communicating it: we call it "acting as if you didn't understand", and it consists in pretending you are pretending[10] you didn't understand the question: it often is a selfironic way of saying you don't want to answer. If somebody asks me "How old are you?", I may reply as a joke:

(32) What? What did you say? I didn't understand ... I really can't hear you!...

As we can see, all of these replies reach the goal of deterring the questioner from insisting on an answer to his question; at the same time, however, such replies have the disadvantage that they probably let you infer at least some information about the answer. At least, in fact, they let you know that the answer would not be a pleasant one to give.

Now we turn to those answers whose goal is not only to avoid answering, but also to hide one's non-answering. The most typical case of a total non-answer is, in this sense, lying. A lying answer is a non-answer, both if you provide your listener with information you don't really believe, and if you say "I don't know" when you do know: both are false answers, and therefore non-answers. The last is not feasible when the question is about some information which it is very implausible that you don't possess, as in the case of your age. Another way of non-answering is to pretend you didn't understand the question's actual goal, and to adhere to another goal you pretend you understood. This is the case in the example given by Ann Weiser (1975) in her "How to not answer a question".

(33) A: "How old are you?"
     B: "Don't worry, they'll let me into Jimmy's."

By not answering in this way, you may avoid letting the questioner understand you don't want to answer; he may think you did not answer, not because you did not want to, but because you could not, as you did not understand the question's real goal. In other words, this way of non-answering shifts the responsibility for the lacking answer from the non-fulfilment of condition "having the goal of answering" to the non-fulfilment of condition "understanding the question". On the other hand, this non-answer is not as effective as lying. When you lie, your reply *sounds* like an answer, so you questioner is satisfied; while, on the other hand, this kind of answer does not sound like an answer to him, precisely because it doesn't adhere to his intended goal; thus, you run the risk that your questioner will put his question again:

(34) A: I mean, I just want to know how old you are.

And this time you'll be forced to answer (or lie). The risk is the same with another non-answer: silence. If you keep silent, the questioner may think you didn't hear his question, and repeat it: so you will have to answer then, for if you keep silent again, your questioner may understand you do not want to answer, and infer at least part of the real answer. On the other hand, silence may belong to that kind of non-answer where you do have the goal of communicating you do not want to answer. In such a case, that would be more a case of reticence than bare silence. As we said, according to Vincent and Castelfranchi (this volume), reticence implies that you implicitly communicate that, and why, you cannot or do not want to answer. If this is the case, a reticent silence adopts the questioner's goal of knowing whether the conditions of answering are fulfilled, and therefore we would call that kind of silence a reply.

Answers

Thus far, we have seen answers as opposed to replies and reactions. Now we shall look at four different kinds of answers, varying as to directness and as to whether they are an adhesion to the questioner's goal or supergoal.

1. Answers to the goal

When the top goal of our questioner is simply his question's literal goal (that is, when that goal is not a means towards any supergoal) then two types of answers are possible: a direct and an indirect one.

We define as an indirect answer a speech act which inferentially answers a question. Here is an example of a direct answer to the goal:

(35)   A: Is John leaving tomorrow?
       B: Yes, he is.
(36)   A: How old are you?
       B: I'm twenty seven.

We represent such a simple question-answer structure as in Figure 2. The goal of B's sentence is to answer (to adhere to) the goal of A's sentence.

An example of an indirect answer to

(37)   A: When will they let me out of jail?

is

(37a) B: Tomorrow we'll drink to your health ....

as opposed to

(37b) B: They'll let you out tomorrow.

The structure of indirect answering is represented in Figure 3. B's goal in saying (37a) is simply to say (37a), but his supergoal is to let A infer (37b).

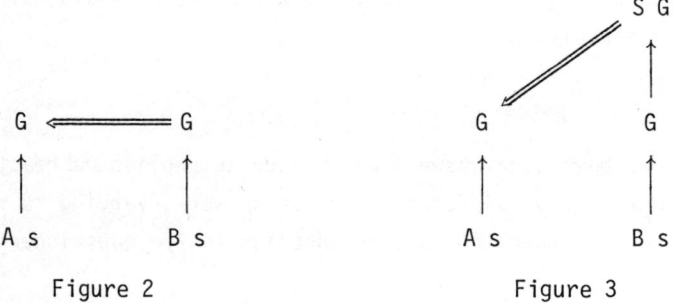

Figure 2   Figure 3

1.1 Direct answers to the goal

Now we shall see some subtypes of direct and indirect answers to the goal. When you directly answer a question, you may or may not add further information besides what was requested. If you do, we may speak of an "additional answer", as in

    (38a)   A: Is John leaving tomorrow?
                B: Yes, with Mary.

or

    (39a)   A: Who's leaving?
                B: John .... tomorrow.

as opposed to simply answering, respectively

    (38b)   B: Yes.

and

    (39b)   B: John.

As we see, we may have an additional answer both to yes-no questions and to Wh-questions. However, there is a problem as far as yes-no questions are concerned. Any "yes-answer" with something added is always an additional answer, but this is not always true of a "no-answer". This is because as you answer "yes", you always provide the requested information, like in these examples:

    (40a)   A: Is Benjamin Britten alive?
                B: Yes.
    (41a)   A: Is John twenty?
                B: Yes.

But when you answer "no", this is not necessarily the case. Let's take these examples:

    (40b)   A: Is Benjamin Britten alive?
                B: No, he died in 1977.
    (41b)   A: Is John twenty?
                B: No, he's twenty one.

In fact, "no" as an answer to questions (40a-b) sounds more informative than "no" questions (41a-b), as if only to say "no" were already a sufficient answer for (40), but not for (41). So, (40b) looks like a "more additional" answer than (41b) does.

If we want to explain this fact, a brief digression is necessary. What's the main cognitive difference between Wh-questions and yes-no questions? When you put a yes-no question you are "taking risks", in a sense, because you are hazarding a hypothesis about the information; and your interlocutor is only supposed, not to give you the right piece of information itself, but simply to confirm or disconfirm your hypothesis about it: this is what to say "yes" or "no" means.[11] Furthermore, we have to distinguish two subtypes of yes-no questions. We may say that the information requested by (40) is a kind of polar or binary piece of information: people can be either alive or dead, tertium non datur. Therefore, whether you say "yes" or "no", the questioner will easily assume the information he wanted. But the information requested by (41) is not of a binary kind: if John is not twenty, he might be twenty one, or twenty two, or nineteen, and so on. Thus, when the questioner is presented the answer that John is not twenty, he just excludes one possibility, but he still does not know how old John is. For this reason, if A's communicative supergoal was actually to know John's age, then that supergoal is not reached: the answer "no" is not adequate, and the "added" information is not in fact additional but just sufficient to satisfy the question. On the other hand, suppose A is looking for exactly twenty, and not twenty or nineteen year old people: then the information he wants to get can be considered to be of a binary kind: what he really wants to know is whether John is twenty or not, and if he's not he doesn't care how old John is. If this is the case, then (41b) can be considered an additional answer.

An additional answer is often a very adoptive answer, since it gives further information so that the questioner need not put other questions. But an additional answer is adequate in so far as it adheres to the questioner's real goal, that is, if it is to the point and it is not redundant.

Other subtypes of answers are those which add some preciseness to the answer proper. We call them "de-centered", "in-centered" and "conditional" answers. Here are the three examples, of the three subtypes respectively:

(42a) A: Is John leaving tomorrow?
       B: According to Mary, he is.
(42b) B: As far as I know, he is.
(42c) B: He is, if the train strike is over by then.

People usually need reliable information: so, when you give information you're not quite sure of, or which is conditioned by some event, it is a very sincere and adoptive act to show the limits within which that information is reliable.

1.2 Indirect answers to the goal

Let us see now some subtypes of indirect answers, that is, speech acts which inferentially adhere to a request for information. A first example is an indirect speech act like:

(43) A: May I leave?
      B: Why not?

Strictly speaking, an idiomatic sentence like this belongs to the set of indirect answers, since its literal meaning is not an answer but a question itself. But if we consider such a sentence from the point of view of its idiomatic meaning, we find it means "Yes", and therefore we should classify it among direct answers.

A very common type of indirect answer is what Parisi and Castelfranchi (1976) call "relying on the support". Here is an instance:

(44) A: Are you going to John's?
      B: He's helping me in my translation.

Such a type of answer is perfectly adoptive since it anticipates a further question the questioner might probably put ("Why are you going to John's?") and by doing this it shortens the eventual interaction sequence. At the same time, this answer is doubly informative: instead of simply giving a positive answer, B gives a reason (a support) which explains the positive answer, and therefore permits A to infer it. Furthermore, this is an economic way of answering, for it gives two pieces of information by means of one speech act only: the support. If you are to perform but one of two speech acts, to choose the support of the assertion is more informative than to utter the assertion itself: to explain why you are going to John's implies you go to John's, while to say you are going to John's does not explain why you are. The frequent occurrence of this "relying on the support" strategy, then, is due to its being a particularly informative and economical one.

Another way of indirectly answering is by "denying the presupposition":

(45)   A: Are you having sugar in your coffe?
       B: I'm not having coffee.

A question like this is doubly adoptive: on the one hand it indirectly adheres to the request for information, since it lets A infer B is not having sugar. On the other hand, this answer also adopts A's fixed goal of "getting adequate assumptions about the world": in fact an answer like this sounds like a notice to A to correct his own incorrect assumption about B's having coffee.

Finally, another way of indirectly answering is by putting a new question which implies a certain answer:

(46)   A: Have you got tea?
       B: Milk or lemon?

This is also a way of shortening the interaction. With his question, B starts another "adjacency pair", and thus lets A infer that the answer to his question is positive. A further goal of indirect answers, beyond that of being short, is to make your answer more effective and to cause a better recall. Of course, an answer like the following is more effective and easier to remember than a simple "no".

(47)   At a public examination, two candidates are talking.
       A: Will they tell us the results soon?
       B: A girl I know sat the exam when she was still engaged:

by the time she got her results, she had a daughter of
four ....

Evidently, the more inferences you're forced to make by an answer, the better you understand and remember it. This is surely one of the reasons why indirect answers are so frequent in everyday conversation.

2. Answers to the supergoal

2.1 Direct answers to the supergoal

We are now going to examine answers to the supergoal. Let us start with direct answers to supergoals. In theory, two choices are possible: you may directly (by speech) adhere to the supergoal and indirectly (by inference) to the goal, as shown in Figure 4. Or you may just directly answer to the supergoal while not answering to the goal at all, as in Figure 5.

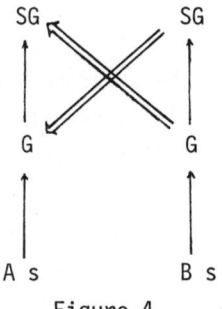
Figure 4

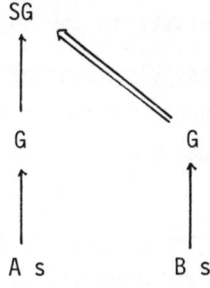
Figure 5

In fact, the second case seems possible only when the supergoal is not a request for information but just an action request - a command performed indirectly by a question - like in the following example:

(48) A: Aren't you sleepy?
B: Okay, I'll go home.

Here, A's supergoal was inviting B to leave, and B adheres (or rather, he says he's going to adhere) to that supergoal. Nonetheless, he does not let A know or infer whether he *is* sleepy or not.

On the other hand, when both the goal and the supergoal are questions, it seems to us that it is not possible to directly answer to the supergoal without indirectly answering the goal. This is the case in the next example:

(49) Mother is going to polish the floors with the electric polisher and she asks her daughter: Is there a wallpoint in your room?
Daughter: Not a 220 one.

Literally - that is, at the goal level - mother is not asking for a particular wall-point - she is just looking for one. However, the daughter knows her mother needs a 220 volt socket for the floor polisher, so she directly answers to her real goal, the supergoal of knowing whether a 220 socket is there. Meanwhile, she also indirectly answers to the literal goal, since from her daughter's sentence the mother may understand there *is* a wall-point in her room, even if not a 220 one.

2.2 Indirect answers to the supergoal

There are two possible types of indirect answers to the supergoal, depending on whether or not at the same time you also simultaneously directly answer the goal. This is an example of the first type (see Figure 6):

(50) A, after explaining the problem, asks B: Did you understand?
B: I did understand, the question ...

In this situation, A's supergoal was to ask "Can you tell me what the solution is to this problem?". A answers the question goal affirmatively; but, at the same time, she explains more precisely: "I did understand the question", and thus indirectly answers to the supergoal, since she lets A infer: "No, I have no solution".
And now an example of the second type (see Figure 7):

(51) Mother: How much money are you getting this month?
Son: Listen, my dear, with that money I am to pay the mechanic and my registration fee ....

The goal of mother's question is not at all adhered to by that answer:

the son does not say how much money he is getting this month. Still, the supergoal of his answer clearly adheres to the supergoal of the question.

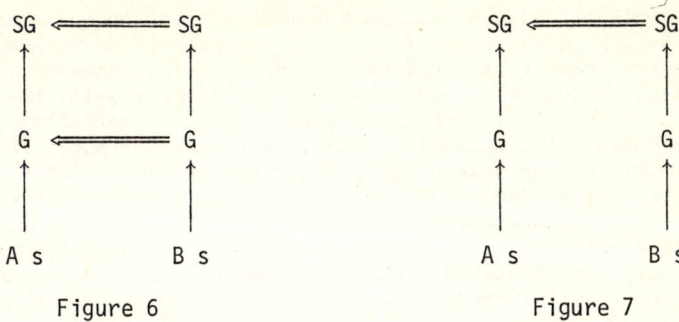

Figure 6   Figure 7

FOOTNOTES

1. In this sense, our position is quite different from the ethnomethodological too empirical view which, in its most extreme formulation, sounds like this: "Finding an utterance to be an answer, to be accomplishing answering, cannot be achieved by reference to phonological, syntactic, semantic, or logical features of the utterance itself, but only by consulting its sequential placement, e.g., its placement after a question". (Schegloff and Sacks 1973: 299, quoted in Goffman 1976: 293.) In our view, for an utterance to be an answer, its being uttered immediately after a question is neither a necessary nor a sufficient condition. It's not a sufficient condition because a sentence uttered by B may follow a question just put by A, still not being an answer at all. For example, A might ask B: "What time is it?" and B might immediately afterwards say: "I saw a wonderful movie yesterday!", which we could not very easily see as an answer. The utterance following A's question may also "make a conversation" with it (say, if A asked for the time in order to know whether it's time to go, B may say: "Come on, let's go.") and still not be an answer. On the other hand, if Schegloff and Sacks' notion of an answer, unlike ours, is intended to include all that may "make a conversation" (with a question or another kind of utterance), then their definition coincides with the trivial postulate that an utterance just uttered by B cannot be ignored by A. Furthermore, the above condition is not necessary to make a pair of utterances a question-answer pair. In fact, a case as the following is possible (which is even a real case, reported to us by Luisa Maffi). Luisa and Michele are talking by phone about a movie they saw together, in which there appeared some hussar soldiers with their hair shaped into a bunch of close little plaits. Luisa asks: "I wonder why those hussars wore such little plaits ...." This sentence, which is clearly an indirect question, is not answered at all, at the moment, and the conversation goes on about other topics. Some days after, Michele calls on Luisa and starts: "Hi. Oh, you see ... they used to wear those plaits in order to keep their face from sword cutting blows". This, indeed, looks like an answer, despite of its not immediately following the question. That's why we don't find the ethnomethodologists' view acceptable. A more correct position is Merritt's (1976: 329): "There is [...] a tension between a questioner's predisposition to hear whatever follows a question as an answer to that question, and his semantic monitoring of what follows to decide whether or not it is 'really' an answer".

2. Our notions of answer, reply and reaction are defined in a different way from Goffman's (1976) answer, reply and response.

3. About "blame questions" (domande-critica), see Crisari (1975).

4. See Parisi and Castelfranchi, this volume.

5. See Vincent and Castelfranchi, this volume.

6. Sometimes I really would not like to answer, but I finally make the decision to answer. In such cases I have the goal of answering only because of the supergoal of avoiding pain or punition, as in power relations (say, torture), but still I do have the goal of answering. (About "power", see Parisi and Castelfranchi 1978).

7. For a discussion on this fact, see Poggi, Castelfranchi and Parisi (1978: 39-44).

8. See Weiser 1975.

9. See Vincent and Castelfranchi, this volume.

10. See Vincent and Castelfranchi, this volume.

11. See Crisari 1975.

ON KRIPKE ON DONNELLAN*

François Recanati

1.   In his influential article of 1966,[1] Donnellan distinguished between two uses of definite descriptions. "A speaker who uses a definite description attributively in an assertion states something about whoever or whatever is the so and so." For example, suppose that we come upon Smith foully murdered. "From the brutal manner of the killing and the fact that Smith was the most lovable person in the world, we might exclaim, "Smith's murderer is insane"". This, Donnellan says, is an attributive use of the description "Smith's murderer": we do not refer to any given particular object, but we mean to say in general that *whoever* killed Smith is insane. "A speaker who uses a definite description referentially in an assertion, on the other hand, uses the description to enable his audience to pick out whom or what he is talking about and states something about that person or thing. [...] For example, suppose that Jones has been charged with Smith's murder and has been placed on trial. Imagine that there is a discussion of Jones' odd behaviour at this trial. We might sum up our impression of his behaviour by saying, "Smith's murderer is insane"". The description, in that case, is used referentially: the speaker intends to refer to a given individual, namely Jones, and he uses the description "Smith's murderer" because he believes, and believes his audience believes, that Jones, the intended referent, *is* Smith's murderer; but if that belief is mistaken and *Martin* actually killed Smith, still the speaker has referred to Jones, though by means of an inappropriate description. (Martin's

actually fitting the description does not imply that Martin has been referred to.) So we see that, while in the attributive use "the description might be said to occur essentially" because "the attribute of being the so-and-so is all-important", it is not the case in the referential use: "in the referential use the description is merely one tool for doing a certain job — calling attention to a person or thing — and in general any other device for doing the same job, another description or a name, would do as well."

This last feature of referential descriptions — the relative unimportance of their descriptive content — reveals some affinity between them and Russell's logically proper names. Logically proper names have no descriptive content: they are used to refer to particular objects without describing them, and this amounts to saying that they refer to these objects *themselves*, not in so far as they fall under any description. Referential descriptions, on the other hand, *have* a descriptive content, but they function as if they had none; they are used simply to refer to some particular object, and their apparently ascribing properties to what they refer to is a mere trifle (indeed, whether that property is rightly or wrongly ascribed does not really matter). "When a definite description is used referentially", Donnellan concludes, "a speaker can be reported as having said something *of* something. And in reporting what it was of which he said something we are not restricted to the description he used, or synonyms of it; we may ourselves refer to it using any descriptions, names, and so forth, that will do the job. Now this seems to give a sense in which we are concerned with the thing itself.... That is, such a definite description comes closer to performing the function of Russell's proper names than certainly he supposed." (1977: 64-65)

Interest in Russell's theory of logically proper names has recently been revived through the semantical doctrines held by such authors as Kripke and Kaplan. According to Russell, the distinction of sense and reference or denotation — the sense being the mode of presentation of reference — does not apply to logically proper names, which represent their reference directly; their reference, as it were, directly enters the proposition expressed (such propositions are, in Kaplan's (1975: 724) terminology, *singular propositions*, i.e. "propositions which contain individuals as immediate constituents"). Now Kaplan thinks that sentences containing demonstratives express singular propositions, so that demonstratives are akin to logically proper names. That is not to deny that, when an individual is demonstrated, there is a "mode of presentation" of the demonstration's intended reference. When I say "I am bald", I, the intended reference, am not referred to in the same way as I am if pointing to me you say "he is bald" (if you speak to some third person) or "you are bald" (if you speak to me). But "the varying *forms* which such a demonstration can take are not reflected in the content of the utterance (i.e. the proposition). The demonstration "gives us" the element of the proposition corresponding to the demonstrative. But *how* the demonstration gives that individual to us is ... irrelevant to the content of the utterance" (Kaplan 1978:230). — Why not, then, if demonstrations are construed as logically proper names although they are given both a sense and a reference, treat Donnellan's referential use as a *demonstrative use of descriptions*, i.e. as a use such that the sense, or descriptive content, of a description so used is simply irrelevant to the proposition expressed, which the reference enters directly as a constituent? That, indeed, is Kaplan's move in his famous paper "Dthat", and it fits Donnellan's description of the referential use quite well.

Russell, as is well known, thought of ordinary language as containing no logically proper name except a few demonstratives like "this" and, maybe, "I". More specifically, ordinary proper names were thought not to be genuine proper names in the "narrow logical sense". Kripke has forcefully argued to the contrary. In "Naming and Necessity" (1972), he shows that ordinary proper names are genuine names and not, as in Frege's or Russell's views, disguised descriptions. This is true, Kripke says, even when a name is introduced to designate an individual known only by description. (For example, we might decide to call "Charlie" the next President of the United States.) Such a description has a rather inessential function, that of *fixing the reference of the name*; although it is given to us only via the description, the individual *itself* is designated by means of the name, and not in so far as it fits the description. Accordingly, if we speak of a counterfactual situation (a possible world) where that individual no longer fits the description, we still speak of *him* in using that name, and not of any other individual who happens to fit the description in that possible world. To put it in a nutshell, names are *rigid designators*, they stick to a certain object which they designate in every possible world. Incidentally, Kaplan's demonstrations also are rigid designators, in so far as what they refer to is a particular object itself, not an object under some description. The contingent properties of an object, and so the descriptions it fits, are liable to vary across possible worlds, so that, if the reference of a designator is dependent upon some description the designatum has to fit, this expression can designate different objects in different possible worlds; but if the object itself, as opposed to a mere bundle of properties, is what the designator refers to, the designation cannot be nonrigid. Let's try to imagine what it would be for such a designator to be nonrigid. Call "D" the designator, "O" the object. O itself (not whatever has O's actual properties) is what D refers to. D is nonrigid if and only if it does not refer to the same object in every possible world. Granted that O itself is what D refers to, D is nonrigid if and only if O itself is not the same thing in every possible world. Since in our world O = O, there must be, for D to be nonrigid, a possible world where O ≠ O. But this world is not a possible world: it is an impossible world. Identity between objects is not a contingent relation, it is a relation which, if it holds in our world, holds in every possible world. Hence D, referring to O itself, cannot be nonrigid.

It is a contention of Donnellan's that, when we use a definite description referentially, we say something of the object itself that is being referred to, and not of this object *qua* its fitting the description. That being so, it seems that referential descriptions are related to Kripke's names no less than to Kaplan's demonstrations. To begin with, referential descriptions are rigid. The statement, "Smith's murderer is surely insane, he behaves so oddly" is about a given individual, say Jones, even if Jones is not Smith's murderer. A possible answer to that statement is, "He is surely insane, but maybe he didn't kill Smith", which does not mean that the man who killed Smith maybe did not kill Smith. Here, we admit that the individual we refer to by means of a description may not, in our wold, fit that description; *a fortiori* do we admit that he may not, in some other possible world, do so. Still we refer to *him* by means of the description, whatever possible world we are speaking of and whatever properties he has in the possible world under consideration.

The statement that referential descriptions are rigid may seem puzzling for two reasons. (A) A rigid designator is commonly defined as a designator that denotes the same object with respect to all possible worlds. A designator "- - - -" denotes an object a with respect to a world w if it is true of a that with respect to w it is - - - -. For example, the designator "Quine" denotes Quine in our world because it is true of Quine that, with respect to our world, he is Quine; and the designator "The U.S. President in 1979" denotes Carter in our world because it is true of Carter that in this world he is the U.S. President in 1979. If it were true of Carter with respect to *every* possible world that he is the U.S. President in 1979, then "The U.S. President in 1979" would be a rigid designator; but it is not, because in some counterfactual situation Carter is not the U.S. President in 1979. On the other hand, someone cannot be Quine in our world without also being Quine in every possible world where he exists, and for that reason "Quine" is a rigid designator. Likewise, "The square root of 25" is a rigid designator because it is true of 5 with respect to all possible worlds that it is the square root of 25. According to that definition, we cannot say that referential descriptions are rigid designators; for even if we use "Smith's murderer" to refer to Jones and Jones has killed Smith, still Jones might have been innocent: the designator "Smith's murderer" does not denote Jones with respect to *every* possible world.

We may, however, say that a designator is *rigid upon one occasion of use* if, whatever possible world is under consideration, we use it to refer to what it denotes in our world, as when we say "The U.S. President in 1979 might never have entered politics": in other words, a designator is rigid upon one occasion if on that occasion it is given the largest possible scope. (B) Even in that sense, referential descriptions cannot easily be construed as rigid; for if I use "Smith's murderer" to refer to Jones and Jones is innocent, I do not refer to what the designator "Smith's murderer" denotes in our world — say, Robinson. Still, I refer to what I *believe* the description denotes in our world, and if I am talking about a counterfactual situation, that gives a sense in which the description, although inappropriate, is used rigidly: the speaker's referent is, as it were, *rigidly misreferred to* by means of the description. To account for rigid misreference, we must admit that what a designator is used to designate rigidly upon one occasion need not be what it actually denotes in our world, but may be what it *putatively* denotes in our world. In that sense at least, it seems that we can say of a referential description that it is rigid.

Kripke, however, has made the counter-claim, that this approach to referential descriptions via their rigidity and their name-like character is fundamentally misguided. To account for Donnellan's referentiality, he says, it is sufficient to invoke the pragmatic distinction between word-meaning and speaker's meaning. Specialized to referring expressions, this distinction becomes that of semantic reference and speaker's reference, and specialized to definite descriptions, it becomes Donnellan's distinction between attributiveness and referentiality. That being so, Kripke (1977) concludes, "it would be wrong to take Donnellan's "referential" use, as he does, to be a use of a description as if it were a proper name";[2] for the distinction between speaker's reference and semantic reference applies to proper names just as well as to definite descriptions. It would be no less wrong to equate referentiality with rigidity, for clearly there are rigid attributive descriptions.

In this paper, I shall criticize Kripke's pragmatic account of Donnellan's distinction. My conclusion will be that this account is either basically inadequate, or supports the very thesis Kripke rejects — the thesis, namely, that referential descriptions are descriptions used as if they were proper names. Within a pragmatic framework like Kripke's, this thesis amounts to saying that proper names, as opposed to definite descriptions, are *semantically referential*, and that in the same way as an interrogative sentence like "Can you pass the salt?" can be used to do the job of an imperative sentence, definite descriptions can be used to do the work of proper names; thus used, definite descriptions are only *pragmatically* referential. At the end of the paper, I shall inquire into how referentiality, whether semantic or pragmatic, could be defined, and I'll show that it should not be confused with rigidity.

2. Here is now the passage where Kripke first introduces the pragmatic apparatus by means of which, he claims, Donnellan's distinction can be accounted for:

> In a given idiolect, the semantic referent of a designator (without indexicals) is given by a *general* intention of the speaker to refer to a certain object whenever the designator is used. The speaker's referent is given by a *specific* intention, on a given occasion, to refer to a certain object. If the speaker believes that the object he wants to talk about, on a given occasion, fulfills the conditions for being the semantic referent, then he believes that there is no clash between his general intentions and his specific intention. My hypothesis is that Donnellan's referential-attributive distinction should be generalized in this light. For the speaker, on a given occasion, may believe that his specific intention coincides with his general intention for one of two reasons. In one case (the "simple" case), his specific intention is simply to refer to the semantic referent: that is, his specific intention *is* simply his general semantic intention. (For example, he uses "Jones" as a name of Jones — elaborate this according to your favorite theory of proper names — and, on this occasion, simply wishes to use "Jones" to refer to Jones.) Alternatively — the "complex" case — he has a specific intention, which is distinct from his general intention, but which he believes, as a matter of fact, to determine the same object as the one determined by his general intention. (For example, he wishes to refer to the

> man "over there" but believes that he *is* Jones.) In the "simple" case, the speaker's referent is, *by definition*, the semantic referent. In the "complex" case, they may coincide, if the speaker's belief is correct, but they need not. (The man "over there" may be Smith and not Jones.) [...] My hypothesis will be that Donnellan's "attributive" use is nothing but the "simple" case, specialized to definite descriptions, and that the "referential" use is, similarly, the "complex" case.

From now on I shall use the terms of art "K-attributive" and "K-referential" as an abbreviation of "attributive in Kripke's sense" (= the simple case) and "referential in Kripke's sense" (= the complex case).

Although Kripke does not say much of definite descriptions in that passage, I think we can state his account of Donnellan's distinction as follows. The general intention of a speaker S is to refer, whenever a definite description of the form "the F" is used as a subject-term, to an object x, whatever it is, such that (1) x is F and (2) for every y, if y is F then $y = x$. (This, probably, should be qualified in the light of what Kripke says on p. 271.) Thus, S uses a description of the form "the F" K-attributively if his specific intention is simply to refer to an object x, *whatever it is*, such that the above-mentioned conditions are fulfilled. If his specific intention is different — if, for example, he intends to refer not to whatever object satisfies these conditions, but to some particular object which he believes happens, as a matter of fact, to satisfy these conditions — then the description is used K-referentially.

It is easy to see that this view of the matter fits Donnellan's examples fairly well. The important point here is the parenthetical comment "whatever it is" supposed to be part and parcel of the speaker's specific intention in the K-attributive case. In both K-attributive and K-referential uses, the speaker's specific intention is to refer to an object x such that $F(x)$ and $(y) (F(y) \supset y = x)$. The distinguishing feature of Donnellan's attributive cases, as Kripke notices (p. 257), "is the legitimacy of the parenthetical comment". In the attributive case the speaker could have said, "Smith's murderer, whoever he is, is insane", while in the referential case he couldn't. Kripke's analysis explains why this is so. For the semantic reference of a definite description is not (like the semantic reference of a proper name) a particular object given once for all; it is whatever fits the description, according to how things are. So if, in the K-attributive case, semantic reference and speaker's reference are to coincide by definition, the speaker must intend to refer to whatever fits the description, and not to any particular object given independently of the description. Even if the speaker thinks he knows which object does fit the description, he must be talking about whatever fits, if he is to use the description K-attributively.

Kripke's account, however, won't do. Remember a quotation from Donnellan I gave in the first part of this paper: "when a description is used referentially, a speaker can be reported as having said something *of* something... This seems to give a sense in which we are concerned with the thing itself...". A referential description refers to a particular object as such, and not to the indeterminate substratum of some uniquely instantiated property; now some K-referential descriptions *do* refer to the indeterminate substratum of some uniquely instantiated property. Kripke's K-referentiality, therefore, does not satisfactorily account for Donnellan's referentiality. Let me give an example of such a non-referential K-referential description.

A definite description of the form "the F" is used K-attributively if the speaker has the specific intention of referring to whatever object x satisfies the following conditions: $F(x)$ and (y) $(F(y) \supset y = x)$. If it is not the case, if the speaker does not have this specific intention, the description is used K-referentially. Suppose now that, coming back home, I find out that my house has been broken into. My money and all my valuables have been stolen; moreover, the furniture has been savagely destroyed. Looking to the curtains torn to pieces, I exclaim, "The robber must be insane!". What is, here, my specific intention?

We may suppose that I have no idea who did the deed; I just think that one must be mad to tear curtains into pieces gratuitously. So, here, the parenthetical comment seems in order: "the robber, whoever he is, must be insane". That, however, is misleading, and it would be wrong to treat that case as K-attributive; for some further evidence might establish that the man who robbed me of my money and my valuables, and the man who destroyed my furniture so savagely, are not in fact the same man. The robber, the police might tell me afterwards, came first, broke into the house, took everything valuable and left; then a vandal, seeing the door opened, came in and destroyed the furniture. I am not so naive as to think that one must be mad to steal; so I didn't mean to say of whoever actually robbed me that he must be mad. I intended, rather, to refer to whoever destroyed my furniture; for *that* suggests insanity. Had I said, "the man who destroyed my furniture (whoever he is) must be insane", my use of the definite description would have been genuinely K-attributive, as the legitimacy of the parenthetical comment shows. But I didn't say that. I said, "The robber must be insane", and as I intended to refer not to *whoever* robbed me (absolutely speaking), but to whoever robbed me *in so far as he also destroyed my furniture*, my use of the definite description was K-referential.

Such a K-referential use is clearly not referential in Donnellan's sense, for what is referred to is not a particular object as such, but whatever has a given property. Indeed, it does not satisfy, or at least, not very well, one of the requirements Donnellan imposes on referential descriptions:

> When a definite description is used referentially, not only is there in some sense a presupposition or implication that someone or something fits the description, as there is also in the attributive use, but there is a quite different presupposition; the speaker presupposes of some *particular* someone or something that he or it fits the description. In asking, for example, "Who is the man drinking a martini?" where we mean to ask a question about that man over there, we are presupposing that that man over there is drinking a martini — not just that *someone* is a man drinking a martini. When we say, in a context where it is clear we are referring to Jones, "Smith's murderer is insane", we are presupposing that Jones is Smith's murderer. No such presupposition is present in the attributive use of definite descriptions. There is, of course, the presupposition that someone *or other* did the murder, but the speaker does not presuppose of someone in particular — Jones or Robinson, say — that he did it. (Donnellan 1977:50.)

What happens when I use the description "the robber" K-referentially in the robber-vandal example? I do not presuppose of someone in particular — Jones or Robinson — that he robbed me. True, I do not presuppose simply that *someone or other* robbed me (and that's why the use is K-referential, not K-attributive); I presuppose, more specifically, that *someone, namely*: the man who destroyed my furniture, robbed me. But if this someone is a "someone-namely" and not a completely general someone ("someone or other"), he is not a particular someone either. I presuppose, not of Jones or Robinson, but of *whoever* destroyed my furniture, that he is the robber; and the not-completely-general someone of whom I presuppose that he robbed me, thus, is the completely general someone of whom I presuppose that he destroyed my furniture.

This example shows that Donnellan's distinction is not as simple as Kripke thought it was, and cannot be handled just in terms of speaker's reference and semantic reference. I shall now introduce a few notions which will help us to account for its complexity.

3. In *The Theory of Speech and Language*, Gardiner calls "incongruent" a sentence used to convey the meaning of another sentence: the sentence "Can you pass the salt?", to take one of Gardiner's examples, is incongruent when it is used to convey the meaning of "Pass the salt". This notion of incongruence applies, in particular, to reference. If I see Smith talking with some man and I say, "I've already met the man Jones is talking with", I mean that I've already met the man *Smith* is talking with; I've simply mistaken Smith for Jones, and I do not intend to refer to some other man *Jones* might be actually talking with. In that example, both the name "Jones" and the description "The man Jones is talking with" are incongruent: what they are used to refer to is not their semantic referent, but the semantic referent of some other name or description. The next example is borrowed from David Kaplan (1978: 239): Suppose that without turning and looking I point to the place on my wall which has long been occupied by a picture of Rudolf Carnap and I say: "that is a picture of one of the greatest philosophers of the

twentieth century". But unbeknowst to me, someone has replaced my picture of Carnap with one of Spiro Agnew. Here again, what I say is not what I mean: I mean to say of a picture of Carnap that it pictures one of the greatest philosophers of the twentieth century, but I actually say so of a picture of Agnew. The demonstration, in that case, is incongruent.

Let's now distinguish between *essential congruence* (e-congruence) and *potential incongruence* (p-incongruence). A description is potentially incongruent if it is used in such a way that it might turn out to be incongruent; and it is essentially congruent otherwise. This distinction is nothing else than Kripke's distinction between K-referentiality and K-attributiveness. A description is essentially congruent if its semantic reference cannot but be identical with the speaker's intended reference; and this identity is logically guaranteed just in case the speaker intends to refer to whatever his words refer to, to whatever is the semantic referent. If, on the other hand, the speaker wants to refer to something and chooses a description because he believes it suits what he intends to refer to, then it might turn out that he is wrong in this belief; it might turn out that, as a matter of fact, the description is incongruent and does not apply to the intended referent. The description, in that case, is potentially incongruent.

Besides that distinction between e-congruence and p-incongruence, there is another one, between *indefinite reference* and *identifying reference*. Indefinite reference is what the quantified variable performs in the sentence, "Someone is tall": no particular individual is mentioned as being tall, the sentence just says that there is such an individual; the sentence "John is tall", on the other hand, goes further and mentions or identifies a particular individual, John, as being tall. Now a definite description may be used to refer indefinitely or identifyingly. When I say to a charming lady, "Your husband must be very happy", I do not mention any particular man as being her husband and thus very happy; I presuppose that some man is her husband, and say that he (whoever he is) must be happy. On the other hand, if I say to her, "I met your husband at the station", I mention a particular man, namely, the man who, as far as I know, happens to be her husband. I do not, here, simply presuppose that someone (someone or other) is her husband; I presuppose of some particular man, whom I could further describe, that he is married to her, and I say of him that we met at the station.

Whether indefinitely-referring or identifying a definite description may be congruent or incongruent. In the example given above, "The man Jones is talking with" is used identifyingly: a particular man, who could be further described, is talked about by means of that (incongruent) description. If, by substituting "Smith" for "Jones", we make the description congruent, it will still be used to refer identifyingly to some determinate individual, namely the man Smith is talking with. In the example discussed in the second section, on the other hand, the description "the robber" or "the person who robbed me" is used indefinitely to refer to whoever destroyed my furniture, and it is incongruent, given that the robber is not identical with the vandal. Had the description "the vandal" or "the person who destroyed my furniture" been used, the same indefinite reference would have been performed by means of a congruent description.

The question, whether the vandal is identical with the robber, is plainly an empirical one. So when the description "the robber" is used to refer to whoever destroyed the furniture, it may be congruent or incongruent according to how things are. A description so used, therefore, is potentially incongruent, although it is indefinitely-referring. This shows Kripke's equation of potential incongruence (K-referentiality) with referentiality to be untenable, for if there are, as in the robber example, indefinitely-referring potentially incongruent descriptions, still *no* indefinitely-referring description can be referential in Donnellan's sense. Indefinite reference is no reference, according to Donnellan. To refer to whatever is the F is not to refer at all, if to refer is always to refer to some particular object. Thus if a speaker says, four years before Goldwater's election as the Republican candidate, "The next Republican candidate for President will

be a conservative", he does not refer to Goldwater nor to anybody else.
"If there is anything which might be identified as reference here",
Donnellan says, "it is reference in a very weak sense — namely reference to whatever is the one and only one ϕ, if there is any such"
(1977: 65). But to deserve the label "referential", a description must
be used to refer, in the *strong* sense, to some particular object capable of being further described; it must be used to refer identifyingly,
not indefinitely.

Kripke's account fails because not all potentially incongruent descriptions are identifying: some, which Kripke overlooked, are indefinitely-referring. Donnellan himself seems to have overlooked the possibility of a description's being both potentially incongruent and indefinitely-referring; he obviously thinks that all potentially incongruent descriptions must be identifying. Let me quote the relevant
passage in full:

> A person who said, "The United States Chamber of Deputies contains
> representatives of two major parties", would be allowed to have
> said something true even though he has used the wrong title.
> Strawson thinks (...) that what we do in such cases, "where the
> speaker's intended reference is pretty clear, is simply to amend
> his statement in accordance with his guessed intentions and assess
> the amended statement for truth or falsity..."
> The notion of an "amended statement", however, will not do.
> We may note , first of all, that the sort of case Strawson has in
> mind could arise only when a definite description is used referentially. For the "amendment" is made by seeing the speaker's intended reference. But this could happen only if the speaker had
> an intended reference, a particular person or thing in mind, independent of the description he used. The cases Strawson has in
> mind are presumably (...) cases in which a description is used
> because the speaker believes, though he is mistaken, that he is
> correctly describing what he wants to refer to. We supposedly
> amend the statement by knowing to what he intends to refer. But
> what description is to be used in the amended statement? In the
> example, perhaps, we could use "The United States Congress". But
> this description might be one the speaker would not even accept
> as correctly describing what he wants to refer to, because he is
> misinformed about the correct title. Hence, this is not a case
> of deciding what the speaker meant to say as opposed to what he
> in fact said, for the speaker did not mean to say "the United
> States Congress". If this is so, then there is no bar to the

"amended" statement containing any description that does correctly pick out what the speaker intended to refer to... But this means that there is no unique "amended" statement to be assessed for truth-value. And, in fact, it should now be clear that the notion of the amended statement really plays no role anyway. For if we can arrive at the amended statement only by first knowing to what the speaker intended to refer, we can assess the truth of what he said simply by deciding whether what he intended to refer to has the properties he ascribed to it (Donnellan 1977: 55-56).

Donnellan's argument is as follows. When someone says something by means of an incongruent description — a description the intended referent does not fit — we do not, Strawson thinks, assess the literal statement for truth-value; rather, we amend the original statement by putting a congruent description instead of the incongruent one, and we assess the amended statement. But the amendment is made by seeing the speaker's intended reference, Donnellan says, and "this could happen only if the speaker had an intended reference, a particular person or thing in mind, independent of the description he used". The hearer amends the speaker's original statement by substituting for the incongruent description another one which correctly describes the particular person or thing referred to. Any such description will do. But then, why bother to find any such description? To assess the intended statement for truth-value, we have just to check whether the speaker's referent itself, independently of any particular description, has the properties the speaker ascribed to it.

The core of Donnellan's argument is the idea that, when the speaker's intended reference is not by stipulation what his words refer to — especially when it is something else than what his words refer to — then it is a particular object he has in mind. Either the speaker intends to refer indefinitely to whatever his words refer to, or he intends to refer identifyingly to a particular object given independently of the description he uses and independently of any other description that could be used to pick it out. Now that is precisely what my example shows to be false; for the speaker, in this example, refers neither to whoever fits the description used, nor to a particular person he has in mind. The description he uses is neither identifyingly-referring, nor essentially congruent: it is both indefinitely-referring and p-incongruent. Donnellan is thus wrong in thinking that p-incongruence implies identifyingness, and his attack on Strawson's notion of an amended statement rests upon this error. The description "The robber", in my example, "is used because the speaker believes, though he is mistaken, that he is correctly describing what he wants to refer to": he wants to refer to whoever destroyed the furniture, and mistakenly believes that whoever destroyed the furniture also robbed him. Owing to his mistake, his intended reference is something else than what his words refer to, and his statement has to be amended, according to Strawson, before we assess it for truth-value. The amendment is made by seeing the speaker's intended reference, *but this is an indefinite reference, not an identifying one*. Contrary to what would be the case if Donnellan were right, the speaker has no particular person or thing in mind although the description he uses is incongruent; his intended reference is independent of the description he uses, but it is not independent of any description that could be used — it is at least dependent upon the description "the person who destroyed the furniture", and the notion of an amended statement raises no difficulty here: the amendment is made by putting "the person who destroyed the furniture" instead of "the robber".

If all incongruent descriptions were identifying, Donnellan would be right in rejecting the notion of an amended statement; for an identifying description refers to a particular object as such, and there are countless ways of correctly describing a particular object, so that there can be no unique amended statement to be assessed for truth-value; what we do when an identifying description is incongruent is rather, as Donnellan says, to check whether the object referred to — independently of any particular description — has the properties the speaker ascribes to it. But not all incongruent descriptions are identifying, and Donnellan is wrong when he says that "the sort of case Strawson has in mind could arise only when a definite description is used referentially"; for Strawson has incongruent descriptions in mind,

and not all incongruent descriptions are referential, because not all
are identifying, whereas all referential descriptions are.

4. Donnellan's distinction is not, contrary to what Kripke says,
identical with the distinction between e-congruent and p-incongruent
descriptions, for some p-incongruent descriptions are indefinitely-
referring, whereas all referential descriptions are identifying. By
the same token, it cannot be identical with the distinction between
identifying and indefinitely-referring descriptions, for some indefinitely-referring descriptions are p-incongruent, whereas all attributive descriptions are e-congruent. What, then, can Donnellan's distinction be, once we've recognized the possibility of a definite description's being both indefinitely-referring and p-incongruent?

How we answer this question depends, it seems to me, on whether we
think it possible or impossible for a definite description to be both
e-congruent and identifying. Suppose we think it impossible; then
Donnellan's distinction can be equated with the distinction between
e-congruent and *identifying* descriptions. Such a distinction makes
sense only if e-congruence is incompatible with identifyingness, so
that an e-congruent description can't fail to be indefinitely-referring, and an identifying description to be p-incongruent; to draw a
distinction between identifying (= referential) and e-congruent (= attributive) descriptions is thus a way of claiming that there is such an
incompatibility, as far as definite descriptions are concerned, between
their being e-congruent and their being identifying. Suppose, on the
other hand, we think there can be e-congruent identifying descriptions.
Then Donnellan's distinction is just a distinction between those e-congruent descriptions that are also indefinitely-referring, and those
p-incongruent descriptions that are also identifying.

Such a distinction as the latter is no more interesting and no
less arbitrary than a distinction between blue circles and red squares
in a universe where there are also red circles and blue squares; for if
there is no special link between the shape of a circle and the colour

blue, and between the shape of a square and the colour red, what is the point of drawing such a distinction? Similarly, what is the point of distinguishing between identifying p-incongruent descriptions and indefinitely-referring e-congruent descriptions, if there is no special link between identifyingness and p-incongruence, and between indefinite reference and e-congruence? Such a link can't be that p-incongruence implies identifyingness, or that indefinite reference implies e-congruence, for the robber-vandal example sufficiently shows this to be false: there are p-incongruent indefinitely-referring descriptions. If, moreover, we think there are e-congruent identifying descriptions, then the link can't be that e-congruence implies indefinite reference or that identifyingness implies p-incongruence. In that case, I believe, no satisfactory link can be found to vindicate drawing a distinction between p-incongruent identifying descriptions and e-congruent indefinitely-referring descriptions; Donnellan's distinction so interpreted should thus be eliminated as pointless, and replaced by two different distinctions, between p-incongruent and e-congruent descriptions on the one hand, and between identifying and indefinitely-referring descriptions on the other.

Some philosophers have argued that this actually should be done. Kaplan, for example, believes there are e-congruent identifying descriptions. According to Kaplan, a description can be used, demonstratively, for "showing" what is being spoken of. By means of such a description, we say something *of* the object itself that is being referred to, and the descriptive content of the description is a sort of contextual factor helping the audience to understand which object the utterance is about. In any case, the descriptive content is irrelevant to the proposition expressed, which proposition consists merely of the object referred to and what is said of it. Kaplan uses a prefix "Dthat" to indicate that a description is being used demonstratively (i.e. identifyingly), as in (1):

(1) Dthat (your husband) was at the station

Now the object demonstratively referred to by means of an identifying description need not, according to Kaplan, be such that it might turn out to be different from what the description semantically denotes; it need not to be the speaker's intended referent as distinguished in principle from the semantic referent. A speaker, Kaplan holds, may well use a description demonstratively for referring to whatever it denotes, as in (2):

(2) Dthat (the first child to be born in the twenty-first century) will be bald (Kaplan 1978:241).

The description, here, is identifying, although it is e-congruent. What this shows is that there is no special link, for Kaplan, between identifyingness and p-incongruence. More generally, Kaplan's distinction between demonstrative and non-demonstrative uses of descriptions is independent of the pragmatic distinction between speaker's reference and semantic reference, and he criticizes Donnellan for having confused the issue:

> My demonstrative use is not quite Donnellan's referential use... When a speaker uses an expression demonstratively he *usually* has in mind — so to speak — an intended demonstratum ... Donnellan and I disagree on how to bring the intended demonstratum into the picture. To put it crudely, Donnellan believes that for most purposes we should take the demonstratum to be the intended demonstratum. I believe that these are different notions that may well involve different objects (Kaplan 1978: 239).

Only when a description is p-incongruent is there an intended referent, distinct in principle from the semantic referent; to say, as Kaplan does, that the intended referent need not enter the picture when the demonstrative (identifying) use of descriptions is being discussed, is to say that identifyingness does not imply p-incongruence, so that there is no bar to a description's being both identifying and e-congruent. Kaplan thus rejects Donnellan's referential/attributive distinction as ambiguous between two different distinctions which are independent from each other and should be carefully told apart; as a matter of fact, any philosopher who admits e-congruent identifying descriptions is likely to reject Donnellan's distinction as confused, arbitrary or ambiguous (see e.g. B. Loar 1976b:364).

As soon as e-congruent identifying descriptions are admitted, Donnellan's distinction as it stands appears quite indefensible. Donnellan, therefore, seems to me deeply committed to the opposite view, that a definite description can't be both identifying and e-congruent. Kripke also seems to me committed to this view, for he wants to account for Donnellan's distinction rather than to replace it; moreover, Kripke's account would be a complete failure, if this view were to be given up. For suppose there *are* identifying e-congruent descriptions; then "attributive" means "both e-congruent and indefinitely-referring", and "referential" means "both p-incongruent and identifying". Kripke's account, which equates referentiality with p-incongruence and attributiveness with e-congruence, is thus basically inadequate; it confuses Donnellan's distinction with one of the two distinctions out of which it is built, and leaves out the fact that a referential description refers to the thing itself, whereas it is not the case in the attributive use. If, on the other hand, we hold that there *can't* be any identifying e-congruent description, then Kripke is right at least in equating attributiveness with e-congruence; to make his account plainly satisfactory, we have just to say that referentiality (i.e. identifyingness) is not, as Kripke thought, *equivalent* to p-incongruence, but merely *implies* it.

In the following section, I shall explore the possibility of defending the view, that no description can be both identifying and e-congruent. We shall see that, to defend this view, we have to construe the semantics of definite descriptions in such a way, that our pragmatic apparatus in its turn will have to be slightly modified to fit in the new framework. As a result of this modification, the notion of e-congruence itself will be dispensed with, and the view we'll show to be actually defensible will be the view that no description can be both congruent and identifying. This view is the core of Russell's theory of descriptions, an it will be pointed out that Kripke, by virtue of his being committed to this view, is also committed, *nolens volens*, to this theory. Finally, it will be shown that accepting Russell's theory and giving a pragmatic account of referential descriptions amounts to saying that they are descriptions used as if they were proper names.

5. The notions of congruence and incongruence are closely related to that of semantic function. A linguistic form, we might say, is congruent if it is used in accordance with its semantic function, and incongruent otherwise. So to know the semantic function of a linguistic form is to know when it is congruent and when not; conversely, to know that a given linguistic form is congruent or incongruent when used in such and such a way is already to know something of the semantics of this linguistic form. Owing to this link between congruence (or incongruence) and semantic function, it should be possible to defend the view, that an identifying description must be somehow incongruent, just by construing the semantics of definite descriptions in a certain way.

The semantic function of a linguistic form in a language is given by a general intention of the speaker of that language to do a certain thing whenever that form is used. For example, the semantic funtion of the interrogative mood is given by a general intention of the speaker to ask a question whenever he utters a sentence in this mood, and such a sentence is congruent if it is used with the specific intention of doing so. Now the semantic function of a proper name, say "Jones", is given by a general intention of the speaker to mention a particular individual, viz. Jones, whenever it is used. The name "Jones" is thus congruent when used to mention Jones, and incongruent when used to do something else. It may, for example, be used to mention somebody other than Jones; but it may also be used to do something other than mentioning anybody. It seems to me possible to imagine a context where, as a result of some conversational process à la Grice, the sentence "Jones can't swim" is used to assert indirectly that *someone* can't swim. We have here an interesting case of incongruence: an indefinite reference is performed by means of a linguistic form the semantic function of which is to refer identifyingly.

Still more interesting for us would be a case of incongruence, where an *identifying* reference is performed by means of a linguistic form the semantic function of which is *not* to refer identifyingly. The sentence "Someone can't swim", for example, could be used in a given context to assert indirectly that *Jones* can't swim; similarly, the sentence "Someone knows my secret, no one else knows my secret, and whoever knows my secret should be killed at once" might be used indirectly to order that Jones be killed at once. We can even imagine, Strawson says, "an elaborate game in which one never used an expression in the uniquely referring way at all, but uttered only uniquely existential sentences, trying to enable the hearer to identify what was being talked of by an accumulation of relative clauses" (1950:18). All these uniquely existential sentences would be incongruent, for part of the semantic function of such sentences is to perform an indefinite reference, so that if they are used to identify an individual and say something of it, they are not used in accordance with their semantic function.

Kripke points out that "the notion of speaker's reference [can] be extended to include cases where existential quantification rather than designation is involved" (1977: 264):

> When a speaker asserts an existential quantification, $(\exists x)(\phi x \wedge \psi x)$, it may be clear which thing he has in mind as satisfying "ϕx", and he may wish to convey to his hearers that that thing satisfies "ψx". In this case, the thing in question (which may or may not actually sastisfy "ϕx") is called the "speaker's referent" when he makes the existential assertion (1977: 266).

To handle such cases, however, we cannot use the pragmatic apparatus previously developed for designators; we have to amend it. A designator is congruent when used to refer to its semantic referent, and incongruent otherwise; moreover, it is potentially incongruent when used in such a way that it might turn out to be incongruent, and essentially congruent otherwise. For example: if the speaker wishes to refer to the man over there and uses the designator "Jones" because he believes that the man over there is Jones, his use is congruent provided his intended referent (the man over there) *is* Jones; but even so, it is p-incongruent, for the man over there might have turned out not to be Jones, in which case the designator "Jones", being used to refer to someone else than Jones, would have been incongruent. Such a use, therefore, is congruent without also being e-congruent. Now a sentence of the form "Some F is G" is congruent if and only if it is used, in accordance with its semantic function, to convey the proposition that there is at least one F that is G, no matter which object, if any, satisfies "F(x)" and "G(x)". If the speaker has an object in mind as satisfying "F(x)" and wishes to convey that this object satisfies "G(x)", there are two possible cases: either the object actually satisfies "F(x)", or it doesn't. Even if it does, however, we cannot say, as previously, that the sentence is congruent without being essentially so, i.e. that it is just *potentially* incongruent; we must say that it is actually incongruent, because it is not used in accordance with its semantic function. To preserve the distinction between cases where the speaker's referent satisfies "F(x)", and cases where it doesn't, the only thing we can do is to say that, in the former case, the existential quantification is weakly incongruent (w-incongruent), and strongly incongruent (s-incongruent) in the latter case.

Pragmatic apparatus for designation:

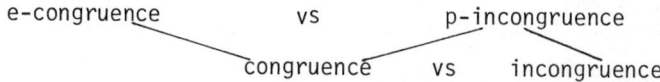

Pragmatic apparatus for existential quantification:

Now what is interesting about these cases, where an existential quantification is used identifyingly to say something *of* an object, is that their construal as congruent uses of existential quantification is ruled out: as far as existential quantification is concerned, identifyingness implies incongruence *by definition*. In the light of this result, it should be clear that, if Donnellan had been concerned with the different uses of existential quantification, his distinction between referentiality and attributiveness would raise no problem. A "referential" existential quantification would be a sentence of the form "Some F is G" used indirectly to say of a particular thing, identified as being F, that it is G. Consider the following example, borrowed from George Wilson:

> There is a certain man at a party who is paying oversolicitous attention to your younger sister. He is a man whom I know you know to be a convicted embezzler. I wish to inform you of the nasty situation and so, perhaps nodding in the direction of the man in question, I say that
>
> > (3) A convicted embezzler is trying to seduce your sister.
>
> Clearly, in saying this, [...] I mean to be making a more specific claim than merely that
>
> > (4) At least one convicted embezzler is trying to seduce your sister.
>
> Rather, I mean to be saying what would equally be conveyed by
>
> > (5) *This person* who is a convicted embezzler is trying to seduce your sister.
>
> if this were said of the relevant man at the party. (5) is a partially more explicit paraphrase of my imagined utterance of (3) in that the phrase "This person" functions as a verbal signal of an intention to be speaking of a certain man — here, the man that we've been observing. What I mean to be doing, in uttering (3), is to identify this man as a convicted embezzler and to say of him that he is trying to seduce your sister... (1978: 57-58).

The referential/attributive distinction as applied to cases of this type raises no problem, because the semantic function of an existential quantification is such that, if it is used to identify a particular object and say something of it, it is necessarily incongruent. Identifyingness and congruence thus being incompatible, we can straightforwardly equate referentiality with the former and attributiveness with the latter. But with definite descriptions, the picture is different. If we construe them as designators on a par with other referring expressions and assign semantic reference to them, we have to use the pragmatic apparatus for designation, and say that they are e-congruent when they are used to refer to whatever is their semantic referent. That being so, we'd like to equate, as far as they are concerned, attributiveness with e-congruence and referentiality with identifyingness; we cannot, however, do so unless it has been demonstrated that there can't be identifying e-congruent descriptions, i.e. descriptions used to say something *of* whatever they denote. But how shall we demonstrate this?

To begin with, I'd like to point out that there is *no* incompatibility between e-congruence and identifyingness with respect to designators in general. Suppose a high school teacher has broken a leg and is replaced by someone else. The new teacher, facing the pupils in the classroom for the first time, looks at a sheet of paper where their names are listed and says, "Jones will now tell me what the previous lesson was about". The designator "Jones" thus used is e-congruent, for the speaker intends to refer to Jones, whoever he may be; but it is nonetheless identifying, for the speaker refers to a particular pupil, viz. Jones, of whom he says that he will tell him what the previous lesson was about. Although the new teacher doesn't know which particular pupil he is speaking of, yet he does identifyingly refer to one of them. Acquaintance with the referent surely is not a necessary condition of identifying designation.

Well, it might be replied, if there is no incompatibility between e-congruence and identifyingness with respect to designators in general, still there may be such an incompatibility as far as definite descriptions are concerned. After all, most philosophers think there is a difference between proper names and definite descriptions; why not, then, say that it is the semantic function of the former to refer identifyingly, and that of the latter to refer indefinitely? Suppose we put the semantic difference between names and descriptions that way; then a definite description is congruent if it is used indefinitely to refer to its semantic referent. A definite description used identifyingly, therefore, can be neither congruent nor (*a fortiori*) e-congruent; even if it is used to refer to whatever is its semantic referent, it is incongruent, provided it is identifying.

What does this move amount to? It amounts to saying that the logical form of a sentence of the type "The F is G" is closer to that of an existential sentence than to that of a subject-predicate sentence with a proper name as subject-term. For indefinite reference is associated with existential sentences like "Some man is tall" or "A man is tall", where no particular object is identified and talked about. Such sentences express *general* propositions, whereas a subject-predicate sentence with a name as subject-term expresses a proposition about the particular object identifyingly referred to by the name. To say that the semantic function of a definite description is to refer indefinitely is thus to say that a sentence of the form "The F is G" expresses a general proposition, like a sentence of the form "An F is G". That is the gist of Russell's theory of descriptions: "The only thing that distinguishes "the so-and-so" from "a so-and-so", Russell says, "is the implication of uniqueness" (1979: 176). "The F is G" means no more and no less than "There is one and only one F, and every F is G" (or "There is one and only one F, and it is G"); so the definite description in such a sentence is congruent if the sentence is used to convey that there is a unique F and that it is G, and it is incongruent otherwise — if, for example, the sentence is used to convey that there is a unique H and that it is G (cf the robber-vandal case), or if it is used to convey that a determinate individual is G. If we accept Russell's theory, therefore, we can equate referentiality with identifyingness, and attributiveness with congruence, with respect to definite descriptions. The notion of e-congruence can be dispensed with altogether, for definite descriptions are no longer construed, in Russell's theory, as designators.

Kripke claims, rightly, that his pragmatic account of Donnellan's distinction would not suffer from accepting Russell's theory of descriptions, for it can be extended to cases where existential quantification rather than designation is involved. But he also thinks that his pragmatic account does not force him into accepting Russell's theory; he thinks that, whether we accept Russell's theory as the correct one or not, this account holds anyway. If, rejecting Russell's theory, we assign semantic reference to definite descriptions and take them to be primitive designators, then, Kripke says, "the general apparatus previously developed [i.e. in terms of e-congruence (K-attributiveness) and p-incongruence (K-referentiality)] seems fully adequate" (1977: 266). But I have shown that, to be adequate, it should be modified so as to have referentiality equated with identifyingness rather than with p-incongruence; this modification, moreover, requires to be operative that identifyingness be demonstrated to be incompatible with e-congruence, and such a demonstration, it seems to me, would amount to accepting Russell's theory and using the pragmatic apparatus for existential quantification instead of the apparatus for designation. That being so, I think we can say that a pragmatic account à la Kripke commits one to accepting Russell's theory of descriptions. Now to accept this theory is to admit that to refer in the strong sense, i.e. to refer identifyingly, is the job of (genuine) proper names, *not* of definite descriptions, so that a referential description is a description used to do the work of a proper name or, more picturesquely, a description used "as if it were" a proper name.

6. Against the conclusion, that within a Russellian framework a referential description can't be but a description used as if it were a proper name, the following objection might be raised. A sentence is incongruent when it is used to convey the meaning of another sentence, and we can say that an incongruent sentence is used as if it were that other sentence, the meaning of which it conveys. Now the sentence where a referential description occurs is used to convey, not the general proposition it literally expresses according to Russell's theory, but the proposition it would express if, instead of the description, a genuine designator (e.g. a proper name) did occur; so we can say that such a sentence is used as if it were that other sentence, which results from the description's being replaced by a proper name of the intended referent. But this does not enable us to say, without further ado, that the *description* itself is used as if it were a proper name.

To meet this objection, I shall introduce the notion of *localized incongruence*. Incongruence is localized when a sentence is used to convey the meaning it would have, if a restricted part of this sentence were replaced by something else. For example the sentence, "I like this man", displays a localized incongruence when used ironically, i.e. when used to convey the meaning of the sentence which results from replacing the verb "like" by an antonym. In such cases, not only is the whole sentence used as if it were another sentence; the restricted part, whose replacement would make the conveyed meaning literally expressed, may also be said to be used as if it were the replacing part. This restricted part is responsible, as it were, for the whole sentence's being incongruent.

Accepting the notion of localized incongruence enables us to say that the definite description, in the robber-vandal example, is used as if it were another definite description; that the indefinite description, in George Wilson's example, is used as if it were a demonstrative; and that a referential description is a description used as if it were a genuine designator, i.e. as if it were an expression the semantic function of which is to refer identifyingly, like a proper name. This notion of localized incongruence surely has to be refined — I do not wish to count, for example, "Can you pass the salt?" as a case of localized incongruence, on the grounds that it conveys the meaning it would express if "Can you" were replaced by "Please"; but however problematical this notion may appear, I don't think it is empty. What follows is an argument to the effect that it is not.

It has been pointed out (by Morgan 1978b: 263) that an expression like "to go to the bathroom" now literally means, in some American dialects, what it was first used to convey by means of conversational implicature. The bearer of a conversational implicature, however, is commonly taken to be the whole incongruent sentence-token, and without a notion such as that of localized incongruence we cannot account for the fact that sometimes an implicature is conventionalized as the literal meaning of an *expression* like "To go to the bathroom". On the contrary, that it is so provides evidence that, before the conventionalization happened, not only was a *sentence* like "John went to the bathroom" used as if it were another sentence, the meaning of which it was intended to convey; the *predicate* in this sentence also was used as if it were another predicate, the meaning of which it eventually acquired. Now if this argument actually shows that the notion of localized incongruence is not empty, it also shows that this notion applies to referential descriptions. For it happens quite often that a definite description, as a result of its being used referentially to mention a given object, becomes a proper name of this object. Strawson (1950: 24) mentions "the class of quasi-names, of substantival phrases which grow capital letters, and of which such phrases as 'the Glorious Revolution', 'the Great War', 'the Annunciation', 'the Round Table' are examples". These quasi-names are definite descriptions whose referential use is being socialized or institutionalized: for any such description, there is an object x such that it is common knowledge within a certain society that, when a speaker utters a sentence where this description occurs, he has x in mind as satisfying the description and wishes to say something of x. There is but a short step from referential descriptions, which are a matter of individual use, to these embryonic names, and from them to genuine names. A socialized referential description becomes a genuine name when its meaning is no longer relevant to its referring role, either because the words no longer mean what they once meant, or because the thing referred to no longer satisfies the description it used to fit. Thus "le Pont-neuf" once was a definite description, suiting the new bridge that had just been built in Paris; nowadays it is the name of that bridge, which is, of course, no longer new. The important point here is that it would not, today, be a genuine name, if previously it hadn't been used, as if it were one, to mention a particular bridge.

7. What I've shown so far is that, to make Kripke's account tenable, we must equate Donnellan's referentiality with identifyingness and

accept Russell's theory of descriptions, according to which the semantic function of definite descriptions is not to refer, or at least (if we think that to refer indefinitely is still to refer), not to refer identifyingly. Thus we must distinguish both between the semantic function of descriptions and that of proper names — proper names are, and definite descriptions are not, semantically referential —, and between the attributive use of definite descriptions, which is conform to their semantic function, and their referential use, which is not. We shall now inquire into how referentiality (i.e. identifyingness) could be defined, and how it is related to rigidity.

An expression is semantically referential if its semantic function is to mention a particular object; and an expression is used referentially if, whatever its semantic funtion may be, it is used to do so. Now we have seen that a description is necessarily rigid when used referentially, and Kripke has suggested, in "Naming and Necessity", that the distinguishing feature of proper names as opposed to definite descriptions is that they are rigid designators. Isn't it possible, then, to equate referentiality with rigidity, and to say that a referential description is a description rigid upon one occasion of use, i.e. a description used as if it were a rigid designator?

Some have argued along these lines (see P. Cole 1978: 3), but if they were right, there could be no rigid attributive description. Now there are such descriptions, as one of Kripke's examples shows:

> Suppose I have no idea how many planets there are, but (for some reason) astronomical theory dictates that that number must be odd. If I say, "The number of planets (whatever it may be) is odd", my description is used attributively. If I am an essentialist, I will also say, "The number of planets (whatever it may be) is necessarily odd", on the grounds that all odd numbers are necessarily odd; and my usage is just as attributive as in the first case (Kripke 1977: 258).

This usage, moreover, is clearly rigid: I say that whatever is the number of planets in our world is odd in every possible world; so there is no incompatibility between rigidity and attributiveness. A description is used attributively if the speaker intends to convey a general proposition of the form "there is an object x such that x alone is F and ..."; now such a description may well be rigid if, considering a counterfactual situation, the speaker means that there is *in our world* an object x such that x alone is F and such that, in that counterfactual situation, x is G. For the description to be nonrigid, on the other hand, the speaker should mean that, in the counterfactual situation, there is an object x such that x alone is F and x is G. In neither case does the speaker mention the particular object, if any, that happens to fit the description in our world or in the possible world under consideration; in neither case is the description used referentially.

There being rigid attributive descriptions sufficiently shows that referentiality should not be confused with rigidity. If a description used referentially cannot be but rigid (upon that occasion of use), the converse is not true. Analogously, if a semantically referential expression, like a proper name, cannot be but a rigid designator, still not all "rigid designators" are semantically referential; for some definite descriptions are rigid designators in Kripke's sense, while we suppose that no description is semantically referential. Although Kripke sometimes suggests that what distinguishes proper names from definite descriptions is their being rigid designators, he gives examples of definite descriptions, like "the square root of twenty-five", which are rigid designators, and admits that, because of these examples, the semantic difference between proper names and definite descriptions must consist in something else than the latter's being rigid designators. He does not say what this difference actually consists in, but he insists that there is such a difference "even in cases where the notion of rigidity versus accidentality of designation cannot be used to make out the difference in question":

> Let me give an example. π is supposed to be the ratio of the circumference of a circle to its diameter. Now, it's something that I have nothing but a vague intuitive feeling to argue for: it seems to me that here this Greek letter is not being used as short for the phrase 'the ratio of the circumference of a circle to its diameter'.... It is used as a name for a real number, which in this case is necessarily the ratio of the circumference of a circle to

its diameter. Note that here both 'π' and 'the ratio of the circumference of a circle to its diameter' are rigid designators... (Kripke 1972: 278).

"π" is not used, Kripke says, as short for the description "the ratio of the circumference of a circle to its diameter"; although the latter is used to fix the referent of "π", still "π" does not refer to 3.1416... *qua* satisfying the description: it directly refers to that real number, of which it is a name. In general, a name directly refers to a particular object, whereas a description may be said, at best, to refer, in a *weak* sense, to whatever it suits. So the semantic difference between names and descriptions Kripke has in mind seems to be the difference between identifying reference and indefinite reference, or between referentiality and nonreferentiality. Being referential, a proper name cannot be but a rigid designator, for a referential expression refers to a particular object, and a particular object is the same in all possible worlds where it exists; hence, a proper name is a rigid designator even when the description (if any) that is used to fix its reference is not a rigid designator. In such cases the name is a rigid designator, unlike the description, because it is, unlike the description, referential, and the difference between rigid and accidental designation can be used to make out the deeper difference between referentiality and nonreferentiality. In other cases, where the description that fixes the reference also is a rigid designator, the distinction between rigidity and nonrigidity cannot be used to reveal the deeper difference; but even then the name is referential, whereas the description is not. Consider the following sentence:

> The square root of 81 must be some number smaller than 10, for 10 is the square root of 100.

The definite description at the beginning of the sentence is a rigid designator in Kripke's sense; and it is, here, used attributively. What the first part of the sentence says is that there is a unique object x such that the product of x by itself is 81, which object is a number smaller than 10. The number 9, it seems to me, is not thereby referred to. What is expressed is a general proposition verifiable, in principle, by any number's being both the square root of 81 and smaller than 10; it is not a proposition about 9. A proper name, on the other hand, if we construe it as referential, i.e. as directed toward a particular object, cannot be used attributively to state a general fact. We cannot use "nine" without mentioning the number nine; and Kripke probably thinks that we cannot use "Jones" as a name without mentioning Jones — even if we don't know who Jones is.

The problem is that the notion of referentiality remains intuitive, and is still to be defined. This intuitive idea is that of a term's tagging an individual and contributing to the meaning of the sentence simply by standing for its bearer. This idea may be found in Mill's, as well as in Russell's, writings, and I understand Kripke's distinction between fixing the reference and giving the meaning in its light. Mill says that proper names have no "connotation", Russell says that genuine names have no sense besides their reference, and Kripke says that a name like "π" has not even the meaning of the description which is used to fix its reference. The latter example clearly shows that the intuitive notion of referentiality should not be confused with the relatively well-defined notion of rigidity. Still, many philosophers have thought of Kripke's notion of a rigid designator as accounting for Mill's and Russell's intuitive notion of a term's being semantically referential, i.e. used merely to stand for its denotation. For example, Christopher Peacocke offers a criterion of rigid designation which avoids quantifying over possible worlds, and then he proceeds to say:

> This criterion of rigid designation can be seen (...) as merely a more explicit formulation of an idea variously expressed as that of term's (...) "tagging" an individual (Marcus [1961]), or in general of an expression's being "used to enable... individuals to be made subjects of discourse" (Mill [1843]); and the view that proper names are rigid designators in our sense seems a natural elucidation of Miss Anscombe's remark that the proper name contributes "to the meaning of the sentence precisely by standing for its bearer" (Anscombe [1958]) (1975: 3).

But no criterion of rigid designation can capture the intuitive idea of a term's being referential, for referentiality is not the same thing as rigidity, although it implies rigidity.

Roughly, Peacocke's definition runs as follows. A singular term t is a rigid designator in a language L free of both ambiguity and indexicals if there is an object x such that for any sentence $G(t)$ in which t occurs, the truth-conditon for $G(t)$ is that $<x>$ satisfy $G(\ )$. "We are here", Peacocke says, "basing rigid designation on the idea of a certain object entering the truth-conditions of all the sentences of the language in which t occurs. What a rigid designator designates is just the object that so enters the truth-conditions" (1975: 110). The object itself, as such, enters the truth-conditions; does not that criterion of rigidity capture the intuitive idea of referentiality? Doesn't it allow us to distinguish between semantically referential terms, like proper names, and definite descriptions? It seems that it does; for the truth-condition of "9 is odd" is that a given object, 9, satisfy "x is odd", whereas this condition is neither sufficient nor necessary for the truth of "The number of planets is odd": it is not sufficient because, for the latter sentence to be true, 9 must also satisfy "x numbers the planets"; and it is not necessary, since the sentence would be true if some other object both numbered the planets and were odd.

Peacocke's criterion of rigidity, however, does not capture the intuitive idea of referentiality. The truth-conditions of "9 is odd" and "the square root of 81 is odd" are the same, viz. that 9 be odd. This condition is necessary and sufficient even for the latter sentence to be true; it is no use saying either that 9 must also satisfy "the product of x by itself is 81", or that some other number's being both the square root of 81 and odd would verify the sentence as well, for 9 alone satisfies "the product of x by itself is 81", no matter how things are. Still, while the two sentences have the same truth-condition, "9" alone is a referential term; the description "the square root of 81" is rigid, but it is not referential, as we have seen.

That is not to say that 9 does not enter the truth-condition of "The square root of 81 is odd"; obviously it does, as it does enter the truth-condition of "9 is odd". So we should admit that a term's being referential is not equivalent to its denotation's entering the truth-conditions of every sentence in which it occurs as subject. I tentatively propose the following[3]: for a singular term to be referential, its denotation must enter *something other* than the truth-condition of the sentence where that term occurs. The denotation's entering the truth-condition is a criterion of rigid designation, but not of referentiality; to account for referentiality, we must go beyond truth-conditions, and invoke propositional attitudes.

That it is possible to use "the square root of 81" attributively shows that one can understand the sentence "The square root of 81 is odd" without knowing *which number* is the square root of 81; and by the same token, one can know that 9 is odd without knowing that this verifies "The square root of 81 is odd", even if he understands that sentence. To understand a sentence, therefore, is not to know its truth-conditions; or, if it is to know its truth-conditions, it is to know them *under a certain description, in a certain light* or *from a certain point of view*. Let us call what is to be known in order to understand a sentence its *perspectival truth-condition*, as opposed to its (absolute) truth-conditions. Rigidity is a matter of (absolute) truth-conditions, but referentiality is a matter of perspectival truth-conditions. To understand "9 is odd", we must know that this sentence is true if 9 satisfies "x is odd"; but to understand "The square root of 81 is odd", we needn't know that this sentence is true if 9 satisfies "x is odd": for we can understand this sentence without knowing which number is the square root of 81. The number 9, therefore, enters the (absolute) truth-condition of "The square root of 81 is odd", but it does not enter its perspectival truth-condition. We have thus a criterion of semantic referentiality:

t is referential in L if there exists an object x such that for any sentence $G(t)$ in which t occurs, the perspectival truth-condition for G(t) is that <x> satisfy G( ).

Descriptions like "the square root of 81" are not referential by this criterion, whereas proper names are. What must be the case for the sentence "the square root of 81 is odd", as well as for the sentence "9 is odd", to be true, is *that 9 be odd*. The number 9 enters the truth-conditions of both sentences. But, for the sentence "The square root of 81 is odd" to be understood, what must be known of what is required for it to be true is, *that there be one, and only one, x such that $x^2 = 81$, and that x be odd*; whereas, for the sentence "9 is odd" to be understood, what must be known of what is required for it to be true is, *that 9 be odd*. The number 9 enters the perspectival truth-condition of the latter sentence (i.e. the sentence where a name occurs), but not of the former.

If we accept this definition of referentiality in terms of perspectival truth-conditions, we shall be committed to the thesis, that although one can mention a particular object without knowing which object he is mentioning (cf. the teacher example), still one could not be said, in such a case, to understand his own utterance; for to understand a sentence-token is to grasp its perspectival truth-condition, and the referent of a proper name enters the perspectival truth-condition of any sentence where it occurs as a name. This thesis, I think, could be admitted; there is a sense in which the new teacher, in my example, does not understand what he says when he utters "Jones will now tell me what the previous lesson was about", whereas his pupils do. Even if we are ready to admit this thesis, however, the notion of perspectival truth-condition raises difficult problems, and conflicts with the orthodox view, according to which the sense of a sentence is its truth-condition, and the reference of a sentence its truth-value. Taking seriously the notion of perspectival truth-condition would lead us, rather, to construe the perspectival truth-condition of a sentence (= the way its truth-condition is presented) as its sense, and therefore to return to what is in any case the intuitive, attractive view that the truth-condition of a sentence (the state of affairs it describes) is its reference. Now there are some reasons to view this proposal with a cold eye, and many philosophers, I believe, would show some reluctance to accept it. Whether they would be right or wrong is not the issue I addressed myself to in this paper, and I won't go into it. What I wanted to do just was to point out that, even if, like Kripke, we favour a pragmatic account of Donnellan's distinction, we cannot discuss it without bringing major semantic problems, like that of the difference between proper names and definite descriptions, into the picture.

FOOTNOTES:

* I am indebted to J.L. Mackie and B. de Cornulier for many helpful suggestions.

1. Unless otherwise indicated, the quotations are from the 1977 reprint of Donnellan's article, pp. 46-47.

2. Unless otherwise indicated, the quotations are from S. Kripke (1977: 264).

3. My proposal is very similar to that of Michael Lockwood (1975: 485-88), who also takes as his point of departure Peacocke's criterion of rigidity.

PHENOMENOLOGICAL ANALYSIS OF LANGUAGE AND ITS APPLICATION TO TIME AND TENSE

Helmut Schnelle

1. *Morphological and syntactic problems of tense analysis*

In order to get a clear picture of linguistic analysis of tense let me briefly remind you of some well-known linguistic facts. Tense is one of the morphological categories that may be marked by morphemes in connection with verbs. In most languages there are further categories marking the verbs. In analysing these verbal categories, it turns out that some of these categories such as person, number, perhaps gender a.o. can be easily and clearly separated morphologically and semantically from the category of tense. There are some other verbal categories, however, that are intricately related to the category of tense, namely the classical categories of aspect and mood - both in the broad sense.[1]

More recently, attention has been drawn to another category intricately connected with the verb, namely (communicative) mode, such as the historical and experiential presentation of sentences in texts.[2] Tense is so narrowly connected with these three other categories that Lyons can write: "Indeed, it is no exaggeration to say that there is probably no tense, mood, or aspect [or mode] in any language whose sole semantic function is the one that is implied by the name that is conventionally given to it in the grammars of the language. Furthermore, it is undoubtedly the case that the terms conventionally used to describe the functions of tenses, moods and aspects in certain languages are very misleading." (Lyons 1977: 682). The connection between these categories has been so strong that "in the later development of Greco-Roman grammatical tradition, which has influenced, and in many ways distorted the grammatical analysis of the majority of the world's better-known languages and the way they are taught in our schools and universities, the terms 'perfect' and 'imperfect' (which derive from the latin translation of 'complete' and 'incomplete') came to be used in collocation with 'tense'" (Lyons 1977: 704). In other words, where this classical tradition is still relevant, we shall have to distinguish between tense in the broad sense - including perfective and imperfective aspects - and tense in the narrow sense. This shows that the analysis of tense is difficult indeed and cannot be undertaken independently from the analysis of aspect, mood, and mode.

Structural analyses of the last ten years usually try to solve the linguistic problems syntactically, i.e. by relying on the interaction of lexical, morphological, or syntactic categories with other categories, i.e. grammatical relations of various sorts. Two such relations are prominent: The interaction of verbal categories and verb subcategories[3] on the one hand and adverbials, such as temporal, frequency and modal adverbials, on the other.

The discussion of the interaction between tense, aspectual characters of verbs, and adverbials or their specifiers has been very fashionable and in some respects very fruitful in the last ten or fifteen years. One gets indeed a more sophisticated characterization of what are the conditions of the uses of tenses by analysing sentences in which such adverbials and clearly aspectually determined verbs are present.

There are, however, problems with this analysis on two respects. First, the analyses tacitly assume that the characteristics of tenses analysed relative to external determinations, such as adverbials, remain nevertheless properties of tenses when these are used without adverbial context. Second, one often makes use of extremely specific classes of adverbials for diagnostic purposes - sometimes even of particular words -. This imports grammatically ad-hoc distinctions into the analysis since these classes are not distinguished grammatically apart from their contribution to tense. The first assumption, however, is easily refuted. It often happens that a tense occurring at an isolated verb has another temporal meaning than the same tense with an adverbial. This may sometimes be explained by saying that the adverbial shifts the temporal meaning of the tense. But Wunderlich (1970) has given good arguments to determine first the meaning of the adverbial, if there is one, and then, the tense of the verb; which sometimes depends on the meaning of the adverbial.

Consider the following German sentences:

(1) Ich habe mein Manuskript geschrieben.
    'I have written my manuscript.'

(2) Ich habe mein Manuskript bis morgen geschrieben.
    'I shall have written my manuscript by tomorrow.'

(3) Ich habe an meinem Manuskript geschrieben.
    'I've been writing my manuscript.'

(4) Ich habe bis gestern an meinem Manuskript geschrieben.
    'I was writing my manuscript up till yesterday.'

Sentence (1) says that the speaker has finished his manuscript by now whereas the adverbial *bis morgen* (by tomorrow) expresses that the speaker will have finished his manuscript by tomorrow implying that he has not yet finished it. Clearly, the meaning of the tense is shifted by the addition of the adverbial. The shift cannot be applied into the past; adverbials such as *bis gestern* (until yesterday) cannot be added to (1). For (3) it is the other way round. Without further context an utterance of (3) means that the speaker was working at his manuscript a moment ago. An utterance of (4) says that he was working at his manuscript up to yesterday, implying that he was not writing a moment ago. Again, the adverbial shifts the meaning of the tense.

The fact that tense distinctions that do not allow shifting are required in English but not in German is not a peculiar fact of German. On the contrary, the phenomenon is rather common among languages.

In addition to the argument that there are uses of tensed forms whose interpretation differs when used with or without certain adverbials there is the further argument that certain features of tense are well established for very small children who have not yet clear command of adverbials, in particular not of those adverbials that have a very strict temporal meaning. To their language the analyses relying on the interaction with adverbials is not applicable.

The conclusion to be drawn from this account is that reference to a semantic structure with respect to which the categories of tense, mood, aspect, and communicative mode could be discussed is indispensable. It turns out, however, that the basic semantic structure used for tense analysis, namely the time-line and its mathematical explication, is unsatisfactory. Indeed, it was the unsatisfactory status of this semantics of tense that caused me to study the problem of tense more carefully. I discussed these problems ten years ago with Wunderlich during the preparations for his dissertation.[4] The dissertation lists a number of important arguments in his paragraph about personal time versus public time (ibid, § 1. 4) without, however, making use of these arguments in its semantics, which is still based on the Jespersen-Reichenbach-Montague analysis and that of their followers. My arguments against this analysis have been given elsewhere.[5]

What is needed is a semantic basis that has psychological relevance and is not physicalistically biased. In considering psychological analysis of possible semantic bases, introspection should not necessarily be excluded as I have argued in another article.[6] It seemed natural therefore to investigate the results of introspective and empirical evidence about temporal structures. In comparing empirical results from psychology with phenomenological analyses the former are often more elaborated and empirically substantiated than their philosophical counterpart. On the other hand, most psychological analyses isolate only one or two features of temporality to the exclusion of others. This is problematic because the various features are interdependent. It is therefore necessary to obtain a systematic framework for these features.

Phenomenological analyses as reported by Husserl and other phenomenologists are therefore to be preferred in spite of their difficult and sometimes obscure presentation. I shall try to give a short account of what I found.

2. *The two subsystems of phenomenological analysis*

My account of the phenomenological analysis of time tries to present the results in a systematic way. I shall refer mainly to what can be found in the book "Erfahrung und Urteil", a script of Husserlian lectures published after Husserl's death in the thirties.[7] It is true that Husserl has written at several places about time - there is even a published script of lectures on the experience of time,[8] but I think that the view presented in "Erfahrung und Urteil" is the most elaborate version.

Let me warn you, however. Husserl does not present his view on time in a particular chapter; the various aspects of the notion of time are discussed at various places in the book. Moreover, the style of Husserl's writings is good German philosophical style, i.e. it is almost incomprehensible to someone who is not accustomed to that style. Because of this a careful philological exegesis of what Husserl really meant would have to go into a lot of details. In contrast to this, my intention is less to follow faithfully Husserl's arguments and phrasings, but rather to give an outline of the procedural and structural aspects of the experiential system uncovered.

The aim of Husserl's analysis of time is to explicate how our notion of an *objective* time as a structure ordering all objects and events of the real world *emerges* on the basis of our own personal experiences, i.e. of what is given in an austere phenomenological analysis. The explication starts from the discussions of simple experiences with temporal aspects and procedes to more complicated levels.

It turns out that an appropriate analysis will have to distinguish different domains of temporal order and to separate them from objective time. Let us list these domains as follows:

a. immediate time aspects,
b. episodic time order,
c. subjective time order,
d. objective time order,
e. quasi-time order.

In addition to these, one has to consider

f. subjective time measure (subjective durations), and
g. objective time measure.

Each of these domains is further structured, containing various subfeatures of temporality.

Before entering into the discussion of the temporal systems, we shall have to discuss the basic structure of the experiential system as it presents itself to phenomenological introspection since the basic time aspects or time orders emerge as organisational features of this experiential system.

From a systematic point of view the experiential system must be subdivided into two subsystems and an interrelation of the two subsystems. The two subsystems may be called the passive and the active subsystem.[9] The interrelation is usually specified by saying that the passive subsystem affects the active one and that the active one has a certain "freedom" to follow the affection or not.[10] The passive subsystem contains those experiential processes which are not necessarily under direct control of consciousness, but may affect conscious processes whereas the active subsystem comprises those experiential processes and procedural results that are under such a control. In a sense, the active subsystem consists of acts of consciousness and a central element of control - the ego center - which can be conceived as the center of activity. At each moment these acts of the active subsystem occur in the context (horizon) of automatized or other unconscious acts some of which affect the active subsystem.

Consider for instance the acts of thinking through a theoretical problem while driving a car on a smooth highway. The processes determining the driving are not under conscious control. Still they are ongoing processes. At times where the situation may become dangerous the perceptions of the occasion may affect the conscious subsystem and cause it to leave its intellectual problem for a while and pay attention to the situation on the highway; it may require reactions that are not automatized.

It should be quite clear that the passive subsystem is not passive in the sense of being only receptual or perceptual. Automatized action belongs to the passive system. This is as it should be for, as M. Arbib argues in his book "The Metaphorical Brain":

> ... for most of the perception of most animals and much of human behaviour, it is more appropriate to say that the animal perceives its environment to the extent that it is *prepared* to interact with that environment in some reasonably structured fashion (Arbib 1972: 16).

In other words:

> ... the primary purpose of recognizing objects is not to classify them, but to be prepared to interact with them (Arbib 1972: 17).

This seems to be an aspect too often neglected in philosophical analyses. Husserl is no exception. But this defect of actual analysis does not concern the primary distinction between the active and the passive field of experience.

Before going into further detail, let me present some methodological reflection whose conclusion will be helpful in our context. Most terms and phrasings used by Husserl for rendering the results of his introspection are metaphors, as elsewhere in philosophy. This is not accidental since language has not developed primarily to talk about the particulars or about the general structure of our internal processing, but about the ways the internal processing is acted upon the outside world and about the ways of appropriate reactions. Since then Husserl and other philosophers analysing human experiences in detail must use metaphor and nobody else will be able to render the relevant insights non-metaphorically; we may feel free to use another kind of metaphor that seems to be praticularly fruitful in our context of research, namely the cybernetic metaphor.[11]

Let me emphasize immediately that in spite of its outlook the cybernetic metaphor has not intrinsically a physicalistic interpretation. The processes determined by the application of subprograms or rules in the artificial intelligence approach and the networks of operative elements, such as formal neurons, are primarily defined as formal procedural elements; they are as such neutral with respect to an interpretation as a physical process on the one hand or as a psychological process on the other. This neutrality is the great advantage of the metaphor: It may serve as a descriptive means for stating the results of introspection and neurophysiology alike.

Now, in trying to represent the results of phenomenological analysis in terms of this metaphor we are led to postualte a combination of two subsystems, one of them, the passive one, being a network of operative elements (such as formal neurons), the other, the active one, being a system determining sequences of operations controlling in each step the modification of a small subsection of the (usually vast) field of data.

(Figure 1: see next page)

The internal structure and the interrelation of the two subsystems may perhaps be pictured as in figure 1 copied from Eccles and Popper (1977)[12] with a slight modification. The upper circle (WORLD 2 or conscious self) represents the active subsystem and everything else, with the exception of the dotted base, represents the neural system, i.e. the passive subsystem. According to Popper's explanation, WORLD 2 is the system of mental states that interact with our bodies. He mentions painful sensations, knowledges, ambitions, determination to act in a certain way, as examples of mental states. Part of the system of mental states are the states characterizing rational actions and among them are those determining rational moves in argumentation or computation. These latter have been carefully analysed by Turing[13] with the result that the main components are:

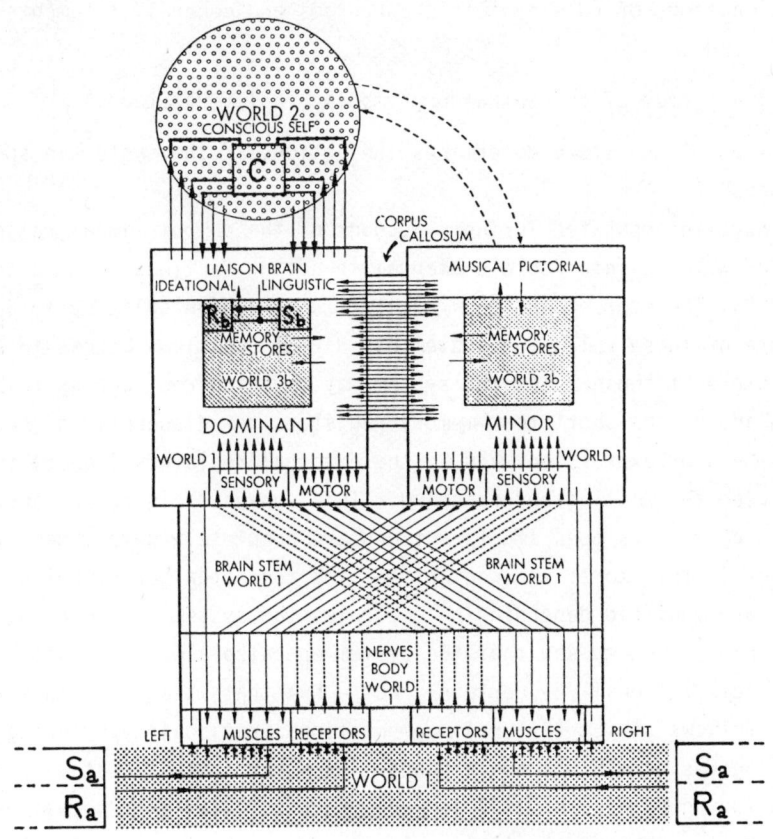

Figure 1   Schema representing the operational parts of the nervous system. The two subsystems are the circle (World 2) on the one hand, and the black boxes for the brain on the other.

(C) a control head determining the moves and the switches of awareness and attention,

(S) a store of rule systems or programs and general statements, and

(R) a system of conceptual or symbolic registers (tapes).

The filling of the store determines the actions of the system in specific ways.

I have incorporated Turing's account of the computational rationality of WORLD 2 into Eccle's diagram in adding sections for the three components. The store S and the registers R have been split up to S_b, the store of those rules the system has direct conscious access to and S_a the store of those rules the system may have indirect access to by reading and R_b the short term memory registers for alphabetic or numerical symbols or expressions and R_a the external registers (paper) that may be used for writing and reacting. This subsystem is to act just as a Turing machine does if its actions are completely determined by the rules in the store: the contents of the conceptual or symbolic registers are modified depending on the rules the system is operating upon. This is not to say that the system operates always in this way when it acts rationally - certainly not - but that it acts in this way when it follows strict (literal) computational rationality. Turing's analysis gives some hints how a subpart of WORLD 2 may operate. In reading Turing's paper of 1937 it becomes quite clear that he was partly aiming at a phenomenological analysis of computational rationality.[14]

In the incorporation into Eccle's diagram as proposed above, I should like to add another feature to the control head. Not only does it determine the "move" and modification of the contents of the internal and external registers, but it is also affected by other parts of the neural system. If the actual features of these other parts arrive at some specific configuration the computational process will have to be suspended and awareness turned to these other parts.

Such a situation might be illustrated by a suddenly dangerous situation occurring after driving on a smooth highway and pondering simultaneously a computational or argumentative problem.

As I said already, there is introspective evidence for each of the two subsystems. The introspective evidence for the active subsystem comes from authorities in the analysis of computing processes, namely Turing and Post. Let me emphasize again that they derived their special systems of state sequence or rule governed programming on the basis of phenomenological introspection.[15] Their methods have been further developed by programming theory and theories of artificial intelligence and they have been applied, as is well-known, in the formal theories of grammars.

The introspective evidence for the passive subsystem comes from Husserl himself. Though introspection can operate only when consciousness and hence the active subsystem is involved, the analysis of the introspective operation may *uncover* those aspects stemming from the underlying passive subsystem. In the course of his analysis Husserl distinguishes *several levels* of the synthesis; with respect to the passive subsystem we need to concern ourselves only with the basic level and the level next to it. The basic level is the level of *austere apprehension* (schlichter Erfahrung) containing the paradigmatic case of austere *perceptual* apprehension. On this level, it is the function of the passive system to present the impressions received, to present retentions and to order them. We shall come back to this (cf. H, p. 75).

The next level is *primitive or general association* (in a specific phenomenological sense[16] or synthesis of coverage (Deckungssynthese). On this level various pieces of experience are interrelated by being of the same or similar nature.

These two levels interrelate pieces in the field of potential experiential data by rousing (faktische Weckung), as Husserl says (cf. H, p. 207). Pieces of experiences rouse other pieces that are similar or contrasting to it. Particular cases in point are remembrances, but Husserl wants to understand the term association in a more general sense in which *every* stretch of experience is potentially related to other experiences to which it bears the relation of sameness or similarity on the one hand, or contrast on the other. This relational network of sameness and contrast over "memory", as we might call the system of all potentially available experiences, is a secondary system of relations added over their temporal orderings in which they have been recorded in short-term and long-term memory.

It is very obvious, then, that Husserl's introspective analysis of the passive subsystem points to an operative network of elements which are interrelated by connections of temporal or associative type, such that activating a connection leads to an activation of a related element. Activated elements are those that affect the active subsystem. If they are sufficiently salient the active subsystem will take account of them. Affection and taking-account-of affecting elements govern the interrelation of the two subsystems.

The picture that emerges from the introspective analysis of Husserl matches quite well with that resulting from neurophysiological analysis as presented for instance by Eccles,[17] though neurophysiological evidence is obviously much more detailed concerning the passive system. What has been said on the affection of passive systems on the active system matches equally well with what Eccles says on liaison brain. I shall not go into the details here.

The situation is different for the active subsystem. Here the neurophysiologist (Eccles) remains almost completely silent whereas the introspective analyst can say quite a lot, at least on the different types of operations.

In Husserl's writings, we can distinguish:

1. plain apprehension and plain consideration
   (schlichte Erfassung und Betrachtung, H. 114),

2. explicating consideration
   (explizierende Betrachtung, H. 139 ff),

3. active impression
   (sich-einprägen, H. 136),

4. imagination
   (anschauliches Ausmalen in der Phantasie, H. 144),

5. remembrance
   (wieder aktualisierte Erkenntnis oder Erfahrung, H. 144-45),

6. grasping of the general
   (Erschauung der Allgemeinheiten),

and furthermore

7. various forms of judgement and inference
   (Urteilen und Schließen)

In contrast to this complex systems of activities uncovered by Husserl's phenomenological analysis, Turing and Post have been mainly concerned with certain activities of rule governed judgement and inference. Their insights developed into well established methods of controlling the processes of computation and inference. Less is known on the other levels and almost nothing is known about a further level that might be mentioned, namely

8. creative imagination and inference.

I shall not go further into the details of these subactivities. Let me return to our topic of the temporal structures established by the interaction of the passive and the active system.

3. *Temporal stucture uncovered in plain apprehension*

On the first level of Husserl's analysis of temporal notions, the passive subsystem plays an important role. Husserl tries to gather introspective evidence on the structure of this subsystem by discussing the perceptual experience in hearing a continuous sound remaining the same in intensity and pitch for some period of time (H, p. 116 ff). What he wants to uncover is the "absolutely rigorous regularity [within the frame of the pure passivity] that occurs without the participation of the activity radiation emanating from the center of ego. It belongs to the regularity constituting the immanent temporality in which every impressional datum of some original momentary Now continually changes into the still-consciously-available of the same in the mode of the just-passed-Now. This retentional result undergoes again retentional modification etc. This shows that what presents itself to consciousness in a concrete presence must comprise a retentional stretch of the past, and that, when the concrete presence ends, a concrete, flowing retentional past must follow." ("... sie spielt sich nach einer absolut starren Gesetzmäßigkeit ohne jede Beteiligung der vom Ichzentrum ausstrahlenden Aktivität ab. Sie gehört zur Gesetzmäßigkeit der ursprünglichen Konstitution der immanenten Zeitlichkeit, in der jedes impressionale Bewußthaben eines originalen momentanen Jetzt sich stetig wandelt in das Noch-bewußt-haben desselben im Modus des So-eben (soeben gewesenes Jetzt). Diese Retention unterliegt selbst wieder der retentionalen Modifikation usw. Es zeigt sich dann, daß das Bewußtsein einer konkreten Gegenwart ein Bewußtsein einer retentionalen Vergangenheitsstrecke in sich schließt, und daß, wenn die konkrete Gegenwart zu Ende ist, eine konkrete strömende retentionale Vergangenheit sich anschließen muß" (H, p. 122).[18]

What has thus been discussed for a particular sound must apply to any perceptually recorded entity. Its recording is continually changed into a record of the just past, which in turn is transformed into weaker and weaker records. Since we are discussing the complete field of perceptual data or stimuli that affect the ego center and not the question which of these data the ego center turns to, we may have, at any moment, a field of such stimuli recording the presence of certain features of the auditory (or visual or other) field together with a sequence of short-term memory data of the features that were present a short time before. In Husserl's terms, we shall have for each feature perceived an impression and a sequence of retentions. The status of these patterns of impressions and retentions determines the regularity of the immanent temporality.

It seems to me that we may slightly modify this picture. The decrease of retentions is probably not the same for all features recorded. There are features that turn out as relevant in the contextual processing and these features may be kept longer in retention than others that do not get enforcement by relevance. Therefore, the interaction among various retentions and their interaction with further processing that is related to these data may increase considerably the period of retention.

Eccles considers this prolonged retention in short-term memory a case in point for interaction between the self-conscious mind and the neural modules. He writes:

> the continued activity of the modules can be secured by continuous active intervention or reinforcement by the self-conscious mind, which in this way can hold memories by processes that we experience and refer to as either verbal or non-verbal (pictorial or musical, for example) rehearsal. As soon as the self-conscious mind engages in some other task, this reinforcement ceases, that specific pattern of activities subsides and the short-term memory is lost (Eccles and Popper 1977: 388).

The last sentences must not be taken in the strict sense: as long as the task in which the self-conscious mind engages is closely *related* to what is contained in the memory it is often kept there even if it is not strictly rehearsed explicitly, as in the case of memorizing a phone number by rehearsing it by inner speech.

Now it is very easy to capture the results of Husserl's introspection in an operative network system. The systems obtained are the same as those I introduced elsewhere as a semantical basis for the most primitive level of the semantic analysis of tense.[19] I shall therefore not go into the details here. I shall turn instead to discussing the role of the active subsystem.

Husserl writes:

> ... the active (receptive) apprehension of the sound ... is itself continually persisting - persisting "as long as" the sound is heard. But the apprehending view is not directed toward the *phase* of the sound just now presented, as if it were the sound in this momentary Now, which were apprehended. On the contrary, to apprehend such a now, such a phase of enduring experience as a moment, and to take *it* as an object, is already the result of a more complex

apprehension. Apprehending the persisting sound, in short "this sound", we are not directed toward the momentary but continually changing present (the present sound phase) but, looking through this change, we are directed to the sound as a unity, presenting itself essentially in this change, the flow of experiences. More precisely ... the primary beam of apprehension of the ego transcends the central moment of the originary Now and turns to the experiential moment of the sound ... This moment remains in the active grasp in the continuity of the changing appearance. In this way the modifying activity of the grasp passes through the pasts joined to the present in a continuous way.

(... aktive (rezeptive) Erfassung des erklingenden Tons ist ... selbst eine kontinuierlich dauernde ... dauernd, "solange" der Ton erklingt, d.i. vernehmlich ist. ... Aber nicht auf die jeweils jetzt erklingende Phase ist der erfassende Blick gerichtet, als ob der Ton in diesem doch nur momentanen Jetzt der Ton schlechthin wäre, der erfaßt würde. Ein solches Jetzt, eine solche Phase der Dauer als Moment herausfassen und für sich zum Gegenstand machen, ist vielmehr eine Leistung einer eigenen neuartigen Erfassung. Den fortdauernden Ton, kurz gesagt "diesen Ton" erfassend, sind wir nicht auf die momentane und doch kontinuierlich sich wandelnde Gegenwart (die jetzt erklingende Phase) gerichtet, sondern durch sie in ihrem Wandel hindurch auf den Ton als Einheit, die sich wesensmäßig in diesem Wandel, diesem Fluß von Erscheinungen darstellt. Genauer besehen, richtet sich ... der primäre Erfassungsstrahl des Ich durch das zentrale Moment des originären Jetzt (auf das in dieser Form erscheinende Tonmoment) ... So geht die *modifizierte Ativität* des Noch-im-Griff durch das Kontinuum der Vergangenheiten, wie es an das lebendige Jetzt angeschlossen ist, stetig hindurch.) (H, p. 117-18).

In further explicating this analysis, Husserl makes it clear that the constitution of the continuously present future is the same as in the case of the constitution of a visual patch. In this case also, awareness is at each moment directed to some stretch in the field of the patch. But the active ego apprehends the patch in its entirety on the basis of a synthesis of coverages (Deckungssynthesen). As far as the feature of color present in the different spans of perception remains the same we have one and the same patch. This synthesis of coverages is a central principle in constituting units, namely extended pieces in space and time, in the range of which a perceptual feature does not change. The range of the coverages ends where the common features of all coverages end. This constitutes the unity of one sound and the unity of objects in general. But just as we see consciously in the case of visual perception a patch of color and not the various ranges of color on which we focus one after the other, we hear a sound and not just a sequence of adjacent or overlapping impressions or retentions of the sound.

Husserl's text and analysis is rather difficult and not completely clear. In particular, it is not quite clear whether the center of ego constitutes the unity of the patches or the complete sound or whether this constitution as such may still be considered part of the passive subsystem, though not of impression or retention, such that the active system can turn directly only to this part of the analysis.

I should prefer the latter analysis that can be easily reconstructed in terms of the cybernetic metaphor of the brain. Let us assume that the impression of the sound under discussion is rendered by the firing of a formal neuron and the sequence of retentions is rendered by the firing of formal neurons delayed with respect to the first. We may now conceive of another neuron (c) related to each neuron in the sequence as indicated in figure 2. If the center of ego usually addresses this last neuron, the neuron is directly understood as representing not the presence of an impression of a sound or the presence of its retention, but the continuous presence of the impression and retention. In any case, we must conceive of the integrating neuron as having priority in its access to the center of ego.

This idea could even be combined with the proposals of Eccles. Obviously, the formal neurons represented in figure 2 may be considered to form a module or part of a module. If, as Eccles claims, the self-conscious mind reads the states of the modules and not of single neurons, it is plausible that an experience of a continuous sound grasps it as a unit rather than a complex of present impression and retention.

(Figure 2: see next page)

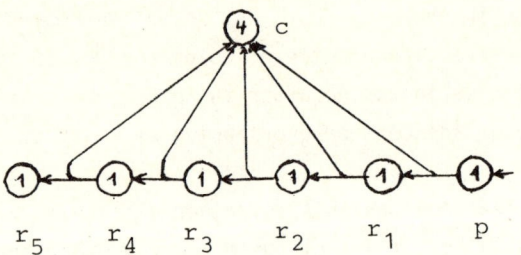

Figure 2 The firing of p represents the presence of some perceived event, the firing of $r_1 - r_5$ the retention of the event, the firing of c the presence of an event of "retentional lenght" 4

Husserl's analysis has been applied only to hearing a persisting sound. The same analysis is easily applied also to the termination of the sound. At the termination of the sound we will obviously have the following pattern: there is still some retention of the sound, but there is no longer the impression of the sound.

Again, if attention focusses on this situation, it sees it as one event: the stopping of the sound. It is correlated with three aspects: retention of a state of where the sound were present, the retention and impression of a lack of that sound, which has also the character of a persisting state and the switch between impression and lack of impression.

We see that we would have two different basic experiences in plain apprehension: the durative experience and the terminative experience. If, however, the event we attend to is a very short event we would have the experience of a momentary event in retension. These three cases could be rendered schematically as in figure 3.

(Figure 3: see next page)

To a linguist it is quite clear what to conclude from this discussion: impression and retention are closely connected to what I have discussed under the heading of Pre-tense. It is connected to the pos-

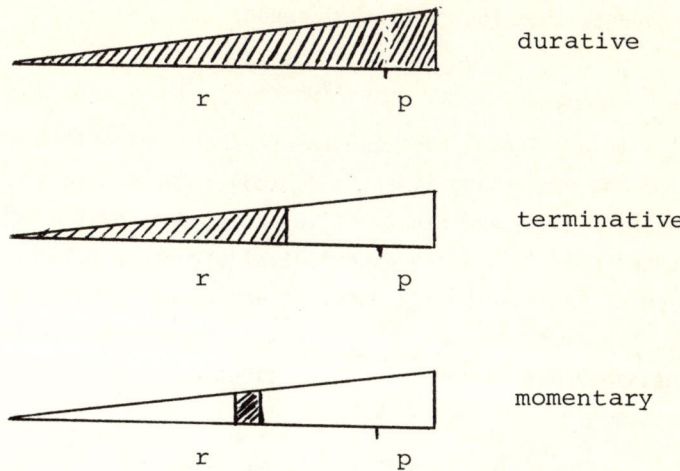

Figure 3   The patterns over a "retentional sequence" representing primitive aspects.

sibility of some experience of something just passed. The attention to the possible patterns over impression and retention make a distinction of an aspectual character of an event: durative, terminative, momentary (punctual).

The terminative obtains a particular importance in connection with actions leading to a definite result, such as accomplishments. In this case, the termination results in the accomplished state. Then, the terminative is called the perfective and the enduring experience is called the imperfective.

In any case, we may conclude from this analysis that the experiences to which the notion of aspect are related are indeed among the most primitive ones for perceptual events, as many linguists have claimed already, since they operate over the fields of immediate impression and retention only. This matches quite well with the insight of many linguists that aspect is more basic than tense in the narrow sense since it is ontogenetically prior and it can be found in more languages than the marking of tense.

4. *Subjective time, objective time, phantasized times*

In developing his analysis further, Husserl contrasts objective time and subjective time (H, p. 183). Subjective time is the time of the perceptual and other active experiences of the ego. It has two subaspects: first, the experiential structure related to the constitution of an experiential unit, an enduring, terminating or momentary event - such as sound, the resulting moment of a push, and a click - and, second, the complex of conscious experiences of events. Husserl writes:

> All experiences of an ego have their temporal unit; they are constituted in a flow of internal experience of time. In it they have their absolute position and singularity, their singular occurrence in an absolute Now, and their subsequent retentional fading away. Obviously, this time of experiences is not the time of the objects referred to (meant) ... as determined by the absolute position in objective time. In disregarding this [intended objective localization, it remains true that] the experiences have, as experiences, their absolute temporal position in the consciousness of inner time, [they have] their earlier and later. The same is true of the phantasized experiences, occurring in the stream [of inner consciousness], whilst the objects intended in the phantasy do not have an absolute, identifiable temporal position.
>
> (Alle Erlebnisse eines Ich haben ihre zeitliche Einheit; sie sind konstituiert im absoluten Fluß des inneren Zeiteinbewußtseins und haben in ihm ihre absolute Lage und Einmaligkeit, ihr einmaliges Auftreten im absoluten Jetzt, worauf sie retentional abklingen ... Natürlich ist diese Zeit der Erlebnisse die Zeit der in den Erlebnissen intentionalen Gegenständlichkeiten, ... sie sind vermeint als bestimmte durch ihre absolute Lage in der objektiven Zeit. Sehen wir hier davon ab, so haben außerdem die konstituierenden *Erlebnisse als Erlebnisse* im inneren Zeitbewußtsein ihre absolute zeitliche Lage zueinander, ihr Vorher und Nachher. Das gleiche gilt von den Phantasieerlebnissen, die in diesem Strom auftreten, während die in ihnen vermeinten Phantasiegegenständlichkeiten keine absolute, identifizierbare Zeitlage haben.) (H, p. 205-6).

Husserl takes care to make a clear contrast between subjective and objective time. He is quite explicit, however, that objective time is a complex structure relative to which objects are conceived as positioned, a structure, however, that is itself constituted by some complicated process on the basis of the individual experiences. The precise nature of this constitution has not yet been completely clarified. Husserl writes:

> Those difficult problems, in particular how the apprehension of absolute temporal determination of objects or the constitution of their position in objective time comes about, and how this structure of objective absolute time appears in subjective times of experience, are the central theme of a phenomenology of temporal consciousness.
>
> (Diese schwierigen Probleme und insbesondere das, wie es zur Erfassung von absoluten Zeitbestimmungen der Gegenstände, zur Konstitution ihrer Lage in der objektiven Zeit kommt, und wie überhaupt dieser Zusammenhang objektiver, absoluter Zeit sich in den subjektiven Erlebniszeiten bekundet, sind das große Thema einer ... Phänomenologie des Zeitbewußtseins.) (H, p. 194).

It is quite clear that in this constitution we have to distinguish the objective time of the real, one and only world, and the times of phantasized "worlds", the worlds of stories etc. and the temporality of conceptual entities (H, p. 303 ff). The subjective time is also called the time of givenness. Any object has, when it is conceived, by this very fact of being conceived, a time of givenness. But it has also, depending on its character, an intended localization in another time: objects intended as real objects are localized in objective time of nature, phantasized objects are located - usually by the process of phantasizing or the story presenting the objects - in the time of some phantasized context. But conceptual entities and general statements are not localized in any such time. Husserl thinks that the non-temporality of such entities and statements is essentially omnitemporality.

I shall not discuss the details further. The details of Husserl's discussions of plain apprehension and of more complex apprehension are rather complicated and sometimes conceptually and stylistically rather difficult. In the present context it is sufficient to get a rough picture of the interrelations of the various notions of temporality.

The systematic organisation underlying these notions is best analysed in terms of the cybernetic metaphor. It seems that explanations using this metaphor are much more flexible and intuitive than the ordinary language metaphors used by Husserl. The details of the cybernetic outline may well differ from the details presented by Husserl, but a detailed discussion of these differences does not seem to advance further empirical or theoretical research and would at most serve the purposes of philological exegesis.

It should, therefore, be sufficient here to localize the various aspects of time introduced above (see beginning of § 2) relative to the framework of the analysis presented by figure 2. When the self-conscious mind (or the control head) concentrates at a particular module of the Liaison brain, we have to consider the various factors of *immediate time*. *Episodic time order* determined by the order of memory traces in the memory stores. Episodes may be read out following that order. In this case, we get simple narrative structures. Or they may be read out by switching back and forth. In order to achieve this, we need more complicated linguistic means, namely temporal conjunctions and prepositions; the read out results in more complex narrative structures.

Subjective time order is nothing more than the sequence of the directions of attention of the self-conscious mind (or of the "moves" of the "control head" of computational rationality). *Objective time order* is not directly given, but implied by the "world view" incorporated in general statements, rules etc. stored in the internal store. It is part of the "theory" of the world which the organism "has". However, it has the contents of theories in another manner than it has its stored memories of episodes and memorized facts. These latter may be part of the contents of theories, but the theories usually transcend these particular knowledges.

Quasi-time-order is a time order of fictional "worlds"; it is similar to the objective time order, except that the order applies to "worlds" unrelated to our one and only world. It is still unclear to me whether "worlds" of this type are not completely determined by texts; if so, it seems that quasi-time order could be identified with episodic time order of the episodes reported by the texts and possibly memorized in memory stores.

In the beginning of § 2, I also referred to time measures. Often time is only discussed with respect to time *measures* presupposing the ordering and partitioning of time as obvious. Time measures have to be related to clocks or processes used in determining the time measure. In this case, the *subjective time measure* is related to certain inner processes in the organisms experiencing the measure[21] whereas the *objective time measure* has to be related to some publicly observable process, viz. that one that yields the simplest form of the laws of nature.[22] In any case, subjective time mesure should be related to some *aspects of the experiential system* itself whereas the objective time measure is rather *implied* by certain decisions on the role of publicly observable periodic phenomena as references for time measurements. The relation between objective and subjective time measures corresponds to the relation between objective and subjective time order. I think that these indications may suffice as a first indication on the status of the various aspects of the notion of time relative to the procedural system uncovered by phenomenological and neurophysiological research alike.

Conclusion

In my recent article Pre-tense I have argued that an appropriate semantic basis for tense analysis would require us to distinguish seven notions of time:

1. Pre-tense, 2. Simple Aspectual Tense, 3. Simple Narrative Tense, 4. Complex Narrative Tense, 5. Complex Aspectual Tense, 6. General Tense, 7. Time-Line Tense.

These distinctions derived from linguistic considerations can be backed up by reference to phenomenological experience. As we have seen, Pre-tense correlated well with the combination of impression and retention discussed by Husserl and Simple Aspectual Tense comes about due to the conscious apprehension of wholes (durative, terminative or momentary). Both, Pre-tense and Simple Aspectual Tense, can be underpinned by the phenomenological analysis of plain apprehension. Simple Narrative Tense is related to the reading out from memory governed by temporal and categorial associations. Complex Narrative Tense with its use of temporal conjunctions - such as after, before, when, etc. - requires more sophisticated reading out procedures involving conscious switching back and forth in the associative memory. Complex Aspectual Tense is connected with various features not discussed by Husserl. Time-Line Tense is shown to result from generalizations produced by the construction of embracing theories for the one and only world in which we live. These notions must necessarily come rather late in the development of a child (5-7 years) and are not at all required in each use of language. In fact, they are probably only relevant in expressions containing explicit reference to dates and clock readings. The differences between the different modes of temporal experience can be specified precisely by reference to a model of experience involving an interaction of a passive and active system, as correctly pointed out by phenomenological analysis.

FOOTNOTES:

1. Lyons (1977: 708 ff.).
2. Lyons (1977: 688) and the literature referred to there.
3. Such as state, event etc., called by Lyons the (aspectual) character of verbs.
4. Wunderlich (1970).
5. Schnelle (1979a, 1979b).
6. Schnelle (1979c).
7. Husserl (1939). It will be referred to by H, where the page numbers refer to the fourth edition of "Erfahrung und Urteil" (1972).
8. Husserl (1966). The reader should also consult the excellent book E. Holenstein (1972) who places Husserl's temporal analysis in the context of his conception of association (see esp. § 12).
9. The terms 'active' and 'passive' are taken from Husserl.
10. This seems to be closely related to Campbell's distinction between *cryptic* activity and *phenic* activity. See his contribution in this volume.
11. See my arguments in (1979c).
For an exposition of the metaphor, Arbib (1972).
12. Eccles and Popper (1977: 375).
13. Schnelle (1979c).
14. Schnelle (1979c).
15. As I have shown elsewhere. Schnelle (1979c).
16. Husserl (p. 77).
17. Eccles and Popper (1977).
18. Here, as well as at other places, Husserl conceives of protention in analogy to retention. Protention is related to expectation. However, since I'm persuaded that protention - and expectation - is a more complicated phenomenon than retention I shall not discuss it here.
19. Schnelle (1979b).
20. Note that "possible worlds" referred to by conditionals refer to *alternatives* to our world and are thus related to it.
21. Ornstein (1969; 1972).
22. Carnap (1966: 84).

COHERENCE AS A PRAGMATIC CONCEPT

Viggo Sørensen

Textual coherence is often considered a property of audible or written traces of text (as captured on tape or paper), - a property attached to definite lexico-syntactic signals or to some semantic intersentence network. But this view is clearly inadequate and has to be modified pragmatically, as can be seen from the following example.

At supper John tells his father all sorts of things, e.g. this:

(1) a. We had no school to-day.
b. Bruce was really $\begin{cases} (b_1) & \text{depressed.} \\ (b_2) & \text{content.} \end{cases}$

In lack of any lexico-syntactic or semantic clue, the father will hardly question the coherence of utterance (1) - unless a specific criterion is at hand, say a considerable pause, broken eye contact, or a new posture between (a) and (b). Coherence - unspecified, as opposed to non-coherence - appears to be a property we simply assign to each other's continuous action, under normal circumstances. In the domain of communicative action it is a principal reflection of Grice's cooperative principle or Habermas' anticipation of ideal speech situation.[1]

Moreover, the definite sort of coherence intended by John - whether (b) is to count as a cause or an effect of (a) - will normally be obvious to his father, on basis of contextual clues derived from their shared knowledge, values and expectations. The father recognizes Bruce as the name of a teacher or one of John's schoolfellows, or he identifies the person by the characteristic trait of depression. The rest of the way he can go on culture specific 'truths' like these:

(2) A teacher's (but not a school boy's) depression (but not contentment) is liable to cause (but not to be caused by) cancellation.

(3) A school boy's (but not a teacher's) contentment (but not depression) is a likely effect (but no likely cause) of cancellation.[2]

So, coherence types - as opposed to each other - must be looked upon as constituant acts of textualization, signalled or not in the text product according to the demands of the situation. Informing a less close person John would certainly have dropped some semantic clue, by referring to Bruce as *the teacher*, *my bench mate Bruce* or the like, or by specifying the aspecto-temporal relation between (b) and (a):

(1) b_1'. Bruce had become really depressed.
    b_2'. Bruce got really content.

And wishing to inform 'upstream' against current expectations, say about a cancellation actually caused by the teacher's contentment, or actually depressing a pupil, John would also tend to use more or less specific coherence markers:

(4) a. We had no school to-day,
    b. $\genfrac{}{}{0pt}{}{as}{for}$ Bruce / the teacher was really content.
(5) a. We had no school to-day,
    b. $\genfrac{}{}{0pt}{}{and}{so}$ (my bench mate) Bruce was / got really depressed.[3]

The reclassification of textual coherence has obvious consequences for the research strategy. A typology of coherence must be established as part of action theory - instead of grammar, building a new framework for the empirical study of coherence patterns and marking conventions in various text and context types. This process of pragmatization has been started already,[4] and I shall use the rest of the present paper to make some - theoretical as well as empirical - contributions to the enterprise.

Unable as yet to put it in safe action theoretical terms, I dare propose a bi- or tripartition of ways in which to present a topic - ways implying different main types of coherence, and each of them dominating great provinces of speech and literature. First, you can present your topic as a fact, with some ready-made interpretation pinned to it by the definite phrasing. What may be further needed in this case will be in the nature of improving the move made, through rewording, elaboration, legitimation, or the like - all of this giving rise to pure logical types of coherence. The resulting - so-called systematic[5] - texts dominate all fields of description, listing, etc.

The second way of presenting a topic is accumulative and suggestive, in as much as you add step by step to a complex picture that can only be fully appreciated and interpreted at the end. The single parts will bear significance according to their elucidation of each other in a temporal perspective superimposed by such coherence patterns as cause and effect, purpose and means, etc. The outcome is narration, which dominates a vast field from everyday report to history and fiction. Replacing temporality and causality with contrast, you get the third - and somewhat dubious - candidate for representation: one dominating if anything a good part of poetry. For practical reasons I shall here regard it as no more than a subtype of systematic textualization.[6]

Even in the fields with one dominating coherence dimension, the other one is likely to show up in embedded forms. A story, e.g., will normally contain features of description and may also hold features of author's comment. Whereas a portrait or a request, basicly systematic constructions, may include illustrating and motivating features of narration, resp. So we shall have to study not only 'linear' coherence and coherence signals, but also phenomena of dimensional transition.

Of course such transition figures especially in text fields without any clear coherence dominance. Take for an example review or literary analysis where you are supposed to serve two purposes at a time - calling for different coherence dimensions: rendering more or less of a paraphrase (organized along the temporal and causal dimension), and coming up with an evaluation or interpretation (organized along the systematic dimension). My sample texts A and B (in appendix 1 and 2, resp.) are just the type, being papers by 18 year old students on Hans Andersen's fairy-tale The Steadfast Tin-Soldier.[7]

You may wonder at this specific choice, since authors of that age can hardly be called fully experienced, and since their motivation for writing such papers would seem rather derivated - say the wish for a good mark, exam training, or the like. Well, for one thing I consider a defective text production fully as instructive as a sophisticated one. Conventions are never so conspicious as when violated. For another thing, most of us are - directly or indirectly - engaged in teaching young people home or foreign language command. Which is a good reason to study their special difficulties.

How differently the authors of text A and B try to cope with the conflicting demands of coherence can be seen from the diagrams of appendix 3-4. The numbered boxes represent speech acts corresponding to the text parts of appendix 1-2 bracketed by the same numbers.[8] And the arrows with single letters or letter combinations attached to them reflect different coherence types, the narrative dimension marked horizontally and the systematic one (more or less) vertically.[9] A list explaining the type abbreviations in such everyday terms that I use myself when teaching students can be found at the bottom of appendix 4.

Now consider the over-all structure of paper A. The author has arranged his topic systematically, taking up one aspect of the literary work after the other: genre (part 1-3), 'surface' plot (4-23), 'deep' stages (24-36), actant structure (37-46), characters (47-56), style (57-76 except 67-69), dating (sic!) (67-69), main themes (77-99).[10] The narrative string of Hans Andersen's story is only reflected coherently in connection with plot and first theme, cf. the embedded horizontal structures; whereas in the rest of the paper the fairy-tale events are torn apart and used almost singly as examples, points of reservation, etc. Undoubtedly following some scheme of analysis introduced by the teacher, the author of A has given priority to interpretation and evaluation at the expense of paraphrase.

Just the opposite with paper B. Except for an initial characterization of the protagonist (part 1-6), and a final indication of second theme (82-89), the author of this paper has taken over Andersen's narration as framework, first in full scale (7-71), then summarized (73-81). A personal contribution is the synthesizing beforehand (e.g. 27, 62) of some action sequences. Onto this paraphrase are then stuck - at intervals and normally coinciding with natural pauses - interrupting elements of interpretation, from simple statements to mere exegesis (such as 37-45). Without going into particulars I should call this choice of disposition partly responsible for the boring repeatedness of paper B.[11]

And now let me pass on to the expressions of coherence used in text A and B, in so far they serve to illustrate what might be called 'mainstream' conventions. Following Meyer (1975) I have distinguished in appendix 3-4 between thematizing, specific, vague, and no coherence marking, shown by doubleshafted, full singleshafted, broken singleshafted, and dotted arrow, respectively.[12] Each individual marker is underlined in appendix 1-2.[13]

Inside purely narrative strings (such as A 14-20, B 33-36, B 57-60, B 74-76) the closely related coherence types N (= next step) and EF (= effect) appear 'unmarked' ones that need no or just vague marking (and if so especially relativization, like A 16, or downgrading, like A 12, A 23). More specific marking (cf. B 8) or thematized coherence (cf. B 64) seem to reflect emphasis. The rest of the narrative types tend, on the contrary, to be marked more or less distinctly: T (= turn) by adversative particle (see A 20, B 78), L (= later step) by some time adverbial (see B 68).[14]

If instead we stick to purely systematic strings (such as A 39-42, A 91-98, B 16-22, B 49-53) a similar picture emerges. The closely related coherence types C (= concretion), E (= elaboration), and ID (= identification) all seem to be 'unmarked'. Relativization (like A 6) or downgrading (like B 5) are maximal signals. Whereas the other systematic types tend to claim a more or less distinct marking - such as quotation marks (cf. A 60), adversative particle in modifying (= R) function (cf. A 41), the monotonous thematizing formulae for IT (= interpretation) in paper B, etc. Non-marked IT (like A 89) or vaguely marked IM (= implication) (like A 54) are, at any rate, liable to cause decoding troubles.[15]

Finally a third set of 'marked' vs. 'unmarked' coherence types appear in the (systematic) branchings of my diagrams (see especially appendix 3). Coherence type A (= aspect) is so vaguely marked that you may prefer to speak about formal and semantic clues, that is to say by means of paragraph and thematic parallelism, respectively. The latter term is to cover the author's circling - explicitly as well as implicitly - around the notion of 'fairy-tale' in the paragraph starts of paper A (cf. A 4,24,37,47,57,67,70,77, all of them 'heads' of the major boxes of appendix 3; further, maybe by overdoing, A 31,62). As opposed to type A, we have the types P (= parallel) and OP (= opposition) with more or less distinct markers. The non-marked P of A 91 seems, at least to me, a mistake.[16]

The three above subsystems of coherence marking might be expected to get into conflict in case of coherence transition. The demands for specific marking would seem to be intensified at the points of dimension contact so as to counteract ambiguity. But no such convention can be traced in text A and B: the coherence types N, EF, C, E, ID, and A are marked just as vaguely in mixed contexts as in the pure ones considered up till now. I can see two reasons for that.

First, the coherence types in branching should not be distinguished from the other systematic ones. When appearing in non-branching structures (such as A 20-22 or B 83ff) P and OP show unchanged expressions, and so do the types C, E, EG (= example), and EX (= exception) when - conversely - engaged in branching (cf. A 48ff, B 2ff, A 58ff,

A 26ff). When you come down to it the crucial type A may even be considered a branching subtype of C, and no more.

So what is different with the branchings is not the presence of specific coherence types or changed marking conventions for single types, but rather the work of a general superimposed convention which you might call a principle of bracketing and put this way: The first member of a branching set should be marked the normal way for its coherence with its primary; the rest of the members should be so only indirectly, via normal marking of their paratactic relation to the preceding member(s). This principle is followed on two levels in A 47-56 and A 57-75. When exceptionally adding to the regular pattern a marker of coherence between second member of branching and primary, the author runs the risk of suggesting the start of a new - embedded - branching (cf. A 28: *yet*). Just as unsatisfying is omission of paratactic marker (see A 91).

The second reason why you can combine dimensions of coherence without intensified marking is the presence of semantic clues. For instance, a transition from narration to comment (as made over and over again in text B) will normally be reflected in a change from 'dynamic' to 'static' verb phrase - the latter notion covering such aspects as true state (e.g. B 17), habit (e.g. B 50), and perfect (e.g. B 61). Of course a transition 'back home' manifests itself reversely (cf. B 15-17, B 31-33, A 12f, and involving a hypothetical sort of 'state': B 25-27). Alternatively, reference to the poet or just some element attached to the act of production (cf. B 79) will suffice as stamp of systematic textualization.[17]

Another kind of transition pertaining especially to text B is that from abstract mention to concrete narration (such as B 27f, B 62ff - but also A 13ff, A 82ff). A current clue to this is the change in lexemic extension. Compare e.g. the sudden concretion as to action and elements in A 14 with the vague formulation of the preceding text part, or consider the whole to part relation between the two time adverbials of B 20-21. Again no intensified coherence marking is called for, and if present (cf. A 10: *as*) tends to falsely suggest a punctual elaboration (by A 10 alone) instead of a coming string of concretion.[18]

Let me stop here. After all, the observations made and principles sketched in this paper are meant as no more than incitements for further empirical studies on a broad front. And even if some of it may prove adequate on a broader scale, we shall certainly have to map a variety of subconventions according to shared horizon, register, genre, etc.

FOOTNOTES:

1. Cf. Grice (1975) and Habermas (1971). -- The so-called 'syntagmatic substitution' of Harweg (1968) et al., e.g. the reference from a pronoun to its antecedent, seems to me nothing but one special sort of semantic key.

2. As for the argumentative status of such 'truths' and related types of warrants, cf. Sørensen (1979) (with further references). --The culture specific character can be easily illustrated: Think of some village in an African state recently liberated from colonialism. In spite of difficulties they have succeeded in building a school and getting hold of a teacher. Now the children (and some of the adults) are taught reading and writing their native tongue, reckoning, history, and a few more things. Would they - children or adults - acknowledge (3) as a natural 'truth'? I'll say (3) is a product of welfare life.

3. Analogously he might use some 'break marker' if wanting to give (1a) and (1b) as separate informations (with separate sets of implication), but fearing - at the premature utterance of (1b) - that his father should erroneously connect the two informations: (6) (a) *We had no school to-day.* (b) *By the way, Bruce was really depressed/content.*

4. Cf. Ehlich and Rehbein (1972), Sandig (1973), Huth (1975) - just to mention a few early works from which I have profited myself.

5. Cf. Stierle (1975).

6. A previous (and more 'psychologically' worded) version of the bipartition will be forthcoming in Papers from the 5th Scandinavian Conference of Linguistics (at Lund, April 1979). A comparison is made to the sentence connecting relations of Meyer (1975).

7. The translations into English of text A and B are partly based on Andersen (1968), especially as to the direct quotations from the fairytale.

8. To my knowledge nobody has so far succeeded in defining a 'natural' level of simple or constituent speech acts. In the present paper I have found it convenient to base my partition of the text on the sentence and clause structure. Yet some parts have been allowed to grow 'over sentence level' (holding closely connected neighbour sentences such as B 11 and B 51), while other parts have been reduced 'under clause level' (cf. such down-gradings, discussed later on, as A 23 and B 5). As for the clauses, I have not considered noun clauses or restricting relative clauses parts in their own right, whereas the other types (including parenthetical relative clauses) are made separate parts.

9. Of course I have used every kind of clue - from lexico-syntactic over semantic to contextual ones - in categorizing the coherence types of text A and B. Yet, needless to say, I have come in doubt many a time. Just consider the P of B 9 and the EF of B 60: couldn't they just as well be reversed as to dimension, figuring as N and P, respectively? And you can find more complicated cases for yourself. The most important reinterpretation I have made from a previous version of appendix 3-4 concerns B 11-26. I had originally mapped this section as a set of OP-related boxes paratactically joined to B 9. The present arrangement is based upon a 'dynamic' interpretation of B 11, B 16-17, and B 23 (cf. note 17). -- When confronted with 'odd' connections I have as far as possible abstained from making reinterpretations (e.g. B 57 where you would expect L instead of N just as text A has it). In a few cases, however, I simply had to reinterpret, thereby accusing the author of disorder (e.g. A 72-76, B 2-6) or wrong expression (which will be exemplified below). -- By the way, all relations registered in appendix 3-4 come under the headings of semantic specification or (concerning CF) evidence. The other main categories of speech act relations established in Sørensen (1976) are not represented in the text type at issue.

10. Admittedly some of these 'chapters' are rather loosely organized (cf. the major boxes of appendix 3 with empty 'heads', that is A 24ff, A 57ff, and A 77ff). I take the position of a sympathetic reader, e.g. the author's teacher.

11. This last impression is further enhanced by the extensive use of long and stereotyped interpretation markers, whether common or (partly) private. The latter are marked in appendix 3 by a stroke across the arrow shaft (see e.g. B 6).

12. In practice you cannot make a sharp distinction between vague and specific coherence marking; you are rather faced with a continuum where you must feel your way. Yet this should be no source of worry here, since the most important conventions (to be illustrated below) seem to base themselves on specific vs. no marking. Vague marking may well appear in the nature of indirection when closer inspected.

13. I have included among the markers contrastive stress though the medium does not allow for registration of it. Once more I am the sympathetic teacher reconstructing the production process (including its likely oral elements).

14. In Gülich (1976) such time adverbials are reckoned among the 'episode markers'. -- As for non-marked T, in my opinion a flaw, cf. (outside a pure narrative context) A 82.

15. Quite another source of confusion is distance between an interpretation and the part(s) interpreted, cf. A 74-76 or B 3-6 (the latter simply causing laughter).

16. The author of B uses paragraph in two other functions: partly as something like an 'episode marker' (cf. note 14) introducing a new step

of the story (cf. B 23, B 57); and partly as a marker of extensive concretion or interpretation to come (cf. B 63, B 37).

17. The rather handy distinction of 'event' vs. (pure) 'state' is, unfortunately, blurred by the possibility of indirection, viz. presenting an event in its proper context through some motivation, effect, implication, or the like. In this version of my paper (cf. note 9) I have taken B 11, B 16-17, and B 23 to be indirect formulations, corresponding to these if directly worded: (B 11') *Der viser sig dog en hindring* .... = *However, there appears to be one obstacle* ...; (B 16'-17').... *at han sætter alt ind på at overvinde hindringen.* = ... *that he concentrates on overcoming the obstacle*; (B 23') *Dog dette får ikke lov til at ske upåagtet* = *But this is not allowed to pass off unheeded*. These readings might seem confirmed by B 62 where the author uses *betyder* = *means* instead of *medfører* = *leads to*.

18. A transition 'back home' from concrete narration to some mainstream of story (e.g. B 48f, B 66f) can hardly be established with any precision, owing to the fact that the final member of an embedded string will - at the time of its utterance - have somehow resumed its primary so that no 'gap' is felt in the story.

APPENDIX 1

Stil A:
⁰Analyse og fortolkning af "Den standhaftige Tinsoldat"⁰

¹"Den standhaftige Tinsoldat" er et eventyr, hvori der indgår en levendegørelse af døde ting.¹ ²Legetøjsfigurer udstyres med tankevirkomhed og andre menneskelige egenskaber,² ³af hvilken grund eventyret må regnes for en fantastik fortælling.³

⁴Eventyret tager sin begyndelse ved en børnefødselsdag,⁴ ⁵hvor en dreng får 25 tinsoldater forærende,⁵ ⁶hvor af den ene har en skavank.⁶ ⁷Denne tinsoldat er vor hovedperson eller helt om man vil,⁷ ⁸og han mangler et ben.⁸ ⁹Den følgende morgen bliver skæbnesvanger for tinsoldaten,⁹ ¹⁰idet han på uheldigste vis[er] falder ud af et vindue,¹⁰ ¹¹således at han nu er kommet bort fra sit trygge værelse.¹¹ ¹²Via gaden hvor han lander¹² ¹³får han en endnu ulykkeligere skæbne.¹³ ¹⁴To drenge sender ham i en papirsbåd ned af rendestenen.¹⁴ ¹⁵Herfra sejler han ind under et rendestensbræt,¹⁵ ¹⁶hvor båden forulykker¹⁶ ¹⁷og han sluges af en fisk.¹⁷ ¹⁸Denne fisk fanges og sælges¹⁸ ¹⁹og på denne måde kommer han tilbage til det selvsamme værelse som han kom fra.¹⁹ ²⁰Men ulykkeligvis kaster en dreng ham ind i [en] kakkelovnen²⁰ ²¹og her smelter han til et tinhjerte.²¹ ²²En papirsjomfru, som han i eventyrets første fase havde forelsket sig i blæses også ind i kakkelovnen²² ²³og efterlader kun en sortbrændt paillet.²³

²⁴Eventyrets 'første fase er i det store og hele præget af harmoni:²⁴ ²⁵barneglæde, nydelige slotte, en smuk papirsjomfru og tinsoldatens kærlighed til hende.²⁵ ²⁶Kun tinsoldatens manglende ben kan virke forstyrrende på harmonien,²⁶ ²⁷men H.C. Andersen undgår dette ved at lade tinsoldaten "stå så fast på sit ene, som de andre på deres to".²⁷ ²⁸Dog er en legetøjstrold i en snustobaksdåse også med til at bringe uro.²⁸ ²⁹Om aftenen forstyrres harmonien også tildels ved legetøjets levendegørelse,²⁹ ³⁰men her er forholdet mellem tinsoldaten og papirjomfruen uændret.³⁰

³¹I eventyrets 'anden fase, uden for værelset er situationen ændret totalt.³¹ ³²Forvirring, ængstelse og tragedie præger billedet,³² ³³og tinsoldaten føler at hans sidste time er kommet.³³

³⁴Da tinsoldaten så i den 'sidste fase kommer "hjem" igen, har‹vi› næsten samme situation som i første fase.³⁴ ³⁵Men da tinsoldaten og papirjomfruen ryger i kakkelovnen bliver situationen uholdbar.³⁵ ³⁶Historien munder så ud i noget nær en modsætning, nemlig tinhjertet og den sortbrændte paillet.³⁶

³⁷Legetøjet / personerne optræder med forskellige forhold til hinanden indbyrdes.³⁷ ³⁸Tinsoldaten skiller sig lidt ud fra mængden af kolleger alene ved sit manglende ben,³⁸ ³⁹men også ved hans kærlighed til jomfruen.³⁹ ⁴⁰Denne kærlighed, som til dels kan tilskrives at han tror at hun er i samme fysiske kondition som han selv (etbenet).⁴⁰ ⁴¹Tinsoldaten er dog klar over den sociale forskel mellem den fine

Paper A:
⁰Analysis and interpretation of "The Steadfast Tin-Soldier"⁰

¹"The Steadfast Tin-Soldier" is a fairy-tale including an animation of inanimate objects.¹ ²Toy figures are endowed with mental activity and other human characters,² ³<u>why</u> the fairy-tale must be considered a fancy story.³

⁴The fairy-tale commences at a child's birthday⁴ ⁵<u>where</u> a boy is given 25 tin-soldiers,⁵ ⁶one <u>of which</u> has got a disability.⁶ ⁷This tin-soldier is our protagonist or, if you like, our hero,⁷ ⁸<u>and</u> he lacks one leg.⁸

⁹<u>The following morning</u> proves fatal to the tin-soldier,⁹ ¹⁰<u>as</u> most unfortunately he falls out of a window,¹⁰ ¹¹<u>so that</u> he has now lost his safe room.¹¹ ¹²<u>Via</u> the street where he lands¹² ¹³he gets an even more unhappy fate.¹³ ¹⁴Two boys send him down the gutter on a paper boat.¹⁴ ¹⁵<u>From here</u> he sails under a gutter-boarding,¹⁵ ¹⁶<u>where</u> the boat is wrecked¹⁶ ¹⁷<u>and</u> he is swallowed by a fish.¹⁷ ¹⁸This fish gets caught and sold,¹⁸ ¹⁹<u>and thus</u> he returns to the very same room he came from.¹⁹ ²⁰<u>But</u> unfortunately a boy throws him into the stove,²⁰ ²¹<u>and here</u> he melts into a heart of tin.²¹ ²²A cardboard maiden, with whom he had fallen in love in first stage of the fairy-tale, is blown into the stove, <u>too</u>,²² ²³<u>and</u> nothing remains but a spangle burnt coal-black.²³

²⁴'First stage of the fairy-tale is very largely characterized by harmony:²⁴ ²⁵child's joy, nice castles, a pretty cardboard maiden, and the tin-soldier's love for her.²⁵ ²⁶<u>Only</u> the tin-soldier's lacking leg may seem to disturb the harmony,²⁶ ²⁷<u>but</u> Hans Andersen avoids this by making the tin-soldier "stand just as firm on his one leg as the others did on their two".²⁷ ²⁸<u>Yet</u> a toy goblin in a snuff-box is <u>also</u> a party to causing unrest.²⁸ ²⁹<u>In</u> the evening the harmony is <u>also</u> partly disturbed by animation of the toy,²⁹ ³⁰<u>but</u> here the relationship between the tin-soldier and the cardboard maiden remains unchanged.³⁰

³¹In the 'second stage of the fairy-tale, outside the room, the situation has been reversed completely.³¹ ³²Confusion, anxiety, and tragedy dominates the picture,³² ³³<u>and</u> the tin-soldier feels that his last hour has come.³³

³⁴When in the 'last stage the tin-soldier <u>then</u> returns "home" we have got almost the same situation as in stage one.³⁴ ³⁵<u>But</u> as the tin-soldier and the cardboard maiden get into the stove the situation turns precarious.³⁵ ³⁶<u>Then</u> the story ends up with something very close to a polarity, that is the tin heart and the coal-black spangle.³⁶

³⁷The toy / persons act in various relationships to each other mutually.³⁷ ³⁸The tin-soldier is a little different from the body of colleagues if only for his lacking leg,³⁸ ³⁹but <u>also</u> because of his love for the maiden.³⁹ ⁴⁰This love which can be partly ascribed to his belief that she is in the same physical condition as himself (one-legged).⁴⁰ ⁴¹<u>Yet</u> the tin-soldier fully realizes the social difference

jomfru og han, soldaten⁴¹ ⁴²og han ved hvad han må ‹kunne› byde hende for at [kunne] gøre hende til ‹sin› kone.⁴² ⁴³Om 'hun gengælder hans følelser kan ikke afgøres.⁴³
⁴⁴Som en [en] modsætning til ovennævnte relation står tinsoldatens forhold til trolden i snustobaksdåsen.⁴⁴ ⁴⁵Trolden truer ham og er muligvis impliceret i at han blæser ud af vinduet.⁴⁵ ⁴⁶Ligeledes fremgår det at [at] trolden må[tte] være skyld i at tinsoldaten blev kastet i ovnen.⁴⁶
⁴⁷I eventyret fremtræder det gode og det onde adsklit.⁴⁷ ⁴⁸Andersen udstyrer det onde med visse dårlige egenskaber og benytter mere eller mindre negative ord i sine beskrivelser af ting - legetøj / personer og dyr.⁴⁸ ⁴⁹Således er trolden lille og sort og har en truende attitude⁴⁹ ⁵⁰og repræsenterer dermed det onde.⁵⁰ ⁵¹Det samme gør en vandrotte⁵¹ ⁵²som Andersen har ladet virke skræmmende og magtfuld.⁵² ⁵³Pa'pirsjomfruen, derimod, står for det gode og skønne⁵³ ⁵⁴og der er brugt mange positive ord til beskrivelsen af hende.⁵⁴ ⁵⁵'Tinsoldaten er beskrevet i et nogenlunde neutralt ordvalg,⁵⁵ ⁵⁶men den brave holdning Andersen har givet ham bevirker nok de flestes sympati.⁵⁶
⁵⁷Andersens ordvalg og hele sprogbrug stemmer ganske godt overens med handlingen,⁵⁷ ⁵⁸f.eks. i starten af eventyret, hvor han beskriver tinsoldaterne.⁵⁸ ⁵⁹Til beskrivelsen benytter han sig af en fyndig og hurtigtlæselig skrivemåde:⁵⁹ ⁶⁰"Geværet holdt de i Armen, Ansigtet satte de lige ud; rød og blå, nok så dejlig var Uniformen".⁶⁰ ⁶¹Da det går på pa'pirjomfruen er beskrivelsen anderledes blid og let.⁶¹
⁶²Det sprog Andersen bruger i eventyret er sikkert normalt sprog, som det blev benyttet på hans tid.⁶² ⁶³Omend det vides at visse udtryk er blevet modereret i lidt senere udgaver,⁶³ ⁶⁴virker sproget tilpas dannet.⁶⁴ ⁶⁵Andersen er også til tider tvetydig og ynder at benytte at lade flere muligheder stå åbne til løsning af problemer i eventyret⁶⁵ ⁶⁶(ex: "Couleurerne vare rent gået af ham, om det var sket på rejsen eller det var af sorg kunne ingen sige‹")›.⁶⁶
⁶⁷Hvornår eventyret udspilles lader sig ikke tidsfæste nøjagtigt,⁶⁷ ⁶⁸men intet tyder dog på at eventyret ikke er samtidigt med H.C. Andersen,⁶⁸ ⁶⁹bortset dog selvfølgelig ‹fra› eventyrets begyndelse: "Der var engang."⁶⁹
⁷⁰Sproget er iøvrigt let tilgængeligt⁷⁰ ⁷¹og de få tilfælde af udbrud og direkte tale der forekommer er blot med til yderligere at give et stemningsbillede.⁷¹ ⁷²Man lægger mærke til at hverken papirjomfruen eller tinsoldaten siger en eneste replik i eventyret.⁷² ⁷³Dette får da også følger for tinsoldaten,⁷³ ⁷⁴som føler at det er under hans værdighed at råbe om hjælp når han er i uniform⁷⁴ ⁷⁵(situationen hvor pigen og drengen leder efter ham).⁷⁵
⁷⁶Den før omtalte lidt klodsede værdighed og standhaftighed kan fra Andersens side være et hib til militærets stivsindethed (og standhaftighed).⁷⁶
⁷⁷Et af de større temaer i eventyret omhandler afvigeren, den der er anderledes.⁷⁷ ⁷⁸Denne repræsenteres af tinsoldaten, som skiller sig ud fra mængden ved sit manglende ben.⁷⁸ ⁷⁹Det manglende ben får ham ikke i egne øjne til at føle sig helt anderledes.⁷⁹ ⁸⁰Han forsøger dog at opnå kontakt med ligestillede,⁸⁰ ⁸¹her som han tror, papirjomfruen.⁸¹

between the noble maiden and himself, the soldier,⁴¹ ⁴²<u>and</u> he knows what he must be able to offer her in order to make her his wife.⁴² ⁴³Whether '<u>she returns his feelings or not is anybody's guess</u>.⁴³

⁴⁴<u>As a contrast to</u> the relation above we have got the tin-soldier's relationship with the goblin in the snuff-box.⁴⁴ ⁴⁵The goblin threatens him and is possibly implicated in his blowing out of the window.⁴⁵ ⁴⁶<u>Likewise</u> it appears that the goblin must be guilty when the tin-soldier was thrown into the stove.⁴⁶

⁴⁷<u>In</u> this fairy-tale good and evil appear separate.⁴⁷ ⁴⁸Andersen provides evil with some bad qualities and uses more or less negative words in describing things, toy / persons, and animals.⁴⁸ ⁴⁹<u>For instance</u>, the goblin is little and black and shows a threatening attitude⁴⁹ ⁵⁰<u>and consequently</u> represents evil.⁵⁰ ⁵¹<u>So</u> does a water-rat,⁵¹ ⁵²<u>which</u> Andersen has made appear frightening and powerful.⁵² ⁵³The 'cardboard maiden, <u>on the contrary</u>, stands for good and beauty,⁵³ ⁵⁴<u>and</u> many positive words have been used to describe her.⁵⁴ ⁵⁵The 'tin-soldier is described in a rather neutral wording,⁵⁵ ⁵⁶<u>but</u> the brave conduct Andersen has provided him with will probably cause most people's sympathy.⁵⁶

⁵⁷Andersen's wording and whole style is fairly well suited to the story,⁵⁷ ⁵⁸<u>e.g.</u> in the start of the fairy-tale where he describes the tin-soldiers.⁵⁸ ⁵⁹In the description he makes use of a terse and readable style:⁵⁹ ⁶⁰"They carried rifles on their shoulders, they held their heads up and looked straight ahead. Their uniform was red and blue, very fine indeed."⁶⁰ ⁶¹When referring to the 'cardboard maiden the description is differently soft and light.⁶¹

⁶²The idiom used by Andersen in the fairy-tale is probably normal speech as used in his days.⁶² ⁶³<u>Even if</u> we know that some expressions have become moderated in more recent editions,⁶³ ⁶⁴the style seems suitably made.⁶⁴ ⁶⁵At times Andersen is ambiguous, too, and likes to profit by leaving open various possibilities of solving problems in the fairy-tale⁶⁵ ⁶⁶<u>(e.g.</u>: "His bright colours had completely gone - no one could say whether this had happened on his travels or whether it was the result of his sorrow.<u>")</u>⁶⁶

⁶⁷It cannot be dated exactly when the fairy-tale took place,⁶⁷ ⁶⁸<u>but</u> nothing seems to show, <u>however</u>, that the fairy-tale should not be contemporary with Hans Andersen,⁶⁸ ⁶⁹of course <u>with exception of</u> the beginning of the fairy-tale: "There were once."⁶⁹

⁷⁰The diction is rather easily understood, <u>by the way</u>,⁷⁰ ⁷¹<u>and</u> the few samples of exclamation and direct speech just help to further produce a lyrical picture.⁷¹ ⁷²One observes that neither the cardboard maiden nor the tin-soldier makes a single remark through the fairy-tale.⁷² ⁷³<u>In fact</u>, this causes troubles for the tin-soldier,⁷³ ⁷⁴<u>who</u> feels it to be beneath him to cry out for help when in uniform⁷⁴ ⁷⁵<u>(the situation where the maid and the boy are looking for him)</u>.⁷⁵

⁷⁶The somewhat clumsy dignity and steadfastness just mentioned may be a dig on Andersen's part at the military stubbornness (and steadfastness).⁷⁶

⁷⁷One main theme of the fairy-tale treats the deviationist, the one who is different.⁷⁷ ⁷⁸This one is represented by the tin-soldier

[82]Kontakten synes ikke at etableres.[82] [83]Det dårlige og onde kommer ind i billedet i form af trolden,[83] [84]og tinsoldaten skubbes helt ud af den trygge tilværelse[84] [85]- jfr. han falder ud af vinduet.[85] [86]Tilværelsen forværres for tinsoldaten og han har mindre og mindre styr over tilværelsen,[86] [87]og langsomt må han til sidst bukke under[87] [88]- jfr. papirbåden synker,[88] [89]hans grundlag opløses under ham.[89] [90]Hans tilbagevenden til den trygge tilværelse får en brat ende da han kastes i kakkelovnen.[90] [91]Hans og papirjomfruens skæbne som henholdsvis tinhjerte og en sortbrændt paillet kan tolkes som hans kærlighed der aldrig svigtede.[91] [92]Han var den skramlede tinsoldat af lavere herkomst[92] [93]og viste sig dog at være af større værdi inderst inde,[93] [94]i modsætning til den fine papirsjomfru fra slottet,[94] [95]som blot [blot] havde en nydelig facade at skjule sig bag.[95] [96]Under denne facade viste der sig ikke noget positivt.[96] [97]'Hun gengældte ikke hans kærlighed,[97] [98]mens 'hans var opretholdt.[98] [99]Og endelig var det måske [var det] hendes straf for dette at hun blæstes ind i kakkelovnen.[99]

Signs: [ ] = cancelled by VS
         ‹ › = added by VS
         x x = text part no x
               (corresponding to a speech act, cf note 8)
         ___ = coherence marker
               (esp: ' = contrastive stress,
                     x̄ = thematic parallelism)

who differs from the multitude by his lacking leg.⁷⁸ ⁷⁹The lacking leg does not make him feel completely different in his own opinion.⁷⁹ ⁸⁰Yet he tries to get in touch with equals,⁸⁰ ⁸¹<u>in this case</u> the cardboard maiden, for all he knows.⁸¹ ⁸²No contact seems to become established.⁸² ⁸³Bad and evil gets into the picture in the shape of the goblin,⁸³ ⁸⁴<u>and</u> the tin-soldier is pushed entirely out from his secure existence⁸⁴ <u>⁸⁵-</u> <u>cf.</u> he falls out of the window.⁸⁵ ⁸⁶The existence deteriorates for the tin-soldier, and he has ever less control of the existence,⁸⁶ ⁸⁷<u>and</u> slowly he must go under at last⁸⁷ ⁸⁸- <u>cf.</u> the paper boat goes down,<u>⁸⁸</u> ⁸⁹his foundation breaks up.⁸⁹ ⁹⁰His return to the secure existence comes to an abrupt end when he is thrown into the stove.⁹⁰ ⁹¹His fate and the cardboard maiden's, as tin heart and a coal-black spangle, respectively, can be interpreted as his love that never failed.⁹¹ ⁹²He was the scratched tin-soldier of humble birth⁹² ⁹³<u>and yet</u> proved to be of greater value in his heart,⁹³ ⁹⁴<u>as opposed to</u> the noble cardboard maiden from the castle,⁹⁴ ⁹⁵<u>who just</u> had a pretty facade to hide behind.⁹⁵ ⁹⁶Beneath this facade nothing positive appeared.⁹⁶ ⁹⁷'She did not return his love,⁹⁷ ⁹⁸<u>whereas</u> 'his was preserved.⁹⁸ ⁹⁹<u>And finally</u>, to be blown into the stove might be her punishment for this.⁹⁹

Note: All idiomatic errors have been preserved in the translation.

APPENDIX 2

Stil B:
⁰Den standhaftige Tinsoldat.⁰

¹Hovedpersonen i denne tekst er tinsoldaten.¹ ²Soldaten lever i ret trange kår,² ³hvilket er symboliseret ved, at han lever i en æske sammen med 24 andre tinsoldater.³ ⁴Ydermere er denne tinsoldat ramt af en "grum" skæbne⁴ ⁵ved kun at have et ben.⁵ ⁶Det er klart, at soldaten kommer fra samfundets nedre lag.⁶
⁷Da tinsoldaten kommer ud af æsken, opdager han slottet og danserinden (jomfruen).⁷ ⁸Han bliver straks forelsket i hende⁸ ⁹og mener, at hun må være den rette kone for ham.⁹ ¹⁰Han tror nemlig, at hun kun har et ben.¹⁰ ¹¹Der er dog en hindring for kærligheden. Hindringen er klasseforskellen.¹¹
¹²Sol'daten kommer fra en æske,¹² ¹³mens danser'inden lever i et slot.¹³ ¹⁴H.C. Andersen viser her, at klasseforskellen har meget stor betydning for sexualiteten og dens udfoldelse.¹⁴ ¹⁵Soldaten kan ikke åbenlys‹t› erklære sin kærlighed overfor danserinden.¹⁵
¹⁶Hans kærlighed er dog så stor og ægte,¹⁶ ¹⁷at han vil overvinde hindringen.¹⁷ ¹⁸Han er klar over hindringen,¹⁸ ¹⁹men som han siger: "Dog må jeg se at gøre bekendtskab."¹⁹
²⁰Det er klart, at her vil soldaten bryde normerne.²⁰ ²¹Han vil sætte sig op mod det bestående.²¹ ²²Dette kan han gøre fordi hans kærlighed er ægte.²²
²³Dog kan dette ikke ske upåagtet.²³ ²⁴Soldaten må ikke gøre oprør mod det bestående eller bryde normerne.²⁴ ²⁵Sker det,²⁵ ²⁶vil han blive straffet.²⁶
²⁷Dette sker i løbet af natten.²⁷ ²⁸Da natten falder på, bliver alt legetøj levende,²⁸ ²⁹og de foretager sig ting, som de ikke gør om dagen.²⁹ ³⁰Det er kalrt, at nattens "udskejelser" skal symbolisere, at når mørket falder på, kommer drifterne frem.³⁰ ³¹Om dagen undertrykkes drifterne,³¹ ³²men om natten kommer de frem.³²
³³Midt i nattens udskejelser dukker der pludselig en trold op.³³ ³⁴Denne siger til tinsoldaten, at han skal holde øjnene ved sig selv.³⁴ ³⁵Da tinsoldaten ikke svarer,³⁵ ³⁶siger trolden: "Ja, bi til imorgen."³⁶
³⁷Det er klart, at trolden skal symbolisere en øvrighed eller formynder.³⁷ ³⁸Soldaten bryder normerne,³⁸ ³⁹og det må han ikke.³⁹ ⁴⁰Trolden advarer ham,⁴⁰ ⁴¹men da soldaten ikke adlyder,⁴¹ ⁴²kommer straffen.⁴² ⁴³Soldatens kærlighed til danserinden er i strid med samfundets normer,⁴³ ⁴⁴og det kan ikke tolereres.⁴⁴ ⁴⁵Soldaten skal fortrænge sin seksualitet.⁴⁵
⁴⁶Næste dag kommer straffen.⁴⁶ ⁴⁷Tinsoldaten bliver blæst ud af vinduet og falder ned på gaden.⁴⁷ ⁴⁸Her kommer han ud for mange begivenheder.⁴⁸
⁴⁹Han lader sig dog ikke kue.⁴⁹ ⁵⁰Lige meget hvor farlig og spændt hans situation er, fastholder han sin kærlighed til

Paper B:
^{0}The steadfast Tin-soldier.^{0}

^{1}The protagonist of this text is the tin-soldier.^{1} ^{2}The soldier lives in rather straitened circumstances,^{2} ^{3}<u>which is symbolized by</u> his living together in a box with 24 other tin-soldiers.^{3} ^{4}<u>Furthermore</u> this tin-soldier has been overtaken by a "cruel" fate^4 ^{5}<u>having</u> got only one leg.^{5} ^{6}<u>It is obvious that</u> the soldier comes from the lower classes.^{6}

^{7}<u>As the tin-soldier comes out from the box</u> he sees the castle and the dancer (the maiden).^{7} ^{8}He falls in love with her <u>at once</u>^{8} ^{9}<u>and</u> thinks that she must be the right wife for him.^{9} ^{10}<u>For</u> he believes that she has got only one leg.^{10} ^{11}There is one obstacle to his love, <u>however</u>. That is the class barrier.^{11}

^{12}The 'soldier comes from a box,^{12} ^{13}<u>while</u> the 'dancer lives in a castle.^{13} ^{14}<u>Hans Andersen shows by this that</u> the class barrier is of great importance for sexuality and its development.^{14} ^{15}The soldier cannot openly make a declaration of his love to the dancer.^{15}

^{16}<u>However,</u> his love is <u>so</u> grand and true^{16} ^{17}<u>that</u> he wants to overcome the obstacle.^{17} ^{18}He fully realizes the obstacle,^{18} ^{19}<u>yet</u> quoting him: "But I can try to make her acquaintance."^{19}

^{20}<u>It is obvious that</u> here the soldier wants to break the norms.^{20} ^{21}He wants to challenge the established order.^{21} ^{22}He can do so because his love is true.^{22}

^{23}<u>But</u> this cannot pass off unheeded.^{23} ^{24}The soldier must not rebel against the established order or break the norms.^{24} ^{25}<u>If</u> that should happen^{25} ^{26}he will be punished.^{26}

^{27}So it occurs <u>during the night</u>.^{27} ^{28}At night-fall all toy come to life,^{28} ^{29}<u>and</u> they do things they do not do by day.^{29} ^{30}<u>It is obvious that</u> the nightly "excesses" <u>are meant to symbolize that</u> at nightfall the sexual instincts break through.^{30} ^{31}At day the sexual instincts are suppressed,^{31} ^{32}<u>but</u> at night they break through.^{32}

^{33}<u>In the middle of</u> the nightly excesses a goblin suddenly appears.^{33} ^{34}This one tells the tin-soldier to keep his eyes to himself.^{34} ^{35}<u>As</u> the tin-soldier does not respond^{35} ^{36}the goblin says: "Just you wait till to-morrow!"^{36}

^{37}<u>It is obvious that</u> the goblin <u>is meant to stand for</u> some public authorities or some guardian.^{37} ^{38}The soldier breaks the norms,^{38} ^{39}<u>and</u> he is not allowed to do so.^{39} ^{40}The goblin warns him,^{40} ^{41}<u>yet as</u> the soldier does not obey^{41} ^{42}punishment lies ahead.^{42} ^{43}The soldier's love for the dancer is contrary to social norms,^{43} ^{44}<u>and</u> that carnot be tolerated.^{44} ^{45}The soldier is under an obligation to suppress his sexuality.^{45}

^{46}<u>The following day</u> discloses the punishment.^{46} ^{47}The tin-soldier is blown out of the window and falls down onto the street.^{47} ^{48}<u>Here</u> he meets with a lot of events.^{48}

danserinden.50 51Det er klart, at H.C. Andersen vil vise, at intet kan knække den rene og ægte kærlighed. Det er det, tinsoldaten er et symbol på.51
    52Stående i papirbåden under rendestensbrættet tænker han: "Ak sad dog den lille jomfru her i båden, så måtte her gerne være engang så mørkt endnu!".52 53Det er her tydeligt, at han ikke vil fortrænge sin seksualitet.53
    54Rejsen, som han kommer ud for, er straffen.54 55Han skal fortrænge sin kærlighed til danserinden. Dette er rejsens formål.55 56Det lykkedes dog ikke at få soldaten til at fortrænge sin sexualitet.56
    57Han kommer tilbage til legeværelset igen,57 58hvor danserinden stadig er.58 59Igen kan han ikke få øjnene fra hende,59 60og han elsker hende stadig lige højt.60 61Det er altså ikke lykkedes at få ham til at fortrænge sin sexualitet.61 62Dette betyder tinsoldatens undergang.62
    63Han har endnu engang sat sig op imod normerne.63 64Det resulterer i, at han bliver kastet ind i kakkelovnen,64 65hvor han begynder at smelte.65
    66Danserinden blæses ind i kakkelovnen,66 67hvor hun brændes op.67 68Det eneste, der er tilbage af hende den følgende dag er pailletten, der er brændt kulsort.68 69Tinsoldaten er derimod smeltet om til et tinhjerte.69 70Dette skal igen vise, at tinsoldaten‹s› kærlighed og følelser er ægte.70 71Intet, selv ikke døden, kan kue kærligheden.71

72Konklusion72

    73Det er klart, at et af de centrale temaer i denne tekst er sexualiteten og fortrængningen af samme.73 74Tinsoldaten elsker danserinden til trods for alle barrierer.74 75Dette kan dog ikke tolereres,75 76og efter forgæves at have prøvet på at få soldaten til at fortrænge sin sexualitet,76 77udslettes han.77 78Hans følelser kan dog ikke udslettes,78 79hvilket er symboliseret i tinhjertet.79
    80Gennem hele historien fremhæver H.C. Andersen tinsoldatens ægte og rene følelser.80 81Det er dette, der gør tinsoldaten til noget særligt.81
    82Et 'andet tema er også forholdet mellem "det fine" - overklassen og underklassen.82 83Danser'inden lever i fine og smukke omgivelser,83 84men det eneste der er tilbage af hende i kakkelovnen er den kulsorte paillet.84 85'Tinsoldaten kommer fra de nedre lag,85 86men er i besiddelse af rene og ægte følelser,86 87og han ender som et tinhjerte.87 88Det er tydeligt, at H.C. Andersen her siger, at det ydre har ingen betydning,88 89men det har derimod det indre.89

Signs: [ ] = cancelled by VS
       ‹ › = added by VS
       x x = text part no x
             (corresponding to a speech act, cf note 8)
       ___ = coherence marker
             (esp: ' = contrastive stress,
                   x̄ = thematic parallelism)

⁴⁹He is not cowed, <u>however</u>.⁴⁹ ⁵⁰No matter how dangerous and tense is this situation, he persists in his love for the dancer.⁵⁰ ⁵¹<u>It is obvious that Hans Andersen wants to demonstrate that</u> nothing can break pure and true love. <u>That is what the tin-soldier symbolizes.</u>⁵¹

⁵²Standing in the paper boat under the gutter-boarding he thinks: "Ah, if only the little maiden were here in the boat, it might be twice as dark for all I'd care!"⁵² ⁵³<u>Here it is obvious that</u> he does not intend to suppress his sexuality.⁵³

⁵⁴The travels that he meets with is the punishment.⁵⁴ ⁵⁵He is to suppress his love for the dancer. This is the purpose behind the travels.⁵⁵ ⁵⁶<u>Yet</u> the soldier could not be made suppress his sexuality.⁵⁶

⁵⁷He returns to the play-room,⁵⁷ ⁵⁸<u>where</u> the dancer still lives.⁵⁸ ⁵⁹Again he cannot take his eyes from her,⁵⁹ ⁶⁰<u>and</u> still he loves her just as dearly.⁶⁰ ⁶¹<u>Then</u> the soldier has not been made suppress his sexuality.⁶¹ ⁶²<u>This means</u> the ruin of the tin-soldier.⁶²

⁶³He has rebelled once more against the norms.⁶³ ⁶⁴<u>The result is that</u> he gets thrown into the stove,⁶⁴ ⁶⁵<u>where</u> he starts to melt down.⁶⁵ ⁶⁶The dancer is blown into the stove,⁶⁶ ⁶⁷<u>where</u> she is burnt up.⁶⁷ ⁶⁸The only trace of her that is left <u>on the following day</u> is the spangle burnt coal-black.⁶⁸ ⁶⁹The tin-soldier, <u>on the contrary</u>, has been remeltet into a tin heart.⁶⁹ ⁷⁰Again <u>this is meant to show that</u> the tin-soldier's love and feelings are true.⁷⁰ ⁷¹Nothing, not even death, can subdue love.⁷¹

⁷²Conclusion⁷²

⁷³<u>It is obvious that</u> one of the central themes of this text is sexuality and suppression of the same.⁷³ ⁷⁴The tin-soldier loves the dancer in spite of all barriers.⁷⁴ ⁷⁵This cannot be tolerated, <u>however</u>,⁷⁵ ⁷⁶<u>and after</u> having tried in vain to make the soldier suppress his sexuality⁷⁶ ⁷⁷he is destroyed.⁷⁷ ⁷⁸<u>Yet</u> his feelings cannot be destroyed,⁷⁸ ⁷⁹<u>which is symbolized by</u> the tin heart.⁷⁹

⁸⁰Throughout the story <u>Hans Andersen emphasizes</u> the true and pure feelings of the tin-soldier.⁸⁰ ⁸¹This is what makes the tin-soldier something exceptional.⁸¹

⁸²A'nother theme is <u>further</u> the relations between "the nobs" - the upper classes and the lower classes.⁸² ⁸³The 'dancer lives in a distinguished and beautiful environment,⁸³ ⁸⁴<u>but</u> the only trace of her left in the stove is the coal-black spangle.⁸⁴ ⁸⁵The 'tin-soldier comes from the lower classes,⁸⁵ ⁸⁶<u>but</u> is in possession of pure and true feelings,⁸⁶ ⁸⁷<u>and</u> he finally becomes a tin heart.⁸⁷ ⁸⁸<u>It is obvious that Hans Andersen here claims that</u> appearances are of no importance⁸⁸ ⁸⁹<u>but</u> so are, <u>on the contrary</u>, intrinsic values.⁸⁹

Note: All idiomatic errors have been preserved in the translation.

PRAGMATICS AND CAUSAL THEORETIC ASPECTS OF SEMANTICS

Dennis W. Stampe

If we are to understand the "limits of pragmatics", we shall have to understand where pragmatics ends and semantics begins.[1] We shall have to understand the nature of the relationships between the pragmatic properties of expressions and their semantic properties. This paper explores those relationships. How we understand these matters will be determined by the way we understand the respective sets of properties. One emerging theory of the basic semantic properties (reference and meaning) is the so-called "causal theory". I shall be particularly concerned with what this causal theory might reveal regarding the relationships between the semantic and the pragmatic properties of expressions.

Language attaches to reality at its *names*. (Or so philosophers have long been pleased to believe. Beyond that it is merely a matter of building constructions--sentences--out of names.) But what attaches a name to its object? What makes this name the name of that object, and not another one instead?

The simple answer is this: in the first place, the name of a thing in just what the thing is called. The name "attaches" to this object because it is what this object (but not the other one) is called. And that is just to say that it is what people call this object. That is all there is to it. Well, perhaps there is *something* more to it, for sometimes a thing is called the "wrong" name, by a name that doesn't belong to it. So perhaps there are some conventions that enter to it. But all these conventions do is determine what people are supposed or *expected* to call by what name. The attachment of name to object is still a matter of the object's being called by the name, and the name's being what the object is called.

People call this thing by that name, whether rightly or wrongly. Calling something something is an act that people perform, something we do. These acts that people perform, of calling this thing by that name, are what constitute the name's naming the thing.

On this resolutely simple view of the matter, a certain semantic property of an expression is bluntly *identified* with a certain pragmatic property of that expression. "Both" properties are relational ones. The semantic relation is one holding between two terms -- a piece of language (a name) and a piece of the world (an object) -- to wit, the relationship whereby the former is what the latter is called. This is designation. The pragmatic relation, with which this is identified, is a relationship holding between three terms -- between speakers, an object, and a name -- to wit, that relationship wherein the first call the second by the third. Assuming, as we may, that when a person calls a thing by a name, he is using the name to do something (perhaps to refer to it, perhaps to describe it), we may regard this three-termed relationship as a genuine pragmatic one. Thus it may appear that the semantic character of a name is nothing other than a certain pragmatic property of it, a property consisting in its being used in a certain way by its speakers.

That conclusion about designation may be joined with a parallel thesis about meaning: that the meaning of an expression is merely what people use the expression to mean.[2] Together these propositions suggest an hypothesis about the relationship between semantic theory and pragmatic theory. Perhaps semantic theory will turn out to be *reducible* to pragmatic theory, i.e. derivable from it, just as the thermodynamic theory is reducible to the kinematic theory of gases.[3] That classical instance of intertheoretical reduction involved the hypothesis that certain thermodynamic properties of gases are identical with certain kinematic properties of their constituents, e.g. that the temperature of a gas is nothing other than the mean kinetic energy of its constituent molecules. The derivation of the laws of thermodynamics from the kinematic laws demonstrated the identity of those properties, and indeed constituted the actual discovery of what temperature is. Perhaps in the future the same kind of reduction relationship can be shown to hold between semantics and pragmatics, and we shall in the same way discover what designation is and what meaning is. But we are far from being able to show that today. We are at the stage of conjecture.

But if this is the right way to conceive the matter, and I think it is, we should recognize that the reduction of semantic properties to pragmatic ones is *not* a thing that can be accomplished by conceptual analysis, however suggestive such analysis may be. As explanation is the business of theory, the question of the relation between semantics and pragmatics, and thus between semantic and pragmatic properties, is ultimately the question of the reducibility of one *theory* to another. On the basis of a priori analysis we may reasonably conjecture that semantic properties are nothing more than a subset of pragmatic properties. But such propositions will in the end be confirmed -- if they are to be confirmed -- by their role (as "bridge laws") in the derivation of the laws of general pragmatics from the laws of general semantics.

These identifications of semantic with pragmatic properties will serve the purpose only if the pragmatic properties *explain* the attribution of semantic ones. To show that the semantic property reduces to the pragmatic property we should have to show that a term is said to have the former *because* it has the latter, and not the other way around; it is in that sense that the pragmatic property must be the *basic* one.[4] (Thus we ascribe temperature to a gas because its constituent molecules are in a certain motion; it is not the other way round, that such a motion is attributed to its constituents because the gas is at that temperature.)

And in the case of these semantic properties one *can*, rightly or wrongly, look at it the other way round. That is, one can hold that the fact that people call a certain town "Urbino" (that pragmatic fact) is explained by the semantic fact that this town is named Urbino. Compare the question, What is that property of a road, whereby it leads to Rome? There is nothing more to it, someone might say, than that people use that road to get to Rome. Well, so they do, but that is surely because it leads to Rome. It is not, in *this* case, the other way around.

The property of leading to Rome is apparently not explained by and does not reduce to the property of being used to get to Rome. For one thing, the road would lead to Rome, whether anyone ever used it to get there or not. But would terms have the semantic properties they do, even if they did not have the pragmatic properties they do? Intuitively it seems clear that the name "Urbino" would not designate this town, if people never called it "Urbino". But again, intuition carries no ultimate weight in the matter. What does is the possibility of explaining one property in terms of the other. A tentative effort in that direction is finally offered here, but not, I fear, until the final turn in the argument.

With that prolegomenon, let us revert to our opening question, introduce the causal theory, and get to work. What is it for a name to designate an object? One answer is this: for a name to designate a given object is for that name and that object to stand in a certain *causal* relation to one another. A theory erected upon this thesis is called a "causal theory". If, as was ventured in the opening remarks, a name's designating an object is a matter of people using the name to designate the object, then the causal thesis might suggest that the causal relation in question is one whereby an object, a speaker's *utterance*, and a name stand in a certain causal relation: perhaps, e.g., that the object causes the speaker's utterance to contain the name.

For instance, consider the name "fire". On the one hand we have the set of sentences, and thus a set of actual or possible utterances, in which the name occurs, including the sentences "Fire!" , "Fire burns", "Fire?", etc. On the other hand we have a set of events or states of affairs in which the thing -- fire -- figures. One of these is the situation in which a fire starts in the kitchen, an event which may well cause the utterance of the sentence "Fire!". Another utterance of that same sentence might cause fire to be brought, where the speaker is issuing an order. And so on.[5] The designation of the object by the name is a matter of there being such a system of causal relationships between the two. So here is a picture from which one variety of causal theory might proceed.

One should want to know, from any causal theorist, exactly what the terms (the "relata") of this causal relation are supposed to be. (Versions of the causal theory may differ, one from another, in their responses to this question.) Presumably causal relations hold primarily between events or states of affairs, and derivatively between the objects that figure in those events or states of affairs. (Thus viruses cause colds, in that the invasion of tissues by viruses -- or some such *event* -- causes the occurrence of a cold.) The proposal that designation is a causal relation might, accordingly, be filled out as follows: on the one hand we have those events or states of affairs in which the name occurs -- i.e., *utterances* of sentences in which the name occurs; on the other hand, we have various events or states of affairs in which the object figures. And the proposal is that the designating of the object by the name consists in there being a certain kind of causal relation between the two, i.e. between the two kinds of events. The proposal therefore presupposes an important truism: that ordinarily or ideally our broadly indicative utterances are caused by the states of affairs about which we speak, and our imperative utterances cause, result in, the states of affairs we specify. (These causal connections are plainly contingent upon the functional properties of utterances, their illocutionary character and so forth; so the involution of pragmatic factors in semantic relations begins to emerge.)

Now the picture we have begun to sketch can already be seen to be rather unlike that associated with the best known rendition of the causal theory, namely that of Kripke.[6] Kripke's picture goes like this: a thing is given a name; that is, by baptism or other means, it is determined that the thing is to be called by a certain name. This name, then, is passed along from speaker to speaker, each one of whom intends to use it as did the person from whom he learned it. Generations later, the name will designate the thing originally given it, because its history traces back from link to link along that historical or causal chain to that thing. It is owing to that historical or causal linkage between object and name that the name names the object. In particular, it is owing to that fact, rather than because only that thing fits some description or concept that is associated with the name. (For, so the argument goes, there need be no relevant description or concept that fits the person at all, much less uniquely -- none, that is to say, which suffices to fix the reference of the name.)[7]

It may be observed that in Kripke's sketch, there is no suggestion of a connection between the causal account and *pragmatics* in particular (whereas the present essay is devoted to promoting such a connection). In Kripke's picture the salient causally-related events are events in which names are given, and subsequent events in the *acquisition* of the name by speakers, thus events in the entrance of the name into ideolects and dialects. His thesis is that the causal relations among such events determines what object or objects the name refers to. In the picture I have drawn, by contrast, the crucial thing is not the acquisition of the term, not its coming to exist in a certain person's language, but rather its occurrence in actual and possible speech acts. (Of course, the circumstances of a term's acquisition are not irrelevant, for they normally exercise causal influence upon its occurrence in utterances.)

That the account should not be framed in terms of acquisition is suggested by the following thought experiment. Suppose, contrary to the facts of the matter, that the lexicon of a language were innate, so that there was no such thing as the acquisition of terms by individual speakers. We do not, I think, want a theory on which innate terms would have no referents. Suppose for instance that the name "Mama" were innate, in the usual sense that upon adequate maturation any child will call its mother "Mama", and later still will refer to her thus. Surely such facts about the use of the term would suffice to make the term refer to her. It would not lack a referent just because there would be no causal chain linking the child's mother with the existence of the term in its language. The operative thing would seem to be instead the causal relations between his mother and his use of the term, i.e. its occurrences in the child's actual and possible utterances. That fits with our initial picture, which, in any case, is what I shall proceed to develop.

It should be pointed out that causal theories are by no means a new thing in philosophy. It has for instance been recognized traditionally that the difference between perception and imagination is a causal one. One who is dreaming of a fire and one who is seeing a fire might be in internally indistinguishable states of mind, the "contents" of their respective experiences being precisely the same. The difference between them lies in the fact that the experience of the seer is necessarily caused by a fire (and caused in a certain way) while that of the dreamer need not be caused by a fire (and if it is, it is caused in a different kind of way). The difference lies in their etiologies. This idea is ancient, well-worn, and indeed correct.[8] Consequently I think it is a good plan to begin with this paradigm of a causal theory -- the causal theory of perception -- and then to see whether a causal account of language doesn't take shape satisfactorily within the mold provided. I am inclined to think it does. And the shape that it will take will be one in which the occurrence of linguistic elements in speech, and thus pragmatic phenomena, are dominant features.

A sentient organism is a device that generates perceptual representations of the world. The things that it perceives are just those objects or states of affairs that cause these perceptual states to arise within it. Jim sees a cat: that is, some cat causes Jim to be in a certain perceptual -- visual -- state. Being in this state involves being presented with a visual representation (an image, if you like) of the situation before him. What Jim sees, the object of perception, is not that image or representation, of course, but the thing represented, presented, to him, *by* the representation. And the thing that is so represented is the thing that happens to *cause* that representation. Notice that it is a certain fact about the object itself -- the cat -- that determines that *it* is the thing being seen; it is the fact, namely, that it is the thing that caused the visual representation. It is not some other or independent fact about the representation, that makes the cat the thing that is seen. Compare a photograph of a cat, and the question, What makes this a photograph of this particular cat, Felix? It is a fact about Felix: namely that he caused the impression on the film, and not some other cat. It is not some other or independent fact about the representation itself, that determines what it is that is represented by it.

In particular, it is not the "content" of the representation (whether photograph or visual image) that determines that this object is the one represented. If the content of a visual state is roughly a matter of (or is specified by a specification just of) how it looks to the seer, then this is obviously so.[9] For one may be seeing a cat, namely the cat Felix, even though it looks to one exactly as if one were seeing a certain furry *hat*. And there, where that happens, it is obviously nothing in the content of the experience that determines that the thing being seen is a cat, still less that it is the particular cat Felix.

A related point concerns knowledge. A seer's knowledge, or ignorance, of what he is seeing has nothing whatever to do with the matter. He needn't know that he is seeing a cat, in order to see one, obviously -- any more that he needs to know that what he is stepping on is a cat in order to step on one.

We may draw a picture of speech analogous stroke for stroke to this picture of perception.

A speaker is a device generating (not perceptual but) linguistic representations of the world -- the percept*ible* representations called sentences. The things about which the speaker speaks are just those objects or states of affairs that *cause*[10] these representations, these statements, to be emitted. Jim speaks of a cat: that is, some cat causes Jim to utter a certain sentence, "The cat just croaked", thus to make the statement that the cat has croaked. Making this statement involves presenting a certain linguistic representation (a sentence) of the situation involving the cat. What Jim speaks of, the object of his remark, is what is represented therein as having croaked. Notice that it is a certain fact about the object itself -- the cat -- that determines that it is the thing being spoken of, being given this representation. It is not some other or independent fact about the sentence, or the linguistic representation, that makes it the object of the remark. What does do so is the fact that *it*, the cat, was what caused the utterance of the sentence.

There is the analogy. The meaning of an expression is to its referent as the content of an experience is to the object experienced. If that is true, if the meaning of an expression *is* just like the content of an experience, then we should never have thought that the meaning of an expression determines its reference. For no one thinks that the content of a perceptual experience determines what object it is that is being perceived. No one thinks that *just* the content of his visual state -- the way it looks to him in that state -- determines what cat he is seeing, or indeed that it is a cat that he is seeing and not just something that looks exactly like one. If the analogy is sound, neither will the meaning of an expression determine its referent. Of course, the meaning of the expression "the cat" does not determine what particular cat it is that is being referred to, as everyone agrees. But neither will it be the case that the *meaning* of the phrase determines that the thing being referred to is a cat at all, *any* cat -- if, that is, the analogy is complete.[11]

But it may be objected that the analogy completely breaks down on the crucial matter of *knowledge*. For it may seem that while one can see a cat without knowing what he is seeing, he cannot speak of a cat, without knowing what he is speaking of. After all, while perceptions obtrude upon our consciousness willy nilly (no matter what we do or do not know about their causes), speech is wholly different. For we *choose* to speak of this thing or that, and it seems impossible that we should make such choices without knowing what it is that we are intending to do, and therefore without knowing what it is that we are speaking of.

This is not just a matter of knowing what one is speaking of, but also a matter of one's knowledge of the character of the representation he produces. For one chooses to speak of a certain object, and must then choose the means whereby to speak of it. One has to choose his words, as well as his subject. In perception, by contrast, even where you do decide what you want to see, and aim your eyes accordingly, the way it will appear to you is determined entirely by the object.[12] So it is true, in that instance, that the content of the representation is determined by the object, and not the other way around. But that is just the difference. In speaking, you select the word to use from a repertoire of terms of which you have a certain command. You produce a token of an expression-type, knowing the representational capacities (i.e. the content) of expression of that type. Since the content or meaning of the expression determines that choice, its meaning *does* determine its referent, in a way that the content of a percept does not determine its object. So it may be said.

But I will defend the analogy. What *is* this knowledge that one must have of an object in order to refer to it? I grant that one must have it. But what does it amount to? This paper opened with the thought that for a name to refer to an object is just for that name to be what people call that object. The property of the object, whereby it is referred to by the name, is just: that of being referred to by the name. The property of the name whereby it refers to the object is just: that of being used to refer to the object. Now suppose that one knows, regarding the name, that it has that property. He will *therein* know what the thing is to which the name refers. And that is all he needs to know in order to refer to that object.

Isn't that circular? No. I am not here offering an analysis of referring, by circular employment of the idea of referring. I am discussing what one must *know*, in order to refer to an object with a term. I say it is enough that he knows, regarding the object, just that it is the thing that is called by that name, or indeed that he *then* calls it by that name. There is no circularity in that. So far as the analysis of referring goes, *that*, according to the causal theory, will *not* be given in terms of what is known about the term on the one side and the object on the other. The term's referring to the object does not consist in the identity of those two sets of properties -- the ones "known in" (contained in) the term and those possessed by the object. According to the causal theory, again, the term's referring to the object consists instead in the existence of certain causal connections between actual and possible utterances containing the term, and actual and possible states of affairs involving the object. What we do or must know about the object or term is ancillary to the existence of that causal connection.

And there is, on second thought, something analogous to that bit of knowledge (sc., that the thing I am referring to is the thing I am now calling "such and such") in perceiving too. For if I know that I am seeing something I know this much about it: it is the thing that now appears to me in such and such a way. So the parallel holds up rather well.

One must know who or what it is he is speaking of. *Knowing who* (what, where, etc.) is a notoriously difficult concept, pliable to the point of promiscuity. It seems on the one hand as if virtually anything and everything must be known about a person in order to know -- really know -- who that person is.[13] Then again, it may seem as if any little scrap of knowledge will do, regardless how trivial. In view of this, it seems reasonable to regard knowing-what sentences as having an indexical element, in their analysis, pinning their truth conditions to some purpose that is relevant in a given context in which someone is said to know or not know who someone is. (Lycan and Boër have worked out a view of this kind in full detail.)[14] But for any bit of knowledge about a person it is probably true that there is *some* purpose, such that that bit of knowledge is sufficient to that purpose, and thus for knowing who the person is. This may explain why it may seem as if knowing who someone is requires knowing virtually *everything* about him.

Now consider the application of this account of "knowing wh." to the principle in question -- that a speaker is semantically competent with respect to a name only if the speaker knows who or what that name is the name of. Whether one does or does not know this will turn on the "relevant purpose in the context". The context is one in which we are concerned merely with the speaker's competence with respect to the *term*. Presumably, therefore, the relevant purpose or purposes are those for which the term is used. That purpose is presumably to make reference to the thing that the name names. If so, then all one needs to know, in order to "know who or what the name names" is to know some fact about the thing the knowledge of which is sufficient for that purpose -- i.e. for making references to that thing. And what *does* one need to know to do that? It is enough, surely, to know what it is called. If the purpose in question is that of referring to some person, it is enough, for that, that you know what to call that person. Indeed, that seems to be *the very thing* you need to know.

If this is correct, then this condition on competence regarding the name "Aristotle", say, requires no more than that one know, regarding Aristotle, that he is called "Aristotle". You do not need to know anything else about him -- that he was a philosopher, or any thing of the sort. That this in fact *suffices* for referential competence is indicated by the fact that knowing just that much, one can quite intelligibly say "I have no idea who or what Aristotle was", and be making competent reference to Aristotle, and saying that you do not know who he was. (You need not be referring just to the *name* "Aristotle".)[15]

Of course names have functions other than that of making reference, and we would have to see whether they too require no more knowledge of their designata than that are designated by that term. In particular names are used to say who someone is, or what something is -- in a descriptive or classificatory role, as well as a referring role. Consider "That is a tiger". Anyone who has command of the common name "tiger" understands what is being predicated of the thing referred to; he understands it to predicate the property of being a tiger to that thing.

What property is that? We may hope to discover it by looking back to the referential use, and to that one property of tigers which anyone competent with respect to that use of "tiger" must know tigers to have -- i.e. that of being things of the kind called "tigers". When I say "That is a tiger", then, all I need know is that that is a thing of the kind that is called a "tiger". That will suffice for me to have predicated, of the thing, the property of being a tiger. I need not know or believe or have any idea that a tiger is a big yellow and black striped feline. I need have no more idea what a tiger is than just, the kind of thing that is called a "tiger". (I need not have any "stereotype" of a tiger either.)[16]

It is easy to get confused here, and to think that the property being attributed to this thing, when I say it is a tiger, is a linguistic property. But it is not. I am not saying of it that it is the kind of thing called a "tiger". I am saying that it is a tiger. Being a tiger is not a linguistic property, it is a biological one. But this biological property may perfectly well be described, and represented, and known, in all sorts of ways: as Hilary Putnam's favorite property; or as the property of being the sort of thing that is called a tiger.

Of course tigers might not have been called "tigers". So the property of being a tiger might not have been identical with the property of being the sort of thing that is called a "tiger". So the knowledge required of that property for mastery of the predicate "is a tiger", is knowledge merely of an *accidental* property of the property of being a tiger. *But that is precisely what is ideal about it*. We don't know what is essential to being a tiger, but we can know, easily enough, that it is being the kind of thing that is called a "tiger". And anyone who has command of the term does know that much.

What we gain, when we learn a language, is a marvellously *facile* device for making representations of things, even in ignorance of the nature of the things of which we speak. So long as there merely is something that a thing is called, and we know what it is that it is called, then we may blithely represent the thing as: the thing so called. (That is what we do when we refer to it by that name.) And that determines a property that may be represented with equal ease, as: the property of being the kind of thing so called. With that we have the wherewithall to predicate properties of things, by uttering some names in a row: "Felix is a cat". This utterance constitutes a presentation of a thing, to wit the one called "Felix", and a property, to wit the one of being the sort of thing that is called a "cat". That is, it constitutes a presentation of this thing and that property provided that the utterance of "Felix" is caused in a certain way by the thing, and that of the utterance of "cat" is caused in a certain sort of way by that property. (This is just slightly simplified.) And it constitutes a representation of the thing *as having* the property, provided the causal history of their joint occurrence in the complex utterance event "Felix *is a* cat" is of the appropriate sort.

This causal process is of course enormously complicated; and it must meet certain conditions before it will be true to describe this utterance as involving the speaker's "referring" to the thing and "saying" of it that it has that property, and before it will be true to say that the whole utterance is the utterance of something that has a "meaning". But the fundamental facts lie in this skeleton, that the utterance is some kind of representation, and causally linked, through sets of intentions, caused by certain beliefs, beliefs about this utterance itself and other utterances too. This causal process involves, certainly, the speaker's choosing his words, thus forming certain intentions, on the basis of such knowledge as he has of the terms on the one hand and the objects on the other. But notwithstanding this intervention of the will, and the knowledge that it requires, the process whereby an object gets spoken of is very like the process whereby an object gets seen. For if the object spoken of is determined by the speaker's intention to speak of it, thus to utter the thing it is called, what determines that that intention is to speak of *it*, is the causal relation between that object and that intention. It is *not* determined *by* the knowledge that is ancillary to the formation of those intentions. It is not determined, as it were, from *within* and by the content of the term, no more than what we are seeing is determined from within us, by the content of the percept. So much, then, for the knowledge of and intentions regarding the object. The speaker must have such knowledge of the object as to know, of it, that it is called a certain thing; and he must know, of the thing that it is called, that it is what that object is called.

But now, on this other side of the coin, what determines that the thing, the name, he elects to utter is in fact what the object is called? What property of the term "tiger" are we talking about when we speak of its "being what tigers are called"? What is the property of the name "Felix" of *being what Felix is called*? Is it, in particular, a semantic or a pragmatic property of the name?

If it is a semantic property of some kind, it is not, I am sure, what is correctly called "the meaning" of the term. It would not be true to say, that the meaning of the term "tiger" is: *what is called a "tiger"*. Of course proper names are not said to have meaning, and I know of no good reason to say that common names have meaning either. ("Having meaning" is a very particular kind of semantic property belonging only, I think, to constructions. But I will not pursue that here.)

However, it may be said to be a semantic property of some more general kind. For instance, the property of being what tigers are called might be identified with the property of having a certain *sense*. And this is perhaps harmless, and even true, if "sense" is taken in Frege's minimal sense, of that whereby a term constitutes what he calls a "mode of presentation". [17] But while we may cautiously accept this, we have learned from Putnam and Kripke what it can*not* mean. The mode of presentation need *not* consist in some set of properties that are necessary and sufficient for the object's being what it is, where those properties *exclude* the linguistic properties of the object -- such as the very property in question, of being what is called by that name. The mode of presentation which a name constitutes is just, the way the object is presented by being called by the name. And the way in which the *name* "Felix" presents the cat Felix, is essentially *just as* the thing called "Felix". Or so I have been saying. If that is accepted as a semantic property, then the name's property of being what Felix is called just is the property of constituting the way in which Felix is presented -- i.e., as the thing called "Felix".

Now if that is a semantic property, it is, I submit, also and equally a *pragmatic* property of the term. For being what something is called is the same thing as being what people call something. Since calling something something is an act that people perform, the property of being what people call something qualifies as a pragmatic property. And if our general picture of the matter is even roughly right, we may also say that this property is a *causal* property of the term.

By the "causal properties" of something, I mean its power to cause certain effects, under certain conditions -- its "active powers", but also (in a Hobbesian phrase) its "passive powers" -- i.e. its being such as to result from certain causes. (Ice, for instance, can cause the temperature of an ambient substance to fall; and ice is such as to result from the cooling of water.) Consider the term "tiger". Its causal properties, its "passive powers", will include its being such as to *occur* -- i.e. to be uttered -- as the result of certain causes.

These causes include states of affairs in which tigers figure.

The term "tiger" has a propensity to be caused to occur in the context of certain utterances, by states of affairs in which tigers figure. That property, of the term "tiger", is I suggest nothing other than the pragmatic property the term has, of being used by speakers to make references to tigers.

The prospects of the causal theory depend on the success with which we specify the causal relationship which holds between term and object (or percept and object), by virtue of which the object is the one the term refers to (or the object is the one that is *seen*). For it is a fiction, of course, that there is such a thing as *the* cause of the percept or of the utterance in which the term figures. There are instead indefinitely many events, and objects, in its causal history. This fact creates a general problem for the treatment of intentional states via any plausible theory of representation, such as causal theory.[18]

To illustrate: the visual representation of a cat (cf. a photograph of a cat) constitutes a representation not just of the cat, but of the pattern of radiation entering the eyeball, the real image on the retina, the pattern of neutral excitation thereby aroused. All these things are causes of the percept, and the percept, which consequently contains information about each of them, constitutes a representation of each of them. (And yet it is the cat that is being seen, not these other things. The causal theory of perception must explain why this is so.)

Similarly the utterance, "The cat is on the mat" is causally related to, and contains information regarding indefinitely many states of affairs involved in causing the utterance utterance of the sentence -- including, *inter alia*, the movements of the speaker's articulatory apparatus, the neutral events that cause those movements, the intentions that cause those movements, the beliefs that cause those intentions, and perhaps the perceptions that cause those beliefs. Everything in that complex causal chain is represented by the utterance of the sentence "The cat is on the mat". Information regarding each of those events is present in the utterance. (It is there, no matter whether we have the capacity or desire to gather that information from the utterance, or not.) And yet there is one paticular state of affairs, one particular set of objects, among all these, that constitutes the *proper* object, so to speak, of the utterance, and of the sentence uttered; there is one particular state of affairs (the cat's being on the mat), and one particular set of objects (the cat, the mat) that pertains to the semantic properties of the sentence. The causal theory must specify the properties of the causal relation which makes it the case that it is that state of affairs (and not the others) that satisfies the truth condition of the sentence, and that objects of that set are the referents of the terms of the sentence.

Now it is the pragmatic aspect of this project on which we are here trying to focus. We may begin by observing that from the utterance of that sentence various bits of *pragmatic* information are made available to us -- information about the presuppositions, implications and illocutionary force of the utterance; information regarding various things expressed by the utterance, but not asserted. We come by the information that the speaker has certain intentions (e.g., that we should think that the cat is on the mat) and beliefs (e.g., the belief that the cat is on the mat, the belief that the whereabouts of the cat is of some conversational pertinence, etc).

This information is the stuff of pragmatics. It is available to the hearer of course just insofar as the hearer is capable of understanding the utterance -- that is, of understanding that event, in the way that the occurrence of events *are* understood, through their *causes*. Pragmatic information -- information about what a speaker is doing or trying to do by uttering a certain sentence -- is available to the hearer only through the causal inferences that he may make from the occurrence of the utterance. If he can infer that the utterance was caused by a certain belief on the part of the speaker, then he can recognize the *presuppositions* of the utterance. (Only her believing that John has at least three children would cause the utterance "All John's children are bald" to issue from her lips.) If he can infer that the utterance must have been caused by certain intentions, he can recognize the conversational *implicatures* of the utterance. (Only her intending it to be recognized that she could not honestly praise his relevant qualities could explain her writing "His handwriting is excellent", in a letter of recommendation; etc.) Similar inferences enable hearers to identify the *illocutionary force* of an utterance. (He said, "You will report at noon": given that it was not otherwise determined what I should do at noon, the utterance must have been caused by his intention to bring it about that I report at noon, and to do so by his saying that I would: thus the speaker must be *ordering* me to report at noon.) Much of the interest of the framework of this causal theory of linguistic representation to pragmatic theory lies in tracing out the intricate causal pathways by which facts result in utterance, and utterances in facts, leading through patterns of causally connected desires, beliefs, and intentions, underlying and specific to various illocutionary acts. Just for an example, consider the act of making a promise. The crucial necessary condition for making a promise, I think, is this: I promise that I will do x only if I give it to be understood that I will do x, if only because I said that I would. In explicitly causal language, this becomes something like this: I intend it to be believed that my uttering, today, "I will do x on Monday", is caused by an intention to do x on Monday, which intention is such that on Monday it will be or could be caused just by the fact that I uttered "I will do x Monday" today (with the intention that it should be believed that all that is true).

But we should not be diverted from the main course of the inquiry. What is relevant to that inquiry is not the fact that pragmatic inference is causal inference. That is, or ought to be, clear enough. The relevant thing is the involution of such information in semantics. It is, or I say ought to be, relatively clear that pragmatics is the study of certain regularities in the causation of utterance, underlying the practical functions that are served by utterance. What is however not clear is whether the same thing is somehow true of semantics.

Someone utters the sentence "The cat is on the mat". The task given the hearer is that of understanding this acoustical event. He reckons its causes, the speaker's intention that he should believe that the cat is on the mat, this perhaps caused in turn by the speaker's belief that the cat is on the mat. But these things -- the expression of that belief, the implementation of that intention -- constitute pragmatic properties of the sentence uttered. These do not give us what is being said. (For he is not saying that we should, or even that he does, *believe* that the cat is on the mat, but that it *is*.) To recognize what is being said is to recognize the cause -- or the putative cause -- of the belief that the speaker expresses: the fact that the cat is on the mat. That is what is the case, if the truth condition of the sentence is satisfied, and the unique relation of the sentence to *that* state of affairs is what is pertinent to its semantics. The things that figure in that state of affairs -- the cat, the mat -- are what are being referred to, not the various ideas or other representational elements that make up the beliefs and intentions that are expressed by the utterance. If we are to supply a causal theory of semantic properties and relations we must give a *causal* characteristerisation of the *unique* relationship in which the sentence stands to the fact that the cat is on the mat, the fact that ideally stands at the far end of the lineage of perceptions, beliefs, and intentions that yield the utterance of the sentence.

It is the *meaning* of the expression that determines the "relevant" cause. So what is wanted is, in effect, a causal theory of *meaning*, correlative to the causal theory of reference. We must develop a conception of meaning, as I have suggested, as a causal property of expressions. My suggestion is that the "relevant cause" is the object or state of affairs which is that it would be capable of causing (etc.) the expression to be uttered under certain ideal conditions, and such that under those conditions *only* it would cause that utterance. The meaning of an expression will be, roughly, that property of the expression owing to which its utterance could be caused (etc.) by that object or state of affairs, and only by it, under those conditions. Other, e.g., intermediate, causes may vary, under those conditions, but the "relevant" one may not.

The conditions in question are in the simplest case conditions which function to permit the relevant object -- the "proper" object -- to result in the appropriate utterance of the expression. And they also prevent anything but that object from causing such utterances. The conditions are, then, conditions under which the device -- the speaker -- is functioning with ideal competence. Whether these conditions ever in fact hold does not matter. They are parallel in some respects to the idealizing assumptions underlying the typical statement of natural laws. (Such assumptions are, incidentally, essential to the derivation of the gas laws from statistical mechanics.)

This adumbrates the idea of a causal theory of meaning. And here an adumbration will have to do. The meaning of an expression is a property of it that determines the proper causes and consequences of the utterance or entokening of that expression. Such objects are the referents of expressions. In that attenuated sense, the meaning of an expression "determines its referent". To know the meaning of an expression is to be in possession of an hypothesis about the cause of any entokening of the expression: the hypothesis that if certain conditions prevail, then the utterance of the expression in a certain context could be caused only by (or could result only in) such and such a fact about the reference. I will not attempt to work this idea out here but only illustrate it in a simple case. Take the sentence "Snow is white". To know the meaning of that sentence is to identify a certain state of affairs with which any utterance of that sentence is causally connected, provided that that utterance occurs under certain optimal conditions. The character of that connection and of those conditions vary with the speech act being performed. Suppose the sentence is uttered in the act of making a statement. Knowing that, one who knows the meaning of the sentence is in possession of an hypothesis about the state of affairs that might cause that sentence to be uttered; indeed one knows that under optimal conditions of utterance, *only* that state of affairs would be capable of causing the utterance of that sentence.[19] For in saying that snow is white the speaker represents himself as *knowing* that it is so. This hypothesis is the sum of two causal hypotheses, both of which I must greatly oversimplify. First, that under ideal *epistemic* conditions, only the fact that snow is white would cause the speaker to believe that snow is white. (Thus he would not believe it unless it were true.) And secondly, that under conditions of absolute *pragmatic* rectitude, only his believing that he knew it could cause him to utter that sentence in the performance of that act. (Thus, taking the two together: he wouldn't say it, if he didn't believe it; and he wouldn't believe it if it weren't true.)

This second hypothesis, and the notion of conditions of pragmatic rectitude, is what is most pertinent to our present concerns. What is required under this heading will differ from illocutionary act to illocutionary act. In performing a given illocutionary act, one gives it to be understood that his utterance has a certain character, what might be called a certain *causal profile*, being caused in certain ways and being intended to cause certain effects. Pragmatic rectitude requires that what is thus given to be understood should be *true*. (And that in turn determines certain requirements on the cognitive status of underlying psychological states.) Thus such conditions as that prescribed by the so-called Maxim of Quality and other maxims of conversational property are among these conditions.

The key thing is this. While the particular conditions that are required by pragmatic rectitude vary from speech act to speech act, they will all be such as to connect the utterance, in their various ways, with that state of affairs which is identified by the meaning of the sentence. That connection is the constant thing. To know the meaning of the sentence is to identify that state of affairs which stands in some particular such causal connection to the utterance of the sentence under the relevant conditions of pragmatic rectitude. And the sentence would not stand in such a hypothetical causal relationship as that to that state of affairs were it not for these pragmatically determined connecting links.

Well, perhaps so. Perhaps pragmatic facts are essentially and inextricably bound up with semantic facts in that way. If semantic relations are indeed hypothetical causal relations -- causal connections that would obtain under certain pragmatic and cognitive conditions -- then it must be so. But again, the fact that semantic facts *involve* pragmatic facts does not indicate that semantic facts are *reducible* to pragmatic facts. For if semantic facts essentially involve pragmatic facts, the converse is also true: pragmatic facts essentially involve semantic facts. The constraints that govern what sentences are uttered under what conditions, themselves presuppose and consult the truth conditions of sentences. One does not make the statement "Snow is white" unless he has a certain belief; but what belief is it that he must have? It is the one which is true if and only if *the truth conditions of the sentence* he utters are satisfied. So while semantic facts involve pragmatic facts, the converse also holds. *Reduction*, however, requires an asymmetry in the order of explanation.

I wish to end by sketching a line of argument which might possibly indicate that the pragmatic facts of the matter are the fundamental ones, and the semantic ones derivative. This argument concludes that certain specific, but fundamental, semantic facts are explained by certain pragmatic facts about those constructions, and not *vice versa*.

There are, notoriously, a number of phenomena that can be treated either from pragmatic principles or alternatively from semantic principles. Illocutionary force is one of these phenomena. One hypothesis is that the force of a sentence is determined by pragmatic features, like the speaker's intentions in uttering it. The alternate hypothesis is that its force is determined by semantic properties of the sentence. A promise made by saying "I will come" invites the pragmatic treatment; a promise made by saying "I promise that I will come" invites the semantic treatment. But there is a general principle which favors having one kind of account for both cases. This general principle motivates both, e.g., the deleted performative or Searle-type semantical treatment of the force of "I'll come", and *also* a pragmatical treatment of the force of "I promise I'll come". The former kinds of view take the force of "I'll come" to be determined by the meaning of some underlying element in its makeup, or of some associated illocutionary force indicating device. The pragmatic treatment postulates no such element, but extends the application of the account given of the force of "I'll come", where it makes a promise, to the sentence "I promise I'll come". Thus the head of the construction, the performative preface, is demoted from the role of *making* the remark a promise, to the ordinary role simply of *saying* what the speaker doing in saying "I'll come". (On this view, the sentence would be more perspicuously represented, "I'll come; I promise it".) I have argued for the pragmatic treatment of illocutionary force in another place;[20] here I am interested just in the general character of that argument.

On the latter account, notice, a pragmatic property of the sentence "I'll come", sc. its being such that a promise may be made by its utterance, gets elevated to the status of a semantic property of a construction in which that sentence occurs: "I promise I'll come". For it is a semantic property of that sentence that it is true, only if a promise is being made by the utterance of it. The phenomenon which interests me, then, might be called the "transmutation" of pragmatic properties into semantic ones.

Another instance of the phenomenon, possibly, is one discussed by my colleague Fred Dretske.[21] Sentences with differing *foci*, like "Clyde *killed* the donkey" and "Clyde killed the *donkey*" differ in their pragmatic properties. They do not, however, differ in their semantic properties, for the two sentences have the same truth conditions. The difference between the two has to do with the relevance (e.g. novelty) of the information represented by the focused element, and that, of course, concerns the pragmatics of the two sentences. What appears to happen, however, is that that pragmatic difference gets transmuted into a semantic difference when the simple sentences are embedded in certain larger contexts. For the sentences "It was unfortunate that Clyde *killed* the donkey" and "It was unfortunate that Clyde killed the *donkey*", having *different* truth conditions, *do* differ in their semantic properties.

Now an instance of central importance concerns psychological sentences, where, arguably, the same thing happens. Consider the relations between the sentence "Snow is white" and the sentence "John believes that snow is white". The sentence "Snow is white", of course, *expresses* the speaker's belief that snow is white but it does not *ascribe* that belief to him, does not *assert* that the speaker believes it. The property of identifying a certain belief, which the speaker may be expressing, is a pragmatic one, a property it has by virtue of the way it is or may be used. Now consider the occurrence of that sentence in the context, "John believes that snow is white", where the belief that snow is white is *ascribed* to the subject. Here the pragmatic property of the constituent sentence (whereby a certain belief is identified) is transmuted into semantic property of the larger construction. For it is, of course, a truth condition of "John believes that snow is white" that the belief that might be expressed by the utterance of the complement clause should be a belief that John has.

I am inclined to say that the pragmatic property of the embedded sentence *explains* the semantic property of the construction in which it occurs. In particular, it seems to explain a certain well-known fact about the "logic" of "S believes p", namely that p *implies* q and S *believes* p does *not* entail that S *believes* q. The actual rule seems something like this: S *believes* p implies that S *believes* q if and only if "q" and "p" would *express* the same belief *for* S. It has been held, of course, that the rule might be stated solely in terms of the semantic property of *synonymy* without recourse to the pragmatic concept of *expression*. The putative semantic rule would be: S *believes* p implies S *believes* q if the sentences "p" and "q" have the same *meaning*. But in fact synonymy does not seem to be sufficient. For suppose that John believes that Sally will be away for fourteen days. Now "Sally will be away for fourteen days" and "Sally will be away for a fortnight" have precisely the same meaning. But suppose that John does not know that "fortnight" and "fourteen days" have the same meaning, and in fact thinks that a fortnight is forty days. In that case it will *not* be true that John believes that Sally will be away for a fortnight. Why not? I suggest that it is because John would not himself *use* the sentence "Sally will be away for a fortnight" to express his belief that Sally will be away for fourteen days. This is of course merely a fact about how John would or would not use certain terms -- a pragmatic fact about the terms. And the thought is, that it is therefore certain *pragmatic* properties of the sentence whereby a belief is ascribed -- facts about what beliefs that sentence would or would not be used to *express* -- that explain the semantic facts in question about the sentence in which that belief is *ascribed*. The semantic capacity of a sentence "p" to *ascribe* a belief to someone -- as it does in the context "S believes p" -- is explained by the pragmatic capacity of that sentence to *express* a belief -- as it does when S says just "p", therein making a statement that p.

I float that argument without great confidence; if the argument can be defended, it appears to suggest that this phenomenon I have called the transmutation of pragmatic into semantic properties provides a case in which pragmatic facts about sentences *explain* semantic facts. "Transmutation" of course is metaphorical; my suggestion is not that the pragmatic properties *change into* semantic ones, but rather that these semantic properties of constructions are shown to *be*, in reality, nothing but pragmatic properties of their constituents.

FOOTNOTES:

1. This paper was delivered to the Urbino Conference on "The Possibilities and Limitations of Pragmatics", in July 1979. I should like to thank Berent Enç and Elliott Sober for many helpful discussions.

2. Cf., e.g., H.P. Grice (1957).

3. The standard discussion of intertheoretic reduction in the philosophical literature is in Ernst Nagel (1961: chapter 11).

4. Cf. Berent Enç (1976).

5. For some discussion and support of a causal treatment of representations even of future states of affairs, see the appendix of my "Show and Tell" (Stampe 1975a).

6. S. Kripke, "Naming and Necessity" (1972).

7. Kripke's suggested causal picture is offered as something to replace a "descriptions theory" of names, which he subjects to withering criticism. (Some say if withered away to nothing, others that while severely withered, the theory survived and lives on; if so, it lives quietly and obscurely.) To understand the advent of causal theories of names and references, the reader must have some acquaintance with this criticism of the main alternative philosophical views of the matter; and also -- just as importantly -- Hilary Putnam's longstanding campaign against wrongheaded theories of reference. See Putnam (1975: volume 2).

8. For just one example, compare Thomas Hobbes, *Leviathan*, Part I, Chapter 1, "Of Sense".

9. "How it looks", that is, irrespective of the way things might actually *be*, whether things are as they appear, or not. The idea of "content" is the idea of those properties of the representational state or entity which are *independent* of the actual state of affairs external to that state or entity, but by virtue of which that external state of affairs is represented, and has a certain (intentional) "existence *in*" that state or idea.

10. Or is in another relevant way causally connected with the utterance, e.g., involved in a state of affairs to be *caused by* the utterance; or in a state of affairs caused by the cause of the utterance (as in prediction).

11. I am not here alluding just to the point that the speaker may be using the term wrongly, referring to what is in fact a dog as a "cat". The important point concerns even the case where there is no performance error, where the term is used with full competence to refer to

what is in fact a cat. The contention is that what determines that that thing *is* its proper referent (that the reference is one competently made) is not the meaning of the term, not anything that might reasonably be thought to be part of the content of the term. For suppose that that it is part of the meaning or semantic content of the term "cat" that a cat is an animal. (One may well doubt whether that is the case. But suppose it is.) Now suppose that it should turn out, that what we had all called cats are (to our astonishment) discovered not to be animals at all, but clever robots, it would nonetheless be correct to call and to have called these machines "cats". Therefore the fact, if it is a fact, that being an animal is some part of the semantic content of the term "cat" cannot be the thing that makes it the case that it is correct to call a cat a "cat". (The argument, and the example, are Putnam's.) There are two diverse conclusions that may be drawn about the meaning of "cat", from Putnam's observation. If one assumes that the meaning of a term is just *whatever* determines its extension, one will be inclined to *enlarge* one's conception of meaning so that it includes the relation between the term and its extension, with Putnam's result, that "meaning is not in the head". The alternative is to argue that, since there is nothing that could *reasonably* be regarded as the meaning or content of the term that also determine its extension, the term *has* no meaning or content. (This is the conclusion I draw.)

12. "Entirely", that is, apart from the contribution of the sensory apparatus of the organism.

13. It is easy to think of things that you might find out even about the person you know best, which would make you say that you had had no idea who that person was -- if e.g. your wife turned out to be the daughter of Anastasia, or Wonder Woman; or if you yourself turned out to be someone very surprising -- the heir to the English throne, say -- you might say that you had not known who *you* were. But in the right context probably any fact about a person could assume that sort of overweening importance. The fact that knowing wh. can seem to involve such complete knowledge is at the source of many important philosophical doctrines, ranging from some kinds of holism to the doctrine that knowing the meaning of a term, or the knowledge required for command of a term, actually requires knowing what is necessary for the thing's being what it is: its essential properties. (This doctrine was, I believe, discussed by Charles Travis at the Urbino Conference.)

14. See Steven Böer and William Lycan (1975).

15. The view I am expressing here is of course a radical one. I am saying, e.g., that if I open up the phone book, as I now do (being in an experimental frame of mind), and put my finger down at random on the name (as it happens) "Harriet Shapiro", I have acquired the ability to use that name with perfect competence to refer to the thing or person to whom the name refers. This does depend on the truth of an assumption that I make about the phone book and thus the etiology of that

list of names. But if that assumption is true, nothing more seems to be necessary. (If I had made up the name, then I would not be in the same position; suppose I had made it up, but had forgotten that I did so, and later found the name in my notes. If I then uttered the sentence, "I wonder who Harriet Shapiro is?", I would not be posing a question about Harriet Shapiro, or referring to the person -- if there should happen to be one -- so named.)

I shall stop short of asserting that the ability to make competent reference is sufficient for what might be called *full* semantic competence regarding the name. In an earlier discussion, I took the view that (1) there was a theoretically interesting thing called semantic competence regarding a term, and (2) that to have it, one had to know what *kind* of thing it was that it is called by the name. On this more moderate view, if the name "Harriet Shapiro" is in fact the name of a boutique, and not a person, I would not have acquired full command of the name. This would explain the fact that I would not know whether such a sentence as "She shops at Harriet Shapiro" was or was not an acceptable *sentence*. On this view, to have full command of "tiger", one would have to know that "tiger" is the name of a certain kind of countable entity; otherwise I might say *"There is lots of tiger at the zoo" (cf., "There is lots of dirt on the floor"). I cannot attempt to decide between the two views on this occasion. Cf. my "On the meaning of nouns" (1972).

16. Putnam maintains that speakers are required to have some stereotypical idea of a tiger in order to count as having acquired the word 'tiger', where this idea need not be accurate, but must be shared by competent speakers. See his "The Meaning of 'Meaning'" (in Putnam 1975). It is simply not true that we would not count a person as having command or the word 'tiger' if he did not associate with the word the stereotype of a *striped* animal, as Putnam maintains (p. 250). With some difficulty we could develop a world class expert on tigers, while carefully keeping from him the fact that tigers have stripes and that stereotypical tigers have stripes; will we refuse to count this person -- the author of several learned monographs on tigers -- as having acquired competence regarding the word "tiger"? But the fact of the matter is that in this theoretical framework, the notion of semantic competence regarding a word, or command of a term, is depleted of much of the intuitive content it might have been thought to have. Consequently, the proper evaluation of this or any other proposal about what we ought to count as semantic competence involves the question whether the notion characterized is one of significant theoretical utility or not.

17. See G. Frege, "Über Sinn und Bedeutung" (1892); in English, see *Translations from the Philosophical Writings of Gottlob Frege* (P. Geach and M. Black, eds.), Oxford, 1952.

18. Cf. my paper "Toward a Causal Theory of Linguistic Representation" (1979). The idea of a causal account of meaning, presented only sketchily below, is developed somewhat more fully in that paper.

19. Relative however to another illocutionary force, this particular linkage is not necessary, but another one is. For instance suppose I say, inquiringly, "The cat is on the mat?", wanting to know, presumably, whether the cat is on the mat or not. Here it is not a condition of pragmatic rectitude that I should believe that the cat is on the mat, but rather, perhaps, that I should want my utterance to elicit an affirmative response only if that response is duly caused by the belief that the cat is on the mat where the cause of *that* belief is that the cat is on the mat. This is the sense in which (as I said earlier) the "intermediate" stages in the causal linkage between states of affairs and utterance may vary, while the state of affairs of unique semantic relevance is invariant. (The case of inquiry is of course quite complicated; there is in fact no causal relation required even under optimal conditions between the utterance "Is the cat on the mat?" and the cat's being on the mat; rather, the causal connection is between an utterance which the inquirer intends to cause the respondant to emit, on the condition that the cat is on the mat, and the cat's being on the mat.) This will suffice to indicate that the present view will have to deal in causal relations that travel from utterance to utterance, and sentence to sentence, as well as simply up and down from utterance to fact.

20. See Stampe, "Meaning and truth in the theory of speech acts" (1975b).

21. See Dretske, "Contrastive Statements" (1972).

HOW TO BE A REFERENT

Charles Travis

0. *A plausible story*

One day, Sam (Browne) enters Harry's office for a chat, lowers himself into Harry's swivel chair, and in doing so, sits on Harry's hat. After Sam's departure, Harry finds Max, and says to him, 'You know what just happened? Sam crushed my hat.' What he said was that Sam (Browne) crushed his hat. So, when, in the speaking of those words the name 'Sam' was spoken, a reference was made - and it was quite clearly and unmistakeably a reference to Sam. One way of identifying that reference is as the reference Harry made on that occasion, or, for short, Harry's reference.

Suppose we ask in virtue of what Harry's reference was so clearly a reference to Sam. Why is it correct to say that that reference, on that occasion, was a reference to Sam, and not correct to say that it was to Harry's desk, or the potted palm in the foyer, or Harpo Marx or Sam Cooke? One might think of the following plausible story: By its nature, Harry's reference is a reference for which there is a certain condition - call it C - such that to make that reference is thereby to establish C as the condition to be fulfilled by anything that would count as the referent of it. That is, given that it is the reference it is, something would count as what was thereby referred to if and only if it (uniquely) met C. So Sam qualifies as the referent of

Harry's reference by meeting C. In general for any reference there is some condition such that to make that reference is to impose that condition on potential referents. A reference may be identified and distinguished from others by identifying the condition it imposes - different conditions identify different references. And the way to be the referent of any given reference is to satisfy the appropriate condition - the one identifying that reference.

There is also a psychological side to the story. Max understood perfectly well what Harry said. *Inter alia*, he understood the reference made *via* 'Sam'. Thus, he can recognize that Harpo, the palm and Sam Cooke do not count as what was referred to, whereas Sam Browne does. Otherwise, we would not say that Max understood what was said. If there was a condition imposed in the making of Harry's reference, Max can distinguish between what satisfies it and what does not. So he must, at least implicitly, recognize what that condition is. But Max has finite intellectual capacities, which suggests that the condition must be a stateable one. If it is stateable, one way of doing so is by giving a description which must fit anything which is to count as the referent. Let us call such a description the descriptive backing carried by the reference. Plausibly, every reference carries its own descriptive backing and may be identified by saying what backing that is.

Like most plausible stories, this one is all too apt to appear trivial precisely where it is not. This one, however, *has* come under heavy suspicion in recent years, largely under the prompting and guidance of Saul Kripke.[1] Though one might well suspect the story, I believe that most of the attention thus far has been directed at the wrong points. Before showing this, however, a few preliminaries are called for: first a few words on what I am calling reference here, and then a discussion of two distinct types of interest one might take in the plausible story, and two corresponding things that might be called theories of reference.

1. *What is a reference?*

I will want to speak in what follows of the making of references, and of references as that which is thereby made. The easiest way to explain what I will mean by this is to begin indirectly and via a special case. Consider first the closely related notion of making a reference to some thing, and a special case where such is done in the course of saying something potentially either true or false. In fact, let us begin with the yet simpler special case where some such thing is said *via* a sentence of the form SP, where the reference in question is made via the expression S. For example, consider Harry's 'Sam crushed my hat.', and the contribution made by 'Sam' to what is thereby said. First, in Harry's words it was said of someone that that person crushed Harry's hat. Second, what was thereby said is to count as true if, and only if *that* person crushed Harry's hat. The function of 'Sam' is to pick out or identify which individual what was thus said was said *of*. 'Sam' specifies, that is, which individual was said to have crushed Harry's hat. In the simple case, then, X is what was referred to in the words N, occurring in the words W, just in case what was thereby said is true just in case something was thereby said of someone, and what was thereby said of someone is true of X.

First generalization: Specifying an individual of which something is being said, as just described, is one way in which some words may be to be understood. For some ways in which words may be so understood, and for some words to be understood in some of those ways, there will in fact be no individual which can be said to be the one they specify as being spoken of. For example, I may say, 'My postman leads a lonely life.', believing myself to have a unique postman, where, either because I have too many, or none at all, I cannot be said to have said of anyone that *he* leads a lonely life. Where words are so to be understood, so that if there were an appropriate individual, they would make the contribution to truth evaluations described above, I will speak of a reference having been made, even where there is no X of which it will be correct to say that reference was made to X. Though this is a natural way of speaking, particularly given the plausible story, such cases will play no crucial role in what follows.

Second generalization: Not everything which is said is to be evaluated as either true or false. Some of what is not contains words which make the same sort of contribution to its evaluations as reference-making words do in the simple case. Not all of what makes such contributions occurs in the same grammatical postion as the S expressions in the simple case. For example, for some words, 'the man on the corner', and for some X, the words may be to be evaluated as referring to X or not. How the evaluation goes depends, *inter alia*, on what, if anything, is picked out by the words 'the corner', which are embedded in the larger noun phrase. To capture such cases, let us factor out various remarks that might be made about how 'Sam', as spoken by Harry above, is to be understood. First, it is to be understood as part of Harry's words, 'Sam crushed may hat.' - a particular instance of saying something to be evaluated as true or false. Second, it is to be understood as specifying that individual of whom something either true or false is being said. Third, it is to be understood in some way in virtue of which various individuals can correctly be said either to be that individual thereby spoken of or not. Whatever such a way may be, to be understood in some such way is a feature shared by words in other cases where I will want to say reference occurs. So, in the general case, I will say that a reference is made where some words are to be understood in some way such that were they to be understood in that way, and were they, so understood, to occur in the S position in some utterance of a sentence covered by the simple case, they would count as words in which a reference was made. For example, in 'the man on the corner', a reference is made *via* 'the corner' just in case, understood as it is to be understood there, but occurring in some other words, e.g., 'The corner isn't safe any more.', a reference would be made via it, which for any corner either would be to that or not.

Do words or people refer? It seems equally right to talk in either way. On either way of speaking, reference may be connected with evaluations in the desired way. I will speak in both ways. What I say is always meant to hold for either. However, each way requires a *caveat*.

Where there is talk of words referring, it is important to distinguish between *someone's* words, or a piece of actual text or discourse, i.e., words in which something *was said*, and, e.g., English or Spanish words, or proper names like 'Napoleon' or 'Esmeralda' as such. If Sam says 'Myron eats Frites.', 'Myron' in what he said may refer to Myron de Quincy. The name 'Myron' certainly does not. In what follows, I will always speak of someone's words, and never the L-ish words or the name N. I do not think it is a property of linguistic expressions or names as such that *they* refer to anything. One can only think, e.g., that the name 'Kaplan' refers to David Kaplan if he is a philosopher attending to his own present uses of it. And, even philosophers like Kripke, who claim to think otherwise, actually discuss what someone *would* be referring to if *he* used such-and-such a name under given circumstances. However, rather than argue the substantive point at length, I simply make the above stipulation.

Where we speak of people referring, it is important to distinguish between perfect and imperfect aspects of the verb - between, e.g., what someone *referred to*, and what he *was referring to*. Imperfect aspects are generally applicable in a wide variety of cases where the deed in question was not actually done, as in 'Smith was leaving the room when he realized there was still drink, so he stayed.' This suggests that it may be correct to say that someone was referring to X in cases where no reference was actually made to X. And that may suggest in turn that there is some phenomenon, called 'speaker reference', which has no essential connection with the truth of what is said. If there is, I do not mean to speak of it. So, to avoid misimpressions, I will confine attention to references that are made, and avoid consideration of those others, if there are any, which someone merely may have been making.

2. *Identification theories*

Suppose that the plausible story is correct and that in fact Harry's reference imposed a certain condition, C, on a potential referent. One thing one might ask is in virtue of what it is the case that Harry made a reference imposing condition C rather than one imposing some other condition, or, under what circumstances one *would* make a reference imposing C rather than some other reference. What is the condition for C being the condition imposed on a referent? This question might be asked in general for any condition that might be imposed in the making of a reference. A general answer to it is one thing that might be called a theory of reference. The answer might also be restricted to a specified range of cases, e.g., references to be made via ordinary proper names. A possible theory of this sort for English definite descriptions, for example, might claim that where a referance is made *via* a description D, C is the condition imposed on a referent if and only if to satisfy C is to be correctly and uniquely described by D. Such a theory would be in a Russellian spirit. Or, for ordinary proper names, one theory of this sort would claim that, where a reference is made via a name N, C is the condition imposed on a referent if and only if to satisfy C is to be as the referrer would describe what he is referring to were he asked.

I will call theories of the sort just described *identification theories* because their aim is to say, for actual or potential historical episodes of reference making, what factors would identify the references made on those occasions as one or another, within a given range, of the references it would be possible to make - given the plausible story, as a reference imposing one condition rather than another. The aim is to state necessary and sufficient conditions for doing things of specified sorts within acts of saying things. A paradigm of this conception of a theory is a Gricean theory of meaning, where a theory is taken to be, not something which says what any words or expressions *do* mean, but rather a statement of conditions for words meaning something at all, and if anything, then one thing rather than another.

When an identification theory provides a condition, S, for a condition C being imposed on a referent, it aims to isolate those factors in reference makings on which referenthood may depend - those factors referred to in stating S. Whatever these factors are - whether the meanings of the words used, or speaker's intentions, or causal connections - they must be identifiable as present or absent in a reference making situation without first having to identify what reference was in fact made, or what condition it imposes on referents, and without appeal to a prior intuitive understanding of what making such-and-such a reference would come to. If the theory is to be informative, it cannot say, for example, that the condition for C being the condition imposed is that a reference be made imposing C, or that that is what people who know what reference is would say. The very idea of an identification theory carries with it, then, the supposition that the phenomenon of making a particular reference - say, one carrying a particular descriptive backing - is analyzable in terms of independent and antecedently recognizable phenomena. In other words, identification theories aim to reduce the phenomenon of reference to other phenomena, with all the usual problems inherent in such an exercise.

The notion of an identification theory is in principle independent of the plausible story. Call Harry's reference R. Suppose it is not a property of a reference that it carries a descriptive backing, or imposes any kind of a stateable condition on referents. Whatever properties in fact do individuate R, we can still ask under what condition R rather than some other reference would have been the one made. An answer to this question *need* not tell us what it would be to be a referent of that reference. Traditionally, though, people who have been interested in identification theories have been fundamentally interested in questions of what makes something a referent. They have not been interested in identifying occurrences of references as an end in itself. Attention has not been directed to the problem of how to know how to take a particular speaking of 'Sam', but rather, without first having solved that problem, to what it would be to be a referent of it. This double problem is perhaps most neutrally represented by characterizing the theories at issue as concerned with identifying occurrences of referent-reference pairs. That is, suppose <R,X> is a pair where R is a reference within the scope of the theory and X is any object. Then the theory aims to state conditions for R having been made to X on an occasion, that is, some condition S such that R will have been made to X if and only if S.

I have discussed identification theories at some length primarily for the purpose of setting them aside in the bulk of what follows. Though so far they have been the primary center of philosophical attention, most interesting issues about the logical structure of what is said can be discussed - and more clearly - independently of them.

3. *Theories of reference identity (generative theories)*

Harry's reference was in fact a reference which, on the plausible story, imposed a condition, C, and thereby was to Sam. But that is only one of many references that Harry might have made at that time and place in saying 'Sam'. For example, Harry and Max might be mutually acquainted with six different Sams. Then, given appropriate background, Harry might have referred to any of them, depending on how his words were to be taken, or on exactly which reference he made. Another thing, then, which might be called a theory of reference is something which says what the different references are which there are to be made within a given domain - for example, what references there are for Harry possibly to have made in saying 'Sam', or more generally, what references there are to be made in speaking an ordinary proper name. Such a theory would specify, e.g., the different ways in which 'Sam' might be taken as referring, or the different ways in which someone's referring words may be to be understood. Such a theory would specify, within the intended domain, the different identities that a *reference* might bear. It would do so by providing characterizations of references - characterizations adequate for distinguishing between one reference and another. That is, it aims to provide two distinct characterizations where and only where there are two distinct references to be made which differ from each other by just those properties the respective characterizations represent them as having. I will call such a theory a theory of reference identities, or, since it generates descriptions of references, a generative theory of references.

Again, the notion of a generative theory is independent of the correctness of the plausible story. But if the story is correct, then one property of a reference is that it imposes a condition on referents, where this condition is stateable in terms of a particular descriptive backing. A further plausible hyphotesis in that case is that such descriptive backings individuate references. In that case, a generative theory might describe *references* by providing descriptions of what *referents* of them must be like. If the plausible story is not correct, then, of course, a generative theory must specify reference identities along some other lines.

How we individuate references will naturally have important consequences for what properties references may be said to bear. For example, one thing true of Harry's reference is that it *was* to Sam. That may suggest that being to Sam is one property of Harry's reference. But that all depends. Suppose we individuate references in terms of descriptive backings. Then the same reference - i.e., one carrying the same descriptive backing - may be made on more than one occasion. Depending on the backing, what it picks out on one occasion may differ from what it picks out on another. And this is more than likely to be true if we consider counterfactual possible occasions as well as actual ones. Then the property of being to something would have to be a property of a reference as made on an occasion, and not one of a reference *tout court*.

Whether or not being to something is a property of a reference, there are certainly other properties it may reasonably be assigned. For example, there is the property that it, or the words in which it is made is (are) to be understood or taken as referring in some particular way, as opposed to others in which references may be taken. There is

also the property that is made in such-and-such words. For present
purposes, I stipulate that these are both properties of references, so
that if a reference, R, as made on an occasion, differs from a reference R' as made on some occasion either in that they are made in different words, or that they are to be understood differently, then they
are to count as distinct references, even if, as may well be, they are
both references which, on the occasion, at least, are to the same
thing. This leaves it open for the present whether references which,
made on distinct occasions, are to distinct things must be counted as
distinct references.

Identification theories and generative theories can be compared as
follows: generative theories specify certain classes of abstract objects, viz., some references there are to be made. As such, they need
carry no commitment about what identifies occasions on which (instances
of) one or another of these objects occur. Suppose that on a given occasion some reference is made. A generative theory need say nothing
about what determines which reference this is. If the reference falls
within the intended range of the theory - if, for example, the theory
is one of references to be made via ordinary proper names, and this is
a reference *via* such a name - then we know that the reference fits some
characterization provided by the theory. But so far we may well have
no method of determining which characterization this is. (Perhaps it
is useful here to think of another sort of generative theory, viz. a
syntax of English. This aims to specify what the sentences of English
are. But such a characterization is highly unlikely to say anything
about how to determine, for an occasion on which some English words are
uttered, which if any of these sentences was thereby produced.)

Suppose we have an adequate generative theory for a given domain -
e.g., references *via* proper names. Then an identification theory for
the same domain would specify, for each of the items characterized by
the generative theory, some necessary and sufficient condition for its
having been produced on an occasion. For the issues that will concern
us in what follows, we are interested only in what is true given that

a particular reference was made on an occasion. It is of no intrinsic interest what brings it about that it was that reference rather than some other. Therefore, in what follows, we will be concerned with descriptive backings as they might function in a generative theory, and not as they might function (*or* be explained) in an identification theory.

4. *Reference and necessity*

Reference, and with it the hypothesis that references carry descriptive backings, has been implicated by some philosophers in an account of what makes individuals necessarily one way or another. The basic idea is this: suppose N is a name which we use to make a reference (or certain references) to an individual, n. Suppose that the reference (or those references) carries a certain descriptive backing, D, where D determines what being what is referred to comes to for that reference. Then, for any property P, n has P necessarily - that is, n, if it existed couldn't have failed to have P - if, and only if fitting D entails having P.

Where would anyone get such an idea? Perhaps from reasoning like this: Suppose, for example, I use the name 'Aristotle' to refer to Aristotle. Suppose my reference(s) carry a certain descriptive backing, D. Now, first, suppose fitting D entails having a certain property P. Then nothing would count as what I was referring to unless it had P, since, by definition, it is exactly the function of descriptive backings to determine what could or couldn't so count. But what I am referring to is Aristotle. So nothing could count as Aristotle unless it had P. But then, Aristotle, if he existed, could not have failed to have P. So P must be a necessary property of Aristotle. Second, suppose that having P is not entailed by fitting D. Then there must be some possible circumstances under which something would count as the person I am talking about when I say 'Aristotle' even though it didn't have P. But what I am referring to when I say 'Aristotle' is Aristotle. Hence, something could count as Aristotle without having P. So

P cannot be a necessary property of Aristotle. On the other end, suppose P is a necessary property of Aristotle. Then under no possible circumstances could anything both be Aristotle and lack P. But then under no possible circumstances could anyone be who I am referring to when I say 'Aristotle' and lack P. But then, having P is a necessary condition for being the referent of my references via 'Aristotle'. So it must be entailed by D. Finally, if P is not a necessary property of Aristotle, then there must be some possible circumstances under which Aristotle would not have had P. But then, under those circumstances, the person I refer to when I say 'Aristotle' wouldn't have had that property. So someone might be the person I am referring to and not have that property. But then, having that property could not be a necessary condition for being the referent of my references *via* 'Aristotle'. So it could not be entailed by fitting D.

If references carry descriptive backings, and if the connection between reference and necessity is as stated above, then for any individual n, there will always be some description such that what is necessary of n is exactly what is necessary for fitting that description, viz., whatever description backs our (or my) current references to n (by name, at least).

Against this position, some philosophers - notably Leibniz[2] and more recently Kripke[3] have argued for the principle, roughly, that being a particular individual cannot be equivalent to fitting any stateable (mere) description. There couldn't be a (mere) description, for example, such that something is Aristotle if and only if it fits that description. To make this idea precise, one would, of course, have to say for exactly what kinds of descriptions it is meant to hold. Being Aristotle surely is equivalent to fitting *some* descriptions - e.g., 'being that individual who is Aristotle'. The ways in which Leibniz would be more precise differ in certain respects from those in which I think Kripke would be. At least what each argues is slightly different. Nevertheless, there is a common idea here, which, for whatever class of descriptions it might be applied to, I propose to call the Leibniz-Kripke principle.

Suppose that the Leibniz-Kripke principle holds for a wide enough class of descriptions - one containing, at least, those that might plausibly serve as descriptive backings for references. Then if references do carry descriptive backings, those backings cannot determine the necessary properties of the individuals those references are to. Either what is necessarily true of an individual cannot be the same as what is necessary for qualifying as the referent of any particular reference to it, or references do not carry descriptive backings at all. Some philosophers have been attracted to the latter conclusion, reasoning, I suppose, somewhat as follows: consider any plausible descriptive backing for *our* references *via* 'Aristotle'. That backing will describe the referent of those references as having some property P. But since fitting that description cannot be equivalent to being Aristotle, either something could be Aristotle without having P, or something could have P without being Aristotle. Suppose the first alternative first. Then we ought to be prepared to recognize that there are some possible circumstances under which Aristotle wouldn't have had that property. But then there are some possible circumstances under which the referent of our references *via* 'Aristotle' wouldn't have had that property. (so far so good.) From this, it might be thought to follow that there are some possible circumstances under which our references *via* 'Aristotle' would be to something without the property P, or under which, when we said 'Aristotle', we would be talking about something without the property P. To put the inference another way, the individual we refer to *via* 'Aristotle' is such that, under some possible circumstances, something would count as that individual without having P. Therefore, under some possible circumstances, something would count as what we were referring to when we said 'Aristotle' without having P. What we are referring to, under some possible circumstances, wouldn't have P. Therefore, under some possible circumstances we would be referring to something that lacked P. The descriptive backing in question, then, cannot be appropriate for backing our references *via* 'Aristotle'. Now suppose the second alternative. Then, under some possible circumstances, something could satisfy the descriptive backing but not be Aristotle. But if that backing were the correct one for our references *via* 'Aristotle', then under some possible circumstances, *our* references *via* 'Aristotle' would be something other than Aristotle. But surely nothing other than Aristotle could count as the referent of the reference I just made when I said 'Aristotle'. So, once again, that descriptive backing cannot be the right one for my references *via* 'Aristotle'. But then there could not be a right one.

I hope to show that this sort of reasoning is not correct in either direction, and that in fact the right conclusion to draw from the Leibniz-Kripke principle is given by the first disjunct - that conditions for being the referent of a given reference, if there are such, do not determine what could or couldn't be true of any particular individual. What could possibly be true of a given individual, and what could possibly be the referent of references to that individual are questions to be settled in quite different ways. I think we can see that this must be so by considering a few examples. Compare the following pairs of questions:

(1) a. Could Aristotle have been a Martian?
  b. Could our references via 'Aristotle' have been to a Martian?
  (By 'Martian' here, I mean a member of some indigenous Martian race, and not merely an inhabitant, perhaps human, of Mars.)

(2) a. Could David Kaplan have been a linebacker for the Los Angeles Rams?
  b. Could our references *via* 'David Kaplan', such as the ones I make in this essay, have been to a linebacker for the Rams?

Question (1a) might be taken in several ways. But on one way, it might be discussed something like this: Aristotle was in fact a certain man. Could a man have been a Martian (in the stipulated sense)?[4] Well, how important is membership in a species? What about Kafkaesque metamorphosis, for example? Suppose that such things are impossible and that membership in a species is a necessary property. Then *Aristotle* couldn't have been a Martian. If they are possible, then perhaps he could have been.

Now for (1b). Suppose that it were published next week in the *New York Review of Books* that, at a certain distant date, a Martian came to earth and masqueraded successfully as a human being. He called himself 'Aristotle', wrote a number of books on philosophy, known to us as Aristotle's *opera*, pretended to be a student of Plato (though he really knew it all already), taught Alexander the Great, and, for good measure, it is stories about him, passed from mouth to mouth down the generations, that are responsible for our using the name 'Aristotle' as I am now doing here. Then I think it would be correct to say of our references *via* 'Aristotle' that they were to a Martian - at least if the NYRB revelation is true. Since all this is at least possible, it appears that our references via 'Aristotle' could have been to a Martian.

As for (2a), as far as logical possibility goes,[5] it seems clear that Kaplan could have been a Ram linebacker rather than a philosopher. Consider the following story: at the age of 12, Kaplan considered a career in philosophy, for about 15 minutes, but decided it sounded boring. He then undertook a strenuous program of physical training, culminating in an athletic scholarship to USC. Having used up his eligibility with still a year and a half to go for his degree in commerce, he showed up at a Ram training camp, where he beat out the ten year veteran at right linebacker and went on to a stellar career. I can see nothing in this story that is logically impossible. Kaplan didn't do these things, but under some other rather remote circumstances, he might have. That is enough for the answer to IIa to be yes.

For (2b), things look quite different. I have already made a number of references to Kaplan above. Could these have been to someone who was a Ram linebacker rather than a philosopher? First, as things are, there are, I believe, a number of David Kaplans in the Los Angeles telephone directory. For all I know, one of these may be a linebacker for the Rams. I have not referred to any of these in the above mentioned references except (if he is listed) the well-known philosopher. If David Kaplan did not exist, I would still not have referred to any of these other Kaplans. Now, I suppose it is possible that David Kaplan may be leading a double life, and actually *is* a Ram linebacker, or that a certain Ram linebacker has deluded us all into believing that he is a philosopher (though this is very hard for me to imagine). In that sense, my refernces via 'David Kaplan' might *be* to a linebacker. But now suppose the only David Kaplan in the world is a Ram linebacker, and he is not even someone we falsely believe to have written on the logic of demonstratives, etc., etc., but merely an ordinary sort of Ram linebacker, and the unique bearer of the name 'David Kaplan'. All our beliefs, about 'David Kaplan' are just delusions, plain and simple. Then I think I would not have referred to that linebacker. Roughly, I think, to be the referent of my present references via 'David Kaplan', a David Kaplan must either be the philosopher who did such-and-such, e.g. wrote 'Bob and Carol and Ted and Alice' or at least the person we (practicing philosophers) generally take to have done such.[6]

It is not my intention here to take sides on specific questions of necessity and possibility. I do not claim that Kafka described possibilities or that he didn't. Nor need I even claim that under no bizarre circumstances whatever could my references *via* 'Kaplan' have been to a linebacker. What the examples illustrate, I think, is that discussion of the paired questions must proceed in quite different ways, and thus that each raises quite distinct issues. Further, the prospects look quite different for one sort of question than for the other. *If* there are essential properties at all, then it may well be that Aristotle couldn't have been a Martian (if he was a man), whereas *our* references *via* 'Aristotle' could have been to a Martian. Conversely, David Kaplan could well have been a linebacker-rather-than-philosopher, while *my* references here *via* his name could not have been to a linebacker-rather-than-philosopher.

The following general observations appear in order: suppose I is an individual and R is some reference *via* I's name to I. Then, first, something may be a necessary property of I without being a necessary condition for being what was referred to in making R - i.e., without its being necessary of *R* that it be to something with that property. Nothing about R may impose the requirement that it not be to a Martian - particularly not any descriptive backing it might carry - while, if it is in fact to a man, it may well be to what couldn't have been a Martian. R may in fact come to be to I in virtue of features that are quite incidental to I. Conversely, If it is a necessary property of R that if it is to anything at all it is to something meeting a certain condition C, it by no means follows that it is a necessary property of *I* that it meets C. These conclusions needn't follow because, even though R is in fact to I, it needn't be a necessary property of I that it was referred to in some making of R, nor of R that on some making it was to I. It isn't a necessary property of Kaplan that my references via 'Kaplan' be to him, which is already enough to show that any conditions my references may impose on referents do not dictate what is necessary of him. And it isn't a necessary property of my references *via* 'Kaplan' that they be to Kaplan. Had he chosen the linebacker career, they wouldn't be.

Second, I might be different than it is in any number of ways, were various counterfactual circumstances to obtain. But it needn't be true that R would have been to I under all of those circumstances. If Kaplan had grown up to be a linebacker, he wouldn't have grown up to be the referent of my references via 'Kaplan'.[7]

Third, if references impose conditions on being a referent of them, then - at least for the sorts of references we have been discussing - the function of those conditions is to distinguish a referent from other things, given the circumstances that in fact obtain. It is not to say what that referent could or couldn't be under all possible circumstances in which it might be found. The function of the condition, or of a descriptive backing that might express it, is to specify what being referred to in the making of that reference comes to. That is a quite different thing from specifying what being a given individual comes to, even where that individual is in fact what was referred to in the making of that reference. For those with an inclination to talk about possible worlds, the point can be put like this: references (at least of the present sort) do not pick out the same thing in every possible world in which it exists, nor do they pick out different things in different possible worlds. They only aim to pick out things in *this* world. If those things exist in other possible worlds, then, of course, they are still the things that *were* referred to in this one. But whether they do or not has nothing to do with the nature of the reference made.

In many respects, the above view may not differ from that actually stated in "Naming and Necessity". However, it does counter a certain misimpression which seems to have gained some currency, namely the misimpression that the Leibniz-Kripke principle, or any considerations about what it is to be an individual, counts against a backing-of-descriptions view of what it is to be a given *reference*. If references do carry descriptive backings, their function is not to say what it is to be any particular individual. It is rather to say what would make an individual appropriate for being what was referred to.

The misimpression has been fostered, I think, by a certain natural, but hardly inevitable view of references. That is the view that it is a property, and furthermore a necessary property of a reference, or of a particular referring use of a name, that it is *to* such-and-such e.g., to Aristotle or to Kaplan. So, it is thought, for any counterfactual story on which that very reference was made, the property of its being to such-and-such must be preserved. If it was a reference to Aristotle, then, whatever else we imagine being different, it must remain a reference to Aristotle. In that case, since descriptive backings are to determine what could count as a referent, they must determine what it is to be that individual which actually was referred to. And by the Leibniz-Kripke principle, mere descriptions couldn't do.

Kripke himself sometimes seems to take such a view of references. Perhaps it provides part of the motive for his anti-descriptive backings views. He says, for example, "When I say that a designator is rigid, and designates the same thing in all possible worlds, I mean that, as used in *our* language, it stands for that thing, when *we* talk about counterfactual situations. I don't mean, of course, that there mightn't be counterfactual situations in which in the other possible worlds people actually spoke a different language . .... Then we are describing a possible world or counter-factual situation in which people, including ourselves, did speak in a certain way different from the way we speak. But still, in describing that world, we use *English* with *our* meanings and *our* references. It is in this sense that I speak of it as having the same reference in all possible worlds."[8]

According to the observations I have made above, the references *I* now make, using standard English, and using names like 'Kaplan' and 'Aristotle' in normal ways have the property that under some possible circumstances, *they* would not be to those individuals they in fact are to, even were those individuals to exist under those circumstances.[9,10] This is a remark about speaking standard English as we now do, with our meanings, and making the references we now do. I do not know whether Kripke would disagree with this or not. It is not covered under either of the alternatives he poses. It is not a remark about our currently speaking *about* counter-factual situations, but rather about our speaking as we now do, but *in* counterfactual situations. But that, I claim, is the phenomenon at issue if one is interested in whether or not references carry descriptive backings, since it is in that way that counterfactual stories might show what, if anything, those descriptive backings might be.

The counterfactual properties of references, of course, depend on the properties by which they are to be identified as having been made in counterfactual situations. On the present view, if, for example, I say, 'Aristotle ...', I will have made a reference which has the property of being to be understood in a particular way, and whatever properties correspond exactly to that. For example, if a descriptive backing view is a tenable one, it will have the property of carrying a particular descriptive backing in virtue of being to be understood as it is. And I can be spoken of as having made *that* reference as long as my speaking of the name 'Aristotle' was to be understood in precisely that way, regardless of what other differences there might be in the world in which I made it. On that view, we can say, as intuitively we might, that my references *via* 'Aristotle' could have been to a Martian, even if Aristotle could not have been a Martian. Such a view suggests both a use for discriptive backings - viz., that of distinguishing one way of being understood in referring from another - and a possible criterion for determining what the backing would be in any particular case.

As the examples indicate, this way of speaking about references is the way we naturally *do* speak about them in discussing what *our* references could be to. One could, of course, *stipulate* that he will count references in a different way - e.g., in terms of what they are to, so that a particular reference couldn't be made at all in any situation where it wouldn't be to what it in fact is to. Obviously, not all the above observations about reference and necessity will hold good on this way of speaking. But equally obviously, such stipulation is no argument against a backing of descriptions view. Unless it is shown why one mustn't count references in the way I have suggested here, one might as well do so. And it is a way on which backings of descriptions can be seen to have a point. At any rate, the Leibniz-Kripke principle, plausible as it may be, doesn't provide any reason for abandoning such talk.

5. *Reference and the a priori*

A more serious problem for a descriptive backing hypothesis is this: consider how we would describe, e.g., the person we are referring to when we say 'Aristotle'. We might say, 'A certain Stagirite', 'A teacher of Alexander the Great', 'the author of the *De Caelo*', and so on. Any such description, even if it happens to pick out a necessary property of whatever possesses it, is such that we are prepared to discover that it is in fact false of Aristotle. That means that we are prepared to recognize, under some possible circumstances, that when we say 'Aristotle', we are referring to someone who doesn't fit that description. Further, Aristotle is a somewhat special case, in that we *are* prepared to describe him in some way or other which might possibly individuate him. Often, where we use a name to refer to someone, this is not the case. As Kripke puts it, "Consider Richard Feynman, to whom many of us are able to refer. He's a leading contemporary theoretical physicist. Everyone *here* (I'm sure!) can state the content of one of Feynman's theories so as to differentiate him from Gell-Mann. However, the man in the street, not possessing these abilities, may still use the name 'Feynman'. When asked, he will say: well he's a physicist or something. He may not think this picks out anyone uniquely. I still think he uses the name 'Feynman' as a name for Feynman."[11]

It appears, then, that there are in general no ordinary descriptions of the things we are referring to that might serve as the descriptive backings for the references we in fact make. What should we conclude from this? Kripke comments, "What's going on here? Can we rescue the theory? First, one may try and vary these descriptions - not think of the famous achievements of a man, but, let's say, something else, and try and use that as our description. Maybe by enough futzing around someone might eventually get something out of this."[12] But Kripke doesn't really think so. What he really thinks is, "the examples show not simply that there's some technical error here, or some mistake there, but that the whole picture given by this theory of how reference is determined is wrong from the fundamentals. .... What

I am trying to present is a better picture."[13]

For Kripke, the descriptive backing hypothesis is connected with a certain account of how a particular description comes to be the one which does in fact back that reference which was made on some given occasion, or at least it is the overall story that he argues against. In addition to the existence of descriptive backings, this story states, roughly, that the descriptions which serve to back a reference are those the referrer would give of what he was referring to. *That* view of where descriptive backings come from one would do well to have no part of. But a generative theory of references, in positing descriptive backings, carries no commitment about what makes one fit on any occasion. And the idea behind descriptive backings as such really suggests a quite different view. That idea is basically this: corresponding to every reference to be made, there is a describable distinction to be drawn between what would be appropriate for being what was thereby referred to and what would not, where for different references, different such distinctions are to be drawn. The descriptive backing in any particular case is that which draws the distinction correctly, that is, which correctly states what being appropriate would come to for the reference in question.

Given this view, why think that a *referrer* could say what the correct descriptive backing for his reference was? One *might* reasonably take the view that *understanding* a reference entails having or acquiring a competence for drawing the right distinction - an ability to say of some range of objects, given sufficient information, which if any was appropriate for being what was referred to. Of course, it may be that either a speaker or a hearer or both fail to understand what reference was made. But suppose the speaker does understand his reference correctly. That means he can say correctly of various objects, 'That's not what was referred to', and perhaps of some object, 'That is what was referred to' - an ability he would lack if he didn't know what reference was made. Is it also reasonable to expect him to be able to explicitly state the principles according to which he is able to draw this distinction? If it is anything like most of the distinctions most of us are able to draw - that between what is and isn't a chair or a door, for example - the answer is, of course not. Just as a correct description of the application of a word like 'door' is a task for serious semanticists, finding the correct specifications of the descriptive backings of given references ought reasonably to be a task for serious generative theorists of reference.

For illustration, let us consider how some such investigation might go. Suppose a man in the street named Fred meets a philosopher at a cocktail party, and, wishing to impress him, says, 'Aristotle was a Stagirite'. The philosopher lets the remark pass, and after a few comments on the dryness of the martinis, the two part company for ever. I think we can conclude without further ado that Fred referred by 'Aristotle' to Aristotle.

If Fred *were* asked to whom he was referring, he would have said, 'Aristotle is some philosopher. I'm sure I've heard that.'. If asked what a Stagirite was, he would have said, 'Well, uh ....' and wandered off. But he never was asked. In some cases, perhaps, he should have been - at least if anyone was seriously interested in knowing to whom he was referring. But in other cases, he should not have been. Not only would it be unnecessary to ask, but at least quite misleading. Consider, for example, the following dialogues:

- A. 'President Carter has trouble with the oil industry.' 'Which President Carter do you mean?' 'Good God! How many are there?' 'Two at least.' 'Really?' 'Yes. There's a president of local 173 of the AF of M named Carter.'
- B. 'Daddy, Mother says to tell you she's at the neighbors.' 'Who do you mean by "mother"?' 'Mother!' 'Yes. But who *is* this "mother"? To whom are you referring?' 'What! Don't you know?' 'No. At least I don't know who *you're* talking about.'

Like the cases imagined here, the above is one of those where the philosopher needn't have asked. What Fred would have said doesn't matter anyway, as is shown by the fact that no further ado was required.

Now, what properties does Aristotle have in virtue of which he is appropriate for being what was referred to when Fred said 'Aristotle'? Here is an hypothesis: first, let me introduce a rough and ready notion, to be refined, perhaps at some future date, which I will call 'preeminence'. To say that someone is the preeminent bearer of a name N relative to a given group and/or occasion is to say, roughly, that if you used the name within that group, or on that occasion, with no further ado, you would probably be taken to be referring to that particular bearer (or presumed bearer) of the name, and that the relevant people would generally agree, given sufficient information, on whether someone was that person or not. A group or subject matter or etc. may also be preeminent on an occasion relative to a given name in that, if you used that name on that occasion, you would generally be taken to be talking about the preeminent bearer of the name within that group or subject matter. The hypothesis, then, is that the property which qualifies Aristotle for referenthood relative to Fred's reference is being the preeminent Aristotle within the preeminent field relative to the occasion on which Fred made his remark.

Some comments: first, there is no reason to expect Fred, if asked, to have thought up that description of what he was referring to. Second, the sort of property described is not one that could be known to apply to anyone without knowing what other people - in this case, philosophers - would decide about who *they* were referring to when *they* said 'Aristotle'. It certainly doesn't provide anything like an analysis of the notion of reference. It merely serves to distinguish Fred's reference from others that might have been made. Third, the hypothesis in fact conflicts with causal accounts of reference. Suppose that in the distant recesses of his past, Fred was actually told falsely of some obscure Aristotle that he was a philosopher. Though he has forgotten the occasion, this is what explains his using the name as he did above. Then there is no appropriate causal connection between Aristotle and Fred. Nevertheless, on the above hypothesis, Fred's reference was to Aristotle. Here, I think it is the notion of preeminence, and not that of causal connection which is on the right track. Finally, the above hypothesis is more than likely to be at least not quite correct. But it is to be shown wrong, if at all, by thinking up circumstances under which the proposed condition leads to intuitively incorrect results, and not by asking Fred.

Kripke certainly *seems* to be offering an alternative picture to the descriptive backing view. On his picture, when someone makes a reference using a name N, we need to ask, not what descriptions are to be understood as backing the reference, but rather what individual, if any, is connected by an appropriate causal chain to that use of the name. However, I think that this picture only appears to be an alternative. It appears thus because it is never said exactly what being an *appropriate* causal connection comes to. The problem for a causal theory, like any other, is to distinguish between the *different* references that may be made in the use of a name, even where the same individual is referred to throughout. If the causal picture is right, such distinctions are always to be drawn in terms of causal chains. Still, the theory must spell out the different kinds of causal connections that could count as appropriate in each case. And to do so would be to provide for each reference a descriptive backing - in this case a description of how the referent is to be causally linked to the referrer. Causal theories really amount, then, to restrictions on descriptive backing theories, requiring that the descriptions figuring in such theories must always make some references to causes.

To see that the above is the case, consider the following example: Russell told us that George IV wondered whether Scott was the author of *Waverley*. Russell did this, *inter alia* by using the name 'Scott' to refer to Scott. Let us imagine that a formerly Anglophobic literary critic is finally persuaded to read Scott, and makes the remark, 'Scott obviously modelled his style on the brothers Grimm.'. Then he too used the name 'Scott' to refer to Scott. Now suppose the following discovery were to be made and published next week in the *New York Review of Books*: George IV did not wonder whether Scott was the author of

Waverly. The reason he did not is that George IV was the author of *Waverly*, and nearly everything else generally attributed to Scott. His purpose in writing was to create paradigms of style. To that end, he began with an assiduous study of the brothers Grimm, whom he always admired. For reasons of decorum, he persuaded Scott to let the work be published under his name - a secret which Scott took loyally with him to the grave. For reasons of dissimulation, George IV gave out the misinformation that he wondered who the author of *Waverly* was.

Under these circumstances, I think Russell would have aided in passing the misinformation on to us, and he would have done so by still having used the name 'Scott' to refer to Scott. The literary critic, however, could be justly credited with having been the first to observe the influence of the Brothers Grimm on the author of *Waverly*, and he would have done so, *inter alia*, by having used the name 'Scott' to refer to George IV. That is what would be true under certain counterfactual circumstances of references which in fact involve current standard uses of the name 'Scott' to refer to Scott. These facts indicate that there is more than one such reference to be made. These references need to be distinguished in some way or other by any correct generative theory. If the difference between one and another is in terms of what would count as a referent, whether that difference concerns the appropriateness of various causal connections or not, then it is one to be represented by assigning appropriate descriptive backings to each reference.

6. *Backings and conditions*

Considerations of the sort raised by Kripke - considerations involving necessity or *a priori* truth - provide no reason for doubting the thesis that references carry descriptive backings, which function as indicated in the plausible story. There may be other reasons, however, why the story doesn't ring true. I now want to indicate one of these. To begin, notice that, on the story as initially told, descriptive backings have really been assigned three distinct functions.

First, they are to individuate and distinguish between different references - references that might be made by a speaker (or his words) on an occasion in using a particular name or other referring expression. That is, to say which descriptive backing a reference carries is, on the descriptive backing hypothesis, to say which reference it is. Carrying a given backing is to distinguish a reference from any other in that any two distinct references will carry distinct backings (as references are being spoken of here).[14] Second, descriptive backings are to represent something there is to be understood in the correct understanding of a reference - something one would understand in taking the referring words as they were to be taken. Third, a descriptive backing is supposed to provide a necessary and sufficient condition for something being what was referred to on an occasion in the making of that reference. That is, descriptive backings are to be such that, for any reference, made on any occasion, something would be the referent of it if and only if it were, on that occasion, (uniquely) described by the backing carried by that reference.

Either the second or the third requirement might be taken as a criterion for a reference having the property of carrying such-and-such a backing. That is, the backing carried by a particular reference might be determined by what there is to be understood, *or* by what it is to be a referent of it. But why think the two criteria *conjointly* isolate anything - that there is something which is to be understood which also is a necessary and sufficient condition on being a referent? And if not, why think either a) that, for references that are to be made, there are statable backings satisfying requirement three, or b) that such, if statable, would in fact play the role of individuating references?

Within a generative framework, at least, I think these question can be given definite answers. First, let me point out, by brief illustration, a certain sort of thing there is to be said about references.

Example I: Fred says to Bill, 'Max has a new Alfa.', and it is thus said that a certain Max - Fred's neighbour - has a new Alfa. Fred is overheard by Sam and Irving, who are relative strangers to these circles. Sam, however, has been around long enough, and collected enough background information to know what was said, whereas Irving, who has just arrived, does not know this. Then Irving might ask Sam something such as, 'What did Fred say?', or, 'Who did Fred say has an Alfa?' Sam might then answer something as follows: 'Apparently, there is a certain person named Max, a relatively close acquaintance of Fred's, and a mutual acquaintance of Fred and Bill. It seems that there may be several such. This one is supposed to be a neighbour, or something.' (Similarly, given enough ignorance, Sam might be called on to explain, 'An Alfa is supposed to be a certain kind of car - Italian, or something like that. (No - they're not talking about the camera.)'

Example II: In a discussion of temporal aspects of truth, someone says, 'Aristotle held ....', making a remark about the great Stagirite. He is overheard by two strangers to western civilization, Kraal and Thlon. Again, Kraal knows enough to know what was said, but Thlon does not. Then Kraal might explain, 'It appears that there was an important thinker on these problems - a philosopher, or something - named 'Aristotle', and that for these people, he is preeminently so - they agree pretty much in their explanation of who *Aristotle* was - and he's the one who was just said to have held .... (This civilization has certainly produced some queer ideas.)' Or: 'Aristotle appears to have been one of their famous philosophers - the preeminent one named Aristotle.'

In each of these cases, in an important sense, the person being informed does not thereby get enough information to be able to *identify* the person being talked about. Irving, for example, is not in a position to say, 'Ah - now I see who they're talking about. It's ...', where he fills in his own specification of who Max is. In fact, he doesn't know Max, and in one important sense, doesn't know who he is. But he is able to specify what information he would need to find out who this 'Max' is - what is relevant and what is not for deciding that question. Thus, he knows that to find the referent, he must look for acquaintances of Fred's, also known to Bill, and, in the event of discovering several 'Max's', look for a neighbour, or at least someone taken by Bill and Fred to be a neighbour. Among various neighbours - if there is a problem about this - he should look - roughly - for the one they would first take each other to be talking about if they said 'Max', and so on. It is an understanding of this sort that allows Irving to take Fred's reference in one particular way rather than another - as a reference to a particular (though perhaps as yet unknown) person - and the one it in fact is to, and not as a reference, e.g., to Max Beerbohm (by means of which some radically false information would have been conveyed), or to some presumed (though in fact nonexistent) famous baseball player named Max Avunquilar.

Any particular piece of information conveyed in an explanation of the above sort may, of course, turn out to be false of the actual referent of the reference being described. Suppose, for example, that Fred has a neighbour named Arthur, who has been concealing that fact for years by referring to himself as Max. Then, under the right circumstances, Fred's reference *via* 'Max' may have been to Arthur. Similarly, Arthur may not actually be a neighbour, but only a very consistent coffee drinker at the house of Fred's actual (and usually absent) neighbour, Henry. So, explanations of the above sort cannot be to be understood as providing - or even purporting to provide - necessary and sufficient conditions on being a referent of the reference they describre.

In a particular case, the scope of the above sort of remark may extend beyond what, strictly speaking, there is to be understood about what the presumed referent is like. In identifying the presumed referent for his questioner, the informant might use information gathered from a variety of sources, and not just what is conveyed by what was said - an option conspicuously open when the presumed referent exists. For example, Sam may have happened to know that Max was the man who won the pinochle tournament at Ed's bar and grill in 1957 - a fact totally unknown to either Fred or Bill - and, knowing that Irving knows who that champion was, used that fact to identify who was being referred to. He might say, e.g., 'You know that guy who won the pinochle tournament in 1957? Well, Fred just said that *he* has a new Alfa.' On the other hand, references *can* be described in terms of what their presumed referents are to be understood to be like, and it appears that for any reference there is some such thing to be understood about how the words in which it is made are to be taken. For example, one might say that 'Aristotle', in the remark of example II, was to be understood (or taken) as meaning, or referring to a certain Aristotle who was a pillar of western thought, lived in antiquity, and so on. Or, when the speaker said 'Aristotle', Aristotle (or the Aristotle in question) was to be taken to be, etc. Similarly, when Fred said 'Max', that was to be understood as meaning or referring to a contextually preeminent mutual acquintance of the speaker and hearer, named 'Max', with contextually definite close links to the speaker, etc. For any reference, let us call what is thus to be understood about the words in which it was made the *presumptive descriptive backing* carried by that reference.

Presumptive descriptive backings do not, of course, amount to necessary and sufficient conditions on referents. What a referent is to be understood to be like may differ from what the actual referent *is* like. For example, though Fred is to be understood to have referred to someone named 'Max', he may in fact have referred to someone named 'Arthur'. One might then ask, in addition to carrying a presumptive descriptive backing, is it also a property of a reference that it imposes fixed, statable, necessary and sufficient conditions on being a referent of it? The notion of a generative theory suggests one step to an answer. Suppose we describe references in terms of their presumptive descriptive backings. Would there then be a need to add descriptions of such necessary and sufficient conditions in order to individuate references, i.e., to distinguish one reference from others there are to be made? That is, could there be two distinct references, each of which carry the same presumptive descriptive backing, but which still differ in that, for each, different things are to be understood about what the necessary and sufficient conditions are for being the referent of it?

This last question admits, I think, of a definite answer. Suppose we are confronted with a reference like Fred's, and, in looking around for a referent of it, we uncover a certain neighbour of Fred's named Arthur, with given and fixed relationships to the speaker, hearer and reference in question. Suppose, in fact, that Arthur is the only possible candidate for referent. Then we have to decide whether to say that Fred's reference was to Arthur, and thus that some of the understood presumptions about the referent were false about Arthur, or whether the reference was to no one, and the presumptions correspondingly about nobody. Suppose that, in fact, we can establish that Fred and Bill falsely believe *of Arthur* that he is named Max. So far, this is not a conclusion about what was said. But in this particular case, that mutually shared false belief does explain how Fred came to make a reference for which being named Max was part of the presumptive descriptive backing. At this point, different philosophers may have different beliefs about whether mistaken beliefs about someone's name vitiate one's references to that person or not. But the point is that what one says about Fred's reference will be dictated by his beliefs on this point. A stipulation that such a determination is to go one way or the other cannot itself be part of how Fred's words are to be understood. So there cannot be distinct references which share presumptive descriptive backings but differ in the way imagined above. Stating necessary and sufficient conditions on referents would not, then, be part of a correct generative theory of references. It would take a bit more argument to show it, but I think it is clear how to show from this that imposing such-and-such conditions on being a referent is not a property of a reference at all. On this view, then, reference turns out to be on a par with other things done or expressed in words: in general, what words mean or how they are to be understood is not something which, in every case, fixes what they could or could not apply to - what they apply to is not, in every case, determined by something or other about what they are meant or to be taken as applying to. It now emerges that reference is no exception to this rule.

In one respect, the present picture of reference shares an important feature with causal pictures. These can be seen, I think, as an attempt to counter the view that, as it were, when we make a reference, *we* decide what would thereby be referred to and what would not, or to use other jargon, what is expressed in what is said - the instensions of our words, and of referring words in particular - determines *extensions*, or what the words do, and would apply to. On a causal view, such issues are settled not simply by any set of resolutions we might make on some occasion, or intentions we might have about what our words should apply to, but rather by certain sorts of facts - causal facts, as it happens - which are to be uncovered in the world. This sort of theory brings our picture of reference in line with, e.g., the picture of the function of natural kind terms drawn by Leibniz and Putnam and the general view of the underdetermination of extensions by meanings presented by Austin and Wittgenstein. That is to say, in this respect, causal pictures - like the present picture - bring our view of reference more in line with what we know in general about how language functions.

On the other hand, causal theories carry very specific commitments about the kind of contribution the world can make in determining what is to count as within the application of words - such contributions are limited to filling in causal connections between referrers and referents. The present view of reference leaves entirely open how it might be determined, under every possible circumstance, what would and wouldn't count as a referent. It even leaves it open that there is no stateable account of what to do in every eventuality. Where things are not as they are presumed to be, the rule is to ask oneself, 'What kind of mistake (or suprise) *should* I say this is?' Causal connections may often be important in deciding this, but there is no reason why sometimes they shouldn't fail to matter at all.

The extra commitment in causal theories is really a sign of the fact that they are identification theories. *Any* such theory, whether Russellian, intentional or causal, takes on two large extra tasks beyond the scope of a generative theory. Suppose a generative theory provides a description of a reference, R, individuating it in terms of its presumptive descriptive backing. Then an identification theory within whose scope R falls aims, for any pair, <R,X> to state conditions for an occasion of reference making being an occasion of R being made to X. To do that, first, it must state conditions for R being made on an occasion at all - that is for an occasion being one on which a reference is to be taken as R is. Then, second, it must state conditions such that, given that it was R that was made on some occasion, something would count as what was thereby referred to if and only if it met those conditions. On the present view, *neither* of these tasks is part of saying what reference R is. Neither is part of a general theory which aims to describe those things there are to be said. Perhaps some day someone might actually come up with a theory that performs both these extra tasks. But reflection on our general abilities to say what we would do in the face of any eventuality gives little reason to think so.

In studying one aspect or another of things that are to be done in using words, it is all too easy to focus exclusively on identification theories - theories which specify necessary and sufficient conditions for doing a thing of that kind. I hope the present discussion has suggested that there are other interests one might reasonably have. One can also aim, for example, to specify those things for which necessary and sufficient conditions might be asked, and to investigate what properties those things can be said to have, independent of facts about their occurrence or non-occurrence on various historical occasions. By separating off such questions and studying them on their own, one can often, if not always, settle issues about logical properties and relations while avoiding extraneous considerations about what makes particular speech episodes the episodes they are. Sometimes it may be an advantage not to try to do everything at once.

FOOTNOTES:

1. Cf. especially Kripke (1972). Kripke sometimes claims to be interested in something called the 'referent of a name', whatever that might be, rather than the referent of a referring use of a name, which is what I will always be talking about here. For example, he says, "In the text, I take the 'referent' of a name to mean the thing named by the name, even though a speaker may properly be said to use the name to refer to someone else." (footnote 3, p. 343). I must say that I have no idea, e.g., who the referent of the name 'Aristotle', or the name 'Kaplan', or the name 'Sam' might be, though when I use 'Aristotle', I refer to Aristotle, and sometimes when I use 'Kaplan', I refer to David Kaplan. However, I don't think this difference really matters for what follows. For one thing, in giving examples, Kripke consistently talks about what a speaker would be referring to in using a name, e.g., "A speaker who ... has heard about Richard Feynman in the market place or elsewhere may be referring to Richard Feynman even though he can't remember from whom he first heard of Feynman or from whom he ever heard of Feynman" (pp. 298-299), or, "We do in fact refer to Gödel. How do we do this?" (p. 247). However he would specify which uses of a name show what the referent of the *name* really is, the remarks I will make are meant to hold for those uses.

2. Cf. especially Leibniz (1689), sec. 8, and (1967).

3. Kripke (1972).

4. One might also ask whether, since there aren't any Martian species, there possibly could have been. But leave that aside here.

5. Possibility is, of course, a complex business. It might be pointed out, for example, correctly I think, that Kaplan couldn't have been a linebacker even if he had tried, because no one Kaplan's size could ever play in the NFL. In the right context, that might be a correct remark, even though there could have been miracle drugs which altered body structure (or, perhaps from certain points of view, even this is not possible). Any adequate account of modalities must ultimately account for complicating phenomena such as those alluded to. But even with all such complications taken into account, the point remains that what one is considering, e.g., possibilities for Kaplan, is not what it is to be a referent.

6. How we know who 'we' take to have done such-and-such may be a complicated business, but, as will emerge, spelling it out has no essential connection with theories of reference.

7. Nor, perhaps, would anyone else. In that case, I very well might not have made them.

8. Kripke (1972:289-190).

9. If my reference *via* 'Kaplan' is to Kaplan, then Kaplan under other possible circumstances, still being Kaplan, is still the man my reference *is* to. This is a different issue from what my reference *would be* to under other circumstances.

10. Of course, in those counterfactual circumstances, I could still correctly say e.g., 'my references *via* 'Aristotle' are to Aristotle', precisely because when I *used* 'Aristotle' in saying who I was referring to *via* 'Aristotle', I would not be referring to Aristotle, hence not reporting what I now report *via* those words.

11. Kripke (1972:292).

12. Kripke (1972:296).

13. Kripke (1972:300).

ON THE ART OF DECEPTION:
HOW TO LIE WHILE SAYING THE TRUTH[*]

Jocelyne M. Vincent
and
Cristiano Castelfranchi

Introduction

For our discussion of deception and lying we shall be using the framework provided by a model which attempts to analyse human behaviour, including linguistic activity, in terms of agent assumptions, intentions and goals.[1] We shall not be concerned here with how utterances or moves may be deceptive or not independently of a speaker's intentions, nor shall we be concerned with the relationship between what the hearer is made to believe and what is "true" or "false" in the real world. We shall, rather, be viewing the process from the deceiver's point of view and from that of the means he uses to pursue his deceptive goals. From this perspective, what may amount to nothing more than casual or accidental effects of a move, or, indeed, questions concerning the ontological truth of propositions, are irrelevant.

We submit that pragmatics is relevant to the study of deception because of its concern, among other things, with speaker goals and the adequacy of linguistic acts with respect to the goals a speaker is pursuing through them. Indeed, pragmatics might be said to involve the study of those conventions and contexts which link actions to their effects enabling justified rational expectations to be made by agents regarding the effects of their utterances or actions. Deception exploits these conventions as does any communicative activity.

Furthermore, mendacity and deceptiveness are not, we think, properties of sentence meanings as such, but rather of utterances, or moves and their agents in their social and psychological context, thus placing the study of lying and deception in the domain of pragmatics rather than that of semantics.[2]

Moreover, as mentioned above, mendacity and deceptiveness need only be viewed from the point of view of the intent to deceive; whether or not a deceitful move is successful (in that the hearer or addressee is actually deceived) does not alter the fact that a deceitful move has been made, just as the hearer's not believing a lie of the speaker's, does not alter the fact that the speaker lied.

Nonetheless, consideration of the consequences of moves would be crucial for the study of deception in interaction, with its complex strategic plans involving dynamic adjustments as the context thickens with the agents' mutual assumptions and expectations being confirmed or thwarted. However, we cannot hope to consider this aspect here, although, we do of necessity, at least need to consider the speaker's assumptions regarding the hearer's assumptions and goals,[3] if no further. Thus, as far as it goes, we are only concerned with somewhat limited chains of reasoning on the part of the speaker and his manipulation of the contextually relative conventions, which can then be classified as different deception strategies. This, then, is no more than an attempt at a taxonomy of some of the basic notions and types.

The goals analysis model has proven very simple to apply and has helped to handle an otherwise none too tractable subject. It also turned out to be a good heuristic device in that it led us to think of strategies which were not exemplified in our original data, nor immediately obvious to us.

Of course, an intentional analysis of lying and deception was not new when we set out with our research. We need only mention the work of Sts. Augustine and Thomas Aquinas.[4] Furthermore, since our first working paper on the subject (Castelfranchi & Vincent 1977), we have found similar points in contemporary writers, notably the philosophers Chisholm & Feehan (1977), and Herman Parret (1978). We do think our discussion has simplicity to offer.

Before proceeding to our present main concern, lying while saying the truth (see section 3 below), we must, at least briefly, consider some basic notions and our methodological assumptions. In section 1 we shall, thus, run rapidly through the model we mean to use, and then, in section 2 we shall set out the basic notions involved in our analysis of deception, in an attempt to provide, if not perfectly rigorous, at least consistent and intuitively acceptable characterisations of our technical use of such terms as true/false, deception, lying, pretending, acting, insinuation etc. In section 4, we shall briefly consider possible reasons for choosing indirect strategies.

1. Moves, or utterances as actions, may be viewed as governed or regulated by hierarchies of goals; at the first level, by the goal of communicating their propositional content, known as the direct goal of an utterance, and then by various super-ordinate goals (henceforth referred to as super-goals), the top one ("meta") being the objective of the action or utterance, and the lower, relatively subordinate goals (referred to as sub-goals) acting as means, or mediating goals, through which the objective is to be reached.

Goals, of all levels, may be communicated, and/or communicative, or neither; indeed they may be, for example, deliberately concealed. A (to-be-) communicated goal is one which a speaker intends his hearer to understand him as having. A communicative goal is one which a speaker intends to reach thanks to communicating it. In other words, communicating it is the means to reach it.

The direct goals of a linguistic utterance are always communicative, and they are always requests that the hearer do something: assume, move, etc. The speaker counts on the hearer to decide to satisfy the speaker's goals once he has understood what they are, i.e. the speaker counts on the hearer to adopt and adhere to his goals. To adopt another individual's goal is to let oneself be regulated by a goal because it is the other's goal, and this is done with the goal of enabling the other to reach his goal. To adhere to a speaker's goal is to adopt it because the speaker has asked so.

Quite normally, utterance super-goals are conveyed indirectly, the hearer somehow reconstructing them through inference; for example, through the operation, perhaps, of natural, conventional, or conversational implicatures. We shall not, nor can we, go into the details of the mechanisms involved here.[5]

A fixed goal is one that controls entire classes of actions; it does not promote them but simply regulates their manner. A fixed goal of practical actions such as cooking, for instance, would be not to burn oneself. In a conversational exchange, fixed goals would seem to be, for example, adhering to one's interlocutor's goals, so long as there is nothing to the contrary, and, speakers have the fixed goal of asking of the hearer only those things which they know he will, or can, adhere to, and, at least as far as acts of informing go, of adopting the hearer's goals (in other words, of cooperating,[6] which might mean nothing more then giving him relevant and adequate information).[7]

Actions are social when their goals mention other individuals. Social actions are aggressive when their goals are to somehow hinder or prevent someone else from reaching a goal of his. Deception is an aggressive act in this sense; it involves, among other things, hindering or preventing someone else from reaching certain information which is, or might be, if he were aware of it, relevant to that other person.[8]

2.1 We turn, now, specifically to our discussion of deception and lying. We began by saying that a correct definition of deception would involve the notion of speaker intentions and assumptions. In other words, it must involve the speaker's beliefs concerning the truth or falsity of the information he is conveying to the hearer, and his intention to convey either true or false information as such, not the actual truth or falsity of that information.⁹ Indeed, even when a speaker has not actually deceived a hearer as to certain facts, that is, he has not led a hearer to be mistaken about certain facts, because what he believed to be false and intended to be false, "accidentally" turned out to be true to the facts, ¹⁰ the speaker does still deceive the hearer as to his own beliefs. Herein lies the act of aggression, the breach of faith, the shift, on the speaker's part, from coordination to conflict.

We might then, formulate the following tentative definitions: A deceptive move or action, (or object used in it,¹¹ or produced by it) is one which has a goal of getting the hearer to make a false assumption. A false assumption for A is one which he assumes, and intends to be different from that which he assents to, or "believes he believes".¹² An information item x or induced assumption in B may be different (i.e. false) for A when A conveys x to B as if he assented to x, in one of the following ways: A does not believe he believes x (he does not assent to x); he believes he does not believe x (he dissents from x); he believes he has no beliefs concerning x or not-x (he withholds x); he believes he believes not-x (he assents to not-x); he believes he believes x but he believes x to be inadequate to B's goals, he believes x is only part of the information B needs, while inducing B to assume that x is the totality of the information A assumes to be pertinent and necessary for B; A believes he believes x but he believes he believes x is irrelevant to B, he believes x to be misleading in that B will assume x is relevant to him. If it is not "the truth the whole truth and nothing but the truth" it is deceptive.

Indeed, "The truth or falsity of statements is affected by what they leave out or put in and by their being misleading and so on [...] It is essential to realise that 'true' and 'false' [...] do not stand for anything simple at all; but only for a general dimension of being a right or proper thing to say as opposed to a wrong thing, in these circumstances, to this audience, for these purposes and with these intentions" (Austin 1962: 143-144).

Furthermore, we would use the term deceptive move not only in those cases where a speaker tries to contribute causally to a positive false increment in the hearer's belief system, but also when A for instance, conceals the truth, or when he otherwise allows what he believes to be falsehoods to be continued to be assumed by B, etc.[13]

One more general point in this rapid review of some of the main issues involved, we consequently believe that it is not necessary nor, indeed, sensible, to class as deception every single instance of the concealment of true information or the positive giving of false information, etc. if the information concerned is not functional to B, i.e. if it is not, nor would be, in any case, a goal of B's. Or, to put in an other way, if A assents to y, i.e. he believes he believes y, and assumes that y is relevant to B's goals, and if A is able to give y to B or otherwise let B have y, and B is able to assume y, then, if A intentionally tries to prevent B from having y or any part of y or making the assumptions that y and that A assumes y (either by concealing y or by giving x, where x is different from y), then we could say that A is intentionally trying to deceive B.

We come now to a summary exposition of some of the more basic, and simple strategies through which deception may operate.

A first important distinction must be made within the set of deceptive moves, we think, between those where the speaker's goals are communicative and those where they are not. Needless to say, the objective or top goal, that of deceiving the hearer, is never communicative nor communicated in any case.[14]

2.2 Pretending or faking[15]

This is an intentionally deceptive move obtained through counterfeiting that which the hearer is intended to assume. A's goal, that B assume x (when A assumes x is false) is non-communicative; i.e. B must not assume that A wants him to assume x. This is schematically represented in figure 1.

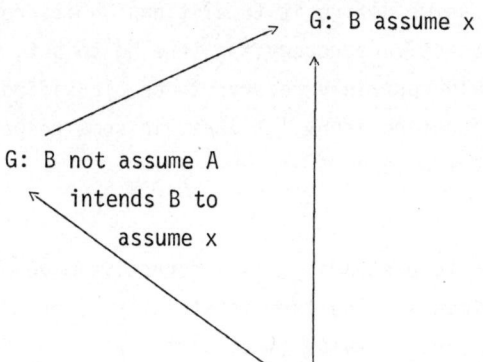

Figure 1

For example, by limping, one can counterfeit lameness; if A's goal is that B assume that A has hurt his leg (usually as part of a larger plan) then he must not let B understand that he is limping on purpose, because if he did, then B would obviously understand that A was not really lame, so he would understand that A was trying to trick him and he could then perhaps even reconstruct what A's objective in tricking him with respect to his lameness might be. Thus, A would end up at a disadvantage with respect to the context before he made his move, he would be vulnerable to B, or "one-down" with respect to B; now if A has the intent to deceive B through his move he will obviously not intend any of the above consequences. Unless, of course, he wants B to see through his hoax as a means to a further goal, but that would no longer be pretending, rather pretending to be pretending.

2.3 Acting

Acting is the non-deceptive sister of pretending. In involves A communicating to B that A is pretending. B and A are accomplices in a game which involves the entertainment of two contradictory worlds: one, the real world, where x is false (a pretense), and the other, a fictional or imaginary world, where x is true.

Although acting, as we define it to distinguish it from pretending, would not be a deceptive strategy, pretending to act, as we shall see (section 3.9), would certainly deserve to be classified as such for obvious reasons. Joking (and irony, at least in some respects) share these characteristics of acting.[16]

2.4 Lying[17]

Lying, as opposed to pretending, is a deceptive move obtained through communicative means. The term is strictly reserved for those cases when A explicitly gives false (i.e. different from that which he assents to) information to B, and does not apply when, for example, true information is concealed by A from B; in other words lying is "positive deception simpliciter" obtained through assertion, "the liar intends to contribute to [...] B's belief that he, the liar, is now asserting something that he accepts." (cf. Chisholm and Feehan op. cit.: 153). It is thus only properly applied to this particular sub-category of deception by commission. It bears repeating that, in saying that it is communicative, we mean that the speaker, A, not only wants B to assume x, where x is false for A, but he also wants him to assume that he assumes x and that he wants him to assume that he wants him to assume x, and this is the means to getting B to assume x.

Linguistic utterances, as we have said, always have communicative goals, but so, often, may non-linguistic moves. Lying, as we have defined it, is not an exclusively linguistic prerogative. However, to distinguish between the linguistic and the non-linguistic lie, the linguistic lie involves double deception, and one of these is a pretense. If A says, for example, "I love you" to B, while not assenting to, or actively dissenting from, his assertion, on the one hand he has the goal that B assume A loves B (and this goal is deceptive), mediated by the goal that B assume that A wants B to assume that A loves B (and this goal is not deceptive, of course), while, on the other hand, the utterance carries the speaker's conventional committment to that which he has asserted,[18] in other words, it has the goal and expected effect of making the hearer assume that the speaker assumes he loves the hearer, and this goal is deceptive too. It is, furthermore, reached through an act of pretending, since A, by asserting that he loves B, acts *as if* he loved B. So, A lies to B if: the general conditions for deception apply; A makes an assertion that x (where x is false for A) by linguistic or other means; A intends B to assume x; A intends B to assume A assumes x; A intends B to assume that A intends B to assume x. This last goal is communicated as the means to get B to assume x - assuming, of course, B's adhesion to the cooperative principle. Figure 2 is a simplified schematic representation.

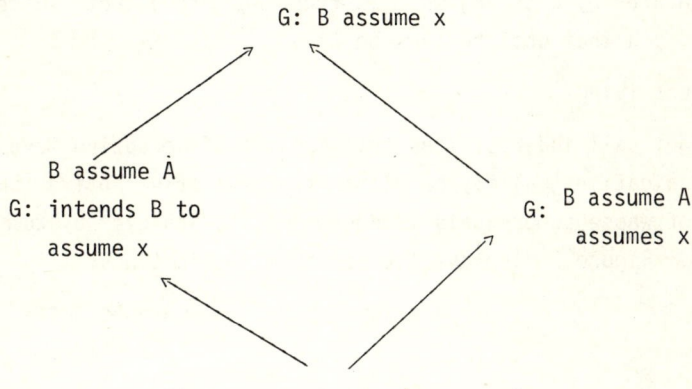

Figure 2

Lying is insincere. Pretending cannot be insincere. Hypocrisy, or insincerity, is intentional deception regarding one's emotions and/or assumptions and/or goals. Non-communicative moves, therefore, cannot be called insincere when they are deceptive. One can talk of sincerity or insincerity only in the case of communicative goals where the hearer is meant to understand that the speaker is committing himself.

Imperative utterances can be insincere, although they cannot be used as lies. For example, a harrassed mother might say to her young child who always does the opposite of what he is told "Don't you dare come near me" in order to get him to come close to her and away from the cliff-edge. She must deceive him as to her true goal, behave as if she wanted him to stay away from her; she must dissemble or conceal her true state of mind and be thus insincere in order to manipulate her contrary child who systematically adheres to an uncooperative principle of interaction with his parents.

3. So far we have discussed what amounts to direct deception strategies. We shall now pass to a brief account of some indirect ones, and, in particular, we shall focus on those where the speaker intends to deceive the hearer by uttering what is true: he intends both to deceive the hearer, and that what he says be true.

3.1 Indirect lying

We might call indirect lies that sub-set of deceptive moves whose first communicative goal may be either truthful or deceptive, but at least one of whose super-goals is deceptive and achieved by communicative means. Figure 3 displays the possible combinations.

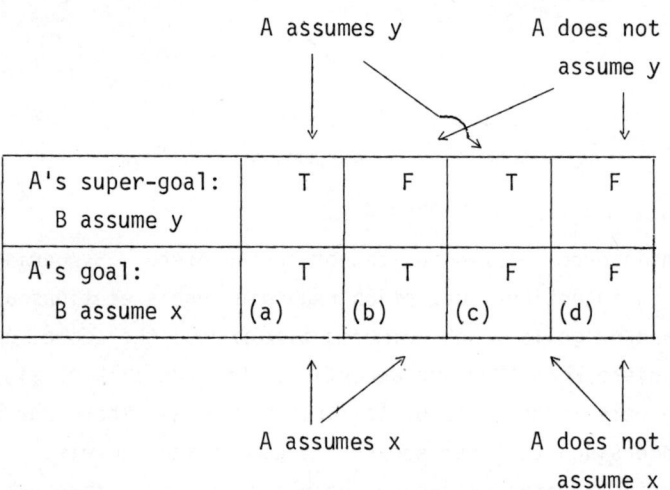

(where T and F stand for true and false for A, respectively)

Figure 3

We shall be concentrating on sub-set (b), where a speaker asserts or directly expresses a proposition he assents to, while having the super-goal that B infer from it a further proposition which A does not assent to, or actively dissents from.

An example of indirect lying by saying the truth might be the following: suppose A wishes to plant in B's mind the idea, y, (which in any of the ways we described earlier, A believes to be deceptive for B, i.e. he believes y to be false) that B's wife is unfaithful to him with a certain other acquaintance of theirs, and in order to do this A makes an assertion x which he intends and assumes to be true. He says something like: "I saw Cassio wiping his beard with Desdemona's handkerchief this morning". Let us assume that Iago is A and Othello B, and that Iago actually saw Cassio wiping his beard with what he (Iago) believes to be Desdemona's handkerchief. (In fact, Iago knows that Cassio has Desdemona's handkerchief because he himself very carefully engineered matters so that Cassio would have it in his possession, and, furthermore, it is very likely that Cassio could have wiped his beard with it, since he does not know that it is a special handkerchief belonging to Desdemona, and would thus have no reason to treat it with more respect than any other handkerchief he happened to have.) So, we can assume that Iago is intentionally saying something which he assumes to be true; yet he is most certainly also conveying something else to Othello which he intends and assumes to be false; through a chain of reasoning with intentionally fallacious links. Thus, ... Desdemona gave the handkerchief to Cassio (false) as a love-token, therefore they are having an affair (false), Cassio shows it little respect, therefore he does *not even* love Desdemona; if one also considers that the handkerchief in question is a very special one, the charmed or talismanic one which Othello was given by his mother and gave as a token to Desdemona when they were married, then one can easily imagine the effect that Iago's words would have on Othello. So, Iago, not unusually for him, accomplishes several objectives at once; one, a collateral, fixed, goal of causing extra suffering to Othello, and the other, the main one here, of making Othello at least suspect that Desdemona is having an affair with Cassio, by making him understand that Iago is implying this. All this as we have seen, moreover, Iago intends to accomplish by saying something which is true.

The above example of a case of indirect lying by saying what is true, also gives us an opportunity to consider the relationship between indirect lies and insinuation, reticence and half-truths.

3.2 Insinuation[19]

If the super-goal that B assume that his wife is unfaithful is communicative, i.e. that A wants B to assume that A wants B to assume it, then the move is also an insinuation; however, not all indirect lies are insinuations, nor viceversa.

An intuitively acceptable definition of insinuation would be, we think, the following. Insinuation is a communicative act with a communicative goal which consists in an implied assumption deliberately involving a negative value-judgment of the relevant referent, fact, or effect on the hearer; however, insinuations need not always be calumnious, i.e. the intended mischief, pejoration or taint, need not be false. And, indirect lying, on the other hand, need not involve anything pejorative; indeed, it is often the case that indirect lying involves amelioration, as in the case where the falsehood is meant to reflect favourably on the speaker, for example. Such a case would be the following, which is also a case of indirect lying while saying what is true: A, an 11-year-old on his first day at a new school says to his desk-mate "My Dad works at the B.B.C." intending B to think that A's Dad is something glamorous or important like a reporter or a cameraman, while the truth behind the truth is that he is a cleaner at the studios.

A further set of examples of indirect lies by means of insinuation might be such as "he's Sicilian ..." or "he's Irish ..." or "è inglese ..." where the speaker lets the hearer infer, by not blocking them with a "but ...", the adherent negative connotations from the current bank of stereotyped prejudices: he's Sicilian and so he must be a greasy mafioso, he's Irish and therefore a stupid drunk, or he's English and therefore an eccentric twit. Although the assertions might all be true in the appropriate contexts, their implications may well not be, for the speaker; in which case he would be insinuating mendaciously, though saying the truth.

3.3 Reticence

There may be points of intersection between reticence and indirect lies but again not all indirect lies will be cases of reticence, nor viceversa.

For reticence to occur it is not enough that something be left unsaid even with the goal that the hearer infer it, nor even that this goal be communicated. We think that reticence might involve at least the following: the speaker lets the hearer understand that he is keeping quiet about something; he makes it clear that he is keeping quiet with a particular goal in mind; he makes it clear what this goal is; he makes it clear that he has the goal of letting the hearer understand that he is leaving something unsaid; he lets the reasons for doing so be understood; he lets the hearer suspect exactly what this something is (helped by the context); he lets the hearer understand that he wants him to understand what it is he is leaving unsaid. As with insinuation, the inferrable information will be somehow negative or hurtful. Indeed, holding back from saying it when what it is is clear to all, also serves to actually taint it, to imply that there is something unpleasant about it in case the hearer had not already realised this.

If the information the speaker is being reticent about and wants B to infer is intentionally false, then naturally we have a case of indirect lying, and, furthermore, if it is to do with something that the speaker assumes the hearer already suspects to be the case, and he wants to recall it to him, then it could be more properly termed an allusion, or rather a lying allusion. Examples such as "he's Sicilian ..." etc., might represent any of these types on given occasions. Shakespeare provides us with an exhaustive repertoire in Iago's moves.[20]

3.4 Half-truths[21]

It is not very clear what this term refers to in everyday usage. It is vaguely and generally used to describe any sort of clever manipulation of the facts, where there is an uncomfortable feeling that, notwithstanding an apparent impeccability of the statement, there is something slippery about it: a trick.

We should like to propose a more restrictive and therefore more useful characterisation of half-truth. With this in mind we propose to relate it to our notions of indirect lying and of lying while saying the truth. A half-lie, or half-truth occurs, then, when a speaker gives part of the truth while concealing another part of it - a part, naturally, which he assumes would be relevant to B - and this would be done with the goal of getting him to make only partially true conclusions, which amounts to false assumptions. In other words, half-truths are misleading. They occur when A does not say everything that is relevant to B's goals, i.e. A intentionally gives B inadequate information: like the school-girl who under interrogation by the headmaster only admits to that part of her misdemeanour which the headmaster has explicitly accused her of; yes she did smoke in the toilets, omitting to tell him exactly what it was she was smoking; or the child who has to admit that he gave a punch to his little sister, when what he actually did was beat her up, i.e. used several punches and kicks.

Half-truths are indirect lies where the inferrable false assumptions are accomplished, or induced it would seem, by the generation of implicatures; for example, from something like Grice's conversational maxim of quantity the hearer will interpret A's utterance as meaning, for instance, one punch and no more.

3.5 Precondition or presupposition faking

Yet another strategy which can be employed for lying indiretly, is that which we shall tentatively call precondition, or presupposition, faking. The general mechanism is sufficiently well known in the literature on presupposition[22] for there to be little need to remind ourselves how it may be used for deceptive purposes. We think it is probably best thought of as a sub-type of pretending, or behaving-as-if, for it involves doing an act or making an utterance which would require certain preconditions for its appropriate use; when, however, these conditions do not exist, the speaker knows they do not exist, and his goal is that the hearer assumes that they do. One example will suffice. Saying something like: "It is rather a pity that Anne and Mark had to be at Burleigh this weekend" to a guest at the speaker's daughter's wedding breakfast in London might well be an example of multiple presupposition faking. For instance, that the speaker knows the two illustrious personages in question well enough to be on first-name terms with them, that the speaker actually invited them to the wedding, that A. and M. would have come but just could not avoid the very important business that took them somewhere else, etc. Some, or all, of these might be false while, of course, it may be true that it is a pity for the speaker, and that H.R.H. and consort are enganged at the time of speaking at the Burleigh horse trials.

The above-mentioned types of indirect lying, where the assertions may be true but the inferrable assumptions false, are not the only ways of lying while saying the truth which we should like to indicate here. We shall, thus, also be briefly discussing the following strategies: deliberate ambiguity; obfuscation; pretending to lie; pretending to act or joke.

3.6 Deliberate ambiguity[23]

Given an utterance with two possible interpretations or readings in a given context, one of which is true for A and one of which is false, A may exploit the ambiguity hoping and intending that B understands the false reading. Of intentional equivocation or deliberate ambiguity used for deceptive purposes, Bolinger (1973) gives us a good example from commercial advertising: "No heat costs less than oil heat". This is trivially true under one reading because not using any heating system will obviously cost less than oil heating, because it will cost nothing at all, whereas, the other reading which is also the most favoured or probable reading, that oil-heating systems are cheaper to run than any other types, needs to be proven, and is at the very least suspiscious if not downright false.

3.7 Obfuscation

The strategy we shall tentatively call obfuscation (borrowing the term form Gowers 1973) might be aptly described as verbal terrcrism, at least in some cases. It involves the speaker is assuming and intending that the hearer will not be able to understand the full import of his utterance. So, he can say the truth, as far as he is concerned, knowing that the hearer will not understand, or will understand something different;[24] which would amount to the hearer not assuming the truth and therefore being deceived. Technical jargon, for example, can be, and is, used in this way by unscrupulous operators. Euphemism, verbal cosmetics, and indeed its opposite disphemism, may also be deliberately employed for the pursuance of deceptive goals. It is well known that governments, advertisers, etc. often manipulate language in this way. Not all prospective fur-coat buyers, for example, will know that "coney" is rabbit (which presumably sounds far too inelegant to be an attraction). And consider how the label "terrorism" is liberally used to describe all kinds of active rebellion when it is particularly uncomfortable to the current institutions; or indeed how symphathetically (to-be-) viewed rebels are called "partisans".

3.8 Pretending to lie

If A says what he believes to be the truth with the intention that B believe he is lying to him then he is doing what we shall call pretending to be lying.[25] A does this with the intent to deceive B because if B believes A is lying to him he will thus assume that what A is saying is false and so, in order to avoid being tricked, B will not assume what A has told him; since what A is saying is true, however, this means that B will not assume the truth, and so is he deceived. This strategy may be resorted to when the speaker needs to pass off a true utterance, or action, as a pretense.

An example of this strategy might occur when a burglar is caught red-handed by the police who know that he always works with a partner, who is nowhere to be seen. The police ask the unfortunate one where his mate has gone; the burglar, assuming that the police will not be expecting him to tell them the truth, could actually say the truth, intending them and expecting them not to believe what he said, i.e. the truth. He will be attempting to deceive them by pretending to be lying. Figure 4 is a simple representation of the strategy in terms of A (the burglar's) goals.

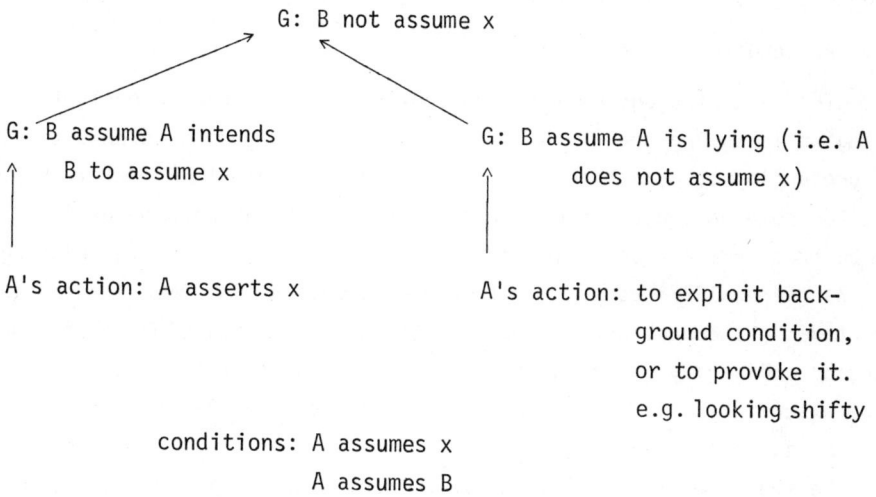

Figure 4

This strategy can obviously only succeed if the burglar stays this one step ahead of the police in the calculation of their mutual expectations. If the policeman is cleverer than the burglar assumes (for example, he credits the burglar with more cunning than the burglar assumed he would) then this very simple strategy could hardly succeed; the success of the strategy would, in other words, depend on the correctness of the strategist's assumptions concerning the hearer's assumptions concerning the strategists' assumptions and intentions, etc. ... We could discuss further countermoves and countercountermoves, based on the interactants' mutual expectations and knowledge, but these would lead us away from the relatively simple strategy of pretending to lie, which operates at a relatively shallow depth of manipulation of mutual assumptions. We are content, here, to limit our discussion to the more elementary ways of lying while saying the truth.

3.9 Pretending to act, or joke

The last strategy we shall be looking at here which amounts to lying while saying the truth, is what we call pretending to be acting, or pretending to be joking. In other words, the agent or speaker passes off (by some manipulation of the context) something which he believes to be true in the real world, as if it were acting, joking (or kidding, cf. Zaefferer 1977) as if, in other words, what he is communicating is not true in the real world. He is pretending to be playful, he is pretending solidarity, pretending complicity in the game by literally or otherwise winking at the hearer; he is pretending to laugh with him, when he is really laughing at him.

We shall let the English proverb "many a true word said in jest" testify for the well established and unexceptional nature of this strategy. Figure 5 illustrates it in terms of A's goals.

(Figure 5, see next page)

It might be interesting to examine the differences between pretending to lie and pretending to joke, by comparing figures 4 and 5. They both have as their objective or highest goal that the hearer assume something different from that which the speaker is asserting; they both either manipulate the hearer's assumptions or involve an explicit collateral action of A's which has the goal of unveiling to B that A is tricking him, i.e. that A does not really assume what he is asserting, and this

ON THE ART OF DECEPTION

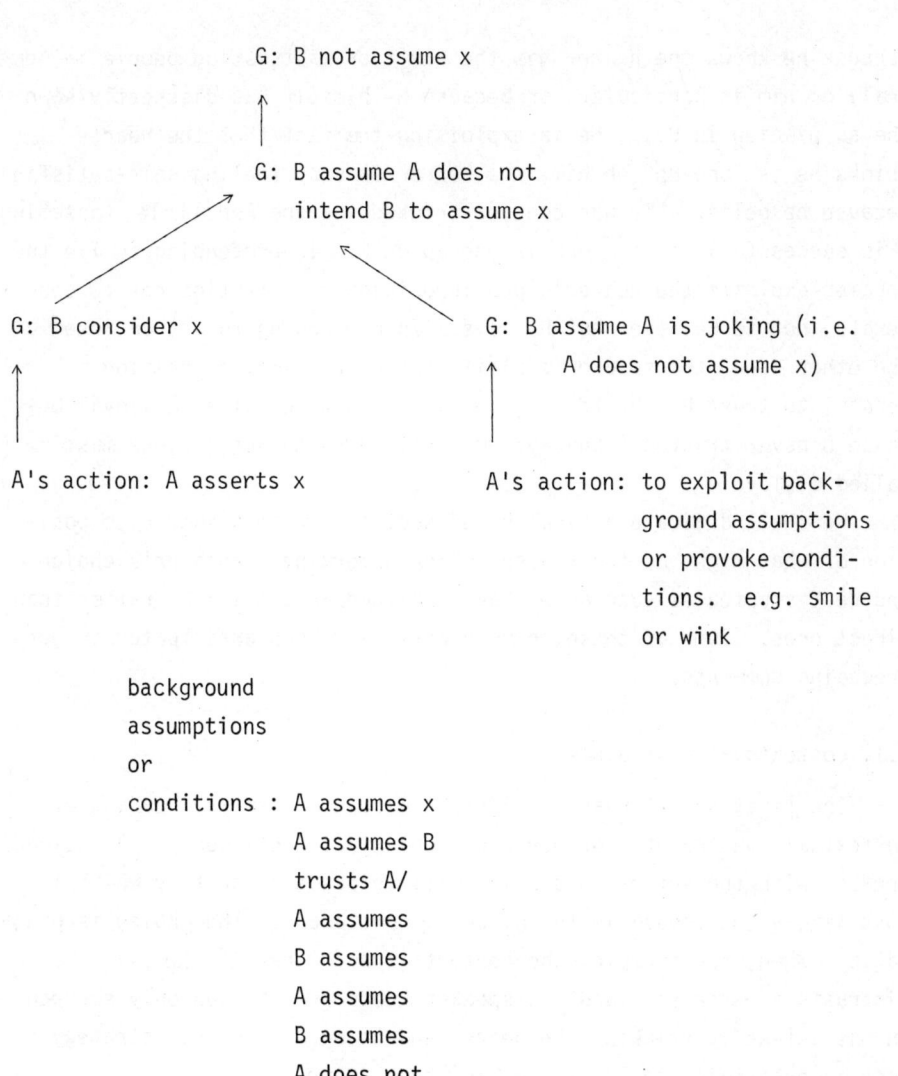

Figure 5

has the goal of making B not assume what A is asserting. In pretending to lie the speaker exploits the fact that the hearer thinks the speaker is trying to trick him (the speaker knows the hearer thinks this either because he knows the hearer has the habit of mistrusting people in general, or him in particular, or because he himself has discreetly sown the suspiscion in B.). He is exploiting the fact that the hearer thinks he is "one-up" on him; the hearer ends up feeling self-satisfied because he believes he has counter-tricked the speaker, while, (assuming A is successful) it is A who is one-up on B. In pretending to lie the speaker exploits the hearer's predisposition or intention not to cooperate, not to believe what he says. In pretending to act or joke, on the other hand, the speaker exploits the hearer's prediposition to cooperate, to trust B. Pretending to lie, cannot be called disloyal because B never trusted A anyway; but pretending to act or joke must be called disloyal.

We shall dedicate a final brief section now to a summary exposition of what might be the reasons which determine a speaker's choice of indirect strategies such as we have examined in section 3, rather than direct ones. Some of these, have necessarily been anticipated in our preceding comments.

4.1 Contextual constraints

The first set of reasons might be grouped under the heading of contextual constraints, or perhaps, contextual contingency. A rational speaker with the intent to deceive will choose the strategy which is most likely to succeed in the given circumstances. The choice is pragmatic. When, for example, the context is such that the hearer mistrusts the speaker, and the speaker knows this, he can only succeed in his intent by tricking the hearer and using an indirect strategy such as pretending to lie as we have seen above.

There may be other contextual features which leave the would-be deceiver no other choice but to employ one of the above described indirect strategies. For example, there might be a third person present who knows that the speaker does not believe x, and who is not a party to, or an accomplice in the deception, and who must not become aware, for various possible reasons, of A's intentions to deceive B. For this reason, among others, Iago has recourse to equivocation or deliberate ambiguity when he says to Cassio "She gives it out that you shall marry her" (Othello: Act IV, sc. i) exploiting the ambiguity or non-uniqueness of reference of the third person pronoun. Cassio, in the context, naturally interprets this as an opening to talk about Bianca, his "whore", and the conversation continues between them in less than respectful terms about "her", much to Iago's delight. Indeed, the point or goal of the operation for Iago, apart from the collateral one of bonomie with Cassio (always useful) is to provide Othello with some "proof" of Desdemona's infidelity; Othello has thus been posted within ear-shot, out of sight; Iago has engineered it that Othello will assume they are talking about Desdemona, and of course this is how he interprets the scene. Iago could not expect Cassio to cooperate willingly, since he knows very well that Cassio and Desdemona are not having an affair and that Cassio sincerely and chastely admires Desdemona. So, he simply uses him without his knowledge and through him tells the lies he could not say directly himself. Thus, in one swoop, providing proof to Othello and playing a very dirty trick on Cassio. Furthermore, it also serves his fixed goal of causing the maximum amount of suffering to Othello since the terms of Iago and Cassio's conversation has cast a rank pall of squalor over the affair: Cassio does not even respect her.

All these goals could not have been served in the circumstances by any direct means; or at least not all together. And Shakespeare gives us example after example of how to fit the deception to the circumstances; Iago almost always finds a way round the external or contextual constraints.

A non-linguistic example of an indirect deception strategy being used because of external or objective constraints which determine the impossibility of simple pretense, for example, might be the case of a lame man who needs, or wants, for some reason, to conceal the fact that he is lame; he cannot avoid limping, of course, but he might be able to reach his goal of concealing his lameness, if the context permits, by pretending to be pretending he is lame, or i.e. by pretending to act lameness.

4.2 Internal constraints

The above-mentioned class of reasons for indirect deception strategies is probably the most important and frequent. However, the following class of reasons may not have a less significant role to play. We call them internal constraints on direct lying. Some speakers may not be able to bring themselves to lie directly, even for "good" reasons, but may kid themselves that some indirect lying strategy or other is not really lying. For example, half-truths, deception by ommission, ambiguity, indeed any of the lying while saying the truth strategies could be used when there is need of a moral alibi. An illusory alibi is of no real value as long as the intent is to be less than truthful and therefore to deceive; also according to Saints Augustine and Thomas Aquinas.

Related, yet qualitatively different to the above type of reason is that of the speaker's sincere tact, delicacy or distaste. He does not like to speak directly of, or name certain matters outright. The use of euphemism might, for example, involve this. Rather than it being the case that the speaker is pretending to be tactful he might sincerely not wish to mention that sort of thing outright. He might even be deceiving himself.

4.3 Further goals

A further set of reasons for choosing to deceive indirectly might be described as strategic, expedient, opportunistic. The super goal which most immediately occurs to us is that of the speaker wanting to avoid eventual responsibility for the deception; by not explicitly committing himself to a proposition a speaker cannot easily or automatically be accused of having conveyed it; even when implicatures are communicated, and deceptive inferences drawn, the speaker might yet be able to get out of having earlier so intended; he did after all, not "say" anything to that effect; if confronted he could even try the counter-strategy of accusing the hearer of having a devious mind.

A further strategic reason for indirect deception would be that it is potentially much more effective than direct deception. This is not always true of course, but it may sometimes be the case. For example, by entrusting to the hearer's imagination the completion of a deceptive picture a speaker's goal may be more surely reached because the hearer may have further crucial information not known to the speaker (or, much more likely, not meant to be known to the speaker) with which to integrate the information the speaker is able to give him. The hearer can thus best convince himself, and thus, in other words, deceive himself. This is clearly interrelated with the first set of reasons mentioned above, that of the need to dodge external constraints. Strategies such as reticence, insinuation and allusion would find an explanation in this.

Furthermore, reticence, or feigned retincence (pretending to be reticent) or even manipulatory euphemism, may be employed when the speaker wants to appear tactful; in other words he pretends tact, and he wants to seem a sensitive, trustworthy friend; this appearing to not want to hurt a friend, to protect him from pain, or seeming to show delicacy towards another, not want to malign someone else, all the more confer credibility to the implied malignities. Iago, for example, uses this in the scene where he is asked by Othello to recount what happened in the street brawl where Cassio disgraced himself.

These strategies are also effective for the successful completion of other later plans. A sensitive, loyal, good-old, honest Iago, cannot be mistrusted easily and, even against the trusting hearer's better judgment, he may thus manage to make him believe otherwise over-audacious falsehoods.

4.4 Finally, the last reason we shall mention here which might help to account for the choice of indirect deception strategies over direct ones, or indeed for any indirect communication device, might be termed rhetorical; the figure termed "affidamento al supporto" (relying on the support) by Parisi and Castelfranchi, can be used, for example, for the sake of brevity. If just giving the support or reason for believing a piece of information is sufficient to convey that information, then one might as well save one's breath. If saying for instance, "I saw so-and-so running away from the scene of the murder with blood on his shirt" is enough to convey that so-and-so did the killing in your opinion, then there is no need to say more.

FOOTNOTES

* The present remarks are a summarised and revised account of some of the main points of an earlier working paper (Castelfranchi & Vincent 1977), focussing, as the sub-title indicates, on one particular aspect. With regard to the terminology of our sub-title, we must say that although "saying the truth" may be collocationally unusual, we can see no other expression which would be more consistent with our discussion. We should like to take this opportunity to thank John Lyons, Steve Isard, Domenico Parisi and the friends and colleagues at this conference for their kind interest and precious comments; any remaining nonsense is, of course, our sole responsibility.

1. The model, called "scopistica" (after the Italian for goal: "scopo") is being developed by Domenico Parisi and Cristiano Castelfranchi at the Psychology Institute of the National Council for Research (CNR) in Rome; cf. Parisi & Castelfranchi (this volume) for a specific exposition of some of the theoretical bases of the model and of the methodological assumptions; cf. also Poggi et al. (this volume) for another application.

2. Cf. Austin (1962: 143-144); cf. also Garfinkel (1977): "a sentence or an entire discourse can be defective in some material way by virtue of its pragmatic appropriateness to the context of the utterance. Truth is not so much a linguistic question as it is a pragmatic question" (136-137).

3. On the depth and limit to reasoning concerning interlocutors' mutual assumptions or presuppositions in conversational exchange cf. Kock & Harder (1976); and cf. Lewis (1969: 52-60), Grice (1975, 1978). Stalnaker (1978: 321-325), Rogers (1978 and 1979) for the notion of presuppositions as common ground between interlocutors, and as their common knowledge and mutual knowledge; cf. also Yorick Wilks (1979).

4. We refer in particular to Augustine's "De mendacio" and "Contra mendacium", and to St. Thomas Aquinas' "De mendacio" (in his "Summa theologiae") which also refers back to Augustine.

5. Although by doing so one would be able to distinguish mechanisms of indirect communication, and therefore, also of deception. However, given the not altogether clear, nor settled, distinctions in the literature between, for example, various types of implicature and their generation (cf. Grice 1975, 1978; Sadock 1978; Morgan 1978b, and Gazdar 1979a, for discussions) it is not clear that this would be at all easy to do as yet. So, a lot is lurking behind this "somehow" of the hearer's reconstruction of a speaker's goals and super-goals; we can, nevertheless say that the mechanisms governing the generation of the hearer's various inferences are contextually relative; they are related to fea-

tures of the context of utterance; for example, Paolo Leonardi and Jens Allwood (personal communications) have stressed the importance of considering such a feature as the respective social stati of the interlocutors in determining a speaker's possible, and/or admissible, super-goals with a particular utterance. Zaefferer (1977), incidentally, proposes an extremely interesting analysis, in terms of decision theory, which describes the contextually bound reasoning of a hearer in deciding upon the reading of, what we should call, the super-goals to attribute to an utterance after having assigned probability values in the particular context to the various possible interpretations. Here, then, we can do no more than mention the importance of the context of an utterance in determining its super-goals, and its degree of deceptiveness, and point to Garfinkel (of. cit.) for a particular examination, from this point of view, of the commercial advertising context. One important last point to be remembered, although not discussed here, and which has also been stressed in conversation with Charles Li, concerns cultural differences in deception strategies; cf. in connection with this, for instance E.O. Keenan's (1976).

6. Cf. for instance Lewis' (1969) notion of convention, and Grice's conversational maxims governed by the cooperative principle, which would seem to be characterisations of fixed goals of conversation. In the case of the maxims put forward by Grice one can discern that these goals may be of at least two types: functional or instrumental to achieving further goals, and collateral.

7. Cf. Grewendorf (this volume) for an interesting proposal for determining degrees of informativeness of answers, and therefore, clearly involving relevance and adequacy of information. Cf. also Brockway (this volume), Sperber & Wilson (n.d.) and Wilson & Sperber (1978),for the notion of relevance. A notion which is of crucial importance here and elsewhere, but of difficult solution, as the discussions referred to reveal.

8. Given our definition of aggression (as any case of preventing someone from reaching a goal), even apparently hearer-protective cases of deception are still "aggressive". Consider, for example, the following situation: A is a doctor, and B a good friend of A's who has consulted him; after the necessary tests have revealed to A that B has a terminal cancer, B asks A is he has cancer, and A tells B that he does not. One might think this lie of A's a protective move, and not, therefore describable as aggressive. However, if A is intentionally preventing B from reaching what he believes is B's goal, i.e. knowing the truth about his condition, this move would have to be called aggressive. Of course, this would depend on B's real goal in asking A, or rather on A's sincere assumptions concerning B's goal. If A thinks B really wants to know the truth about whether he has cancer, then preventing him from knowing what he, A, believes to be the truth, by lying, is aggressive, with regard to B's goal, even though in the short run, it protects him from the pain of the truth. The adherent pain or pleasurableness of a fact is not to be confused with the aggressiveness or solidarity of an

action. To return to our example, A's move is aggressive or non-solidary for the further reason that it deceives B about A's assumptions. On the other hand, if A sincerely believes B would really rather not want to know the truth, if the truth is that he has cancer, then by telling him that he does have cancer would be intentionally non-cooperative, and therefore aggressive, although truthful. Deceptive moves, then, are merely a sub-set within the set of aggressive moves. To sum up this point, by examining the goals of a move at the various levels one could find some were aggressive and others not so. The "protective" lie, then, would have a non-aggressive top-goal or objective, but, as described, some of its sub-goals would be aggressive.

9. This point has now been made by many since Augustine first made it (to our knowledge): "mendacium est enuntiatio cum voluntate falsum enuntiandi" (De mendacio ch. IV); cf. for instance Siegler (1966), Chisholm and Feehan (op. cit.,) who also specifically refer to the notions of formal versus material truth and quote Aquinas in a passage where he distinguishes essential from accidental truth (op. cit.: 148, note 7).

10. Although, the speaker may thus be described as having lied while saying the truth, this is only trivially and accidentally the case. We shall be concerned here with the deliberate use or manipulation of truth with the intention to deceive. The speaker intends to say what is true, and also intends to deceive.

11. For example a gold-plated bracelet worn with the intention of getting others to assume it is solid gold, might properly be called a "fake" upon the discovery of its true nature and of the *wearer's* intentions. If worn without that intention, however, it would not be appropriate, or fair, to call it a fake.

12. Cf. D. Mellor (1978) on assenting as conscious belief; especially important for the determination of a speaker's sincerity, and also for the characterisation of self-deception.

13. Cf. Chisholm and Feehan (op. cit.: 143-146) for their fundamental distinction of four types of deception by commission and four by omission; Cf. Parret (op. cit.) who also adpots their distinctions.

14. Thus, we agree with Herman Parret that speech act theory is not adequate for the study of deception, not even for that of linguistic deception. However, the main reason we would put forward for this is that speech act theory, albeit in considerable depth, deals only with what we call communicative goals or supergoals of utterances, and cannot, thus, deal with acts or moves whose goals are non-communicative or even necessarily concealed. Indeed, Searle's indirect speech acts coincide with the communicative supergoals of utterances, as they are called here; and these are only one of the types of goal which utterances may have. Speech act theory would then have a place as that specific theory which studies one aspect of linguistic action - as a part of a more general theory of linguistic action which would also have to take account of non-communicative goals of utterances.

15. There is not in English, or Italian, a strict lexical distinction between pretending where one does not want it to be understood as such, and pretending where, on the contrary one wants it to be communicated. We have decided therefore, although not entirely arbitrarily, to use the term "pretending" for the first case, and "acting" for the second (see 2.3 below). Furthermore, one cannot fail to refer the reader to Austin's essay on pretending: Austin (1970).

16. Cf. also Augustine in his exclusion of "joci" from deception: "exceptis igitur jocis, quae nunquam sunt putata mendacia, habent enim evidentissima ex pronuntiatione atque ipso jocantis affectu significationem animi nequaquam fallentis etsi non vera enuntiantis" De Mendacio II; cf. also Weinrich (1976: 176-182), on irony; cf. also Sperber & Wilson (to appear in Cole ed.).

17. Cf. Chisholm and Feehan (op. cit., sect. IV especially); Siegler (op. cit.); Weinrich (op. cit.) for definitions of lying, and a history of the notion in the literature. And cf. Coleman and Kay for an investigation into the prototypical characterisation of lying.

18. For a recent discussion on assertion cf. Stalnaker (1978) for instance, and Rogers (1978 and 1979); cf. also Chisholm & Feehan (op. cit., sect. III) for an examination of the place of the notion in the explication of lying.

19. Cf. Parret (op. cit.: 16-17) and Caffi (1979) for viewpoints seemingly at variance with our characterisation of insinuation. However, we distinguish between insinuating an idea into someone's mind by covert means (cf. Parret's example of the doctor and the diet) and doing insinuation. We are concerned with the latter. It is, furthermore, also true that one cannot make an insinuation by using the performative "I insinuate that ..." (cf. Caffi's point about illocutionary suicide) but this does not necessarily mean that insinuation is not to be communicative, rather, we think the point is that this would undermine or compromise the super-goals which characterise the choice of an act of insinuation (cf. sect 4.3 below - avoiding responsibility, for example). And, moreover, surely the speaker's very choice of doing insinuation rather than, say, stating, indicates that there is, or would be, something unwelcome or shameful about the information. Indeed, we see the doing of insinuation precisely as the speaker's means of conveying not only the information but also and especially his negative value judgement of the information, or that it is potentially harmful to the hearer. The hearer, thus, must realise that the speaker is insinuating - the speaker must let the hearer realise this, and that he is letting him understand it, on purpose. This is why we maintain that insinuation is communicative, and that it involves negative value judgements. Parret is not addressing himself, in fact, to the same strategy as we are.

20. Cf. Castelfranchi and Vincent (op. cit.); and Vincent (in preparation) for a more specific discussion of Iago's strategies of deception.

21. Cf. Garfinkel (op. cit.) for a different definition of half-truth; it is, however, only a terminological difference, since what he calls

half-truths would seem to come under our general category of indirect lying through inference, being, furthermore, one mode of doing what we term lying while saying the truth.

22. Cf. for example, Gazdar, Stalnaker, Rogers, (op. cit.), Kock and Harder (op. cit.). And cf. the recent debate on the status of presupposition and its various types, in for example Wilson and Sperber (1977), von Stechow (1978). And cf. Ruth Kempson (1975) and C.K. Oh & D. Dineen (eds.) (1979).

23. Cf. also Ann Weiser (1974, 1975) for related points concerning the deliberate use of ambiguity and other manipulatory strategies for the concealment of requested information.

24. Sam Steele (personal communication) has suggested a related tactic or strategy: the deliberate exploitation of speaker and hearer idiolectal differences.

25. Cf. also Chisholm and Feehan (op. cit.: 154) on "counter deception".

ON A FORMAL TREATMENT OF ILLOCUTIONARY FORCE INDICATORS

Dietmar Zaefferer

0. *Introduction*

What I am going to present here on the topic of a formal treatment of illocutionary force indicators are not so much results but rather a proposal for a framework in which a program of research should be carried out. The general aim of this program of research is to expand existing formal semantics for natural languages like the ones presented for instance by Richard Montague,[1] David Lewis[2] or Max Cresswell[3] in order to encompass not only locutionary indicators, i.e. truthvalue-relevant components of linguistic expressions, but also illocutionary indicators, i.e. those features of linguistic expressions which point rather to how they are to be taken. One of the most important illocutionary indicators is of course sentence mood and so I will illustrate my proposal with a fragment of German including declarative, interrogative as well as jussive sentences. A further type of illocutionary indicators, namely particles, will also be considered in order to show the interaction of different kinds of illocutionary indicators. But before presenting the relevant data, let me first say a few words about how I see the connection between a formal theory of illocutionary meaning and a theory of language use.

1. *The framework of a theory of language use*

I assume that normal use of language or, as I shall say equivalently, normal linguistic behaviour is part of rational behaviour, and that therefore the central aim of a theory of language use is to answer the following question:

> What are the conditions under which it is rational for a possible speaker to use a certain linguistic expression?

It is widely agreed that language has two basic kinds of uses: a dialogical and a monological one or, as Gilbert Harman (1977) puts it, a communicative and a calculative one. I do not object to Harman's claim that "language surely has both uses, and the second is as important as the first",[4] but I do not believe that the theories for both uses should be developed independently nor that a theory of the dialogical use should be based on a theory of the monological one. One argument for following the opposite strategy comes from the ontogenesis of language: no child will calculate linguistically before having learned a language, and he learns language through its communicative use, even if what he learns first is to a large extent a special kind of monologuing. But I do not want to dwell further on the difficult topic of how to explain the monological or calculative use of language, and I will restrict my attention in what follows to the dialogical one. Then a first preliminary answer to our central question can be given as follows:

> It is rational for a possible speaker to use a certain linguistic expression E if he wishes to entitle a possible interpreter to draw certain inferences from his behaviour and if he believes that the use of E is a good means to that end.

Among the inferences a possible interpreter is entitled to draw from a given occurrence of linguistic behaviour are certainly those which constitute what is called a correct understanding of the given occurrence. Thus, like E. von Savigny,[5] I propose to explain linguistic behaviour in terms of a correct understanding of this behaviour. But what are the inferences which constitute a correct understanding? Obviously not all those which are possible. If I hear someone pronounce distinctly "What can I do for you?", I can infere that he has a tongue, but this does not belong to the inferences we have in mind when we are thinking of correct understanding. Why? Because the basis for this inference, the fact that to have a tongue is a necessary condition for behaving as described, is a law of physiology, and not an instance of my knowledge of English. What we are after are inferences of a special subclass of those which intuitively are valid with respect to a given occurrence of behaviour. As a first approximation I propose to define the subclass in question as containing exactly those inferences which depend on the assumption that the speaker knows the language he uses, i.e. that he knows what the correct inferences are which a possible interpreter is entitled to draw.

Some technical considerations are in order before we can proceed. The normal logical means for representing a class of inferences is a sentence: Given a logical system which defines a notion of sentence as well as a notion of inference, a class of inferences with respect to a given sentence S can be identified with the set of those sentences which logically follow from S. Thus if we wish to identify correct understanding with a class of inferences, we can characterize it by a sentence together with a suitable notion of inference. But what is the sentence which determines the correct understanding of a given linguistic utterance? Is it the expression which is uttered? Not every utterance has the form of a sentence, not even an elliptical one (what would e.g. "Wow!" be an ellipsis of?), and those which have are not completely understood if only the expression is understood, but not what the speaker is doing in uttering it. Therefore, I propose to take a description of the linguistic act at the illocutionary level as the kind of sentence we are looking for. And, knowing well the intricacies of the semantics of natural illocution-describing predicates, I propose further to use artificial terms for the formulation of the illocutionary description. If we use a system with indirect interpretation like the one defined in Montague's PTQ,[6] we have no problem in doing this since the intensional logic into which natural expressions are translated provides infinitely many constants of each type besides those which have natural counterparts. Of course, we will have to define those abstract constants, because the class of inferences we are after will depend on them. But then we will be in a position to check the adequacy of our theory in terms of what U. Blau (1978) calls intuitive correctness and intuitive completeness. Our theory will be intuitively correct, if no inference turns out to be formally valid although intuitively it is not. It will be intuitively complete if all inferences which are intuitively valid are valid in their formal reconstruction as well. Accordingly, to refine a theory is to achieve an increasing degree of completeness while trying to keep inside the field of correctness. But first we have to define a notion of entailment on the illocutionary level or, for short, or Il-entailment. And then we can reformulate our answer to the central question in the following decision-theoretic way:

> It is rational for a possible speaker to use expression E in situation S if it is optimal for him with respect to his assumptions and preferences to entitle a possible interpreter to draw those inferences from his behaviour which are characterized by the illocutionary meaning of E in S and the notion of Il-entailment.

2. *Exemplification*

In the first part of this chapter, some data from German are presented which, as far as I can see, can only be handled in an adequate way if not only syntax and semantics proceed hand in hand, as Montague claims they should,[7] but syntax, semantics, and pragmatics in one of its senses or, in my terms, syntax, locutionary, and illocutionary semantics. Then the data are treated formally in the suggested way, i.e. with the help of an intensional model-theory and via the notion of illocutionary entailment.

2.1 *The data*

The data are chosen from German with the intention to show (a) the intuitive relations which hold between illocutions of different type, but with related content, (b) the interaction between ambiguities on the locutionary as well as the illocutionary level, and (c) the interaction between illocutionary indicators of different types. The following four German sentences will constitute our material:

(1) *Wen kennt jeder?*
'Whom does everybody know?'

(2) *Ich frage dich, wen jeder kennt.*
'I ask you whom everybody knows.'

(3) *Sag mir, wen jeder kennt!*
'Tell me whom everybody knows!'

(4) *Niemanden kennt jeder.*
'Nobody is known by anybody/everybody.'

Locutionary ambiguities

On the locutionary level, all four sentences are ambiguous with respect to the scope of *jeder*. (This is why (4) has two English translations.) The wide scope reading of (1) can be paraphrased as (1'), the narrow scope reading as (1"):

(1') For every person x: whom does x know?
(1") For which person(s) x: everybody knows x?

In spoken German (1) is normally disambiguated by stressing *kennt* in the former and *jeder* in the latter case. Note that in its wide scope reading, (1) is equivalent on the locutionary level (L-equivalent) with the so-called multiple question (5):

(5) *Wer kennt wen?*
'Who knows whom?'

It follows that (5) can also be paraphrased by (1'), and this means that *wer* as well as *jeder* can be rendered by the universal quantifier. If we apply the same procedure to *wen*, we get (1'''),

(1''') For every person x and every person y: does x know y?

which is also a good paraphrase of the relevant L-reading of (1) and where no interrogative pronoun occurs at all. This is one of the facts on which my treatment of WH-questions will be based.

Exactly the same scope ambiguity arises with respect to the indirect question clauses *wen jeder kennt* in (2) and (3), and (4) is ambiguous in an analogous way: its wide scope reading can be paraphrased as (4') and its narrow scope reading as (4''):

(4') For every person x: x knows nobody.
(4'') For no person x: everybody knows x.

Illocutionary ambiguities

On the illocutionary level we shall focus on two uses of interrogative sentences, namely the erotetic and the assertive ones.[8] The erotetic Il-reading of (1) aims at an answer regarding either those persons who are known by everybody or those pairs of persons <x,y> such that x knows y, according to which L-reading is chosen. The assertive Il-reading of (1), on the other hand, is a more stylish way of expressing the belief that nobody (or almost nobody)[9] is known by everybody or, much stronger, by anybody, again according to the L-reading under consideration. In German WH-interrogatives, this Il-ambiguity is often removed by introducing the particle *schon* (not to be confused with the adverb *schon* 'already') if the assertive reading is meant. At the same time, the L-ambiguity is removed as well since, at least according to my intuitions, (6) has only the wide scope and (7) only the narrow scope reading.[10]

(6) *Wen kennt jeder schon?*
(7) *Wen kennt schon jeder?*

This fits in with our observation that in spoken German the main stress is on *kennt* for the wide scope reading and on *jeder* in the narrow scope case since, as Krivonosov (1965) has pointed out, only unstressed elements can occur between the main verb and a modal particle.

Sentences (2) and (4) are declarative sentences. In general, declarative sentences have at least two Il-readings, an assertive and a declarational one. The assertive use of a sentence S commits the speaker in some way to the belief that S is true while the declarational use of S makes S true. According to a proposal made by I. Heim (1977), which I shall adopt here, Austin's (1962) so-called explicit performative utterances are a special case of declarations. So the interesting Il-reading of (2) is the explicit performative or the declarational one. On the other hand, with respect to (4) only the assertive reading will be considered. (It seems hard indeed to imagine a situation where (4) can be interpreted as a declaration.)

(3) is a jussive sentence, and here only the directive use will be considered.

Illocutionary relations between (1) - (4)

When confronted with sentences (1) - (4), every native speaker of German will feel that there are strong intuitive relations holding between them. These relations, however, are not locutionary or semantical in nature (as D. Lewis (1970: 205-212) falsely claims),[11] but they are illocutionary relations, since they vary according to the Il-reading under consideration. My claim is that the relations which hold between (1) - (4), and which constitute data to be accounted for, are the following:

> The L-readings of the erotetic reading of (1) are Il-entailed by the corresponding L-readings of the declarational reading of (2) and by the corresponding L- readings of (3). The L-readings of the assertive reading of (1), on the other hand, are Il-equivalent with the corresponding readings of (the assertive reading of) (4).

2.2 *A formal treatment of the data*

2.2.0 *Outline*

My proposal for a treatment of the above-mentioned data rests on the assumptions put forward in Montague (1974b), namely that a formal grammar (in the sense of syntax *and* semantics) of some language L has to define not only the notion of a sentence of L, but also a corresponding disambiguated language L' which provides a syntactic counterpart for each reading of a L-sentence. Here, certain abstract elements like parentheses and indices are introduced which do not occur in L. Furthermore, it has to assign each L'-sentence its meaning (intension) with respect to an interpretation and its denotation (extension) with respect to a model, i.e. an interpretation together with a point of reference. For the sake of perspicuity, Montague uses in PTQ a second artificial language L" into which L' - expressions have to be translated before the meaning-assignment can apply. In the following, I shall adopt this procedure as well as the intensional logic which plays in PTQ the role of L".

2.2.1 *Syntax*

I will first characterize the disambiguated language DG (disambiguated German) in which the above-mentioned readings of (1) - (4) will be represented.

Categories of DG

Cat is to be the smallest set such that
 (i) e, t^n, f^n ε Cat (n ε $\mathbb{N}$),[12]
 (ii) if A, B ε Cat, then $A/_n B$ ε Cat (n ε $\mathbb{N}$).
If n = 0, it will usually be omitted. e is to be understood as the category of entity expressions, t^n as the categories of truth-value-denoting expressions or sentence radicals and f^n as the categories of force carrying expressions or sentences. As indicated above, the distinction between the locutionary and the illocutionary level is reflected in the syntax, the formal means being the distinction between the categories t^n and f^n.

Categories of some basic expressions of DG

Abbreviation: IV := (e/t)

$\{ich, du, jeder, niemand, er_0, er_1,...\} \subseteq B_T := B_{t/IV}$

$\{wer\} \subseteq B_{QT} := B_{t/_1 IV}$

$\emptyset = B_{PQT} := B_{t/_2 IV}$

$\{kenn\} \subseteq B_{IV/_4 T}$

$\{sag_{ob}\} \subseteq B_{(IV/_1 t)/_3 T}$

$\{frag\} \subseteq B_{(IV/_1 t)/_4 T}$

If A is a category, then $B_A \subseteq P_A$, where B_A is the set of basic expressions of category A, and P_A the set of phrases of this category. For mnemonic reasons, I will use the following abbreviations: $P_{Dec}: P_f 1$ are the declarational, $P_{Ass} := P_f 2$ the assertive, $P_{Ero} := P_f 3$ the erotetic, and $P_{Dir} := P_f 4$ the directive DG-sentences.

The language of intensional logic IL

As target language of the translation procedure to be specified below, I take the typed intensional tense logic defined in Montague (1974c: 256f.), with its definitions of types and of meaningful expressions of each type. I also adopt the notational convention of designating those IL-constants which are target expressions of the translation procedure by primed variants of the corresponding DG-expressions, and of marking the extensional counterparts of IL-predicates by a substar.

Translations of the relevant basic DG-expressions[13]

ich	translates into		sp*
du	"	"	ad*
jeder	"	"	$\hat{P}\Lambda x[\text{Pers}(x) \to P\{x\}]$
niemand	"	"	$\hat{P}\neg vx[\text{Pers}(x) \wedge P\{x\}]$
er_n	"	"	$\hat{P}\ P\{x_n\}$
wer	"	"	$\hat{P}\Lambda x[\text{Pers}(x) \to P\{x\}]$
$kenn^o$	"	"	*kenn'*
sag^o_{ob}	"	"	$sag_{ob}{'}$
$frag^o$	"	"	*frag'*

The relevant rules of syntax and translation

The form of a syntactical rule is the following: let A, B, C be any categories. If $\alpha \in P_A$ and $\beta \in P_B$, then $\gamma \in P_C$, where γ is the value of some operation F for the arguments α and β. β can be zero. The form of the corresponding translation rule is as follows: Let A, B, C be as above. If $\alpha \in P_A$, α translates into α', $\beta \in P_B$, and β translates into β', then γ ($\gamma \in P_C$, $\gamma = F(\alpha,\beta)$) translates into γ', where γ' is the value of some operation F' for the arguments α' and β'. I will combine both forms into the following rule scheme:

$$\frac{\begin{array}{ll}\alpha \in P_A & \alpha' \\ \beta \in P_B & \beta'\end{array}}{\gamma \in P_C \qquad \gamma'}$$

The types of the target expressions are determined by the following rule: every DG-phrase of category A translates into a meaningful IL-expression of type k(A) where k, the category-to-type mapping, is that function from Cat into the set of types such that (i) $k(e) = e$, $k(t^n) = k(f^n) = t$ for all $n \in \mathbb{N}$, and (ii) $k(A/_n B) = \langle\langle s,k(B)\rangle, k(A)\rangle$ for all $n \in \mathbb{N}$.

R 1 *Object embedding*

For any $A \in Cat$, $n \in \{3, 4\}$

$$\frac{\begin{array}{ll}\alpha \in P_T & \alpha' \\ \beta \in P_{A/_n T} & \beta'\end{array}}{\alpha^n \beta \in P_A \qquad \beta'(^\wedge\alpha')}$$

R 2 *Indirect question clause embedding*

$$\frac{\begin{array}{ll}\alpha \in P_{IV/_1 t} & \alpha' \\ \beta \in P_t & \beta'\end{array}}{\alpha, ob\ \beta^+ \in P_{IV} \qquad \alpha'(^\wedge\beta')}$$

where β^+ comes from β by replacing all occurrences of (i) γ^{on} by the nth person indicative present tense of γ, (ii) δ^3 by the third case of δ, and (iii) η^4 by the fourth case of η.[14]

R 3 *Subject inserting*

$$
\begin{array}{lll}
\alpha & \varepsilon\ P_T & \alpha' \\
\beta & \varepsilon\ P_{IV} & \beta' \\
\hline
\alpha\ \beta^+ \varepsilon\ P_t & & \alpha'(^\wedge\beta')
\end{array}
$$

where β^+ comes from β by replacing all upper indices o in β by o1 if $\alpha = ich$, o2 if $\alpha = du$, and o3 otherwise.

R 4/R 5 *Declarative sentences with assertive and declarational force, respectively*

$\alpha\ \beta^4\ \gamma^3\ \delta^{on}\ \eta\ \varepsilon\ P_t$ $\qquad\qquad\qquad\qquad\alpha'$
where $\eta \in \{1,2,3\}$ and β^4, γ^3, η may be empty

$$
\left.
\begin{array}{l}
(\alpha\ on_\delta\ 3_\gamma\ 4_\beta\ \eta.)_\omega \\
(3_\gamma\ on_\delta\ \alpha\ 4_\beta\ \eta.)_\omega \\
(4_\beta\ on_\delta\ \alpha\ 3_\gamma\ \eta.)_\omega \\
(\eta\ on_\delta\ \alpha\ 3_\gamma\ 4_\beta.)_\omega
\end{array}
\right\} \varepsilon\ P_\omega,
$$

where $\omega \in \{Ass, Dec\}$, on_δ is the nth person indicative present tense of δ, and 3_γ, 4_β are the third and fourth case of γ and β, respectively.

$Ass(^\wedge sp, ^\wedge ad^*, ^\wedge \alpha')$ if $\omega = Ass$,
α' if $\omega = Dec$.

R 6 *Interrogative sentences with erotetic force*

$\alpha\ \beta^4\ \gamma^3\ \delta^{on}\ \eta\ \varepsilon\ P_t \qquad\qquad \alpha'$
(conditions as above)

$\overline{(on_\delta\ \alpha\ 3_\gamma\ 4_\beta\ \eta?)_{Ero}\ \varepsilon\ P_{Ero}} \qquad Ero(^\wedge sp, ^\wedge ad^*, ^\wedge \alpha')$
(Notation as above)

R 7 *Interrogative sentences with assertive force*

$\alpha \; \beta^{on} \; \gamma \quad \varepsilon \; P_t 1 \qquad\qquad \alpha'$
where $n \quad \varepsilon \; \{1.2.3\}$

$(\alpha \; on_\beta \; \gamma+?)_{Ass} \; \varepsilon \; P_{Ass}$ $\qquad Ass(\hat{\;}sp, \hat{\;}ad^*, \hat{\;}\alpha')$

where on_β is the nth person indicative present tense of β and γ^+ comes from γ by replacing all items with upper indices 3 or 4 in γ by their third or fourth case, respectively.

R 8 *Jussive sentences*

$\alpha \; \beta^4 \; \gamma^3 \; \delta^{o2} \; \eta \; \varepsilon \; P_t \qquad\qquad \alpha'$
(conditions as above)

$(Imp_\delta \; 3_\gamma \; 4_\beta \; \eta!)_{Dir} \; \varepsilon \; P_{Dir}$ $\qquad Dir(\hat{\;}sp, \hat{\;}ad^*, \hat{\;}\alpha')$

where Imp_δ is the imperative form of δ and 3_γ, 4_β are as above.

R 9,n *Quantifying in*
For any $A \; \varepsilon \; \{f^m, t^m\}$, $m \; \varepsilon \; \mathbb{N}$

$\alpha \qquad \varepsilon \; P_T \qquad\qquad \alpha'$
$\beta \qquad \varepsilon \; P_A \qquad\qquad \beta'$

$\beta[\gamma_n/\alpha_n^+] \; \varepsilon \; P_A \qquad\qquad \alpha'(\hat{x}_n \beta')$

where $\beta[\gamma_n/\alpha_n^+]$ comes from β by replacing the first occurrence of an item with lower index n by the corresponding case of α with lower index n.

R 10,n *Term questions*

$\alpha \qquad \varepsilon \; P_{QT} \qquad\qquad \alpha'$
$\beta \qquad \varepsilon \; P_f m \qquad\qquad \beta'$

$\beta^+ \; \varepsilon \; P_f m$, where either $\qquad \alpha'(\hat{x}_n \beta')$

(a) there is an occurrence of *ob* in β and β^+ comes from β by deleting the first item with lower index n in β and by replacing *ob* by the corresponding case of α, or (b) there is an occurrence of an element of P_{QT} in β and $\beta^+ = \beta[\gamma_n/\alpha_n^+]$, the latter being defined as in R 9,n, or (c) there is no occurrence of *ob* or an element of P_{QT} in β and β^+ comes from β by deleting the first item with lower index n in β and by prefixing β with the corresponding case of α.

R 11 *Pseudo-question-terms*

$$\frac{\alpha \quad \varepsilon \quad P_{QT}}{\alpha \quad \varepsilon \quad P_{PQT}} \qquad \frac{\alpha'}{\bar{Q} \; \alpha'(\hat{y}_\neg \; Q\{y\})}$$

R 12,n *Pseudo-term-questions*

$$\frac{\begin{array}{c}\alpha \quad \varepsilon \quad P_{PQT}\\ \beta \; \gamma^{om} \; \delta \quad \varepsilon \quad P_t\\ \text{where } m \; \varepsilon \; \{1,2,3\}, \text{ and } \delta \text{ may be empty}\end{array}}{\alpha^+ \; \gamma^{om} \; \beta^+ \; \delta \; \varepsilon \; P_t1} \qquad \frac{\alpha'}{\beta'} \\ \alpha'(\hat{x}_n \beta')$$

where β^+ comes from β by deleting the first occurrence of an item with lower index n in β and α^+ is the corresponding case of α.

The working of these rules can be demonstrated in a familiar way with the help of analysis trees. The number of the rule in operation is added to the right of the output expression, furthermore, the category of each expression is indicated inside a circle.

Two sample analysis trees:

(1a')   *(wen kennt jeder$_0$?)* Ero (f^3), 9,0

  jeder (T)   *(wen kennt er$_0$?)* Ero (f^3), 10,1

    wer (QT)   *(kennt er$_0$ ihn$_1$?)* Ero (f^3), 6

        er$_0$ er$_1^4$ kenn^{03} (t), 3

    er$_0$ (T)   *er$_1^4$ kenn^0* (IV), 1

        er$_1$ (T)   *kenn^0* (IV/$_4$T)

(3a')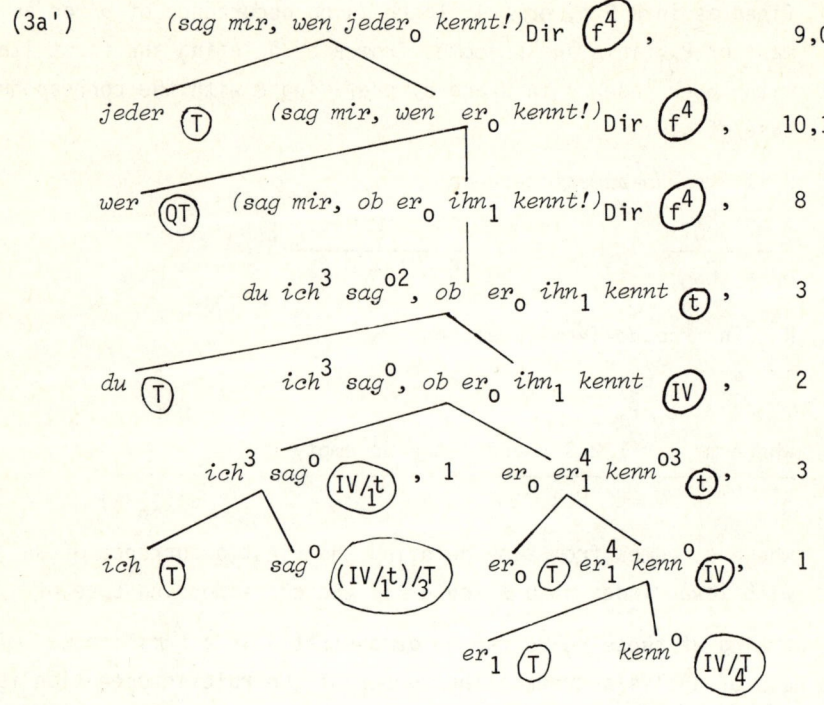

Representation of the relevant readings of (1)-(4) in DG:

The two sample analysis trees should have made clear how to derive the following ten sentences, which are the DG-representation of the readings mentioned under 2.1 above.

(1a) *(wen kennt jeder$_o$?)*$_{Ero}$
(1b) *(wen kennt jeder?)*$_{Ero}$
(1c) *(wen kennt jeder$_o$?)*$_{Ass}$
(1d) *(wen kennt jeder?)*$_{Ass}$
(2a) *(ich frage dich, wen jeder$_o$ kennt.)*$_{Dec}$
(2b) *(ich frage dich, wen jeder kennt.)*$_{Dec}$
(3a) *(sag mir, wen jeder$_o$ kennt!)*$_{Dir}$
(3b) *(sag mir, wen jeder kennt!)*$_{Dir}$
(4a) *(niemanden kennt jeder.)*$_{Ass}$
(4b) *(niemanden$_o$ kennt jeder.)*$_{Ass}$

The ambiguation relation AR:

AR is to be the smallest relation such that $<\alpha,\alpha'> \varepsilon$ AR if and only if $\alpha \varepsilon P_f n$ for some $n \varepsilon \mathbb{N}$ and α' comes from α by capitalizing the first letter and deleting all parentheses and indices in α. The range of AR is called S or the set of G-sentences, where G is the ambiguous counterpart of DG. It is easy to see that (1)-(4) are elements of S according to this definition.

Representation in IL

The application of the translation part of our rules leads to expressions which are equivalent with the following IL-formulas (1a")-(4b").[15] Abbreviations: if α is a formula, then ERO($^\alpha$) := Ero(^{sp}, ^{ad*},$^\alpha$), ASS($^\alpha$) := Ass(^{sp},^{ad*},$^\alpha$), and DIR($^\alpha$) := Dir(^{sp},^{ad*},$^\alpha$).

(1a") $\Lambda u[Pers_*(u) \to \Lambda v[Pers_*(v) \to ERO(^\wedge kenn'_*(u,v))]]$
(1b") $\Lambda v[Pers_*(v) \to ERO(^\wedge \Lambda u[Pers_*(u) \to kenn'_*(u,v)])]$
(1c") $ASS(^\wedge \Lambda u[Pers_*(u) \to \neg \bigvee v[Pers_*(v) \& kenn'_*(u,v)]])$
(1d") $ASS(^\wedge \neg \bigvee v[Pers_*(v) \& \Lambda u[Pers_*(u) \to kenn'_*(u,v)]])$
(2a") $\Lambda u[Pers_*(u) \to \Lambda v[Pers_*(v) \to frag'(^{sp},^{ad*},^\wedge kenn'_*(u,v))]]$
(2b") $\Lambda v[Pers_*(v) \to frag'(^{sp},^{ad*},^\wedge \Lambda u[Pers_*(u) \to kenn'_*(u,v)])]$
(3a")
$\Lambda u[Pers_*(u) \to \Lambda v[Pers_*(v) \to DIR(^\wedge sag_{ob}'(^{ad},^{sp*},^\wedge kenn'_*(u,v)))]]$
(3b")
$\Lambda v[Pers_*(v) \to DIR(^\wedge sag_{ob}'(^{ad},^{sp*},^\wedge \Lambda u[Pers_*(u) \to kenn'_*(u,v)]))]$
(4a") $ASS(^\wedge \Lambda u[Pers_*(u) \to \neg \bigvee v[Pers_*(v) \& kenn'_*(u,v)]])$
(4b") $ASS(^\wedge \neg \bigvee v[Pers_*(v) \& \Lambda u[Pers_*(u) \to kenn'_*(u,v)]])$

2.2.2 *Semantics*

An IL-interpretation is essentially an interpretation in the sense of Montague's PTQ-logic (loc. cit. p. 258), i.e. a quintuple $<E,W,T,\leq,F>$, where E,W,T are nonempty sets (to be understood as the sets of entities, possible worlds and moments of time, respectively), $\leq$ is a linear ordering on T and for every $i \varepsilon I$, $F(i)$ is a function which maps the constants of each type into the set of possible denotations of that type; I, the set of indices, is defined as E x E x W x T. Therefore, for each i ε I, the first and second coordinate of i are individuals and may serve in every interpretation as the i-extensions of the special expressions 'sp' (for speaker) and 'ad' (for addressee). Of course, not all possible IL-interpretations will be interesting for the interpretation of German. With the help of some meaning postulates, I will therefore characterize a more restricted notion of IL-interpretation which I will call G-IL-interpretation (interpretation of intensional logic admissible for the analysis of German) and on which my central definitions of truth and entailment will be based.

Meaning postulates

It would be the task of an explicit theory of morphological meaning to define the abstract constant 'Pers', and of a theory of speech acts to define the abstract constants 'Ero', 'Ass', and 'Dir'. In this paper, however, two of them are only partially characterized, since for the present purposes, even the first two meaning postulates will do.

The Π, i, g-extensions of the following formulas are to be 1 for all G-IL-interpretations Π, all Π-indices i and all Π-assignments g:

MP 1 $\Lambda x \Lambda P \Lambda p [Ero(x,P,p) \leftrightarrow frag'(x,P,p)]$

MP 2 $\Lambda x \Lambda y \Lambda p [Dir(x, \hat{P}P\{y\}, \hat{\ }sag_{ob}'(y, \hat{P}P\{x\}, p)) \to Ero(x, \hat{P}P\{y\}, p)]$

MP 3 $\Lambda x \Lambda P \Lambda p [\delta(x,P,p) \to Ass(x,P,p)]$, where $\delta \in \{behaupt', mitteil', feststell'\}$. ('assert', 'communicate', 'state')

MP 4 $\Lambda x \Lambda P \Lambda p [\delta(x,P,p) \to Dir(x,P,p)]$, where $\delta \in \{aufforder', bitt', befehl'\}$. ('ask', 'request', 'order')

Truth, locutionary, and illocutionary entailment

Let α, β be elements of $P_f n$, for some $n \in \mathbb{N}$.

(1) *Truth-in-a-model.* Let Π be a G-IL-interpretation and i an Π-index. If there is an IL-formula α' such that α translates into α' or Ass($\hat{\ }$sp*,$\hat{\ }$ad*,$\hat{\ }\alpha'$), then α is *true in Π at i* if and only if $\alpha'^{\Pi, i, g}$ = 1 for all Π-assignments g. (Thus, the notion of truth is only defined with respect to sentences with declarational or assertive force, but not with respect to erotetic or directive sentences.)

(2) α *L-entails* β if and only if for all G-IL-interpretations Π and all Π-indices i, α is true in Π at i only if β is true in Π at i. Notation: α $\xrightarrow{L}$ β.

(3) α *IL-entails* β if and only if for all G-IL-interpretations Π, all Π-indices i, and all Π-assignments g, $\alpha'^{\Pi, i, g} = 1$ only if $\beta'^{\Pi, i, g} = 1$, where α' and β' are the translations of α and β, respectively. Notation: α $\xrightarrow{Il}$ β.

2.3 *Results*

The results of our formal treatment of illocutionary force indicators in an illustrative fragment of German are a formal reconstruction of the facts stated at the end of chapter 2.1; the only difference, a mutual entailment in the first two cases instead of a simple one, is due to the rather uninteresting fact that our small fragment neither treats plural, nor indices with more than one speaker or addressee, nor the difference between *du* and *Sie*. Here are the results:

(2a)	$\xleftrightarrow{Il}$	(1a)	(1c)	$\xleftrightarrow{Il}$	(4a)
(2b)	$\xleftrightarrow{Il}$	(1b)	(1d)	$\xleftrightarrow{Il}$	(4b)
(3a)	$\xrightarrow{Il}$	(1a)			
(3b)	$\xrightarrow{Il}$	(1b)			

3. *Discussion*

In this third part of my paper, I will open the discussion myself and give some preliminary replies to several objections that might be raised against my proposal for a formal treatment of illocutionary force indicators.

Objection 1: Isn't that another attempt to reduce pragmatics (in the sense of a theory of language use) to semantics?

Reply 1: Yes and no. Yes in the rather trivial sense that every occurrence of language use can be described, and the semantics of this description can be studied. But this is probably not what you mean. No in the sense that I do not identify the rule for the use of a linguistic expression with either the locutionary or the illocutionary meaning of this expression, rather I regard the locutionary meaning as partly determining the illocutionary meaning and the latter as the central notion in the rule for the use of the expression under consideration.

Objection 2: You propose to distinguish between a rather small number of illocutionary types. Why not just three, corresponding to the three main sentence moods or, with Wittgenstein (1958: §23) infinitely many?

Reply 2: As for the first part of your counterproposal, I hope my examples have already shown that there is no one-to-one correspondence between sentence mood and illocutionary type, at least in German or English. I do not deny that possibly there are natural languages which have unambiguous syntactic devices for distinguishing between illocutionary types. As for the second part, I would say: "Illocutiones non sunt multiplicandae praeter necessitatem." - if we get by with the assumption of a rather small stock of illocutionary types, we should avoid an inflation of this stock. Of course you can think of a continuous transition between e.g. the erotetic and the assertive use of interrogative sentences, but the German language for instance draws a sharp line between them by permitting or forbidding the occurrence of the particle *schon*.

Objection 3: On the level of locutionary semantics we try to distinguish as sharply as possible between vagueness and ambiguity. Your proposal amounts to the claim that primary performative sentences are ambiguous on the illocutionary level. To me it seems more appealing to suppose that they are just vague.

Reply 3: You are right that I claim primary performative sentences to be Il-ambiguous; let me add that I do not exclude explicit performative formulas from that claim. Concerning your vagueness proposal, I have no real knock-down argument against it, but I think the following data constitute at least *some* evidence against the assumption that for instance German declarative sentences are just vague with respect to the declarational or assertive force they can have. I suppose you agree that the reference of indexicals can be vague as well as ambiguous, and that e.g. 'he', used in a situation where the speaker is pointing at two persons, is rather ambiguous than vague. Now imagine the following situation: A, while saying (8), gives a letter to B.

(8) *Hiermit teile ich Ihnen mit, daß Ihr Goldfisch verstorben ist.*
'I hereby inform you of the death of your goldfish.'

hiermit ('hereby') contains an indexical element which, in the given situation, may refer either to the utterance or to the letter. I hope you concede also that in this case *hiermit* is rather ambiguous than vague. But now look at the illocutionary force of (8)! If *hiermit* is interpreted in the first way, then an utterance of (8) constitutes a declaration and the truth of (8) depends among other things on the question whether it is uttered or not. If it is uttered, as supposed, and if all happiness conditions obtain, then (8) is clearly true. If, however, *hiermit* is taken in the second way, then an utterance of (8) constitutes an assertion and the truth of (8) depends on what the letter says. If it says, for instance, that the addressee's goldfish is still alive, then (8) is clearly false. So we have two clear-cut cases: The declarational one with truth of (8), and the assertive one with falsity of (8), and there is no continuous transition between the two and hence nothing which supports the vagueness claim and everything which supports the ambiguity claim.

Objection 4 ... No, now it is your turn!

FOOTNOTES

1. Montague (1974a, b, c).
2. Lewis (1972).
3. Cresswell (1973).
4. Harman (1977: 418).
5. von Savigny (1974, ch. 7).
6. This is the commonly used abbreviation for Montague (1974c).
7. Montague (1974a:210).
8. The latter is also known as rhetorical question.
9. In ordinary language, expressions like 'everybody' are often used in a sloppy sense which can be paraphrased as 'almost everybody'.
10. I am not entirely sure whether (7) has not still both readings, which can be separated in spoken German by stressing either *kennt* or *jeder*.
11. For a critique of his position cf. Zaefferer (1981).
12. $\mathbb{N}$ is the usual notation for the set of natural numbers (including zero).
13. For the details of the IL-expressions such as variable-names, arc- and upstar-convention cf. Montague (1974c:260).
14. For those readers who are not familiar with German morphology, the relevant forms of our fragment are the following:

	ich	*du*	*jeder*	*niemand*	er_n	*wer*
third case	*mir*	*dir*	*jedem*	*niemandem*	ihm_n	*wem*
fourth case	*mich*	*dich*	*jeden*	*niemanden*	ihn_n	*wen*

15. For the equivalence proofs, it is profitable to use the PTQ-principles stated in Link (1979: 179ff., 220).

REFERENCES

Abadan-Unat, N.
  1975 "Educational problems of Turkish migrants' children". International Review of Education 21.311-322.

Abelson, P.
  1975 "Concepts for representing mundane reality in plans". In D.G. Bobrow and A. Collins (Eds.), 1975, 273-309.

Akmajian, A. and R. Jackendoff
  1970 "Coreferentiality and stress". Linguistic Inquiry 1:1.124-126.

Allwood, J.
  1976 Linguistic Communication as Action and Co-operation. University of Göteborg, doctoral dissertation.

ALPAC
  1966 Languages and Machines: Computers in Translation and Linguistics. A Report by the Automatic Language Processing Advisory Committee. Washington, D.C.: National Academy of Sciences and National Research Council.

Alston, W.P.
  1964 Philosophy of Language. Englewood Cliffs, N.J.: Prentice-Hall.

Altham, J.E.J. and N.W. Tennant
  1975 "Sortal quantification". In E.L. Keenan (Ed.), 1975, 46-58.

Andersen, H.
  1968 Fairy Tales. Translated by L.W. Kingsland. Oxford: Oxford University Press.

Anderson, A.R.
  1956 "The formal analysis of normative system". In N. Rescher (Ed.), 1967, 147-213.

Anscombe, E.
  1958 Introduction to Wittgenstein's Tractatus. London: Hutchinson.

Anscombre, J.-C. and O. Ducrot
  1976 "L'argumentation dans la langue". Langages 42.5-27.

  1978 "Echelles argumentatives, échelles implicatives, et lois de discours". Semantikos 2.43-67.

Åqvist, L.
  1975 A New Approach to the Logical Theory of Interrogatives. Tübingen: Niemeyer.

Arbib, M.
  1972 The Metaphorical Brain. New York: Wiley-Interscience.

Atkinson, M. and P. Drew
  1979 Order in Court. London: Macmillan.

Atlas, J.D.
  1973 "Some remarks on presupposition". Ms.

Austin, J.L.
  1962 How do Do Things with Words. Oxford: Oxford University Press.

  1970 "Pretending". In Philosophical Papers. Oxford: Oxford University Press, pp. 253-271.

Augustine, Saint (Bishop of Hippo)
  1968 "De Mendacio" (A.D.395) and "Contra Mendacium ad Consentium" (A.D.420). In J.P. Migne (Ed.), 1968, Patrologica Latina, tom. 40: S. Aurelii Augustini, Opera Omnia 6. Turnholti: Brepols, pp.488-518 and 518-547.

Bailey, C.-J.N. and R.W. Shuy (Eds.)
  1973 New Ways of Analyzing Variation in English. Washington, D.C.: Georgetown University Press.

Ballmer, T.
  1972 "Einführung und Kontrolle von Diskurswelten". In D. Wunderlich (Ed.), 1972, 183-206.

  1976 "Inwiefern ist die Linguistik empirisch ?" In D. Wunderlich (Ed.), 1976, 6-53.

  1978a Logical Grammar. Amsterdam: North-Holland.

  1978b "Analysis and synthesis of linguistic surface". In J. Groenendijk and M. Stokhof (Eds.), 1978, 1-17.

Ballmer, T. and W. Brennenstuhl
  1981 Speech Act Classification. New York: Springer.

Bar-Hillel, Y. (Ed.)
  1971 Pragmatics of Natural Languages. Dordrecht: Reidel.

Bartsch, R.
  1976 "The role of categorical syntax in grammatical theory". In Kasher (Ed.), 1976, 503-540.

Bauman, R. and J. Sherzer (Eds.)
  1974 Explorations in the Ethnography of Speaking. Cambridge: Cambridge University Press.

Belnap, N.D.
  1963 An Analysis of Questions: Preliminary Report. Ms.

1969 "Åqvist's corrections-accumulating question sequences" In J. Davis et al. (Eds.), 1969, 122-134.

Belnap, N.D. and B. Steel
1976 The Logic of Questions and Answers. New Haven/London: Yale University Press.

Ben-Amos, D. and K. Goldstein (Eds.)
1975 Folklore, Performance and Communication. The Hague: Mouton.

Benzon, W. and R. Fritzson
1979 "Tutorial: Machine translation". Postal Service of The Press at Twin Willows 14.5.

Berlin, I. et al.
1973 Essays on J.L. Austin. Oxford: Oxford University Press.

Berliner Gruppe
1975 Sprachliches Handeln: Kategorien, Listen, Modelle. Ms.

Bernal, J.D.
1954 Science in History. London: C.A. Watts.

Bever, T.G.
1974 "The psychology of language and structuralist investigations of nativism". In G. Harman (Ed.), 1974, 146-164.

Biasci, C. and J. Fritsche (Eds.)
1978 Texttheorie-Textinterpretation: Theoretische Grundlagen der kanonischen Repräsentation von Texten. Hamburg: Buske.

Bierwisch, M.
1979a "Utterance meaning and mental states". Ms.

1979b "Semantic structure and illocutionary force". Ms.

Birrley, R., R. Bronaugh and A. Marras (Eds.)
1971 Agent, Action, Reason. Toronto: University of Toronto Press.

Blackburn, S. (Ed.)
1975 Meaning, Reference and Necessity. Cambridge: Cambridge University Press.

Blau, U.
1978 Die dreiwertige Logik der Sprache. Berlin: De Gruyter.

Bloch, N.C.
1978 "Troubles with functionalism". In C.W. Savage (Ed.), 1978.

Bloomfield, L.
1955 "Linguistic aspects of science". In O. Neurath et al. (Eds.), 1955, International Encyclopedia of Unified Science, vol.1. Chicago: University of Chicago Press, pp. 215-278.

Bobrow, D. and A. Collins (Eds.)
1975 Representation and Understanding: Studies in Cognitive Science. New York: Academic Press.

Boër, S. and W. Lycan
    1975 "Knowing who". Philosophical Studies 28.299-344.

Böhme, G., W. von den Daele and W. Krohn
    1974 "Die Finalisierung der Wissenschaft". In W. Diederich (Ed.), 1974, 276-311.

Bolinger, D.
    1973 "Truth is a linguistic question". Language 49:3.539-550.

Borkenau, F.
    1932 "Zur Soziologie des mechanistischen Weltbildes". Zeitschrift für Sozialforschung 1:3.311-335.

Botha, R.P.
    1970 The Methodological Status of Grammatical Argumentation. (= Janua Linguarum, Series Minor, 105.) The Hague: Mouton.

    1973 The Justification of Linguistic Hypotheses: A Study of Nondemonstrative Inference in Transformational Grammar. (= Janua Linguarum, Series Maior, 84.) The Hague: Mouton.

    1976 "On the analysis of linguistic argumentation". In J.R. Wirth (Ed.), 1976, 1-33.

Bransford, J.D. and N.S. McCarrell
    1974 "A sketch of a cognitive approach to comprehension: some thoughts about understanding what it means to comprehend". In W.B. Weimer and D.S. Palermo (Eds.), 1974, 189-229.

Brockway, D.
    n.d. Semantic Constraints on Relevance. University College, London, Ph.D. dissertation.

Brown, P. and S.C. Levinson
    1978 "Universals of language usage: Politeness phenomena". In E.N. Goody (Ed.), 1978, 56-288.

Bruner, J.S.
    1979 "The organization of action and the nature of adult-infant interaction". Paper presented at a meeting on the Organization of Action, Maison des Sciences de l'Homme, Paris, 12th January, 1979.

    n.d. "The pragmatics of acquisition". Ms.

Bühler, K.
    1934/65 Sprachtheorie. Stuttgart: Fischer.

Burt, M.K.
    1971 From Deep to Surface Structure: An Introducing to Transformational Syntax. New York: Harper and Row.

Butterworth, B.
    1979 "Editorial". Linguistics 17:1/2.1-2.

REFERENCES

Butts, R.E. and J. Hintikka (Eds.)
   1977 Basic Problems in Methodology and Linguistics. Dordrecht: Reidel.

Caffi, C.
   1979 "Some cases of illocutionary pathology: How to undo things with words". Paper read at the Conference on Possibilities and Limitations of Pragmatics, July 1979, at Urbino, Italy.

Camaioni, L.
   1979 "Child-adult and child-child conversation: an interactional approach". In E. Ochs (Ed.), 1979, 323-337.

Campbell, R.N.
   1979a "Cognitive development and child language". To appear in P. Fletcher and M. Garman (Eds.), Studies in Language Acquisition. London: Cambridge University Press.

   1979b "On Fodor on cognitive development". To appear in B. de Gelder and P. van Geert (Eds.), Knowledge and Representation. London: Routledge & Kegan Paul.

Campbell, R.N. and P.T. Smith (Eds.)
   1978 Recent Advances in the Psychology of Language (Vol.I). London: Plenum Press.

Carnap, R.
   1947 Meaning and Necessity. Chicago.

   1956 "The methodological character of theoretical concepts". In H. Feigl and M. Scriven (Eds.), 1956, 38-78.

   1966 Philosophical Foundations of Physics. New York/London: Basic Books.

   1968 Introduction to Semantics and Formalization of Logic. Cambridge, Massachusetts: Harvard University Press.

Carnap, R. and R.C. Jeffrey (Eds.)
   1971 Studies in Inductive Logic and Probability, Vol.I. Berkeley.

Carnap, R. and W. Stegmüller
   1958 Induktive Logik und Wahrscheinlichkeit. Wien.

Carswell, E.A. and R. Rommetveit (Eds.)
   1971 Social Contexts of Messages. London/New York: Academic Press.

Castelfranchi, C. and D. Parisi
   1979 Linguaggio, Conoscenze e Scopi. In press.

Castelfranchi, C. and I. Poggi
   1978 "'Bĕh ?' e 'bĕh...': Analisi semantica di un' interiezione italiana". Roma: Istituto di Psicologia, CNR.

Castelfranchi, C. and J.M. Vincent
   1977 "I am not what I am: L'arte dell' inganno". Roma: Istituto di Psicologia, CNR.

Cazden, C.B., V. John and D. Hymes (Eds.)
   1972   Functions of Language in the Classroom. New York/London: Teachers College Press.

Chafe, W.L.
   1968   "Idiomaticity as an anomaly in the Chomskyan paradigm". Foundations of Language 4.109-127.

Chisholm, R.M. and T.D. Feehan
   1977   "The intent to deceive". The Journal of Philosophy 74:3.143-159.

Chomsky, N.
   1957   Syntactic Structures. (= Janua Linguarum, Series Minor, 4.) The Hague: Mouton.

   1976   Reflections on Language. London: Temple Smith.

   1979   "Communicazione: un termine da delimitare". Revista Illustrata della Communicazione 1:1.8-12.

Cicourel, A.V.
   n.d.   "Constructing recent history from interviews: A study of Sephardic Jewish communities". Ms.

   1972   "Basic and normative rules in the negotiation of status and role". In D. Sudnow (Ed.), 1972, 229-258.

Clark, H.
   1979   "Responding to indirect speech acts". Cognitive Psychology 11:1.

Clark, H. and E. Clark
   1977   Psychology and Language. New York: Harcourt, Brace, Jovanovich.

Clarke, D.
   1977   "Rules and sequences in conversation". In P. Collett (Ed.), 1977.

   1978   "The syntax of action". Ms.

Cohen, D. (Ed.)
   1972   Papers from the University of Wisconsin Linguistic Group, First Annual Symposium, on Limiting the Domain of Linguistics. Madison: University of Wisconsin.

Cohen, L.
   1971   "Some remarks on Grice's views about the logical particles of natural language". In Bar-Hillel (Ed.), 1971, 50-68.

   1973   "Speech acts". Current Trends in Linguistics 12.173-208.

Cohen, P.R.
   1978   On Knowing What to Say: Planning Speech-Acts. University of Toronto Ph.D. thesis.

Cohen, T.
   1973   "Illocutions and perlocutions". Foundations of Language 9.492-503.

Cole, P.
1978 "On the origins of referential opacity". In P. Cole (Ed.), 1978, 1-22.

Cole, P. (Ed.)
1978 Syntax and Semantics 9: Pragmatics. New York: Academic Press.

Cole, P. and J. Morgan (Eds.)
1975 Syntax and Semantics 3: Speech acts. New York: Academic Press.

Coleman, L. and P. Kay
1981 "Prototype semantics: The English word *lie*". Language 57:1.26-44.
n.d. "How to lie". Ms.

Collett, P. (Ed.)
1977 Social Rules and Social Behaviour. Oxford: Blackwell.

Conrad, R.
1978 Studien zur Syntax und Semantik von Frage und Antwort. (= Studia Grammatica 19) Berlin.

Conte, A.G.
1962 Saggio sulla completezza degli ordinamenti giuridici. Memorie dell' Istituto Giuridico, Torino.

Cossio, C.
1944 Teoria egologica del Derecho. Buenos Aires.

Coulmas, F.
1977 "Concerning the range of pragmatics". Journal of Pragmatics 1: 3.299-307.

1979 "On the sociolinguistic relevance of routine formulae". Journal of Pragmatics 3:3/4.239-266.

Coulmas, F. (Ed.)
1981 Conversational Routine. The Hague: Mouton.

Cresswell, M.
1973 Logics and Languages. London: Methuen.

Crisari, M.
1975 "Sugli usi non istituzionali delle domande". In D. Parisi (Ed.), 1975.

Darnell, R. D.
1969 The Development of American Anthropology 1879-1920: From the Bureau of American Ethnology to Franz Boas. Ph.D. dissertation, University of Pennsylvania. Ann Arbor, Michigan: University Microfilms.

Dascal, M.
1977 "Conversational relevance". Journal of Pragmatics 1.309-327.

Dascal, M.
1979 "Towards Psychopragmatics". Paper delivered at the Congress of of the International Association of Semiotic Studies, Vienna, July 1979.

1981 "Strategies of understanding". In H. Parret and J. Bouveresse (Eds.), 1981.

n.d. "Two types of functionalism in the philosophy of language". Ms.

Dascal, M. and T. Katriel
1977 "Between semantics and pragmatics: the two types of 'but' - Hebrew 'aval' and 'ela'". Theoretical Linguistics 4:3.143-172.

1979 "Digressions: a study in conversational coherence". PTL: A Journal for Descriptive Poetics and Theory of Literature 4.203-232.

Davidson, D.
1963 "Actions, reasons, and causes". The Journal of Philosophy 60. 685-700.

1970 "Mental events". In L. Foster and J. Swanson (Eds.), 1970.

1971 "Agency". In R. Birrley et al. (Eds.), 1971, 3-26.

Davidson, D. and G. Harman (Eds.)
1972 Semantics of Natural Language. Dordrecht: Reidel.

1975 The Logic of Grammar. Encino, CA: Dickenson.

Davis, J. et al. (Eds.)
1969 Philosophical Logic. Dordrecht: Reidel.

Davis, M. (Ed.)
1965 The Undecidable. New York: Raven Press.

Diederich, W. (Ed.)
1974 Theorien der Wissenschaftsgeschichte. Frankfurt a.M.: Suhrkamp.

Dijk, T.A. van
1977 Text and Context. London: Longman.

Dijk, T.A. van (Ed.)
1976 Pragmatics of Language and Literature. Amsterdam: North-Holland.

Dittmar, N., H. Haberland, T. Skutnabb-Kangas and U. Teleman (Eds.)
1978 Papers from the First Scandinavian-German Symposium on the Language of Immigrant Workers and their Children. ROLIC-papir 12 (Roskilde Universitetscenter).

Donnellan, K
1966 "Reference and definite descriptions". Philosophical Review 75.281-304. Reprinted in S. Schwartz (Ed.), 1977, 42-65.

Dowty, D.
1972 Studies in the Logic of Verb Aspect and Time Reference in English. Department of Linguistics, University of Texas.

Dreske, F.
1972 "Contrastive statements". The Philosophical Review 81:4.411-437.

Dressler, W.U. (Ed.)
1978 Current Trends in Text Linguistics. Berlin: De Gruyter.

Ducrot, O.
1972   Dire et ne pas dire - Principes de Sémantique Linguistique.
        Paris: Hermann.

1973   La Preuve et le Dire. Paris: Mame.

DUDEN
1973   Grammatik der deutschen Gegenwartssprache. Mannheim: Bibliographisches Institut.

Eccles, J.C. and K.R. Popper
1977   The Self and Its Brain (Part II by J.C. Eccles). Berlin/London/
        New York: Springer.

Edes, E.
1968   "Output conditions on anaphoric expressions with split antecedents". Ms.

Ehlich, K. and J. Rehbein
1972   "Zur Konstitution pragmatischer Einheiten in einer Institution:
        Das Speiserestaurant". In D. Wunderlich (Ed.), 1972, 209-254.

Eisenberg, P.
1976   "Kommentar zu Lang". In D. Wunderlich (Ed.), 1976, 299-300.

Eisenberg, P. and H. Haberland
1972   "Das gegenwärtige Interesse an der Linguistik". Das Argument
        14:72.326-349. Reprinted as Argument-Studienheft SH 27, 1979.

Ekegren, E., D. Hecht and S. Hansen
1979   Forskere, mellemmaend, boligaktivister: Rapport om forskerrollerne; et aktionsforskningsprojekt blandt fremmedarbejere i
        København 1975-1979. København: Nyt fra Samfundsvidenskaberne.

Ekstrand, L.H.
1978   Bilingual and Bicultural Adaptation. Bulletin from the Department of Educational and Psychological Research, School of Education, Malmö, no.66.

Enç, B.
1976   "Identity statements and microreductions". The Journal of Philosophy 73:11.261-282.

Ervin-Tripp, S.
1976   "Is Sybil there ?: the structure of some American-English directives". Language in Society 5.25-66.

Ervin-Tripp, S. and V. Miller
1977   "Early discouse: some questions about questions". In M. Lewis
        and L.A. Rosenblum (Eds.), 1977, 9-25.

Evans, G.
1973   "The causal theory of names". Proceedings of the Aristotelian
        Society, Supplementary Series 47.

Evans, G. and J. McDowell (Eds.)
1976   Truth and Meaning. Oxford: Oxford University Press.

Feigl, H. and M. Scriven (Eds.)
    1956   The Foundations of Science and the Concepts of Psychology and Psychoanalysis. Minneapolis: University of Minnesota Press.

Feys, R.
    1937   "Les Logiques nouvelles des modalités". Revue Scholastique de Philosophie 40.217-252, 517-553.

FİDEF
    1978   Bericht zur Bildungssituation türkischer Kinder in der BRD, dem Kongress zur Bildungssituation türkischer Kinder in der BRD am 11./12. Februar 1978 in Gelsenkirchen vom Bundesvorstand der FİDEF vorgelegt. Fidef yayınları 5.

Field, H.
    1972   Tarski's theory of truth. Journal of Philosophy 59.

Fink, H.
    1973   The Analysis of Goodness. D.Phil. thesis, Oxford.

Fodor, J.A.
    1975   The Language of Thought. Hassocks, England: Harvester Press.

Foster, L. and J. Swanson (Eds.)
    1970   Experience and Theory. University of Massachusetts.

Fotion, N.
    1971   "Master speech acts". Philosophical Quarterly 21:84.232-43.

Franck, D.
    1980   Grammatik und Konversation. Königstein: Scriptor.

Franck, D. and H. Houtkoop
    1979   "Beurten als practische en analytische eenheden in spontane gesprekken". Ms.

Franz, F.
    1975   "The legal status of foreign workers in the Federal Republic of West Germany". In R.E. Krane (Ed.), 1975, 46-60.

Freed, B. et al. (Eds.)
    1975   Forms of Representation. Amsterdam: North-Holland.

Frege, G.
    1892   "Über Sinn und Bedeutung". Zeitschrift für Philosophie und philosophische Kritik 100.25-50.

French, P., T. Uehling and H. Wettstein (Eds.)
    1977   Studies in the Philosophy of Language. (= Midwest Studies in Philosophy 2.) Minneapolis: University of Minnesota Press.

    1979   Contemporary Perspectives in the Philosophy of Language. Minneapolis: University of Minnesota Press.

Fries, U.
    1977   "On a typology of answers". Ms.

Fritz, G.
1978 "Kohärenz: Grundfragen der Dialoganalyse". Ms.

Furberg, M.
1971 Saying and Meaning: A Main Theme in J.L. Austin's Philosophy. Oxford: Basil Blackwell.

Gardiner, A.
1932 The Theory of Speech and Language. Oxford: Oxford University Press.

Garfinkel, A.
1977 "Truths, half-truths and deception in advertising". Papers in Linguistics 10:1/2.135-149.

Garfinkel, H.
1967 Studies in Ethnomethodology. Englewood Cliffs: Prentice-Hall.

Gazdar, G.
1976 "On performative sentences". Semantikos 1.37-62.

1979a Pragmatics: Implicature, Presupposition and Logical Form. London: Academic Press.

1979b "Speech act assignment". In A.K. Joshi et al. (Eds.), 1979.

Gazdar, G. and E. Klein
1977 "Context-sensitive transderivational constraints and conventional implicature". Papers from the 13th Regional Meeting, Chicago Linguistics Society 13, 137-146.

Geach, P.T.
1956 "Good and evil". Analysis 17.33-42.

Gelder, B. de
1979 "Questions on representation". In B. de Gelder and P. van Geert (Eds.), 1981.

Gelder, B. de and P. van Geert (Eds.)
1981 Knowledge and Representation. London: Routledge and Kegan Paul.

Gelman, R. and M. Shatz
1977 "Appropriate speech adjustments: the operation of conversational constraints on talk to two-year olds". In M. Lewis and L.A. Rosenblum (Eds.), 1977, 27-61.

Giuliani, M.V. and F. Orletti
1977 "Aspetti dell' ironia linguistica". In G. Mosconi and V. D'Urso (Eds.), 1977.

Givón, T.
1978 "Negation in language: Pragmatics, function, ontology". In P. Cole (Ed.), 1978, 69-112.

Gochet, P.
1978 Quine en perspective. Paris: Flammarion.

1980 Outline of a Nominalist Theory of Proposition. Dordrecht: Reidel

Goffman, E.
　1974　Frame Analysis: An Essay on the Organization of Experience. New York: Harper and Row.
　1976　"Replies and responses". Language in Society 5:3.257-313.

Goldman, A.
　1970　A Theory of Human Action. Englewood Cliffs, N.J.: Prentice-Hall.

Goody, E.N. (Ed.)
　1978　Questions and Politeness. Cambridge: Cambridge University Press.

Gordon, D. and G. Lakoff
　1975　"Conversational postulates". In P. Cole and J.L. Morgan (Eds.), 1975, 83-106. (Previously published in 1971, Papers from the 7th Regional Meeting, Chicago Linguistic Society 63-84).

Gowers, E.
　1973　The Complete Plain Words. Harmondsworth: Penguin.

Green, G.M.
　n.d.　"Linguistics and the pragmatics of language use. What you know when you know a language". Ms.

Greenberg, J.H. (Ed.)
　1978　Universals of Human Language (4 volumes). Stanford: Stanford University Press.

Gregory, R.L.
　1972　Eye and Brain - The Psychology of Seeing. London: Weidenfeld and Nicolson.

Grewendorf, G
　1978　"Probleme der logischen Analyse von Fragen". Papiere zur Linguistik 19.5-57.

Grice, H.P.
　1957　"Meaning". Philosophical Review 66.377-388.
　1975　"Logic and conversation". In P. Cole and J. Morgan (Eds.), 1975, 41-58. Also in D. Davidson and G. Harman (Eds.), 1975, 64-75.
　1978　"Further notes on logic and conversation". In Cole (Ed.), 1978, 121-128.

Groenendijk, J. and M. Stokhof (Eds.)
　1976　Proceedings of the First Amsterdam Colloquium on Montague Grammar and Related Topics. University of Amsterdam.
　1978　Proceedings of the Second Amsterdam Colloquium on Montague Grammar and Related Topics. University of Amsterdam.

Grossman, R.E., L.J. San and T.J. Vance (Eds.)
　1975　Papers from the Parasession on Functionalism. Chicago: Chicago Linguistic Society.

Grossmann, H.
1935 "Die gesellschaftlichen Grundlagen der mechanistischen Philosophie und die Manufaktur". Zeitschrift für Sozialforschung 412.161-231.

Gülich, E.
1976 "Ansätze zu einer kommunikationsorientierter Erzähltextanalyse (am Beispiel mündlicher und schriftlicher Erzähltexten)". In W. Haubrichs (Ed.), 1976, 224-256.

Gumperz, J.J.
1974 The Sociolinguistics of Interpersonal Communication (= Working Papers No.33). Urbino: Centro Internazionale di Semiotica e di Linguistica.

Gumperz, J.J. and D. Hymes (Eds.)
1972 Directions in Sociolinguistics - The Ethnography of Communication. New York: Holt, Rinehart and Winston.

Gunderson, K. (Ed.)
1975 Language, Mind, and Knowledge. Minneapolis: University of Minnesota Press.

Gustafson, D.
1973 "A critical survey of the reasons vs. causes arguments in recent philosophy of action". Metaphilosophy 4:4.269-297.

Haberland, H. and J.L. Mey
1977 "Pragmatics and linguistics". Journal of Pragmatics 1:1.1-12.

Habermas, J.
1971 "Vorbereitende Bemerkungen zu einer Theorie der kommunikativen Kompetenz". In J. Habermas and N. Luhmann, 1971, 101-141.

Habermas, J. and N. Luhmann
1971 Theorie der Gesellschaft oder Sozialtechnologie. Frankfurt am Main: Suhrkamp.

Halle, M. et al. (Eds.)
1956 For Roman Jacobson. The Hague: Mouton.

Halliday, M.A.K.
1975 Learning how to mean. London: Edward Arnold.

Halliday, M.A.K. and R. Hasan
1976 Cohesion in English. London: Longman.

Hammer, O.
1976 De Nye Danskere: Om Udenlandske Arbejdere i Danmark. København: Mellemfolkeligt Samvirke.

Hancher, M.
1979 "The classification of cooperative illocutionary acts". Language in Society 8:1.1-14.

Hanson, G.

1979 The position of the second generation of Finnish immigrants in Sweden: The importance of education in the home language to the welfare of the second generation immigrants. Preprint, Symposium on the position of the second generation of Yugoslav immigrants in Sweden, Split (Yogoslavia), October 30th- November 1st, 1979. Swedish Commission on Immigrant Research (EIFO).

Hanssen, E. and G. Wiggen (Eds.)
1973 Målstrid er Klassekamp. Oslo: Pax.

Hare, R.
1970 "Meaning and speech acts". Philosophical Review 79:1.3-24.

Harman, G.
1973 Thought. Princeton: Princeton University Press.

1976 "Katz' credo". Synthese 32:3/4.387-394.

1977 Review of Linguistic Behaviour by Jonathan Bennett. Language 53:2.417-424.

Harman, G. (Ed.)
1974 On Noam Chomsky - Critical Essays. Garden City: Doubleday.

Harweg, R.
1968 Pronomina und Textkonstitution. München: Fink.

Haubrichs, W. (Ed.)
1976 Erzählforschung I. Göttingen.

Hausser, R.
1978 "Surface compositionality and the semantics of mood". Amsterdam Papers in Formal Grammar 2.174-193.

Heim, J.
1977 "Zum Verhältnis von Wahrheitsbedingungen - Semantik und Sprechakttheorie". Papiere des SFB 99 (Konstanz).

Hessen, B.
1931/71 "The social and economic roots of Newton's Principia". In Science at the Crossroads: Papers presented to the International Congress of the History of Science and Technology held in London from June 29th to July 3rd, 1931, by the delegates of the USSR. London: Frank Cass & Co., pp.149-212.

Heutiges Deutsch: Texte gesprochener deutscher Standardsprache III.
1975 München: Hueber.

Hindelang, G.
1978 Auffordern: Die Untertypen des Aufforderns und ihre sprachlichen Realisierungsformen. Göppingen: Kümmerle.

Hintikka, J.
1962 Knowledge and Belief. Ithaca, N.Y.: Cornell University Press.

1973 Logic, Language Games and Information. Oxford: Oxford University Press.

1974 "Questions about questions". In M.K. Munitz and P.K. Unger (Eds.), 1974, 103-158.

1975 "Answers to questions". In The Intentions of Intentionality and Other New Models for Modalities. Dordrecht: Reidel, pp.137-158.

Hiż, H.
1962 "Questions and answers". Journal of Philosophy 59.253-265.

1978 "Difficult questions". In H. Hiż (Ed.), 1978.

Hiż, H. (Ed.)
1978 Questions. Dordrecht: Reidel.

Hockett, C.F.
1956 "Idiom formation". In M. Halle et al. (Eds.), 1956, 222-229.

Holenstein, E.
1972 Phänomenologie der Assoziation. The Hague: M. Nijhoff.

Horn, L.R.
1972 On the Semantic Properties of Logical Operators in English. U.C.L.A., Ph.D. dissertation. Distributed by Indiana University Linguistics Club.

Hunt, E.B.
1975 Artificial Intelligence. New York: Academic Press.

Husserl, E.
1966 Zur Phänomenologie des inneren Zeitbewuβtseins, Vorlesungen 1893-1917 Husserliana. The Hague: M. Nijhoff.

Huth, L.
1975 "Argumentationstheorie und Textanalyse". Der Deutschunterricht 27:6.80-111.

Hymes, D.
1975 "Breakthrough into performance". In D. Ben-Amos and K. Goldstein (Eds.), 1975, 11-74.

Invandrarna och Utbildningsväsendet
1979 Invandrarna och Utbildningsväsendet: Handlingsprogram för SÖ:s arbete med invandrarfragor. Förslag. Stockholm: Skolöverstyrelsen.

Irvine, J.
1974 "Strategies of status manipulation in the Wolof greeting". In R. Bauman and J. Sherzer (Eds.), 1974.

Isard, S.
1973 "Changing the context". In E. Keenan (Ed.), 1975, 287-296.

Jackendoff, R.S.
1972 Semantic Interpretation in Generative Grammar. Cambridge, Mass. MIT Press.

Jacobs, R.A. and P.S. Rosenbaum (Eds.)
1970 Readings in English Transformational Grammar. Waltham, Massa-

chusetts: Ginn and Company.

Jefferson, G.
1972 "Side sequences". In D. Sudnow (Ed.), 1972, 294-338.

1974 "Error correction as an interactional resource". Language in Society 3:181-199.

Jeffrey, R.C.
1967 Logik der Entscheidungen. Wien/München.

Joshi, A.K., I.A. Sag and B.L. Webster (Eds.)
1979 Proceedings of the Pennsylvania Workshop on Computational Aspects of Linguistic Structure and Discourse Setting. New York: Cambridge University Press.

Just, M.A. and P.A. Carpenter (Eds.)
1977 Cognitive Processes in Comprehension. Hillsdale: Lawrence Erlbaum Associates.

Kachru, B.B. et al. (Eds.)
1970 Papers in Honor of Henry and Renée Kahane. Urbana: University of Illinois Press.

1973 Issues in Linguistics. Urbana: University of Illinois Press.

Kalinowski, G.
1975 "Du métalangage en logique". Documents de Travail 48 (Urbino).

Kamp, J.A.W.
1975 "Two theories about adjectives". In E.L. Keenan (Ed.), 1975, 123-155.

Kanngiesser, S.
1976 "Spracherklärungen und Sprachbeschreibungen". In D. Wunderlich (Ed.), 1976, 106-160.

Kaplan, D.
1975 "How to Russell a Frege-Church". Journal of Philosophy 72.716-729.

1978 "Dthat". In P. Cole (Ed.), 1978, 221-243.

Karlsson, F. (Ed.)
1976 Papers from the 3rd Scandinavian Conference of Linguistics. Turku: Academy of Finland.

Karmiloff-Smith, A.
1978 "The interplay between syntax, semantics and phonology in language acquisition processes". In R.N. Campbell and P.T. Smith (Eds.), 1978.

1979 A Functional Approach to Child Language. London: Cambridge University Press.

Karttunen, L. and S. Peters
1975 "Conventional implicature in Montague grammar". Proceedings of the 1st Annual Meeting of the Berkeley Linguistics Society, 266-278.

Kasher, A.
1974 "Mood implicatures: A logical way of doing generative pragmatics". Theoretical Linguistics 1.6-38.

1976 "Conversational maxims and rationality". In A. Kasher (Ed.), 1976, 197-216.

1977 "Foundations of philosophical pragmatics". In R.E. Butts and J. Hintikka (Eds.), 1977, 225-242.

Kasher, A. (Ed.)
1976 Language in Focus: Foundations, Methods and Systems. Reidel: Dordrecht.

Keenan, E.L. (Ed.)
1975 Formal Semantics of Natural Language. Cambridge: Cambridge University Press.

Keenan, E.L. and R. Hull
1973 "The logical presuppositions of questions and answers". In J. Petöfi and D. Franck (Eds.), 1973, 441-466.

Keenan, E.O.
1976 "The universality of conversational postulates". Language in Society 5:1.67-80.

Keller, E.
1979 "Gambits: Conversational strategy signals". Journal of Pragmatics 3:3/4.219-238.

Kelsen, H.
1925 Allgemeine Rechtslehre. Berlin.

1943 General Theory of Law and State. Cambridge, Mass.: Harvard University Press.

1960 Reine Rechtslehre. Wien.

Kempson, R.M.
1975 Presupposition and the Delimitation of Semantics. Cambridge: Cambridge University Press.

1977 Semantic Theory. Cambridge: Cambridge University Press.

Khatchadourian, H.
1974 "Conditions of illocutionary acts". Philosophical Studies 26. 1-22.

Kirshenblatt-Gimblett, B.M.
1975 "A parable in context: A social interactional analysis of storytelling performance". In D. Ben-Amos and K. Goldstein (Eds.), 1975, 105-130.

Kock, C. and P. Harder
1976 The Theory of Presupposition Failure. Copenhagen: Akademisk Forlag.

Krallmann, G. (Ed.)
1979 Theorie der Frage. Mannheim: IdS-Schriften.

Krane, R.E. (Ed.)
   1975   Manpower Mobility Across Cultural Boundaries. Leiden: Brill.

Kripke, S.
   1972   "Naming and necessity". In D. Davidson and G. Harman (Eds.), 1972, 253-355.

   1977   "Speaker's reference and semantic reference". In P. French et al. (Eds.), 1977, 255-276.

Krivonosov, A.
   1965   "Die Rolle der modalen Partikeln in der kommunikativen Gliederung der Sätze in Bezug auf die Nebensatzglieder". Zeitschrift für Phonetik, Sprachwissenschaft und Kommunikationsforschung 18.487-503.

Kummer, W.
   1973   "Pragmatic implication". In J.S. Petöfi and H. Rieser (Eds.), 1973, 96-112.

   1975   Grundlagen der Texttheorie. Reinbeck: Rowohlt.

Kuno, S.
   1975   "Three perspectives in the functional approach to syntax". In R.E. Grossman et al. (Eds.), 1975, 276-336.

Kuusela, J. and T. Skutnabb-Kangas
   1978   "The situation of foreign workers in Sweden". N. Dittmar et al. (Eds.), 1978, 79-84.

Labov, W.
   1972   "Rules for ritual insults". In D. Sudnow (Ed.), 1972, 120-169.

Labov, W. and D. Fanshel
   1977   Therapeutic Discourse - Psychotherapy as Conversation. New York: Academic Press.

Lakoff, G.
   1970   "Some thoughts on transderivational constraints". In B.B. Kachru et al. (Eds.), 1970, 442-452.

   1971a "Presupposition and relative well-formedness". In D.D. Steinberg and L.A. Jakobovits (Eds.), 1971, 329-340.

   1971b "On generative semantics". In D.D. Steinberg and L.A. Jakobovits (Eds.), 1971.

   1972   "Linguistics and natural logic". In D.D. Davidson and G. Harman (Eds.), 1972, 545-665.

   1974   "Syntactic amalgams". Proceedings of the 10th Regional Meeting, Chicago Linguistic Society, 321-344.

Lang, M.
   1976   "Thesen zur Wissenschaftsentwicklung der Linguistik". In D. Wunderlich (Ed.), 1976, 281-293.

Laver, J. and S. Hutcheson (Eds.)
1972 Communication in Face-to-Face Interaction. Harmondsworth: Penguin.

Lee, P.A.
1976 "Impositive speech acts". Working Papers in Linguistics (Ohio State University) 21.99-144.

Leech, G
1977a Language and Tact. Trier: Linguistic Agency University Trier.

1977b "Natural language as metalanguage: An approach to some problems of semantic description in English". Transactions of the Philological Society 1976-77.1-31.

1980 Explorations in Semantics and Pragmatics. (= Pragmatics & Beyond 5) Amsterdam: John Benjamins.

Leibniz, W.
1686 Discourse on Metaphysics.

1967 The Leibniz-Arnauld. Ed. and translated by H.T. Mason. Manchester: Manchester University Press.

Lemmon, E.J.
1957 "New foundations for Lewis' modal systems". Journal of Symbolic Logic 22.176-187.

1965 "Deontic logic and logic of imperatives". Logique et Analyse 8.39-71.

Levin, S.R.
1976 "Concerning what kind of a speech act a poem is". In T.A. van Dijk (Ed.), 1976, 141-160.

Levinson, S.C.
1978 "Some pre-observations on the modelling of dialogue". Ms.

1979 "Activity types and language". Linguistics 17:5/6.365-399.

1980 "Speech act theory: The state of the art". Language Teaching & Linguistics: Abstracts 13:1.5-24.

Lewis, C.I. and C.H. Langford
1951 Symbolic Logic. New York: Dover Publications.

Lewis, D.K.
1969 Convention: A Philosophical Study. Cambridge, Mass.: Harvard University Press.

1972 "General semantics". In D. Davidson and G. Harman (Eds.), 1972, 169-218.

Lewis, M. and L.A. Rosenblum (Eds.)
1977 Interaction, Conversation and the Development of Language. New York: John Wiley.

Lieb, H.-H.
1971 "On subdividing semiotic". In Y. Bar-Hillel (Ed.), 1971, 94-

119.
1977 "Outline of integrational linguistics". Linguistische Arbeitsberichte, Berlin.

Link, G.
1979 Montague-Grammatik. München: Fink.

Loar, B.
1976a "Two theories of meaning". In G. Evans and J. McDowell (Eds.), 1976.

1976b "The semantics of singular terms". Philosophical Studies 30.353-377.

Lockwood, M.
1975 "On predicating proper names". Philosophical Review 84.471-498.

Lorenz, K.
1973 "Rules versus theorems: A new approach for mediation between intuitionistic and two-valued logic". Journal of Philosophical Logic 2.352-369.

Lorenzen, P.
1961 "Ein dialogisches Konstruktivitätskriterium". In Infinitistic Methods. London: Pergamon Press.

1962 Metamathematik. Mannheim: Bibliographisches Institut.

1969 Normative Logic and Ethics. Mannheim: Bibliographisches Institut.

Lyons, J.
1968 Introduction to Theoretical Linguistics. Cambridge: Cambridge University Press.

1977 Semantics. Cambridge: Cambridge University Press.

Maas, U.
1976 Kann man Sprache lehren ? Frankfurt a.M.: Syndikat.

Makkai, A.
1972 Idiom Structure in English. The Hague: Mouton.

1978 "Idiomaticity as a language universal". In J.H. Greenberg (Ed.), 1978, (Vol.3), 401-448.

Malcolm, I.G.
1979 "The West Australian aboriginal child and classroom interaction: A sociolinguistic approach". Journal of Pragmatics 3:3/4.305-320.

Manninen, J., and R. Tuomela
1976 Essays on Explanation and Understanding. Dordrecht, Holland: D. Reidel Publishing Company.

Marcus, R.
1961 "Modality and intensional languages". Synthese 27.303-323.

Margalit, A. (Ed.)
1979 Meaning and Use. Dordrecht: Reidel.

Martinich, A.P.
  1975 "Sacraments and speech acts II". The Heythrop Journal 16:4.406-408.

Marx, K.
  1970 Capital: A Critique of Political Economy, Vol.I. London: Lawrence and Wishart. First German edition 1867.

Matthews, P.H.
  1979 Generative Grammar and Linguistic Competence. London: Allen & Unwin.

McCawley, J.D.
  1971 "The applicability of transformations to idioms". Papers from the 7th Regional Meeting of the Chicago Linguistic Society, 198-205.

  1976 "Causatives". In M. Shibatani (Ed.), 1976.

  1978 "Conversational implicature and the lexicon". In P. Cole (Ed.), 1978, 245-260.

McDowell, J.
  1977 "On the sense and reference of a proper name". Mind 86.

  1978 "Physicalism and primitive denotation: Field on Tarski". Erkenntnis 13.

Mchoul, A.
  1978 "The organization of turns at formal talk in the classroom". Language in Society 7:2.183-214.

Mead, G.H.
  1924/34 Mind, Self and Society. Chicago: University of Chicago Press.

Mellor, D.H.
  1978 "Conscious belief". Paper presented at the Meeting of the Aristotelian Society, London, 9th January 1978.

Merritt, M.
  1976 "On questions following questions in service encounters". Language in Society 5:3.315-359.

Mey, J.L.
  1979 Pragmalinguistics: Theory and Practice. The Hague: Mouton.

Meyer, P.G.
  1975 Satzverknüpfungsrelationen. Tübingen: Gunter Narr.

Meyer-Ingwersen, J., R. Neumann and Matthias Kummer
  1977 Zur Sprachentwicklung türkischer Schüler in der Bundesrepublik. 2 Bände. Kronberg i. Ts.: Scriptor.

Mill, J.S.
  1843 System of Logic. London: Longman.

Mitchell-Kernan, C. and S. Ervin-Tripp (Eds.)
  1977 Child Discourse. New York: Academic Press.

Mitchell-Kernan, C. and K. Kernan
  1977a "Directives in black children's role playing". In C. Mitchell-

Kernan and S. Ervin-Tripp (Eds.), 1977.

1977b "Pragmatics of directive choice among children". In C. Mitchell-Kernan and S. Ervin-Tripp (Eds.), 1977, 189-208.

Molony, C., H. Zobl and W. Stölting (Eds.)
1977 Deutsch im Kontakt mit anderen Sprachen/German in Contact with Other Languages. Kronberg i. Ts.: Scriptor.

Montague, R.
1974 Formal Philosophy: Selected Papers of Richard Montague. New Haven: Yale University Press.

1974a "English as a formal language". In Montague 1974, 188-221.

1974b "Universal grammar". In Montague 1974, 222-246.

1974c "The proper treatment of quantification in ordinary English". In Montague 1974, 247-270.

Montague-Smith, P. (Ed.)
1979 Debrett's Correct Form (Revised Edition). London: Debrett's Peerage with Futura Publications.

Morgan, J.
1973 "Sentence fragments and the notion sentence". In B.B. Kachru et al. (Eds.), 1973.

1978a "Towards a rational model of discourse comprehension". In D. Waltz (Ed.), 1978.

1978b "Two types of convention in indirect speech acts". In P. Cole (Ed.), 1978, 261-280.

Morpurgo-Tagliabue, G.
1967 Linguistica e Stilistica di Aristotele. Roma: Ed. Dell'Ateneo.

1972/73 "J.L. Austin tra logica e linguistica". Rivista critica di storia della filosofia 1972:4, 1973:1.

1975 "Lineamenti di una analitica del pensiero assiologico". In Studi in Onore di G. Bontadini. Milano: Vita e Pensiero, pp. 150-226.

1978 "Chomsky: Linguistica e filosofia". Studi di Grammatica Italiana 7.

1980 "Un'eredità di J.L. Austin: i performativi". Lingua e Stile 1980:1.

Morris, C.W.
1938 "Foundations of the theory of signs". In O. Neurath (Ed.), 1938, International Encyclopedia of Unified Science 1. Chicago: University of Chicago Press, pp.77-138.

1946 Signs, Language and Behavior. Englewood Cliffs, New Jersey: Prentice-Hall.

Mosconi, G. and V. D'Urso (Eds.)
1977 Psicologica e Retorica. Bologna: Mulino.

Munitz, M.K. and P.K. Unger (Eds.)
1974 Semantics and Philosophy. New York: New York University Press.

Nagel, E.
1961 The Structure of Science. New York: Harcourt, Brace and World.

Newmeyer, F.J. and J. Emonds
1971 "The linguist in American society". Papers from the 7th Regional Meeting, Chicago Linguistic Society, 285-303.

Öberg, K.
1979 "Samverkan och/eller konflikt". Ms.

Ochs, E. (Ed.)
1979 Developmental Pragmatics. New York: Academic Press.

Oehrle, R.T. and L.G. Shiman
1976 "An analytic grammar for vision and natural languages". Ms.

Oh, C.K. and D. Dinneen (Eds.)
1979 Syntax and Semantics 11: Presuppositions. New York: Academic Press.

Olson, D.R.
1970 "Language and thought:Aspects of a cognitive theory of semantics". Psychological Review 4.257-273.

Ornstein, R.
1972 The Psychology of Consciousness. San Francisco: Freeman.

Parisi, D.
1975 "Appunti per la construzione di una macchina che risponde alle domande". Roma: Istituto di Psichologia, CNR.

1978 "Affetto". Giornale Italiano di Psicologia 5:1.127-142.

Parisi, D. (Ed.)
1975 Studi per un Modello del Linguaggio. Quaderni della Ricerca Scientifica, CNR.

1979 Per una Educazione Linguistica Razionale. Bologna: Mulino.

Parisi, D. and C. Castelfranchi
1976 "Discourse as a hierarchy of goals". Documents de Travail 54-55 (Urbino).

1977 "La conversazione come adozione di scopi". In Studi di Grammatica Italiana. Firenze: Accademia della Crusca.

1978 "Potere". Rassegna Italiana di Sociologia 19:4.555-592.

Pariso, D., C. Castelfranchi and G. Lariccia
1976 "Tipi di domande alle quali si sa rispondere dopo aver letto un brano". Roma: Istituto di Psicologia, CNR.

Parret, H.
1975 "La pragmatique des modalités". Documents de Travail 49 (Urbino).

1978 "Eléments d'une analyse philosophique de la manipulation et du mensonge". Documents de Travail B:70 (Urbino).

Parret, H. and J. Bouveresse (Eds.)
1981 Meaning and Understanding. Berlin/New York: Walter de Gruyter.

Peacocke, C.
1975 "Proper names, reference, and rigid designation". In S. Blackburn (Ed.), 1975, 109-132.

Peirce, C.S.
1931-35 Collected Papers. Cambridge, Mass.: Harvard University Press.

Perrault, R., J. Allen and P. Cohen
1978 "Speech acts as a basis for understanding dialogue coherence". In D. Waltz (Ed.), 1978.

Petersen, R.
1978 "A Greenlandic problem of lack of intermediate persons". Paper presented in advance for participants in Burg Wartenstein Symposium, "Indigenous Anthropology in Non-Western Countries", July 15-24, 1978. Wenner-Gren Foundation for Anthropological Research, no.78.

Petöfi, J.S.
1979 "Written, spoken, and face-to-face verbal communication: Some philosophical aspects of the investigation of natural language". Paper presented at the Fourth International Wittgenstein Symposium (Kirchberg am Wechsel, August 28th to September 2nd, 1979).

Petöfi, J.S. and D. Franck (Eds.)
1973 Präsuppositionen in Philosophie und Linguistik - Presuppositions in Philosophy and Linguistics. Frankfurt am Main: Athenäum.

Petöfi, J.S. and H. Rieser (Eds.)
1973 Studies in Text Grammar. Dordrecht: Reidel.

Phillips, J.R.
1973 "Syntax and vocabulary of mother's speech to young children: age and sex comparison". Child Development 44:182-185.

Piaget, J.
1923 Le langage et la pensée chez l'enfant. Neuchâtel: Delachaux et Niestlé.

Piovesan, P. (Ed.)
1972 Ricerche di Filosofia Linguistica. Firenze.

Poggi, I., C. Castelfranchi and D. Parisi
1978 "Risposte, repliche e reazioni". Roma: Istituto di Psicologia, CNR.

Poggi, I., R. Conte and D. Parisi
1979 "Proposte per un curricolo sugli aspetti scopistici del lin-

guaggio". In D. Parisi (Ed.), 1979.

Pomerantz, A.
1978 "Compliment responses: Notes on the co-operation of multiple constraints". In J. Schenkein (Ed.), 1978.

Pope, E.
1973 "Question-answering systems". Papers from the 9th Regional Meeting, Chicago LInguistic Society, 482-492.

1977 Questions and Answers in English. The Hague: Mouton.

Popper, K.R.
1972 Objective Knowledge: An Evolutionary Approach. London: Oxford University Press.

Power, R.
1977 "A model of conversation". Pragmatics Microfiche 2:6.A2-F1.

Pratt, M.L.
1977 Towards a Speech Act Theory of Literary Discourse. Bloomington: Indiana University Press.

Putnam, H.
1973 "Meaning and reference". Journal of Philosophy 70.

1975 Mind, Language and Reality: Philosophical Papers. Cambridge: Cambridge University Press.

Raskin, V.
1977 "Literal meaning and speech acts". Theoretical Linguistics 4: 3.209-225.

Reinhart, T.
1976 The Syntactic Domain of Anaphora. MIT doctoral dissertation.

Rescher, N. (Ed.)
1967 The Logic of Decision and Action. Pittsburgh.

Rieck, B.-O. and I. Senft
1978 "The situation of foreign workers in the Federal Republic of Germany". In N. Dittmar et al. (Eds.), 1978, 85-98.

Rieger, C.
1976 "An organization of knowledge for problem solving and language comprehension". Artificial Intelligence 7.89-127.

Rist, R.C.
1979 "On the education of guest-worker children in Germany". School Review 87.242-268.

Robinson, J. and J. Hobbs
1978 "Why ask ? Interpreting questions in context". SRI technical note, Menlo Park, California.

Rogers, A.
1978 "Remarks on the analysis of assertion and the conversational role of speech acts". Proceedings of the Fourth Annual Meeting of the Berkeley Linguistics Society 190-201.

1979 "Taking speech acts seriously". Paper read at the Conference on Possibilities and Limitations of Pragmatics, July 1979, at Urbino, Italy.

Rogers, A., B. Wall and J.P. Murphy (Eds.)
1977 Proceedings of the Texas Conference on Performatives, Presuppositions, and Implicatures. Arlington, Virginia: Center of Applied Linguistics.

Rohrer, C. (Ed.)
1979 Time, Tense and Quantifiers. Tübingen: Niemeyer.

Rosenberg, J.F. and C. Travis (Eds.)
1971 Readings in the Philosophy of Language. Englewood Cliffs, N.J.: Prentice-Hall.

Ross, J.R.
1970 "On declarative sentences". In R.A. Jacobs and P.S. Rosenbaum (Eds.), 1970, 222-72.

1973 "A fake NP squish". In C.-J.N. Bailey and R.W. Shuy (Eds.), 1973, 96-140.

Rumelhart, D.E.
1975 "Notes on a schema for stories". In D. Bobrow and A. Collins (Eds.), 1975, 211-236.

n.d. "Toward an interactive model of reading". Paper presented at Attention and Performance VI International Symposium, Stockholm. Ms.

Russell, B.
1919 Introduction to Mathemantical Philosophy. London: Allen and Unwin.

Ryan, A.
1970 The Philosophy of the Social Sciences. London: Macmillan.

Ryle, G.
1930/31 "Are there propositions ?". Proceedings of the Aristotelian Society 30.91-126.

Sacks, H.
n.d. Transcribed lectures (1967-1972), with index prepared by Gail Jefferson. University of California, Irvine, mimeo.

Sacks, H. and E. Schegloff
1974 "Opening up closings". In R. Turner (Ed.), 1974.

Sacks, H., E.A. Schegloff and G. Jefferson
1974 "A simplest systematics for the organization of turn-taking for conversation". Language 50.696-735.

Sadock, J.M.
1978 "On testing for conversational implicature". In P. Cole (Ed.), 1978, 281-298.

Sandig, B.
 1973 "Beispiele pragmalinguistischer Textanalyse (Wahlaufruf, Familiäres Gespräch, Zeitungsnachricht)". Der Deutschunterricht 25:1.5-23.

Savage, C. Wade (Ed.)
 1978 Minnesota Studies in Philosophy of Science IX. Minneapolis: University of Minnesota Press.

Savage, C.W. (Ed.)
 1954 The Foundation of Statistics. New York.

Savigny, E. von
 1974 Die Philosophie der normalen Sprache. Frankfurt a.M.: Suhrkamp.

Sbisà, M.
 1972 "Il problema della classificazione degli Atti illocutori". In P. Piovesan (Ed.), 1972.

Schaerlaekens, A.-M.
 1973 The Two-Word Stage in Child Language Development. The Hague: Mouton.

Schank, R.
 1975 Conceptual Information Processing. Amsterdam: North-Holland.

Schegloff, E.A.
 1968 "Sequencing in conversational openings". American Anthropologist 70:6.1075-1095. Reprinted in J. Laver and S. Hutcheson (Eds.), 1972.

 1972 "Notes on a conversational practice: Formulating place". In D. Sudnow (Ed.), 1972, 75-119.

 1976 "On some questions and ambiguities in conversation". Pragmatics Microfiche 2:2.D8-G12.

 1978 "On some questions and ambiguities in conversation". In W.U. Dressler (Ed.), 1978, 81-102.

Schegloff, E.A. and H. Sacks
 1973 "Opening up closings". Semiotica 8.289-327.

Schegloff, E.A., H. Sacks and G. Jefferson
 1977 "The preference for self-correction in the organisation of repair in conversation". Language 53:2.361-382.

Schelling, T.
 1960 The Strategy of Conflict. Cambridge, Mass.: Harvard University Press.

Schenkein, J. (Ed.)
 1978 Studies in the Organization of Conversational Interaction. New York: Academic Press.

Schnelle, H.
 1976 "Circumstances and circumstantial expressions". In J. Groenendijk and M. Stokhof (Eds.), 1976, 231-252.

1979a "Circumstance sentences". In A. Margalit (Ed.), 1979, 93-115.

1979b "Pre-tense". In C. Rohrer (Ed.), 1979.

1979c "Introspection and the description of language use". Ms.

Schwartz, S. (Ed.)
1977 Naming, Necessity and Natural Kinds. Ithaca: Cornell University Press.

Searle, J.R.
1969 Speech Acts: An Essay in the Philosophy of Language. Cambridge: Cambridge University Press.

1975a "Indirect speech acts". In P. Cole and J.L. Morgan (Eds.), 1975, 59-82.

1975b "A taxonomy of illocutionary acts". In K. Gunderson (Ed.), 1975, 344-369.

1976 "A classification of illocutionary acts". Language in Society 5:1.1-23.

1978 "Literal meaning". Erkenntnis 13.207-224.

Searle, J.R. and D. Vanderveken
n.d. Foundations of Illocutionary Logic. Ms.

Seuren, P.A.M.
1978 "Grammar as an underground process". In A. Sinclair, R. Jarvella and W.J.M. Levelt (Eds.), 1978.

Shatz, M. and R. Gelman
1973 The Development of Communication Skills: Modification in the Speech of Young Children as a Function of Listener. Monographs of the Society for Research in Child Development, 152, Vol.38, No.5.

Shibatani, M.
1973 A Linguistic Study of Causative Constructions. Bloomington: Indiana University Linguistics Club.

Shibatani, M. (Ed.)
1976 The Grammar of Causative Constructions. New York: Academic Press.

Shiman, L.G.
1978 "The law of perceptual stability: Abstract foundation". Proceedings of the National Academy of Sciences 75:4.2049-2053.

Siegler, A.
1966 "Lying". American Philosophical Quarterly 3:2.III.128-136.

Sinclair, J. McH. and R.M. Coulthard
1975 Towards an Analysis of Discourse: The English Used by Teachers and Pupils. London: Oxford University Press.

Sinclair, A., R. Jarvella and W.J.M. Levelt (Eds.)
1978 The Child's Conception of Language. Berlin: Springer.

Skutnabb-Kangas, T.
1978 "Vad vet vi om den andra generationen ? Erfarenheter fran förskolan och skolan". Paper given at a symposium on the second generation of Finnish immigrant children in Sweden, Hanasaari (Finland), February 1978.

1979a "Invandrarbarnens utbildning - forskning och politik". In Papers from the Second Nordic Conference on Bilingualism. Stockholm: Akademilitteratur, pp.158-178.

1979b "Bilingualism as an unrealistic goal in minority education". Preprint, Symposium on the position of the second generation of Yugoslav Immigrants in Sweden, Split (Yugoslavia), October 30th - November 1st, 1979. Swedisch Commission on Immigration Research (EIFO).

Smaby, R.
1975 "Ambiguous coreference with quantifiers". Ms.

Snow, C.E.
1972 "Mothers' speech to children learning language". Child Development 43:549-565.

Sørensen, V.
1976 "Textuality - a pragmatic approach". In F. Karlsson (Ed.), 1976, 381-391.
1979 "The argumentative status of modality." In W. Vandenweghe and M. Van de Velde (Eds.), 1979, 273-284.

Sperber, D. and D. Wilson
1979 "Irony and the use-mention distinction". Ms.
n.d. Foundations of Pragmatic Theory. Ms.

Spohn, W.
1978 Grundlagen der Entscheidungstheorie. Kronberg.

Stalnaker, R.C.
1972 "Pragmatics". In D. Davidson and G. Harman (Eds.), 1972, 380-397.
1978 "Assertion". In P. Cole (Ed.), 1978, 315-332.

Stampe, D.W.
1972 "On the meaning of nouns". In D. Cohen (Ed.), 1972, 54-71.
1975a "Show and tell". In B. Freed et al. (Eds.), 1975.
1975b "Meaning and truth in the theory of speech acts". In P. Cole and J.L. Morgan (Eds.), 1975, 1-39.
1977 "Towards a causal theory of linguistic representation". Mid-West Studies in Philosophy 2.
1979 "Towards a causal theory of linguistic representation". In P. French et al. (Eds.), 1979, 81-102.

Stechow, A. von
 1978 "Presupposition and context". Pragmatics Microfiche 3.6,A2.

Stegmüller, W.
 1964 "Remarks on the completeness of logical systems relative to the validity concepts of P. Lorensen and K. Lorenz". Notre Dame Journal of Formal Logic 5.81-112.

 1973 Probleme und Resultate der Wissenschaftstheorie und Analytischen Philosophie, vol.IV: Personelle und Statistische Wahrscheinlichkeit. Berlin/Heidelberg/New York: Springer.

Steinberg, D.D. and L.A. Jakobovits (Eds.)
 1971 Semantics: An Interdisciplinary Reader. Cambridge: Cambridge University Press.

Stierle, K.
 1975 "Geschichte als Exemplum - Exemplum als Geschichte". In Text als Handlung. München: Fink, pp.14-48.

Stölting, W.
 1977 "Die Sprachpolitik an deutschen Schulen für ausländische Kinder". In C. Molony et al. (Eds.), 1977, 213-236.

 1978 "Teaching German to immigrant children". In N. Dittmar et al. (Eds.), 1978, 99-109.

Stoutland, F.
 1976 "The causal theory of action". In J. Manninen and R. Tuomela (Eds.), 1976, 271-304.

Strawson, P.F.
 1950 "On referring". Mind 59:235.320-344. Reprinted in Logico-Linguistic Papers. London: Methuen, 1971, pp.1-27.

 1964 "Intention and convention in speech acts". Philosophical Review 73.439-60. Reprinted in Logico-Linguistic Papers. London: Methuen, 1971.

Sudnow, D. (Ed.)
 1972 Studies in Social Interaction. New York: The Free Press.

Swetland, C.
 1979 The Ghetto of the Soul. Paris: UNESCO.

Tarski, A.
 1956 "The establishment of scientific semantics". In A. Tarski, 1956, Logic, Semantics, Meta-Mathematics. Oxford: Oxford University Press.

Thomas, Saint (Aquinas)
 1972 "De Mendacio". In Summa Theologiae, vol.41, 2a2ac, Quest.110. Edited by T.C. O'Brien. Latin text and English translation. London: Blackfriars, in conjunction with Eyre & Spottiswoode.

Thomson, J.J.
 1977 Acts and Other Events. Ithaca: Cornell University Press.

Tomberg, F.
1973 Bürgerliche Wissenschaft. Frankfurt a.M.: Fischer Taschenbuch Verlag.

Travis, C.
1971 "A generative theory of illocution". In J.F. Rosenberg and C. Travis (Eds.), 1971, 629-645.

Turing, A.M.
1937 "Computable numbers, with an application to the Entscheidungsproblem". Proceedings of the London Mathematical Society 42. 230-265. Reprinted in M. Davis (Ed.), 1965.

Turner, R. (Ed.)
1974 Ethnomethodology. Harmondsworth: Penguin.

Vandeweghe, W. and M. Van de Velde (Eds.)
1979 Bedeutung, Sprachakte und Texte. Tübingen: Niemeyer.

Vendler, Z.
1967 Linguistics in Philosophy. Ithaca: Cornell University Press.

Vennemann, T.
1973 "Topics, sentence accent, ellipsis: A proposal for their formal treatment". In E. Keenan (Ed.), 1975, 313-328.

Verschueren, J.
1978a Pragmatics: An Annotated Bibliography. Amsterdam: John Benjamins. (Annual Supplements in the Journal of Pragmatics.)

1978b "Reflections on presupposition failure: A contribution to an integrated theory of pragmatics". Journal of Pragmatics 2:2. 107-151.

1979 What People Say They Do With Words. University of California, Berkeley, Ph.D. dissertation. (Fully revised and expanded version to be published in The Hague by Mouton.).

Vincent, J.M.
n.d. "The witcraft of Iago". Ms.

Vogt, H.
1973 "Målvetskap og målstrid". In E. Hanssen and G. Wiggen (Eds.), 1973, 89-94. (Written in 1935.)

Vonnegut, K.
1969 Slaughterhouse 5. Frogmore: Panther Books.

1975 Breakfast of Champions. Frogmore: Panther Books.

Waltz, D.
1978 TINLAP-2 (Theoretical Issues in Natural Language Processing, Second General Convention). Urbana: Co-ordinated Science Lab.

Warnock, G.J.
1973 "Some types of performative utterances". In I. Berlin et al., 1973, 69-89.

Weimer, W.B. and D.S. Palermo (Eds.)
  1974 Cognition and the Symbolic Process. Hillsdale: Lawrence Erlbaum Associates.

Weinrich, H.
  1976 "La linguistica della menzogna". In Metafora e Menzogna: La Serenita dell'Arte. Bologna: Il Mulino, pp.133-191.

Weiser, A.
  1974 "Deliberate ambiguity". Papers from the 10th Regional Meeting, Chicago Linguistic Society, 723-731.

  1975 "How to not answer a question: Purposive devices in conversational strategy". Papers from the 11th Regional Meeting, Chicago Linguistic Society, 649-660.

Wellman, C.
  1961 The Language of Ethics. Cambridge, Mass.: Harvard University Press.

Widgren, J.
  1975 Migration to Western Europe: The social situation of migrant workers and their families. UNESCO working paper, UN/SOA/SEM/60/WP/2.

  1978 "Some major issues in Swedish migration policy". Ms.

Wierzbicka, A.
  1976 "Particles and linguistic relativity". International Review of Slavic Linguistics I:2-3.

Wilks, Y.
  1979 "Computer models of speech acts *must* explicate something". Paper presented at the Conference on Possibilities and Limitations of Pragmatics, July 1978, at Urbino (Italy).

Wilson, D. and D. Sperber
  1977 "A new approach to presupposition". Pragmatics Microfiche 2.6, A2.

  1978 "On Grice's theory of conversation". Pragmatics Microfiche, August 1978.

  1979 "Ordered entailments: An alternative to presuppositional theories". In C.K. Oh and D. Dinneen (Eds.), 1979.

Wilson, G.
  1978 "On definite and indefinite descriptions". Philosophical Review 87.48-76.

Winograd, T.
  1972 Understanding Natural Language. New York: Academic Press.

  1977 "A framework for the understanding of discourse". In M.A. Just and P.A. Carpenter (Eds.), 1977, 63-88.

Wirth, J.R. (Ed.)
1976   Assessing Linguistic Arguments. Washington/New York: Hemisphere.

Wittgenstein, L.
1958   Philosophical Investigations. Oxford: Basil Blackwell.

1966   Lectures & Conversations on Aesthetics, Psychology and Religious Beliefs. Compiled from Notes taken by Yorick Smythies, Rush Rhees and James Taylor. Edited by Cyril Barrett. Oxford: Basil Blackwell.

1967a Philosophische Untersuchungen. Frankfurt a.M.: Suhrkamp.

1967b Zettel. Oxford: Basil Blackwell.

1969   Notebooks 1914-1916. Oxford: Basil Blackwell.

Wright, G.H. von
1951   "Deontic logic". Mind 60.

1957   Logical Studies. London: Routledge and Kegan Paul.

1964   "A new system of deontic logic". Danish Year-Book of Philosophy 1.173-182.

Wunderlich, D.
1970   Tempus und Zeitreferenz im Deutschen. München: Hueber.

1974   Grundlagen der Linguistik. Reinbek: rororo.

Wunderlich, D. (Ed.)
1972   Linguistische Pragmatik. Frankfurt: Athenäum.

1976   Wissenschaftstheorie der Linguistik. Kronberg i.Ts.: Athenäum.

Zaefferer, D.
1977   "Understanding misunderstanding: A proposal for an explanation of reading choices". Journal of Pragmatics 1.329-346.

1979   "Fragesätze und andere Formulierungen von Fragen". In G. Krallmann (Ed.), 1979.

Ziff, P.
1972   Understanding Understanding. Ithaca: Cornell University Press.

INDEX

ABADAN-UNAT,: 303

ABDUCTION: 108, 117-18

ABELSON, P.: 164

ACCENT, CONTRASTIVE: 519-26. See also: INTONATION; PROSODY

ACCEPTABILITY: 65

ACT, CONTROL: 199-203, 206-08. See also: CONTROL; DIRECTIVE; GOAL, CONTROL

ACT, ILLOCUTIONARY: 215, 223; 251-52, 256-57; 334-47; 415, 419; 478; 493-97, 508; 701, 704; 781, 783, 786. See also: EFFECT, ILLOCUTIONARY; FORCE, ILLOCUTIONARY

ACT, LOCUTIONARY: 226; 252-53, 259; 345; 493-94; 783, 785-86, 794-95

ACT, PERLOCUTIONARY: 344, 357; 431; 478, 481; 493-96. See also: EFFECT, PERLOCUTIONARY; INTENT, PERLOCUTIONARY; PURPOSE

ACTING: 751, 755-56, 766, 769

ACTION: 84, 88, 92; 105; 186-93; 195-208; 211-12; 239, 243-44, 249; 332; 380-84, 387; 477, 479; 552-54, 565; 571-73, 579; 637-38, 640, 649, 657; 749, 752. See also: ACTIVITY; BEHAVIOR; SEQUENCE, ACTION

ACTION, AGRRESSIVE: 752-53, 774-75

ACTION, BASIC: 188-90

ACTION, INTENTIONAL: 186-88, 190-91; 240, 247

ACTION, LINGUISTIC: 17, 54; 332-33; 443; 554; 570. See also: ACTIVITY, LINGUISTIC; SPEECH ACT

ACTION, NON-INTENTIONAL: 186-88

ACTION, PARALINGUISTIC: 117

ACTION THEORY: See: THEORY OF ACTION; THEORY OF ACTION, CAUSAL

ACTIVITY: 205-07; 216; 636-40, 642-43, 645, 647, 650, 654. See also: INTERPRETATION, 1

ACTIVITY, CONVENTIONAL: 142

ACTIVITY, CRYPTIC: 98; 655. See also: PROGRESS, CRYPTIC

ACTIVITY, EVERYDAY: 141-42. See also: INTERACTION, FAMILY

ACTIVITY, LINGUISTIC: 100; 217-23; 749. See also: ACTION, LINGUISTIC

ACTIVITY, PHENIC: 98; 655. See also: PROCESS, PHENIC

ACTOR: 201, 202, 205; 323; 380

ADDRESSEE: 17; 196, 198; 235; 496; 576-78; 794-95. See also: HEARER

ADJUSTMENT: See: SPEECH ADJUSTMENT

"AFTER ALL": 59, 62, 64-66, 73-76

AGENT: 184, 186, 192; 395; 749-50, 766. See also: CASE

AKMAJIAN, A.: 528, 530

ALLEN, J.: 488

ALLWOOD, J.: 490; 774

ALSTON, W.P.: 158

ALTHAM, J.E.J.: 359

AMBIGUITY: 24, 34, 41, 47-48; 97, 99; 145; 230, 234; 504, 507; 626; 662; 763, 769-70; 783-85, 793, 796-97

ANALYSIS, CONVERSATIONAL: 226, 233, 235; 343, 356; 464; 531

ANAPHORA: 510, 525-26. See also: IDENTIFICATION, ANAPHORIC

ANAXAGORAS: 494

"AND": 75. See also: CONSTANT, LOGICAL

ANDERSEN, H.: 660-61, 665

ANDERSON, A.R.: 499

ANSCOMBE, E.: 625

ANSCOMBRE, J.-C.: 362

ANSWER: 106; 248; 264-82; 339; 423, 433; 447-53, 455-65, 469-70; 474, 479, 482, 484; 569, 571-91. See also: REPLY; RESPONSE; SEQUENCE, QUESTION-ANSWER

"ANYWAY": 59, 62, 64-65, 76

APPROPRIATENESS: 8; 79, 90-92; 423; 443; 452; 505; 703; 737-38; 763. See also: SPEECH ADJUSTMENT

ÅQVIST, L.: 264-66, 268, 283-84; 447, 458

ARBIB, M.: 637, 655

ARBITRARINESS: 416

ARGUMENTATION: 362, 364, 366; 454; 565-66; 665

ARISTOTLE: 6; 503-06

ARTIFICIAL INTELLIGENCE: 15; 18; 164; 371-72, 384, 393-94; 487-89; 638-43, 645, 647-48

ASPECT: 631-32, 634, 649, 653-54; 717

ASSERTION: 84; 252, 259; 350, 352; 367-68; 430; 443-47, 450-52, 455-56, 459, 461-62, 467, 470; 483-84; 495; 593; 756, 759, 763; 784-85, 789-90, 794, 796-97. See also: DECLARATIVE; REPRESENTATIVE; STATEMENT

ATKINSON, M.: 491

ATLAS, J.D.: 177; 490

ATTITUDE, PROPOSITIONAL: 126-28; 320; 376-80, 385, 391; 627. See also: STATE, INTENTIONAL; STATE, MENTAL

ATTITUDE, PROPOSITIONAL (ASCRIPTION OF): 126-33, 135, 137. See also: BELIEF (ASCRIPTION OF); INTENTION (ATTRIBUTION OF); STATE, MENTAL (ASCRIPTION OF).

AUDIENCE: see: HEARER

AUGUSTINE (SAINT): 751, 770, 773, 775

AUSTIN, J.: 128

AUSTIN, J.L.: 167, 176; 219, 252-55; 357; 493, 497, 508; 744; 753, 773, 776, 785

AUTHOR: 507; 660-62. See also: WRITER

BACH-PETERS PARADOX: See: PARADOX, BACH-PETERS

BALLMER, T.: 7, 8, 11; 29, 33, 48, 51, 53; 291

BAR-HILLEL, Y.: 1; 154, 176; 287

BARTSCH, R.: 18; 263

BEHAVIOR: 111; 477, 488; 551-54; 571; 749. See also: ACTION; ACTIVITY

BEHAVIOR, INTENTIONAL: 241-49

BEHAVIOR, INTERACTIONAL: 83-84

BEHAVIORISM: 19-20; 167; 237; 407

BELIEF: 48; 57-59, 68-73; 105; 126-29, 131-33, 136; 155; 196; 229; 269-72, 279-80; 374-77, 379, 383, 385-88, 391, 395-97; 402, 404, 406; 426, 432, 434-38; 463; 493; 571, 580; 593, 598, 604, 608, 614; 696, 699-702, 704-05, 707-08, 712; 743; 749-50, 753, 764, 768, 771; 780, 784-85

BELIEF (ASCRIPTION OF): 126-27, 131-32; 249; 707-08. See also: ATTITUDE, PROPOSITIONAL (ASCRIPTION OF); INTENTION (ATTRIBUTION OF); STATE, MENTAL (ASCRIPTION OF)

BELNAP, N.D.: 265, 283; 447, 449, 453, 457-59, 467

BENNET, R.: 210

BENZON, W.: 312

BERNAL, J.D.: 286

BERNSTEIN, B.: 290

BET: 211-17

BEVER, G.: 157

BIASCI, C.: 330

BIERWISCH, M.: 1; 103

BILINGUALISM: 294, 304-07, 309

BLACK, M.: 154; 711

BLAU, U.: 782

BLOCH, N.C.: 238

BLOOMFIELD, L.: 167, 176

BOËR, S.: 694, 710

BÖHME, G.: 291

BOLINGER, D.: 763

BORGES, J.L.: 153

BORKENAU, F.: 286

BOTHA, R.P.: 333-34

BRANSFORD, J.D.: 177

BRENNENSTUHL, W.: 48

BROCKWAY, D.: 2, 8, 14, 16; 77, 78; 774

BROUWER, L.E.J.: 446

BROWN, P.: 441; 488, 490-91

BRUNER, J.S.: 5; 239-41, 245-47

BRUNNER, G.: 368

BÜHLER, K.: 22

BURGE, T.: 708

BURT, M.K.: 339

"BUT": 59, 75; 158; 361, 364; 562

BUTTERWORTH, B.: 286

CAFFI, C.: 776

CAMAIONI, L.: 5, 8; 80

CAMPBELL, R.N.: 5, 6; 94; 655

CARNAP, R.: 177; 283; 285, 292, 310; 404, 410; 509; 655

CARROLL, LEWIS: 145

CARSWELL, E.A.: 165, 177

CASE: 46-48; 377

CASTELFRANCHI, C.: 8, 12, 13; 554; 569-70, 581, 585, 590-91; 751, 771, 773, 776

CATAPHORA: 43-44

CATEGORY, GRAMMATICAL: 391-92, 394, 396-98; 786-87

CATEGORY, LOGICAL: 501-04

CATEGORY, VERBAL: 631-32

CAZDEN, C.: 293

CHAFE, W.L.: 143, 145

CHISHOLM, R.M.: 751, 756, 775-77

CHOMSKY, N.: 154, 176; 310; 332-33; 488, 492

CICERO: 505-06

CICOUREL, A.V.: 7, 8, 15; 111, 116; 546

CLARK, E.: 96

CLARK, H.: 96

CLARKE, D.: 473, 490

CLAUSE, SUBORDINATE: 42-43

COHEN, L.J.: 159, 176

COHEN, P.: 488

COHEN, P.R.: 374-76, 379, 389-90

COHEN, T.: 494

COHERENCE: 14; 116-17; 235; 353, 356; 362, 367-69; 383-84, 393-94; 473, 484; 516; 657-64. See also: COHESION; UTTERANCE, COHERENT

COHESION: 486; 534-36; 566. See also: COHERENCE

COLE, P.: 1; 622; 776

COLEMAN, L.: 776

COMMAND: 252-55, 257-58; 495. See also: DIRECTIVE; IMPERATIVE; ORDER

COMMENT: See: TOPIC/COMMENT

COMMISSIVE: 214, 220

COMMITMENT, SPEAKER'S: 58; 214; 419, 435; 496; 756, 770; 785

COMMUNICATION: 17, 30; 94, 96; 107; 140, 146; 197, 201; 215; 225-27, 229, 235; 315-16, 321; 336; 343, 345-46; 371-73; 480; 506; 526; 531, 533, 538; 554-55, 557-59, 561-63, 565; 570, 573, 575, 577-81; 750-51, 754, 756-58, 760-62, 766, 770-71; 780. See also: COMPETENCE, COMMUNICATIVE; MODE, COMMUNICATIVE

COMMUNICATION, METALINGUISTIC: 95. See also: METACOMMUNICATION

COMPETENCE, BILINGUAL: 141

COMPETENCE, COMMUNICATIVE: 81-82, 88-89; 156-57; 304

COMPETENCE, DISCOURSING: 373

COMPETENCE, LINGUISTIC: 94; 142, 149; 555, 559, 562-63

COMPETENCE, SEMANTIC: 694, 703

COMPREHENSION: See: UNDERSTANDING

CONDITION, FELICITY: 222; 227, 229, 231; 385-86, 395-96; 429, 431-32, 470; 762-63

CONNECTIVE: 75-76; 377; 515, 524

CONSISTENCY: 383; 515

CONSTANT, LOGICAL: 445, 454-55

CONSTRAINT, SEMANTIC: 63, 73-4

CONSTRAINT, TRANSDERIVATIONAL: 59-61, 77

CONTE, A.G.: 499

CONTENT, PROPOSITIONAL: 79; 218, 222; 252-53, 257, 259; 393-94, 396-98; 422-23, 426-27; 483-84; 516-17, 520-21, 523-25; 751. See also: PROPOSITION

CONTEXT: 8-9; 69, 72-77; 79-83; 107-08, 110; 142-44, 147, 148; 153-69, 173-75; 202, 207-08; 230-32; 314, 324; 372-74, 378; 404-06; 424-27, 429, 431, 434-36; 444, 461, 468; 482; 496-97, 503; 533, 544; 555-57; 610, 613-14; 632-33, 636, 645; 657-58, 662; 694, 697, 699, 703, 707; 749-50, 761, 763, 768-69

CONTEXT, ACTION: 269

CONTEXT, DISCOURSE: 512-13, 522, 524

CONTEXT, ETHNOGRAPHIC: 107, 118

CONTEXT, POLITICAL: 286, 295

CONTEXT CHANGE: 7, 11; 17-54; 229-30; 381-82, 386-88

CONTEXT DEPENDENCE: 59-61, 67-68;

156, 171, 175; 231, 233; 367

CONTEXT OF INTERPRETATION: 324-26

CONTEXT OF PRODUCTION: 324-26

CONTEXT OF RECEPTION: 324-26

CONTRADICTION: 458; 497, 502-03. See also: PRINCIPLE OF NON-CONTRADICTION

CONTROL: 88, 92; 97; 162; 195-96; 542; 636-37, 640, 652. See also: ACT, CONTROL; GOAL, CONTROL

CONVENTION: 60; 79; 208; 344-45; 388-92, 394-98; 415-18, 428, 431; 497; 621; 658, 650-61, 663, 666; 684; 749-50, 774. See also: RULE, CONVENTIONAL

CONVERSATION: 75; 79; 147; 161-62; 225-29, 235; 473, 475, 479, 482, 486-89; 531-33, 537-38, 542, 544; 551, 563-66; 569-72, 587, 590; 752. See also: ANALYSIS, CONVERSATIONAL; INTERACTION; SEQUENCE, CONVERSATIONAL

CONVERSATION, MAXIMS OF: 60-61, 63-64; 97-99; 173; 233; 429-35, 441; 468-70; 573, 575; 704; 762. See also: PRINCIPLE, CO-OPERATION; PRINCIPLE OF RELEVANCE

COOPER, D.E.: 3, 4

COOPERATION: 98, 101; 173; 207; 211-12, 214, 219; 233; 278-80, 284; 350; 389-90; 463-64; 485, 488; 752, 768-69

COORDINATION: 372-73, 388; 463; 487-88; 753

CORNULIER, B. DE: 630

COSSIO, C.: 501

CO-TEXT: 154-56, 162

COULMAS, F.: 13, 15; 141, 151

COULTHARD, R.M.: 91; 198; 473, 481, 490; 546

CRESSWELL, M.: 123, 124; 779, 798

CRISARI, M.: 590-91

CRUSIUS, C.A.: 502

DARNELL, R.D.: 288

DARWIN, C.: 370

DASCAL, M.: 9; 161, 164, 169, 176, 177; 311

DAVIDSON, D.: 133-34; 174; 187, 189-90

DAVIS, S.: 11, 15

DECEPTION: 505; 749-73, 775. See also: LYING

DECISION THEORY: See: THEORY, DECISION

DECLARATION: 220; 785, 789, 794, 796-97

DECLARATIVE: See: DECLARATION; SENTENCE, DECLARATIVE; STATEMENT

DEMETRIUS: 506

DEMOCRITOS: 502

DESCRIPTION, DEFINITIVE: 593-613, 616-24, 626-29; 718

DESIGNATOR: 596-98, 614-19, 622-26; 731

DIALOGUE: 54; 233-24; 444-45, 447, 454, 461, 464, 468-69; 473-78, 482-90; 780

DIJK, T.A. VAN: 116; 165

DINNEEN, D.: 777

DIODORUS CRONUS: 504

DIOGENES LAERTIOS: 494

DIRECTIVE: 195-205; 214, 220; 335; 349, 354; 375; 534, 546; 787. See also: IMPERATIVE; REQUEST

DISCOURSE: 14-15; 147; 215; 343-44, 346, 349, 353-54, 356; 371,

383-84; 468-71; 486; 509-26; 534, 545; 551, 559-64, 556; 569; 717. See also: COMPETENCE, DISCOURSING; CONTEXT, DISCOURSE; DISCOURSE ANALYSIS; GENRE OF DISCOURSE; INFORMATION, DISCOURSE

DISCOURSE ANALYSIS: 107-08, 116; 275

DONNELLAN, K.: 3; 528; 593-96, 598-603, 605-12, 615, 618, 621, 629

DOUBLE BIND: 383

DOWTY, D.: 179, 181-83

DRETSKE, F.: 706, 712

DREW, P.: 491

DUCROT, O.: 161; 362

DUMMETT, M.: 446

ECCLES, J.C.: 638, 640, 642, 645, 647, 655

EDES, E.: 36

EDUCATION OF IMMIGRANT CHILDREN: 294-95, 299, 301-08

EFFECT, ILLOCUTIONARY: 215, 218, 220; 494. See also: ACT, ILLOCUTIONARY; FORCE, ILLOCUTIONARY; POINT, ILLOCUTIONARY

EFFECT, PERLOCUTIONARY: 12; 344-45, 347; 495-96. See also: ACT, PERLOCUTIONARY; INTENT, PERLOCUTIONARY; PURPOSE

EFFECT OF UTTERANCES: 750, 759

EHLICH, K.: 665

EISENBERG, A.: 210

EISENBERG, P.: 291, 311

EKEGREN, E.: 311

EKSTRAND, L.H.: 306

ELLIPSIS: 208; 230; 423; 781

EMONDS, J.: 289-90

ENÇ, B.: 709

ENGLISH: See: LANGUAGE, ENGLISH

ENTAILMENT: 71; 182, 185; 522; 794-95

ENTAILMENT, ILLOCUTIONARY: 782, 785, 795

ERVIN-TRIPP, S.: 5, 12, 13; 80; 195, 198

ETHNOMETHODOLOGY: 165; 235; 590

EVANS, G.: 132

EVERYDAY LIFE: See: ACTIVITY, EVERYDAY; INTERACTION, FAMILY; KNOWLEDGE, COMMON

EUPHEMISM: 143; 764, 770-71

EXPECTATION: 90-92; 146, 148; 195, 197-98, 203-08; 234; 281-82; 435-36; 482, 486; 493-94, 504, 507; 655; 657-58; 684; 750, 756, 765-66

EXPLOITATION: 300-01

EXPRESSIVE: 220

FANSHEL, D.: 161-63; 473, 481; 490, 492

FEEHAN, D.: 751, 756, 775-77

FELICITY CONDITION: See: CONDITION, FELICITY

FEYERABEND, P.: 469

FEYS, R.: 500

FIELD, H.: 138

FILLMORE, C.J.: 149

FINK, H.: 364, 366

FIRTH, J.R.: 167, 176

FITCHETT, J.: 368

FOCUS: 514; 705

FOCUS, ATTENTIONAL: 205-07

FODOR, J.A.: 102

FORCE, ILLOCUTIONARY: 157-58; 211,

215-16, 220-230; 253, 257-58; 319-20; 344, 353; 419, 431; 477, 481-83; 494, 497; 516-18, 526; 687-88, 700-701, 705-06, 711; 783, 786, 789-90; 794-97. See also: ACT, ILLOCUTIONARY; EFFECT, ILLOCUTIONARY; INDICATOR, ILLOCUTIONARY FORCE; POINT, ILLOCUTIONARY

FORM, LOGICAL: 425; 445, 447

FOTION, N.: 12, 14; 357

FRAASSEN, B. VAN: 446-47

FRAME: 164-65, 177; 346; 372-76, 382-97

FRANCK, D.: 4, 10; 236

FRANZ, F.: 298

FREGE, G.: 177; 252-53; 501; 595; 698, 711

FRENCH: See: LANGUAGE, FRENCH

FREUD, S.: 370

FRITSCHE, J.: 330

FRITZ, G.: 357

FRITZSON, R.: 312

FURBERG, M.: 357

GALILEI, G.: 311; 499

GAME: See: LANGUAGE GAME; THEORY, GAME.

GAME THEORY: See: THEORY, GAME

GARDINER, A.: 603

GARFINKEL, A.: 773-74, 776

GARFINKEL, H. 146; 429

GAZDAR, G.: 59-60, 77; 254; 480-81, 490; 773, 777

GEACH, P.T.: 27; 364; 711

GELDER, B. DE: 5, 12; 250

GELMAN, R.: 80, 82, 92

GELPHMAN, S.: 210

GENRE OF DISCOURSE: 505

GERBINO, W.: 81

GERMAN: See: LANGUAGE, GERMAN

GIVÓN, T.: 431

GOAL: 105-07, 115, 116-17; 196-97, 199-202, 208; 245; 345-47, 349-50, 353-54, 356; 372-76, 382-97; 484-88; 551-67; 569-89; 749-75

GOAL, CONTROL: 564, 566; 570, 572, 577, 579

GOAL, FIXED: 752, 759, 769, 774

GOAL ANALYSIS: 8, 12; 551-67; 569-91; 773

GOCHET, P.: 13, 16; 261

GOFFMAN, E.: 155, 165, 176; 479, 490-92; 538, 590

GOLDMAN, A.: 187

"GOOD": 340; 365

GOOD, D.: 490

GORDON, D.: 210; 418; 481, 491

GOWERS, E.: 764

GRAMMAR: 4, 15; 105, 116; 150; 225, 235; 263; 291, 293; 331, 333-34, 336, 338-40; 371, 373-76, 384; 411; 415, 417-19; 493-94, 504, 507; 545; 631, 641; 658

GRAMMAR, GENERATIVE: 18; 263. See also: GRAMMAR, TRANSFORMATIONAL

GRAMMAR, MONTAGUE: 389; 786

GRAMMAR, STORY: 115, 118

GRAMMAR, STRUCTURALIST: 331, 340; 632

GRAMMAR, TEXT: 165

GRAMMAR, TRANSFORMATIONAL: 293; 331, 334, 340; 410; 415. See also: GRAMMAR, GENERATIVE

GRAMMAR BOOK: 331-34, 339-40

GREEK, ANCIENT: See: LANGUAGE, ANCIENT GREEK

GREEN, G.M.: 195, 116, 119

GREGORY, R.L.: 177

GREWENDORF, G.: 2, 6, 12, 14; 283; 774

GRICE, H.P.: 5, 6, 10, 14; 60, 63, 64; 98; 124; 142; 158, 161, 173, 177; 233; 413, 415-16, 420, 430-31; 464, 467-71; 494, 505-07; 518; 537; 613; 657, 665; 709; 718; 762, 773-74

GROSSMANN, H.: 286

GÜLICH, E.: 666

GUMPERZ, J.J.: 165, 176

GUSTAFSON, D.: 187

HABERLAND, H.: 7, 11; 285, 293, 311

HABERMAS, J.: 657, 665

HALLIDAY, M.A.K.: 141-42; 368

HAMMER, O.: 299

HANCHER, M.: 211-15, 217, 219

HANSEN, S.: 311

HANSON, G.: 307

HARDER, P.: 773, 777

HARE, R.: 252-53

HARMAN, G.: 9; 168-69; 780, 798

HARWEG, R.: 665

HASAN, R.: 368

HAUSSER, R.: 254-59

HAYS, D.G.: 290-91, 309

HEARER: 22; 57-58, 67-70, 72; 79; 116, 118; 154-55;195-201, 205-07; 211; 226, 229-31, 233-34; 323; 334; 344-45, 347, 349-50, 353; 367; 383. 385, 391, 395; 419-20, 428-38; 496-97, 506, 508; 534; 554-62; 570-73, 576; 593, 607, 610; 700-02; 734, 742; 749-54, 756-71. See also: ADDRESSEE; INTERLOCUTOR; INTERPRETER

HECHT, D.: 311

HEIM, I.: 785

HENDRIX, G.: 376

HESSEN, B.: 286

HEYDRICH, W.: 5, 14

HEYTING, A.: 446

HILBERT, D.: 446

HINDELANG, G.: 15; 342

HINTIKKA, J.: 6; 379-80, 385; 444, 447, 451, 459-62, 467; 499

HIŻ, H.: 447, 459-60, 467

HOBBES, T.: 698, 709

HOBBS, J.: 484

HOCKETT, C.F.: 143-44; 309

HOLENSTEIN, E.: 655

HOLES, C.: 491

HORN, L.: 97-99

HOUTKOOP, H.: 236

HUBIEN, H.: 261

HULL, R.: 267; 440

HUME, D.: 192; 504

HUNDSNURSCHER, F.: 12, 14

HUNT, E.B.: 420

HUSSERL, E.: 635, 637, 641-48, 650-52, 654-55

HUTH, L.: 665

HYMES, D.: 106; 165

HYPOTHESIS, PERFORMATIVE: 16; 157-58; 253-55; 414; 481-82; 706

IDENTIFICATION: 604-21; 713-15, 718-20, 722-23, 741, 745

IDENTIFICATION, ANAPHORIC: 510-15, 518, 524-26. See also: ANAPHORA

IDEOLOGY: 296, 300, 306-07; 501

IDIOLECT: 93-94, 97, 100; 688

IDIOM: 139-51; 417; 585

ILL-FORMEDNESS: 156; 423, 425. See also: WELL-FORMEDNESS

ILLOCUTION: See: ACT, ILLOCUTIONARY; ENTAILMENT, ILLOCUTIONARY; FORCE, ILLOCUTIONARY; INDICATOR, ILLOCUTIONARY FORCE; POINT, ILLOCUTIONARY; PREDICATE, ILLOCUTION DESCRIBING; SEMANTICS, ILLOCUTIONARY

IMPERATIVE: 195, 201. See also: DIRECTIVE; SENTENCE, IMPERATIVE; SENTENCE, JUSSIVE

IMPLICATION: 507. See also: ENTAILMENT; IMPLICATURE

IMPLICATION, PRAGMATIC: 71-73

IMPLICATION, SYNTHETIC: 71

IMPLICATURE: 97, 99; 158-59; 419, 430-32, 434-35, 437; 468, 470; 762, 770

IMPLICATURE, CONVENTIONAL: 158, 161; 752

IMPLICATURE, CONVERSATIONAL: 147; 158, 161, 164; 413, 416, 420, 430; 505; 613, 620; 701; 752

INDEXICALITY: 171-72; 231-32; 325; 405-06; 509; 626; 694; 796-97

INDICATOR, ILLOCUTIONARY FORCE: 223; 251, 259; 390, 394, 396; 706; 779, 783, 795. See also: SENTENCE, PERFORMATIVE; VERB, PERFORMATIVE; VERB, SPEECH ACT

INFERENCE: 96-97, 99-101; 106, 108, 117, 120; 126-27, 130, 132, 134-35, 137; 141-43, 147-48; 419; 562; 567, 579, 582, 585, 587; 643; 700-01; 752, 759-63, 770; 780-82

INFORMATION: 1. INFORMATIVENESS: 69-71; 200, 205, 208; 265-78, 283; 318-20, 325; 393; 429-31; 583-86.   2. GIVING-, ASKING FOR -: 83-84, 88-89; 354; 429-30, 432-33, 436; 554, 559, 561-64; 573-80, 584-87; 752-54, 756, 761-62, 771.
         3. IN SOCIAL RESEARCH: 106-11, 116-20

INFORMATION, CONTEXTUAL: 323, 327; 334; 384, 393; 420. See also: INFORMATION, SITUATIONAL; KNOWLEDGE, 2

INFORMATION, DISCOURSE: 511

INFORMATION, OLD-NEW: 514; 706

INFORMATION, PRAGMATIC: 701

INFORMATION, SITUATIONAL: 142-43

INFORMATION, SOCIAL: 199-201

INSINUATION: 751, 760-61, 771; 776

INTELLIGENCE, ARTIFICIAL: See: ARTIFICIAL INTELLIGENCE

INTENT, PERLOCUTIONARY: 12; 477-78, 480, 487-88; 495-97. See also: ACT, PERLOCUTIONARY; EFFECT, PERLOCUTIONARY; GOAL; PURPOSE

INTENTION: 105-07; 124, 130-31, 136; 155; 186, 192; 196, 200, 202; 226, 231; 239-49; 334; 371, 376-77, 379-82, 385-91; 416; 478, 482; 493, 495, 497; 593, 600-02, 604, 607-08, 611, 613-15, 621-22; 696-97, 699-702, 705; 749-68

INTENTION (ATTRIBUTION OF): 242-44, 248-49. See also: ATTITUDE, PROPOSITIONAL (ASCRIPTION OF); BELIEF (ASCRIPTION OF); STATE,

MENTAL (ASCRIPTION OF)

INTERACTION: 22; 146; 225-30, 233, 235; 238-41, 243-49; 345-47, 353-54; 531, 545; 585-86. See also: BEHAVIOR, INTERACTIONAL; CONVERSATION

INTERACTION, ADULT-CHILD: 79-82, 85-87, 89-92; 196-97, 204-05; 239-41, 244-49

INTERACTION, ASYMMETRICAL: 88-89, 92; 248; 540-41, 544

INTERACTION, CHILD-CHILD: 79-82, 85-92; 200-01

INTERACTION, CLASSROOM VERBAL: 531-46

INTERACTION, FAMILY: 202-03

INTERACTION, INSTRUMENTAL: 19-22

INTERACTION, SYMMETRICAL: 91

INTERACTION STYLE: 81-82, 85-88, 91-92

INTERLOCUTOR: 80-84, 88-92; 373, 375, 382-83, 389-90; 424; 493-95, 506, 508. See also: ADDRESSEE; HEARER; INTERPRETER

INTERPRETATION: 1. - of activities: 109; - of an expression: 23, 25, 39-40; 141-45, 148-49; 228; - of a narrative: 106-10, 115-18; - of a sentence: 414, 416, 423-24, 428-39; 511, 513, 522, 526; - of a text: 317, 321-22, 324-28; - of objects as signs: 313; - of phonetic properties: 525; - of speech acts: 231; - of utterances: 55-77; 153, 155, 156, 160-66; 195-96, 198-99, 202-03, 206, 208; 227, 233-35; 367; 373; 763. 2. - of a formal language: 31-32; 128-29, 135; 378-79; - of intensional logic: 786, 793-94. 3. - of action goals: 202; - of intentions: 241-42; - of speaker and hearer: 195, 201; - of the situation: 540

INTERPRETER: 313-19, 322-29; 372-76, 384-85; 780-82

INTERROGATION: 421, 427. See also: QUANTIFIER, INTERROGATIVE; QUESTION; SENTENCE, INTERROGATIVE

INTERVIEW: 106-20

INTONATION: 80-81; 200, 207; 318; 510, 513-14, 518-20; 558; 783-84. See also: PROSODY

INTUITIONISM: 446-47, 449

IRONY: 20; 507; 620; 756

IRVINE, J.: 484

ISARD, S.: 18; 773

ITALIAN: See: LANGUAGE, ITALIAN

JACKENDOFF, R.S.: 528

JACQUARD, F.: 288

JAMES, W.: 237

JAMIESON, P.: 77

JAVANESE: See: LANGUAGE, JAVANESE

JEFFERSON, G.: 96; 487-88, 491; 531-32, 537, 546

JEFFREY, R.C.: 284

JESPERSEN, O.: 634

KAFKA, F.: 727-28

KALINOWSKI, G.: 499-500

KAMP, J.A.W.: 360

KANNGIESSER, S.: 291

KANT, I.: 502, 504-05

KAPLAN, D.: 594-96, 603, 610-11; 717

KARMILOFF-SMITH, A.: 95-96

KARTTUNEN, L.: 59

KASHER, A.: 385, 463-64

KATRIEL, T.: 161, 176

KATZ, J.: 169

KAY, P.: 776

KEENAN, E.L.: 267; 440

KEENAN, E.O.: 774

KEENE, S.E.: 410

KELLER, E.: 146

KELSEN, H.: 499, 501

KEMPSON, R.: 360, 777

KERNAN, K.: 199; 546

KHATCHADOURIAN, H.: 158, 173

KIEFER, F.: 1

KIRSHENBLATT-GIMBLETT, B.M.: 106

KLEIN, E.: 59-60, 77

KNOWLEDGE: 1. 84, 88, 90, 92; 118-20; 229; 264-66, 269-71, 278-81, 283; 376-77, 379, 385-86; 459-60, 462-63; 502, 504; 555, 557-59, 561-65; 570-73, 577-79, 587; 627-28; 638, 652; 690, 692-97, 703-04; 740-41; 781. 2. - used in interpretation processes: 19-20; 68-69; 141-43, 148; 164-65, 169, 171; 197; 203, 205, 207-08; 327-28; 740-41; 767-68

KNOWLEDGE, COMMON: 146-47; 227; 468; 621; 657

KNOWLEDGE, MUTUAL: 388; 766

KNOWLEDGE, SHARED: See: KNOWLEDGE, COMMON

KOCK, C.: 2, 14, 15; 773, 777

KOLMOGOROFF, A.N.: 284

KRIPKE, S.: 3; 124; 594-95, 598-601, 603-06, 609, 612, 614, 618-19, 621-25, 629, 630; 688, 698, 709; 714, 717, 724-25, 730-34, 737-38, 746-47

KRIVONOSOV, A.: 784

KUMMER, W.: 12, 14, 15; 18; 374, 385

KUMMER, M.: 302

KUNO, S.: 530

KUUSELA, J.: 297, 305

LABOV, W.: 161-63; 293; 473, 481, 490, 492

LAKOFF, G.: 59, 77; 190; 418; 478, 481, 491; 521

LAMBERT, J.H.: 502

LANG, M.: 291, 308

LANGUAGE, ANCIENT GREEK: 259

LANGUAGE, ENGLISH: 25; 93-94, 96-97; 149-50; 197-98; 259; 332; 420-21; 633; 717-18, 722, 731; 766, 776; 781, 783, 796

LANGUAGE, FORMAL: 376-78; 448; 486, 490; 786-93. See also: INTERPRETATION, 2; LOGIC, INTENSIONAL

LANGUAGE, FRENCH: 95; 112; 254, 259

LANGUAGE, GERMAN: 25-26, 42; 299, 301-04; 633; 782-85, 794-96

LANGUAGE, ITALIAN: 543; 776

LANGUAGE, JAVANESE: 150

LANGUAGE, SPANISH: 112-14; 717

LANGUAGE, SWEDISH: 198, 305-07

LANGUAGE ACQUISITION: 1-6; 19-20; 80-81; 93-96, 101; 239, 249; 780

LANGUAGE GAME: 10; 331-34, 339-40; 400, 406-09; 447, 453, 463, 467; 483

LANGUAGE USE: 105, 111, 120; 218, 220; 232, 235; 257, 259; 285; 413-14; 445, 462

LATRAVERSE, F.: 4, 10

LEAR, B.: 612

LEBLANC, S.: 4, 10

LEE, P.A.: 335

LEECH, G.: 5, 8, 10, 13-15; 419, 440

LEIBNITZ, W.: 724-25, 730-32, 744, 746

LEMMON, E.J.: 500

LEONARDI, P.: 6, 8, 10, 12; 467; 774

LEONTJEW, A.A.: 393

LEVIN, S.R.: 414

LEVINSON, S.C.: 8, 11, 14, 16; 440-41; 482-83, 487-88, 490-92

LEWIS, C.I.: 252; 500

LEWIS, D.K.: 254-55; 388; 494; 773-74; 779, 785, 798

LEXICON: 142-44, 148-49; 181; 327; 391-92, 297; 555; 577; 687

LI, C.N.: 774

LIEB, H.H.: 263; 410

LINGUISTICS: 176; 234; 286-93; 308-10; 332-34; 370; 403-04, 410

LINK, G.: 798

LISTENER: See: HEARER

LOAR, B.: 127

LOCKWOOD, M.: 630

LOGIC: 6-7; 18; 360; 423, 425-26, 428, 433, 439; 444-47, 457 -58; 493, 498-504, 507; 659. See also: CATEGORY, LOGICAL; CONSTANT, LOGICAL; FORM, LOGICAL

LOGIC, ASSERTORIC: 450-51

LOGIC, CONTEXT-CHANGE: 7; 30-33, 51-53

LOGIC, DEONTIC: 499-501

LOGIC, INTENSIONAL: 782, 786

LOGIC, MODAL: 6; 499-500

LORENZ, K.: 444, 446, 454, 467

LORENZEN, P.: 6; 444, 446, 454, 467

LYCAN, W.: 694, 710

LYING: 172-73; 575, 580-81; 749-52, 756-70

LYONS, J.: 156-57, 159, 176; 363-65; 631-32, 655; 773

LYSENKO, T.D.: 308

MAAS, U.: 291

MACKIE, J.L.: 630

MAFFI, L.: 590

MAKKAI, A.: 142-43

MALCOLM, I.G.: 293

MANNINEN, J.: 250

MARCUS, R.: 625

MARRIAGE: 217

MARTINICH, A.P.: 221-22

MARX, K.: 288

MATHEMATICS: 446; 503

MATTHEWS, P.H.: 103

MC CARREL, N.S.: 177

MC CAWLEY, J.D.: 139; 177; 182

MC DOWELL, J.: 138

MC HOUL, A.: 546

MEAD, G.H.: 237-38

MEANING: 3, 9; 21; 59-62, 65, 74; 98; 111, 119; 123-25, 129; 140-44, 150; 156-69, 175-76; 181, 183, 188-92; 231, 233, 235; 253, 257; 274; 360-69; 405-09; 414, 428; 445-46, 459, 461, 468-69; 474; 506-07; 559; 570; 598, 603, 619-21, 623, 625; 633-34; 683-84, 691-92, 696, 702, 703-04, 706-08, 710; 718, 731, 742-44; 750, 762; 786, 795-96

MEANING, COMPOSITIONAL: 149

MEANING, IDIOMATIC: 143, 145-47

MEANING, INTERACTIONAL: 227, 230

MEANING, LITERAL: 141, 143, 145-47, 149; 163-64, 166, 169-75; 235; 406; 468; 481-82; 585; 620

MEANING, MORPHOLOGICAL: 794

MEANING, SOCIAL: 201-02

MELLOR, D.H.: 775

MENK: 304

MENTALISM: 5; 129; 237, 239, 243-44, 248; 402-03. See also: MIND; STATE, MENTAL

MERRITT, M.: 491-92; 590

METACOMMUNICATION: 201; 232. See also: COMMUNICATION, METALINGUISTIC

METAPHOR: 20; 147-49; 507; 637-38, 647, 652

MEY, J.: 1; 285, 293, 311

MEYER, P.C.: 661, 665

MEYER-INGWERSEN, J. 302

MILL, J.S.: 625

MILLER, V.: 80

MIND: 129, 133-34; 237-38, 242, 244, 248-49; 347; 424; 461; 564; 607-08, 615, 621; 645, 647, 652. See also: MENTALISM; STATE, MENTAL

MINSKY, M.: 165

MITCHELL-KERNAN, C.: 199; 546

MODALITY: 75; 319-20; 377-78. See also: LOGIC, MODAL; QUESTION, MODAL

MODE, COMMUNICATIVE: 631-32, 634

MONTAGUE, R.: 255-56; 389; 634; 779, 781-82, 786-87, 793, 798

MONTAGUE-SMITH, P.: 417

MOOD: 253-57; 631-32, 634

MOOD, INDICATIVE: 337

MOOD, SENTENCE: 779, 796

MOOD, SUBJUNCTIVE: 337

MORGAN, J.: 1; 479, 488; 620; 773

MORPHOLOGY: 338; 371, 391-92, 395, 398; 510; 631-32. See also: MEANING, MORPHOLOGICAL; RULE, MORPHO-SYNTACTIC

MORPURGO-TAGLIABUE, G.: 5-6, 13; 494, 497, 505

MORRIS, C.W.: 98-99; 105; 138; 404, 407

MOTIVATEDNESS: 415-18

MURPHY, J.P.: 1

MYERS, T.: 410

NAGEL, E.: 709

NAME: 683-84, 686-88, 692-98. See also: DESIGNATOR; REFERENCE

NAME, PROPER: 594-96, 598-99, 601, 613, 617-29; 697; 717-18, 720, 722-43. See also: DESIGNATOR; REFERENCE

NARRATION: 106; 206; 383; 652-54; 659-61, 663. See also: GRAMMAR, STORY; INTERPRETATION, 1

NECESSITY: 498-504; 723-25, 727-32, 738

NEGATION: 421-22, 426-27, 431-32. See also: CONSTANT, LOGICAL

NEGOTIATION: 82, 92; 94; 106, 118; 200; 213; 227; 540-41

NEUMANN, R.: 302

NEWMEYER, F.J.: 289-90

NORM, IMPLICIT: 363-68

ÖBERG, K.: 296

OCKHAM'S RAZOR: 129

O'CONNER, C.: 210

OEHRLE, R.T.: 2, 15; 529

OFFER: 196-97; 213-14, 216; 227; 351; 419, 436; 474, 476, 482-83

OH, C.K.: 777

OLSON, D.R.: 9; 103; 167-68

ORDER: 478; 496; 701. See also: COMMAND

ORLETTI, F.: 15

ORNSTEIN, R.: 655

OWEN, M.: 490

PAILLET, J.-P.: 410

PARADOX, BACH-PETERS: 7; 28, 32-33

PARADOX OF EPIMENIDES: 497

PARAPHRASE: 660-61

PARISI, D.: 8, 12-13; 554; 569-70, 585, 590-91; 771, 773

PARRET, H.: 103; 502; 751, 775-76

PEACOCKE, C.: 625-26

PEIRCE, C.S.: 4; 108, 117, 118; 137

PERCEPTION: 17, 54; 117-18; 246; 641, 643-44, 646-48, 650; 689-93, 699

PERFORMANCE: 17; 100; 167. See also: THEORY OF PERFORMANCE

PERFORMATIVE: See: HYPOTHESIS, PERFORMATIVE; SENTENCE, PERFORMATIVE; UTTERANCE, PERFORMATIVE; VERB, PERFORMATIVE

PERLOCUTION: See: ACT, PERLOCUTIONARY; EFFECT, PERLOCUTIONARY

PERRAULT, R.: 488

PERSUASION: 344; 352; 368; 505

PETERS, S.: 59

PETERSEN, R.: 299, 309, 311

PETÖFI, J.S.: 5, 14; 330

PHENOMENOLOGY: 4; 634-43, 650-54

PHILLIPS, J.R.: 80

PHYSICALISM: 129, 133-35; 634, 638

PIAGET, J.: 79

PLAN: 105, 107, 118; 235; 485, 487-88; 750

PLANNING, VERBAL: 372-76, 384, 388-89, 392-98

PLATO: 259

"PLEASE": 59; 559

POETRY: 659

POGGI, I.: 12; 591; 773

POINT, ILLOCUTIONARY: 344-46; 420; 516-18, 526. See also: EFFECT, ILLOCUTIONARY; FORCE, ILLOCUTIONARY

POLITENESS: 201, 209; 227; 391; 417, 424, 436-39. See also: EUPHEMISM; PRINCIPLE OF POLITENESS

POMERANTZ, A.: 483

POPPER, K.R.: 416; 444, 456; 638, 645, 655

POSSIBILITY: 498-501, 503-05; 725-32, 746

POST, E.: 641, 643

POULAIN, J.: 410

POWER, R.: 473, 488-89

PRAGMATICISM: 4. See also: PRAGMATISM

PRAGMATISM: 1-10; 17-18, 54; 59-64, 76-77; 98-101; 105-06, 109-110, 116-20; 123-25, 127, 138; 140, 149-51; 153-54, 157-60, 166, 169-77; 193; 201; 225, 231, 233; 239; 256, 258-60; 263-64, 267-68; 285-86, 309-10; 314, 324-26; 331, 334; 343, 346; 366; 392; 399-409; 413-21, 428, 438-40; 443-47, 453, 464, 467; 493-94,

496-99, 501, 504, 507; 509, 527; 531, 545; 551, 566; 569, 575; 598-99, 610-15, 619, 629; 657-58; 683-86, 688, 697-701; 704-08; 749-50, 768; 782, 795

PRAGMATICS, GENERATIVE: 256-57

PRAGMATICS, LOGICAL: 443

PRAGMATICS OF ACQUISITION: 245, 247

PRAGMATICS OF GRAMMAR: 331, 334, 339-40

PRAGMATISM: 136-37

PRATT, M.L.: 430

PRAYER: 212, 220

PREDICATE: See: PREDICATION

PREDICATE, ILLOCUTION DESCRIBING: 781. See also: VERB, PERFORMATIVE; VERB, SPEECH ACT

PREDICATION: 182-84; 364; 394, 396-98; 422, 427; 448; 695-96

PREDICATION, LEVEL OF: 107, 115, 118, 120

PREEMINENCE: 736, 740, 742

PRESUPPOSITION: 173; 448-49, 451, 467; 483; 503-05; 602-05; 700; 762-63, 773

PRETENDING: 751, 754-57, 763-71, 776

PRINCIPLE: 8; 98; 105; 413, 415; 469; 482

PRINCIPLE, COOPERATION: 101; 173; 233-34; 415-16, 431, 438-39, 441, 464, 468-69; 657; 757; 774. See also: CONVERSATION, MAXIMS OF; COOPERATION

PRINCIPLE OF NEGATIVE UNINFORMATIVENESS: 431, 435

PRINCIPLE OF NON-CONTRADICTION: 501-04

PRINCIPLE OF POLITENESS: 417, 436, 438-39, 441

PRINCIPLE OF RELEVANCE: 63

PRINCIPLE, UNCOOPERATIVE: 758

PRINCIPLES, CONVERSATIONAL: See: CONVERSATION, MAXIMS OF

PRINCIPLES OF CONVERSATIONAL RHETORIC: 418, 420

PROBLEM SOLVING: 8; 105, 107, 115; 228, 234; 373-74, 376, 393-95; 420, 439

PROCESS, CRYPTIC: 95-103. See also: ACTIVITY, CRYPTIC

PROCESS, INTERPRETATION: See: INTERPRETATION, 1

PROCESS, PHENIC: 95-103. See also: ACTIVITY, PHENIC

PROCESS, PRODUCTION: See: PRODUCTION

PRODUCTION: - of discourse: 371; - of linguistic expressions: 17, 25; 692; - of texts: 660, 663; - of utterances: 153, 155, 161; 371-74, 384-85. See also: CONTEXT OF PRODUCTION

PROMISE: 196; 211; 232; 349; 385-88; 419; 495-96, 498; 701, 705-06

PRONOUN: 23-25; 96-97; 198; 447; 510, 512, 514-15, 524; 769

PROOF: 446

PROPOSITION: 13-14; 68-76; 181-82; 251-60; 270-71, 275, 277-79; 397; 422-23, 426-28, 431-35, 461; 493, 497, 506; 519-26; 595, 610 615, 618-19, 623, 625; 759, 770. See also: CONTENT, PROPOSITIONAL

PROPOSITIONAL ATTITUDE: See: ATTITUDE, PROPOSITIONAL

PROSODY: 2; 510, 517-18, 520, 526-27. See also: INTONATION

PSYCHOLINGUISTICS: 5; 393

PSYCHOLOGY: 17, 23; 94, 102; 127, 133-35; 237-39, 249; 347; 410; 634, 638; 665; 704, 707; 714

PUN: 144-46

PURPOSE: 195; 275-76, 278-80, 284; 496; 537; 694. See also: GOAL; INTENT, PERLOCUTIONARY

PUTNAM, H.: 3; 138; 463, 467; 695, 698, 709-11; 744

PYTHAGORAS: 502

QUANTIFICATION: 359, 369; 444; 604

QUANTIFICATION, EXISTENTIAL: 614-16, 618-19. See also: QUANTIFIER, EXISTENTIAL

QUANTIFIER, ADJECTIVAL: 361, 364-68

QUANTIFIER, ADVERBIAL: 361-64

QUANTIFIER, EXISTENTIAL: 451, 462. See also: QUANTIFICATION, EXISTENTIAL

QUANTIFIER, INTERROGATIVE: 447-48, 451, 470

QUANTIFIER, UNIVERSAL: 451; 783

QUESTION: 106, 109; 118; 201, 203-04; 232; 248; 252-53, 257-59; 264-81; 339; 422-24, 432-38; 447-65, 469-70; 474-76, 478, 482-84; 569-89. See also: INTERROGATION; SENTENCE, INTERROGATIVE; SEQUENCE, QUESTION-ANSWER

QUESTION, CONDITIONAL: 458-59

QUESTION, EXAMINATION: 432, 440; 451, 453-54

QUESTION, MODAL: 195, 197-98

QUESTION, WH-: 423; 448-49, 455; 583-84; 784, 790-92

QUESTION, WHO: 395-98; 459-60, 462-63

QUESTION, YES-NO: 423, 432-33, 438; 448-49, 452-53, 455; 583-84

QUINE, W.V.O.: 258

RAMSEY, F.P.: 135

RASKIN, V.: 177

RATIONALITY: 98, 101; 133; 248; 498; 638, 640, 652; 768; 780, 782

REACTION: 19-22; 229, 235; 344, 347, 353; 364; 373; 546; 571-72, 578-79; 637

READER: 118; 340-41; 361, 368; 507; 563

RÉCANATI, F.: 3, 13; 77

REFERENCE: 3, 13; 22-37, 43-44, 54; 123-25, 128-32, 134-35; 501; 510-11, 522, 525, 528; 593-629; 683-84, 691-96, 699-700, 703-710; 713-47; 786, 796

REHBEIN, J.: 665

REICHENBACH, H.: 252; 634

REINHART, T.: 528, 530

RELEVANCE: 57, 62-64, 69, 71-74, 77; 116-17; 132; 275; 383, 389, 393; 453, 465; 544; 694, 702-03, 706; 740; 762. See also: PREEMINENCE

RELEVANCE, TYPES OF: 62, 66, 75-76

REPLY: 83-84, 88-89, 91; 569, 571-72, 576-81. See also: ANSWER; RESPONSE

REPRESENTATION: 1. Linguistic -: 691-92, 696, 699-701; mental -: 244-45, 248-49; semantic -: 179-87; 414; 577; visual -: 690, 699. 2. - of the context: 375; - of the interpreter: 375. 3. - in intensional logic: 792-93; - in TeSWeST: 314, 317-30

REPRESENTATIVE: 220; 375

REQUEST: 81, 83-84, 88-89; 163; 195, 197-99; 227-28, 232; 241-42, 246; 344-45, 349-50, 354; 374-75, 390-92; 419, 431; 479, 481, 485; 534, 542; 571, 573, 575-79, 585-87. See also: DIRECTIVE

RESPONSE: 57, 66; 213-14; 226; 459, 462; 474, 476-79, 483-85; 494, 496-97, 507. See also: ANSWER; REACTION; REPLY

RHETORIC: 4-5; 225, 233-35; 493, 504-07; 771

RHETORIC, CONVERSATIONAL: 413, 415, 418, 420

RIECK, B.O.: 298, 301

RIEGER, C.: 165

RIST, R.C.: 303

ROBINSON, J.: 484

ROGERS, A.: 1; 201; 491; 773, 776-77

ROLE: - in a game: 444-45, 451-52, 454-63; - in the interaction: 80-81, 89-92; 203-05; 541, 544; 566; social -: 162; 204; 537, 540-41

ROMMETVEIT, R.: 165, 177

ROSENBLATT, P.: 531

ROSS, J.R.: 253; 418

RULE: 8; 17; 105; 165; 234; 248; 343-44; 413, 415-18, 431, 439; 443, 445-47, 451-55, 465, 469-70; 473, 481-82, 484, 486, 488; 511-12, 523-26

RULE, CONSTITUTIVE: 8; 331-32, 334, 339; 415; 463

RULE, CONVENTIONAL: 60; 415-16; 482

RULE, GRAMMATICAL: 389; 415-17; 497

RULE, MORPHO-SYNTACTIC: 394

RULE, PRAGMATIC: 61

RULE, REGULATIVE: 8; 248; 415

RULE, SEQUENCING: 474, 478, 482-83, 486-88

RULE, TURN-TAKING: 531-33, 536-37, 543-44

RULES OF CLASSICAL RHETORIC: 505-07

RULE OF USE: 148

RUMELHART, D.E.: 115, 117-18

RUSSELL, B.: 453; 594-95, 612-13, 618-19, 622, 625; 718, 745

RYAN, A.: 430

RYLE, G.: 258

SACKS, H.: 96; 235-36; 464-65; 476-77, 479, 482, 487-89; 531-32, 546; 590

SADOCK, J.M.: 158; 773

SANDIG, B.: 665

SANTAMBROGIO, M.: 6, 8, 10, 12; 467, 471

SAUSSURE, F. DE: 416

SAVIGNY, E. VON: 780, 798

SBISÀ, M.: 494

SCALAR TERMS: 97-99

SCHAERLAEKENS, A.-M.: 93

SCHANK, R.: 18; 165

SCHEGLOFF, E.A.: 96, 103; 198; 236; 464-65; 476-77, 482, 487-89; 531-32, 537, 546; 590

SCHELLING, T.: 492

SCHENKEIN, J.: 165; 487; 531; 546

SCHIFFER, S.: 388

SCHNELLE, H.: 4, 16; 18; 655

SEARLE, J.R.: 1, 8, 9, 10, 11; 169-75; 211-12, 215, 217, 219-20;

236; 252-53, 256-57, 259; 334-35; 357; 375; 406; 413-15, 418-20, 422, 429-32, 436, 440; 481, 490-91; 494-95, 508; 534; 706; 775

SEMANTICS: 1-4; 43-44; 59-63, 76-77; 98-99; 123-37; 140, 149, 151; 157-60, 164, 166-72; 231-32, 235; 258; 263-64, 266; 285; 336-37; 400, 402-08; 413-15, 418-19, 421, 422-28, 438-39; 443, 446, 467-68, 471; 488; 493-94, 496-97, 499, 504, 507; 509, 517, 519, 522, 527; 599, 601, 603-04, 611-20, 622-23, 625-29; 631, 633, 645; 657-58, 663, 665; 683-86, 688, 694, 697-98, 700, 705-08; 750; 782, 785-86, 793-95

SEMANTICS, FORMAL: 7; 128, 135; 251, 255-57; 779

SEMANTICS, GENERATIVE: 179, 181; 256

SEMANTICS, ILLOCUTIONARY: 782

SEMANTICS, INDEXICAL: 263

SEMANTICS, LOCUTIONARY: 782, 786

SEMANTICS, NON TRUTH-CONDITIONAL: 60; 362-69

SEMANTICS, TRUTH-CONDITIONAL: 60, 77; 359-61, 366-67, 369

SEMIOTICS: 53; 400, 404; 527

SENFT, I.: 298, 301

SENSE: 166; 493, 501; 594-95, 625, 628; 698

SENTENCE: 41, 45-48, 54; 161, 169-70, 174; 215, 218; 225, 230, 232; 251-55, 258-59; 343; 383, 392-94, 398; 421-28, 439; 443-45, 461; 479, 481-82; 513-14, 526; 554-59, 561; 569; 603, 619-21, 628; 631-32; 665; 683, 687, 691, 700, 703-05, 707-08; 715-16; 750; 781, 786. See also: INTERPRETATION, 1

SENTENCE, CAUSATIVE: 182-86, 192. See also: VERB, CAUSATIVE

SENTENCE, DECLARATIVE: 232, 255; 369; 421-28, 439; 779, 785, 789, 796. See also: ASSERTION; MOOD, INDICATIVE

SENTENCE, IMPERATIVE: 232; 255, 258. See also: SENTENCE, JUSSIVE

SENTENCE, INTERROGATIVE: 232; 421-28, 439; 447-48, 461; 779, 784, 789-90, 796. See also: INTERROGATION; QUESTION

SENTENCE, JUSSIVE: 779, 785, 790. See also: SENTENCE, IMPERATIVE

SENTENCE, NEGATIVE: 421-28, 439. See also: NEGATION

SENTENCE, PERFORMATIVE: 258; 334; 481; 796. See also: UTTERANCE, PERFORMATIVE; VERB, PERFORMATIVE

SEQUENCE, ACTION: 380, 383; 661

SEQUENCE, CONVERSATIONAL: 473, 477, 479; 537-41

SEQUENCE, QUESTION-ANSWER: 464-65; 475, 483, 486

SEQUENCE, SELF-DEFEATING: 385, 396

SEQUENCE, SPEECH ACT: 54; 343, 349-56; 384; 473, 485, 487; 534

SEUREN, P.A.M.: 27; 99, 100

SEXTUS EMPIRICUS: 504

SHAKESPEARE, W.: 761, 769

SHATZ, M.: 80, 82, 92

SHEFFER, H.: 252

SHIBATANI, M.: 180-83

SHIMAN, L.: 529-30

SIEGLER, A.: 775-76

SIGNIFICANCE: 161, 166, 172, 175

SIGNIFICANCE, PRAGMATIC: 275-78, 280-82

SILENCE: 155; 204; 293; 479; 493;

579, 581

SINCLAIR, J. McH.: 91; 198; 473, 481, 490

SKUTNABB-KANGAS, T.: 7, 11; 295, 297, 300, 305

SMABY, R.: 77

SNOW, C.E.: 80

SOBER, E.: 709

SOCIOLOGY: 119-20; 141; 165; 238; 500

SØRENSEN, V.: 14; 665-66

SPANISH: See: LANGUAGE, SPANISH

SPEAKER: 62-63, 68-70, 77; 79, 81; 106, 116, 118; 123-38; 140, 146; 154-55; 195-201, 205-07; 212-14; 226-29, 231-35; 323; 334-35; 344-47, 349, 353; 361, 367; 372-76, 383-85, 389-91, 395, 398; 419-20, 428, 444, 451 -52, 454-63, 468; 477; 496-97, 506, 508; 532-37, 541, 543-44; 554-58, 560-63, 566; 570, 573, 575; 593, 598, 600-01, 603-04, 607-08, 611, 613-15, 617, 621- 23; 684, 686-89, 691, 694, 696 -97, 699-700, 702-05, 707; 717, 734, 739, 742; 749-54, 756-71; 780-82, 785, 794, 797. See also: COMMITMENT, SPEAKER'S

SPEAKER, NATIVE: 785

SPEAKER, NON-NATIVE: 141-42, 148 -50

SPEECH ACT: 54; 105, 107, 115; 126; 195, 199, 202, 207; 211- 20, 223; 257-58; 328; 334, 338 -40; 343-46, 353; 375, 383, 391, 393, 397-98; 413, 415, 418-19, 430-31; 473, 478-81; 509; 551; 569, 571, 582, 586; 660, 665; 688, 703-04

SPEECH ACT, INDIRECT: 20; 197-98, 203-04; 226, 228, 232; 257; 414-14, 417, 438; 474, 476, 480-81, 491; 534; 551; 585

SPEECH ACT, INITIATIVE: 346, 348- 50, 353-55

SPEECH ACT, REACTIVE: 346, 348

SPEECH ACT CLASSIFICATION: 11; 48- 51; 107; 211; 334-35; 497

SPEECH ACT SEQUENCE: See: SEQUENCE, SPEECH ACT

SPEECH ACT THEORY: See: THEORY, SPEECH ACT

SPEECH ACT TYPE: 11-12; 226-27, 231-32; 343, 349; 385-87, 390; 474-75, 477, 480, 483, 486, 490. See also: ANSWER; ASSERTION; BET; COMMAND; MARRIAGE; OFFER; ORDER; PRAYER; PROMISE; QUESTION; REPLY; REQUEST; RESPONSE; SUGGESTION

SPEECH ACT VERB: See: VERB, SPEECH ACT

SPEECH ADJUSTMENT: 79-82, 90, 92. See also: APPROPRIATENESS

SPERBER, D.: 63-64, 67, 70, 77; 774, 776-77

SPOHN, W.: 283-84

STALNAKER, R.C.: 155; 773, 776-77

STAMPE, D.W.: 3, 13; 124; 709, 712

STATE, INTENTIONAL: 402-05; 699. See also: ATTITUDE, PROPOSITIONAL; STATE, MENTAL

STATE, MENTAL: 229; 237-38, 244, 250; 638; 689; 758. See also: ATTITUDE, PROPOSITIONAL; STATE, INTENTIONAL

STATE, MENTAL (ASCRIPTION OF): 128; 248-49. See also: ATTITUDE, PRO- POSITIONAL (ASCRIPTION OF); BE- LIEF (ASCRIPTION OF); INTENTION (ATTRIBUTION OF)

STATEMENT: 128, 135-36; 201; 232; 252, 259; 361-63, 368; 422, 428- 32; 478; 506; 607-08; 703-05, 708; 753, 762. See also: ASSER- TION; REPRESENTATIVE

STATEMENT, GENERAL: 651-52

STATUS: 79-81, 90; 546

STECHOW, A. VON: 777

STEEL, B.: 449, 467

STEELE, Sam: 777

STEELE, Susan: 530

STEFANI, L.: 81

STEGMÜLLER, W.: 283-84; 444, 467

STEREOTYPE: 695, 711

STIERLE, K.: 665

STÖLTING, W.: 301-02, 304

STOUTLAND, F.: 250

STRAGE, A.: 210

STRATEGY: 4, 6, 8; 229, 233; 245; 417, 420, 439; 457, 461-63, 470; 488; 750-51, 754, 756, 762-71

STRATOS, G.: 210

STRATTON, G.M.: 177

STRAWSON, P.F.: 123; 391; 467; 494; 606-08, 614, 621

STRESS: See: ACCENT, CONTRASTIVE; INTONATION; PROSODY

STYLE: 79-80; 505, 507

STYLE, INTERACTION: See: INTERACTION STYLE

SUBJECTIVE PROBABILITY THEORY: See: THEORY, SUBJECTIVE PROBABILITY

SUGGESTION: 335-38, 342; 351, 354

SUMMARIZATION: 118, 120; 333; 661

SUPER-GOAL: 553-63; 572-75; 577-78, 581-82, 584, 587-89; 751, 758-60, 770

SWEDISH: See: LANGUAGE, SWEDISH

SYNONYMY: 254-55, 258-59; 337; 364; 707-08

SYNTAX: 1-2, 4; 28-29, 38-39, 41-48; 98-99; 139; 149, 151; 235; 253, 255, 259; 263-64, 266; 289-90; 338, 343; 371, 391-92, 395, 398; 400, 404; 413, 415, 419, 421-23, 425, 439; 447-50; 475; 504; 509, 516, 517, 519, 527; 555; 577; 632; 657; 722; 782, 786-93, 796

SYNTAX, EROTETIC: 449

TACT: 770-71

TARSKI, A.: 129

TENNANT, N.W.: 359

TENSE: 631-34, 645, 648, 650, 653-55

TEXT: 114-16; 155-56; 313-17, 324, 326; 343; 563; 631, 653; 657-60, 663, 665; 717. See also: INTERPRETATION, 1

TEXT GRAMMAR: See: GRAMMAR, TEXT

TEXT THEORY: See: THEORY, TEXT

THEME: 514; 542; 661-62

THEORY: 249; 292; 408; 652, 654; 718-19; 782

THEORY, DECISION: 264, 272-84; 774; 782

THEORY, GAME: 6; 388; 444-45, 447, 451-59, 461-65, 468-71; 488

THEORY, SPEECH ACT: 10-11; 157-58, 176; 225-33; 251, 258-59; 263; 325; 338; 343-46; 480, 482, 484, 492; 775; 794

THEORY, SUBJECTIVE PROBABILITY: 264, 270-72, 280-84

THEORY, TEXT: 313-30

THEORY, TEXT-STRUCTURE WORLD-STRUCTURE: 314, 318, 326, 330

THEORY OF ACTION: 658-59

THEORY OF ACTION, CAUSAL: 244, 250

THEORY OF DESCRIPTIONS: 618-19, 622

THEORY OF LANGUAGE USE: 779-82, 795

THEORY OF MEANING, CAUSAL: 3; 683, 700-703

THEORY OF MEANING, GRICEAN: 718

THEORY OF PERCEPTION, CAUSAL: 689-690, 699

THEORY OF PERFORMANCE: 157, 159-60, 166-67

THEORY OF REFERENCE, CAUSAL: 124-25, 129, 132; 683, 686-88, 693, 699-702, 709; 731, 736-37, 744-45

THEORY OF REFERENCE, GENERATIVE: 721-23, 734-35, 738-39, 742-43, 745

THOMAS AQUINAS (SAINT): 751, 770, 773, 775

THOMSON, J.J.: 191

TIME: 635-36, 643-45, 650-53

TITLE: 563

TOMBERG, F.: 286, 308, 311

TOPIC: 483-84, 488; 534-37, 544; 564; 579; 659-60

TOPIC/COMMENT: 514

TRANSLATION, MACHINE: 292-93, 309, 311-12

TRAVIS, C.: 13; 256; 710

TRUTH: 123; 410; 444-46, 461, 470; 504-05; 565; 658, 665; 704; 715-17, 726, 738, 740; 749, 751-56, 758-62, 764-66, 770, 773; 785, 794, 797

TRUTH CONDITION: 170, 173-75; 406; 626-28; 694, 700, 702, 705-07. See also: SEMANTICS, TRUTH-CONDITIONAL

TRUTH VALUE: 123, 136-37; 174; 253, 255; 607-08, 628; 786

TUOMELA, R.: 250

TURING, A.M.: 638, 640-41, 643

TURN: 474, 488; 531-39, 541-42, 544

TURN-TAKING: See: RULE, TURN TAKING

UHLENBECK, E.M.: 177

UNDERSTANDING: 96, 98, 100; 117-19; 144, 146; 162, 164-65, 175; 207-08; 314-15, 319; 371, 373, 384-85; 555, 563; 575, 577-78, 581; 610, 627; 700, 702; 715-16, 721-22, 734, 737, 739, 741-43; 751-52, 755, 764; 780-81

USE: - of a name: 684, 688, 693, 699; 737-39, 745; - of a sentence: 708; 785; - of a word: 59, 74-75; 690; - of an expression: 780, 782, 795-96. See also: LANGUAGE USE; THEORY OF LANGUAGE USE

UTTERANCE: 174; 228-30; 374; 473-76, 479-80, 488; 496; 514, 517-19; 686-87, 696, 700, 704; 750-51, 762; 781, 797. See also: INTERPRETATION, 1

UTTERANCE, COHERENT: 397-98

UTTERANCE, PERFORMATIVE: 213, 220; 226, 232; 419; 706; 785

UTTERANCE, SECOND INSTANCE: 425-26, 433-34, 440

VAGUENESS: 173; 188; 231-32; 359, 363, 366-67; 661-62, 666; 796-97

VANDERVEKEN, D.: 256-57, 259

VENDLER, Z.: 497

VENN, DIAGRAM OF: 502

VENNEMANN, T.: 18

VERB: 631-32

VERB, CAUSATIVE: 179-93

VERB, PERFORMATIVE: 157-58; 419; 497. See also: PREDICATE, ILLOCUTION DESCRIBING; VERB, SPEECH ACT

VERB, SPEECH ACT: 335; 353; 419.
  See also: PREDICATE, ILLOCUTION
  DESCRIBING; VERB, PERFORMATIVE

VERSCHUEREN, J.: 11

VINCENT, J.M.: 12; 581, 590-91;
  751, 773, 776

VOGT, H.: 287-88, 290-91, 293

VONNEGUT, K.: 139, 145

WALL, B.: 1

WARNOCK, G.J.: 494

WATSON, J.B.: 237

WEINRICH, H.: 776

WEISER, A.: 580, 591; 777

WELL-FORMEDNESS: 60, 77; 150,
  173; 245; 327; 377, 392-93,
  398; 417. See also: ILL-FORMED-
  NESS

WELL-FORMEDNESS, RELATIVE: 59

WELLMAN, C.: 335

WIDGREN, J.: 295-297

WIERZBICKA, A.: 77-78

WILKS, Y.: 773

WILSON, D.: 63, 64, 67, 70, 77;
  774, 776-77

WILSON, G.: 616, 620

WINOGRAD, T.: 18, 27; 371

WITTGENSTEIN, L.: 10; 168; 370;
  406-09, 411; 445; 744; 796

WOODS, W.: 490

WORD ORDER: 393, 398

WORLD: 8; 18; 105; 123, 129, 133
  -34; 191-93; 313-17, 319, 323-
  24, 329; 431; 444; 598, 622-23;
  637, 651-52, 654, 689, 691;
  730, 744; 749, 755, 766

WORLD, BELIEF: 379, 383

WORLD, DISCOURSE: 53-54

WORLD, FICTIONAL: 651-53; 755

WORLD, INTENTION: 379

WORLD, KNOWLEDGE: 379

WORLD, PERCEPTUAL: 144

WORLD, POSSIBLE: 155; 182; 255;
  596-98, 622-25; 655; 730-31,
  793

WRIGHT, G.H. VON: 499-500

WRITER: 339-40; 364. See also:
  AUTHOR

WUNDERLICH, D.: 286; 633-34, 655

ZAEFFERER, D.: 7, 15; 766, 774;
  798

ZIFF, P.: 163